Praise for

THE LUCKIEST MAN

"A moving and lucidly written memoir . . . Mr. Salter's admiration for his old boss is profound, but he is aware, too, of McCain's complexity. . . . Reading Mr. Salter's fine memoir, I am confirmed in an old opinion: that it is one of the great tragedies of our politics that John McCain was never elected president. America was just unlucky, I guess."

—*The Wall Street Journal*

"Franklin Roosevelt had Louis Howe and Harry Hopkins, JFK had Ted Sorensen and Arthur Schlesinger Jr., and John McCain had Mark Salter. In this compelling, honest, and much-needed book, Salter, McCain's longtime coauthor and adviser, captures the raucous, resilient, and invigorating spirit of the late war hero and legendary senator. McCain wasn't always right, but he was always decent, and Salter's terrific account reminds us of what public service—and public servants—ought to be like."

—Jon Meacham

"One of John McCain's key staffers turns in an affecting memoir. . . . Salter gives a highly readable, blow-by-blow account . . . One of the best fly-on-the-wall political memoirs in recent memory. Highly recommended."

—*Kirkus Reviews* (starred review)

"Salter's psychological portrait of McCain is informed and convincing . . . McCain may have considered himself 'the luckiest man on earth,' but we too are lucky to have counted him among our leaders and to have this intimate biography that will keep his memory bright."

—*The Washington Post*

THE LUCKIEST MAN

— LIFE WITH JOHN McCAIN —

MARK SALTER

Simon & Schuster Paperbacks

NEW YORK   LONDON   TORONTO
SYDNEY   NEW DELHI

Simon & Schuster Paperbacks
An Imprint of Simon & Schuster. Inc.
1230 Avenue of the Americas
New York, NY 10020

First Simon & Schuster trade paperback edition November 2021

SIMON & SCHUSTER PAPERBACKS and colophon are registered trademarks of
Simon & Schuster, Inc.

For information about special discounts for bulk purchases, please contact Simon &
Schuster Special Sales at 1-866-506-1949 or business@simonandschuster.com.

The Simon & Schuster Speakers Bureau can bring authors to your live event.
For more information or to book an event, contact the Simon & Schuster Speakers
Bureau at 1-866-248-3049 or visit our website at www.simonspeakers.com.

Interior design by Paul Dippolito

Manufactured in the United States of America

1   3   5   7   9   10   8   6   4   2

Library of Congress Cataloging-in-Publication Data has been applied for.

ISBN 978-1-9821-2093-1
ISBN 978-1-9821-2094-8 (pbk)
ISBN 978-1-9821-2095-5 (ebook)

For Diane, Molly, and Elizabeth

To suffer woes which Hope thinks infinite;
To forgive wrongs darker than death or night;
To defy Power, which seems omnipotent;
To love, and bear; to hope till Hope creates
From its own wreck the thing it contemplates;
Neither to change, not falter, nor repent;
This, like thy glory, Titan, is to be
Good, great and joyous, beautiful and free;
This is alone Life, Joy, Empire, and Victory

PERCY BYSSHE SHELLEY,
PROMETHEUS UNBOUND

CONTENTS

THE LUCKIEST MAN

REMINISCENCES

In my memory of that warm July day in 1989, there are half a dozen staffers milling around his subterranean office in the Russell Building, including an intern who was shadowing him for the day. It was casual. The men were in shirtsleeves, ties loosened. Everyone called him John, not "sir" or "Senator." Those formalities were reserved for responses when he was angry with you or with a colleague or with himself. There were two or three conversations happening at the same time. He introduced me to the intern, whom I sat next to on the leather sofa. It was a little hard to hear him over the hum of multiple conversations. Many years have passed, and I have an old man's memory, but I recall his instruction to me going something like this:

"Look, Lorne is leaving. I want you to fill in. Most of the job will be Central America and Southeast Asia, but I want you to do a lot of the writing around here. Go talk to Chris about the money."

Lorne was Lorne Craner, his foreign affairs aide, son of air force colonel Bob Craner, who had occupied the cell next to the senator's when they were held in solitary confinement in Hanoi. Lorne had accepted a job in George H. W. Bush's State Department. Chris was Chris Koch, McCain's administrative assistant, which is what head staffers in Senate offices used to call ourselves before we inflated our title to chief of staff.

I hadn't expected him to offer me a position on his staff, and I asked him for a little time to consider it. I thought I would appear overeager to jump at it, even though I knew instantly I wanted the job. He looked puzzled and a little put out by my response, and he paused for a second before asking, "Whaddya need, a couple hours?" I mumbled something noncommittal in reply, and he dismissed me with, "Yeah, okay, think about it. But not too long. We'll have fun. Talk to Chris about the money."

I talked to Chris about the money. Then I walked back to my office wondering how long an interval I should let lapse before I accepted. I didn't want to risk offending him, but having asked for time, I thought it would look silly if I got back to him that day. And I first had to break the news to my employer, former UN ambassador Jeane Kirkpatrick, who was vacationing in France at the time. I decided to call Kirkpatrick in the morning and then call Chris to accept the senator's offer precisely twenty-four hours after he had extended it. The recollection of my overthought, dorky propriety makes me laugh now, which is appropriate. Derisive laughter was the typical response to most examples of formality in the notoriously informal McCain world.

Twenty-eight years to the month later, I found myself in his office—a more spacious one, a floor above his first suite of rooms, with a fine view of the Capitol—searching again for the right reaction to another unexpected and, in this instance, unwanted turn of events. It was just the two of us, a few days after McCain had returned to the Senate, and less than two weeks since he had been diagnosed with terminal brain cancer. We talked about his priorities for the time that remained to him. There was urgency in his attitude, but not a great deal more than the urgency he usually brought to new predicaments. He lightened the conversation with wisecracks and irony, his trademark response to adversity. His response to success, too. His response to everything, to fate, to human folly, to the physical laws of the universe: *It's always darkest before it's totally black*. I tried to behave likewise, kidding that I expected him to outlive me. "You're giving the eulogy at my funeral," I insisted. "I've already written it for you. It's very moving."

I suddenly felt myself losing composure. Nothing had seemed to precipitate it. One moment we were joking around, and then, as if I had been startled by something, I asked him, "What are we going to do about this?" He held up his hand to stop me from going further and said, "We're going to man up, you and me. That's what we're going to do about it."

The nearly three decades that had passed between my introduction to the life of John McCain and his declaration of how he intended to face its end were purposeful, exhilarating, and, as he had promised, fun. I was exposed to people and events that shaped the course of history, to national politics at the highest level, to world affairs as conducted in corridors of power, and to the struggles of human beings for security, autonomy, and respect. I went to work for him when I was thirty-four years old. Before then, I had not traveled outside the continental U.S. except for a brief trip to Canada. My exposure to national politics was limited to conversations with friends who worked for politicians. McCain was a man with causes. They were causes I was obligated to serve by my responsibilities to him, for which my previous experiences had not prepared me, and they gave my life greater purpose than I had expected it to have. My life likely would have been a lot less interesting and rewarding had I not worked for him. A lot less fun, too.

In the course of our long association, we became friends, and I am obligated, too, by bonds of friendship to defend his reputation, as I did in one capacity or another while he was alive. I won't present a false portrait of the man, puffing up his virtues and denying his defects. He was not someone who was particularly guarded about his reputation. I don't mean his reputation didn't matter to him. It certainly did. But he didn't think his reputation—or anyone's, for that matter—should be so delicate a thing that it couldn't admit to failings, rough edges, and contradictions. What mattered was that you acted honorably in service of something more important than yourself, and you treated people fairly. He didn't believe politicians had to adhere to strict rules of decorum that put their personalities in a straitjacket. He believed if you maintained your honor, which could be a demanding commitment, you didn't have to sweat the sillier stuff of politics, the conventions on how to act and speak in public, the cautious image-making that made you appear as though you had been born middle-aged or the affected folksy modesty of the phony populist. He thought most voters could see through that stuff. You could be yourself, he believed—mostly, anyway.

He was himself most of the time, in private and public, a man, his mother observed, who "has no sides," one personality for some people and another for others. He was lousy at posing. It's not that he didn't attempt it occasionally. Any of his staffers can attest to witnessing an overdose of fulsome charm accorded someone he was trying to impress, a visiting celebrity he admired or a profile writer. Those occasions were not many, mercifully, and were always comically unconvincing. You could tease him about it afterward, when he had relaxed, and the next time you caught him buttering up a new acquaintance and gave him a look, he'd likely flash a grin to acknowledge it and take it down a notch. But in his public persona, for most people, most of the time, he kept it real to a degree unusual for a politician. And most people seemed to appreciate it.

My responsibilities, as a friend, to defend his honor don't require me to polish his image any more than he did, to smooth out his rough edges or clean up his language or refuse to acknowledge failings that he acknowledged. His reputation didn't depend on those pretenses, not the reputation he cared about. "Nobody gives a shit, boy," he typically responded when I urged him to tone it down a little, "if I don't act like . . ." The ellipses represent a rotating cast of fellow politicians whom he felt were phonier than the job required. He often gave them an expletive for a middle name.

He was usually willing to cop to his flaws to voters, reporters, colleagues, to perfect strangers sometimes. He'd be embarrassed for himself and for me if I didn't have the same confidence about what is really important and what isn't. This account of him, of the public man seen from the private vantage point of an aide and friend, respects his wishes. Although he mentioned in an interview that he wanted me to write his biography, we never discussed the project in any detail. His time was too short by then, and we were racing to finish our last collaboration, his memoir, *The Restless Wave*. But I approached this book with his standard admonition to me squarely in mind: "Cut the crap."

His prideful insistence on permitting as small a gap as possible between the public and the private John McCain was the essence of his charisma with voters, with the press, and with his friends. It was also, as you would expect, a recipe for regular trouble for a public figure with presidential ambitions because the quality most obviously shared by both the private and the public McCain was the habitual wiseass's delight in getting a laugh. And wiseasses in politics, however entertaining they might be, can make their own lives a lot harder by making their rivals' lives easier.

It often fell to me to remonstrate with him when his devil-may-care authenticity threatened to cause political problems or harm important relationships. During my tenure as his administrative assistant, I could be blunt with him, to the point of rudeness sometimes, and could even get away with nagging him when he refused to follow my advice. He might argue with me, both our voices raised. He might snap at me to drop it. He might just laugh at my concerns or ignore me. To my astonishment, he might say, "You're right. I'll fix it." The record of when such concessions were meant sincerely and when they were meant to get me off his back is mixed. But there were enough of the former occasions that I didn't give up trying.

He loved appearing on the late-night talk shows. He loved doing any shows hosted by comedians. He delighted in guest-hosting *Saturday Night Live*. He enjoyed trading insults with Jon Stewart. He eagerly agreed to offers of cameo roles in movie and television comedies. He fancied himself an amateur stand-up comedian, beginning every town hall appearance and even more formal public addresses with a litany of jokes he had been collecting, refining, and repeating forever. Before every turn on a comedy talk show, he would come up with a "routine," canvassing friends and staff for new jokes to mix with his standards, and cram as many of them as he could into his exchanges with the host even if they had little relevance to the topics being discussed. He insisted on the approach despite protestations from the shows' professionals that he should improvise his humor within the flow of the conversation.

In 2005 he was beginning to give serious consideration to running for president again. That same year he had appeared in a brief, inoffensive scene in the R-rated movie *Wedding Crashers*, which Matt Drudge had hyperbolically denounced as a "boob raunch fest," after noting the senator's appearance in it. McCain was scheduled to do *The Tonight Show with Jay Leno* the next day; anticipating a question about the Drudge thing, he came up with a line, or someone gave him a line, to make a joke of it. "In Washington, I work with boobs every day," he told an appreciative Leno, earning loud laughs and applause from the studio audience.

There was at the time resentment among some of his colleagues over the frequency of his media appearances, and not just cable news hits but the Sunday-morning shows and, increasingly, entertainment media. The resentment was compounded by his tendency to get laughs at their expense. A senator with whom he was not on the friendliest of terms was once heard to exclaim to several appreciative colleagues that he had a "great Sunday." "You know what makes a great Sunday?" he asked before answering his own question. "A Sunday when McCain isn't on TV." Someone relayed the comment to McCain, who laughed it off: "He wishes he could get five minutes on cable on a Saturday." Still, he knew that not all of his colleagues were as thrilled by his comedic stylings as he was, and "McCain Calls Colleagues Boobs on Leno" stories weren't going to help matters.

He had returned to Washington on the red-eye the morning after that show. I walked into his office not long after he arrived, and I shut the doors, which indicated that I was about to gripe about something, and he looked at me expectantly. I told him the next time he decided to make a joke at his colleagues' expense, he might remember that should he decide to run for president again, he would be asking many for their support. Few Senate Republicans had signed on to his first campaign, in 2000, and he needed to do better to be the front-runner for the Republican nomination in 2008.

"John, you can't make fun of people on *Leno* at night and then ask them for their endorsement in the morning," I objected. He graciously conceded the point. "You're right, boy, you're right. I'm sorry. I'm sorry. I'll be better."

While we were talking, his telecommunications counsel, Lee Carosi, was waiting outside the office to accompany him to a conference committee meeting, and she tried to hustle him out the door as soon as I opened it. As he left with her, he called over his shoulder to me, "Goodbye, Mark, I'm going to meet with a bunch of boobs right now." I could hear him cackling down the corridor as he walked to the elevator.

We agreed I would go with him to New York the first time he hosted *Saturday Night Live,* in 2002, and stick close by him throughout rehearsals. My charge from his other political advisors was to make sure he didn't agree to sketches that were so embarrassing he would elicit more ridicule from detractors than laughs from fans. I was to be especially vigilant, we all agreed, about any suggestion that he dress in drag, as Rudy Giuliani had agreed to do in his first appearance on the show.

The writers and cast convened in Lorne Michaels's office on Monday evening to start tossing around sketch ideas, which the writers would start to flesh out the next day. Most were half-baked concepts and would never make it into the show, but all of them, predictably, made the guest host laugh. Happily, none of them tripped my censor alarms. By Wednesday, all the proposed sketches were written and read aloud in front of the entire cast and crew, and by Friday, the list had been pared down to a few more than could fit in the ninety-minute live show. The final cut would take place just after the live dress rehearsal Saturday evening. I reported to my colleagues that we could relax. While some skits were funnier than others, we didn't need to worry that any would prove too embarrassing or controversial.

We were reading the newspapers in his dressing room on Friday afternoon between rehearsals. I was a cigarette smoker in those days, and as we had a half hour or so before his next rehearsal, I excused myself to go outside for a smoke. It took about twenty minutes and two elevators to exit the building, smoke a cigarette, pass through security, and get back to the floor where his dressing room was located. When I returned, I discovered the dresser helping him squeeze into a pair of snug fishnet stockings.

"What's going on?"

"This is his costume for the CD cover," the dresser responded.

"What CD cover?" I asked.

"The CD cover in the Streisand bit."

The bit he was referring to was a pretend TV ad that had him dressed like a hotel lounge singer performing a medley of Barbra Streisand songs in his genuinely awful singing voice to promote a *McCain Sings Streisand* CD as payback for the outspoken liberal's criticism of Republicans. In between murders of Streisand classics, the ad cut to the CD cover. For the cover photo, someone had decided to dress him in Streisand's costume from *The Owl and the Pussycat;* she'd played a prostitute in the film. The costume in question was a tight-fitting dress with handprint appliques over the breasts and a pair of fishnet stockings. It looked better on Streisand.

"We agreed no drag," I protested.

"It's not for the sketch. It's just for the CD cover," the dresser replied.

"Yeah, it's just the CD cover," the agreeable McCain confirmed with one leg in fishnets and the other still bare.

"No drag, no fishnets, no dresses, no women's attire of any kind. We agreed," I practically shouted.

"But—" the dresser tried to interject.

"But—" his confederate implored.

"You can't, John," the killjoy aide persisted.

"I guess I can't," the crestfallen amateur comedian conceded.

In the end, they posed him awkwardly in a long T-shirt with a Superman emblem and a pair of white shorts, a facsimile of the Streisand costume on her *Superman* album. It wasn't drag, technically. Everyone agreed the Streisand bit was the funniest sketch in the show.

He was a fascinating character to study at close quarters, capable right until the end of surprising you with qualities you hadn't thought could fit compatibly in one personality. He was a great bunch of guys, staffers used to joke. He was romantic and cynical, hopeful and fatalistic. Having seen humanity at its best and worst in the same experience, he expected to see good and evil in every conflict, martial and political. He believed there were always, in every fight, good guys fighting bad guys on behalf of little guys. But his romanticism didn't ignore reality.

He saw the gray between the white of his convictions and the black of their antitheses. He was worldly, widely traveled, well informed, pragmatic, and familiar with all kinds of actors in all kinds of conflicts. He assured American soldiers in Iraq and Afghanistan that they were fighting forces of darkness. In Libya, he pleaded with an Islamic militant militia commander to join the provisional government in the hope that his presence would dissuade other jihadist militia leaders from attacking it.

His romanticism might seem naive at times or an expression of his orneriness because he was so tenacious. That tenacity, like others of his qualities, resided in his extraordinary capacity to hold on to hope in the grimmest situations. He rarely gave up because he rarely lost hope, no matter the setbacks he suffered. For all his chronic impatience, he would persevere for years, decades, in pursuit of a goal he believed was right and just. And he was drawn to people who did likewise, people who refused to accept permanent defeat, who held on to hope when experience taught them hope was for fools. He sponsored three comprehensive immigration bills, introduced over a span of eight years. Two passed the Senate with the support of incumbent presidents George W. Bush and Barack Obama. But they all ultimately failed. They were big, time-consuming, exhausting efforts that McCain had poured his heart and soul into. They made him vulnerable to damaging attacks from rivals for the Republican presidential nomination. He risked a lot and fought as hard as he could to get them to the president's desk. Their failure was extremely discouraging to the bill's advocates, especially the defeat of the last effort, which had passed the Senate by a super-majority and died in the House before it could be signed by President Obama because House Republican leaders wouldn't take it up. And yet, in the months after his brain cancer diagnosis, he was able to attend the last session of Congress and, despite a reluctant Republican congressional leadership and a hostile Republican president, discuss with staff and colleagues how to get negotiations started on a fourth immigration bill. He wanted to make one more attempt at putting together a coalition to solve a problem that "shouldn't be this damn hard to solve." "We can get it started, anyway," he explained, sensing his listeners' skepticism, "even if I'm not around to see it finished."

A key provision of his signature campaign finance legislation, McCain-Feingold, formerly titled the Bipartisan Campaign Reform Act of 2002 (BCRA), was overturned by the Supreme Court's *Citizens United* decision in 2010. The decision disheartened supporters who had toiled for nearly a decade to get the law passed. It upset McCain, too. He chewed out one of the lawyers on the legal team representing Citizens United, Ted Olson, for the hypocrisy of representing the plaintiff after having successfully defended the law before the Court in 2003, when he was solicitor general in the Bush administration. Olson had assured McCain at the time that he believed in the constitutionality and necessity of the law, having been convinced by the evidence that the current campaign finance system was corrupting lawmakers. McCain remained angry with those responsible for weakening the law. Anytime you mentioned the subject to him, he would repeat his disdainful observation about the justices who had ignored or rejected evidence of corruption. "Not one of them ever ran for anything," he scoffed. But as was often the case when disappointment infuriated him, it also fueled his determination to find another way to accomplish his goal. Realistically, the political composition of the Court will have to change before real campaign finance limits are again established in law. But that didn't stop him from seeking other ways to make political campaigns more transparent and politicians less corruptible.

He hated to quit. No matter how steep the climb. You could defeat his attempts to summit, but you couldn't defeat his drive to keep trying, to explore new routes to get there. I never speculated with him about the psychological reasons for his tenacity. He would've laughed at me had I tried. But I suspected his refusal to give up causes that appeared hopeless was connected at least in part to the trauma that had humbled him more than any other experience, the one time when he gave up, when he truly lost hope, the lowest moment of his imprisonment, when he gave his captors a taped confession. Did the memory of the despair he had felt then, and the guilt he always felt for yielding to it, breed his fierce aversion to giving up? I assume so, but he probably would have mocked the suggestion, and undeniably, there were plenty of examples in his life before Vietnam of what might be described as his dogged refusal to face facts and give up.

He could be impatient in the calm and steadfast in adversity. When he decided on a course of action, he wanted to start on it immediately. The tobacco bill he sponsored in 1998 and pushed through committee could have rightly been assigned somewhere other than Commerce, Science, and Transportation, which he happened to chair at the time. But once he began meeting with interested parties and had grasped the dimensions of the problem, he saw how he might move a bill through his committee and just started acting like it was his problem to sort out. He pestered and cajoled Majority Leader Trent Lott to give Commerce the sole responsibility for a bill, while he was already in negotiations with the White House and with committee members, many of whom had conflicting interests on the outlines of a compromise. Before Lott officially acquiesced, John had staff planning a markup of a bill that had yet to be written, and was already starting in on Lott about how much floor time he could have to get it through the full Senate. The bill that the committee would send to the full Senate was mostly written during markup, as John negotiated with one member after another on scores of amendments, accepting some, revising others, and rejecting a few, until he had not only enough votes to report out the bill but a nearly unanimous consensus. Only one committee member voted against it.

To the observer unfamiliar with his methods and personality, the action around McCain could appear chaotic and his conduct impulsive. Both were often true. But the observation missed how well he thrived in those conditions. Bustling with energy and optimism, he might appear impatient and unfocused, but he had a goal, and he launched himself toward it day after day, until he won or lost. He was indefatigable. In all that action and appearances to the contrary, he was, in his peculiar fashion, relaxed. "Steady strain," he admonished his overloaded staff when an important project was advancing or floundering and emotions were running high. It was a phrase he borrowed from his navy days that refers to the optimal condition of lines holding two ships together at sea.

He was the most restless person I ever knew, and there was a manic quality to that restlessness. You suspected he was worried he would lose something important if he didn't cram more into his day than anyone else would cram into theirs. Twelve-to-fourteen-hour workdays were the norm. Crisscrossing the country almost every week, sometimes twice a week. Campaigning all over the country for almost anyone who asked for his help. Overseas trips were referred to as "McCain death marches" by exhausted colleagues and staffers who traveled with him. I remember one trip to Asia that included stops in five countries in eight days. We once flew to Hanoi for a single day of meetings, just days before his 1992 reelection. His weekends could be as busy as his weekdays. Racing around the state, holding town halls and press events, meeting with local officials, visiting military bases, frequent trips to Native American reservations.

He was an unusually hardy soul. He never seemed as tired as you were when you traveled with him or shared his long workday. He could nap anywhere to restore himself and was an especially sound sleeper on flights notable for heavy turbulence that had other passengers fingering their rosaries and looking at pictures of their kids. His dietary habits were a curious mix of high and low cuisine, at home in a Michelin-starred restaurant or in one of his favorite barbecue joints, coffee shops, or Mexican cafés. When he ate lunch in his office, which was most days, his usual fare would be familiar to an eighth-grader—a hot dog, a bag of potato chips, and for dessert, a package of Chuckles. His weight seldom varied: He was blessed with a metabolism that, like his energy, ran at more RPMs than most people could boast. But occasionally, he would add a couple pounds to his normally slim build and, noticing a tightness at the waistband, would go on a quick health kick, announcing to his personal assistant that he was "on a diet." When she asked what he wanted for lunch, he answered, "No hot dog. I'll have a baloney sandwich on white bread." Did he still want chips and Chuckles? "Sure."

The one place he reserved for relaxation, if you can call it that, was his and Cindy's place in northern Arizona, euphemistically referred to as "the cabin" (when they purchased it, a single cabin was the only habitation on the property, and then they started expanding). He was totally unguarded there, which, since he wasn't very guarded in public, was evident mostly in his dress: Cindy made sure the public John McCain was nicely attired. But in private, no one could save him from his indifference to the clothes he wore. At the cabin, you found him in ratty jeans, T-shirts, flannel shirts, and sweatshirts. "I Got My Crabs at Joe's" was a favorite.

There he would begin his mornings, usually earlier than guests who were visiting, with a cup of coffee, seated at his favorite spot on a bend of Oak Creek, waiting for others to wake. He might watch the birds while he sat there, especially the pair of rare black hawks and their offspring if they were in residence. He wouldn't have the newspapers yet, and if you watched him unobserved from the window of a guesthouse, he appeared lost in thought or, to the untrained eye, idle. He was at peace. Or as much at peace as his restless nature could bear. It wouldn't last long. Soon the papers would arrive, breakfast would be cooked and consumed, and the day's activities would commence. They would end in the evening meal that he slowly grilled for hours while nursing one or two vodkas on ice. He'd hike the steep hills surrounding the hidden valley to an Indian cave or a point with a panoramic view. He would "swim" in his creek, a tributary of the Verde River that carves a spectacular canyon as it descends from Flagstaff; it can be a raging torrent in the spring after the snowmelt. In the drier months, it was a shallow stream that might be waist-deep in spots where rocks formed pools. A reporter once asked McCain how he got exercise, and he ran through his activities at the cabin. "I hike and swim a lot there," he bragged. When asked if the creek was deep enough for swimming, he conceded that wasn't always the case. "I wade," he added, "I wade." The answer became an inside joke among campaign staff, repeated when an ambitious response to a press query had to be modified following a subsequent disclosure.

Of all the images that come most readily to mind when I think of him, the most frequent is of him hustling down a hallway some minutes behind his crowded schedule, setting a brisk pace with that stiff-legged gait, staffers jogging to keep up as they hurriedly briefed him for whatever meeting or vote he was racing to, bounding down stairways at a controlled lurch, letting gravity do the work that his broken knee made difficult. Famously, he couldn't elevate his arms above his shoulders for more than a few seconds. If his hair was out of place, he would pause wordlessly and bend at the waist while a staffer patted it down.

"What else? What else?" His incessant question to staff, to colleagues, to friends, to strangers. To the world. What else do you have to tell me, teach, reveal, entertain, provoke, summon? What else? "I got nothing, John" was my signal to terminate the conversation, at least my end of it. A quick look of disappointment invariably followed, and then off he went in search of another conversation to keep stimulated a mind that required little rest.

He was sentimental and more easily moved to tears than most people imagined. I once awoke from sleep on an overnight flight to Japan to observe him, seated across the aisle from me, watching the final scene of the movie *Ghost*, tears rolling down his cheeks as Demi Moore kissed goodbye the apparition of Patrick Swayze. It was easy to plant lines in a speech that would choke him up a little, triggering a memory of loss or sorrow or sacrifice. It might embarrass him, but it made a powerful impression on his audiences. If it got to me when I wrote it, I knew it would get to him. "Dammit, you did it again," he would complain after. But we both knew it was affecting.

He was hard-nosed and a soft touch. I knew a couple of navy aviators who had been his students in Meridian, Mississippi, where he was a flight instructor in the early 1960s. "You never got over it," one of them told me, "flying with him in the back seat, yelling at you the whole time, banging his clipboard on the canopy, on your helmet. Jesus." I never asked him about it. I assumed he was trying to simulate the stress of flying in combat, although at that time he had yet to experience the real thing himself.

If he thought a witness before his committee was being evasive or lying to him, he would barrage the offender with hard-edged questions until he or she was visibly rattled, and, were it a confirmation hearing, while the witness's family and friends in the audience watched with alarm. But if he thought a witness was being treated unfairly, he would fly to their defense.

He was capable of abusing and sympathizing with someone in the same set of circumstances. He was a leading critic of the Clinton administration's policy concerning North Korea's nuclear buildup. On a trip to South Korea, he had a moderately contentious discussion with the general commanding U.S. forces there, urging him to make clear to Congress the reservations he had about the policy: "That's your duty, General," he snapped. But he knew, too, that the general was in a tough spot. He was making his reservations clear to his superiors in the Pentagon and to the National Security Council; were he to be totally open with Congress, it would cost him influence within the administration. Politics would inevitably threaten his position anyway. He came to see McCain months later, in advance of a hearing where he knew he was likely to catch hell from some Republican members who planned to go after him in order to disparage the administration. "Don't worry about them," McCain advised him. "They couldn't carry your mess kit. If it gets out of line, I'll step in."

McCain derided the Clinton administration's "feckless" approach to negotiations with North Korea, complaining that every time the North Koreans crossed a line we had warned them not to cross, talks were suspended only to be resumed by the administration without conditions and with new incentives offered to Pyongyang. In speeches, interviews, and op-eds, he denounced the "all carrot, no stick" policy as "appeasement," and rebuked the administration for "reinforcing failure with failure." Chief negotiator Robert Gallucci, an intelligent and seasoned diplomat, occasionally came in for special abuse. Gallucci asked to meet with McCain. I sat in on the meeting, which was manageably tense as Gallucci briefed a skeptical McCain on the progress of negotiations, pausing patiently for questions and criticism. When Gallucci appeared to have finished, he asked if he could have a few minutes alone with John, and I left the meeting.

I was on the phone and didn't see Gallucci leave a few minutes later. When I hung up, I walked into John's office to ask what Gallucci had wanted. I found him writing an apology to Gallucci's adolescent son, praising his father. Gallucci had told him that his son had asked him at the breakfast table the other day to explain why John McCain had called him an "appeaser." John had apologized to the father and asked for his mailing address. He explained what he was doing and asked me to help draft it. "How apologetic?" I asked. "Groveling," he replied. He showed me what he had written so far and told me what else he wanted to say. I revised a few lines, but the letter was undeniably his. "I spoke with your father the other day," it began,

and he told me you had seen a recent comment I made about your dad and his work. I want you to know that I very much regret that remark. I have apologized to your father, and I apologize to you.

Your father and I disagree about the problem he spends so much time working on—the problem of North Korea. Although we disagree about how to solve that problem, we both love our country, and are trying our best to do our duty as God has given us light to see that duty. Your father is an honorable man, who is trying hard to act in the best interests of the United States.

Your father works hard because North Korea is such a difficult and dangerous problem. I admire his patience and his dedication to his work. He knows that your well-being, my children's well-being and the well-being of everyone's children may be seriously affected by how well he does his job. That's why he works so hard, and feels so strongly about the problem.

I feel strongly about it, too, and sometimes in the heat of debate, people personalize a disagreement. I did that recently in my disagreement with your father. That was a mistake I regret very much, and I hope he and you will accept my apology. I give you my word, should I disagree with your father in the future, I will do so respectfully.

He kept his promise. Thereafter, although he remained a vocal critic of the policy, he kept the invectives to a minimum and avoided calling Mr. Gallucci anything harsher than "mistaken."

McCain could be quick to anger and quicker to feel bad about it. Working on landmark legislation to protect the Grand Canyon, he was on the phone one day trying to persuade another western senator, the late Malcolm Wallop, to release his hold on the bill. He tried pleading and cajoling. He tried promises to address Wallop's reservations in subsequent legislation, all to no avail. Suddenly, his demeanor changed from supplicant to avenging angel, and he erupted, spitting invectives at Wallop for thirty seconds or so. "It's the Grand Canyon, Malcolm! Don't you get that? The! Grand! Fucking! Canyon! It's only our greatest national treasure, and you don't give a shit about it!"

He slammed the phone down and, in the next instant, looked across his desk at me and another aide, John Raidt, as we stared at him slack-jawed. Arching his eyebrows to express uncertainty, he asked meekly, "Too tough?" Before we could answer, he had gotten Wallop back on the phone. "Malcolm, I'm sorry, my old friend, I'm sorry. I don't know what got into me. I apologize." Not a minute had elapsed since he had excoriated Wallop, who, as far as Raidt and I could tell, said nothing in response to this rapid turn of affairs.

That his temper was notorious, a feature of profiles and commentary, had much to do with the fact that its outbursts were usually directed at his peers and other powerful people, many of whom weren't used to receiving abuse from a colleague. I never observed him lose his temper with a president. But several times I overheard him give the commander in chief a dose of "straight talk," criticizing an administration decision or action as "stupid," "foolish," "naive," and other unflattering adjectives, often punctuating the criticism with "See what I mean?" But he always stood up to take the call and punctiliously addressed his listener as "Mr. President" throughout the conversation.

He would bark at staff, scold us, and argue with us, sometimes at high volume, but rarely would he really blow up at one of us and deliver a memorable dressing-down. There were a few times. But it wasn't until the months before his cancer diagnosis when staff started to notice he was getting much shorter with them, harsher in disagreements, and unwilling to drop the matter when the staffer had yielded with a "Yes sir, will do." They had started to worry then that there was something wrong with him, and a few staffers mentioned their concerns to Rick Davis and me. But in the almost three and a half decades preceding that trying time, he had been a demanding, blunt, teasing, profane, fair, funny, sometimes difficult, and often inspiring boss. The tenure for McCain staff was years longer than the average tenure for Hill staff. Most of his staff loved him. All of them respected him.

He teased us constantly, introducing us to VIPs as people with checkered backgrounds. He introduced a junior staffer to General David Petraeus as a parolee in a work-release program, and the young man was rewarded with a sincere "Good for you, son" from the general. Or we might be a recovering [fill in the blank] addict just out of rehab. The eccentric character actor Gary Busey visited the office once, and McCain declared that the aide staffing the meeting was "just back from Betty Ford's." The actor's face lit up as he announced, "Me too!" and asked, "What were you in for?"

McCain was cheap, out of ignorance, partly. He didn't need to worry about money, and while he understood things like inflation rates and cost-of-living increases in the abstract, he paid less attention to their effects on real prices and wages. Once a year, as his administrative assistant, I met with him to go over proposed fiscal year-end bonuses and salary raises, holding a sheet of paper listing all the staff, their current salaries, and the bumps I thought they had earned. In every one of those meetings, McCain was surprised about the salaries we were paying, which were, I assured him, no more than the average, and modest in a city as expensive as Washington. He donated to charity every salary raise he received, and I don't think he had any idea how much he was being paid. He would have considered it a fortune, as he did the salaries of his senior staff. "How much are we paying him?" he'd ask with a look of astonishment and, when I confirmed the amount he was staring at, "Good God!" Yet not once did he refuse my recommendation.

He regularly encouraged others to adopt his parsimony. An aide was tasked with purchasing a new sound system for the television in John's condo, which John was having trouble hearing clearly. As the staffer stood in line at the Best Buy register, he noticed a stack of *Saving Private Ryan* DVDs on sale for $9.99. Thinking the movie's opening D-Day sequence was ideal to demonstrate the quality of the senator's new surround sound, he added a copy to the purchase. After installing the system and leaving detailed operating instructions next to the remote, he informed John that it was all set up and ready to go.

"Oh, and they had copies of *Saving Private Ryan* on sale, so I picked one up for you."

"Who told you to do that?"

"Um, no one, but I know you liked it, and I thought what a great movie to watch with the surround sound."

"Take it back."

"I can't, it was on sale."

"Don't do that again."

With that, the exasperated aide reached in his wallet and pulled out a ten-dollar bill, explaining, "Fine, I'll buy it, then." John nodded and took the money.

Seated next to him on a flight to California, his friend and longtime fund-raiser Carla Eudy purchased the airline's Wi-Fi service so she could respond to emails on the flight. A skeptical McCain observed the transaction. "How much did you just pay for that?" he asked. "Eight dollars," she replied. "That's a waste of money," he rebuked her, "why don't you just read a book?" Carla shot him a look of irritation and snapped, "It's my money, and I'll spend it on whatever I want. I've got work to do." Among her emails during that flight was one from the Senate office, asking her to tell McCain that Vladimir Putin had included his name on a list of Americans forbidden to travel to Russia, which it delighted him to learn. He immediately began dictating emails he wanted Carla to send, asking for more information. "I guess I won't be spending spring break in Siberia this year," he told her, a line he would repeat again and again to reporters and other audiences, cracking himself up each time.

Yet for all his frugality about expenses, he was one of the more generous people I've known. He tipped generously and never failed to pick up the check at dinner, no matter the size of the party. He was an easy touch for panhandlers. He gave liberally to charities. He was bighearted. He never refused his help to a friend or former aide struggling with a serious problem. If a former staffer lost a job or was miserable in one, McCain would make call after call recommending him or her for a new position. If none could be found, he'd call me into his office and instruct me to try to find a place for the person back on staff.

He split evenly with me the royalties from the books we collaborated on, an uncommon arrangement, to say the least. When his presidential campaign went broke in the summer of 2007, senior campaign staff had to stop taking salaries and agree to become volunteers for the remainder of the year. I had two mortgages, two kids in private school, and a spouse who had given up her job to raise them. McCain knew it would be hard for me to work for free for six months. He called his literary agent and instructed her to assign to me all of the remaining advance we were owed for his soon-to-be-published new book. He said nothing to me about it. I found out when I received the check. When I went to thank him, he cut me off with "You did the work," and then he changed the subject.

He was an avid sports fan. He often joked that he would stay up late to watch "the bed wetters play the thumb suckers" if there were no other games available. He was a devoted follower of all Arizona's teams, college and professional. The Coyotes, the Cardinals, the Diamondbacks, the Suns, the Sun Devils, the Wildcats, the Grand Canyon University Antelopes all claimed him as their number one celebrity fan. He went to their games whenever he could. Games he couldn't attend in person, he watched on TV or checked the scores on his phone, doing it surreptitiously only when he was chairing a hearing or occupied with some other official duty. He rarely felt it necessary in social settings to disguise the fact that he was more interested in how his guys were doing than he was by the company he was in. He became friends with some of the players and particularly close friends with

Larry Fitzgerald of the Cardinals, Luis Gonzalez of the Diamond-backs, and Shane Doan of the Coyotes.

McCain wasn't a "political" fan. He was a fan's fan, intense, loyal, knowledgeable, cheering on his guys with his injured arms thrust straight out in front of him, thumbs up, booing bad calls, expressing without any thought to appearances all the joys and disappointments of a sports nut. When the L.A. Dodgers celebrated clinching their division title in 2013 by jumping in his beloved Diamondbacks' pool, McCain reacted like any other Diamondback fan with access to social media. He denounced the insult on Twitter, calling it "a no-class act by a bunch of overpaid, immature, arrogant, spoiled brats!" Adding, for good measure, "The Dodgers are idiots." He could walk into a ballpark and not be booed, although probably not in Dodgers Stadium. More often than not, he received an ovation, one of very few politicians regularly accorded that courtesy. Fans knew he was one of them. He took care to make sure he was. He talked to anyone who approached him at a game, took pictures, signed autographs, engaged in brief discussions of the game.

The sport he loved most was boxing. He was a passionate fight fan, as he had once been an amateur fighter at the Naval Academy. He always described himself as a mediocre high school and college athlete, but, as with all things he cared for, in his youth and in his old age, he brought intensity to the pursuit, almost a ferocity that seemed to come naturally to him and partially compensated for limitations in skill. The late journalist Bob Timberg, in his insightful book *The Nightingale's Song*, captured McCain's style in the ring, the style he brought to other contests as well. "Unschooled as a boxer," Timberg wrote, "McCain's style was to charge to the center of the ring and throw punches until someone went down."

He had an acute sense of fairness that was actuated by the exploitation of fighters. For years, he and filmmaker Ken Burns pleaded with presidents of both parties to pardon posthumously the legendary fighter Jack Johnson, whose only crimes had been to have a larger-than-life personality and become the heavyweight champion of the world. Fairness drove McCain's efforts to protect fighters from unethical promoters, especially journeyman fighters, many of whom ended their boxing careers broke and broken, without pension or prospects. His sense of fairness provoked reactions to the fights themselves when he felt the judges had robbed a fighter of a decision.

He was at the classic 1997 welterweight title fight between Pernell Whitaker and Oscar De La Hoya and was beside himself at the decision. Everyone ringside, including De La Hoya promoter Bob Arum, heard him yelling that Whitaker had been robbed. And by the next day, everyone he knew in the sport, and a good many people who had a merely passing interest in it, if any, had heard from him on the subject.

His sense of fairness was alert even to small examples of thoughtlessness. Late in his public life he finally agreed to let an aide drive him. He had always had an aide designated to drive with him. For many years it was his longest-serving staffer, Joe Donoghue. Most of the time Joe rode in the passenger seat, taking the wheel only when John arrived at his destination, couldn't find a parking spot, and let Joe sort it out. After the 2008 election, aides convinced him he was too distracted to drive, as he was constantly talking on his phone while at the wheel. When you drove him, you had to get him through Washington's notoriously sluggish traffic to reach his destination more or less on time even though he had put off leaving fifteen minutes longer than he should have. You had to get him through the traffic without, as many drivers did, cutting in front of a line of cars waiting to pass through a bottleneck. You got a lecture if you did, a stern one. "See those people, that guy right there giving you the finger? You deserve it. You see all those people behind him? See them? You just screwed them. Don't. Do it. Again."

He disliked the coddling he and his colleagues received, the routine perks of senatorial life that he thought were intended not just as conveniences or security precautions but to elevate them as a privileged class. In the spring of 1994, McCain exited the old terminal at National Airport after arriving from Phoenix. He walked with an aide to the parking lot reserved, free of charge, for members of Congress, Supreme Court justices, and foreign diplomats, conveniently located mere steps from the terminal. He noticed a young, very pregnant woman struggling with her luggage shooting him a disdainful look as she cut through the VIP lot on her way to some more distant lot, where she no doubt had been charged a fee to park. "Goddammit," he muttered, "that's not right." When he arrived at the office, he instructed staff to prepare an amendment to whatever bill was pending before the Senate, which would open to the public airport parking lots reserved for senators and charge the same fee to everyone who used them, U.S. senator and expectant mother alike. To his chagrin, his amendment was defeated 53 to 44, after causing considerable ill will among colleagues in both parties, a few of whom had the courage to debate it on the Senate floor.

He didn't like any accommodation reserved for "senators only," including the elevators in the Capitol Building off-limits to unaccompanied staffers, custodial workers, lobbyists, journalists, and the throngs of tourists who, in pre-9/11 days, were allowed to wander most of its halls without supervision. He went out of his way to beckon passersby to share an elevator with him. After stepping into an elevator in the Russell Building once, he motioned to two guys in blue shirts with mops and rolling buckets to ride with him. "No, thanks, Senator. We'll get the next one," they declined politely. "C'mon, guys," he shot back, "whatever you're doing is more important than what I'm doing," and with a nod of thanks, they joined him. A family of sightseers was welcomed into the paneled sanctuary of a senators-only elevator in the Capitol with the encouragement to "act like you own the place. Because you do."

When he became chairman of the Senate Commerce, Science, and Transportation Committee in 1997, one of his first instructions to aides was to hang on the hearing room walls the official portraits of as many past committee chairmen as they could locate in the Senate archives. The collection grew to around fifty by the time they were done. He had them all reframed and hung in chronological order. He loved to walk constituents or reporters down the marble hallway from his senate office to the hearing room, where he would point at the portraits, asking, "Remember this guy? No, well how about this guy?"

He would go in that fashion until he had selected ten or so of his forgotten predecessors. "You know, these guys thought they were really big deals."

He was generous with his time and stopped to talk with anyone who wished to shake his hand or exchange a few words or take a picture with him in hallways and airports and at sporting events. He was usually running late to catch a flight and talking on his cell phone. But he would almost always pause to take a selfie with anyone who stopped him, answer their questions, and ask them a few in return. "This will all be over someday," he routinely reminded himself and aides who were accompanying him, "and no one's gonna give a shit who I used to be." He knew that whatever inconvenience his celebrity might cause him, he would miss all of it when it was gone. Once in a great while he would be irritable when importuned, if he was focused on a game or hurrying somewhere with his family or engaged in conversation with someone else. But that was very rare. He knew who he worked for, and he accepted that they were entitled to his time and attention, no matter how little of it he had available. He was usually willing to accept abuse as well. His town halls in Arizona were attended by detractors and often featured lengthy complaints about a position he had taken and a few loud jeers from the crowd. He didn't accept opprobrium meekly. He gave as good as he got, but he didn't resent it, either. He began almost every town hall promising to speak briefly, after which he would open it up "for your questions, comments, and insults," and he meant it. Voters were allowed to give him a hard time, he said. And he was obliged to take it.

John Raidt recalls watching a woman tear into McCain for five minutes at the Arizona State Fair on the issue of abortion. He silently nodded throughout her diatribe. She was so aggressive that Raidt made a couple of attempts at intervening, only to be waved off by the senator. Appreciating his forbearance, the woman eventually moderated her tone and they settled into a good, candid discussion. After they had finished and she had walked away, he didn't make any smart remarks about the encounter. He told Raidt he had appreciated his attempted intercession, but she had a right to express her views as forcefully as she wanted to, and he had a duty to listen. He admired the courage of her convictions, he added.

He hated motorcades. He hated the fuss, the procession of motorcycles and squad cars and black SUVs with tinted windows. He hated the inconvenience imposed on people trying to go about their business in a traffic jam caused by him. He didn't dwell on his disappointment the night he lost the election for president, but chose to look on the bright side. "No more motorcades," he rejoiced moments after being told he could go ahead and deliver his concession speech. After a campaign event in Winston-Salem, while riding in a long line of black SUVs carrying the candidate, campaign staff, and Secret Service to the airport, he noticed all the exits to the airport had been closed until his motorcade passed, with traffic backed up at each one. He was beside himself. "How many people are going to miss their flight because of me? How many?" he yelled to no one in particular. The head of his Secret Service detail explained that he hadn't ordered the closings; local law enforcement had taken the unnecessary precaution upon themselves.

"Well, dammit, Billy, don't let them do that."

"They don't always ask, sir. But we'll make sure they know how you feel about it."

"Make sure they know how I feel about it before they do it, okay?"

"Yes, sir."

Motorcades were part of living in the bubble. And he hated the bubble, hated its constraints, its barriers to normal experiences. He wanted to be in the world, not protected from it. He wanted to go to the ball game or the movies, eat in a restaurant, buy a cup of coffee, shop at the grocery store, browse a bookstore without an intervening force preventing incidental human contact. He put off accepting Secret Service protection as long as he could in 2008, until his pleading family and senior aides wore down his resistance. On election night, he dismissed his detail with genuine gratitude but firmly when the plan had been to continue protection for another week or so. The next morning, surprised Phoenicians encountered him as he happily walked with Cindy to their neighborhood Starbucks to get his morning cappuccino, "with no more protection than a little sunscreen," he recalled.[1]

He disliked being stuck in someone else's security bubble as much as he did in one of his own. He resented what he thought were the excessive precautions the Secret Service took with the president's protection, and when he was a candidate for that office, he frequently swore that should he win the election, the first thing he would do was "cut out half this shit." Sometimes he expressed his disapproval by refusing to defer to security precautions, which could be a hair-raising experience for staffers accompanying him. He and a Republican group of senators were scheduled to have dinner with Obama at a Washington hotel one night during the president's first term. He was a little late getting there, and the Secret Service and D.C. police had already sealed off a perimeter around the hotel in advance of the president's arrival. As McCain's driver at the time, Jake Terrell, approached the cordon, a policeman some distance from the car held a hand up to stop him and motioned for him to turn around. John instructed him to keep driving: "Just run it, Jake."

"Stop the car," the cop demanded.

"Keep going, Jake."

"I said stop!"

"Go on, go on."

"Driver, stop the car now!"

"No guts, no glory, Jake. Go on."

The policeman, who was jogging toward the car now, shone his flashlight at Jake, put his hand on his sidearm, and shouted, "STOP! THE! VEHICLE! NOW!" as Jake remembered thinking, "I'm going to get shot for thirty-eight thousand dollars a year."

The cop reached the car, hand still on his gun, and shouted, "Do you not hear me, driver? Are you stupid?" which prompted an intervention: "What did you say?" asked the familiar white-haired man in the passenger seat.

The cop looked at him, registered his identity, offered a quick "Oh, sorry, Senator, I didn't see you," and arranged to escort the car down Sixteenth Street to the hotel. The senator appeared otherwise undisturbed.

He wanted the same freedom when he traveled overseas and discouraged overt protection except in war zones and once in Colombia during the height of the cartel mayhem in the 1990s. When he had a spare hour or two, he wanted to visit a marketplace or tour a museum or choose a restaurant at random or, as he did in Prague one pleasant evening, just wander the streets of a beautiful foreign city in the company of Czech revelers celebrating their first post–Cold War free election.

I traveled with him and Phil Gramm on his first visit to Ukraine after the dissolution of the Soviet Union, which included a trip to the Crimean Peninsula. He wanted to see the Soviet naval base in Sevastopol, which the Russians were insisting remain in their possession. We spent the night and part of the next day in the historic Black Sea resort town of Yalta, a place he had always wanted to visit. We had the afternoon off before we were scheduled to fly to Latvia. We toured the czar's summer palace, where the famous World War II conference had been held. We ate lunch at a seaside restaurant. Afterward, he said he wanted to walk around the docks, where he tried to strike up conversations with several boat owners until he found one who could speak passable English. Within minutes, we were boarding the boat, and John was handing the captain a wad of bills. We spent an enjoyable few hours on the Black Sea, ten miles or so offshore, swimming in our skivvies, sipping a local whiskey that tasted of petroleum, and attempting conversation with the skipper and his one crewman. We discovered in due course that our hosts were Turkish smugglers who were planning on returning that evening to whatever port they called home. They hadn't any idea who their passengers were other than Americans with money. McCain was thrilled to have fortuitously fallen in with fascinating company, and would recall the adventure years later, embellishing it a little—the boat described as less seaworthy and the captain and crew more swashbuckling—for the sake of his listeners' amusement.

He was the last to leave the office after congressional office buildings were ordered evacuated on 9/11; he waited until all staffers had left. He was calm and casual, talking and joking around with us as if nothing frightening were happening. When he at last left the building, Joe Donoghue informed him that the Capitol Police were waiting to

take him to "the bunker," the undisclosed secure facility prepared for
senior members of Congress in the event of a national emergency; its
rumored location was West Virginia.

"The what?"

"The bunker, John."

"Joe, I'm not going to sit in a fucking bunker with Trent Lott."

It wasn't the prospect of Senator Lott's company that deterred
him. He and Lott had disagreements from time to time, as he had
with every Senate leader, Republican or Democrat, but they were on
friendly terms. It was the idea of hiding in a bunker that repelled him.
Again, the temptation to play armchair psychoanalyst is strong, and
the amateur diagnosis is obvious: A man deprived of his liberty and
subjected to physical and mental abuse for five years would of course
balk at the idea of surrendering any of his independence even to a
benign authority. Probably. But again, there were plenty of incidents
prior to his imprisonment when he refused to submit to the authority of institutions that had reason to expect his deference. There was
something in him from the start that made it harder for him to follow
than to lead.

That terrible September morning there would be no sheltering in
an undisclosed location for him, huddling with colleagues to com-
prehend the savage act and its consequences. He walked out into the
sunshine with the masses of people exiting the Capitol and its surrounding office buildings. Some were running; some threw themselves to the ground when they heard the sonic boom caused by air
force jets that had been scrambled out of Andrews. Traffic was at a
standstill, so we abandoned his car and made our way on foot to the
nearby apartment of a young staffer, Sonya Sotak. She wasn't expecting
company and was embarrassed as she hurriedly straightened up her
one-bedroom walk-up, while John fiddled with the rabbit ears on her
non-cable-equipped television to get a clearer picture of news reports.
When he asked for water, her only clean glass was a giant wine goblet,
which she filled from the tap and brought to him. Our press secretary
managed to reach his mobile phone and patch him through to a few
reporters. A camera crew from a cable or broadcast network I can no

longer recall found us, and John talked to them standing in front of her apartment building. In each interview, he expressed his sympathy and resolve and offered repeated reassurances that we would prevail against enemies who target the innocent in the name of God, not just because we were more powerful but because we were just. Eventually, we made our way to a popular Capitol Hill tavern in search of food and cable TV. When he walked into the crowded Hawk and Dove, the patrons applauded. He was where he wanted to be, free in the world and happy to be of use.

"His courage," I wrote after his passing, was "quick, heedless, defiant, and quite a thing to witness."[2] He and his wife, Cindy, and I traveled to Russia to observe the parliamentary elections in 1993. Late one night, we were being driven to our hotel when we encountered three men severely beating each other with rifle butts on an otherwise deserted street. McCain yelled at the driver to stop. The driver refused. "I said stop," McCain repeated. "Nyet," the driver responded. "Stop, dammit, stop," he insisted, and he started to slide open the door as if he were going to jump from the moving van. The driver sped up as I reached over the seat and held McCain's arm tightly until we were blocks away from the scene. He glared furiously at me as I stated the obvious: "Those guys had guns, John," but he said nothing in response. He didn't say anything at all to me for the rest of the night.

He tried to act honorably and fairly in all circumstances where he believed honor and fairness were involved, and when he fell short of that standard, which wasn't often, it ate at him. He would seem extra restless and distracted, worried and intemperate, until he either rectified the offense or confessed it publicly and chastised himself. He never forgave himself for his false confession in prison, which anyone with intelligence and humility considered excusable in such dire circumstances. "I failed. I failed," he repeated, brushing away routine assurances to the contrary. Failed to be tough enough. Failed to suffer as others had. Failed to uphold his code of honor and his family's.

Despite resenting their restraints on his individuality, he valued his schools' honor codes. They informed his own, as did the examples of his father's and grandfather's "Never lie, cheat, or steal" creed, and

the values he discerned in the literature he loved, especially Hemingway's odes to courage and self-sacrifice. The occasions when he acted
in accord with his conscience, often at risk to his own interests, are
numerous. The times when he tried to ignore his conscience are van-
ishingly few. He wanted to prove himself a person of integrity and
moral purpose. He intended that his service in public office should do
good in the world, and he mostly stuck to it. His mistakes were of the
head but rarely the heart.

I joined him in Arizona in August 2017 to work on our last book
and assist with interviews for *60 Minutes* and an HBO documentary
about him produced by Kunhardt Films. It had been a little over a
month since he'd had a glioblastoma tumor removed from his frontal
lobe, and we were all still in the shock-and-awe phase of coming to
terms with his diagnosis. He had been the most poised and upbeat
among us that weekend, and in both interviews he was easygoing,
funny, and honest. But it's fair to say that off camera he was more wistful and quieter than we were used to seeing him. He hiked with his
daughter Meghan to the top of the hill above their little valley, and
they sat quietly on a bench there to take in the familiar panorama.
We talked about his prognosis that night while he grilled ribs, what
he hoped to achieve in the time left to him, and how he didn't want to
upset his family, but neither did he want to deceive them or himself
about his chances. He did most of the talking as I murmured banal
reassurances. I poured him a vodka, and he tapped his glass against
mine and said, "Here's to you, pal. Who knows, maybe I'll get lucky
again, but if not, no complaints. I'm eighty-one years old. No one's
cheated me." He turned his attention to the Diamondbacks game on
the television before coming back to the subject on all our minds. "I've
had a great life. Seriously. Who's had a luckier life than me? Nobody."

We drove down to Phoenix the next afternoon. It was a drive he
had made a thousand times, and he was far away in his thoughts. He
had grappled with the reality of mortality many times in his life, but I
suspect on this occasion he might have found his reserve of hope insufficient. He and Cindy invited me to their Phoenix condo for dinner
that night. When I arrived, I found him sitting at their kitchen table

while Meghan prepared the meal; he was calling the family of each of the ten sailors who had perished when the USS *John S. McCain* collided with an oil tanker off the coast of Singapore. To each father, mother, or spouse, he offered his condolences and asked how he could help them. He gave each of them his cell phone number and invited them to call him if they needed anything. Each time he hung up, he called a staffer in Washington and gave instructions on how to help. He was not the commander in chief. He wasn't in the sailors' chain of command at all. But the ship was named for his father and grandfather, and as he struggled to come to grips with his own crisis, he felt a responsibility to provide the bereaved what assistance he could.

He called himself, variously, "the luckiest man on earth," "the luckiest man you'll ever meet," or "the luckiest man you know," and he believed it. He lived an adventurous, eventful, influential, and exciting life. He never stopped feeling that he had been blessed by providence more than most people were. His rebellious teenage years, his lackluster performance at the Naval Academy, his early mixed reputation in the navy, the crashed airplanes, the close scrapes with death, a disaster at sea, and five and a half years in prison where he almost died, all of that was followed by his rise to a position of national and international prominence from which he could do good in the world and help make history. "Unbelievable," he would say when he finished reciting the examples of bad behavior and narrow escapes that had not thwarted his ambitions. "Fifth from the bottom of my class, and the Republican nominee for president. Unbelievable." Even at the end he genuinely marveled at his good fortune. He was superstitious and perhaps not entirely conscious of the fact that he had, for the most part and sometimes in dire circumstances, made his own luck.

PROLOGUE

The society column in the August 31, 1936, edition of the *Panamanian American,* an English-language newspaper for Americans stationed in Panama, carried the brief announcement.

Lt. and Mrs. J.S. McCain Jr., of the Submarine Base, are the parents of a son born Saturday afternoon at the Submarine Base Hospital.

He was christened John Sidney McCain III. He should have been the fourth. His great-grandfather, a landowner and local eminence in Carroll County, Mississippi, was the first John Sidney McCain. For reasons never explained to me, the McCains didn't start counting John Sidneys until his grandfather came along.

His people on both his father's and mother's sides were southerners. He had ancestors of Scots-Irish and English descent in Mississippi, North Carolina, South Carolina, Virginia, Arkansas, Texas, Tennessee, Kentucky, and Alabama. The McCains were from Mississippi by way of North Carolina and Northern Ireland. McCain was kin to the novelist Elizabeth Spencer, his father's cousin, who grew up in Carroll County. She describes the Mississippi McCains in the early twentieth century in her memoir, *Landscapes of the Heart:*

Absorbed in their affection for one another, close to the point of clannishness, knowing pride as a rightful attribute, valuing honesty, integrity, and intelligence. They were all "smart," that is to say, even after a lost war, they could regroup and go on with their liveliness of intellect, their unquestioned traditions of manners and friendliness. They were welcoming people.[3]

John Sidney McCain III said that because of his itinerant childhood, he never felt particularly southern, even though the McCains' Mississippi plantation was in the family's possession throughout his boyhood. He spent summer vacations there, fishing and riding horses. He briefly resided there during one of his father's deployments, and he attended the area's one-room schoolhouse. He remembered affectionately his uncle Joe, Joseph Pinckney McCain—his grandfather's younger brother who ran the place—as a peppery, wisecracking smart aleck, qualities that would in time describe the McCain I knew. I've seen accounts that suggested alcoholism and depression afflicted the uncle who appeared so lively and gregarious to his nephew. His wife had died young in 1938. As would he, fifteen years later, from an accidental shotgun discharge. "Could've been suicide," the senator suggested while we were collaborating on our first book, *Faith of My Fathers*, "although I don't know that for a fact."

"I'm not from anywhere," he remarked with a note of regret. He hadn't felt "part of what people with hometowns and regular families had," he said. "We were a navy family." When I asked him for a list of places he had lived prior to high school, he looked puzzled, as if he couldn't understand why anyone would be interested in the details of his nomadic childhood. He ticked off a few places without much thought, seemingly bored by the effort. "Panama, where I was born, but I don't remember it. Pearl Harbor. New London. San Diego for most of the war. Jacksonville. Portsmouth. Portland, Oregon, for a while." His thoughts trailed off, and I moved on to another question. He had spent a couple of elementary school years and gone to high school in Alexandria, Virginia. He lived in Alexandria as an adult, too, including during his first term in the Senate. I once suggested to him that if you totaled the years he had resided there, Alexandria was the closest thing he had to a hometown, a southern hometown at that, if you can consider a Washington suburb southern. He laughed and gave me a variation of a line he had used to great effect in his first race for Congress: "That would probably be Hanoi, then."

During the 2000 presidential campaign, McCain told Jake Tapper, who was reporting a story for *Salon* magazine about slaves owned by the antebellum McCains, that he considered himself a military man, not a southerner. It would be "ridiculous," he said, to campaign in South Carolina as some kind of "good ol' boy."[4] The dismissal didn't imply an aversion to his southern roots or indifference to his family history. He was interested in it, intrigued by it, proud of the distinguished military careers it produced—four McCains risen to flag rank and buried in Arlington National Cemetery—and often amused by it. However, he had a kind of detachment from it, which didn't appear to be based on anything more than the fact that he had grown up not in one location, among an extended family, but all over the place and with a frequently absent father. I think he felt that to fake an intimacy with people he hadn't lived with or known very well would tarnish the relationship with falseness.

When asked by Tapper and other reporters how he felt about his family's slave-owning past, McCain offered an appropriate acknowledgment of slavery's iniquity. Privately, he was nonplussed. Why should he be expected to feel differently about slavery or the antebellum South than any of his questioners? He wasn't nostalgic for Old Dixie. He wasn't even a southerner. "Your ancestors owned slaves and fought for the Confederacy," I said, defending the press's interest in the subject. "It's part of your family history."

"Well, I didn't," he replied, "it's not part of my history."

"In a way, it's like the military tradition in your family history. It's an interesting part of your background, and people want to know about it."

"Yeah, but I served in the military. That's the difference."

He visited the family elders in their environs, was familiar with their stories, and was charmed by much of it, but felt himself more an observer than an intimate member of their clan. Still, the attitudes of his southern forebears, and of ancestors in earlier generations who distinguished themselves in war, offer parallels to qualities in his own personality. No doubt those qualities derived in part from the person-alities of his father and grandfather, who were steeped (especially his grandfather) in the traditions of the Mississippi McCains. Certainly, his high-spiritedness, literary enthusiasms, and craving for adventure were an inheritance from the McCains and from his mother.

Elizabeth Spencer again, explaining the decision by her uncles Bill and Sidney, McCain's great-uncle and grandfather, to leave Mississippi:

> What could they do around farms and small towns in an im-poverished area, not yet healed from a civil war? The law? The church? Nothing there seemed to challenge them.
>
> I wonder if their dreams were fed by their reading. They fa-vored bold adventure stories and poems—Kipling, Scott, Ste-venson, Henty, Macaulay, Browning. Stuck away in trunks in the attic in Carrollton, school notebooks I came across . . . were full not only of class notes but also original verses that spoke of heroism and daring deeds. Their Latin texts with Caesar's Gallic Wars were in our bookshelves. They were cavalier.[5]

Another observation interjected a note of foreboding in Spencer's narrative: "All his boys"—meaning J. S. McCain's four sons—"had a weakness for drink" and were a "constant worry" to her mother, their sister.

The McCains, including the Canadian family that founded McCain Foods, are descended from a fifteenth-century Scottish Highlander, Mac Eáin.[6] Many of his descendants are believed to have been promi-nent supporters of Mary, Queen of Scots, who absconded to Ireland to escape the wrath of Queen Elizabeth. The senator's branch is believed to have fled Scotland for Ulster in the seventeenth century, and from there in the next century to colonies in America, bearing variations of the McCain name. The first American of his patrilineal forebears, Hugh McCain, with his wife, Agnes, and six children, emigrated in 1778 from County Antrim to Caswell County, North Carolina, and built an estate there.

Hugh's grandson William Alexander McCain moved the family to Mississippi in 1848 and acquired a landholding that encompassed two thousand acres of delta flatland spread beneath the low hill where he built his manor house. When the original house burned down in 1889, the family confiscated a house on the property that belonged to a former slave and enlarged it. William's wife, Mary Louisa, admired the novels of Walter Scott and wanted to name the place Waverley. But the name that stuck was the old Choctaw name for the area, Teoc, which meant Tall Pines.

In time, William McCain would acquire more than a hundred slaves to work his cotton and corn fields, although another estimate put the number at fifty-two. Many of them shared the surname McCain, and some continued to work the land after the Civil War as sharecroppers. The descendants of two former Teoc slaves, Isom and Lettie McCain, refer to themselves as the "black McCains." Country blues legend Mississippi John Hurt was born on the plantation to former slaves, Mary Jane McCain and Isham Hurt.

William McCain died in 1863 or 1864 defending slavery either as a private in the 5th Mississippi Cavalry Regiment or in a Mississippi militia company.[7] William and Mary Louisa had six children. Their oldest son, Joseph Warren McCain, enlisted in the 20th Mississippi Infantry Regiment and was reported to have fainted at the sight of blood in his first battle, and been left for dead on the battlefield. Their second son, the original unnumbered John Sidney McCain, born in 1851, tried to enlist, too, but as he was only fourteen in the war's last year, he was rejected for being underage. With his mother and an uncle, he managed Teoc in his father's and older brother's absence.

The fifth child, Henry Pinckney McCain, was the first McCain to make a career in the U.S. military. A graduate of West Point, class of 1885, he was assigned his first post as a second lieutenant at a western fort in Montana. He saw service in the Philippines near the end of the Spanish-American War and was present for the Battle of Manila in August 1898. He was made adjutant general of the army in 1917 and has been called "the father of the selective service" for organizing the draft in World War I. As a major general, he commanded an infantry regiment training for service in Europe that had yet to deploy by the war's end. After he retired from the army in 1921, he ran the Old Soldiers' Home in Washington, the hilltop retreat that Abraham Lincoln had used to escape the summer heat during the Civil War. Henry is buried in Arlington National Cemetery. The army's Camp McCain in Grenada, Mississippi, is named for him.

John Sidney McCain married Elizabeth Ann Young, "Miss Lizzie," in 1877 and brought her to live at Teoc. The McCain genealogy is teeming with warrior forebears and includes eminent martial ancestors such as William the Conqueror and Charlemagne. One ancestor who mattered to Senator McCain more personally than other long-ago relations was his sixth great-grandfather Captain John Young, a progenitor in Miss Lizzie's family line. He was born in 1737 and emigrated from Northern Ireland as a child, settling in Augusta County, Virginia, near what is today the town of Staunton. He fought with the Virginia militia in actions against local Indian tribes. The late journalist and McCain biographer Robert Timberg unearthed a colorful story about Young that the captain's sixth great-grandson hadn't heard and was delighted to learn. In 1764, John and his older brother, Thomas, fought a battle with Indians in southwestern Virginia, remembered as the Battle of Back Creek. Thomas was killed and scalped. John Young tracked the culprits for three days, fought them again, recovered his brother's scalp, and brought it home to bury with his body.

Young was an officer in a Virginia militia company at the outbreak of the Revolution. He later served as an officer in the Continental Army, where he managed to impress General Washington, who placed him on his staff. That service entitled Captain Young's male descendants to membership in the Society of the Cincinnati, which is limited to one male descendant of a Continental Army officer at a time. It was several years after his father's death, while he was serving in the House of Representatives, when John S. McCain III became aware that he was entitled to membership as the eldest son of a deceased member, and he applied. He wasn't typically proud or even interested in social distinctions that he had done nothing himself to merit. I'd heard him on numerous occasions make a sarcastic remark after someone who, apropos of nothing, had made sure to inform him of his or her family's ancient social prominence. "*Mayflower* my ass," he had said about one such acquaintance's affectation, laughing; "Mayflower moving van, maybe." Uncharacteristically, he seemed gratified to be a member of the Virginia chapter of the Society of the Cincinnati. I'm not aware that he attended many if any meetings or other functions at the Massachusetts Avenue villa that serves as the society's headquarters. But he was genuinely pleased to have an ancestor who had given distinguished service in the Revolutionary War.

John Sidney and Miss Lizzie had six children, four boys and two girls. He was elected to two terms as Carroll County's sheriff in the 1890s, and later served on the county's board of supervisors. Elizabeth Spencer, who was the daughter of his fourth child, Mary James McCain, writes of him affectionately: As Carroll County Sheriff, "Mister Johnny was said to have dealt justly with black and white alike and to have been averse to violence—lynching and any such lawlessness."[8]

It's important to note that, whatever virtues were observed in John Sidney McCain's character during his tenure as sheriff, Carroll County had one of the worst records for racial violence in the state of Mississippi. A conservative estimate records twenty-nine racially motivated killings between the years 1877 and 1950, a span that encompassed McCain's terms in county office. Twenty-five of the murders, however, were reported to have occurred during one bloody month in the winter of 1886, some years before McCain was elected sheriff, all related to an incident remembered as the Carrollton Courthouse Massacre. Justice for African-Americans was a scarce commodity in Jim Crow Mississippi, and no less so in Carroll County during the time of the McCain family's prominence there, irrespective of any white official's rectitude.

Miss Lizzie died in 1922, leaving John Sidney a widower for the next twelve years. He lived at Teoc with his youngest son, Joseph Pinckney McCain, and died in 1934. John McCain III was born two years later and never knew him. He didn't recall hearing many stories about him from his McCain relatives; he knew John Sidney had tried to enlist in a Confederate militia company and had been a sheriff. He read with interest Elizabeth Spencer's account of him. Trent Lott once showed him a document noting that his great-grandfather had endorsed a Lott ancestor for some county office. But he mostly regarded him as the father of the two McCains who intrigued him the most.

He liked best the stories about unorthodox, high-spirited behavior in his family, and none offered more entertainment than stories about his great-uncle William Alexander McCain and his grandfather John Sidney McCain Sr.

Bill was the oldest, born six years before Sidney, who was called by his middle name to avoid confusion with his father. They looked alike in old pictures, a lot like their father and "Uncle Pink," as they called Henry Pinckney McCain. Rail-thin, slight stature, long neck, and a narrow face that bears a trace of mirth even in formally posed portraits. Yet you could see in Sidney's Naval Academy yearbook photograph how his youthful face could, by middle age, under the strain of dangerous service and what he laughingly referred to as his "riotous living," be described as wizened.

Bill was called "Wild Bill" for his "daring horsemanship," it was said, and, one assumes, for conduct exemplified by the manner in which he asked his girlfriend's father for permission to marry her, by riding his horse onto their veranda. He attended Ole Miss for a year before receiving an appointment to West Point. He graduated in 1902 and was commissioned a second lieutenant in the 8th Cavalry and posted to Fort Riley. He served several tours in the Philippines and at various forts on the western plains, commanding one of the most remote, Fort Washakie in Wyoming. He went to artillery school and in 1915 was posted to Camp Furlong, near Columbus, New Mexico, when relations with Mexico were growing tense due to the actions along the border by bandit and revolutionary Pancho Villa. Bill had brought his wife and daughter with him to New Mexico. On March 9, 1916, a band of Villa's guerrillas, numbering as many as four hundred, raided Columbus and Camp Furlong. The McCains were forced to abandon their hacienda and hide in a nearby mesquite grove, where they were joined by another officer. One of the marauders discovered them by accident. Bill pointed his shotgun at the man's chest and pulled the trigger, but the gun had been loaded with birdshot and the blast didn't kill him. Author Max Boot, in his 2002 book, *The Savage Wars of Peace: Small Wars and the Rise of American Power*, gives a bloody account of what happened next:

> The men grabbed the wounded Mexican and realized he had to be silenced before he could give the alarm. They tried to cut his throat with a pocketknife, but it proved too dull. They finally killed him by hammering his head with a pistol, as a distraught Mrs. McCain and her little girl watched in horror from only a few feet away.

I happened to read a copy of the book that had been sent to the senator by the publisher. I showed it to him and then wrote Boot a note informing him that his subject was the senator's uncle. I received a one-line reply: "That is one fighting family."[9]

Wild Bill rode with General Pershing into Mexico to punish the raid and capture Villa. They didn't achieve the latter objective, but the army gained valuable training for their next expedition, to Europe the following year, where Wild Bill, promoted to lieutenant colonel, again served under Black Jack Pershing's command, this time as an artillery officer in France. He fought at St. Mihiel and in the Meuse-Argonne offensive, and received the Distinguished Service Medal. After the war, he served in military intelligence before transferring to the Quartermaster Corps, taking command of the Philadelphia Quartermaster Depot after a polo accident left him permanently injured. He retired in 1942, at the rank of brigadier general, after forty years in an army uniform. He died in Doylestown, Pennsylvania, in 1960 at eighty-one, a very old age for a McCain of his generation, and is buried in Arlington next to his younger brother, Sidney, who preceded him in death by eighteen years.

John Sidney McCain Sr. was "Slew" to friends and acquaintances made after he left Mississippi. At his brother Bill's suggestion, he took the Naval Academy entrance exams to practice for the West Point exams. But when he did well enough to be surprised with an

appointment to Annapolis, he took the bird in the hand and joined
the United States Naval Academy class of 1906, the first of four John
Sidney McCains to enter those gates. It appears he acquired "Slew" at
Annapolis; it was one of several nicknames his classmates bestowed
on him. I asked his grandson why he was called that. "No idea," he
said, shrugging. His mother and brother couldn't enlighten me, either,
other than to suggest it might have been an obscure reference to his
Mississippi roots.

Like his son and grandson, Slew was an academic underachiever
at Annapolis and an overachiever when it came to rules infractions
and accumulating disciplinary demerits, 189 in his first year alone.
Most of them were for minor offenses, sloppiness, smoking, card
playing, and other common misbehavior; one punishment was for a
more serious offense, disrespect to a superior officer. Slew was popular among his fellow midshipmen and his instructors, who perceived
his leadership qualities. He suffered a serious hearing loss his junior
year. The medical officer who diagnosed his condition recommended
he be dismissed from further service. The academy superintendent
successfully appealed to the surgeon general to approve a waiver of
the physical requirements until his final physical examination before
graduation the following year. The ailment must have resolved itself,
as there is no mention in that subsequent examination of any disqualifying deficiency.

He reported to the USS *Chesapeake* for his first summer training
cruise at the Naval Academy. There he met Midshipman William
Frederick Halsey Jr., class of 1904, called Bill by his family and friends,
and Bull by the press corps who would cover him in World War II. It
was the beginning of a lifelong friendship between the two comrades
in arms.

He graduated seventy-ninth in a class of 116, an undistinguished
rank, to be sure, but higher than his son and grandson would attain.
He shipped out to the Philippine Islands after graduation. He served
on a battleship, a cruiser, and a destroyer—earning the ire of one of his
skippers for poor discipline—before he reported as executive officer to
the USS *Panay,* a gunboat patrolling the southern Philippine Islands,

with Ensign Chester Nimitz, USNA class of 1905, in command. The future commander in chief of the Pacific Fleet in World War II and his subordinate, the future commander of a fast carrier task force in the fleet, remembered their service on the *Panay* as the time of their lives. "Those were great days," Nimitz wistfully recalled.

Slew McCain returned to the United States in 1909 on board the USS *Connecticut,* the flagship of Teddy Roosevelt's Great White Fleet. Defying Congress, the headstrong president (and hero to Slew's grandson) had ordered the fleet halfway around the world as a demonstration of American power projection, then left it to Congress to appropriate the funds needed for it to steam home.

That same year, Slew married Katherine Vaulx of Fayetteville, Arkansas, six years his senior. Kate, as she was known, had been one of his instructors at Ole Miss. They were an example of opposites attracting, to an extent. She was self-disciplined and well mannered. Slew was not. But they shared a love of literature and often read aloud to each other selections from favorite authors. She tolerated with grace the demands on their family imposed by her husband's career and his long absences. And though she is said to have remonstrated with him over their effect on his health and their circumstances, I never heard her described as terribly censorious about Slew's vices, the cigarettes, bourbon, gambling, and chronic profanity he so enjoyed. She was charmed by his vivacity, likely against her better judgment. They were, by all accounts, devoted to each other. Two years after their wedding, on January 17, 1911, the McCains welcomed their first child, John Sidney McCain Jr., called Jack. His father was at sea, and Katherine had been visiting her sister in Council Bluffs, Iowa, when she went into labor.

Her grandson remembered Katherine McCain as punctiliously formal. When he stayed at her home in Coronado, he was summoned to tea and dinner by a maid ringing a bell at exactly four and seven every day. If he took more than a few minutes to respond, she'd send him away. But politely. "She always mentioned she had looked forward to seeing me," he recounted.

The John S. McCain III of my experience didn't go in for that kind of formality. On the contrary, he scorned it. But when he talked about his grandmother, it was easy to detect his affection for her, and his respect. He avoided displays of starchy decorum in his own life and, whenever possible, the company of people who exhibited it. But there was something about Kate McCain—perhaps her intelligence or her equanimity in the face of adversity or her obvious comfort in her own skin while living with a husband with a distinctly different style—that made her propriety impressive to him. "She had standards," he recalled, "and by God, she stuck to them." Considering the rowdy family she had joined, maybe her gentility made her in his eyes something of a nonconformist, a personality type he usually found irresistible.

Perhaps, too, his memories of her were tinged by nostalgia for the days he spent with her, sleeping in his absent father's old room amid the volumes his father had treasured in his boyhood, books by Stevenson, Twain, Cooper, Tarkington, and Burroughs, works that his son read and reread in his grandmother's house and loved as much as his father had. John told me a few times about his days in Kate McCain's decorous home when he discovered he and his father shared the same taste in literature. Maybe he forgot he had told me the story or maybe the memory was such a fond one, an enduring connection to the old man, that he liked to summon it regularly.

While Wild Bill was chasing Pancho Villa with Black Jack Pershing, Slew McCain was serving as executive officer on an armored cruiser patrolling Mexico's Pacific coast. And while Bill commanded field artillery in France, Slew served on a cruiser escorting convoys across the treacherous, U-boat–infested Atlantic. Their paths diverged after the war. Bill took up intelligence work before transferring to the Quartermaster Corps. Slew was assigned to the navy's Bureau of Navigation and later graduated from cruisers to battleships. He assumed his first command in 1926, of an old freighter the navy had pressed into service as a transport ship. He attended the Naval War College in Newport, Rhode Island, in 1928, while his son, to his delight, was preparing for a career of his own at the Naval Academy. There he studied the classics in naval strategy and tactics, especially the works of Alfred Thayer Mahan, among others, a favorite of Teddy Roosevelt's as well as Jack's.

He studied naval aviation, too, still in its early days, but he realized its growing importance. He wrote two theses at Newport, both foreign policy treatises, which I discovered only recently when reading William Trimble's *Admiral John S. McCain and the Triumph of Naval Air Power.*[10] When I read that he had chosen foreign policy as the subject of his theses and, in one of them, offered a prescient warning about Japan's ambitions, I imagined how much that would have pleased his grandson, who devoted much of his public life to debating, influencing, and conducting foreign policy.

Slew's "riotous living" had ruined his health by the age of fifty. He suffered acutely from ulcers. His teeth were gone, and a set of ill-fitting dentures clicked and caused a whistle when he spoke. He was recalled by some acquaintances as an anxious man. He was also known as a brave, considerate, and inspirational leader. He had a high-pitched cackle for a laugh, a gambling den or horse track in every port, and a bourbon and branch water in hand. He wrote unpublished works of fiction under the pen name Casper Clubfoot. He didn't wear shoes in his office, and he favored a notably irregular navy aviator's cap with its crown removed. He loved the navy and believed it was the best way of life a man could find. He was almost a caricature of an old salt, skinny, stooped, cussing, animated, and funny. Sailors who served under him, and revered him, called him behind his back—but with affection—"Popeye the Sailor Man." His grandson remembered him as a lively, ebullient character who "looked older but acted younger than his age." He rolled his own cigarettes, Bull Durham, one-handed, and messily, and always had one dangling from the corner of his mouth. He gave his empty tobacco bags to his grandson, the child he played with, teased, praised, and appeared to favor whenever they were in each other's company. The child's mother, Roberta, recalled her father-in-law announcing one night when the child was an infant, "That boy has the stamp of nobility on his brow." They entertained each other, and their act entertained the rest of the family. "Each other's favorites," Roberta called them.

It was when Slew McCain reported to Pensacola Naval Air Station in 1935 that his legend acquired one of its most colorful stories.

Fifty-one years old, a navy captain, he had decided he was going to be an aviator. A new navy regulation required prospective aircraft carrier skippers to learn to fly. And so he did, even if he never learned to do it well. "The base prayed for his safe return each time he flew," one subordinate recalled. But he stuck it out through the regulation training, accumulated the necessary hours flying solo and cross-country, pulled off sea landings, carrier landings, catapult launches, and earned his wings after fourteen months. He had just turned fifty-two, younger by six months than his friend Bill Halsey had been when he earned his wings, and robbed Slew of the distinction of being the oldest navy officer to do it.

That same year Slew assumed command of the naval air station at Coco Solo on the Atlantic side of the Panama Canal Zone, where, by happy coincidence, his son Jack was stationed as executive officer on a submarine. They both attended the christening ceremony for John Sidney McCain III—Johnny, the family called him. There is a well-known photograph of the occasion, with both men seated on a bench, Johnny's father in a white flannel suit, a slight smile on his closed lips, and his grandfather wearing his navy whites, holding the child in his christening gown, grinning from ear to ear. The following year, the smiling grandfather took command of the USS *Ranger*, the first navy ship built to be an aircraft carrier.

The first command of Rear Admiral John S. McCain Sr. in World War II was of all land-based airpower in the South Pacific at the advent of the Solomon Islands campaign and the invasion of Guadalcanal, an operation that naval historian Samuel Eliot Morison described as one of "the most bitterly contested in [U.S.] history." The admiral oversaw air attacks against the Japanese fleet in naval battles for the island. He shipped planes to Henderson Field, the air base that the 1st Marines fought hand to hand to control. He put himself in harm's way, flying in B-17s, leading convoys of fighter planes to Henderson. He was said to have wept, his grandson told me, over the casualties suffered by his pilots and the marines counting on them for protection, ammunition, gasoline, and other supplies. He held the command for a little over five months before he was summoned to Washington in October

1942 to run the Bureau of Aeronautics. The fight for Guadalcanal continued another four bloody months. He would return to the island in the campaign's last weeks to confer with Halsey and Nimitz. One of the first stories his grandson told me concerned a notorious incident during that last visit. Japanese bombers attacked Henderson the night when the three admirals were there. They had received the same treatment the night before on Espiritu Santo, indicating that Japanese military intelligence knew their itinerary. The attack at Henderson occurred after the admirals had gone to bed. Halsey and McCain fled their huts together and jumped into different trenches. Slew chose a latrine ditch. The latrine had been moved earlier that day, but the trench had yet to be filled in with dirt. He spent the night there, up to his waist in waste. The story quickly spread around the navy—an amused Halsey made sure of that.

As head of the Bureau of Aeronautics, Slew was the navy's air boss, overseeing the production and maintenance of all naval aircraft and the training of their crews. He rushed Avengers and Wildcats to the Pacific, found the personnel to fly and maintain them, and spent his nights at the Army and Navy Club in downtown Washington, drinking and playing cards.

He returned to the Pacific theater as a vice admiral for the last year of the war, where he commanded two fast carrier task forces, the first one in the Fifth Fleet and the second in Halsey's Third Fleet. In that capacity, he was one of a handful of flag-rank contemporaries who transformed naval aviation from a tactical force to a strategic power. He is credited with important innovations in the use of attack carriers. With his talented, innovative operations officer and navy ace Commander John "Jimmy" Thach, Slew helped design new tactics for carrier-launched operations, including a defense against kamikaze attacks, "the big blue blanket," that was adopted by all carriers in the Pacific theater. When Slew's grandson and I collaborated on *Faith of My Fathers*, he tried to explain one of Thach's innovations to me—using his hands as aviators do to illustrate—an air combat formation called the "Thach Weave," which the senator had flown in Vietnam.

McCain's carriers launched strikes against the Marianas, the Philippines, Formosa, Okinawa, and the Japanese home islands. His assaults on Japanese airfields on Formosa destroyed more than five hundred enemy planes. A Japanese counterstrike crippled two of his cruisers, the USS *Canberra* and *Houston*. Rather than order them abandoned and scuttled, Slew steamed his task force toward the attacking Japanese force and used his ships to provide a protective screen around the cruisers as they were towed to safety, encountering fierce resistance from waves of enemy sorties. His planes continued operations against the airfields on Formosa before finally scattering the Japanese ships. Halsey decorated him with the Navy Cross for his actions.

One of the most memorable episodes in Slew's combat command concerned a battle he wasn't supposed to be in. Elements of two navy fleets, the Third and the Seventh, participated in the Battle of Leyte Gulf under separate commands. When Halsey was baited into taking his Third Fleet on a chase after a Japanese decoy force, he left a Seventh Fleet carrier group protecting the American landings at Leyte, code-named Taffy Three, vulnerable to attack by a larger Japanese force. The ensuing Battle of Samar, named for a nearby island in the Philippines archipelago, would prove the deciding brawl in the battle for Leyte Gulf, which itself would prove to be the last significant stand by the Imperial Japanese Navy. Facing a superior force, Taffy Three's commander, Rear Admiral Clifton Sprague, asked Halsey, whose fleet was far to the north, for help, as did the Seventh Fleet commander, Vice Admiral Thomas Kinkaid. Halsey replied that he would dispatch Task Force 34 to steam to Sprague's aid. Sprague's ships fought the Japanese force as gamely as they could, but the situation grew dire, with no Third Fleet task force in sight. Nimitz sent Halsey a blunt message: "WHERE IS, RPT, WHERE IS TASK FORCE 34?" After a few minutes, an incensed Halsey signaled back, "I HAVE SENT MCCAIN." Slew McCain's task force was 350 miles to the east, headed for a refueling station. But the old man had monitored Kinkaid's messages to Halsey and, on his own initiative, had already turned his carriers around and was steaming at top speed toward the fight. He realized he wouldn't get there in time, and after receiving Halsey's order, he launched his aircraft, knowing they had enough fuel to reach the battle but not enough left to return to their carriers; they would have to land in the Philippines or on Seventh Fleet carriers. The planes helped turn the tide of the battle. The admiral commanding the Japanese force was interviewed after the war and allowed that he had decided to retire from the battle when he received intelligence that a large, unexpected air strike was on its way. He had nearly reached the American landing force when he broke off the attack.

As he was during his first combat command earlier in the war, Slew was popular with the men who served under him, officers and enlisted. He worried about them, and they seemed to know it. He was said to wait anxiously for the return of his aviators from every strike, leaning on a rail chain-smoking and looking toward the horizon, counting the number of planes returning in the hope he hadn't lost any. He often waited on the flight line to greet the returning pilots, asking them questions, giving them attaboys. "Whenever a pilot was lost, it was not just a sad thing," John Thach said of him, "it seemed like a personal loss to him, and it took a lot out of him." Secretary of the Navy James Forrestal described him as "a fighting man all the way through." Halsey called him "not much more than my right arm."[11]

Near the end of the war, a typhoon killed six sailors and damaged four carriers and destroyed many planes. Both Halsey's and Slew McCain's decision-making in their efforts to avoid the storm were found wanting by a navy court of inquiry. Halsey was too popular with the American public to fire, but Slew was expected to retire from the navy. He was distressed by the decision, though he was subsequently informed that he would be appointed the first head of the new Veterans Administration in Washington. He was sixty-one years old and looked much older. Subordinates closest to him believed him to be ill. Some thought he'd had a heart attack at sea and pretended it was his ulcers. He didn't want to attend the surrender ceremony, but Halsey ordered him to be there. He was his usual manic, funny, and profane self on the USS *Missouri*, where, to all appearances, he seemed to enjoy himself. He is seen in photographs of the ceremony standing in the first row of flag officers. Visitors to his grandson's Senate office were often treated to a tour of its memorabilia by the senator, which invariably included a look at the famous photograph, the tour guide pointing at the gaunt, stooped figure with head bent, informing them, "That's my grandfather, right there."

After the ceremony, Slew made his way to a submarine tender anchored in Tokyo Bay, the USS *Proteus,* to meet his son Jack, who had brought a captured Japanese submarine into port. Slew and Jack McCain, who were as close as any father and son ever were, would never see each other again. Slew arrived home at Coronado four days later. The next night, Kate arranged a welcome-home cocktail party, where he dropped dead of a heart attack. His obituary ran on the front page of the *New York Times,* contending that he "fell as he might have fallen in battle." Chief of Naval Operations Ernest King maintained the same, that Slew had been "killed by the stress and strain of war." President Truman sent condolences, and many of the most senior military brass headquartered in Washington attended the funeral. A popular radio network broadcaster of the time remembered Slew as "one of the world's greatest carrier task force commanders, an outstanding example of American manhood at sea."

Senator McCain kept a photograph of the reunion on the *Proteus* on his office desk. When I walked into his office for our first interview on the book we were to write about his family, he was seated on his leather couch, holding the picture in his hand. "Let's start with this," he instructed, and we did. The book begins with: "I have a picture I prize of my grandfather and father, John Sidney McCain Senior and Junior, taken on the bridge of a submarine tender, the USS *Proteus,* in Tokyo Bay a few hours after World War Two had ended."[12]

He was nine when his grandfather passed away, and he remembered it as a shock that sapped the family's vitality. "It hung over us for a while," he said, "especially my dad." When he was some years older, his mother told him she had returned to California from the funeral to find his father waiting for her on the tarmac, weeping. He had tried but failed to make it back from the Pacific in time for the funeral. He confessed he was glad he hadn't been there. "It would've killed me," he told her.

In our interviews for the book, John twice recalled one particular memory. In 1953 the navy commissioned a new destroyer, built at Bath Iron Works, and named it for Slew, the *John S. McCain.* Admiral Halsey was scheduled to speak at the commissioning. The McCain family was in attendance. As Halsey started to tell of his friendship with Slew, he broke down, and he kept sobbing until he gave up trying to speak and sat down. At the reception afterward, an embarrassed Halsey made his apologies to the family, who reassured him that they understood and were grateful for his attendance. After a minute or two, while hailing a waiter, the old admiral asked seventeen-year-old Johnny McCain to drink a toast to his grandfather with him. "What do you drink?" he asked. The underage teenager muttered something noncommittal in reply. "Well, your grandfather drank bourbon and branch water. Get the boy a bourbon and branch water."

The regard John Sidney McCain III had for his grandfather was uncomplicated. Whenever he told me a story about him, there was humor and warmth in his reverie that wasn't always evident in reminiscences of his father. There was not as much time spent with his grandfather as he would have liked. Slew died when John was quite young, and he had been at sea or otherwise occupied with the demands of a senior military command for most of the nine years their lives intersected. But I never detected a trace of lingering resentment over absences and preoccupations in musings about his grandfather that you could sense when he discussed his father. Both Slew and Jack were navy legends, and about each man and his legend, the man who bore his name said, "I admired the hell out of him," and he did, genuinely. But he seemed to be more of an enthusiast of his grandfather's legend than his father's. The most likely reason is that he knew the Slew McCain legend better than he knew the man himself. It was the reverse with his father. He was quick to tell you that James Michener had written about Slew in *Tales of the Pacific,* or that the crew of his flagship, the *Shangri La,* believed his funny-looking cap was their good-luck charm, or how nonchalant Slew was during a kamikaze attack, leaning on a railing as he smoked his hand-rolled cigarettes, watching his gunners destroy the diving planes. All true stories, but parts of a legend that were recounted and admired by others, too. His recollections of his father included illustrations of his legend—an angry outburst toward a senator who had insulted his sense of honor, for example. But John often talked about them as if they were lessons in leadership rather than chapters of an exciting adventure story, the way he viewed Slew's. His grandfather "loved the navy." His father "lived for the navy." That those meant different things to their namesake was clear in the elaboration he offered after the first declaration and the silence that usually followed the second.

On the same wall as the surrender ceremony photograph and the picture of John McCain Senior and Junior aboard the *Proteus,* to his right as the senator sat at his desk, hung three portraits, one of Slew, one of Jack, and one of another man, who will be discussed in an upcoming chapter. The photo of Slew could be a still from a movie. The old man is seen in profile, on board his flagship, jaw jutted, crushed cap set at a rakish angle, khaki shirt open at the collar, gaze fixed on some distant point, looking every inch the old salt. The photograph of Jack McCain was an official navy portrait, posed in his blue dress uniform, left hand on his hip, looking straight into the lens, four stars on his shoulder; the only sign of irreverence, the enormous cigar his fingers held.

However complicated were his feelings for his father, the senator honored him as reverentially as he honored his grandfather for what he considered the central act of both men's lives, the act that, in his eyes, redeemed them from their flaws and foibles. The fact that they both sacrificed their lives for the country—one actually, the other practically—was "the defining thing," he told me. "They gave everything they had—strength, courage, health, everything—to the navy and the country," and that, in their namesake's eyes, made them men of special character and conviction. They had principles, taught from father to the son, as the son's son recounted word for word. "An officer must never lie, cheat, or steal; he keeps his word. Never give a man a duty that's yours. Never let someone take the blame for your mistake." An officer's most solemn responsibility is never to risk the lives and reputations of enlisted men under his command for an order that serves his interests, not the country's.[13]

"Some officers get it backwards," Jack McCain criticized. "They don't understand that we are responsible for our men, not the other way around. That's what forges trust and loyalty."

"Mr. Seapower," navy contemporaries and appreciative audiences called Jack McCain for the practiced lecture emphasizing the navy's central importance to the West's defense in the Cold War that he regularly delivered as the navy's chief liaison officer to Congress. He had a wide social circle that included senior members of Congress. But his son described him to me as shy and insecure, ill at ease in social settings. "I think that was part of the reason he had a drinking problem," he surmised, "so he wouldn't feel uncomfortable at parties."

In our conversations, McCain stressed repeatedly how glamorous and important navy social life was in the 1930s, especially in the navy community in Hawaii when Jack McCain was a young officer and he and his vivacious wife, Roberta, were just starting their family. "The navy was a small world back then," he explained, "and the submarine service was even smaller. All the officers knew each other. Most of them had gone to the academy. You did something that hurt your reputation, everybody heard about it, and your career could be permanently damaged."

He talked as if he were a witness to the whirl of his parents' social engagements in the era that he couldn't have remembered, either because he had not been born yet or would have been too little to have memories of them. "Did you ever read Wouk's *The Winds of War*?" he asked me more than once. It was one of his favorite novels, and the way navy society is portrayed in the book, he said, "is the way it was when my parents lived there." He described the elaborate etiquette of the era as if he had practiced it. I suspect he acquired the memories from his mother, who recounted for him the rituals of calling cards and tea dances at the Royal Hawaiian Hotel and formal dinner parties, the women in white gloves and hats, the men in tailored uniforms or dinner jackets. "My dad wore his dress uniform or black tie, and my mother wore an evening gown for dinner every night, if they were going to someone's home or to a ball or if they were dining alone at home."

Jack McCain kept his feelings to himself. His manner was ordinarily gruff and direct and no less so when suffering personal anguish. When friends and well-meaning acquaintances expressed their concern for his son after he was reported missing in Vietnam, and during the five years he was held a prisoner of war, they were cut off with the same one-line response, "I pray for the boy every night," followed by silence. Some would be warned ahead of time by the admiral's aides, "The admiral doesn't discuss his son." Even his youngest son, Joe, received little paternal guidance when his parents called him with the news that John had been shot down before later reports announced he had been captured alive. "What do we do now?" he asked his father. "We pray for him," Jack answered. The McCains had received the call from Washington in their London home as they were dressing for a dinner party. Roberta asked what they would say to friends that evening. "Nothing," he instructed her, and then they left for the party. When they returned home that night, Jack took a call from his friend Admiral Tom Moorer, the chief of naval operations, who broke the news that his son likely had not survived. His plane was destroyed, and no one in his squadron had seen a parachute. Jack thanked him for the call and hung up so he could call John's first wife, Carol.

"He did pray for me," the senator recalled, "every night on his knees, aloud, my mother says." For most of his captivity, his father was CINCPAC (commander in chief, Pacific), the commanding officer of all U.S. military forces in the Pacific, including those fighting in Vietnam. He arranged for his change-of-command ceremony to be held on the *Oriskany*, the carrier his son had been serving on when he was shot down. As CINCPAC, the admiral frequently traveled to Vietnam. He usually ate Thanksgiving dinner with marines at one of the firebases near the DMZ. After dinner, he would excuse himself and walk alone toward the base's northern perimeter, then spend ten minutes or so gazing in the direction where his son was held prisoner. Years later, the subject of his father's contemplation would regularly receive letters to his Senate office from marines who had witnessed his father's practice. They usually ended with some variation of "I thought you would want to know your father was thinking of you then." He did want to know, and he was clearly touched by their accounts. But he wouldn't elaborate or show emotion himself when he mentioned them to me. I think he, too, wanted to respect the old man's privacy.

He thought his father's suppressed emotions were another contributing factor to his alcoholism. "Maybe it was his only way to let off steam when things got to be too much for him," he theorized. By "things," he usually meant the strain of a wartime command, as well as whatever it was that caused his father's feelings of insecurity. But I think he meant, too, his father's worries for his children.

Jack wasn't a man who declared "I love you" to his wife and children very often. His son Joe recalled him using the third person to express his affection: "You know your old dad loves you." I don't think any of them doubted he loved them, even if his oldest son seemed to carry some unsettled business into adulthood—not quite a grudge but an unanswered question, why had his father's love for the navy been more apparent than his love for them. "My father worked every day," he told me, "even when he was home with us, even on Christmas. After we opened our presents, he'd go upstairs, put on his uniform, and walk to his office."

Jack McCain was a binge drinker. His son was always circumspect with descriptions of his father in a state of drunkenness, but he made clear that he abhorred it. "It changed him" is all he would usually offer. "How so?" I'd ask. "Completely," he answered, "a completely different person. I didn't recognize him when he was drunk." I never succeeded in getting much more on the subject from him than that, other than an acknowledgment that his mother had acted heroically in unspecified ways to protect his father from doing permanent damage to his career. There is a well-known anecdote about Jack McCain that always gets a laugh. As the story goes, he was once asked by a reporter how could he tell his wife and her identical twin sister, Rowena, apart when, as was frequently the case, Rowena was traveling with them. "That's their problem," he answered. Funny. When people brought up that story to John, he would nod and smile a little, but in a bored way, as if he had heard it a million times, which of course he had. When I mentioned it once while we were working on the book, he cut me off sharply and blurted out with vehemence, "What my mother put up with, what she did for him . . ." Then he stopped and changed the subject.

He wasn't without sympathy for his father's struggle. He credited him for good-faith efforts to quit drinking, the long stretches of sobriety that preceded the next binge, praying to God for strength, almost sweating with anguish. He tried to understand and never stopped trying even after he thought he had identified the main culprits, the social insecurity, the strangled emotions, and World War II, when submarine skippers and their crews on R&R in isolated locations were encouraged to relieve the terror and strain of combat with tremendous amounts of booze.

I noticed a change in his tone when he talked about the war experiences his father needed to drink to recover from. It went from a matter-of-fact description to something more effusive, something close to awe. One of John McCain's most enduring wartime memories of his father—a memory he returned to again and again when he talked about his father or his father's generation of military officers—occurred on Pearl Harbor Day. The McCain family, including five-year-old Johnny, were in the front yard of their New London, Connecticut, home. A black sedan slowed down as it passed their house. The driver, a navy contemporary of Jack's, rolled down the window and shouted, "Jack, the Japs have bombed Pearl Harbor." His father went into their house wordlessly, his son recalled, "packed a bag, and went to the [submarine] base, and I didn't see him for a long time." That wasn't true, as McCain readily acknowledged when pressed. Jack McCain stayed in New London until the fall of 1942, when his submarine guided landing craft in Operation Torch, the American invasion of French Morocco. "Remember, I was pretty young at the time," he said, explaining his faulty memory, "and I really don't remember seeing much of him until the war was over. I know he was in New London for a while. But he was at the base all the time, and if he came home, it was usually late. I know we saw him before he went to the Pacific, and he was home on leave at least once. But in my memory, he left the house that Sunday morning without saying anything to us, and he didn't come back for four years. I remember seeing my grandfather a bunch of times. But I really don't remember seeing my dad."

The reason his memory of that Sunday was so clear and real, and still impressed him sixty years later, he explained to me once, was because it was the first time he was conscious of experiencing history. The urgency in the driver's voice and his father's swift, silent reaction conveyed a sense that something extraordinary had happened. "I knew right away that it was an historic day. At that age, I probably didn't know what history was. I just knew that something really big had happened, something we'd remember." He paused for a moment to relish the memory, and then added, "Looking back on it, it's like that black car was history, and it stopped at my house to take my dad."

The hazards his father braved in the war were many and serious, but on that Sunday in December, John Sidney McCain III thought his father, Lieutenant Commander John Sidney McCain Jr., was the luckiest man he knew for being summoned to his duty by history. Maybe it was only an intuition then, but it kept the memory vivid, and when Johnny McCain was old enough to understand the concept of history, he dreamed of his own summons. Until his last days on earth, the U.S. senator, nominee for president, and world statesman believed that to play a role in history, to be allowed to influence its course, was the best luck a person could have in life. Perhaps his father had believed the same.

Jack McCain skippered two submarines during World War II. He was captain of the *Dentuda* in the last year of the war. But his longest, most daring command was the USS *Gunnel*, which, after its service in Operation Torch, was ordered to join the Pacific Fleet in the summer of 1943. The eight officers and seventy-three enlisted men who served on the *Gunnel* called him "Captain Jack" and, according to the *Gunnel's* executive officer, "would do anything for their skipper." He was an aggressive commander and enough of an inspirational leader that his crews emulated rather than dreaded his aggression. In the more than two years McCain was the *Gunnel's* captain, it would survive four treacherous combat patrols, sink three freighters—sending seventeen thousand tons of cargo to the bottom of the sea—and endure multiple counterattacks with depth charges and grapnel hooks, some lasting many hours, from warships escorting the convoys the submarine attacked. He was one of the few submarine skippers to attack an enemy aircraft carrier twice. A long-distance shot, his torpedoes missed their targets, but the action was considered audacious, as the *Gunnel* didn't hunt in packs, and in a fight with a carrier and its escorts, it was decidedly overmatched. Following the second attempt at a carrier, the *Gunnel* suffered a sustained depth-charge attack as retaliation for its skipper's audacity.

After his service in the war, for which he received a Silver Star for "bravery under fire and aggressive fighting spirit," Jack didn't talk in specifics about his experiences except with men he served alongside or who had served in like circumstances. John remembered lying beneath the dining table when his parents were entertaining, and soaking in details as Jack and his contemporaries swapped war stories. But he brushed off inquiries from his youngest son, Joe, by quoting Sherman's "War is hell." One afternoon when John was on leave from the Naval Academy and contemplating his own future in the navy, he knocked on the door of his father's study, entered, and asked him to tell him about his war. Jack closed the book he was reading and spent the rest of the afternoon describing, in a matter-of-fact tone but in detail, what he had gone through, beginning with his one combat patrol off North Africa and ending with his presence in Tokyo Harbor for the surrender and his last meeting with his father.

He recounted the story of his attack on a convoy in the East China Sea that resulted in three Japanese destroyers hunting the *Gunnel* for a day, after it had already endured several depth charges that detonated uncomfortably close to the sub and shook it severely. The sub's crew had listened to the chains of a grapnel hook as it dragged along the *Gunnel*'s port side, "rattling slowly and excruciatingly," the skipper recorded in his captain's log. They dove to a depth of three hundred feet and stayed there while the destroyers searched for them with their sonar. When they drew close, the crew of the *Gunnel* could hear sonar pinging, and they prayed. After sixteen hours, they surfaced and spotted a Japanese destroyer five thousand yards to the east. The *Gunnel* tried to escape, running at full speed in the opposite direction, but the destroyer was faster, and when it had closed to within half the initial distance, its guns fired fused shells that barely missed. Jack gave the order to fire the stern torpedo tubes, then dove his submarine. Two torpedoes hit their target, sinking the enemy ship. Seconds later, the first depth charges exploded off the *Gunnel*'s stern. The sub descended again to three hundred feet as more depth charges detonated. It surfaced six hours later, needing to recharge its batteries and fill its air banks, and was immediately spotted by the two remaining destroyers. Jack took her down once more and stayed down this time for eighteen hours, running without auxiliary engines in order to keep as quiet as they could. It was hot, the temperature in the sub well over a hundred degrees, and humid; the air was fouled and unbreathable. Most of the crew had been ordered to lie in their bunks and breathe slowly. They were scared, Jack told John, "some of the younger boys were crying," and a few were delirious. That night, with no more than an hour of life left in their batteries and their air gone, Jack gave his officers two choices. The first was to surface as quietly as they could, go to battle stations, and, while running away, slug it out with whatever was waiting for them above. The other, which he opposed, was to destroy all classified materials on board, surface, and scuttle ship, then jump overboard in the improbable hope that the Japanese were feeling merciful that night and would rescue them. The officers unanimously preferred the first option. When they surfaced, ready to fight, the Japanese destroyers were spotted far in the distance. The relieved skipper and crew of the *Gunnel* steamed at full speed in the other direction.

Ten days later they arrived at Midway Island for a month's rest. Jack described the island to his son as a "bleak, inhospitable place, with more gooney birds than people." There was nothing to do there for the officers and crews but to drown the trauma of combat with liquor. And they did, tearing up the officers' club one night and driving a jeep, the skipper at the wheel, through the front door of the hotel where officers were quartered. Jack told of other strange, remote places where they had recuperated from combat patrols: the submarine base in Fremantle, Australia, for instance, where officers were assigned bungalows stocked with cases of beer and liquor, and where some idiot once threw a box of bullets into the fireplace, forcing men to dive behind furniture when the rounds started cooking off. Jack didn't regale his son with those kinds of antics; John heard those details from other sources. His father offered observations that noted the histories and unusual conditions of the places where they rested between patrols, and he gave accounts of his battles that were clear and striking but not overstated. "He told me about his war and let the facts speak for themselves," John said.[14] Any lessons from those accounts that could prove useful to the son's future navy service were left implied, not spelled out. "My dad taught me the rules of personal honor," he explained, "never lie, cheat, or steal and that kind of stuff. And he told me a navy career was the best job you could have. He used my grandfather as a role model. But he let me work out the rest for myself."

I had the sense that unsaid but implied in that reflection was gratitude for his father's discretion: He appreciated the respect it implied for him. That discretion was generous but not without limits. Jack would let his son conduct himself however he saw fit. He could be headstrong, a cutup, a rebel; he could mouth off, bend, break, or ignore rules and be punished when caught, as long as he didn't violate rules of honor or, importantly, make impossible those decisions his parents did impose on him, indirectly. They were few, the most important of which, he would still object to fifty years later, was his attendance at the United States Naval Academy. "I would have liked a say in where I went to school," he complained. He dreaded going to the academy. He dreaded worse not going and disappointing his parents, exempting himself from the family tradition, and bringing an abrupt end to the legend of the fighting John S. McCains.

"My parents never told me I had to go to the Naval Academy," he allowed, "they just told everyone else I was going." His parents introduced him to new acquaintances with "This is Johnny. He's going to the Naval Academy." He heard that "a million times." It was such an established fact that "they didn't bother discussing it with me, and I resented it."

He was bothered by other facts of his life, too, that were not nature's impositions but his family's. He read to me a passage from Elizabeth Spencer's memoir. It recalled the time his grandfather and his brothers returned to Teoc from their far-flung adventures when their father, the first John S. McCain, was ill and thought to be dying: gathered together in their father's bedroom, playing games, teasing, clearly delighting in each other's company. It intrigued him. He hadn't known that kind of tight-knit closeness in his family, and he was sorry he hadn't. John had met most of them, spent time with them, especially his uncle Joe and, of course, Slew. But the first John Sidney was dead by the time he was born, and by the time he was an adolescent, other McCains were gone, too, the survivors scattered and absorbed in their occupations. He was allowed only a privileged glance from a distance. He knew the legend of the clan, and he knew he would be pressed into its service. But I think he would have liked it to have been a more intimate experience than it was.

He regretted some effects of his itinerant childhood, although I don't recall him expressing serious misgivings about the dozen or more schools he attended, and the substandard education he received at some of the base schools. He resented having to make friends in a hurry, using his tenacity in sports and willingness to fight to attract a crowd, only to say goodbye in a year or sometimes in just a few months. He wasn't happy, either, about having been sent without being consulted to a boarding school in Virginia in the hope of improving his irregular education. But he didn't seem to feel he had suffered a learning deficiency that put him at a disadvantage.

He had looked to his parents, especially his mother, for instruction. He read books from his father's library, styling his own education, and ever after was something of an autodidact. The things he needed to know but that bored him, he left to formal instruction. The things that interested him, that thrilled him and fed his imagination, history, literature, politics, he undertook the study of himself from newspapers, magazines, biographies, histories, and novels. He carried favorite books around with him for years, dog-eared story collections, accounts of famous lives, tales of empires, their pages marked by coffee and food stains. Decades after it had happened, he still spoke with amazement about the day he discovered Hemingway's *For Whom the Bell Tolls,* and how he idolized ever after the book's protagonist, Robert Jordan, who had sacrificed his life in a cause he knew was lost for the sake of people he had come to love. John was eleven or twelve when he found a four-leaf clover in the yard, rushed into his father's library to press it in a book, and pulled the Hemingway novel set during the Spanish Civil War off a shelf. The book fell open to an account of a war atrocity, and it grabbed his attention. He started reading and didn't stop until he finished the book. He would read it many times again over his life. When I asked him once for a list of his childhood heroes, Robert Jordan was one of the first names he mentioned. "He's fictional," I observed. "I know," he replied, "but he's important to me."

He knew more than a little about lots of things and would surprise you all the time with a reference to an obscure fact or incident relevant to the subject under discussion. A McCain foreign policy aide, Richard Fontaine, recounted a trip to Malta with the senator. The visit included a brief tour of Malta's Grand Harbour. "McCain," Fontaine remembered, "waxed poetic" about the Great Siege of Malta in the sixteenth century, when the Knights Hospitaller defended the island from Ottoman invaders. "He seemed to know more details about the siege than the tour guide did." He would occasionally misattribute a quote to the wrong historical figures or assign them a history they hadn't lived; sometimes he did it intentionally, a quirk of his sense of humor. As a young navy lieutenant, he had appeared on the venerable television game show *Jeopardy!* and won. And he would have won the next night, too, but he misunderstood the "Final *Jeopardy!*" question. The category was famous literature, and the clue was something like "Cathy loved him." He scribbled down, "What is *Wuthering Heights*?" The correct response was "Who is Heathcliff?"

His father worked in Washington after World War II, before commanding a submarine squadron in the Pacific. Promoted to captain, he deployed to the Korean War as executive officer on the cruiser *St. Paul*. A series of commands at sea followed. His family lived in Washington, D.C., while he was at sea. His oldest son had accepted his destiny, an appointment to the Naval Academy, but appeared to be sabotaging his chances of graduating by accumulating a great many demerits that necessitated paternal cautions between sea deployments. His father urged him to keep his antics within limit. Jack made rear admiral in

1958, the year his troublemaking son managed to graduate, fifth from
the bottom of his class. Jack ran the navy's congressional liaison office, establishing friendships with leading members of both houses
of Congress, a political network he tended to assiduously, and which
gave him a measure of political influence in the nation's capital not
usually possessed by a one-star. In 1962 he was made chief of naval
information, another job that fostered political connections. In 1965,
as commander of all amphibious forces in the Atlantic Fleet, he commanded the invasion of the Dominican Republic. He was promoted to
full admiral in 1967, given the prestigious command of all U.S. naval
forces in Europe, and went to live in London, where he was when his
son was shot down over Hanoi and made a prisoner of war. In the
spring of 1968, on the advice of the CNO and Jack McCain's friend
Tom Moorer, President Johnson gave Jack McCain the biggest combatant command in the United States Armed Forces, commander in
chief, Pacific Command, CINCPAC.

In moments snatched when John was back from school and his father wasn't at sea or working fourteen-hour days at the Pentagon, the
older McCain could still be a distant and inscrutable patriarch. He
wasn't stern or incapable of praising his children or giving them some
of the attention they wanted from him. "He was just always working or
preoccupied mentally with work." But the grievance didn't blind John
to his father's uncommon drive and integrity. "I knew he was special,"
he acknowledged. "He became a powerful person and did it honorably."

The first time I traveled overseas with Senator John McCain, we
stopped for two days of meetings with officials in the Taiwanese government and military. On the first day, a group of Taiwanese flag officers, perhaps as many as thirty, some on active duty but most of them
retired, hosted a lunch for John. We sat at an immense round table. It
went on for hours, the conversation interrupted every five minutes or
so as one after another old man stood up, raised his glass of a Chinese
liquor that looked like some kind of whiskey, nodded at John, and
shouted, "To your father!" The others would jump to their feet and
echo the toast. Every one of them saluted John S. McCain Jr. They had
all known him when he was CINCPAC, and they obviously held him

in high regard. John smiled, stood up, and pretended to sip his drink with each toast. So did I, although I actually did take a sip each time and was a little drunk when the lunch mercifully concluded. On our way to his next appointment, I said something to him about our hosts' effusive tributes to his dad. "Happens all the time," he responded, "whenever I'm in Asia."

For intimacy in a childhood relationship, he had to look elsewhere. Fortunately, a beautiful, bright, adventurous, high-spirited, resilient presence who gave him enough attention was usually close at hand—his mother, Roberta Wright McCain. She is the daughter of a wild-catter with a notorious past, an identical twin who seemed always to be at the center of whatever social world she occupied, and John McCain was in many respects his mother's son. Roberta imparted to her son her humor, curiosity, candor, and a lively intellect that needed constant stimulation. He told me when we were working on our first collaboration that his mother had taught him "the joy of living" and that he thought he possessed "variations" of her qualities. "She was loquacious," we would write, "and I was boisterous. Her exuberance became rowdiness in me." He said she had an irrepressible spirit "that wouldn't yield to adversity," a quality she imparted to him, "as fine a gift as any mother ever gave her children."[15]

Roberta connected him to a family with as colorful a history as the McCains'. The Wrights were a southern family, too, and shared a common ancestor with George Washington, which made John the founding father's cousin many times removed. Her father, Archibald Wright, known as Archie, was born in Mississippi and moved at the turn of the century to Muskogee, Oklahoma, where he earned a repu-tation for running a gambling den raided by the authorities, and boot-legging, for which he was arrested.[16] He was described in the local press as "a well-known debonair dead-game sport." He acquired a par-cel of land from Native Americans; some of his neighbors suspected he had won it in a card game. When he struck oil on it, which made him a wealthy man, he and his wife, Myrtle, moved their family to Los Angeles, where he never worked another day in his life. Instead, he devoted himself to raising their children.

Their twin girls, Roberta and Rowena, were born in 1912 and lived in Oklahoma for their first decade. While Roberta talked in detail to her children about her upbringing in Los Angeles and her travels with her father, she didn't talk about their years in Muskogee. I doubt it was because of her father's shady past there. Anyone who knows Roberta knows she wouldn't mind having rascally relatives; it would delight her, as so much of her life did. The Archibald Wright who quit working to raise her was a doting father who told her made-up stories about fictional relatives with checkered pasts as a warning to steer clear of low behavior (though I suspect, knowing Roberta, he might have made it sound fun).

John didn't talk about Archie Wright as much as he talked about Slew McCain, but he liked him, and knew him for more years than he knew his paternal grandfather. Archie and Myrtle both died in the early 1970s, while their grandson was imprisoned in Hanoi. He was entertained by the stories Roberta told him of life in L.A. with Archie and Myrtle, and all the places to which Archie had escorted his daughters as he saw to their education in manners, morals, culture, and history. He took them to dance classes and etiquette lessons, to museums and galleries. The Wrights were inveterate travelers and took their children every summer to visit a natural wonder or two. They raised Roberta to be confident and independent and to speak her mind, and she always has.

Roberta and Rowena were two of the most pursued debutantes in Los Angeles, with crowds of boys vying for their attention. But until Roberta met Jack McCain, "I had never teamed up with any man," she said. They met on the battleship he served on, the *Oklahoma*, which was homeported in Long Beach. A friend of Jack's had escorted her aboard, and they encountered Jack McCain shaving in front of a mirror. "He had these two red cheeks," she recalled, "like apples." And she was smitten. So was he. They had courted for a little over a year when Jack proposed and Roberta accepted. Archie and Myrtle refused to give their permission. Myrtle especially was opposed to the idea of a sailor for a son-in-law. Archie, I suspect, just didn't want to give up his daughter. The two eloped in 1933 to Tijuana and were married in the room above Caesar's Bar, where the Caesar salad was invented. The only relative in attendance was Slew, who pronounced himself very pleased with the match. It was the start of a close, affectionate relationship between Roberta and her father-in-law. Archie and Myrtle got over it.

A story John liked to tell of his parents' early years of marriage concerned a discovery his grandfather had made when looking at his son's fitness report filed with navy records: Jack had been admitted to the hospital after suffering dramatic weight loss. Tuberculosis was suspected. When asked by doctors what might have caused him to lose so much weight, he suggested his diet: "My wife doesn't know how to cook and my meals are very irregular." Slew kept a copy of the report, showed it to friends, and was reported to have laughed as hard as he did the first time each time he got to the punch line.

When John talked about his mother for the first book, he did so with warmth and affection. He did stress many times that his father's career came first with her, too, even before their children. But he didn't betray any anger about it. Not a trace ever. I think he understood how much his father had needed her help. He didn't feel cheated of time spent with her. She was a single parent most of the time, in charge of moving them from one base to another, which often involved cross-country trips by car with three squabbling children for company. John remembered fighting in the back seat with his sister, Sandy, during one interminable drive west. Roberta chucked her metal thermos at John, hitting his head and denting the thermos. She drove time-consuming routes that were plotted to take them past natural, historical, and cultural landmarks, spectacular canyons and caves, rivers and Great Lakes, the bluffs at Natchez, the Petrified Forest, famous cathedrals, Mount Vernon, their itinerary meant to be a tutorial, just as her father had supplemented her education.

John was very fond of her, and proud of her, and he sometimes seemed to be as starstruck in his regard for her as most people were. "The joy of her life is learning about people and places," he wrote, "and coming to know them as well as she can; she never loses the desire to know them better. She has a remarkable capacity for delight. Life, all its adventures and many interests, thrills her as much in her late years as it did in her childhood."[17]

He was much like her. Except for one attribute—his temper. Roberta could be cantankerous but not often hot-tempered. Her son, by the time he was two, was given to raging fits where he would hold his breath until he passed out. His parents sought a medical opinion. A doctor advised dropping him in a bathtub of cold water when he lost control of himself, which they did repeatedly, until he could govern his temper a little better. Not that it didn't flare up every now and again, throughout his childhood and beyond.

He would be his own man in time, he insisted, but the influence of his extraordinary family was evident in his habits, his judgment, and the sprawl of his own adventurous life. Their respect for him, he would readily confess long after his father and grandfather had passed away, "remained the most lasting ambition" of his life.

ON THE RUN

S omeone, a campaign aide or a local reporter, tagged John "the White Tornado" for the frenetic energy he exhibited in his early years in politics. He didn't seem to like the title. He didn't say anything if you used it in his presence, but you might get a quick, unsmiling stare for your impertinence. Nevertheless, the term stuck among aides and close associates who had been with him since his first campaign, which I had not been. By the time I met him, he was a veteran politician, twice elected to the House of Representatives and serving his first term in the Senate. But I know the nickname was appropriate. I saw the prodigious energy and single-minded intensity he brought to subsequent political battles. Campaign staff, including my wife, who was a volunteer, say that nothing compared to the "superhuman" drive he had in his first campaign and years in the House, as he worked—"frantically," in the words of one—to get to know his constituents and how to represent them in Congress.

He and Cindy moved to Arizona, her home state, on March 27, 1981, five days after his father had died suddenly on a westbound transatlantic flight. They had buried him at Arlington that morning. The last thing John had done before boarding the airplane to Phoenix was turn in his navy ID. Thereafter, he was Captain John S. McCain III (Retired). Three such weighty events occurring in a single day must have made for some of the most emotionally fraught hours of his life—or I assume they did, even though his descriptions of the events in response to my prompting as we worked on another book were mostly spare and dispassionate. He mentioned the music and liturgy chosen for the funeral at Fort Myer's Old Post Chapel, and the high-powered names in attendance. His brother, Joe, had given a eulogy. John had recited from memory a Robert Louis Stevenson poem he and his father admired, "Requiem":

> *Under the wide and starry sky,*
> *Dig the grave and let me lie.*
> *Glad did I live and gladly die,*
> *And I laid me down with a will.*
>
> *This be the verse you grave for me:*
> *Here he lies where he longed to be;*
> *Home is the sailor, home from sea,*
> *And the hunter home from the hill.*

Some of the music and readings, including "Requiem," would be included in his own funeral services nearly four decades later. I know the day had to have been among his most meaningful, but for whatever reason, he tried to keep that to himself. Only twice did I detect a trace of emotion: once, when he recounted meeting the air force C-5 his parents had been traveling in when his father had his fatal heart attack. His mother had been very composed when she informed him, "John, your father is dead," and he looked over her shoulder at his father's body lying behind the passenger seats, a blue blanket covering him, his brown shoes sticking out. When he got to the detail about the brown shoes, his voice cracked.

The other small change in demeanor was a smile registering admiration for his mother's conduct at the reception following the funeral, when she had whirled about their spacious apartment, greeting guests and enlivening conversations, as always the charming hostess. She had "devoted her life," he said, to his father, but she is a stickler for maintaining a dignified comportment in adversity. The country would witness that resolve at the memorial services for her son decades later, ancient, wheelchair-bound, eyes looking straight ahead, lips pressed together, giving her granddaughter's hand a comforting squeeze, tears discreetly shed, dignified. McCain inherited much of his sense of humor from his mother. She would later joke to a reporter about her son's transition from naval officer to politician: "He started all the trouble. We were okay until he came along."[18]

When I pressed him for a recognition that the day had lasting significance to him, asking him how he felt about burying his dad and leaving the navy on the same day, he answered with something like: "Yeah, it occurred to me it was the first time in a long time that there wasn't a McCain in the navy."

"Did you regret that?" I followed up.

"Maybe a little."

"What were you feeling?"

"Tired. I felt tired."

He was forty-six years old and running for Congress the moment he set foot there, even before he knew where exactly he was running. He took a job as a public relations executive at his father-in-law's Budweiser distributorship, Hensley & Company. He had some talent for the work. Considering that his last job in uniform had been the navy's liaison to the U.S. Senate—in effect, the service's principal lobbyist to members of the Senate Armed Services Committee—you could argue he brought compatible experience to the job. But no one thought he would remain at Hensley long, not McCain, his father-in-law, or Cindy. Months earlier, the best man at his wedding, Senator Bill Cohen, had put him in touch with his chief political consultant, Jay Smith, who also advised John Rhodes, Arizona's longtime congressman and leader of the Republican minority in the House. Smith had advised McCain to be discreet about his political intentions but to start making the rounds of Republican groups, business organizations, and Rotary clubs.

John spoke about national defense mostly off the cuff or from a card with a few notes scribbled in his indecipherable hand. He included stories from his service in Vietnam, which was what his audiences were most interested in hearing, and which he delivered with humor and irony that seemed to come to him effortlessly when he talked about himself in public. His unpretentious presentation and his jokes, delivered with impeccable timing, made for a winning performance. He was charismatic. You almost suspected he had professional training somewhere along the line. He wasn't a great orator and never would be. But he had a naturalness, disarmingly candid and self-effacing, that conveyed authenticity, the most potent quality a candidate can have. He wisecracked his way to the culmination of every prison story, which always ended with a story of another POW's heroism, never his own. He demurred when he was called a hero, joking that he had merely "intercepted a surface-to-air missile with my own airplane." He praised the sandals issued by the Vietnamese that had been made from old tires. "I highly recommend them," he would say. "One pair lasted my entire time in prison." The story of his refusal of early release from prison was not part of the performance. He had talked about it publicly when he first returned home from Vietnam. I'm sure he knew its potency as part of a campaign message. I know some of his memories of it were fraught with regret and painful. Other people talked about it, though, and he didn't object. He was shrewd about how he used the war. He understood his audiences viewed his experience as the context for whatever message he delivered. He didn't need to be heavy-handed about drawing their attention to his patriotism. They knew his sacrifice. He used Vietnam to communicate other parts of his appeal, his humility and idealism.

For a time, it appeared he wouldn't have anywhere to use his natural campaign skills. He had planned to be a candidate for Congress in the 1982 midterm elections, counting on a new district being created in Maricopa County after the 1980 census. Instead, the new district was located mostly in the Tucson area. He knew that as a brand-new arrival to the state, he would have to deal with carpetbagger accusations were he a candidate for any office. An abrupt move from Phoenix to Tucson would make it harder to mount an effective defense against the charge. He wasn't disappointed for long. John Rhodes had voluntarily given up the minority leader's job in 1981, and insiders in Washington and Arizona speculated he wouldn't run for reelection in Arizona's First District, which encompassed parts of Phoenix and its suburbs. Rhodes's consultant, Jay Smith, was certainly aware of the speculation, as was his newest client, John McCain.

Rhodes called a press conference in January 1982 and confirmed the speculation. That same day, John and Cindy, who had been living just outside the district in north-central Phoenix, bought a house in Tempe in the First District. Two months later, John announced he was running to represent his new neighbors in Congress.

Before Rhodes's announcement, Jay Smith asked Grant Woods, a young public defender, to meet with McCain. Like other Arizona Republicans at the time, Grant was initially skeptical and offended by the presumptuousness of a "guy who just moves here and starts running for Congress first thing." "Let him run for the legislature," Grant remembered telling Jay. Nevertheless, he agreed to meet the prospective candidate.

"I'd never met anyone like him, his enthusiasm, his humor," he recalled. "His knowledge of issues was complete. He had done his homework. I told Jay, 'I'm in.'" Grant introduced McCain to his parents, Joe and Nina Woods, influential Republicans from Mesa in Maricopa's East Valley, who had the same reaction, as would most people once they met the candidate with the cinematic backstory and infectious energy and confidence. Grant became his closest campaign aide. McCain liked having him around; a shared irreverence cemented their friendship. Having a sharp sense of humor was a virtue to John McCain, one of the most important. After the election, Grant agreed to serve as McCain's first administrative assistant for two years, after which he would return to practicing law. He would become a prominent attorney and political figure in his own right, serving two terms as Arizona's attorney general. But he jokes, as scores of old McCain hands do, that McCain's world is the Hotel California—once you check in, you can't ever check out. Their friendship would have its rough patches, as many friendships do, but Grant was still a close McCain friend and confidant at the end.

McCain was an indefatigable campaigner. He had to be. That first campaign would always be remembered as his toughest Arizona race, the only one where he started as a decided underdog. The district was heavily Republican. The only real race was for the party's nomination. McCain was pitted against three better known, more experienced Republicans: Donna Carlson West, a state legislator from Mesa; Jim Mack, a state senator from Tempe; and the front-runner, Ray Russell, a veterinarian and Republican activist who was very popular in the East Valley's large, influential Mormon community. Each opponent had strong support in the more established parts of the district. McCain had to concentrate on areas that attracted newcomers like him— Phoenix's east side, parts of Tempe, and most important, Scottsdale.

He had to raise more money than his opponents, and he did. He raised over three hundred thousand dollars for the primary, half of it money he and Cindy loaned the campaign. He was not and never would be a prodigious fund-raiser. There were various reasons why he wasn't good at raising money. One of them was simple: He didn't like doing it, and donors could tell he didn't. He had a hard time feigning enthusiasm for a task he considered drudgery and a little embarrassing. I don't remember him ever refusing to do a fund-raiser, although it was harder to get him to make fund-raising calls, the awkward necessity of a politician's life. Sometimes he would call a prospective donor and end up discussing the news of the day without ever asking for money. He didn't complain too much about appearing at fund-raising events. He knew they were necessary, that the election loser was usually the one who had been outspent. But he didn't show the enthusiasm for the money side of a campaign that he did for its more performative functions, town hall meetings and press interviews, for example, meeting the voters in person or through the media.

He was the least known of the candidates, and Jay advised him how to increase his name recognition enough to be competitive. He met voters and raised his name ID the old-fashioned way: He knocked on their front doors. The primary was scheduled for the first week in September, which meant peak campaigning would happen in the hottest months of an Arizona summer. Grant, who often walked with him, remembers twenty consecutive days when the temperature was 115 or warmer. McCain knocked on doors six days a week for six or more hours a day, never complaining, never wilting, giving his pitch at the last stop of the day, equal parts funny and earnest, with the same energy he had given it at the first stop that morning. By the end of the campaign, he had knocked on twenty thousand doors and gone through three pairs of shoes. Cindy had one pair bronzed.

Supplementing retail politics were the upbeat, polished ads and mailers that Jay produced. "A new leader for Arizona," went the tagline. They invoked McCain's POW history and cut to a picture of him in the company of prominent senators, whom he had gotten to know as the navy's liaison officer to the Senate, and a photo with Ronald and Nancy Reagan. He had been a favorite of the Reagans since the days when the president had been governor of California, and John and his first wife, Carol, attended a prayer breakfast the Reagans had held for the returning POWs. By the time McCain ran for Congress, he believed he was still in good standing with President Reagan. "But Nancy wasn't speaking to me," he ruefully acknowledged. Mrs. Reagan was close to Carol McCain, who worked in the White House, and she was steamed about their divorce. The estrangement lasted years but wasn't permanent. They would be on friendly terms again after the Reagans left the White House. In both his campaigns for president, Mrs. Reagan went out of her way to be helpful to him.

His other relationships in Washington were helpful as well. Senators Bill Cohen and Gary Hart gave him useful advice and, in the case of the former, national Republican connections. Hart, of course, is a Democrat; he had managed George McGovern's presidential campaign and was preparing to run for president in 1984. He wasn't in a position to introduce John to political and financial contacts. But they were good friends, and Hart was a trusted source of private political advice. The senator who proved the most helpful, however, was a navy veteran and chairman of the Senate Armed Services Committee, John Tower of Texas. Tower was a nationally known Republican with an extensive national network of political friends and donors. He had been a mentor to Captain McCain and formally endorsed him shortly after he announced his candidacy, breaking a personal rule never to endorse a candidate in a Republican primary outside of Texas.

No prominent figure in Arizona—with the exception of Cindy, who campaigned as diligently as her husband—was more instrumental to McCain's success than the Republican mayor of Scottsdale, Herb Drinkwater. Ever after, McCain regarded Drinkwater with great affection and gratitude, and marveled that the immensely popular mayor had supported him in the first place, crediting his endorsement as the most important of the election. Scottsdale was key to success in the primary, and Drinkwater was routinely reelected its mayor by margins unseen outside of autocracies. He won 87 percent of the vote in one reelection and was puzzled why 13 percent had voted for the other candidate. John asked for a meeting with little hope of support, expecting to be politely brushed off with a genial noncommitment. But he gave his pitch on why he was the right candidate to represent Scottsdale in Congress, and to his surprise, Drinkwater responded, "All right, I'll endorse you. You're a good man." By the next week, Drinkwater had persuaded every member of the Scottsdale city council to follow his lead and endorse the newcomer. McCain was stunned and delighted, reflecting years later, "Herb didn't anguish about political decisions. He liked to give you an answer, yes or no, right away."

Drinkwater was also the model for McCain's accessibility to his constituents. He wanted to write about Herb in one of our books, and recounted example after example of how Herb, who used to ride around town on horseback, would stop to talk to anyone who wanted a word. He treated every Scottsdale resident as a friend and benefactor. He was happy to give even tourists a courteous audience, seeing them as future winter residents of the city he loved. One story about Herb that McCain never tired of retelling was the account of how a constituent once called the mayor at home at two o'clock in the morning. Herb heard the man out and promised to get back to him with an answer within twenty-four hours. True to his word, he called the guy back at two o'clock the next morning, apologizing for the late hour, and adding, "I knew you'd be up."

McCain made other important friends in the district whose support would give him an advantage over his opponents. The *Arizona Republic*, the state's leading newspaper, and its sister publication, the afternoon daily the *Phoenix Gazette,* endorsed him that summer. Editorial endorsements were more impactful in those days, and scoring the *Republic's* approval was considered a coup. At the time the paper had a conservative lean. The Pulliam family owned it, and its publisher, Darrow "Duke" Tully, was one of the most powerful men in the state, a self-described air force ace, two-war veteran, and colonel in the Air Force Reserve. John had been introduced to him prior to announcing his candidacy, and the two had hit it off. McCain would later concede the obvious—that there had been an element of opportunism in his friendship with Tully. Tully was a swaggering, imperious presence in the newsroom, where he was resented, and he talked more about his wartime heroics than combat pilots are typically known to do. He wasn't the type of character who normally appealed to McCain, who described him to me as "kind of full of himself." But he insisted he had liked the guy anyway, and enjoyed his company. Two years after they became friends, John and Cindy would ask Tully to be godfather to their daughter Meghan.

Just before Christmas in 1985, Tully resigned suddenly from the paper. A Maricopa County attorney, who had been accused of impropriety in a *Republic* editorial, discovered Tully had invented his military biography. He had never served in any war. He was never in the air force. It was an immense scandal and, of course, humiliating to its subject. John was stunned, he said, although years after the fact, he would describe Tully to me in a way that suggested he had a vague suspicion the man might have been exaggerating his war record. Nevertheless, as Tully was widely scorned for his make-believe heroism— nowhere more so than in the *Republic's* newsroom—John remained sympathetic to the ruined ex-powerbroker, sensing in his downfall more tragedy than outrage. This despite the fact that authentic combat veterans resent few misdeeds more than they resent acts of "stolen valor," the contemporary term for inventing a war record.

"I felt bad for the guy," he allowed, "to make up something like that, and talk about it all the time, something so easy to find out, it doesn't make sense. Something had to have happened that screwed him up." That was one of several instances when I noted McCain's reaction contrasted with the attitude of many veterans. He was right about Tully. There was a tragedy at the root of his disgrace. Tully's brother had been a marine pilot, killed in action in World War II. Their father was so destroyed by grief that he killed himself. John knew none of that at the time but had sensed that something more disturbing than egotism had caused the man's humiliation. He wasn't always the best judge of character, but he could surprise you with an intuition about someone that hadn't been apparent.

If he had an intuition about Charles Keating, he didn't share it with anyone. His friendship with Keating was another helpful association with an Arizona VIP that would not have been obtainable for most newcomers to the state's political scene. As chairman of the American Continental Corporation (ACC), Keating was one of the wealthiest real estate developers in Arizona and a heavyweight donor to state, local, and federal candidates. McCain was introduced to him at a Navy League dinner in 1981, and Keating, who had a genuine military background as a naval aviator in World War II, spontaneously offered his support, which would turn out to be considerable. Keating and his family and associates would donate well over a hundred thousand dollars to McCain's two House races and his first Senate campaign. The two men quickly became friends, and the McCains were frequent guests at Keating's Cat Cay vacation home in the Bahamas, flying there on Keating's corporate jet and enjoying day trips on Keating's yacht.

Charlie Keating had a highflier's reputation for lavish parties and extravagant gestures of largesse to his employees and friends. He was sincerely philanthropic, donating huge sums to worthy causes, especially Mother Teresa's charities. He was also overly confident of his talents as a businessman and the integrity of his business practices. There is little doubt that he genuinely admired McCain's military background and liked him personally. The two had compatibly conservative views. But Keating also gave money to candidates who didn't share his political philosophy, and he considered campaign contributions an investment for which he expected a return. When American Continental acquired a troubled California savings and loan a few years later, the investments Keating had made in the careers of five

U.S. senators, including John McCain's, would prove a disaster for all parties concerned.

By midsummer, McCain was gaining traction and creeping up in the polls. By August he was, if not the candidate to beat, not the afterthought people had expected he might turn out to be. The well-liked, genial Ray Russell still appeared to be the favorite, but he wasn't a sure thing any longer. Another opponent, Jim Mack, tried to blunt John's rise in the polls by calling Carol McCain to solicit dirt. Carol hung up on him and called John. At their next candidate joint appearance, McCain went up to Mack and informed him, "If you ever try to hurt a member of my family again, I will personally beat the shit out of you." Mack was "totally terrorized" by the encounter, Grant Woods recalled. "John meant it, too. And Mack believed he meant it."

McCain's biggest handicap in the race remained the carpetbagger label. Reporters and local pundits questioned him about it repeatedly, and he often seemed a little sheepish in reply. Why hadn't he spent a few years getting to know the state? Why hadn't he set his sights on a state or local office first? Shouldn't candidates for Congress have previous experience in office and more of a history in their district? You've only been here a year. What do you know about the issues that matter most to Arizonans? Finally, in the last candidate forum of the primary, when the carpetbagger question was raised again, McCain snapped. I suspect he had thought in advance about a more forceful answer, but witnesses recall him speaking with genuine irritation verging on anger: "Listen, pal," he began as he pointed out that he had served for twenty-two years in the navy and was raised in a navy family, which had necessitated frequent relocations. And then he gave what a veteran political columnist called "the most devastating response to a potentially troublesome political issue I've ever heard."[19] He hadn't "had the luxury," McCain explained, "of growing up and spending my entire life in a nice place like the First District of Arizona, but I was doing other things. As a matter of fact, when I think about it now, the place I lived longest in my life was Hanoi." The ovation that followed not only proved the potency of John McCain's backstory but revealed he had real chops as a campaigner.

He was "bouncing off the walls" on primary day, according to one eyewitness. He would be anxious on every subsequent Election Day, even the ones that were a foregone conclusion. Some election nights he was over-caffeinated, pestering aides for exit poll numbers and tidbits of information about turnout. Other elections—the close ones, usually—he was tight-lipped and withdrawn, giving the impression he was worried that if he said anything or betrayed any emotion, he might jinx his chances. The night of the South Carolina primary in his 2008 bid for the Republican presidential nomination, he was wound tight as a golf ball, believing the contest was a must-win for him. He was unusually grim-faced as he watched the returns, and he became annoyed when friends who had gathered in his suite began celebrating prematurely. "Stop it," he commanded, "I want to hear this," and returned his attention to the television.

The afternoon of his first election, he was so wound up, he knew he needed a distraction. He decided to go see a movie, one of the *Star Wars* sequels, starting an Election Day superstition that continued the rest of his career. He won the primary by a margin of three thousand votes over his nearest rival, Ray Russell. As expected, he strolled through the general, although he kept knocking on doors to the end. John Tower called him the day after the primary to offer congratulations and some encouragement: "Don't let your shirttail hit you in the ass," Tower exhorted.

McCain was elected in a miserable year for congressional Republicans. A recession had provoked voters to send the Reagan administration a message by adding twenty-six seats to the Democrats' House majority. The margin of the Democrats' majority surpassed one hundred members. It was not a very big freshman class of Republicans who entered the House that year, just twenty-one new members. But it was a talented group of politicians: In addition to McCain, it included future highly regarded members of the House Sherry Boehlert, Nancy Johnson, Barbara Vucanovich; and future senators or governors Tom Ridge, John Kasich, Connie Mack, Mike DeWine, and Jock McKernan. When they came to the Capitol for freshman orientation the month before their swearing-in, John brought Grant and had him attend some new-member meetings without him while McCain lobbied fellow freshmen in one-on-one meetings, asking them to elect him president of their class, which they did, overwhelmingly.

Given John McCain's reputation as a maverick, one might assume he was not the type to be interested in official leadership positions. That was the prevalent view of him, in and out of Congress. And he did operate more effectively as an informal and idiosyncratic leader. That said, he craved the responsibility of leadership, formal and informal, and sought the former with the same energy he invested in the pursuit of the latter. After all, he ran for president twice. He sought an elected leadership job in his first Senate term, too, running for chairman of the Senate Republican campaign committee, often the first rung on the Senate leadership ladder. He lost that race and wasn't happy about it. If you asked him what part of his navy record he was proudest of, he would unhesitatingly answer his command of VA 174, a replacement air group squadron (RAG), the largest squadron in the navy, based in Jacksonville, Florida. Not his years as an attack pilot flying off carriers, or as a prisoner of war in Vietnam, or as a popular navy captain consorting with senior members of the U.S. Senate, learning how to acquire and wield power. He was proudest to have been the skipper of a navy squadron, a formal leadership job in which he helped restore the reputation and morale of his command.

Among the new congressman's duties that fell to Grant during freshmen orientation week was choosing a numbered chip from a wooden box in the lottery for office space. Grant picked chip number 2. They would have one of the larger offices available, 1123 Longworth, where John McCain began his thirty-five years of service in the United States Congress.

After persuading Grant Woods to leave his law practice and be his administrative assistant, McCain hired the entire staff for the district and Washington offices without consulting him. Woods recalls expressing surprise and McCain joking, "Don't worry, you'll have to fire half of them." The staffers he had recruited included a woman hired as his liaison to the Hispanic community, who, Woods soon discovered, "couldn't speak Spanish." "He didn't need any help in Washington,"

Grant remembers. "He knew what he was doing. That wasn't the case in Arizona."

McCain had gotten to know his congressional district well enough to be elected its representative, but he was still a stranger to most Arizonans. He knew Washington better than he knew his state, and he focused his zeal on remedying the deficiency. He did not intend to remain in the House of Representatives for long. Arizona's senior senator, Barry Goldwater, was serving the last term of his illustrious career and would retire in 1986. McCain was running to succeed him from the moment he arrived at the Capitol. His ambition was an open secret in Washington and Arizona, encouraged by friends in high places in both locations, but resented by some Republican stalwarts in Arizona, including, apparently, Goldwater himself.

McCain went home nearly every weekend, a ten-hour round trip that would exhaust most people who had to do it every week. It never appeared to faze him. Staff tried to convince him to ease the strain by flying first class. "No one cares if you're in coach," Grant argued. "They elected you to go to D.C., not come home every week stuffed in a middle seat in the back of the plane. We'll make sure everybody knows you're paying for your ticket." McCain stubbornly disagreed. He would show the same stubbornness years later, when the *Washington Post* criticized him for helping an Arizona-based airline get nonstop flights between Phoenix and Washington's Reagan National Airport. An editorial suggested he had done it as a convenience to himself. Fuming, he vowed he would never take the flight, a commitment he honored for the better part of two decades before staff finally convinced him the statute of limitations on his promise had expired. Woods set up meetings for him with farmers, ranchers, businesspeople, lawyers, doctors, anyone he could persuade to spend an hour or so with the new congressman. "You just had to get them to agree to the meeting," Woods recalled, "once they talked with him, they were sold."

State party activists were another matter—not all of them but enough to be a potentially serious problem. In those early days, McCain's problem with the Republican base in Arizona was almost entirely attributable to the fact that he lacked a political pedigree in the state. Arizona's explosive postwar population growth has seen whole communities double and triple in size every decade as new residents flooded there from other states. The state is teeming with new arrivals to its workforce, professional ranks, schools, media, and politics. But ambitious newcomers are still liable to be objects of suspicion, even hostility, to people who have volunteered years of their lives building the party. Obviously, that kind of resentment eventually dies down if the newcomer can stick it out enough years to become a familiar figure. But McCain would always have a lingering problem with the base, partly because he was seen by more militant conservatives as a moderate on certain issues. Another contributing factor was that McCain seemed to grow in stature nationally as quickly as he did in Arizona politics, aggravating a grievance among some Arizonans that he was America's or the Washington press corps's senator before he was Arizona's. His opposition to the Far Right's favorite governor, the rash and tactless Evan Mecham, was another mark against him in their eyes. McCain had supported the state's Senate majority leader, Burton Barr, in the 1986 gubernatorial primary. After Mecham won and was elected governor, he proceeded to lurch from one controversy to another and was ultimately impeached. In the midst of all the turmoil, McCain called for him to step down. Many Mecham supporters never forgave him, and they formed the core of the McCain opposition within the state party. Finally, McCain's leadership of comprehensive immigration reform in the 2000s, the bête noire of Arizona fire-eaters—in partnership with Ted Kennedy, no less—was an unpardonable apostasy.

McCain was never one to let opposition from one or another quarter deter him from making a case to voters willing to hear him out. He never quailed at the prospect of a hostile town hall audience; he faced quite a few in his time, and he often appeared to relish it. In those early days, he was going to steam ahead and convert or wear down suspicious Republicans. It was harder than he expected but not so formidable it couldn't be done. Most of the resistance to him in the beginning was related to his apparent interest in succeeding Goldwater, and the fact that many party regulars felt the honor belonged to Bob Stump, a native Arizonan and longtime Arizona legislator, then serving his fifth term as a member of Congress. Stump began his career as a conservative Democrat but had switched parties the same year McCain was sworn in to the House, earning the gratitude of many Republicans in return. One of them, Barry Goldwater, was rumored to prefer Stump as his successor; certainly, his chief aide, Judy Eisenhower, tried to do what she could to thwart McCain's ambitions, and didn't bother to be discreet about it. McCain conceded to me that he hadn't expected Goldwater to be cool to him. He knew him from his navy liaison days and believed Goldwater, who had been a friend of Admiral McCain, liked him. "I knew Barry wouldn't be happy about retiring," he recalled. "But I really didn't think he'd object if I ran for his seat. Someone was going to."

Speculation about which Democrat would run to succeed Goldwater focused on the popular retiring governor, Bruce Babbitt, who would be a formidable candidate at a time when Democrats were quite competitive in statewide elections. "I figured Barry might think I had the best shot at beating Bruce and holding the seat," McCain said. "I guess I was wrong." Goldwater's reservations didn't appear to concern anything other than the short time McCain had spent in Arizona politics. He never expressed—nor, McCain believed, did he privately harbor—personal hostility toward him, and John was careful not to give him reason to do so. He paid Goldwater the respect he was due, not only because it suited his interests to avoid a public breach but because he genuinely respected him as an elder statesman and an Arizona legend. McCain was captivated by stories of the families who had settled the Arizona territory and gone on to dominate the state's politics. The Goldwaters were one of those families, and McCain's interest in their history and unfailing courtesy to his predecessor after he left office eventually warmed Goldwater to him. He regularly sought Goldwater's advice about politics and defense issues. He defended Goldwater when far-right conservatives in the state attacked him for his stance on social issues. They grew quite close in the older man's last years, and John and Cindy were good friends with Susan Goldwater, Barry's wife. When Goldwater was dying in

1998, Susan invited them to their home on Camelback Mountain to say goodbye. They spent an hour or more with Goldwater, who was conscious and didn't want them to leave. He died the next morning. When asked about it years later, McCain was still moved by the memory, and impressed that Goldwater had exited the world just as he had wanted to, "in the place he loved, looking out at the mountain, the beauty of Arizona right there."

It was another scion of an Arizona pioneer family and political legend, though, whom McCain credited more than any other Arizonan with helping him learn his state and his profession—the liberal icon with the lively wit Morris K. Udall. "No one did more for me politically in Arizona than Mo," McCain insisted, "no one." We were discussing his relationship with Udall as a subject in the second book we wrote together. "I loved him," McCain had begun the conversation.

Udall was a self-described "one-eyed Mormon Democrat from conservative Arizona" and the senior member of Arizona's House delegation. By the time McCain made his acquaintance, Udall was a veteran legislator and the powerful chairman of the House Interior Committee. McCain's affection for him began with gratitude for Udall's generosity to the newest member of Arizona's congressional delegation. "He didn't have to help me," McCain reflected, "I was nobody compared to him, a Republican nobody." He soon came to admire Udall for his wit and intelligence, for his integrity, and for his open-minded, pragmatic bipartisanship in pursuit of his goals, a style McCain would consciously emulate as he acquired seniority.

Udall had attained his status as a senior statesman without following the established route of deference to party leaders while quietly gaining seniority. He had been a leading member of the Young Turks, a coalition of reform-minded Democrats who, in the 1960s and '70s, challenged the authority of conservative Democratic chairmen. He had run for Speaker and lost decisively in 1969. He lost a closer race for majority whip two years later, despite assurances of support from a majority of his colleagues. He quipped afterward, "I've learned the difference between a cactus and a caucus. With a cactus, the pricks are on the outside." Udall lost the 1976 Democratic presidential nomination to Jimmy Carter, after which he declared, "The people have spoken, the bastards!" He called himself "old second-place Mo."

Southern Democrats ran most of the committees in the 1960s, and House barons viewed Mo as their principal antagonist. But by the mid-1970s, buttressed by a large post-Watergate class of reformers, power had shifted to the left. Committee chairmanships in the House were no longer awarded strictly on the basis of seniority but by a vote of the caucus. In 1977 Democrats chose Udall, an outspoken conservationist, as chairman of the Interior Committee. For the next decade and a half, Udall was one of the most powerful members of the House, and he used his chairmanship to pass one landmark environmental bill after another.

He was one of the best known, most popular politicians in Arizona, a favorite son on par with his friend Barry Goldwater. The Udall and Goldwater families had been close since territorial days. Mo Udall and Barry Goldwater were Washington giants and Arizona icons who represented not only their constituents but the state's character and history. McCain revered their stories, as he revered stories of other prominent figures in Arizona's frontier history. I don't know if John McCain imagined in 1983 that he would ever be as important to Arizona's future as Udall and Goldwater were to its past and present, but I know he craved that distinction, to have a profile in history as a statesman grounded in his identity as an Arizonan. When he heard from a Udall associate that on election night the chairman had advised him to keep an eye on the newly elected McCain, "he's going places," McCain said he was "never more flattered in my life."

Given the prevalence of land-use and water issues in Arizona politics, and his lack of experience with them, Congressman McCain campaigned hard for a seat on the Interior Committee, where he could acquire experience. He pestered the Republican leadership and the ranking Republican on the committee, Manuel Lujan, "making a nuisance of myself," he remembered, until they relented and assigned him to the committee. At the end of the committee's first hearing that year, Chairman Udall asked to have a private word with the new member of the committee's minority. Udall spent an hour or so going through his plans for the committee that Congress, highlighting legislation affecting Arizona that he hoped John would help him with, assuring him that members of the Arizona delegation cooperated on issues that were important concerns in the state. He and Barry were lifelong friends, he said, and worked very closely together on state issues; he hoped they would, too. To that end, he welcomed opportunities for joint public appearances in Arizona and would call soon to see if something could be arranged. "I was bowled over," McCain recalled. "I'd always heard what a nice guy Mo was, easy to get along with, but he went way beyond what I expected. I mean, he didn't have to be that nice. He could've just given me a crumb once in a while, and I'd have been happy. He didn't know what kind of congressman I'd turn out to be. He was just a generous, thoughtful guy who believed making friends made it easier to get stuff done than making enemies."

As promised, Udall called a few weeks later to invite him to a press conference he planned to hold in Casa Grande to go over the committee's agenda for the year and how it would impact the state. McCain had aides give him a crash course on the issues to be discussed, but there wasn't time for him to retain enough information to sound like he knew what he was talking about. "I was nervous as hell," McCain remembered. "Honest to God, back then I didn't know a copper mine from a cotton farm. And I thought I'd just defer questions to Mo and say as little as possible."

Mo had other plans. He addressed the issues one at a time, introducing each as another thing "Congressman McCain and I are working on," then pausing to ask his colleague to speak. McCain remembered responding to the invitations by "saying too little to sound smart but not enough to give away how ignorant I was." McCain knew the confidence Mo had in him was based on nothing but the hope that he would turn out to be a hardworking member of the committee and do his best by the state Mo loved. "It was just kindness," he explained, "and I never forgot it."

After the press conference, Mo asked if he and John could drive back to Phoenix together, to get to know each other a little better.

McCain drove while Mo talked, "mostly about himself and his family, about Arizona politics in the early days, and about Barry." Reflecting back years after Mo had died, McCain realized his friend and benefactor had been "trying to teach me Arizona, not just the issues here, but the people, the culture, the history."

Cementing their friendship was their mutual love of a good joke. "Mo," McCain said, "was the funniest guy I ever knew in politics." Decades later, reporters who covered McCain's 2008 presidential race would have T-shirts made that displayed the top ten jokes McCain told and retold on the stump. Half of them were jokes he had stolen from Mo Udall.

Over McCain's first four years in the House, Udall took him all around the state, introducing him to people who were important for an ambitious young politician to know. Years later, McCain would still marvel at his generosity. "Mo knew I was going to run for Barry's seat, and he knew he was helping me by vouching for me like that. He didn't care if it gave me an advantage." Udall had long been a friend to Arizona's Native Americans. Having spent time among them growing up in rural Arizona, he was genuinely sympathetic to their situation. The committee once had a subcommittee on Indian affairs that had been dissolved because few members wanted to serve on it, correctly seeing little political advantage in the assignment. Udall convinced McCain they should form an informal Indian affairs panel, and McCain agreed. They held hearings, sponsored bills, and visited reservations together, and in time, McCain, too, enjoyed a reputation as a sympathetic supporter of Native American interests. Later, he would chair the Senate Committee on Indian Affairs and would often repeat the advice Udall gave him about working with the tribes: "Never lie to them. They've been lied to enough."

Two of McCain's proudest legislative accomplishments for Arizona were bills that Mo Udall persuaded him to cosponsor, putting millions of acres into protected wilderness status. Both bills had divided the Arizona delegation, with the Democrats in favor and the Republicans opposed and two exceptions: Goldwater and McCain were with Mo Udall. The second of the two bills, the Arizona Desert Wilderness

Act, was passed in 1990 and was the last major legislative triumph of Udall's illustrious career.

Udall had been diagnosed with Parkinson's disease in 1980, two years before McCain was elected to Congress. The effects of the disease weren't very noticeable in the beginning of their friendship, but by 1990 the Parkinson's was advanced and debilitating. His tremors were pronounced, and he had difficulty speaking. McCain was solicitous of his friend but careful not to betray anxiety about his condition, worried that it would embarrass Udall. He described to me the incident that made him realize Udall would have to retire. They were meeting in Mo's office in 1990 to discuss the wilderness bill, and Mo leaned forward to reach for his glasses, couldn't stop himself, and banged his head hard on the coffee table in front of him. "I knew he wouldn't be able to hold on," McCain recalled, wincing as if he had just witnessed it again. He was right. Udall resigned his seat the next year, after falling and breaking four ribs.

He convalesced in a veterans' hospital about two miles north of the Capitol and would remain there until his death eight years later. He had been a popular and powerful person in Washington, beloved by many in the capital and in Arizona, but as the years passed and Udall declined and sank into what appeared to be a vegetative state, few could bear to witness how the disease had ravaged the famously charming man. Outside of his family, though, he had one regular visitor. Every week or so when he was in Washington, John McCain would drive the two miles to the hospital and sit for a half hour or so with his silent friend, reading him the news from Arizona, the state Mo had served so well and had taught John McCain how to do the same.

There were few politicians who made a bigger impression on McCain than Mo Udall, or whom he more deliberately emulated. In the years when I knew McCain, his Senate years, I witnessed him time and again reach out to new members of the body, irrespective of their politics, and offer to work on an issue with them or invite them to accompany him on an overseas trip. He had a good intuitive sense about which new members were sincere in their convictions and their desire to be useful members of the Senate. He detected it almost immediately in Russ Feingold of Wisconsin and the late Paul Wellstone,

recognizing in them the same impulses for political reform that motivated him. When he traveled abroad on official business, he liked to
assemble politically diverse delegations. Near the end of his life, when
tribalism in American politics seemed to be approaching a point of
no return, McCain invited members as far apart in their views as the
very liberal Elizabeth Warren and the very conservative David Perdue
to join him, knowing that traveling together in close quarters over
great distances encouraged people to be friendly, and being friendly
often planted the seeds of real friendship between people with different politics.

CODE OF CONDUCT

I

McCain wasn't often impressed by official Washington pomp, but there was one occasion that he would warmly reminisce about years later. At the end of their orientation week, the freshmen members were honored in Statuary Hall, the old House chamber, with an elegant dinner welcoming them to Washington. "It was beautiful, candlelight, strolling violins, the whole thing, beautiful," he recalled. He had lived in Washington and its suburbs before, had gone to school there, and had worked on the Hill just a couple years earlier. His parents had been a part of Washington society, and he knew the city's power structure. It struck me as I listened to him talk about that dinner that the word best describing his state of mind that evening was one he didn't use—contented. Contentment was a quality that no one who knew him well would say was normal for a person as restless as he was. I smiled as he struggled to explain it as if it had been his first encounter with a strange sensation that had mysteriously sneaked up and overwhelmed him: "I don't know, something about the thing got to me. Maybe it was the fifth-from-the-bottom thing, the times I screwed up, I don't know. Now I was on the inside. It wasn't that long since I'd worked in the Senate. Not that long since Vietnam. I'd thought about getting in politics back then. Now I was. At the dinner, I don't know, I guess I was kind of amazed it happened."

The "fifth-from-the-bottom thing" would be a punch line he used throughout his political career, usually as an illustration of the theme

"Anything can happen in America," and often to buttress his conviction that his was an exceptionally lucky life. Not once did I hear him concede regret or embarrassment for graduating so low in his Naval Academy class. I suspect he did, at least a little, but he had such drive, such energy and brash confidence, that you didn't often see him look backward, and when he did, it was usually just nostalgia, not regret, that occasioned the remembrance. He focused on the fun he had, not the bad times. I don't think there were many times in his life when he thought an ambition was beyond his reach. On the few occasions when he had experienced something close to futility, when the thing he wanted or thought he wanted was denied him and he couldn't do much about it, his reaction was a mix of fatalism and truculence.

He arrived in 1951 at Episcopal High School in Alexandria, the venerable boarding school for mostly well-off southern boys, with a chip on his shoulder and experience at facing down attempts to intimidate the new kid. Order was imposed there, as it would be at Annapolis, by upperclassmen, not teachers and administrators. New students were hazed with verbal and sometimes physical abuse. McCain didn't submit to it without a fight. Bob Timberg quoted one of McCain's friends at the school describing him as "a tough, mean little fucker." But by all accounts, as he had in other schools, he used his attitude and athletics to make friends and find a respectable place in the school's social order—if not exactly a leader of his class, not a follower, either, and not an outcast.[20]

Timberg believed McCain's misconduct at Episcopal, for which he was frequently punished, was an attempt to sabotage his admission to the Naval Academy. He chafed over the fact that he did not have a real say in the matter, which curdled into bitterness, as most of his friends there were headed for more glamorous-sounding destinations. "I daydreamed about going to Princeton or Virginia, where my friends were going," he acknowledged, "and studying English literature. And I'd get pissed off that there really wasn't anything I could do to make that happen." I'm not as certain as Timberg about the reason behind McCain's misbehavior; his attitude didn't change once he got to Annapolis. If anything, he was even more insubordinate. But I think somewhere, maybe buried in his subconscious, was the knowledge that he would regret not following his forebears to Annapolis more than he regretted having the decision imposed on him.

There were things about Episcopal and Annapolis that McCain admired, revered even, people as well as traditions. He believed in their honor codes, and he spoke in later years about Episcopal's code with great respect. It mattered to him that whatever misconduct he'd engaged in—going over the wall, drinking, smoking, fighting—he had not done anything that could be construed as an honor-code violation. He knew in the end that was all that would actually matter to his parents. He received a few parental warnings when he was at Episcopal and Annapolis that he needed to moderate his behavior to avoid getting into trouble he could not get out of. But his parents didn't punish him for what, I assume, they considered routine teenage hijinks.

There was one other person whom he didn't want to disappoint: his English master, William B. Ravenel, whose photograph hung next to the pictures of McCains Senior and Junior on the wall next to his desk in his Senate office. "Mr. Ravenel," as he always referred to him with a deference he accorded few people, was a decorated veteran of World War II. He had been a major in Patton's tank corps and was a colonel in the Army Reserves when he taught English literature at Episcopal. He took an interest in young McCain despite the boy's rebel-without-a-cause attitude that McCain would later concede had been "just showing off." Ravenel had him doing yard work to work off demerits. During those afternoons he spent raking leaves and trimming hedges for Mr. Ravenel, the two discussed all manner of subjects, "from the war to sports to Somerset Maugham stories." McCain was grateful that Ravenel's evident regard signaled to his classmates that he wasn't "just some punk" (though "punk" was one of his nicknames at Episcopal).

Most impressive to McCain and his classmates was Ravenel's deftness at guiding their ethical development without seeming to instruct them in the specifics of their moral obligations. "He helped us figure that stuff out for ourselves," McCain remembered as he recounted an experience when Ravenel, coach of JV football, had let McCain and the rest of the team decide the punishment for one of their teammates who had broken training. "We decided to let the guy off because he hadn't signed the pledge not to break training, and he wasn't caught doing it. He told us he did it. Otherwise, it would have been an honor-code violation, and he could have been kicked out of school. I spoke up in his defense, and afterwards Mr. Ravenel told me we had done the right thing, and he was proud of me.

"Praise from him," he started, and then paused, his voice thick with emotion, before continuing, "He was one of the finest men I ever knew." He credited Ravenel with helping shape his personal honor code, which wouldn't supersede the honor codes he observed in school and in the navy but would augment them. He didn't need to be "some straight-arrow, Dudley Do-Right guy," he explained. "I didn't have to obey all the rules all the time. I had to be basically honest, show some guts when I needed to, and treat people fairly." In an appearance on *Monday Night Football*, on the night before he lost the election for president, he recalled the football coach who had been his greatest inspiration. "The most important lesson he taught me," McCain remembered, "was that you've always got to do the honorable thing, even when nobody's looking—because maybe nobody will know, but *you'll know.*"

There would be occasions in the future when McCain wouldn't live up to those principles as well as he knew he should have, and his troubled conscience would show in good ways and bad. But those were rare exceptions in an otherwise honorable life. Even in severe trials, he managed to keep to his code more faithfully than most people could have done. He certainly did in Vietnam. And when he returned from that trial, after reuniting with his family, he most wanted to see Mr. Ravenel. "He was the one guy I wanted to talk to about it, who wasn't there with me. I thought he'd understand what I'd gone through, or maybe I thought I could explain it to him better than I could to someone else, even my family." He wouldn't have the chance. Mr. Ravenel had died of a heart attack at fifty-three years of age, less than a year after McCain was shot down over Hanoi. "I had a hard time accepting it," McCain remarked when asked how he felt when he learned his hero had passed away. "Still do." Decades later, at a fund-raiser for his 2000 presidential campaign hosted by Episcopal classmates, he became emotional again as he talked of how much he had wished he could have seen his mentor again. "I would have liked to ask him what quality he detected in me that remained undetected to others."

In an off-the-cuff speech he made to Episcopal students almost fifty years after he graduated, he told them the great strength of their school was "its adherence to an honor code. It's both a privilege and a burden because, forever, you will have the obligation and the burden that if you do something in your life that is a violation of the honor code, you're not going to be able to get around it, you're not going to be able to rationalize it, you're not going to be able to excuse it."

He began his plebe summer at the Naval Academy in late June 1954. He didn't mind it at first. "It was sort of like a sports camp," he recalled. "We boxed and wrestled, did calisthenics, obstacle courses . . . I made friends right away. They made us march in formation, and some gung ho stuff, but it didn't get bad until later."

Later was the end of summer, when the first- and second-year midshipmen returned and the hazing began. Until then, McCain enjoyed himself and even impressed the junior officers who supervised the plebes that summer. They made him a company commander, the last time academy authorities would recognize him for more than his infractions of the rules and stubborn resistance to becoming a "squared-away midshipman."

No one, not even McCain himself, told the story of his Annapolis years better than Bob Timberg's account in *The Nightingale's Song*. Bob was a great reporter and a gifted writer. He was also a graduate of Annapolis and understood the place and its customs as well as the graduates who were his subjects. He understood the paradoxical sentiment that McCain volunteered in an interview: "I hated the place, but I didn't mind going there."[21] The great challenge at Annapolis, as McCain saw it, was to preserve his individuality against intense pressure to conform and, at the same time, be recognized as a leader within the institution. For all his reservations about the academy, he knew the navy was his most accessible path to a life of adventure and distinction.

He "hated every minute" of his plebe year. "I don't even like to re-member it," he added. He believed the abuse he received from upper-classmen was more than they accorded most other plebes, because "my contempt for it was obvious." He didn't resent merely the haz-ing, which he considered an abuse of authority by the upperclassmen who focused their attention on him. He resented the authority itself, "the idea that I had to take shit from someone just because he was a couple years older than me." He rebelled by provoking the abuse and sneering at it. To a civilian, his offenses seem trivial, but in the power structure of the Naval Academy they were considered perni-cious. He avoided "bilging out"—committing an unpardonable breach that would get him expelled—but he got close. "I didn't cross any lines I thought would cost me more than a few more hours of extra duty," marching on the weekends while his classmates were on liberty, the standard punishment for demerits at Annapolis. Decades later, Mc-Cain's self-deprecating humor often included a reference to all the extra duty he had marched at the Naval Academy, measured in an imaginary round trip to "Baltimore and back," seven or ten or fifteen or twenty times.

In his plebe year, his misbehavior was limited to minor offenses. He left his room in disorder, regularly showed up a few minutes late for morning and noon formation, wore his uniform just sloppily enough to draw attention, performed menial tasks assigned him perfuncto-rily, without the customary "Yes, sir!" gusto. The offenses in his up-perclassman years were more serious. "Going over the wall"—getting his friends to sneak out at night and head for a roadhouse that served them beer—was the most common. As he courted the hostility of up-perclassmen, he built a reputation among fellow plebes for his dar-ing and self-confidence. "People kind of gravitated to him," Timberg quotes Chuck Larson, McCain's best friend at the academy, their class president and future four-star admiral. "They . . . cared about his ap-proval and they cared about what he thought."[22] Over his four years at Annapolis, McCain grew in stature as an informal leader in his class, leading even the most squared-away midshipmen, such as Chuck Lar-son, on rowdy adventures over the wall. "We all still marvel at how much control John had over what we did," reflected Jack Dittrick, another McCain friend who spoke to Timberg.

Listening to McCain reminisce about his years at Annapolis, you got the impression that his favorite activity had been vexing his company officer, a marine major, whom McCain portrayed as a kind of Wile E. Coyote to his Road Runner. Decades later, McCain still delighted in poking fun at his nemesis and recounting the times he had outfoxed him. We included several of those stories in his first book, which was published in 1999, during his first campaign for the Republican presidential nomination. Some reporter tracked the poor guy down in California, where he lived in retirement, and he expressed genuine hurt at being the butt of McCain's jokes. He insisted he had never disliked McCain and added that he planned to vote for him. I showed the article to McCain, and he read it with a pained expression. I smiled in anticipation of some quip, but he handed the clip back to me without comment; all he offered was a slight headshake. I never heard him make fun of the guy or even mention his name again. He did invoke the memory from time to time, but in a self-deprecating way, to question whether he deserved an award or recognition he'd been given, speculating that his "old company officer" might not approve.

McCain had the guts even then to act on his acute sense of fairness and his hostility to people who bullied the helpless, no matter who they were, Vladimir Putin or an abusive first-classman picking on a Filipino steward. McCain witnessed the latter transgression when he was an underclassman. He was seated at the table in the dining hall where the first-year was harassing the steward. He steamed over it in silence until he couldn't stand it any longer. McCain never told the story to me or anyone, as far as I know. His roommate, Frank Gamboa, shared it with Bob Timberg and others. Frank was so impressed by it that he had remembered its details for decades. "Why don't you pick on somebody your own size," McCain had finally exploded at the obnoxious senior, shocking everyone at the table, including the fellow to whom his outburst was addressed. Underclassmen don't reprimand upperclassmen at Annapolis. The consequences can be severe. The chain of command is the chain of command, and those below are not supposed to upbraid those above. You show respect, at least superficially, even if you think the guy is a jerk. But an officer's duty to the men below him is as sacred as his duty to his superiors. That's what John McCain's father had taught him. You owe no less respect to the people who obey your orders than you do to those who give you orders. That was the code of an "officer and a gentleman," and the jackass across the table from him had violated it.

"What did you say?" the first-classman demanded. "I said you're picking on that steward, and he's doing the best he can," McCain shot back. Fortunately, the guy was so stunned by McCain's impudence, or possibly intimidated by it, that all he could do was mumble, "What's your name, mister?" to which he received a prompt response: "McCain. What's yours?"[23] With that, the bully left the table, and McCain didn't remember encountering him again. "Do you know what ever became of the guy?" I asked McCain after reading *The Nightingale's Song*. "No idea," he replied. "Doubt he amounted to much."

Midshipmen all had the same major in McCain's time at Annapolis, electrical engineering, a subject that didn't interest him, and as with all things that didn't interest him, he paid it as little attention as possible, learning the bare minimum to get by and forgetting it as soon as he could. His friends recalled him chronically pestering them for urgent tutoring as he crammed for exams. He was discerning and enthusiastic about subjects that did interest him, however; years later, he could recite whole passages from works he had admired as a student, probably because he routinely reread books that made an impression on him. I remember once sitting next to him on the Senate floor as he debated an issue with Senator Robert Byrd, who prided himself on his oratory. The well-read Byrd liked to decorate his arguments with lines from Shakespeare. McCain, smiling, rebutted with more Shakespeare, until Byrd worked himself up to a windy peroration that ended with a long finger pointing at McCain as he issued an invitation from Macbeth: "Lay on, Mac—" He paused abruptly before the next syllable, which McCain provided before Byrd could: "Duff. Lay on, Macduff." Other senators on the floor paid little attention to the exchange; it had been for their own amusement.

One of McCain's favorite instructors at Annapolis was the eminent historian E. B. Potter, who had written naval histories of World War II that included appreciative mentions of McCain's grandfather. McCain chose Slew as the subject of his term paper for Potter. As part of his research, he wrote to Admiral Nimitz, who was retired and living in California, asking for his impressions. He received a prompt and lengthy reply, which, as hoped, lavished praise on Slew's contributions to winning the war in the Pacific. But what impressed McCain most was that the old admiral had devoted most of his reminiscences to the days when he and Slew McCain had been young officers, sailing around the Philippines on the *Panay*. "It was the kind of life you read about in fiction," McCain mused. It was also the kind of life to which he aspired. Nimitz's letter reminded him that the academy offered more than harassment and humiliation. It offered adventure and honor.

Nevertheless, he remained a nonconformist troublemaker, piling up demerits and coming perilously close to bilging out his last year, when he received an unusually heavy punishment for having left his "room in gross disorder." The normal punishment for the offense was fifteen demerits; he received seventy-five. The new penalty brought him to 165. Ten more and it was automatic expulsion. "There's no way I could've avoided getting ten more. Shit, ten was nothing. I could get that for not shining my shoes." He said he thought about quitting and sent away for literature about joining the French Foreign Legion. Instead, he was summoned to the commandant's office and dressed down after he made the case for why the punishment had been unfair. "You're a spoiled brat, McCain," the commandant accused him. "Whatever you say, sir. It's still unfair." The commandant ordered him to leave his office. Two weeks later, his punishment was reduced to thirty demerits and a week's confinement.

While his grades were underwhelming and disapproving superiors might have despaired of making a good officer out of him, McCain thrived at sea during the summer cruises all midshipmen are assigned. He recounted his first cruise, the summer after his plebe year, with undiminished pride over forty years after the fact. The skipper of the old destroyer he had been assigned to, Lieutenant Commander Eugene

Farrell, had been a student and admirer of his father and took an interest in him. He was a profane, excitable old salt, McCain said. "I liked him right away, and I knew he liked me," despite subjecting McCain to a torrent of abuse every time the midshipman made a mistake on deck. Farrell believed that the best instruction was delivered while shouting insults and inducing as much stress in the pupil as you could, a style that would be familiar ten years later to flight school students at Meridian Naval Air Station who reported to Lieutenant John McCain III. "He'd yell for me to get off his bridge," McCain recalled, "and then call me back and show me what I'd done wrong and let me do it again." Farrell had him take [the conn] and drive the ship. He loved it. In the early 1960s, when he had a reputation in the navy as an unserious playboy who crashed a couple airplanes and knocked down power lines in Spain, he would spend many hours during Mediterranean deployments qualifying as an "officer of the deck underway," capable of commanding an aircraft carrier at sea.

For all his irreverence toward the Naval Academy's rules and customs, and his earlier ambivalence about going there, he was, as he admitted to Bob Timberg, glad he had. Annapolis launched him on an eventful navy career, most of which he enjoyed. It also included him in the traditions of honor it represented and that he respected, just as he respected famous men the school had produced. Navy and Marine Corps legends Dewey, Nimitz, Halsey, Spruance, Lejeune, Burke, his commanding officer in prison, Jim Stockdale, his father and grandfather.

Upon leaving Annapolis, the newly commissioned McCain embarked on the wild, thrill-seeking life he had seemed to be preparing for at Annapolis. He and Chuck Larson roomed together at flight school in Pensacola, where they earned their wings, and again at Corpus Christi, where they continued their training. McCain drove a Corvette, dated a stripper, qualified as an attack pilot, and, as he had at Annapolis, assumed the role of ringleader for a rowdy band of fellow fliers. He crashed a plane in Corpus Christi Bay, sank to the bottom before ejecting, swam to the surface, and went back to his quarters to shower and get ready for Saturday night. He was assigned in 1960 to a squadron in the Atlantic Fleet, serving on two carriers, first the *Intrepid* and then the *Enterprise*. He rented a beach house in Virginia Beach and hosted weekend-long parties that he claimed were the hottest ticket in that navy town. He was a familiar face in Monte Carlo casinos and on the isle of Capri, two of his favorite haunts when on liberty during deployments to the Mediterranean. He was always happy to regale a listener with stories from "my misspent youth," and he looked back on his early navy years, before Vietnam, with wistful fondness. He did, however, repeatedly emphasize that his high spirits weren't necessarily alcohol-fueled. "I liked a good time. But I didn't drink as much as people think I did. I'm sure I was overserved once in a while, but a lot of nights, I'd have a Coke rather than another drink."

The *Enterprise* had just returned to Norfolk, Virginia, from the Mediterranean in October 1962 when his squadron was mysteriously ordered back to sea. After they had steamed south of Cherry Point, Virginia, they were ordered to the wardroom, where they listened to a radio broadcast of President Kennedy announcing a naval blockade of Cuba in reaction to the Soviet Union's ploy to build a nuclear missile base there. The *Enterprise* sailed at full speed under nuclear power and was the first carrier on station. "The first few days were exciting," McCain recalled. "Seemed like we really might go to war. Things settled down, but we stayed there for a couple months, maybe longer, and we flew a lot of missions. Guys started getting hurt, so they gave us four days' leave in Jamaica. That was a lot of fun."

He reported to Meridian Naval Air Station as a flight instructor in 1964, flying out of McCain Field, which was named for Slew. Meridian offered fewer social attractions than Virginia Beach, so officers at the base organized the Key Fess Yacht Club, named for a small island in a nearby swampy lagoon labeled by a marine officer as Lake Fester. The club was notorious among navy aviators. Fliers based on both coasts, including an admiral once, flew to sleepy Meridian to attend one of the club's toga parties or another of its weekend bacchanalia. The members elected John McCain the club's commodore.

Despite his nostalgia for those times, he claimed he had begun to worry that he had a fixed reputation as the profligate flyboy with few prospects for a command. He settled down when he started dating Carol Shepp, the ex-wife of one of his classmates. They married in 1965. He adopted her two sons, Doug and Andy, and they welcomed a daughter, Sidney, the following year. For the most part, he abstained from the kind of antics that had spread his notoriety. He resigned as commodore of the Key Fess Yacht Club, as club membership was limited to bachelor officers. He groused to Chuck Larson that he didn't believe he would ever be taken seriously, and floated the idea that he might get out of the navy, since a career there was starting to look unlikely for him. Larson had left aviation for nuclear submarines in 1963 and was well on his way to eventual flag rank. He was chosen as a White House fellow in 1968, and a year later, he served as President Nixon's naval aide. Twenty years and four stars later, he was nominated by President George H. W. Bush to be CINCPAC. He encouraged McCain to seek an assignment that would give him the chance to prove his suitability for command. Both men agreed the best place to do that was in a combat squadron flying missions over Vietnam. McCain put in for a combat assignment in 1966, when he was still at Meridian, and was transferred to Cecil Field in Jacksonville to start training in the A-4 Skyhawk. In May 1967, eight months after his daughter's birth, Lieutenant Commander John S. McCain III reported to A-4 squadron VA-46 on the USS *Forrestal*, which was conducting training exercises off Guantánamo Bay. A month later, the *Forrestal* steamed for Cape Horn and the Pacific, and on July 25 reached Yankee Station in the Gulf of Tonkin, where McCain would make the first of two fateful decisions, the most fateful of his life, he would later claim.

II

The wayward midshipman and brash aviator had matured by the time he ran for public office. The obvious assumption is the war matured him, but he wouldn't concede the point. "I was thirty-one when I went to Vietnam," he observed. "I wasn't some kid who didn't know what he was getting into." The extravagant personality traits of those younger years were still in evidence in the words and actions of the middle-aged politician, but at a lower register—the headstrong independence tempered by flashes of self-awareness, the outspokenness, the irreverent wit, the infectious enthusiasm that could boil into impetuousness, the pugnaciousness and quick temper. Now added was an uncommon resilience he possessed after five and a half years suffering privation and abuse, which strengthened his capacity for patience, though he would never have an ample supply, and toughened his psychological immune system to failure.

President of his Republican freshman class in the House would be as close as he ever came to an official congressional leadership position. After he ran for and lost the chairmanship of the senatorial committee, he never sought another leadership job. But as always, the magnetism of his wit, guts, and enthusiasm, and respect for his war record, drew colleagues to him, as did his facility with the media. Early on, he was acknowledged as a leader in Congress on national security and foreign policy matters. The authority his biography gave him and the charm of his wit and candor were features in his quick rise to prominence. So was his nose for the spotlight, how good he was elbowing his way into the main event. Last was his willingness to go against the grain for what he insisted were not self-interested reasons, and be believed, because it was often true. And as friends, aides, and reporters who knew him well could tell you, when he wasn't on the level, he would find a way to let you in on it.

During his first term in Congress, he was expected by most observers to be a conventional conservative, a loyal foot soldier for the president he genuinely admired, Ronald Reagan, and for the most part he was. He would regret casting a vote in 1983 against making the birthday of Martin Luther King Jr. a federal holiday. President Reagan had previously opposed the holiday, although he reversed his decision and signed the bill. House Republicans were split on the question, although more voted for it than against it. But all Arizona Republicans in the House voted nay. The measure passed and was scheduled to go into effect in 1986. Not every state would follow suit and recognize the holiday. The Republican-controlled Arizona legislature declined to, but Arizona governor Bruce Babbitt had other plans. He declared it a holiday by executive order. Evan Mecham was inaugurated governor the following year and rescinded Babbitt's order. McCain supported the move.

His reasons for opposing the holiday, he maintained, had been fiscal. But he changed his mind as Arizona became the focus of national resentment over the slight, and as he heard from people in and out of Arizona—including more than a few very emotional exchanges—who made clear to him that the value of memorializing a heroic and hugely consequential American life was more valuable than its cost to public treasuries. In 1990 McCain convinced Ronald Reagan, who had left the presidency two years earlier, to endorse an Arizona referendum reinstating the holiday. The referendum failed, and he supported a second effort the year before that succeeded. Seven years later, as he ran for president for the first time, he conceded he had erred in opposing the holiday, telling NBC's Tim Russert, "We all learn, okay? We all learn. I will admit to learning, and I hope that the people that I represent appreciate that, too. I voted in 1983 against the recognition of Martin Luther King. . . . I regret that vote."

On September 28, 1983, less than a year into his first House term, McCain asked for recognition on the floor of the House to speak in opposition to the pending resolution authorizing the deployment of American marines to Lebanon. The marines were already there, sixteen hundred of them, inserted earlier that month into the bloody complications of Lebanon's civil war. Ostensibly part of an international peacekeeping force intended to enforce a fragile cease-fire, they were plainly a misguided attempt by the Reagan administration to strengthen the Lebanese central government, which was beset by enemies on all sides, as innumerable factions, proxies for Israel, Syria, and Iran, reduced the country to violent bedlam. The administration had made their side clear by dispatching an armada to Lebanon, led by the battleship *New Jersey*, which promptly lobbed shells the size of cars at

Syrian allies in the hills above Beirut. John McCain, who had returned from Vietnam ten years earlier, "knew a quagmire when he saw one."[24]

McCain told Bob Michel his intention. Neither Michel nor anyone else argued or pressured him to change his mind. "I hope you're wrong" was all Michel said after listening to his argument. His opposition had been unexpected but was not worrying. He was powerless to affect the outcome of the vote. Tip O'Neill had committed his caucus's support for the resolution, and it would pass easily. But McCain's points were hard to refute. What are we doing there? he questioned. "It is said we are there to keep the peace, I ask, what peace? It is said we are there to help the government, I ask, what government?"

Seizing the strategic advantage from the Syrians, the main culprits in Lebanon's turmoil, would require vastly more force than the U.S. was prepared to use. McCain disparaged the idea that a small naval force and several hundred marines were sufficient to the task. He closed by emphasizing the folly of sending a force smaller than any one of a dozen factions fighting in Lebanon to force peace on the combatants. "I do not foresee obtainable objectives in Lebanon. I believe the longer we stay, the more difficult it will be to leave, and I am prepared to accept the consequences of our withdrawal. I will vote in opposition to the measure."

He told me he had given the issue a lot of thought in advance, had consulted at length with a friend from the National War College, and had checked the opinions of other military friends, national security professionals, and experts on Lebanon. "Did they persuade you, or did you start off knowing it was a bad idea?" I asked.

"The latter," he answered.

"Did Vietnam influence your thinking?"

"Yes."

"How much?"

"A lot."

His unexpected opposition garnered national media attention for the first time in his young political career. The *New York Times* and the *Washington Post* interviewed him, and he appeared on *The MacNeil/*

Lehrer NewsHour. His judgment was tragically affirmed a month later, when a Shiite terrorist, a proxy for Iran and Syria, blew up the marine barracks in East Beirut, killing 241.

A little over a year later, not long after his 1984 reelection to the House, McCain traveled with Walter Cronkite to the country that had taught him to be wary of uncertain war aims sought with wrongheaded strategies and inadequate means. He was interviewed by Cronkite for a CBS special that aired on the tenth anniversary of the end of the Vietnam War. They walked the grounds of the prison where he had once been confined and broken.

QUESTIONS OF HONOR
(PART ONE)

I

In politics, as in the navy, John McCain ran straight at obstacles to his ambitions, and if they didn't move, he tried to flank them by taking his case to the media and the public, employing candor and irreverence to make his points and convey his authenticity. There really wasn't much difference between his inside game and his outside game, the back room and the public stage. He made the same arguments to his colleagues that he did to the public, usually with the same level of emotion. Sometimes his temper helped him by, if not intimidating opposition, wearing it down when combined with his obstinacy. Sometimes it got in his way and exacerbated whatever difficulty had triggered it.

The things that provoked his temper were a mix of the ordinary and extraordinary. When he lost his temper over small things, the cause was, more often than not, nothing more complicated than fatigue. When he was tired, which was hard to prevent given the schedule he insisted on maintaining, the ordinary frustrations of a legislator strained his self-control, and he was quicker to speak out loud opinions that were best kept to himself. He was usually mindful to be gracious in defeat. But he could also be defiant, which sometimes sounded like anger. He was a gamer. His competitiveness was easily roused and hard to turn off when the contest ended. Staff joked that he was "defiant in defeat, and sometimes in victory, too." His nomination in 2008 was effectively sealed when he won the Florida primary, which set him up to win the biggest prizes on Super Tuesday, after which his closest competitor, Governor Mitt Romney, would drop out of the race. Unfortunately, there was still a debate at the Reagan Library scheduled for the evening after the Florida primary. It should have been a comparatively relaxed and friendly exchange. We had encouraged him to be gentle. Both men knew their contest would soon be over. He would come to trust and admire Governor Romney in the months ahead, and they would become friends. But he came in roaring that night, not so much in triumph from his victory but with game-day ferocity that he couldn't shut off. To the surprise of his staff—and I assume Governor Romney as well—he threw punches from start to finish. Afterward, when aides expressed reservations about his performance, he looked genuinely confused.

His competitiveness could also be roused by partisan fights, a team sport, and get the better of him. Even if he was merely a bystander in a political skirmish, he had a tendency to jump in if he saw an associate abused. It happened early in his first term, when Republican leader Bob Michel, a gentleman of the old school, was uncharacteristically engaged in a heated dispute with Majority Leader Jim Wright on the House floor, while McCain was standing nearby. McCain had no animosity for Wright nor his lieutenant, Illinois congressman Marty Russo, who was also on the floor. On the contrary, he liked both men. But it was a period of intensified hostility in the House, after the Democratic majority had seated the Democratic candidate in a disputed election in Indiana, outraging Republicans. It had strengthened the hand of a group of insurrectionist Republicans led by Newt Gingrich, and had put in a tough spot institutionalists with milder temperaments, such as Bob Michel. McCain saw what he later described as Wright "poking his finger in Bob's chest," and "I decided to get in his face." In the process, he said something to Wright that offended Russo, who had as quick a temper as McCain. McCain wasn't clear about what had set him off, but things took a dramatic turn for the worse when Russo, who was taller, grabbed him by the throat. McCain pushed Russo's arm aside, and the two traded a few shoves and more than a few profanities before McCain suggested they "take it outside." Russo, now exercising more judgment than McCain, declined the invitation. The tempest passed within the hour, when Russo called to apologize and McCain responded in kind.

The most amusing incident of this kind, perhaps because I had the pleasure of witnessing it, occurred in the Senate between McCain and the Senate titan whom McCain loved to spar and work with, Ted Kennedy. McCain and Kennedy both recalled this story so many times, and with unusual similarity in their particulars, that I hesitated to include it in these pages. But the pleasure of describing it is irresistible. Kennedy was reading at his desk on the Senate floor, waiting to talk on another subject, while a debate over President Clinton's surgeon general nominee was getting heated. The principals were Illinois Democrat Carol Moseley Braun and Oklahoma Republican Don Nickles, with a few others on each side chipping in their two cents. Braun was new to the Senate, and Kennedy, who had started paying attention when voices were raised, decided that she was being picked on and jumped into the fray, using his booming Boston brogue to get the chair to recognize him. McCain was passing through the chamber on his way to a meeting elsewhere, but he stopped to see what the fuss was all about when he heard Kennedy shouting. Once Kennedy started to barrage Nickles with demands for regular order, McCain charged to his desk and started barking the same demand of Kennedy. Kennedy objected to McCain's request. McCain objected to Kennedy's, both managing to include various insults in their objections. Years later, McCain would joke at Kennedy's memorial service that they had shared the same creed: "A fight not joined is a fight not enjoyed." Neither of them was completely clear what they were fighting about, but a zest for combat propelled both of them into the kind of furious scrap in which they seemed to forget where they were. The instigators of the fight were now bystanders, watching with alarm as Kennedy yanked his microphone from his lapel and directed McCain to the well of the Senate, where, presumably, he thought they could have a few unamplified words. McCain charged after him. They didn't need the mikes. Reporters hung over the balcony rail to get a better look at the two men and record the perfectly audible exchange.

"Fuck you, Ted."

"Fuck you, John. Why don't you act like a fucking senator?"

"Why don't *you* act like a fucking senator?"

After both senators had exhausted themselves in this way, and reporters had called their respective press offices for comment, they exited the chamber through the same door. I was trailing them at a safe distance of ten feet. I watched as Kennedy threw his arm around McCain's shoulder and burst into laughter. "John, I think we got a little carried away this time, don't you?" Then they began to replay the event, cracking up as they recalled how the original combatants had quietly withdrawn from the scene looking confused and worried.

Nothing disturbed McCain more than having his honor questioned. It was hard for him to control his temper on the rare occasions when that happened. Restraint was also harder for him to exercise when he worried that he couldn't command his circumstances. He would get anxious and exhibit aggressive impatience, pushing constantly to create a new dynamic that would alter the situation. That could appear as anger to some observers, and sometimes the appearance was reality.

The expected marquee race to succeed Barry Goldwater, McCain versus Babbitt, hadn't materialized. Bruce Babbitt's sights were set on the 1988 Democratic presidential nomination, and he passed on the race. So did Bob Stump, the veteran conservative congressman who had been the preference of many party activists in the state. The McCain camp had done all it could to discourage Babbitt and Stump from running. Babbitt might have been interested in campaigning for the presidency as a senator rather than a retired governor, but less appealing was the prospect of a hard-fought, expensive campaign for the Senate, which he might lose. Having visited every town and rural hamlet in the state, and spoken to any group that would have him, McCain made clear that Babbitt would have just such a fight. McCain had raised over a half million dollars for his reelection to the House in 1984, when he had faced a little-known opponent with no money and almost no chance to beat him. He started raising money for the Senate race before he was even sworn in to his second House term. His leave-nothing-to-chance campaign to clear the field succeeded. He faced nominal competition in the primary and easily dispatched his well-regarded but overmatched Democratic opponent, utilities regulator and son of a former state senate majority leader, Richard Kimball, in the general election.

The only real trouble McCain encountered he had made for himself: He was as incapable as ever of restraining his smart-ass id. Speaking in Tucson in the summer of 1986, he exhorted University of Arizona students to exercise their franchise by wisecracking about the high propensity of senior citizens to vote. He referred to Leisure World, the huge retirement community in Mesa, as "Seizure World, where ninety-seven percent of the people who live there come out to vote while the other three percent are in intensive care." A minor brou-haha ensued. "Everybody in the state seems to have a relative there," McCain groused years later. A Democratic Party staffer had been in the audience and recorded the remark. The Kimball campaign shared it with the press and denounced with faux outrage McCain's insensitivity to Arizona seniors. The storm eventually subsided. It would have done so sooner had McCain not insisted on reciting a long list of the things he had done in Congress on behalf of Arizona retirees instead of just apologizing and moving on. Nothing got John McCain up on a high horse quicker than criticism he could construe as an attack on humor generally, and on his personal sense of humor specifically. The more trouble it caused him, the more vociferous his self-defense, at least in private. I didn't know him in those days, but aides of old and recent vintage can all testify to having heard him proclaim at least once in their presence, "It was a joke, goddammit. And I don't care what anybody says, I'm not going to stop having a sense of humor just because other people don't have one."

II

He was a month shy of his thirty-first birthday as he prepared for his sixth combat mission, an alpha strike on military targets in North Vietnam that had been selected in Washington. The *Forrestal* had been on station for five days. Operation Rolling Thunder had been under way with brief interruptions for two years, and pilots were suffering heavy casualties as North Vietnam's air defenses were strengthened with additional surface-to-air missiles (SAMs) and antiaircraft batteries supplied by the Soviet Union. McCain's parents were living in London then, and he and Carol decided she and the kids would live in Europe while he was deployed. He expected to be home by the following spring.

Like most navy fliers, he was superstitious and followed the same preflight protocol before every mission. His parachute rigger, Petty Officer Tom Ott, who had been with Lieutenant Commander McCain since training, performed the last task in the sequence, wiping off McCain's flight helmet visor with a rag. He had just handed the helmet back to the pilot, who was third in line on the port side. He flashed a thumbs-up, and McCain pulled the plane's canopy shut. In the next instant, stray voltage from the engine ignition of an F-4 Phantom on the starboard side fired a Zuni missile across the deck. It struck either the belly fuel tank of McCain's A-4 or the fuel tank of the A-4 next to his, piloted by Lieutenant Commander Fred White, igniting the two hundred gallons of fuel that spilled onto the deck. "I thought my aircraft exploded," McCain recalled. "Flames were everywhere." He never saw Petty Officer Ott again. He pulled open the canopy, scrambled to the plane's nose refueling probe, dropped to the deck, rolled through a wall of fire, patted out the flames that had caught his flight suit, and raced to the starboard side. He saw Fred White come through the fire, engulfed in flames, and ran to help him while Chief Petty Officer Gerald Farrier ran ahead with a portable fire extinguisher. Before they reached the pilot, a thousand-pound bomb knocked loose from his plane cooked off.

The explosion knocked McCain backward and killed Chief Farrier,

Lieutenant Commander White, and others. Small pieces of shrapnel pierced McCain's legs and chest, but none of the wounds was serious. Bloody mayhem ensued. More bombs cooked off, and Zuni missiles streaked across the deck. An immense fireball rolled over the deck and seemed to swallow it. Scraps of metal and body parts rained down on the deck. Planes burned. Pilots pulled their ejection seat handles, and men jumped overboard. Explosions blew craters in the flight deck, and the fire spread below. McCain helped throw some bombs overboard and then went to the ready room, where he watched on the ship's closed-circuit television monitor the crew fighting the conflagration. A little while later, he went to sick bay to have his wounds dressed. He saw men burned beyond recognition draw their last breaths. I was interviewing him about the disaster right after we had both watched grainy film of the fire captured by a camera on the *Forrestal's* deck. He pointed to a small, barely visible figure jumping off the nose of a plane into the flames and billowing black smoke. "That's me, right there." Less than a minute later, the camera shakes after the first bomb explodes, and the firestorm erupts. It's hard to imagine anyone surviving the blast. "A kid I didn't recognize because of his burns said, 'Mr. McCain,' and asked if one of the pilots in our squadron was alive. I told him I thought he was, and he said, 'Oh, thank God,' and he died a couple minutes later."

He paused before continuing, and then, as if he had reconsidered recounting anything more about the day, ended with "I couldn't take it anymore, and I left." I looked at him expectantly for a few seconds, but he was finished. It took twenty-four hours to extinguish the last of the fires. When it was over, 134 men had perished. The *Forrestal* was just barely saved from sinking, and limped its way to Subic Naval Base in the Philippines with huge holes below its waterline.

Later that afternoon, he called me into his office and said, "I forgot to tell you about Johnny Apple. A helicopter flew him and a film crew to the *Forrestal* while we were heading to Subic. That's where I met him. He took me to Saigon with him." The encounter was the beginning of a friendship between McCain and the legendary *New York Times* newsman and bon vivant R. W. Apple Jr. that continued until

Apple's death in 2006. Dispatched as a pool reporter to the *Forrestal*, Apple persuaded McCain's superiors to let the survivor accompany him to Saigon, where he could brief other reporters on the heroism that saved the ship. I believe this was McCain's first exchange with the press, the beginning of another lifelong relationship that, if not accurately described as a friendship, was, for the most part, a mutually beneficial association, if occasionally strained by misunderstandings, not unlike most friendships.

"Start of Tragedy: Pilot Hears a Blast as He Checks Plane," read the headline of the *Times*'s front-page write-up of McCain's account of the disaster. "Commander McCain spoke evenly—and quite coolly—about the explosions and fire aboard the carrier," described *Times* reporter Bernard Weinraub.

At random moments, however, his eyes flickered and his voice softened as he recalled the heroism and death of large numbers of enlisted men.

> "We're professional military men and I suppose it's our war," he says, "and yet here were men who earn $150 a month and work 18 to 20 hour days—and I mean manual labor—and certainly would have survived had they not stayed to help the pilots fight the fire. I've never seen such acts of heroism."

Weinraub included a description of the pilot's comportment that will resonate with reporters who covered McCain the politician: "Commander McCain has a disarming disregard for formal military speech or style. He is wiry, prematurely gray and does not take himself too seriously."[25]

McCain flew back to the *Forrestal* a day later. By his own admission, he was disappointed that his combat tour had lasted less than a week. The carrier would be in dry dock for repairs for the next seven months, and the pilots were told they would board flights for home once the ship reached the Philippines. Before they did, an officer from the USS *Oriskany*, which was just coming off Yankee Station for a few weeks, appeared in the ready room of McCain's squadron, asking for

volunteers. The *Oriskany's* attack squadrons had suffered heavy casualties that month, and one squadron, VA-163, "the Saints," which
had a reputation for aggressiveness, was especially shorthanded. By
the time President Johnson announced the end of Rolling Thunder
in 1968, thirty-eight *Oriskany* pilots had been shot down and killed
or captured. Sixty planes had been lost, twenty-nine of them A-4s.
The Saints had the highest casualty rate. One-third of their pilots were
dead or prisoners of war. McCain and a few other pilots volunteered.
"Not my best decision," he joked years later.

He didn't have to report to his new squadron until the end of September. He flew to Europe to spend a few weeks vacationing with
his family, and help move them to Orange Park, Florida, where they
would wait for him to come home from the war. He came on board
the *Oriskany* on September 30, 1967, and flew his first combat mission
with the Saints two days later.

The squadron was equipped with new smart bombs. Their greater
accuracy reduced civilian casualties and helped convince Washington
to escalate the air war that for two years had failed to break the will of
the North Vietnamese. McCain, like the rest of his squadron, disparaged Washington's restrictive target lists. "They had us hitting the same
shit over and over," he complained. He recalled one of their targets, a
military barracks that had "been bombed twenty-seven times, while a
half mile away, there was a bridge with truck tracks that we couldn't
touch. Senseless." He approvingly quoted James Stockdale, who would
be his senior ranking officer in Hanoi and had commanded the *Oriskany's* air wing in 1965. "We were making gestures with our airplanes,"
he repeated. "We'd see them offloading SAMs in Haiphong and truck
them in broad daylight to missile sites, and we couldn't do a goddamn
thing about it. We could only hit the sites if they were shooting at
us." He recounted the time they had lost a pilot over Haiphong and
another pilot in the squadron had bombed the SAM site he believed
was responsible for killing his friend. When they got back to the ship,
the pilot was grounded for dropping his ordnance on an unapproved
target. McCain still had anger in his voice as he recalled the incident.

He liked the other pilots in his squadron. He liked the Saints' reputation for aggressive tactics and their record of success. Before McCain joined the squadron, the Saints had destroyed every bridge at the port of Haiphong. The previous August, they had flown their first mission to Hanoi and destroyed a thermal power plant there. The squadron's skipper, Commander Bryan Compton, had been decorated with the Navy Cross for his actions that day. McCain held Compton in high esteem, "the bravest guy in the squadron," he called him, "and the best pilot." And he respected the commander of the carrier's air wing, Commander Burt Shepard, astronaut Alan Shepard's brother.

He had "a great day" on October 24, when he destroyed two MiGs parked at an airfield outside Hanoi. "I was fired up," he remembered. "I was still the new guy, and I wanted to impress them." The same impulse led him to pester the Saints' operations officer, Jim Busey, to include him in a big alpha strike, involving two attack squadrons and fighter escorts from two F-8 squadrons, scheduled for October 26. The target was the same Hanoi power plant the Saints had destroyed two months earlier, when Compton had earned a Navy Cross. It had been rebuilt. McCain smirked as he repeated Busey's nickname for him, "Gregory Green Ass, that's what he called me. He was a really good pilot, who had a Navy Cross, too, and he had the typical older guy's attitude about new guys. But I really wanted to go on this one, and after I took out the two MiGs, I think he thought I was up to it."

It would be McCain's first mission to the enemy capital. Burt Shepard would command it, and McCain would fly as Shepard's wingman. The strike operations officer told him he expected casualties and warned McCain to be careful. "You don't need to worry about me," he recalled responding. "I'm not planning to be killed." At the time, Hanoi possessed the strongest air defenses in the history of warfare. The city was protected by three concentric rings of SAM sites, and antiaircraft artillery, "triple A." Vietnamese gunners waited for the Americans to fly within range of their antiaircraft batteries as they tried to evade the SAMs. "Like flying telephone poles," was how McCain described the missiles, "scary-looking, but it was the triple A that got most guys." The mission was different from any other he had flown. "As soon as we turned inbound on the target, our warning lights started flashing and alarms started. It was so loud I had to turn the volume down. I saw these big clouds of dust and smoke on the ground where they fired SAMs. We usually kept pretty good radio silence, but that day there was a lot of chatter, guys calling out missiles. The closer we got, the worse it got. It was the first time I saw a lot of flak, I mean a lot, it was like a World War II movie. One of the F-8s got hit, and the pilot ejected. Charlie Rice, good guy."

McCain recognized the target from the intelligence briefing photos, and as he dove to drop his bombs, the alarm went off signaling he was being tracked by a SAM. He released his bombs at about thirty-five hundred feet and had pulled back the stick to begin a steep climb when the missile tore his right wing off. "That's when you realize why your training is so repetitive. You don't think in that situation. You'd die while you're thinking. You do what they told you to do. You radio, 'I'm hit,' and go, eject. My plane was upside down when I ejected and I hit it."

The Vietnamese who witnessed him fall into a small lake said his parachute had barely opened before he hit the water. He had been knocked unconscious and came to when he hit the water, and touched bottom. He tried to pull the toggle to inflate his life vest and discovered his arms wouldn't work. He used his teeth. A year after his capture, the Vietnamese had him write down basic biographical details and a list of his injuries. The Vietnamese government sent it to him in 2017, an inventory of broken bones written in a hand recognizable as his to anyone familiar with his handwriting:

Broken right leg
Broken right arm (three breaks)
Broken left shoulder.

A group of locals waded into the shallow water to retrieve him, floating him on bamboo poles. Over the years, he received several letters from various Hanoi residents, each claiming to be the one who rescued him. They might or might not have been on the level. In photographs of his capture, about a dozen men are pulling him out of the water. An angry mob gathered on the shore to greet him. Someone stuck him with a bayonet in the ankle and groin. "I think I was going into shock or something," he recalled, "I didn't feel that much pain right then. But I was scared as hell." To his relief, an army truck arrived, and "a woman jumped out of the back and started shouting at the people to back away from me. Then she pretended to give me tea, and somebody else took a picture of it. Then they loaded me in, and drove me to Hoa Lo. It was about a five-minute drive." Hoa Lo was the nineteenth-century, French-built, trapezoid-shaped prison that took up an entire block in the very center of Hanoi. The Americans held there called it "the Hilton."

They set his stretcher down on the floor of a cell in the part of the prison the POWs had named the Desert Inn, stripped him to his skivvies, covered him with a blanket, and left him there. "I was out of it most of the time, unconscious, for at least a day or two. When I woke up, they'd carry me to another room and try interrogating me. I couldn't even understand half of what they were asking. I gave them name, rank, et cetera, and they'd hit me where they knew my fractures were."

He pleaded to be taken to the hospital. They ignored him. His treatment alternated between neglect and abuse. They left his broken bones as they were, and when he became feverish and couldn't keep his food down, they let him lie in his own vomit and waste. When he was conscious, they interrogated him and beat him until he blacked out. After three or four days—he was never certain how many had elapsed—he saw that his right knee was badly swollen and discolored. "I remembered a guy in Meridian who broke his leg—his femur— when he ejected. The blood pooled in his leg, and he went into shock and died. I was scared the same thing was happening to me."

He begged the guards to take him to the hospital. "I'll die if you don't." They fetched an English-speaking officer, a man the POWs called "Bug." McCain bargained with him: "Take me to the hospital and I'll give you the information you want." Bug sent for a medic, who took his pulse and shook his head. "It's too late," he declared. Desperate, McCain argued, "Take me to the hospital and I'll get well," only to be told again, "It's too late." They didn't ask him any more questions or hurt him. They left him to his fate. He felt a surge of panic, he said, and then "I kind of fell apart." He passed out soon thereafter, which "was probably for the best." I assume he meant that he hadn't wanted to be conscious when he died, but I never pressed him on the point.

He was roused sometime later by an excited Bug. McCain wasn't sure how much time had passed since he'd been left to die, but he didn't think it was longer than an hour. "Your father is a big admiral," Bug shouted. "Now we take you to the hospital."

On October 28, two days after he had been shot down, the *New York Times* ran a front-page story written by R. W. Apple Jr.: "Adm. McCain's Son, *Forrestal* Survivor, Is Missing in Raid." It probably saved his life. "The Vietnamese read the main American newspapers," McCain explained to me. "They pretended they didn't, but they'd quote stuff from them in propaganda broadcasts. . . . I didn't know about Johnny's story, but I bet that's how they found out who I was."

The story included a few details about the shoot down and quoted from a Vietnamese radio broadcast that described the capture. But most of the piece was based on quotes from Apple's conversations with McCain after the *Forrestal* fire. "It was almost three months ago, that the young, prematurely gray Navy pilot sat sipping a Scotch with friends," it began, "and recalled the holocaust he had managed to live through." In the third paragraph, Apple quoted McCain offering an unexpected sentiment for a man who had been disappointed when he thought his combat tour was going to be cut short: "It's a difficult thing to say, but now that I've seen what the bombs and napalm did to the people on our ship, I'm not sure that I want to drop any more of that stuff on North Vietnam."

Apple explained McCain's decision to transfer to the *Oriskany* through a quote invoking his navy heritage: "I always wanted to be in the Navy," McCain had insisted. "I was born into it, and I never really considered another profession. But I always had trouble with regimentation."

His hospital room was "filthy," he remembered, and dank, with water on the floor, mosquitoes, and rats. "I was mostly out of it in the beginning, but they gave me a transfusion and glucose, and I started coming around after a couple days." Once his condition had stabilized, they started interrogating him again. He said he gave them the name of his ship and squadron number but not much else. "They asked for the names of the other guys in my squadron, so I named the Packers' offensive line." When his interrogators tried beating information out of him, "I screamed as loud as I could," he said. "I think they were worried about the medical staff getting annoyed, not that I remember many doctors or nurses taking much interest in me."

He had been in the hospital about a week when he met the commandant of North Vietnam's prisoner-of-war camps, "a real dapper guy, well educated"—the POWs called him "the Cat"—who informed McCain that a French television journalist was coming to interview him. Cat warned him that he needed two operations on his right leg that they would not give him if he refused to cooperate. Before his visitors arrived, a doctor had spent ninety minutes manipulating McCain's right arm, trying to set his multiple fractures, before giving up and slapping a body cast on him. "Without any anesthesia," McCain emphasized.

The interview with François Chalais, which has been seen by thousands if not millions of people over the years, always embarrassed McCain. He begins the interview as gamely as he can, his voice shaky, as is his left hand, holding a cigarette. He is clearly struggling to keep his composure. But he holds himself together for most of the interview, even joking about the food. Near the end, he struggles to fight back tears after Chalais asks if he wants to say something to his family. "I would just like to tell my wife," he responds, "that I will get well, and I love her, and hope to see her soon. I'd appreciate it if you'd tell her that."

McCain saw the interview many times in documentaries about the war and profiles of him. It's compelling viewing. But it bothered him every time he saw it. He thought he looked weak, and you couldn't convince him otherwise. I tried. Once, in exasperation—because we wanted to use a clip of the interview in a campaign ad, and he was resisting—I sarcastically dismissed his reservation: "Nobody comes away from seeing it, John, and says, 'Boy, that McCain's a wimp.' Trust me." He didn't. When I informed him a few years ago that documentarian Ken Burns was using the interview in a ten-part series on the Vietnam War, John urged me to make sure the film explained that, minutes before the interview, doctors had clumsily tried to set his fractures "without anesthesia. Not even an aspirin."

The Cat had instructed McCain before the interview that he was expected to thank the Vietnamese doctors and people for the "humane and lenient" treatment he had received. McCain did allow, when asked, that he had been "treated well by the people and doctors here." He also added that he was waiting for an operation on his broken leg and another cast for his left arm. When McCain ended the interview, one Vietnamese officer told him to say he could receive letters and pictures from home. And the Cat demanded that McCain say he wanted the war to end soon so he could go home. He refused, and Chalais intervened when they repeated their demands: "I think what he told me is sufficient."

They operated on his leg in December and botched it, severing the ligaments on one side of his knee. "There was a film crew in the operating room," he added, "no clue why." The cast they had put on his chest and right arm was unlined, and the plaster "wore two holes in my arm down to the bone." He never got the cast for his left arm. He suffered from chronic dysentery and lost a lot of weight; the sixteen-year-old who guarded him ate most of his food. He reckoned he had dropped to no more than a hundred pounds by December, and he was running a high fever. Medical staff must have informed the prison authorities that he was failing. The Bug showed up one day and declared, "The doctors say you are not getting better." McCain asked to be taken back to prison and put in a cell with other POWs. "Put me with Americans," he implored, "and I'll get better."

They brought him on a stretcher to a camp that was formerly a film studio; the Americans called it "the Plantation." The Plantation was intended for propaganda purposes to be, if not exactly a showcase prison, at least one suitable for foreign peace delegations to visit and confirm its humane conditions. When the Vietnamese discovered

McCain was an admiral's son and started referring to him as the "Crown Prince," they knew his potential value as a propaganda object was greater than that of any other prisoner they held. They gave him to two U.S. Air Force majors, George "Bud" Day and Norris Overly. Day suspected they brought McCain to them not in the hope that the two Americans could nurse him back to health but, rather, to have scapegoats to blame when McCain died. He was filthy, covered in grime, unshaved, with food particles in his beard and hair and waste staining his legs. "He was a skeleton with white hair, his face was red with fever and bug-eyed. He smelled rotten," Day remembered. "I thought he'd die in a day or two." McCain, however, was "overjoyed. I couldn't stop talking. I told them everything I could remember about being shot down and captured and how I'd been treated since. They told me their stories. Bud had escaped and almost made it to a marine base before they got him. I asked about the camp, how many of us were there, how they were being treated, et cetera. I was so relieved to be with Americans again. I think I started getting better right then.

"I owe them my life," McCain stressed, crediting not only their physical care of him but the restorative effect their company had on his morale. Day's injuries were as severe as McCain's, and beyond offering words of encouragement, he couldn't do much for the injured pilot; Overly did everything. "He was a gentle, uncomplaining guy," McCain recalled. "He cleaned me, fed me, massaged my bad leg, got me on and off the bucket, wiped me, everything. Just a good, good guy."

He slept eighteen to twenty hours a day in the beginning. But after their first week together, Overly had him on his feet, then hobbling around on crutches soon after. He put on a little weight and recovered his humor and irreverence. One day, to the cellmates' amusement, a young English-speaking army officer brought several Communist Party worthies to their cell. After staring at him for a minute, the officer asked McCain, "How many corporations does your family own?" "What do you mean?" a puzzled McCain responded. The officer replied, "Your father is a big admiral. He must have many companies that work for the government."

"We were laughing," McCain recalled, referring to his cellmates' reaction. "And when I told the guy my dad lived on his navy salary, and he translated it for the other guys, they all laughed. A definite culture clash."

After a month or so, their captors suddenly began giving them more to eat. Interrogations weren't demanding, and punishment for not cooperating was mild. McCain remembered the Cat paying several visits to their cell and inquiring about their welfare. "We knew something was up," he said, "but didn't find out what for a few weeks, until Norris told us they were sending him home." That was in early February. Overly and two other prisoners had agreed to the Cat's offer of amnesty and were released on February 16. Overly believed he was chosen because he was in comparatively good condition and could attest that his cellmates had received medical treatment for their injuries. Most, though not all, of the other POWs objected to the three men's decision. Bud Day, whom Overly had nursed back to health as he had McCain, thought he was making a mistake and told him so but didn't resent him for it. McCain told me he, too, had thought "Norris would regret it," but didn't say anything to him. "He was so good to me, I didn't want to be ungrateful." Instead, when the guards came to move Overly to a separate cell, McCain asked him to carry home a note he had written to Carol, and wished him well. "I thanked him, hugged him goodbye, and told him good luck." A few days later, in a ceremony at the Plantation in front of a sizable contingent of foreign press, the three prisoners were handed over to two prominent American anti-war figures.

McCain never spoke disparagingly about Overly in any of our conversations about his years in prison. On the contrary, he never mentioned Overly without acknowledging his debt to him and describing him as an uncommonly decent person. I asked once if he had ever gotten in touch with Overly after the war. He said he had and that the last time they'd spoken hadn't been that long ago. I have no reason to doubt that. But I don't know of a time after that conversation when the two men talked. I likely would have known. I remained his administrative assistant for another ten years and spoke with him every day. But he could keep his own counsel when he thought something was no one else's business, which was certainly the case here.

Day and McCain were still in poor physical shape when Overly left. Fellow POWs teased them as they watched the men hobble to the washroom once a week. They made fun of each other, too. They were both the type who laughed easily and infectiously. They spoke admiringly of each other's resilience. McCain said Day had "an indomitable will to survive" that gave him courage. Day said, "McCain had a fantastic will to live." In April 1968, camp authorities observed McCain getting around on his crutch well enough. They moved Bud Day to a cell in another part of the camp, and not long after to another prison, "the Zoo," intended for hard-core resisters. McCain was moved to another cellblock at the Plantation, a building the POWs called "the Warehouse." With Day's departure began two years of solitary confinement that McCain called the worst two years of his life. He described the miseries of solitary confinement as "worse than torture."

McCain said he felt despair the instant he and Day were separated. "The first weeks are the hardest. Without someone encouraging me, right away I started doubting myself." He was still suffering from severe dysentery, which caused stabbing stomach pains and made it hard to keep food down. Malnourishment left him constantly fatigued. "I became kind of a hypochondriac in solitary," he added. A prison medic checked on him a few times a year, he recalled, but offered nothing more than an exhortation to eat more and exercise, though McCain's injuries made the latter impractical. Left on his own, he confessed to being "paranoid" about common ailments. "I got hemorrhoids from the dysentery, and when they didn't go away, honest to God, I thought it might be fatal.

"You start to get used to it [solitary] after a month," he explained. "You have to come up with ways to keep your mind occupied." He mentioned memorizing the names of other prisoners and details about the camp, guards, and interrogators. He said he prayed more often and more sincerely than he ever had. But he spent most hours reenacting stories from favorite books and films. "I'd get so wrapped up in them some days that I'd get pissed off if something interrupted me." By the early summer, he had even started a limited exercise regime of a few standing push-ups off his cell wall, though "it hurt like hell." Those first weeks "felt like time stopped, like I was living in the same day forever." But as he adjusted, time started to move along again. Repeating a popular prison adage, he said, "The days and hours are very long, but the weeks and months pass quickly."

He was "saved from going nuts" by the guy in the cell next to him, Air Force major Bob Craner. "Bob wasn't as talkative as me," McCain recalled, "and he had a cellmate part of the time we were neighbors. But he knew how much I needed to talk." The two became inveterate communicators, using the tap code devised by the prisoners and, more often, wrapping a shirt around the enamel cup each POW was provided and speaking through the wall. If they were caught communicating, and McCain often was, they were physically punished. "It was worth it," he argued.

They talked about their situation, about their lives before Vietnam, about their families, about sports—both men revered Ted Williams. McCain relayed a story about Craner breaking up with a girl he had avidly pursued because she thought Stan Musial was a better ballplayer than Williams; thirty years later, the story would still have McCain shaking with laughter. They had similar senses of humor, heavy on the sarcasm and irony, and they poked fun at the propaganda broadcasts piped daily into their cells. They gave titles to "patriotic" songs they were made to listen to: "Springtime in a Liberated Zone" and "I Asked My Mother How Many Air Pirates She Shot Down Today." They joked that the Vietnamese had warehouses full of munition cases labeled "Very First Shot," in reaction to the near-daily reports of peasant marksmen who brought down another air pirate "with the very first shot."

Their voices were their presence. Neither knew what the other looked like. But "he was my dearest friend," McCain recalled, "the closest friend I ever had." After the war, Craner described their relationship to a reporter:

My world had shrunk to a point where the figures in my dreams were myself, the guards and a voice . . . and that was McCain. I didn't know what he looked like, so I could not visualize him in my dreams, because he became the guy, the only guy I turned to for a period of two years. We got to know each other more intimately than I will know my wife. We opened up and talked about damn near everything besides our immediate problems— past life, and all the family things we never would have talked about. We derived a great deal of strength from this.[26]

I read the quote to McCain, who hadn't seen it before. "Yeah, well, there's a lot of truth in it. And I'll tell you this, without Bob Craner, I wouldn't have come home, at least not as myself. I wouldn't have come home as myself."

Are there friendships like this formed in ordinary circumstances, or are they only formed in ordeals such as war? I honestly don't know. I asked him if he thought so, and he flattered me with his answer. "You can have close friends outside a war, friends you confide in. You're a close friend. I confide in you." Then he repeated my original question: "Can you have the kind of friendship Bob Craner and I had? No, you probably can't."

An avid communicator, McCain acknowledged he was also one of the least discreet. He said the interrogations—"quizzes," the POWs called them—he was subjected to in his first year of captivity usually followed being caught in the act of talking to or passing messages to other prisoners. He emphasized that the mistreatment he suffered "wasn't as bad as other guys had." And in the months after Norris Overly and the others had gone home, the Vietnamese had been "pretty lenient" with him, often just threatening him with punishment or withholding his cigarette ration when they caught him communicating. One of his interrogators, who spoke good English and affected a friendlier demeanor toward the POWs, had asked McCain that spring if he would like to go home. He didn't take the offer seriously.

Six weeks later, McCain was taken to "the Big House," an ornate, dilapidated two-story mansion that housed interrogation rooms, administrative offices, and a large reception room where visiting anti-war delegations were received and filmed. McCain found himself in the reception room with Cat, seated before a glass-top coffee table and offered tea, cookies, and cigarettes while he listened to Cat's meandering discourse on his experiences running prisoner-of-war camps during the French Indochina War, translated by an interrogator and experienced torturer whom the prisoners called "Rabbit."

The commissar eventually got around to the purpose of the interview. He told McCain he had recently met with two French prisoners he had freed in the last war, and the hale and hearty men had expressed their gratitude. He added that Norris Overly and the two other POWs released in the winter had been warmly welcomed home. Then he asked McCain if he wanted to go home. The offer took McCain by surprise, and he asked for time to consider it. Cat admonished him to consider it "carefully" and dismissed him. The prisoner's code of conduct maintained that prisoners should be released in the order they were captured, and there were a good many Americans who had been held longer than McCain had. Remembering the resentment some of the POWs had felt toward Norris and the other two paroled prisoners, McCain didn't believe Cat's assurances that they had been welcomed home as heroes. However, given his physical condition, "I could have rationalized going home," he explained. He was badly injured, sick with dysentery, malnourished, and underweight. "I knew they'd make me read some kind of propaganda statement, but I probably could've figured some way to screw it up."

He asked Bob Craner for advice. The two men speculated about what the Vietnamese might demand from him in exchange for his release. Finally, noting that the code of conduct allowed for the seriously injured to accept amnesty, Craner advised him to take the offer because his condition made long-term survival in prison questionable.

"Why didn't you?" I asked him.

"Because I knew that wasn't the case. I knew I would survive," he answered.

"Why did Craner feel you couldn't?"

"Because he'd been listening to me complain, I guess."

The two men went back and forth on the question for days. Craner suggested he play along and find out what he would have to do in exchange for being released. McCain didn't believe it would matter "what I said or didn't say. They'll tell all of you, 'We let McCain go because his father is an admiral. But your father's not, and nobody gives a shit about you.'" Unbeknownst to Craner and McCain but not to the Vietnamese, President Johnson had selected Admiral McCain as CINCPAC two months earlier, and the admiral would assume the command in early July.

Craner advised McCain to relay the offer to the senior ranking officer at the Plantation. McCain said he told Craner he would, but I couldn't get him to say explicitly that he had, only that he "wouldn't have gone home without [the SRO's] agreement." He was summoned to the Big House a few days later and declined the offer: "American prisoners cannot accept parole or amnesty or special favors. We must be released in order of our capture, starting with Everett Alvarez."

The Cat told him President Johnson had ordered him home, and McCain asked to see the order. Rabbit handed him a letter from Carol McCain expressing regret that he hadn't been among the prisoners who had been sent home, and Cat ordered McCain returned to his cell. A third meeting was cut short by a bout of dysentery.

He was summoned for a final interview on the Fourth of July. News that three Americans were to be granted amnesty had been broadcast over the camp's loudspeakers that morning, and one of the camp officers—the one with the friendly demeanor whom they called "Slick" or "Soft Soap"—congratulated McCain on being one of the lucky prisoners granted amnesty: "You will have a nice family reunion, Mac Kane."

McCain was brought to see the Cat a few hours later. He would recount the exchange with greater attention to detail than was usually his practice. He was taken to an interrogation room rather than the reception room. He wasn't offered cookies or cigarettes. Cat was seated at a table, a dated copy of the *International Herald Tribune* at hand, opened to an Art Buchwald column. Rabbit instructed him to give "our senior officer . . . your final answer."

"My final answer is no," McCain responded.

Cat snapped the pen he was holding in half, and ink splattered the newspaper. He stood up abruptly, knocking over his chair in the process, and barked in English, "They taught you too well." "Seconds seemed like minutes," McCain remembered, as he and Rabbit stood looking at each other before Rabbit dismissed him with the warning, "Now it will be very bad for you, Mac Kane." Two months later, McCain would discover that his father had assumed command of all U.S. forces in the Pacific that same day.

I never heard him say he was proud he had made such a hard decision. He was too chastened by the experiences that followed to speak of his pride. He would say repeatedly that his choice to remain in Hanoi rather than risk dishonor gave him confidence in his own judgment, confidence that he would do the honorable thing in the worst of trials, confidence that he would retain the rest of his life. He considered it the greatest test of his life, and when he spoke of his reasons for choosing to remain, and how the choice had affected his future and his character, it was not with pride—certainly not a boastful pride—but with relief, as if he had surprised himself by pulling off a narrow escape. I also suspect that he believed the act of self-denial, with all its attendant risks to his life and health, could redeem past sins and future ones. He kept on the wall opposite the photographs of his father, grandfather, and Mr. Ravenel a framed Photostat copy of a State Department cable dated September 13, 1968, sent by Averell Harriman, the Johnson administration's envoy to the early Paris peace talks: "At last tea break," Harriman reported, "Le Duc Tho attended, he mentioned that the DRV had intended to release Admiral McCain's son as one of the three pilots freed recently, but he had refused. According to Tho, Commander McCain feared that if he was released before the war was over, President Johnson might 'cause difficulties' for his father because people will wonder if McCain had been brainwashed."

Two weeks before Harriman sent the cable that mentioned McCain, a forced confession had played from prison loudspeakers and eventually made its way to the attention of the Pacific Command and Admiral John S. McCain Jr. In 2016 a recording of the confession was made public, and McCain-hating Internet trolls denounced it as Songbird McCain's Tokyo Rose moment. Yet John McCain had described to me and many others the statement the Vietnamese had forced him to make, first in a written statement he had signed and then in a tape recording. He discussed it in numerous interviews after the war and in the first book we wrote together. He couldn't remember the precise wording of the statement, but the gist that he described proved to be pretty close to the actual statement:

I, as a US Airman, am Guilty of Crimes against the Vietnamese country and people. I have bombed their cities, towns and villages and caused many injuries, even death to the people of Vietnam.

I was captured in the Capitol of Hanoi while attacking it. After I was captured I was [inaudible] for the hospital in Hanoi where I received very good medical treatment. I was given an operation on my leg which allowed me to walk again and a cast on my right arm which was badly broken in three places. The doctors were very good and they knew a great deal about the practice of medicine. I remained in the hospital for some time and regained much of my health and strength.

Since I arrived in the camp of detention, I have received humane and lenient treatment. I received this good treatment and food, even though I came here as an aggressor and the people who I injured have much difficulty in their living standards. I wish to express my deep gratitude for my kind treatment and I will never forget this kindness extended to me.

He had made the confession following four days of the worst physical abuse he would suffer in prison. The abuse had begun with a question. "Why do you treat your guards disrespectfully?" the camp commander had demanded. "Because they treat me like an animal," McCain had answered, and with that the commander signaled the guards to beat him savagely. He had been trussed in ropes, kept awake for days, repeatedly and savagely beaten, his left arm refractured, his bad knee swollen, his teeth broken, left to lie in his own blood and waste. So despairing was he that at one point he made a weak attempt to hang himself with his shirt. Other prisoners who had suffered similar abuse or worse had been coerced into providing their captors propaganda statements. None of them I knew doubted McCain had done his utmost to resist. And certainly no one who hadn't shared the experience with him, and had an ounce of humility, would fault him for the confession. But he did. He was ashamed of it.

He was angry when the tape recording made the rounds of conspiracy mongers, and angrier still when it was reported in the legitimate press. "It's frustrating," he said, explaining his anger, "they don't know the full story." But he had told the story himself, and with the exception of people who felt extreme antipathy toward him, it was obvious that no rational, fair-minded person thought he had acted dishonorably. I don't think he really believed people would think less of him for his confession. He couldn't pardon himself for it, and he *did* know the full story. I don't think he ever stopped regretting it. "I was disgraced," he said. "No, you weren't," I once responded, and he ignored it. Well-meaning reassurances from people who hadn't been there meant nothing to him. What did we know? "I failed," he repeated again and again. "I failed."

By Christmas, he was finding ways to resist again. At a filmed Christmas service held in the building the prisoners named "the Movie House," McCain made a spectacle of himself by talking loudly to other prisoners and giving the camera the finger. Soft Soap told him to be quiet. "Fuck you!" he shouted back, starting a general uprising as the other POWs started talking and flashing hand signals to each other.

But McCain would remember the year that followed his confession as his worst time in prison. His treatment was now more in line with what other resisters experienced when they were caught communicating or showing disrespect for the guards, offenses McCain was now routinely punished for committing. He would be beaten or left on a stool all night with his arms cinched tightly behind his back until he wrote an apology to the prison authorities. Like other prisoners, he was sometimes made to read "the news" over the camp loudspeakers.

He would read in a stilted fashion, screw up the syntax, invert the meaning of words, and make up facts, to the amusement of his audience. He was "an inventive resister," one fellow POW observed, who "had an uncommon ability to endure abuse and bounce back from it again and again."[27]

That resilience was essential to McCain's survival in prison and a driving force in his political career. It was difficult for him to turn off. He couldn't understand why anyone wouldn't react to trouble or suffering as he did. When he was dumped back in his cell after a night of punishment, he "got right back on the wall," he said, talking to whoever was there to listen. When others returned from a beating, McCain wanted to rally their spirits, get them talking, tell them to hang in there, reassure them they had done well. I once mentioned to his cellmate Orson Swindle that McCain had criticized another prisoner who was returned to his cell after being tortured for communicating: He wouldn't respond to McCain's tapping. "I was trying to find out how he was doing," he explained, "and he wouldn't answer for days." Swindle laughed as he explained to me, "Most guys just wanted to lay low and regroup after getting the shit kicked out of them. John didn't understand that. He was ready to go again." In the McCain mind-set, you weren't beaten until you quit. He could be on the losing end of any number of contests, but the next fight was all that mattered. Speaking on the stump in his 2008 campaign, he expressed a sentiment that could have been his motto: "Hopelessness is the enemy who defeats your will. I felt those things once before. I will never let them in again."

A general crackdown on the POW communications networks was instituted in all the camps early in the summer of 1969, following a daring escape attempt that May by two air force pilots, John Dramesi and Ed Atterberry. After their recapture, Dramesi and Atterberry were savagely beaten, and Atterberry died of his wounds. McCain, who later shared a cell with Dramesi, said the hardened resister "was one of the toughest guys I'd ever met." Cells were inspected frequently. Interrogations were longer and more violent and focused on discovering escape plans; harsher punishment was meted out for those caught communicating. Again, McCain was regularly discovered in the act and subjected to his share of abuse. He recalled that summer being the hottest of his five summers there, and he suffered from heat rash to go along with the dysentery and beatings. Still in solitary confinement, he struggled to keep his "mind focused on other things than how miserable I was." Mainly, he helped to maintain discipline by keeping intact the communication lines to their senior officers. It was perhaps the first experience in his life in which McCain was a committed company man, recognizing that his personal ordeal couldn't be solved separately from the others'. He embraced the creed imparted by his superiors: To get home, the men had to keep faith with God, country, and each other. He was sincere about it, he said. He took comfort in the affirmation. He was full of ideas about new ways to resist and recommended them to his commanding officers. As would be the case in his next career, he could be a little put out when leadership didn't take him up on his proposals, but he followed orders faithfully, "to the letter, if I could," he said, because "it was important there, it was important, to have that kind of discipline. It helped you, and you needed the help in situations when you were dealing with the Vietnamese by yourself. You knew what you could do and what you couldn't do for as long as you could hold out."

America became more to McCain in Vietnam. It wasn't only his home or the side he was fighting on. He told me that he reminded himself often during the worst of the abuse that if the situation were reversed and the Vietnamese were captives, Americans would not treat them as cruelly. That conviction would motivate his opposition to the Bush administration's treatment of detainees. Because America was founded on ideals of liberty and equal justice, to defend the country was to defend its ideals. It ennobled their sacrifice at the lowest points of pain and suffering and humiliation. A country based on ideals wouldn't abandon them and would respect suffering.

McCain spoke little to me about his religious faith. He may have been more forthcoming with others, but I doubt it. He was raised Episcopalian and could quote from *The Book of Common Prayer,* but he found the enthusiasm and informality of services at First Baptist Church of Phoenix more to his liking. I do know that his religious beliefs were never more potent than during his years in Hanoi. He spoke of religious experiences there like they were epiphanies: a Christian guard who was kind to him, drawing a cross in the dirt for them both to venerate; discovering the "Our Father" scratched on the wall of a punishment cell. Both encounters had moved him deeply, and he recalled them with humility. In the later years of his captivity, he undertook, at the request of his fellow POWs, what can fairly be described as ministerial duties. He was appointed chaplain for the big room where he was held with twenty-five other prisoners in the last year of their captivity. He helped organize and conduct an Easter service and even proselytized to a disbelieving interrogator about the meaning of the holiest day on the Christian calendar. He wrote down the story of the Nativity from the Gospel of Luke and read it during a Christmas service in 1972. He recalled weeping as they all sang "Silent Night" to end the service, and he looked out on the wretched congregation of battered, sick, and hungry men. In the nights before and after the service, B-52s dropped their payloads so close that the ground they were standing on shook.

Three prisoners released in a third round of amnesty in the summer of 1969—one had been expressly permitted by his commanding officer, and the other two were severely injured—gave public testimony to the Vietnamese's mistreatment of prisoners. The Nixon administration had reversed Johnson's policy that kept the conditions of their imprisonment subject to quiet negotiations and not public scrutiny. Public opinion was turning more and more against the war, but stories of Americans being tortured threatened to slow or reverse the trend. "The Vietnamese," McCain frequently stressed, "paid close attention to the media and public opinion." The POWs' treatment improved in the fall of 1969, and McCain attributed it to the criticism Hanoi was getting in the Western press for physically abusing prisoners. He said an interrogator had confirmed to him that the North Vietnamese government was aware of and concerned about the media reaction. POWs, including McCain, also suspected that Ho Chi Minh's death in September of that year had something to do with it, ascribing the cruelty of policies regarding POWs to the cruelty of the man they assumed had ordered those policies. That did not prove to be the case, though. By the time of his death, Ho Chi Minh was more a figurehead than the actual head of government. That power belonged to Le Duan, the Communist Party general secretary, who had effectively elbowed Ho to the side years earlier.

Whatever had precipitated it, their treatment continued to improve with each passing year. They weren't routinely beaten for refusing to make propaganda statements. Food rations were more generous. "Some guards even made an effort to be pleasant," McCain remembered. There was an apparent shake-up of prison authorities in October 1969 and a crackdown on the abuse of prisoners. McCain chuckled as he recalled Soft Soap coming to his cell one day. "Even the Russians criticize us. You tell lies about us. You say we . . . make you live in unventilated rooms," he whined to McCain, who was sitting in an unventilated cell. "That was an unexpected reversal," McCain observed as he described the new attitude forced on interrogators and guards. "And not everybody got in line." He was caught communicating in that period and made to stand for two days and nights facing the wall of a punishment room. On the second night, exhausted, he dropped to the floor. An angry guard gave him "a memorable beating," jumping on his bad leg, which forced him to rely on a crutch again.

The Plantation was shuttered in 1970. By then, McCain had been returned to "Little Vegas," the section of Hoa Lo prison where he had been briefly held after his capture. In March 1970, he finally got a cellmate, Air Force lieutenant colonel John Finlay, whom he proceeded to barrage "for days" with questions and an account of his own experiences. "It must have been like drinking from a firehose," McCain remembered. "Fortunately, John was a good-natured guy and put up with it."

The previous Christmas, McCain had welcomed an unexpected visitor. Cat had been demoted in the aftermath of the prisoner abuse controversy. He was no longer commissar of the entire prison system but appeared to still have senior officer status at Hoa Lo. He entered McCain's cell dressed nattily in a well-made three-piece suit. He wore a diamond stick pin in his tie and offered McCain a cigarette from a silver cigarette case. He hadn't brought an interpreter but managed to speak comprehensible English. "He started talking about Christmas and how it was celebrated in his home when he was a kid. His family might have been Catholic, and upper class, for sure." Then Cat began to talk about his experiences in the war, both the war with the U.S. and the French Indochina War. "It was weird," McCain recalled. "Maybe he was doing it because they'd been ordered to treat us better, I don't know. Maybe he thought we had something in common." Cat's father had been a close associate of Ho's during his Viet Minh days, and it seemed to McCain that Cat was trying to relate to him as one son of a powerful father to another. Cat talked about a villa on an island in Ha Long, the beautiful bay near Vietnam's border with China, where his father had once been invited to spend a holiday with Ho. As he got up to leave, he remarked that had McCain accepted his offer of amnesty the year before, "you would be home celebrating with your family tonight."

"You'll never understand why I could not," McCain responded.

"I understand more than you think," Cat snapped, and left the cell.

As McCain recounted the exchange to me, I noticed, not for the first time, that he was able to regard some of his captors, and the North Vietnamese in general, with something that sounded like empathy. If it wasn't empathy, he at least seemed to bear them no ill will. That didn't apply to all of them, of course. I don't think it even applied consistently to the Cat, who had, after all, ordered the torture that had broken and humiliated him. One of McCain's guards, whom he called "the Prick," had struck him when he refused to bow day in and day out; the Prick was no longer posted at the prison after the shake-up. "I loved picturing the fucker on the [Ho Chi Minh Trail] getting pounded by the air force," he offered.

He got in trouble in his 2000 presidential bid for referring to his captors as "gooks," which was dutifully reported by the journalists he said it to. As was often the case with McCain, if he believed something he said was misconstrued or taken out of context, he would get his back up and refuse to budge on the point. That happened in this instance, when he refused to concede that the term "gook" could be considered a racial epithet. "It's not racist," he insisted. "I'm not talking about all Vietnamese. I'm talking about the ones who tortured and killed my friends." He even made reference to a Cuban, an expert on torture techniques who had helped interrogate POWs in Hanoi and was responsible for the death of at least one prisoner. "That Cuban asshole was a gook," McCain declared as he defended his use of the word. In those situations, when he felt his character was in question, it was often best to speak your piece, listen to him protest, and wait for him to adjust to reality of his own accord, which is what happened here. We stopped trying to change his mind, and he seemed to stop using the word, mostly. Unless, of course, he was challenged by a reporter newly arrived to the bus, and then we were off to the barricades again.

For the most part, though, he had an attitude to the people who once were his enemies and his oppressors that ranged from indifferent to benign. Perhaps it was nothing more than a professional military officer's respectfulness toward a battlefield foe. But I suspect it had more to do with the powerful force that propelled McCain through life at breakneck speed. He could be as nostalgic as anyone for past good times, but he didn't think of re-creating halcyon days; he thought it foolish to try when even better times might be had in the future. And bad memories of hardship and humiliation, well, it was best not to look back at all at those, and to put as much distance as possible between then and now.

I asked him once if any memory of the war still bothered him, and he answered, "No, not really." But then he allowed that for some years after he had come home, the sound of keys jangling would set his nerves on edge: It was the sound the turnkeys made when they approached his cell to fetch him for an interrogation. Most of the turnkeys "were peasants," he said. "Some of them were okay," he allowed, but some could be "the meanest guys you had to deal with." During one of his many trips to Vietnam as a senator, he was the guest of honor at a dinner hosted by Vietnam's foreign minister. An American military officer who spoke Vietnamese was seated next to me and informed me that a dinner guest claimed to have been one of McCain's turnkeys. I thought it best to break the news to him myself rather than risk him suddenly recognizing the fellow and possibly reacting undiplomatically. I got up and walked around the table to where he was seated; he cocked his head to his left so that I could whisper the news I was bringing him. I directed his attention to the man in question. McCain stared at him for a few seconds. "Don't recognize him," he said impassively, and he returned his attention to the foreign minister.

I detected a trace of sympathy when he mentioned that the Cat appeared to be suffering from a debilitating illness in McCain's later years of confinement: He had developed a hand tremor and had lost weight. When he told me the story of the Christmas visit, almost thirty years after it had happened, he still seemed intrigued by it. Maybe it was just the novelty of the brief time-out in the war and in a long adversarial relationship. But I imagined at the time that McCain had recognized something familiar in his jailer's psychology. They were both sons of prominent military fathers who had something to prove, and maybe there was something tragic in the Cat's case. I suggested writing a line in the book to that effect, and he rejected the idea. "That wasn't the case?" I asked. "You'd have to ask him," he replied. A little cryptic, but it was all I was going to get.

In 1970 McCain was moved several times within Little Vegas to cellblocks the POWs called the "Golden Nugget," "Thunderbird," and "Riviera." He was also exiled for a three-month stretch of solitary confinement in a filthy six-by-three-feet punishment cell they called "Calcutta." The cell was "pretty bad," McCain said, and "being in solitary again almost drove me nuts. I didn't know if I could hack it again." As at the Plantation, prison authorities had gone to great lengths to disrupt chains of command and lines of communication among the prisoners at Hoa Lo. They had transferred several senior officers and some of the toughest resisters to more isolated cells or to small punishment camps. McCain helped his senior ranking officers at Little Vegas—future U.S. senator Jeremiah Denton and future Naval Academy superintendent Bill Lawrence—rebuild Vegas's communications network. He respected both men immensely, and Lawrence would become a close lifelong friend. Other POWs told me Lawrence had been the one senior officer in prison who could get the rambunctious Mc-Cain to calm down and be more discreet. McCain spoke often about Bill Lawrence, as reverentially as he spoke about Mr. Ravenel. He said Lawrence was an ideal commanding officer, who led by example and quiet authority. McCain and another future member of Congress, Air Force fighter pilot Sam Johnson, were appointed "mailmen" for Thunderbird and Stardust, carrying notes between the cellblocks that were hidden behind a light switch. McCain was sent to Calcutta as punishment after being caught "delivering mail."

Following a failed American raid on Son Tay, a POW camp outside Hanoi, the Vietnamese began to centralize prisoners in the city, and the population at Hoa Lo increased significantly. Near the end of 1970, to accommodate the new arrivals, prisoners were congregated in large cells that could hold twenty to forty men. "Camp Unity," the prisoners called it. "A great day," McCain said, recalling the occasion when he was suddenly living in a room with dozens of POWs. He was soon reunited with Bud Day, who would be his SRO at Unity. "I hadn't seen him in almost three years, since the day they moved him out of our cell," he remembered. "I was overjoyed to see him again." From that point in his prison narrative, his recollections of imprisonment began to favor amusing anecdotes over existential crises; at times, it almost seemed to the listener that McCain enjoyed his remaining years in prison. He described entertaining his cellmates by narrating novels by Hemingway and Maugham, and re-creating his favorite films for "Saturday Night at the Movies," remembering some of the dialogue "and making up the rest." He recalled how one POW, Konrad Trautman, was always the first to take his seat and puff his pipe as he hung on every word of the performance. McCain talked about Sunday-afternoon bridge tournaments and a lecture series in which prisoners shared their expertise on subjects as far-ranging "as physics and meat cutting." He and Orson Swindle taught a class together, "The History of the World from the Beginning," which McCain described as "a work of imagination as much as it was an actual history lesson."

The benefits of Camp Unity were interrupted by a clash with prison authorities over religious services the prisoners wanted to conduct, remembered as "the Church Riot," which resulted in the exile of McCain, Day, Swindle, and twenty-four other prisoners to a run-down prison camp for troublemakers, a place the prisoners called "Skid Row," where they would remain for the next seven months. The cells lacked lights or ventilation, and the camp didn't have bathing facilities. They were initially kept one to a cell. McCain was incensed at being held again in solitary confinement. He shouted insults at the guards, which amused Swindle. "He was an ornery little guy," Swindle remembered. Even Bud Day, who ordered him to knock it off, couldn't get him to quiet down. Eventually, to everyone's relief, the Vietnamese moved him into a cell with another prisoner, Navy lieutenant Pete Schoeffel. "We barely had enough room to stand shoulder to shoulder," McCain remembered. But he was happy not to be in solitary, and he settled down. He never told me how Schoeffel had felt about the new arrangement. Orson Swindle recounted for me how McCain had treated him to a joking insult at Skid Row, which would be familiar to anyone who spent much time around McCain. I would hear him repeat it a hundred times or more.

"Hey, Orson," he hailed the marine flier a few cells down from him.

"Yeah," Orson replied.

"Did I ever tell you I wanted to be a marine?"

"Is that right."

"Yeah. But they wouldn't take me. My parents are married."

McCain, Day, and Swindle were the last to leave Skid Row. They were back at Unity in November 1971 and remained there for all but the last few weeks of their imprisonment. Their treatment continued to be more lenient than in earlier years, but it was not without incidents of cruelty. It was in McCain's last year of captivity that a navy bombardier-navigator from Alabama, Mike Christian, was dragged from their cell and beaten mercilessly for having sewn from scraps of cloth an American flag that the POWs pledged allegiance to every day. The night he was dumped back in their cell, bloody and bruised, his eyes nearly swollen shut, McCain watched him begin to sew a new flag. "He didn't do it for his sake but for ours," McCain remembered. He would tell the "Mike Christian story" on hundreds of occasions, in town halls and stump speeches, at Republican Party national conventions, at annual meetings of veterans' organizations and Rotary Club lunches. Never once did it fail to bring an audience to tears. It would always be the most effective part of any speech, which was attributable to Mike Christian's heroism, of course, and to the sincerity of McCain's gratitude toward him, which was evident in his every retelling.

A little over a year after they returned to Unity, the so-called Christmas bombing commenced, and B-52s again dropped their payloads very near the Hanoi Hilton. The prisoners, McCain included, correctly interpreted the decision to resume bombing as an indication that their captivity was nearing its end. Recently captured B-52 pilots confirmed news that Paris peace negotiations had appeared to be approaching a settlement when they were stalled by Hanoi's obstinacy. The B-52s were intended to get things back on track. And judging from the reaction of the guards, it was working. "For the first time, they looked genuinely scared," McCain remembered, "and we cheered every explosion."

The Plantation resumed operations in early January, and McCain was one of a number of POWs transferred there. On January 28, they were ordered to assemble in the camp's courtyard. They understood what was coming, and their senior officers—who knew the Vietnamese would want to make a propaganda show of it—had prepared them to show no emotion when the peace agreement was announced. As McCain described the day, he spoke of how proud he felt, standing in formation, staying perfectly quiet in front of the cameras as the accords were read. "We hardly made a sound as we broke ranks and went back to our cells. We waited for the cameras to leave, then we started celebrating." A few days before, Henry Kissinger had arrived in Hanoi to initial the final provisions of the accords. The Vietnamese offered to let him take Admiral McCain's son back with him. He refused, asserting that Commander McCain would want to return home with the others, in order of their capture. He recounted the offer to McCain when they met for the first time months later, not knowing how he would react. "He thanked me for saving his honor," recalled a visibly moved Kissinger, who would retell the story many times over the years of their ensuing friendship, the last time in his eulogy for McCain.

The day before he was to be released in the second group of prisoners to leave Hanoi, McCain was summoned by camp authorities and asked if he would like to thank the doctor and people of Vietnam for the operation that had saved his life. Noticing a nearby tape recorder, McCain said he spoke slowly and clearly: "No, I don't think so. But I would like to ask, where the fuck have you been for the last five years."

He described how proud he felt at the airport departure ceremony on March 15, performing the routine courtesies of an American military officer, saluting superior officers present, returning the salute of the escort officer who accompanied him as he limped up the ramp of the C-141, having tossed aside the new crutches provided by the Vietnamese. He cheered along with the rest of them after the plane took off, but he told me that the flight from Hanoi to Clark Airfield Base in the Philippines was "kind of anticlimactic." His mind was moving ahead already. "I wanted to get home and see my family," he recalled, "and catch up on everything I had missed." When he got to Clark, stewards asked him if there was anything they could bring him. He asked for newspapers and magazines.

QUESTIONS OF HONOR
(PART TWO)

"It kind of soured me on the place, for a while, at least," McCain said about the Senate's rejection of his friend John Tower's nomination as secretary of defense. "I thought it was disgraceful." The Tower nomination fight preceded my employment on his staff, but I remember the wounds were still fresh when I started working there in the summer of 1989, and his anger at colleagues he felt were responsible for his friend's disgrace was still raw; relations with one or two were never repaired. He did manage to put aside his grievance to form working relationships and even friendships with several Democratic colleagues whose failure to support Tower's nomination had angered him. In time, he would come to profess respect for Tower's chief antagonist, Senator Sam Nunn.

With the exception of his lost election for a leadership post, McCain's first two years in the Senate had been promising. He was considered by colleagues and Washington luminaries an up-and-comer with a great biography. He got the committee assignment that most mattered to him—the Armed Services Committee—thanks in part to Barry Goldwater, who had lobbied colleagues on his behalf. He got along well with the Republican leader, Bob Dole, who gave weight to McCain's foreign policy views. Dole had appointed him co-chair of a bipartisan Senate group focused on Central American policy as debate on the subject was at its most rancorous. McCain was fast becoming a quotable source for the Capitol Hill press corps. His profile had been elevated to the point that he was rumored to be on George H. W. Bush's short list of VP prospects. A *New York Times* profile in 1988 described him as "not only . . . a key voice on defense and foreign policy issues, but also a rising star in the post-Reagan Republican Party." Vice President Bush's convention manager, Fred Malek, offered McCain a prime-time speaking slot at the 1988 convention, on the same night President Reagan would give his farewell address. I attended the convention and watched McCain speak. He had written the speech himself and closed it with his story about Mike Christian. He had the audience in tears. It was the first time I remember paying attention to him.

His family was growing, too. He and Cindy had welcomed their first daughter, Meghan, in 1984, just a couple weeks before his reelection to the House. John Sidney McCain IV—Jack—followed two years later, while his father was running to succeed Barry Goldwater in the Senate. Jimmy McCain arrived two years after Jack. The McCains would break the pattern of two-year intervals between children when they adopted their second daughter, Bridget, in 1991, after Cindy brought her to the U.S. from Mother Teresa's orphanage in Dhaka, Bangladesh, for an operation.

McCain credited John Tower's support—his endorsement, advice, the donors he directed McCain's way, and the credibility that Tower's seal of approval conferred on him with the national security establishment—as critical to his quick rise in national politics. More personally, Tower's relationship with McCain was described by various observers as close to paternal. Tower had been a sailor in World War II, serving as a seaman first class on landing craft in the Pacific theater. He was proud of his navy heritage, and his choice of military escorts for overseas travel reflected his pride. He preferred that the navy liaison office oversee the logistics of his travel and supply his escort, which in the late 1970s meant Captain John S. McCain III assumed the duty.

Tower had known McCain's father, and knew of his grandfather, and had from the beginning of their association treated McCain with a genial familiarity that wasn't typical of Texas's senior senator. "Tower was a pretty formal guy," McCain remembered, "very courtly, very well mannered." He fit the bill of a seasoned diplomat, dressed in Savile Row suits when meeting with foreign government officials. "He could usually get meetings with heads of state, not just defense and foreign ministers," McCain noted. He was well traveled, experienced, "smart, and he knew it." He didn't suffer fools. He was opinionated, imperious, and quick to deploy a cutting remark in debate. "He didn't have a lot of friends in the Senate—not close ones, anyway," McCain conceded. "Bill Cohen and a few others, but almost everybody respected him, and committee staff were really devoted to him."

As chairman of the Senate Armed Services Committee, Tower was instrumental in authorizing the defense buildup begun in Reagan's first term. "Few senators knew the large strategic premises of national defense and the intricate details of defense policy as well as John Tower understood them," McCain wrote, defending President George H. W. Bush's nomination of Tower to be secretary of defense.

> Few knew the caliber of the men and women, officer and enlisted, who fight for us and the quality of the weapons we give them to fight with as well as John Tower did. And few senators had as extensive contacts with leading international statesmen as John Tower did.[28]

In his protégé's opinion, and in the opinion of most of the national security establishment, Tower was well qualified for the position. He had endorsed Bush in the primary and was assumed by everyone to be on the president-elect's short list for defense secretary. "We were all expecting it," McCain remembered, meaning Tower's nomination, "even though Bush hadn't committed to it and took his time to decide. No one, I mean no one, was worried about his confirmation. We took it for granted. We were only worrying about whether he'd be picked."

McCain conceded that the twice-married Tower had a reputation for womanizing and hard drinking, but he disputed the accuracy of the widespread perception. He told me that Tower's second marriage had been an unhappy one, and volatile, and that "we all had Lilla stories," referring to the run-ins most of Tower's aides and friends had with his second wife. Their acrimonious divorce a few years before had included Lilla's allegations of infidelity, which somehow made their way to newspapers after his nomination was announced. By the time of his nomination, Tower was in a stable relationship with a woman near his age, and "happier than I'd seen him in years." Tower's drinking, McCain insisted, wasn't anything like the incapacitating malady his detractors asserted or insinuated was the case. "He wasn't an alcoholic," McCain emphasized. "I know what a binge drinker looks like, and Tower wasn't one." Among his duties as an escort officer for overseas congressional delegations, McCain saw to the members' meals and drinks. "I traveled all the time with Tower," he reminded me. In Saudi Arabia (where liquor is officially banned), McCain had "to smuggle little mini-bottles of whiskey from the plane, so he and the other members could have a drink at the hotel." But he said he had never seen Tower have more than a glass of wine with lunch or a glass of champagne after boarding a plane. "Nothing more than that during the day," he stressed. "At the end of the day, he liked to unwind with two or three Scotches, Johnnie Walker Black. So what. I maybe saw him tipsy a couple times, tipsy but never out of control, never an embarrassment. Far from it." By the time he was nominated, Tower claimed to have quit drinking Scotch and to have limited his drinking to a glass or two of wine with meals. I asked McCain if that was true, and he answered, "As far as I know, yes."

What bothered McCain the most about the Tower affair "was the fucking hypocrisy" involved; he identified one particular Tower antagonist, a midwestern senator, "as one of the biggest boozers in the place." Tower's nemesis, the guy who appeared to be driving events toward the eventual derailment of his nomination, was the chairman of the Senate Armed Services Committee, Sam Nunn, a serious, thoughtful legislator respected by colleagues on both sides of the aisle, including John McCain. McCain theorized about why Nunn came to oppose Tower's nomination, but never found an answer that satisfied him. He thought it likely that the imperious Tower had slighted

Nunn, "probably more than once," by treating him with, if not disrespect, indifference. He also believed Lilla, Tower's ex-wife, was providing Nunn's staff with unverified accusations and malicious gossip. McCain accepted that Nunn might have been genuinely offended by what he was hearing. "He's a straitlaced guy," he acknowledged. But what McCain couldn't accept was "the unfair process Nunn concocted" to scrutinize the nomination, which McCain believed invited mischief by Tower's enemies and subjected the nominee to a ruthless campaign of humiliation. Breaking with precedent—which restricted access to FBI investigative files on a nominee to the chairman and ranking minority member of a committee—Nunn granted access to all committee members and staff. FBI reports on a nominee contain all manner of false or unsubstantiated allegations, which is why they are handled with such discretion. Once the reports were, in McCain's words, "tossed to the wolves," all sorts of salacious allegations began appearing in the press. The worst of them, McCain insisted, proved to be "a hundred percent bullshit." There were tales of Tower chasing secretaries around an office in Geneva, of a drunk Tower dancing on a piano with a Russian ballerina, of drunk driving and disorderly behavior on airplanes, and a host of other alarming episodes, none of which, McCain said, had been substantiated by multiple FBI investigations. "Not one was true."

Again and again, in our discussions of the Tower nomination fight, it seemed clear that McCain respected the fact that Nunn probably had genuine if misinformed reservations. But Tower "was entitled to fair treatment by the committee he had chaired, and he didn't get it." The facts didn't stop his nomination, the process did. The process was dragged out weeks longer than it should have been to, in McCain's opinion, "give every John Tower enemy and every nutcase looking for attention" a chance to make unfounded allegations. The process included testimony by a controversial figure from what in those days was called the New Right, Paul Weyrich, whom McCain denounced as a "pompous, self-serving son of a bitch."

He mimicked Weyrich's testimony for me, repeating, as the witness apparently had, "I'm a family man. I'm a family man. I'm a family man," a protestation intended to assure Weyrich's listeners that though he was in the vicinity of sin, it was not a location familiar to him. "Over the course of many years," Weyrich testified, "I have encountered the nominee in a condition—a lack of sobriety, as well as with women to whom he was not married." The accusation caused Nunn to gavel the public hearing to a close and question the witness in a closed hearing. McCain recounted how he questioned Weyrich behind closed doors and, in a matter of minutes, "exposed the fat fraud." When Weyrich alleged that he had witnessed Tower engaging in "immoral behavior," McCain instructed him to describe the alleged misconduct. Weyrich replied that he had seen Tower "coming on" to a woman at the Monocle, a popular Capitol Hill drinking establishment.

"What do you mean by 'coming on'?"

"He was holding her hand."

"You mean holding someone's hand is immoral behavior?"

Weyrich assumed the question was rhetorical and "just sat there staring at me."

According to McCain, Weyrich couldn't give the committee any credible evidence that Tower had been intoxicated in his presence, either, and "every member of the committee, no matter which side they were on, was put off by him." McCain and others assumed that Weyrich's public opposition to Tower was based on politics and ideology, not morality. Tower was pro-choice, though solidly conservative on most other issues. He was a skeptic of the New Right and a critic of Weyrich and his allies. McCain was convinced that Weyrich had made up or exaggerated his allegations. "He wanted to show the Bush administration [which conservatives like Weyrich believed was dominated by moderates] that he had power," McCain explained, "and they had to pay attention to him. He should've been deposed and never allowed to testify."

Although McCain was a junior member of the committee, he and Bill Cohen were Tower's chief advocates. "I should've realized sooner," he told me, "that Nunn had made up his mind. He was going to stop the nomination. Once that happened, it was a fight to the finish, and

[Senate majority leader George] Mitchell would get involved and help Nunn get the votes." Nunn was one of the most respected members of his caucus, and few Democrats would oppose his position lightly. McCain understood the predicament most of them faced, and he was selective with whom he singled out for abuse. He was irritated with a few Republicans who, at one time or another, had expressed reservations about Tower, and subjected them to an occasional insulting aside. He had an overactive animus for Bush White House counsel C. Boyden Gray, a somewhat eccentric East Coast patrician with the kind of personality that stirred McCain's deep reserves of sarcasm. Gray had apparently shared with Nunn his dislike of Tower, which could have signaled to Nunn that President Bush—to whom Gray was close—wouldn't fight hard for his nominee. Gray kept trying to curry favor with the chairman long past the point when it was clear that Nunn was determined to kill the nomination, and McCain mocked him to Republican colleagues as an "Ivy League dilettante."

By the end, McCain was publicly and privately chastising other colleagues over what he believed was their violation of basic rules of fairness that should be accorded any nominee for high office, especially one whom they all knew. His anger during the nomination supplied some of the foundational anecdotes for the legend of John McCain's temper. One Democratic committee member from the old school of transactional politics had committed to McCain, who was whipping votes for Tower, that he would break with Nunn and support the nominee. When he didn't keep his word, McCain charged up to him in front of scores of witnesses, "nose to nose," McCain described (although the senator in question was a good six inches taller), "and let him have it." To his credit, McCain allowed, "he took it pretty well." To another—whom he identified as a lead instigator of the anti-Tower mob mentality and who had said to McCain about allegations against Tower, "I know what I know"—McCain shouted, again in front of witnesses, "What you know is a lie, and you're a goddamn liar." He had been in the Senate only two years, and he was dressing down members with greater seniority. He didn't care. He felt his friend was wronged, and he intended to make clear he knew who had wronged him. Though I wasn't around then, I imagine Chris Koch, his administrative assistant at the time, and other aides encouraged restraint. But of his many qualities, good and bad, John McCain's righteous indignation was the hardest to suppress. You wouldn't want to suppress it most times. Even if its expression wasn't always appropriate to the environment, it was usually honest. Many of McCain's closest friends in Washington at the time had worked on the committee staff for Tower. They shared McCain's outrage and urged him on. I doubt he needed the encouragement.

He went to see Tower in his temporary office at the Pentagon right after the Senate deprived him of his life's ambition by voting down his nomination for secretary of defense. The committee had rejected the nomination on a party-line vote, and the vote by the full Senate had been a foregone conclusion. A few Democrats stood by Tower, and McCain would never forget it. He said he was moved by Connecticut senator Chris Dodd's speech on Tower's behalf. He would fight with Dodd over foreign policy issues every year that they were both in the Senate. But ever after, he considered him a friend and enjoyed traveling overseas with him. And he remembered Bill Cohen's speech as one of the "most eloquent" addresses he ever heard on the Senate floor; he brought it up to me often.

He was lost in the emotions of the moment that day as could happen to him, and those emotions are his clearest memories of the affair. He had closed his own speech with an extemporaneous "God bless you, John Tower. You're a damn fine sailor," his voice thick. He said Tower had kept his game face on when they met that afternoon to commiserate over the defeat. "But I knew he was hurt not just by losing the job but to find out that a lot of his colleagues, guys he thought were his friends, didn't think much of him." McCain swore vengeance against the backstabbers as the stoic Tower struggled to keep his emotions in check. McCain said he saw Tower cry as they embraced goodbye. "I'd never seen him cry. I'd never seen him hug somebody, either." McCain left quickly then, he recalled, "before he saw me cry."

Two years later, I was traveling in Asia with McCain when a foreign service officer brought news that John Tower and his daughter had been killed in an airplane crash. McCain looked at the guy incredulously, asking repeatedly, "John Tower? John Tower? John Tower?" receiving a "Yes, sir" each time. He hardly spoke to me or anyone over the next few hours before he caught a flight back to Washington, and then on to Texas to attend Tower's funeral.

Sam Nunn remained Armed Services committee chairman for another four years, and became ranking Democrat on the committee after the Republican victories in the 1994 midterms. McCain was gaining in seniority on the committee, which had jurisdiction over the issues that were most important to him. Though he couldn't afford to have an openly hostile relationship with Nunn, he managed a detached but professional regard. They were never friends. They didn't socialize. He never joked with or kiddingly insulted Nunn, as he did with almost every senator at one time or another. The Tower nomination aside, he respected Nunn's expertise in defense matters and recognized his qualities as a statesman. Nunn retired from the Senate in 1997. McCain happened to be on the floor as he gave his farewell speech, and he remained there until Nunn had concluded, "out of respect," he said. Afterward, he approached Nunn, extended his hand, and told him, "You're a good senator." I asked him how Nunn had reacted. "He seemed to appreciate it" was all he said. I later learned from a committee staffer that Nunn had been surprised and moved.

McCain said it took a long while after the Tower controversy before he could believe "this place was on the level again." And before he could do that, he would have to survive a long, hard fight to save his own reputation. On April 2, 1987, John McCain joined three colleagues, Senators Dennis DeConcini, Alan Cranston, and John Glenn, in a meeting he had decided a few days earlier he should not attend. For the rest of his life, he would regret reversing his decision and his attendance at a follow-up meeting. "Keating Five will be on my tombstone," he frequently lamented. It isn't. But his inclusion in that group of senators posed a greater threat to his political career and his reputation for integrity than any other mistake he made or criticism he faced. Over twenty years after the events in question, McCain would say to a reporter for the Associated Press, "[W]hile my sense of honor was tested in prison, it was not questioned. During the Keating inquiry, it was, and I regretted that very much."[29] That was a refinement on an analogy McCain made in the middle of the controversy, when he called the experience "worse than Vietnam." He quickly revised the answer to allow that suffering in prison had been harder on him than the scandal's effect, but that the attacks on his honor were worse.

Prominent Arizona real estate developer Charles Keating and his family and associates were major donors to John McCain's early campaigns for office, his two campaigns for the U.S. House, and his first campaign for the Senate. Moreover, John and Cindy became personal friends of the Keating family; they vacationed at Keating's home in the Bahamas and were flown there on the private jet owned by Keating's company, American Continental Corporation. McCain used the jet for other travel as well. The use of corporate aircraft by members of Congress is permissible under the rules of the Senate and federal law, as long as the officeholder pays the owner compensation equivalent to the cost of first-class air travel to the same destination, which McCain believed was the case.

Friendship is friendship and business is business, but a successful entrepreneur like Charles Keating didn't always see a distinction between the two. In 1984 ACC had acquired an underperforming California thrift, Lincoln Savings and Loan. The S&L business was booming in those days, along with home construction. The Carter administration had deregulated the industry, and a 1982 law allowed thrifts to make unsecured loans and invest directly in large commercial real estate developments. Flush with success and encouraged by a looser regulatory environment, some S&Ls began to speculate in riskier investments than home mortgages. "Those were heady days of overnight fortunes made in land development deals and brokered deposits," McCain wrote. "Many thrifts were joining in the fun, but Lincoln had not been one of them until Charlie acquired it."[30]

Keating had committed to continue Lincoln's focus on mortgage lending and other safe investments, a commitment the developer didn't keep after the acquisition. Home loans dropped to 15 percent of Lincoln's business as direct investments fueled ACC's riskiest development deals. The brief if attention-getting growth in the thrift's profitability, as with other S&Ls pursuing the same fast-growth strategies, helped eventually to plunge the industry into insolvency, at a cost of $500 billion, to cover federally insured deposits. In 1986 regulators with the Federal Home Loan Bank in San Francisco scrutinized Lincoln's investments and grew alarmed by what they were finding. Keating was a supremely confident businessman and sure that the investments he authorized, like his development projects, were sound and would yield profits to all parties concerned. They included investors of more modest means, many of them retirees, who were among Lincoln's bondholders. He was aggressive with the regulators, which proved to be an imprudent strategy.

He could be aggressive, too, with members of Congress in whose careers he had made an investment. His lobbyists had worked to rally congressional opposition to a new rule promulgated in 1985 that would restrict direct investments to 10 percent of a thrift's portfolio. McCain signed several letters to Ed Gray, chairman of the Federal Home Loan Bank Board (FHLBB), and to other Reagan administration officials, expressing concern about the proposed regulation, and he cosponsored a resolution calling for its promulgation to be postponed. His efforts had little if any effect. The regulation was promulgated on schedule, and Lincoln's application for an exemption was denied. Keating had also pressed McCain to endorse his candidate for a vacancy on the FHLBB: Lee Henkel, a former Keating associate who once shared a flight with the McCains on Keating's jet. McCain demurred but did call a friend and former Tower aide in the White House legislative affairs shop, Will Ball, to inquire about the status of the appointment.

In 1986, not long after Henkel joined the bank board, the San Francisco regulators finished their first examination of Lincoln's investments and reported numerous concerns, including $135 million in losses. Around the same time, Lincoln filed a lawsuit to overturn the new direct investment limits. Henkel had tried to get the board to approve a grandfather clause that would have exempted one thrift, Lincoln, and when the sole beneficiary was discovered, Henkel was forced to resign. The FHLBB announced an investigation into allegations of file stuffing and backdating documents by Lincoln executives. By 1987 Charlie Keating and the Federal Home Loan Banks were at war, which was how John McCain found himself weighing Charlie Keating's request that he and Arizona's senior senator, Dennis DeConcini, meet with Ed Gray to, in Keating's view, get the FHLB off his back.

That wasn't how McCain saw his role. He had defensible reasons for giving attention to Keating's concerns. ACC employed two thousand constituents, and its success was a legitimate economic interest in Arizona. But even before the scandal that would sharpen them, McCain had pretty good instincts about actions that could be judged improper or have the appearance of impropriety. Having been, in effect, the navy's lobbyist to the Senate, he knew where the ethical boundary lines were that distinguished legitimate petitions on behalf of constituents from special pleading on behalf of a benefactor. Near the end of the day on March 17, 1987, DeConcini came to McCain's temporary offices in the Hart Senate Office Building with suggestions that the two meet first with Chairman Gray and then, if necessary, fly together to San Francisco to meet directly with the examiners investigating Lincoln. McCain's internal alarm started sounding.

He had been a member of the Senate for only two months as he listened to DeConcini's proposal. He had brought most of his House staff with him to the Senate, but had increased the staff's size with new hires, aides he hadn't worked with before, including Chris Koch and a young legislative aide whose portfolio included banking issues, Gwendolyn van Paasschen. Both Chris and Gwendolyn had previously served on the staff of Washington senator Slade Gorton, who had not been reelected in the 1986 midterms. Chris was more experienced, and Gwendolyn was quite young at the time. But both were hardworking and discerning aides who, throughout the Keating controversy—which would drag them into a special counsel's investigation and

Senate Ethics Committee public hearings—cautioned their boss to avoid any action, witting or unwitting, which could be construed as an ethics violation.

Before the meeting, Gwendolyn found waiting in her office mail-box a copy of a letter from Lincoln's auditor, Jack Atchison, to the chairman of the Senate Banking Committee, Don Riegle. Atchison claimed he had sent the same letter to DeConcini and McCain, but neither McCain nor his staff had seen it. The letter alleged abuses by the San Francisco bank examiners and offered assurances that Lincoln's practices were sound and the thrift's finances healthy. Chris had Gwendolyn call Jack Atchison and go over his assertions that Lincoln was being unfairly harassed by the FHLBB. She felt he made a credible case. Riegle had met with Atchison a couple of weeks prior to the McCain-DeConcini meeting. The letter addressed to Riegle—who, like McCain and DeConcini, had received campaign contributions from Keating and Keating associates—had been sent to Gwendolyn by an ACC lobbyist. Riegle had once discussed with McCain on the Senate floor ACC's concerns about Lincoln's regulators, and McCain and staff had been regularly apprised of those concerns by Lincoln lobbyists. Riegle would later deny having played any role in urging a meeting between Gray and the Arizona senators.

Eventually, McCain's and DeConcini's relationship would be severely strained. Nevertheless, both men accepted that they had to maintain a working relationship in the interest of the state they represented. And McCain allowed that he found DeConcini and his staff easy to work with and straightforward. By the time the Keating Five controversy ended with the findings of the Ethics Committee in February 1991, the two men were barely on speaking terms, and their relationship would never recover.

Their meeting on April 2, 1987, ended inconclusively. McCain rejected the idea of meeting with the regulators in San Francisco but told DeConcini he would think about meeting with Chairman Gray. Gwendolyn, young and new to the McCain world as she was, worried appropriately about the appearances of a direct intervention in a regulatory dispute on behalf of a McCain donor. She mentioned her concern to McCain, warning him that he shouldn't be "coaxed into" doing something he would later regret. He told her to call his chief political consultant, Jay Smith, to see if he, too, thought the matter could prove politically problematic. She also called Chris Koch, who was out of the office for a few days, to solicit the more experienced aide's views on whether her reservations were overblown. He assured her they were reasonable.

McCain conceded that among his deficiencies was a tendency to procrastinate at times about making a politically difficult decision in the hope that events would overtake the necessity of doing so. That, he confessed, was what he hoped would happen when he ended the meeting with DeConcini without committing one way or another to a meeting with Gray. Nevertheless, after being cautioned by Gwendolyn and Chris, and learning that Jay Smith had concerns as well, and knowing his own instincts agreed with theirs, he had staff contact De-Concini's office to say he wouldn't go to Gray's office or San Francisco. DeConcini responded by suggesting he host a meeting with Gray, and with Senators Alan Cranston and John Glenn, both of whom had benefited from Keating's financial support. Charlie Keating also asked to see McCain. He agreed to both requests.

A DeConcini legislative aide had called Gwendolyn afterward and shared that Keating wanted the senators to propose a quid pro quo to regulators on behalf of Lincoln. In exchange for the FHLB exempting Lincoln from the new direct investment limit, Lincoln would commit to making more home mortgages. Gwendolyn also recounted that Keating had responded to DeConcini's mention of McCain's reservations about the meeting by calling McCain "a wimp" and saying he "would straighten him out" in their meeting that afternoon. She added that her boss had defended McCain. Gwendolyn passed the intelligence on to Chris Koch.

McCain arrived late to the meeting. A visibly agitated Keating and Jim Grogan, ACC's chief lobbyist, were already waiting in his office. Before McCain joined them, Chris had pulled him aside to let him know what had transpired in DeConcini's office a few hours before. The agitated Keating would confront an even more agitated McCain, who, Chris and Gwendolyn would testify, began the meeting before handshakes with an angry rebuke: "Charlie, I'm not a coward. And I didn't spend five and a half years in a Vietnamese prison so that you could question my courage or my integrity." McCain told me he had wanted Keating to apologize, and Keating wouldn't. "He didn't deny it or defend it," he remembered, "but he didn't apologize, either," and both their tempers flared. In intervals when things cooled down, Keating tried to get McCain to agree to represent Keating's proposal to Gray. McCain refused: "It wouldn't do either of us any good for me to negotiate for you." He said he would ask Gray why the investigation was taking so long, and he would raise Keating's complaint that the examiners' appraisals of Lincoln's assets were unfairly low. "But that's all I'll do," he insisted. Keating, McCain recalled, reacted by "just repeating the deal he wanted me to make for him." Tempers rose and subsided several times as they went back and forth to no conclusion. An exasperated Keating finally brought the discussion to a close with an angry "Don't go to the meeting, John. Do whatever you want." McCain countered with "No, I'm going. You're an important employer in Arizona. But I'm not going to negotiate for you." With that, the meeting broke up. The two would never meet again.

The meeting with Gray was held in DeConcini's office on April 2. It was inconclusive or, as McCain described it to Chris Koch, "a dud." Gwendolyn had told DeConcini's aide that McCain would agree only to inquire why the investigation was taking so long and to raise Lincoln's concerns that the appraisals were too low. DeConcini began the meeting by referring to "our friend at Lincoln," an unfortunate choice of words that Ed Gray would subsequently make public. McCain asked the first question: Did Gray feel their meeting was proper, to which Gray replied, "It isn't improper to ask questions." Most of the participants kept their inquiries limited to the investigation's length and to the appraisal dispute. Gray pleaded ignorance, saying he didn't know the answers to their questions. Some of the senators were irritated by Gray's unresponsiveness and said so. The meeting ended after Gray told them that the investigators could answer their questions. McCain asked Gray if he thought meeting with the examiners was appropriate, Gray answered that it was, and at DeConcini's request, he agreed to help arrange it. Later, to the press and to the Ethics Committee, Gray would accuse DeConcini of attempting to negotiate Keating's proposed quid pro quo. DeConcini denied it, and McCain said he hadn't heard his colleague float the proposal. "Do you think he did?" I asked McCain some years later. He answered, "I didn't want to call Gray a liar, but I think I would've remembered if Dennis had done that. I don't think he did."

The meeting with the San Francisco examiners was held a week later, again in DeConcini's office. Senator Riegle joined the other four senators. Riegle had asked DeConcini for a letter from him and McCain asking him to attend. DeConcini provided it and had McCain's name added to it without asking McCain or his staff, which caused considerable consternation when our office learned about it. The meeting began at six o'clock in the evening. One of the regulators took such detailed notes—apparently at Gray's instruction—that when a transcript of the meeting was publicly disclosed, McCain suspected the regulators had surreptitiously taped the meeting. This time DeConcini did attempt to negotiate Keating's proposal with the regulators. The other attendees repeated their questions from the Gray meeting about the investigation's length. McCain characterized them as variations on John Glenn's position: "You should charge them or get off their backs. If things are bad there, get to them. . . . Why has the exam dragged on and on?" McCain was uncomfortable with DeConcini raising the Keating offer, and told the regulators, "I don't want any part of our conversation to be improper." One of the regulators later described him as "Hamlet . . . wringing his hands about what to do."

When all the senators had spoken, the lead investigator, in answer to McCain's question about the propriety of their meeting, said, "This meeting is very unusual, to discuss a particular company." (At that, McCain acknowledged later, "I should have thanked them for coming and left." But he didn't.) DeConcini retorted, "It's very unusual to have a company that could be put out of business by its regulators." The regulators firmly refuted Atchison's analysis and insinuated that Lincoln was on the verge of insolvency and was probably guilty of criminal wrongdoing—"a ticking time bomb," as one them described the thrift. When John Glenn asked if they were going to charge Lincoln with a crime, one of the regulators coolly responded, "We're sending a criminal referral to the Department of Justice. Not maybe, we're sending one." The meeting adjourned briefly so that the senators could go to the floor for a vote. "I shouldn't have gone back," McCain conceded. But he returned with his colleagues, "although we didn't really have anything left to say." Riegle asked if there was anything that could be done to save the thrift, to which one examiner replied that Lincoln "had bet it all on sixteen black in roulette" and destroyed itself, in consequence. "We all scurried back to our offices then," McCain sarcastically recounted. Chris Koch recalled John's demeanor when he arrived back at his office after the meeting: He was whistling through his teeth and raising his eyebrows to signal the import of his news. "Worse than we thought," he informed Chris. "Charlie's in a lot of trouble. We're not doing anything more."

A few weeks later, regulators recommended Lincoln be seized and placed in receivership. Ed Gray had left the chairmanship by then, and his successor ordered a new independent investigation of Lincoln, probably infuriating the regulators who had wanted to send the case to Justice. Two years and two more examinations later, examiners came to the same conclusion about Lincoln, and sent criminal referrals to U.S. attorneys in Phoenix, Los Angeles, and New York. American Continental Corporation filed for bankruptcy in April 1989, and Lincoln was seized the next day. Lincoln's collapse would cost taxpayers $3.4 billion. By then, ACC had unloaded hundreds of millions of dollars of debt in bond sales through Lincoln. Some of the buyers would explain after the thrift's demise that they had been led to believe the bonds were federally insured.

The first story of the unusual meeting between five U.S. senators and regulators for the Federal Home Loan Banks broke in a trade publication, *National Thrift News*, on September 27, 1987. The account was based on an interview with a confidential source, likely one of the examiners. The *Los Angeles Times* picked it up the next day. The *Detroit News* ran two stories some months later, and the *Washington Post* ran one as well. None of them made that much of a stir, but the McCain office was alert to the probability that the story could have legs. It found them in 1989, when ACC declared bankruptcy and Lincoln was seized and the press began to examine whether there was a connection between senators' actions and the damaging delay in seizing Lincoln. The public relations problem anticipated by the McCain office was under way when McCain directed staff to send a letter from him to Ed Gray, asking the former chairman to confirm that their meeting hadn't been improper. McCain assumed Gray would agree, since he had said so at the meeting. McCain assumed wrong: Ed Gray fired off a blunt response, essentially alleging that a quid pro quo had been offered at the meeting to get Keating off the hook. The letter arrived in our office not long after it arrived in the newsrooms of most major newspapers. A follow-up letter, drafted by Chris and signed by John, was sent to Gray the next day, stating, "I regret that we disagree on the events of this meeting, but we do disagree." In a crisis, McCain usually had a bias for action, which didn't always work out the way he planned. In this case, he had thought the Ed Gray of April 1987—who had acknowledged the propriety of the meeting—would be the same fellow two years later, after Lincoln's collapse and the delay in charging Keating. He was not.

Another serious problem was brewing unbeknownst to the press. In March 1989 Jay Smith had copied to Chris Koch a letter he had sent recently to an ACC accountant, informing him that he had instructed the McCain campaign committee to reimburse at first-class airfare rates two trips on the company's jet. The letter didn't set off any alarms for Chris, he said, but it did for McCain when Chris mentioned the letter. At least two flights had not been reimbursed in a timely fashion, and McCain worried whether any others were unpaid. A period of confusion and frantic research ensued as Chris tried to assemble a reliable chain of events to determine any liabilities. He couldn't find payment records for several other flights, and he saw to it that reimbursements were made. Later, he would discover that at least two flights had been paid for twice, but no matter. By this time the press was in hot pursuit of the Keating Five, and a potentially explosive new element would be added to an increasingly problematic narrative of senators bringing undue pressure to bear on regulators to benefit a campaign donor.

The mistake was unintentional. Cindy McCain had either not received or had misplaced invoices. Many of the flights had been reimbursed, and the McCains could easily afford the expense. The office alerted both the House and Senate Ethics Committees to the oversight, and to the recent reimbursements, and asked for a ruling from both. Senate Ethics declined to offer an opinion, claiming it didn't have jurisdiction, as McCain had been a member of the House at the time. House Ethics did the same, claiming it no longer had jurisdiction over his travel since he had left the body, and because he had now reimbursed the flights, it did not require further action by him. But the mistake was now a matter of public record.

On June 13 the *Wall Street Journal* published a scathing editorial referring to the five senators as "Senatorial Shills." McCain remembered, "All hell broke loose after that." He became intensely focused on regaining control. He didn't talk about much else, and I suspected he didn't sleep much, either, but he did seem to realize that allowing a problem, however worrying, to consume him entirely and prevent him from being seen doing his job would end up hurting him more than the damage he was trying to limit. He stepped up his legislative activities. He was a leading supporter and outspoken advocate for the Americans with Disabilities Act, and he authored several of the bill's provisions. He led the fight to repeal an unpopular new surtax on Medicare recipients. He was a prominent voice commenting on the astonishing developments beginning with the breach of the Berlin Wall and Eastern Europe's liberation from the Soviet Union's dominion. He took care to be seen giving as much attention to those and other issues as he did to turning the corner on the Keating controversy.

He worked to get his side of the story into press accounts, and he succeeded for a time. He made clear what he had said in the meetings and, more important, what he had not said, and most stories reflected his position: He had refused to negotiate for Keating, their friendship had ended as a result, and when he had learned that criminal referrals were coming, he had dropped the matter entirely. But some of the other senators implicated were working just as hard to make sure he couldn't extricate himself from the scandal. Riegle maintained that he had attended the meeting only at the request of both Arizona senators, which was not true. And DeConcini commented on McCain's efforts to emphasize he hadn't done anything improper by insisting, "He's in it just like I am."

Fatigue and worry complicated McCain's public relations strategy because they made it difficult for him to control his temper when reporters' interest in the story wouldn't subside. It made for a few tense exchanges and a quite explosive one with two reporters from the *Arizona Republic*, Andy Hall and Jerry Kammer, to whom McCain disclosed the late reimbursements for the ACC flights. The reporters were already working on a story alleging that McCain's ties to Keating were more extensive than previously reported. Cindy's father's company had made a minority investment in a Keating project, a shopping center development called Fountain Square. It wasn't a secret. Cindy was a partner at Hensley & Company, and by law, McCain had to disclose all of his and his spouse's investments in his annual Senate financial report. The reporters merely had to read the public report to learn about the investment. They began to interrogate him about the investment as if he had tried to hide it or had a nefarious motive for acquiescing to Cindy's involvement, referring to it as a conflict of interest. He lost his temper. Epically. With copious profanity employed. At high volume.

He told me later that he hadn't even known about the investment. The accountant who prepared his financial disclosure had dutifully reported it, and he had reviewed the document before signing it, "but I didn't study the damn thing!" he complained. When the story ran two days later under the headline "Kin's Deal, Trips Reveal Close McCain-Keating Tie," it described McCain "angrily" denying the investment had "influenced his actions on behalf of Keating." That contention was true. Had McCain even remembered the investment, I'm confident it wouldn't have influenced his decisions. I never saw him consider the impact of any policy or action on his personal financial interests. I'm not sure of the extent to which he was aware of his family's financial interests. Reporters are paid to be skeptical, and McCain understood that theoretically. But when a journalist's skepticism seemed to raise questions about his integrity, his understanding became more subjective.

He was unapologetic about his intemperate interview with the *Arizona Republic* reporters, but he knew he had made matters worse. He didn't admit it then or later, but his subsequent actions reveal his understanding that transparency and a virtue he usually lacked, patience, rather than hypersensitivity to loaded questions, would help get his side of the story out. He adopted a public relations strategy that he would embrace as a general rule for most of his public life—open access—and it generally worked to his benefit. He resolved to talk to as many reporters as wanted to speak with him about whatever angles of the controversy they were pursuing. He would be suspected, even accused, by other parties involved of leaking confidential information. He denied it publicly and didn't tell me anything different in private. But he agreed to many on-the-record interviews, with almost anyone who asked for one. It began with a press conference in Phoenix that he scheduled a few days after his stormy interview with the *Republic* reporters, around the same time the government watchdog Common Cause filed a complaint with the Senate Ethics Committee, asking for an investigation of the five senators' ties to Charlie Keating. (Common Cause was the first to employ the moniker that would come to be shorthand for the entire scandal: the Keating Five.)

The press conference lasted over an hour, ending when none of the reporters in the room had any more questions. McCain had answered every one as fully and candidly as he could. He maintained throughout that he had not done anything that could be fairly described as improper, but for the first time, he began to concede that he hadn't paid attention to the appearances of his actions, and that he had been inattentive about seeing that his air travel was properly reimbursed. The next day, the *Republic* ran an editorial that praised his forthright acceptance of responsibility for his actions and suggested that he should be "out of the woods."

He knew he had a long road ahead of him to repair the damage to his reputation. It would prove longer than he imagined. In November 1989 the Senate Ethics Committee announced an inquiry into the actions of the Keating Five, which would be conducted by a prominent Washington attorney the committee had brought on as special counsel, Robert Bennett. McCain hired John Dowd, a partner at the law firm of Akin Gump, to represent him. I had joined the staff as a legislative aide three months earlier. My portfolio was confined to foreign policy issues. I hadn't been on staff when the events in question had occurred, and I was yet to become a McCain confidant. I wasn't privy to any internal deliberations on Keating issues. My only involvement in the matter was an occasional minor contribution to the public relations campaign planned and organized by Chris Koch, Jay Smith, and the senator's press secretary, Scott Celley. Every now and then I was asked to write op-eds defending the propriety of his actions. It was hard in those days, however, not to feel the general tension and anxiety that pervaded the office and, increasingly, the attitude of John McCain.

True to form, he wanted to accelerate the process, or at least his participation in it, by offering to appear immediately before the committee's three Democrats and three Republicans to answer any questions they might have concerning his actions. Alas, the investigation would last well over a year and would include televised—and, to John McCain's mind, humiliating—hearings and the committee's excruciatingly slow deliberations about the comparative guilt or innocence of the five senators. He kept it together in public, mostly, but he talked of little else behind closed doors. His popularity in Arizona plunged: His approval rating dropped twenty-five points in one poll, and he was up for reelection in November 1992.

The committee instructed the five to prepare written accounts explaining their actions. McCain's ran to ninety-six pages. In March

1990 he, Chris, and Gwendolyn were deposed by Robert Bennett and associates. For three months, he waited for the inquiry to wrap up and determine his fate. Nothing happened. In June, he requested to meet with all six members of the committee to answer any remaining questions. The committee turned him down. For McCain, few predicaments could be more unnerving than to be trapped in a stasis between salvation or ruin. He felt powerless to affect his fate, and the summer of 1990 was an unhappy one. He would later sheepishly admit to me that he was almost relieved when Saddam Hussein's army invaded Kuwait in August, precipitating a national security crisis for the U.S. and its allies. "I finally had something reporters wanted to interview me about besides Keating."

Bob Bennett gave his report to the committee in September. To McCain's frustration, the committee didn't disclose its contents or render a judgment. Instead, it summoned all five senators for additional questioning and shared some of the special counsel's findings. To his relief, albeit temporary, McCain learned that Bennett had recommended the committee drop his and John Glenn's conduct from further investigation because, counsel believed, they had not attended the meetings as a reward for Keating's campaign donations or to negotiate on his behalf; neither had they tried to hide their actions from the committee. The other three members of the Keating Five were not so fortunate. Bennett recommended the committee proceed with a public examination of their conduct. The committee had deadlocked over the report. The Republican members wanted to accept counsel's recommendations. The Democrats did not, for one reason: John McCain was the only Republican implicated. Without agreement over whether to accede to all or part of Bennett's recommendations, the committee decided to move ahead with a public inquiry into the actions of all five senators.

This was the impasse McCain feared. "After Tower, I knew how ruthless people were here," he explained, "and I could see how I was going to get the same treatment." He was anguished to be stuck in a limbo between political life and death, and infuriated that partisan rivalry might determine his fate, rather than an impartial inquiry or his own decisions. The beginning of the 1990s might be remembered as a less polarized time than today, but politics then, as now, had plenty of examples of careers shortened and reputations permanently damaged by partisanship that didn't value such things as highly as it valued power. To subject the lone Republican to additional embarrassment and hazard was one thing—unfair, to be sure, though not exactly an unheard-of political hit job. But to keep a fellow Democrat, Glenn, in the same predicament because cutting him loose required cutting the only Republican loose? That was cold. Really cold. However, that is exactly what Democratic majority leader George Mitchell, a statesman and, when duty obliged, hard-nosed partisan infighter, made happen. It drove John McCain to boiling frustration and at times to an emotion he tried hard to keep at bay all his life, despair. Senator John Danforth, an Episcopal minister, frequently dropped by in those days to sit with McCain in his office. No one was privy to their conversations, but when I asked McCain about them years later as we worked on a book, he told me that most of the time, the two of them sat together quietly. "And I appreciated it," he added.

Bennett's report was leaked to the press, to McCain's and presumably John Glenn's satisfaction and to the immense irritation of the other three. They suspected McCain or someone on his behalf was the culprit. Again, McCain never acknowledged culpability to me; nor did he adamantly deny it. I suspect he had an idea where the leak originated, but he didn't let on. He did let it be known that he was pleased and relieved that "the truth was out there" for reporters and Arizona voters to judge. It was every man for himself now. That was evident to him with the committee's decision overriding Bennett's recommendation. He wasn't only trying to repair the damage caused by his own mistakes. He was defending himself from the machinations of political adversaries. And he fought the way he always fought: all out.

In late October, he spoke on the Senate floor and assailed the committee for "inexcusably delaying" the investigation's conclusion. Bob Dole spoke on McCain's behalf at his request, and two other Republicans, Slade Gorton and John Danforth, joined him. It was an unorthodox move that most members wouldn't have made, out of concern that it would prejudice the members of the Ethics Committee against them. But it didn't appear to affect their calculations either way. Public hearings were scheduled to begin on November 17. They would continue for most of the next two months. McCain repeatedly described them as a "public humiliation." The five of them seated at small individual tables, draped in green cloth, in a cavernous hearing room, packed with family and friends, spectators, reporters, and cameras. "Prisoners in the dock," McCain remarked. The hearings began with Bennett's presentation of his report's findings, examining each senator's role sequentially. "Of the five senators before you, Senator McCain had the closest personal relationship with Keating," Bennett observed, "[and] was the only one who received personal as well as political benefits from Charles Keating." He then detailed those benefits. Nevertheless, he absolved McCain of improper conduct, which was what mattered most. He noted that McCain's attendance at the meeting did not appear connected to aforementioned benefits. "[W]as there anything improper about Senator McCain's conduct?" Bennett asked rhetorically. "The evidence suggests not."

Had that been the end of it, McCain still would have been upset, but I don't think he would have reached the state of frustration he would eventually suffer as his "public humiliation" continued on and on and on. Cindy sat through all the hearings, as did Roberta McCain and a rotating cast of family and friends. Back in the office, McCain staffers were riveted to television sets, neglecting their responsibilities. Four of the five senators gave public testimony (Alan Cranston was exempt, as he was being treated for prostate cancer), questioned by their own attorneys and by special counsel or his associates and by committee members. Staff members were called to testify as well, including Chris and Gwendolyn. John was, I think, embarrassed to have his staff dragged into the public spectacle. But both aides acquitted themselves admirably on the stand, and he was grateful to them. John Dowd was the first to question him, and even though he elicited answers from his client that built a case for exoneration, McCain was curt and cranky throughout the interrogation. Although he was obviously angry to be stuck in the spectacle, he appeared to some witnesses to be inexplicably annoyed with his own attorney.

Bennett questioned him next and walked him over the same ground, and the senator's mood didn't improve. Then the committee members had their turn, but only one of them—the chairman, Howell Heflin of Alabama—appeared intent on embarrassing him, asking again and again for clarification about why the private flights had been reimbursed so late.

Charges and insinuations of bad faith were leveled by the senators in the dock in sometimes contentious testimony and questioning by one another's attorneys. For all concerned, it was a miserable experience that finally ground to a halt on January 16. The conclusion of the hearings was followed by over a month of continued silence and indecision by the committee before they finally rendered judgment. Bennett had continued to recommend McCain and Glenn be excused without any chastisement. The committee members negotiated decisions that issued serious rebukes of Riegle and DeConcini, the latter for his "aggressive conduct with the regulators." Cranston was to be subjected to further investigation with the strong likelihood that the Senate would be asked to vote on a motion to formally censure him. The committee merely noted that McCain and Glenn had exercised poor judgment by attending the meeting, but absolved them of any impropriety. McCain called the conclusion of his ordeal anticlimactic. "I was so fucking sick of it all by then."

At one point during the interval between the conclusion of the hearings and the committee's final judgment, I accompanied him to the Senate floor. A Central American issue was being debated, and I had drafted a statement for him. We walked from the Russell Office Building to the Capitol in silence. He was lost in his thoughts or his anguish. When he reached his desk on the floor, he motioned to a page to bring a chair for me, and I sat down next to him. He got recognition from the chair and proceeded to read the statement I had written. He didn't say a word when he had finished. He didn't offer whether he thought it a good speech or a bad speech or a middling effort, as he usually would have. He didn't joke. He didn't complain. He didn't smile. He didn't grimace. He seemed drained, a condition he rarely was noticed to suffer. He nodded toward the door, indicating we would return to the office. We continued to walk in silence. We had crossed Constitution Avenue and were about to ascend the staircase to the Russell Building entrance when he stopped and looked at me squarely and, apropos of nothing he or I had said, informed me, "It's not going to be this way forever."

RECOVERY

No matter how many times he retold the anecdote, McCain still had a note of amazement in his voice as he recalled the realization that diverted him from one destiny and opened his eyes to a journey of greater ambition. The navy's liaison to the U.S. Senate is essentially the service's lobbyist to the Senate's Armed Services Committee, the Defense Appropriations Subcommittee, and the Foreign Relations Committee. Commander John S. McCain III was appointed to the post in the summer of 1977, then promoted to captain two years later. He remained in the job until he retired from the navy in 1981. He spent a lot of his time monitoring Armed Services Committee meetings, seeing to it that the navy's requested spending levels were authorized. He attended the markup of the defense authorization bill and watched members of the committee make deals and trade votes, writing amendments on scraps of paper before handing them to aides to turn into legislative language that would affect everything from his captain's pay to how many nuclear submarines the navy would have. It suddenly occurred to him that the senior members of the committee—Stennis, Tower, Goldwater, Jackson, Cannon, Thurmond, and others—had greater influence over the navy's future than most three- and four-star admirals had. "They would tell the president what kind of navy he would have," he marveled. Even junior members of the committee had more sway. "Even committee staff, the top ones, anyway, were treated with deference," he remembered. That was the moment "I think I realized I was going to get out of the navy and into politics."

The truth of that declaration is disputable. He had talked generally about being part of history someday, and specifically about a political career, with navy friends, with his first wife, Carol, and with his fellow POWs. But the liaison job transformed a daydream about a national future ambition into an immediate interest.

His future in the navy was uncertain. Physical limitations from his war injuries caused him to fail his last flight physical. He wouldn't be allowed to command a carrier air group, handicapping his chances for promotion to flag rank. He thought he could probably earn one star, maybe two, if he stuck it out. When he made the decision to retire, then secretary of the navy John Lehman tried to persuade him to remain in the liaison job, assuring him he was on track to make rear admiral. But he knew he would never be a four-star, as his father and grandfather had been. Politics could provide a route to acquiring as much or more influence.

The capital's political scene wasn't unfamiliar to him; nor were powerful congressional committee chairmen. His parents had been friends with Georgia congressman Carl Vinson when he chaired the House Armed Services Committee and was known as the "father of the two-ocean navy." Most mornings when Congress was in session, Vinson stopped at the McCains' Capitol Hill home for breakfast. McCain's parents' wide social circle in Washington included politicians. His father had hawkish and generally conservative views, but while his social relationships with elected officials were mostly with those involved in national security policy, he didn't favor one party's representatives over another. "He never voted," McCain told me. "He didn't think it was appropriate for a military officer to pick a political side."

John McCain was popular on the Hill almost as soon as he arrived. The story of his imprisonment and his refusal of amnesty made him a celebrity before anyone there really knew him. When they did get to know the funny, charismatic navy flier with the long military pedigree and the distinguished war record, who balanced deference toward them with an infectious informality, younger senators became his friends, and the senior members—Tower and Scoop Jackson, especially—treated him like a protégé. The navy's office on the first floor of the

Russell Building became a haunt for senators and senior aides looking to wind down at the end of the day, or McCain was found in the center of a cluster of laughing senators and aides at the Monocle, a popular Capitol Hill saloon. General Jim Jones, future commandant of the Marine Corps and President Obama's first national security advisor, worked with McCain in the liaison office. "John had more influence there than most staffers," he told me, "and he knew it." Jones described McCain as someone at complete ease in his environment. Laughing at the memory, he recalled the time when a powerful Senate aide had been bent out of shape about something McCain had or hadn't done and was threatening retribution. Jones briefed a disinterested McCain, "his feet on his desk, reading the newspaper," on the brewing problem. "I wasn't even sure he was listening," he recalled. "Then he put down the paper, got to his feet, and said, 'Let's go see about that,'" and left to seek not the staffer but the staffer's senator. When he returned, he told Jones he had sorted it out. The next time Jones encountered the aide in question, his attitude was more agreeable.

McCain was a popular choice to escort overseas congressional delegations (CODELs), arranging senators' transportation and accommodations. The experiences helped him forge genuine friendships with his charges, many of whom would still be in the Senate when he was elected to the body in 1986, giving him an advantage over other Senate freshmen, who didn't have old friends waiting to welcome them to the club. Democrat Gary Hart, a two-time presidential candidate, and Republican Bill Cohen, a future secretary of defense, were two of his closest friends and served as groomsmen at his wedding to Cindy. His friendship with senator and future vice president Joe Biden began on an overseas trip. Biden and his wife, Jill, were with him at the reception in Honolulu in 1979 where he first met Cindy Hensley. The three senators were around the same age, and they all had a reputation as serious students of national security policy and foreign affairs. They had earned the respect of veteran senators on the Armed Services and Foreign Relations Committees. They also had the respect of McCain, who was opinionated on those subjects. He was always an avid consumer of international news and as well-informed then as he would be decades later as a senior member of the Senate. He remained close to the three senators for the rest of his life. They were all pallbearers at his funeral. Near the end of his life, he publicly joked about having once had to "carry Joe Biden's luggage" and "resenting it ever since."

He gleaned other valuable observations from escorting CODELs that influenced how he modeled his own Senate career. He saw that diplomacy and the conduct of foreign policy weren't the exclusive preserve of presidents and secretaries of state. Senators, too, could acquire the influence of world statesmen. McCain talked of how John Tower and Scoop Jackson had made such an impression on him. They could get an audience with anyone from Deng Xiaoping to Margaret Thatcher, he said. He was particularly impressed by the reverence that political dissidents had for Jackson and the antagonism he received from their oppressors. He was "a hero to the refuseniks," McCain observed as he recalled Jackson once being mobbed by Russian émigrés to Israel. "They had more respect for him than they had for the president," he claimed, adding approvingly, "and the Soviets feared him."

Finally, McCain observed how CODELs could be incubators for friendships across generations and party lines. Long flights, shared meals, planning meetings, sightseeing trips all familiarized senators with one another, and familiarity doesn't necessarily breed contempt. McCain made an observation when we were discussing his overseas travel for the last book we wrote. "You get to know each other on CODELs. Your staffs get to know each other. If spouses are traveling, you get to know them. You learn about their families, the ages of their kids. You get friendly. You have to. Long hours in close quarters. And it's a helluva lot easier to get something done in the Senate when the people whose help you need happen to be your friends."

McCain's recovery from the Keating fiasco began before the Ethics Committee rendered its judgment. The first phase of Operation Desert Storm, the five-week aerial bombardment of Iraq, began on January 17, 1991, a day after the committee's hearings had concluded. As a senator with a well-known war record, McCain was a popular choice for news show bookers. He was a prominent voice in the Senate debate over a resolution authorizing the use of force against Iraq. In Arizona, he filled his schedule with public appearances wherever he could draw a crowd interested in hearing his take on the war and the astonishing new weapons technologies on display in the conflict. He visited an Army National Guard facility to meet with families of Arizonans who had deployed to Saudi Arabia in the run-up to the war. He assured them the war would be over in a few weeks. He congratulated workers at McDonnell Douglas on the success of the army's Apache attack helicopters, manufactured at the company's Mesa, Arizona, plant. He credited the Apaches with taking out radar facilities in the hours before the initial bombing sorties, the "first shots fired in Desert Storm," he claimed. The ground campaign commenced on February 24 and ended four days later.

Even the experienced former attack pilot was astonished by the rapidness of the success and the ruthless efficiency of the United States Armed Forces. Like others, he saw the success as a vindication of the United States military's ability to achieve its objectives in a war with clear aims and a realistic exit strategy. He did not see it as a redemption of the Vietnam War. The losses suffered in Vietnam, some personal to him, made America's defeat there irredeemable. He attributed defeat in Vietnam to a lack of political will to defeat an enemy prepared to endure a long war with high casualties. "You can't defeat the enemy without occupying its territory," he argued. Casting his own service in the war as an exercise in futility, he added, "And you can't do that from the air." That view was not very different from his father's assessment of the war. But while the Gulf War didn't reverse his view that wars are ultimately won on the ground, it did increase his appreciation for what airpower equipped with smart munitions could do to break an enemy's will to fight.

He saw, in the public's celebratory mood after Desert Storm's success, an opportunity for Vietnam War veterans to receive a belated welcome home, which he encouraged in his public appearances. "Thank them for their service, too," he appealed. "Tell them welcome home." He said he had always felt guilty about the welcome he and his fellow POWs received, the Nixon White House dinner in their honor, and the hundreds of local homecoming celebrations. "We got all that attention, while guys who suffered more were ignored or treated like shit."

In March, McCain traveled with a Senate delegation to Saudi Arabia and Kuwait. Oil wells were burning still, and the carnage of the unprecedented air campaign was everywhere. McCain expressed both disgust for the environmental atrocity and sympathy for the Iraqi soldiers who had proved to be mostly frightened conscripts, poorly led and equipped, who had "no business taking on the most powerful military in the world."

On the military transport plane that carried the senators to and from the Gulf, John McCain and John Kerry had their first extended conversation. Each had been wary of the other. Kerry, a veteran who was a prominent anti-war protestor, likely thought McCain was an unreconstructed hawk. McCain resented that Kerry had joined other veterans tossing their medals at the Capitol during an anti-war protest on the National Mall. I remember when McCain voiced that resentment to me. I don't recall why we were discussing Kerry, but whatever the reason, McCain ended the conversation by pointing in the direction of the Capitol and railing, "Right over there. He threw them away right over there." I don't know what they talked about on the flight to Kuwait or whether they discussed Vietnam; McCain mentioned to me that he had sat next to Kerry and they had gotten along, but he offered no further details. Whether or not they talked about it, Vietnam soon gave two senators who had distrusted each other a common purpose to achieve.

When McCain returned from his 1985 trip to Vietnam with Walter Cronkite, he began reconsidering his support for the status quo in relations between the former enemies. Vietnam had violated the terms of the Paris Peace Accords by launching an invasion of the South and reuniting the country by force of arms. The United States responded by imposing a diplomatic and trade embargo, which put Vietnam in a class reserved for countries such as North Korea. Even Cuba enjoyed some diplomatic relations with the U.S. Each country had "interest sections" in each other's capitals, located in an obliging third country's embassy. We didn't permit Hanoi even that nominal contact.

For some years after the war, it didn't appear as if the victorious North Vietnamese were interested in a normal relationship with the United States. They imprisoned more than three hundred thousand former South Vietnamese military and civilian officials in reeducation camps. They invaded Cambodia in 1978, overthrew the murderous Khmer Rouge regime, ignited a civil war, and occupied Cambodian territory for a decade. Hanoi's ruinous Marxist policies consigned much of the population to desperate poverty and brought the country to the brink of famine by the mid-1980s. The Cambodia invasion prompted China to start a brief border war with Vietnam in early 1979, capturing several towns near the border before the Vietnamese succeeded in fighting them to a draw. While China's invasion failed to compel Vietnam's withdrawal from Cambodia, it did impress on Hanoi that they couldn't rely on their patrons in the Soviet Union to defend them against the colossus to their north.

Vietnam's dire economic straits convinced the leadership to rethink its allegiance to Marxist economics. The politburo approved economic reforms in 1986. Among other initiatives, agricultural cooperatives were no longer mandated. Long-term land leases were given to rice farmers, who were allowed to keep most of the income from the sale of their crops. In consequence, Vietnam quickly went from a near rice famine to becoming one of the biggest net exporters of rice in the world. Private businesses were legalized in 1990. Settling old business with the U.S. and getting the trade embargo lifted became priorities for politburo members who worried that China—and not the U.S.— was the nation's number one threat. The most prominent of them was Vietnam's foreign minister, Nguyen Co Thach, who invested his considerable energy and prestige in pursuit of normal relations with the United States.

McCain and his friend and fellow Vietnam veteran Tom Ridge had cosponsored a resolution in 1986 recommending that the U.S. and Vietnam open interest sections in each country's capital. They were criticized by Reagan administration officials, some veterans' organizations, and the National League of POW/MIA Families, all of whom felt the Vietnamese hadn't done enough to account for America's missing. McCain and Ridge continued to advocate the move until 1988, when Vietnam suspended cooperation with a new POW/MIA initiative begun the year before, after Thach had met in Hanoi with an American delegation led by the retired chairman of the Joint Chiefs General John Vessey. President Reagan had asked Vessey to serve as his special emissary to Vietnam. Thach had agreed to joint field investigations of sites where U.S. pilots were believed to have crashed. Hanoi had also begun unilaterally repatriating the remains of U.S. servicemen, which confirmed suspicions that the Vietnamese had warehoused the remains. Vietnam's leaders, including Thach, were disappointed that the agreement with the U.S. didn't immediately produce a greater thaw in relations. Their complaints focused on the administration's continued opposition to the McCain-Ridge resolution. They decided to show their displeasure by temporarily reverting to the obstinacy that characterized their previous responses to U.S. demands. McCain reacted to the reversal by withdrawing his support for interest sections.

In the fall of 1990, he received a request from Foreign Minister Thach to meet in Washington. Thach, who had been attending the UN's General Assembly in New York, was given permission to travel to Washington by Secretary of State James Baker. Baker and President Bush's national security advisor, General Brent Scowcroft, encouraged McCain to meet with him. Vietnam had withdrawn its forces from Cambodia in 1989 and had resumed cooperating with POW/MIA investigations. McCain agreed to the meeting.

It was his first encounter with Thach. I sat in on the meeting, and I could tell McCain took an immediate liking to the diplomat. Thach was witty and unusually candid for a senior Vietnamese official. He criticized his government's policies as well as U.S. policies for having missed opportunities to improve relations. He spoke fluent English and used American vernacular. He was argumentative, plaintive at times, and aggressive at other times, urging a rapprochement that, his attitude suggested, a fool could see was in our mutual interests. Even when McCain pushed back abruptly—once inserting into the discussion Hanoi's continued detention of hundreds of South Vietnamese officials in reeducation camps—I could tell he was enjoying himself. He punctuated every point with a smile. Thach seemed to enjoy their give-and-take as well. The meeting continued past the point of productivity because each man insisted on having the last word, and because they both appeared to be enjoying themselves.

Thach had joined the Viet Minh as a teenager in the 1920s and had been jailed by the French in Hoa Lo. He had fought the Japanese and been an aide to Vo Nguyen Giap at Dien Bien Phu. He was Le Duc Tho's chief aide at the Paris peace talks. Now he was leading efforts to reconcile with the United States. He fascinated McCain, who viewed his new acquaintance as a person of significance in history, a species of being he considered humanity's most interesting. Thach knew something that many of his colleagues did not appreciate—they assumed Vietnam was still the focus of world attention, as it had been during the war; Thach knew they were not. So did McCain. "He's a realist," he said to me after the meeting. "He knows nobody gives a shit anymore what they do."

Thach was under pressure from his detractors in the politburo to produce results from his diplomatic outreach. Some of them preferred reconciliation with China rather than the U.S. That became more apparent as McCain's relationship with Thach developed into, if not a friendship, a relationship of mutual admiration and trust. Thach was impatient for progress, and American politics—which made support for normalization a politically fraught position in both parties—exhausted what patience he did possess. McCain was seldom the most patient party in a relationship, but he was in this one. I remember subsequent meetings in which Thach was visibly irritated, and McCain would stop the discussion to reassure him, "Look, we can get this done. It won't be easy. But we can," before returning to the point he had been making.

In their first meeting, Thach implored McCain to resume his support for improved relations. McCain said he would consider it but wouldn't take a position until he had an opportunity to come to Vietnam and gauge for himself the extent of cooperation with our POW/MIA investigations. Thach expressed disappointment at McCain's reluctance but extended an invitation to come to Vietnam "when you like."

We traveled there in April 1991, stopping first in Bangkok to get entry visas, since Vietnam didn't have a consulate in the U.S. It was the first of many trips to Southeast Asia I made with John McCain. I traveled the world with him in the 1990s, but his trips to Southeast Asia, especially to Vietnam, are my favorite memories. The country intrigued him for reasons separate from his personal history. He always maintained he had gotten over Vietnam when the plane flying the POWs to freedom landed at Clark Air Base in the Philippines. I don't think he was exaggerating. His memory of Vietnam didn't have a hold on him in terms of lingering resentment or anguish. In the many trips that followed that first one, he saw Vietnam as a beautiful and exotic place with enterprising people who were unexpectedly friendly to him. He recognized something in their society that made him confident of their future. "They'll be the leaders in the region," he predicted on a subsequent trip there, "economically and militarily. And they're going to drive the Chinese crazy. They're the only ones they're not sure they can bully or squash."

McCain's meetings on that first trip were with the top leadership, including Secretary General Do Muoi. Thach hosted a formal dinner for McCain in a French-built villa the ministry owned. Thach's closest associate, Vice Minister Le Mai, the head of the ministry's Americas Department, was as cosmopolitan, shrewd, and friendly as Thach and considerably more patient. Often when McCain challenged a Vietnamese official on some point, he provoked a long lesson on all the invading forces Vietnam had expelled over its history, beginning with Chinese dynasties of ancient times. McCain appreciated that Thach and Mai never subjected him to the same sermon. After sitting through so many on that trip, I watched McCain do something on subsequent visits to Vietnam that he rarely did. He censored himself, avoiding phrasing his points in ways that would trigger the lecture. "I don't think I could survive another one," he said, laughing, after I had mentioned my observation. "Honest to God, if they'd done that to us in prison, we would have cracked immediately."

At McCain's request, he was granted a meeting with Vo Nguyen Giap, the architect of France's defeat at Dien Bien Phu. McCain was like a little kid before the meeting. He had all these questions for Giap, none of which had to do with current events. Most concerned Giap's military decisions, especially at Dien Bien Phu. Some were politically touchy. Had Giap advised against the Tet and Easter Offensives? McCain wanted to hear Giap's views on China, and he even asked if reports were true that he had opposed Vietnam's invasion of Cambodia. Giap, whose demeanor was almost avuncular considering his reputation for tolerating shockingly high casualties in the battles he led, didn't answer any of McCain's questions. Smiling, chuckling, waving his hand to dismiss "all these questions of the past," he kept insisting they focus on the future friendship between America and Vietnam. McCain was crestfallen. It wasn't every day he got to interview such a historic figure, but alas, this one didn't seem interested in history.

En route to Vietnam, McCain had taken a call at the U.S. Embassy in Bangkok from Deputy Assistant Secretary of State Ken Quinn, an experienced foreign service officer with a distinguished record of wartime service in Vietnam. Ken had called to brief McCain on a proposal he was about to present to Vietnamese officials in New York, outlining a series of undertakings the U.S. wanted Vietnam to agree to in exchange for moves that would ultimately lead to the normalization of diplomatic and economic relations. The Vietnamese had already met one condition: They had withdrawn their forces from Cambodia. Most of the other conditions were commitments and progress markers for the fullest possible accounting of our MIAs. Ken wanted McCain to endorse what came to be called "the road map," and discuss it in general terms with the Vietnamese. McCain said he would on the condition that a requirement to release all remaining South Vietnamese officials from reeducation camps be added to the list. Ken agreed.

Having heard Thach's appeal for clarity about U.S. intentions, McCain assumed Thach would be pleased about the road map. But he wasn't pleased at all. Quite the contrary, he disparaged it as a "very big disappointment." The road map, he complained, amounted to a multi-year process, front-loaded with demands on Hanoi, while delaying relief from economic sanctions until much later. His government, he maintained, "has done already many things you have asked of us, and we have received nothing in return." He looked genuinely dejected, and McCain tried again to explain the sensitive politics involved in normalization, as well as the influential interests opposing it, including veterans' groups, MIA families, and conservative commentators. "This process will help us overcome obstacles," McCain stressed. "Maybe it won't be as quick as you'd like, but it can't be done without having an answer for people in a position to stop it." But Thach was concerned with his own political difficulties, a skeptical leadership who greeted the road map as a rebuff rather than a reward. Eventually, his truculence provoked McCain's temper, and their discussion became heated, culminating in a dispute over which country had been first to violate the terms of the Paris Peace Accords, a dead-end argument both men knew better than to waste time waging. Over time, without ever conceding they were doing so, the Vietnamese began providing the cooperation stipulated in the road map. McCain, true to his word, did everything in his power to see that the United States kept its end of the bargain.

A first step, which Thach agreed to in a meeting with General Vessey a week later, was the establishment of a Defense Department detachment in Hanoi to serve as part of Joint Task Force—Full Accounting (JTF—FA), and work with Vietnamese counterparts to investigate the fates of America's missing. American military officials were again posted to Vietnam, sixteen years after the last marines had evacuated Saigon. They were in residence in their official quarters, nicknamed "the Ranch," by the time McCain returned the following year. With their Vietnamese associates, they conducted difficult and dangerous field searches and cleared hundreds of cases over time. We got to know many of the Americans assigned to the Ranch in those early days. The U.S. didn't have an embassy in Hanoi, and there were no diplomats to assist visiting members of Congress. The guys in the Ranch filled in, arranging and escorting us to meetings, sometimes serving as translators. They were smart, tactful, dedicated soldiers whose successors continue their mission to this day. They have suffered casualties over the years, including the loss of life, as they discharged their duty to Americans who had fought and disappeared in a long-ago conflict. Despite popular mythology that America abandoned its missing in Vietnam, the U.S. government and the government of our former enemy have gone to extraordinary lengths. It has been an elaborate, fully resourced, and dedicated campaign. It made a deep impression on McCain and on me as one of the most honorable endeavors I have personally witnessed.

We spent several days in Hanoi on that first trip before traveling to Saigon. It was hard to move in the city without seeing Hoa Lo, aka the Hanoi Hilton. It was a big ocher-colored sandstone building with immense steel doors underneath the legend "Maison Centrale." It sits in the very center of the city, and we passed it every time we left the government guesthouse where we were quartered for meetings in various ministries. It was still a going concern in those days, with a large population of inmates jailed for crimes rather than for political or military purposes. McCain didn't ask to take a look inside. Nor was he offered the opportunity. We must have passed it more than a dozen times. He looked out the window each time we did. Only once, the first time, did he say anything. He nodded at it and said, "That's Hoa Lo," and added that he remembered "the sound of the doors closing behind me like it was yesterday."

One other stop on the itinerary for McCain enthusiasts visiting Hanoi is Truc Bach Lake, where he landed after ejecting from his crippled A-4. It was located about two miles from where we were staying, and at his request, we drove there one afternoon. He had been delighted to discover during his 1985 visit with Walter Cronkite that the Vietnamese government had erected on the lakeshore a cement monument commemorating his shoot down: It depicts an American airman on his knees with his hands up and his head lowered. "USAF" is chiseled on the monument to the figure's left, and a paragraph carved on its right identifies the American air pirate Air Force Major John Sney McKay. It has been remade in recent years to correct the spelling and his service affiliation, owing to the gratitude of the Vietnamese for McCain's friendship and their inability to tell when McCain was ribbing them. Whenever he mentioned the monument in meetings with Vietnamese officials in Washington and Vietnam, he jokingly complained about the insult of being called a major in the air force. Then he groused about the condition of the statue, the weeds that had grown up around it, and the bird shit deposited on it.

We learned later that in those early years of McCain's renewed attention to Vietnam, the government had discussed demolishing the monument, encouraged by some well-meaning pro-normalization Americans. "God, no!" McCain protested when he got wind of it, or whenever a Vietnamese official gingerly suggested that if he was upset by the monument's mistakes and condition, it could be replaced with some more appropriate recognition. "It's the only monument I have in the world. Leave it alone." He became very friendly with a foreign ministry official who, after relations between the two countries were normalized, would be appointed Vietnam's first postwar ambassador to the U.S., Le Van Bang. At the end of a meeting, McCain complained, as usual, about the "weeds and bird crap." After Bang left the meeting, he told a mutual friend who had accompanied him, "Tell the senator my home is very close to the lake. I will see to its maintenance myself."

McCain wisecracked about the USAF mistake and the birds, but the monument clearly delighted him. He drew a crowd while we were standing there. He wasn't the recognizable celebrity in Vietnam that he would be later, when throngs would encircle him as he walked the city, often chanting his name. But he was recognizably American, and in 1991, there weren't a lot of those walking around Hanoi. He asked a local to use my camera to take a picture of us: He's standing at attention, his usual pose in photographs, and beaming. I'm trying to affect a more solemn appearance. He wrote on the photo: "My Friend Mark." I keep it next to photographs of my family, a reminder of the early days of our association, when I traveled the world with John McCain.

It wasn't until we left the monument and returned to our rooms that I realized in the thirty or forty minutes we had stood at the lake, he hadn't mentioned anything about his experience there, not about falling into it with shattered limbs or sinking to the bottom and nearly drowning, not about being pulled out of it or about the angry mob who had assaulted him. Nothing. It was just a funny irony to him. He had nearly died at the spot. Now he was a U.S. senator, looking at a weird cement statue that called him an air pirate and an air force officer.

A few months after we returned from Vietnam, *Newsweek* published a cover story suggesting Americans might still be imprisoned in Vietnam. The magazine had somehow acquired a photograph of three men purported to be MIA in Vietnam. They turned out to be Ukrainian farmers in the 1930s. The story supplied to *Newsweek* was a hoax, one of many involving missing servicemen perpetrated over the years by swindlers and aspiring Rambos. At the time of publication, a majority of the country believed that Americans were still being held against their will and the U.S. government had abandoned them to their fate. It was bullshit. McCain knew it was bullshit, and he was so offended by the perpetuators of the myth that it was hard to restrain him at times from saying so in impolite language. He believed the controversy was the work of conspiracy nuts and charlatans who preyed on families clinging to the hope that their loved ones might come home.

His view was informed by his own experiences as a POW. The Americans had built extensive communications networks in prison, in part to keep count of prisoners held in the North; when they were caught doing it, they were punished. "We went to sleep reciting names of prisoners we knew. And when they moved us to a different prison, we'd share the names from the last place with the guys in the new place." He described his process for keeping a count to a writer for the *New Yorker*:

> You start with the "A"s, and you fill them in to where they are in the alphabet. . . . I would just associate the names: Brudno with "brute"; Baker, and I'd think of a loaf of bread. I would remember the number of names under each letter.

He also had well-informed insights into the behavior of his captors. "The Vietnamese could be cruel," he explained, "but I never knew them to be capricious. There was nothing in it for them to keep any guys after the war. It would have been the one thing that would have brought us back into it." He believed his war record positioned him to be the guy who blew the whistle on the myth, and inoculated him from serious retaliation. There was no political advantage in that role. He might have felt he wasn't taking a big risk, but he didn't expect any reward from assigning himself the role of truth teller to an audience that included people who preferred the myth to the truth. He did it because he believed it was in his country's best interests, in the interests of the reputation of the United States government and armed forces, and, painful as the truth was, in the best interests of the families of the missing.

In reaction to the *Newsweek* cover, support increased in the Senate for the formation of a special select committee on POW/MIAs. It was empaneled in October 1991, charged with investigating evidence that Americans were still captive as well as evidence of the government's neglect or malfeasance in failing to secure their return. It was chaired by John Kerry and Bob Smith, a Republican from New Hampshire. Smith had believed for years that Americans remained in Vietnamese and Laotian prisons, as did many of the staff he recruited. The other committee members included every Vietnam veteran then serving in the Senate and the Senate's only former prisoner of war, John McCain. Thus began a fifteen-month ordeal that consumed most of my and John McCain's attention, during which we were both assaulted, he by accusations of treason, and me the old-fashioned way, at the hands of a former Green Beret. By the end of the experience, the myth of abandoned POWs had been punctured, relations between the United States and Vietnam were on the verge of normalization, and John McCain and I had become good friends.

The first hearings were held in November 1991. The witnesses were Secretary of Defense Dick Cheney and General Vessey. McCain greatly admired Vessey, a World War II veteran who had lied about his age to enlist at seventeen, and received a battlefield commission at Anzio. Vessey was a competent, genial, and modest officer who had been chairman of the Joint Chiefs in Ronald Reagan's first term. He had retired to his childhood hometown, White Bear Lake, Minnesota, a year before his term as chairman expired; he had promised his wife, Avis, they would be home before the next snowfall. McCain was never one to be overawed by the stars on someone's shoulder boards. He had grown up around flag officers. In Armed Services Committee hearings, the higher the witness's rank, the likelier McCain was to be abrupt and contentious. With Vessey, though, he was always deferential and warm. Vessey was volunteering his services in a thankless job for which he was routinely and unfairly criticized. McCain felt honor bound to defend him. More than that, though, Vessey was so plainly decent, a modest man with a fine sense of duty, that McCain held him up as the ideal patriot and was quick to confront his detractors as if they were his own, which they usually were.

The star witness during the second day's hearing was Bui Tin, a former colonel in the North Vietnamese Army who had been famously photographed riding a tank onto the grounds of the presidential palace in Saigon to accept the surrender of the Republic of Vietnam. He had also worked in the army department in charge of Vietnam's prisoner-of-war camps. He became a prominent critic of the regime after the war and was currently living in Paris. He met with McCain the day before the hearing and reminded him they had met when McCain was a POW. McCain told me afterward that he didn't remember the encounter, but it could have happened. "I had a lot of surprise visitors," he recalled, "who wanted to see the admiral's son." Bui Tin testified that a few American deserters had remained in Vietnam after the war, but no Americans had been kept there against their will. That upset the POW truthers and charlatans, and some of the families, who accused the witness of being a plant for Hanoi. They had their doubts about McCain, too, who had promised to keep an open mind but was clearly skeptical that Vietnam was still holding Americans. The doubts were confirmed when Bui Tin embraced McCain as they shook hands after the witness had finished his testimony. Photographs of their hug appeared in newspapers around the country.

McCain's credibility as the only POW on the committee made his hesitancy especially aggravating to the activists. The press and public gave his views more weight than those of other members—for good reason, of course. He had extensive personal knowledge of the subject and had nothing to gain personally from being a skeptic. The same day Bui Tin testified, the committee heard from a self-styled "journalist" convinced that American POWs were held after the war. She reported that one POW had been kept in isolation in Hanoi for three years, and none of the other POWs had known of his existence until they were relocated to large group cells later in the war. The implication was that other prisoners could have remained hidden from the POWs who came home. As soon as she named the mysterious prisoner, Norm Gaddis, John interjected: "I knew Norm, we all knew him." He cited the nickname of the section of Hoa Lo where Norm Gaddis had been held in solitary confinement, Heartbreak Hotel. "None of us were surprised to see him when they moved us," he continued. "Well, that's one side of the story," she retorted. McCain was incredulous that his eyewitness testimony wasn't considered more reliable than rumors and groundless speculation. And those who traded in rumors and groundless speculation were incredulous that McCain didn't defer to them. It was a ludicrous situation that exasperated him and made for a contentious, exhausting test of wills between antagonists. It also convinced him that the best way to put Vietnam and all its effects, the tragic and the ludicrous, behind us was to normalize relations with our former adversary as soon as possible. To do that, someone had to speak the truth to people who earned a living from perpetuating falsehoods and false hopes, and even to people for whom the truth meant abandoning hope of a reunion with their loved ones. He did it unhesitatingly, often sternly, and sometimes angrily.

His main foil was Ted Sampley, an ex–Green Beret who had served two tours in Vietnam. He owned a weekly rag called *U.S. Veterans Dispatch,* which he used to accuse McCain of being the Manchurian Candidate, acting on the Kremlin's orders to help Hanoi hide its continued imprisonment of our boys. He also owned several T-shirt booths located on the National Mall near the Vietnam Veterans Memorial. Though he didn't have a permit for the booths, politically intimidated Interior Department officials declined to order their removal. The people who worked in the booths for Sampley were unpaid volunteers, but the T-shirts were sold for profit with the proceeds going to Sampley. He had married the daughter of an MIA, and they had an infant daughter whom Sampley brought to committee hearings and held aloft when he created disturbances that could get him ejected. He usually sat as close to the front as he could, and in McCain's line of sight. He routinely gave McCain the finger, and McCain routinely gave it back to him from the dais in view of television cameras. Several times McCain left the hearing room and deliberately walked past Sampley and said in an audible voice, "You're scum."

It wasn't the Manchurian Candidate stuff that got McCain so worked up; he didn't like it, but he had been called worse, and he could usually laugh it off. It was his certitude that Sampley didn't believe a word of the conspiracies he promoted that bothered him most. For his own ego and profit, Sampley was deluding families into believing they were going to see loved ones again. "He's got himself a little cult there," McCain remarked. "He tells them ghost stories, and they make him feel like he's a big man." Sampley organized a notorious protest against President George H. W. Bush at a convention of MIA families in 1992, when Bush was in the middle of a difficult reelection race. The normally courteous president was so frustrated by the abuse hurled at him by Sampley and company that he shouted, "Sit down and shut up."

In December of that same year, Sampley came into our front office, carrying a stack of his newspapers with the Manchurian Candidate slander on the front page, and started hassling our receptionist. She called me and asked for help. I ordered him to leave, and he refused. I threatened to call the Capitol Police, and he said he would leave but wanted to talk to me first. I agreed to give him a couple minutes but in the hallway. A couple seconds after I had followed him out the door, he turned on his heel and hit me with a roundhouse to my chest, cracking a rib and stunning me for a moment. He threw another punch that opened a cut beneath my right eye. I had been in fistfights before, but not lately, and not with a Green Beret who was bigger and tougher. In an act of self-preservation, I dove at his legs and knocked him down. I can still hear the "ugh" he emitted when he hit the marble floor. I thought I could survive the experience if I wrestled with him in a clinch until the cops arrived, and didn't give him space to throw another haymaker. That is how it worked out. Two Capitol Police officers arrived a few minutes later and took Sampley away in cuffs. He spent the night in jail. I went to wash the blood off my face and explain to my displeased fiancée, who also worked in the McCain office, why I had been brawling in the Russell Senate Office Building.

McCain had been out of the office at the time of the fight but returned not long after. He was solicitous, first asking me to describe the event and then asking after my condition. "You sure you're okay, boy?" he asked a couple times. Assured that I was, he then offered what was in his mind a defense of my honor: I hadn't lost the fight; I had been cheated. "He sucker-punched you," he insisted. "Caught you off guard. Not your fault." I wasn't as concerned as he was with the embarrassment of losing the bout. "We could've gone to the gym and put the gloves on, and he still would've gotten the better of it," I told him. "Yeah, well, it was still a sucker punch," he answered.

A week later, I took a call from an assistant district attorney who asked if I would drop the charges if Sampley agreed to a restraining order that prohibited him from coming to our office or within five hundred feet of McCain or me. I agreed to the deal. Sampley refused it, and the case went to trial. Sampley was convicted. The judge sentenced him to time served and imposed the restraining order, which kept Sampley from going to hearings or any public event that McCain and I were attending. There were only one or two hearings left by then, but I was relieved that Sampley wouldn't be there. I was a little worried John might say something that would end in him trying his own luck against the guy.

Many of the hearings had a circus-like atmosphere, outbursts from the audience, eccentric witnesses, weird testimony, and testy exchanges between senators and witnesses. The environment behind the scenes wasn't always better. Senator Smith and his staff insisted on investigating "live-sighting reports" as if they were all credible, no matter how outlandish the claim or dubious the source. One weird tale alleged that there was a secret underground prison beneath Ho Chi Minh's mausoleum, which hundreds of people—English-speaking tourists among them—visit every day. McCain burst out laughing when he first heard the claim, exclaiming, "You have got to be fucking kidding me." To his credit, John Kerry kept things from collapsing into chaos, patiently addressing every report and rumor, keeping John calm when he had reached his limit of bullshit for the day, skillfully interviewing witnesses, pressing the Vietnamese for answers. Kerry even got the Vietnamese government to let him and Smith prowl around the basement of Ho's tomb, considered a shrine in Vietnam, searching for the rumored lost prison. It was an impressive performance, and McCain admired Kerry's skill and fairness, crediting him with pulling off the impossible—getting all committee members to sign a report, released in January 1993, which found:

> While the Committee has some evidence suggesting the possibility a POW may have survived to the present, and while some information remains yet to be investigated, there is, at this time, no compelling evidence that proves that any American remains alive in captivity in Southeast Asia.

The previous summer and fall, information had fallen into the hands of a Defense Intelligence Agency asset that helped resolve some of the so-called discrepancy cases, those instances when a pilot was known to have survived an "incident of loss": Witnesses saw a parachute, or the pilot had radioed that he was on the ground or was seen being taken prisoner. Documentation collected by an American whom the Vietnamese allowed to research the archives in Hanoi's Army Museum included photographs of corpses, the apparent victims of executions. Regime officials must have authorized the release of the photographs, although they adopted the pretense that they knew nothing about it. The Bush administration chose not to condemn the Vietnamese for the atrocities but encouraged them to facilitate further "research" that could close more cases. Just two weeks before the election in which both John McCain and President Bush was on the ballot, Bush's national security advisor, Brent Scowcroft, called John and asked him to accompany General Vessey on a mission to let Hanoi know the material was helpful and appreciated, and the United States would welcome more of it.

It was a quick trip, three refueling stops on the way over, twenty-four hours in Hanoi, and back to Washington by way of Elmendorf Air Force Base in Anchorage, Alaska, where we spent a night. General Vessey and his team were all business. When he and John discussed how to approach the officials they were scheduled to see, they used secure communications technology or went for a walk around a nearby lake. The security officers had swept our rooms for bugs, and the detectors had lit up like a Christmas tree. They were cautious and focused on their mission and didn't spend an idle moment until the meetings were over and they had received assurances of further access to the army archives. But when we had dinner in a restaurant that night before departing in the morning, General Vessey was in an expansive mood, entertaining us with funny stories from his postwar service in occupied Germany, as I watched an uncharacteristically mute McCain listen intently. Vessey was a self-possessed man without airs of any kind. I could see why John thought so highly of him. On the flight back to Washington, Vessey pointed out the window as we flew over the lake where he and his wife lived, and told us a story from his first Sunday church service after he had retired. He heard two elderly ladies in the pew behind him speculating about who he was. "His name's Vessey," one whispered to the other, "and he used to be somebody in the government."

When we got back to Washington, Vessey and McCain went to the White House to brief Brent Scowcroft on their trip and recommend that the administration reciprocate Vietnam's cooperation by releasing some Vietnamese assets in the U.S. that had been frozen since the end of the war. Scowcroft promised to raise the issue with the president, who gave it serious if brief consideration before deciding to reconsider it after the election. If President Bush were defeated, as most observers expected at that point, he would leave the normalization of relations between the United States and Vietnam to the new president, who had evaded the draft as a young man and been less than truthful about it during the campaign.

Owing to the Keating controversy, McCain expected to face a difficult reelection race. For a time, Bruce Babbitt was rumored to be considering the race; Evan Mecham planned to run as a conservative independent. Babbitt passed, Mecham didn't. A national anti-incumbent environment grew stronger with every passing month. McCain faced community activist Claire Sargent as his Democratic opponent in an election season that was billed "The Year of the Woman" for the number of female candidates running for Congress. It should've been a harder reelection than it turned out to be. But McCain had worked hard to rebuild his reputation after Keating, so even a more experienced candidate would have had a difficult time defeating him. While Mecham was a nuisance, McCain never counted on support from the 10 percent of the Arizona electorate who identified as hard-right McCain haters. As for Claire Sargent, she was an inexperienced candidate who struggled to raise money. Plus, the expected barrage of negative ads tying McCain to Keating never materialized.

McCain had to postpone a debate with Sargent when he traveled with General Vessey to Vietnam. All he was allowed to say to explain his absence was that the president had asked him to go and the reasons were important but classified. Sargent accused him of making up the whole thing to duck the debate. Senator Bob Kerrey, a fellow Vietnam veteran and member of the POW/MIA committee, had agreed to do a Democratic Party event in Phoenix where he shared the stage with Sargent. After she denounced McCain for dodging the debate, she turned to Kerrey, who she said would confirm her accusation. Kerrey said he was sorry, but he couldn't do anything of the kind. He couldn't reveal the purpose of the trip, but he knew it was urgent, and McCain's participation was important. A few days later, McCain was comfortably reelected with 56 percent of the vote to Sargent's 32 percent and Mecham's 11 percent.

Around this time, McCain's administrative assistant, Deb Amend, announced that she was marrying McCain's state director, Wes Gullett, and moving to Arizona. McCain offered me the job. We had become close over the previous year. I could be honest and direct with him when I felt he was in error. That is essential to a good relationship between a senator and his chief of staff, and to his credit, he allowed me that liberty even when he felt I was pestering him needlessly. Eventually, it became a routine for us, an inside joke, the nagging advisor to the recalcitrant senator. It amused the rest of the staff, whom he often urged, "Don't tell Mark" when they observed him doing or saying something I had cautioned him against. He did, however, think it necessary when he offered me the job to identify a problem that could hamper a successful working relationship. "We're both hotheads," he observed. "One of us should probably work on that." It was obvious he meant me.

After the new Congress convened, McCain viewed lifting the trade embargo against Vietnam as his first item of unfinished business. The lame-duck Bush administration had unfrozen some Vietnamese financial assets, as McCain and Vessey had recommended, but left the question of the trade embargo to the new administration. With President Bush and General Scowcroft out of office, we weren't sure how and to whom to make the case. McCain didn't know the new president; nor did he know many of his aides. He knew the incoming defense secretary, Les Aspin, who had chaired the House Armed Services Committee, and some of Aspin's deputies. But most White House staff were strangers; he didn't even know which aides would have the most influence in formulating Clinton's Vietnam policy. McCain deferred to Kerry to lead the outreach to the new administration, and had me work with Kerry aides Frances Zwenig and Nancy Stetson, as well as an outside advisor to both Kerry and McCain, Virginia Foote, to come up with a plan for convincing the Clinton administration that the time had come for normal relations between former enemies. Another complicating factor was the loss of Nguyen Co Thach, who had been pushed out of the politburo, reportedly for his anti-China views. McCain didn't have as candid a relationship with Thach's successor, Nguyen Manh Cam, so he relied on Vice Minister Le Mai as his intermediary in Hanoi.

I wasn't sure what kind of relationship McCain would have with the new president. He didn't think highly of Clinton in the beginning. He had held President Bush in high regard and was resentful that Clinton had defeated him. While he had occasionally butted heads with Secretary of State James Baker and other Bush administration officials over various issues, McCain considered Baker and the rest of Bush's national security team, Secretary of Defense Dick Cheney, Joint Chiefs chairman Colin Powell, CIA director Robert Gates, and, of course, Scowcroft, to be the best ever assembled, led by a president who had been CIA director, UN ambassador, and ambassador to China. For most of Clinton's first year in office, McCain had serious reservations about the quality of the new national security team. And Clinton staffers had serious reservations about him. McCain had criticized Clinton's draft history evasions during the campaign, and he was close friends with Phil Gramm, a sharp Clinton critic, who planned to run against Clinton in 1996. Gramm and McCain traveled the country later that year to campaign against Clinton's health care proposal, and anonymous White House staffers had already been quoted disparaging Gramm and McCain.

All of this was just the ordinary cut and thrust between political adversaries. But resolving the Vietnam question required McCain to gain influence with the president. He didn't have a plan for that, but he did do something early on that likely started a White House reappraisal of what kind of adversary they should expect John McCain to be. Clinton's draft controversy had sparked speculation that veterans would stage a big protest if he accepted an invitation to lay a wreath and speak at the Vietnam Veterans Memorial on Memorial Day. There was also reported grumbling among active-duty military about their new commander in chief, which bothered McCain. He had been in the navy long enough not to be surprised by soldiers privately grousing about politicians; he had done it himself. But the idea that soldiers wouldn't show Clinton the respect they had showed his predecessor offended him. Respect for the authority of elected officials is the central tenet of the military's sense of duty and honor in a democracy. McCain dictated a note to Clinton, urging him to accept the Memorial

Day invitation and promising to defend him publicly. He even offered to accompany him to the Wall. He had the note faxed to Anthony Lake, Clinton's national security advisor. Lake said later that he rushed the fax into the Oval Office, and Clinton immediately penned a note of thanks to McCain, which was delivered that same day. Clinton did speak at the Wall that Memorial Day, and other than a few signs protesting his appearance, he was received warmly. McCain wasn't there. He had gone to Vietnam with a delegation John Kerry had organized, which included Pete Peterson, another former prisoner of war and member of Congress from Florida, several other senators and representatives, and officials from veterans' organizations. The purpose of the visit was to make a final assessment of Vietnam's cooperation before Kerry and McCain began a public campaign to persuade the administration to lift the trade embargo.

We joined the delegation in Bangkok. The day it departed Andrews Air Force Base, McCain was scheduled to deliver the commencement address to the United States Naval Academy. I had never seen him as anxious about a speech or spend more time practicing one. It was obviously a great honor. His father had given the commencement address twenty years before. The academy's superintendent, Admiral Tom Lynch, who had extended the invitation, was a friend. "That's a hell of a thing for Tom to do," he remarked. He was elated with how the speech was received by the midshipmen. They laughed where he expected them to, at his recitation of his deficiencies as a midshipman and the aggravation he had caused his superiors. They sat in rapt attention as he recounted examples of heroism he had witnessed, and he promised they would see as much or more. When he finished, he received a long standing ovation from the graduates and their families. He was as happy as I'd ever seen him when we left Annapolis that day. He told me afterward, when we were on the plane to Southeast Asia, that there were two moments in his life when he felt he had achieved a distinction that surprised not only his doubters but himself. The first was at the ceremony in Jacksonville when he transferred command of a squadron. His parents had attended, and Admiral McCain had been introduced as "Commander McCain's father." The second time "is today," he said. "Who the hell would've ever guessed I'd give the commencement address at the United States Naval Academy." I had helped write the speech, and he was letting me know how much it had meant to him. I had his complete trust back then, a privilege I appreciated then and in memory.

The Vietnamese gave the delegation access to archival information they had yet to release, and they made available every Vietnamese official Kerry had requested to see, including retired generals who had commanded military regions where missing American pilots had been lost, as well as senior officials in the prison administration system. We met with some of the prison officials in an administrative office next to a courtyard just inside the entrance to Hoa Lo prison. It was the first time McCain and Peterson had been inside the prison since the war. As delegation members milled around the courtyard, Peterson noticed a scrap of railroad iron that had served as a gong to wake the POWs in the morning and order them to sleep at night. "Hey, John, remember this?" he called out as he struck it. Hoa Lo was still an operating prison then, and in one corner of the courtyard, a door with a barred window sealed a corridor with prisoner cells on either side. It was the section of the prison the Americans had named "Heartbreak Hotel," and John had been held in one of its cells. A few curious inmates were looking out the barred window at the visiting Americans. As the meeting wrapped up, Kerry asked our hosts to allow us access to the cells. "Senator McCain was held in one of them," he informed them, "and he would like to see it." They initially refused, but Kerry kept at it. Eventually, one of the officials excused himself, presumably to make a call to his superiors, and returned with permission to enter the corridor. Guards instructed the inmates to go to their cells and close the doors. The door to the corridor was unlocked, and McCain, Peterson, Kerry, and other delegation members entered. McCain didn't appear noticeably affected by his surprise return to the place where he had suffered. He wasn't very talkative and didn't make any wisecracks. But neither was he solemn or tense; nor did he give any indication that he was straining to control his emotions. He was matter-of-fact in speech and demeanor. Kerry asked if the place looked the same, and he acknowledged it did, pointing to the naked light bulb that hung in each cell, and the inch of standing water in the corridor. The only difference, he observed, was that the inmates were crowded two or three to a cell. "They kept us in solitary here."

When they emerged from the corridor and the guards had shut the door, two curious inmates returned to look out the door's barred window. A guard gave the bars a loud rap with his baton to shoo them away. McCain, who was standing about ten yards away with his back turned, heard the sound, wheeled around, and shouted, "Hey, you," at the guard. He pointed a finger and told him, "Remember, humane and lenient. Humane and lenient." Then he thanked the government officials for their time and courtesy and left. He would come back for another visit seven years later with Cindy and his son Jack, but by then the prison was out of commission: A trade office building and actual hotel occupied the spot. All that remained of the Hanoi Hilton were exterior walls, the green iron doors, and a small museum that contained, among other artifacts, McCain's photograph and flight suit.

Kerry arranged for the delegation to meet with President Clinton and administration officials the Friday after we returned to Washington. I went with McCain to the meeting, and we were both surprised to find in attendance not only the president but Vice President Gore, the secretary of defense, the deputy secretary of state, the national security advisor, the veterans affairs administrator, and senior White House staff, including George Stephanopoulos. I would estimate the number of people in the Roosevelt Room to have been more than fifty. Every seat at the long table was occupied, as were all the chairs lining the walls, and some people had to stand. The meeting lasted over two hours. Kerry asked each member of the delegation to speak, and the attentive president questioned or addressed a comment to each of them. Some White House staffers appeared occupied with other concerns, including one staffer who read the paper while noisily chewing ice from a glass of Coke. McCain barely spoke at all, and I could tell that he was agitated: His shoulders were tensed, and he was clenching his jaw. I was seated in a chair behind him, and several times he turned in his seat and gave me a wide-eyed, eyebrows-arched look that asked, "What the hell is going on?" He was used to White House meetings in the Reagan and Bush administrations when an aide would inform him, "You will be escorted into the Oval Office at precisely two-seventeen and the meeting will conclude promptly at two-thirty-three." McCain's Senate office was informal and didn't always run on schedule. But he held the White House to higher standards. He always stood up to take a call from the president, and moments after the conversation began, he would start apologizing for taking up too much of the president's time.

The Roosevelt Room gabfest that Friday afternoon offended McCain's sense of decorum and taxed his patience. He was incredulous that the president remained in his seat all that time and, to all appearances, was completely engaged in the discussion. I could see him getting more and more restless. He had a flight to Phoenix to catch. Cindy was having minor surgery that day, and he had planned to be there when she was released from the hospital. He was waiting for the president to leave before he announced that he, too, would have to go. But the president never left. Finally, an embarrassed McCain stood up and addressed Clinton directly. He apologized that they had taken so much of his time. It was "inexcusable," he confessed, "and I'm sorry. I'm also embarrassed that I have to leave before you do, Mr. President. My wife is in the hospital, and I'll miss my flight if I stay any longer." Clinton was gracious in reply, and we left the meeting. McCain was sputtering mad in the car afterward. "You do not, I repeat, you do not take up that much of the president's time!" He was almost shouting. He complained that Kerry shouldn't have let everyone talk, and he criticized the lack of structure in the Clinton White House. "They need someone there to kick asses, or they're never going to get a goddamn thing done."

Clinton's closest political advisors counseled him against moving quickly on normalization. They feared widespread condemnation from veterans, which would highlight Clinton's vulnerability on the issue. Kerry and McCain succeeded only in persuading the administration to lift U.S. objections to loans to Vietnam from the International Monetary Fund and World Bank. Clinton dispatched an administration delegation to Vietnam in the fall, led by Assistant Secretary of State for Asia Winston Lord, who returned with reports of Vietnam's "excellent" cooperation. Still, the administration continued to hesitate.

Kerry and McCain hatched a plan to pass a Senate resolution that endorsed lifting the embargo. McCain thought he could get twenty Republicans to vote for it, which was deemed sufficient bipartisan cover for the step that Clinton and his advisors were reluctant to take. They introduced the resolution on January 26, 1994. The Senate debated it for two days. McCain's closing statement framed the debate as a two-sided question of honor—whether Americans were keeping faith with their missing warriors and whether the U.S. would keep its word to former adversaries who had kept their word to us. "Let us take such steps that will best honor our commitments, protect our interests, and advance our values," he argued. "There is no dishonor in that." The resolution passed with fifty-eight votes; all but two of the Vietnam veterans in the Senate voted for it. Republican leader Bob Dole opposed it, as did most Republicans. But McCain got the twenty Republican votes he had promised the White House, which lifted the trade embargo the next week.

McCain returned to Vietnam in the spring of 1994. A month or so earlier, he had invited Vice Foreign Minister Le Mai to lunch in the Senate dining room. Le Mai had traveled to Washington for discussions with his State Department counterparts after the end of the embargo had been announced. He and Le Mai had become quite familiar and comfortable in each other's company by then. They talked about the prospects for the full restoration of relations. McCain said he wanted to make another trip to Vietnam, and he would not be traveling with other senators, which was fairly unusual for him; Cindy and I would be coming with him. Le Mai welcomed the visit and asked whom McCain wished to meet with while he was in Hanoi. McCain identified the officials he wanted to see, and a few issues the American POW/MIA investigators at the Ranch had raised with him that he hoped to resolve while he was there. Near the end of the lunch, McCain very casually mentioned that he would like to visit Ha Long

Bay. He understood that Ho had used as a retreat one of the hundreds of islands that dotted the beautiful bay. "I'd like to spend a night on that island, if that's possible," he said. The normally imperturbable Le Mai looked very surprised and asked McCain how he knew this. McCain told him the story of the Cat's Christmas visit, which appeared to amuse Le Mai; he didn't readily agree to the request but promised to raise it with his minister when he returned to Hanoi.

We received no word about McCain's proposed Ha Long visit until we arrived in Hanoi and found in the itinerary that the Foreign Ministry had prepared for us an afternoon and evening of "sightseeing at Ha Long Bay." A few days later, after a long, bumpy ride on red clay roads first to Haiphong and then to Ha Long, we boarded a thirty-foot sightseeing boat, a seaworthy but pretty bare-bones vessel with a crew of four, which cruised the bay past scores of jagged black volcanic islands teeming with monkeys and other wildlife. Small saucer-shaped boats pulled alongside and sold us prawns and other seafood that the crew prepared for our lunch. Since then, the bay has been developed commercially and is one of Southeast Asia's most popular tourist destinations, complete with casinos built by the Chinese for those interested in more sedentary vacations. But in 1994, it was the most exotic place I'd ever been, and the well-traveled McCain pronounced it "one of my top five favorite places."

His enjoyment of Ha Long's charms was heightened all the more when we stepped ashore on an island with three dilapidated villas. A crew of ten or so Vietnamese greeted us. They were there to show us to our quarters and prepare us a memorable feast of fresh seafood. When dinner was finished, John, Cindy, and I spent a half hour in the villa where I was to stay, talking and enjoying the breeze off the bay through the unshuttered windows. The Vietnamese left the island a little before ten o'clock and turned off the generator that supplied power to the villas. We lit candles, and John and Cindy made their way carefully up a slight rise to the villa they had been assigned, the one Ho had used when he had needed a little rest and relaxation from the rigors of expelling the French from Vietnam. John looked as content as I had ever seen him, like a man who had made a bet with himself and won.

The Clinton administration remained reluctant to take the final steps toward full diplomatic normalization. Kerry asked McCain to make another trip to the White House to encourage the president. McCain refused at first: "I won't do it, John. I'm not going down there and taking up hours of Clinton's time again." Kerry assured him it would just be the two of them. "Twenty minutes, John. We won't need more than twenty minutes."

The two of them, accompanied by Kerry's aide Nancy Stetson and me, met at eleven o'clock on the morning of May 23, 1995, in the Oval Office with President Clinton and two of his aides. Kerry gave a succinct summary of the political and diplomatic case for lifting the embargo. When he had finished, the president asked McCain to speak. "Mr. President, I'm not interested anymore in who was for the war and who was against it," he began. "I'm tired of all that. I'm tired of looking back in anger at Vietnam. And I don't want the country to look back in anger anymore. It's time to move on, and if you do this, you will have my full support and gratitude."

That was all he said. It has been twenty-five years since I heard him speak those words. They still move me. It was a purely decent thing for him to do, humane and wise. Clinton was moved, as were, I think, all of us in the room. "You're a remarkable man, John McCain," Clinton responded. John perked up at that. He was as susceptible as anyone else to Bill Clinton's flattery. "I thought it went pretty well," he said in the car on the way back to the office. "What did Clinton say about me again? That I was an amazing man?"

"Remarkable. I think he said you're a remarkable man," I corrected him.

Six weeks later, on July 11, I sat in the East Room of the White House listening to President Clinton announce the full normalization of relations with Vietnam. A group of supporting players stood behind him on the dais, including John Kerry and John McCain. When Clinton finished his remarks, he turned to McCain and they embraced. At a mutual friend's house the following weekend, I asked Clinton advisor Paul Begala how the president was feeling about his decision to normalize. "A lot better since your guy hugged him," Begala replied.

• • •

Staff compiled a weekly reading file for McCain, a collection of articles, memos, and letters we thought he would want to see. It was kept on top of a cabinet just outside my office door, and he would usually look through it every few days or so. I checked its contents every day. A couple weeks after the White House announcement, I came upon a letter in the file from a person whose name I've forgotten. He didn't have a connection to McCain but was writing to praise him for his role in normalization. He was an elegant writer, and the letter was quite touching. He ended it by quoting some lines from Shelley's *Prometheus Unbound*, "which brought you to mind when I read them."

> *To suffer woes which Hope thinks infinite;*
> *To forgive wrongs darker than death or night;*
> *To defy Power, which seems omnipotent;*
> *To love, and bear; to hope till Hope creates*
> *From its own wreck the thing it contemplates;*
> *Neither to change, nor falter, nor repent;*
> *This, like thy glory, Titan, is to be*
> *Good, great and joyous, beautiful and free;*
> *This is alone Life, Joy, Empire, and Victory*

David Ifshin had traveled to Hanoi in 1970, where he made antiwar statements that were piped into the cells of John McCain and his fellow POWs. Campaigning for Ronald Reagan's reelection in 1984, McCain attacked the Mondale campaign for hiring Ifshin as its general counsel. Ifshin approached McCain at an AIPAC conference in Washington two years later and expressed a desire to apologize. McCain invited him to come by the office, which Ifshin did a few days later. He began to speak, but McCain interrupted and offered his own apology for attacking Ifshin in the 1984 election. They agreed to work on human rights issues together, and friendship followed.

Ifshin served as the Clinton-Gore campaign's general counsel in the 1992 election. When President Clinton spoke at the Vietnam

Veterans Memorial, one of the protestors in the crowd held up a sign
that read, "Clinton: Tell us about Ifshin." David had expected to receive an administration appointment, an ambassadorship, but had yet
to be offered anything. The reason, most observers assumed, was that
senior administration officials were worried he wouldn't be confirmed
by the Senate on account of his anti-war activities. When McCain got
word, he went to the Senate floor to speak on David's behalf. He began
by noting the protestor's sign and then went on, "I'll tell you about
David Ifshin. David Ifshin is my friend." Three years later, David Ifshin
died of lung cancer, leaving behind a wife, three children, and hundreds of close friends. John stayed in regular contact with David and
his wife, Gail, throughout the ordeal. I went with him to David and
Gail's house to exchange an emotional farewell shortly before David
died. President Clinton and John McCain were two of the eulogists at
his funeral. John credited David with teaching him about "the futility
of looking back in anger." He talked about learning to see the virtue
in people with whom you had profound disagreements. "David Ifshin
was my friend. His friendship honored me and honors me still." Few
of the mourners would forget hearing the testament to a friendship
between two politicians who lived in a city consumed by politics and
yet had managed to transcend politics. John McCain, of the famous
temper, wouldn't look back in anger because he knew the view would
blind him.

The support he had given the administration on Vietnam policy notwithstanding, McCain was a leading critic of policies on a host of foreign relations and national security issues. The debacle in Mogadishu
in October 1993—barely nine months into Clinton's first term—when
a local warlord attacked two companies of Army Rangers, killing eighteen, wounding seventy, and shooting down two Black Hawk helicopters, left McCain skeptical that the new president had the fortitude for
tough international problems or the capacity to conduct sound, consistent policy. McCain cosponsored a resolution demanding the withdrawal of U.S. forces from Somalia. He told me years later he regretted

having done so. Bob Dole had opposed the resolution, and he had corralled enough Republican votes to defeat it. "Bob was right," he reflected. "We can't let some thug force us out." He explained his action as a vote of no confidence in the administration: "I didn't trust them. They looked like they didn't know what they were doing." Earlier in the year, the administration had become embroiled in a trade dispute with Japan, our main Asian ally; and reversed itself on two issues—Taiwan and human rights—in our relationship with China, our main Asian adversary. McCain enjoyed a friendship with Henry Kissinger, whom he often consulted. Kissinger had complained to him about the administration's strategic incoherence: "Leave it to Clinton," he said, "to stumble into a fight with Japan and China at the same time." The doubts and hesitation exhibited by the administration in confrontations with dictators in Iraq, Haiti, and especially North Korea exacerbated his concerns.

On the same day the president announced the restoration of diplomatic relations with Vietnam, Bosnian Serbs overran a contingent of UN peacekeepers in the town of Srebrenica, and after a couple days established control of the Muslim enclave. NATO air forces supported the UN mission, but by the time they responded to the Serbian assault on the peacekeepers, it was too late to reverse the facts on the ground. The Serbs held dozens of peacekeepers hostage while they rounded up thousands of Muslim men and boys, executed them, and buried them in mass graves. The atrocity, the worst in Europe since the end of World War II, affected McCain's view of the wars in the Balkans, which had been ongoing for four years. It confirmed his opinion that the UN was incapable of enforcing peace among the warring former Yugoslavian republics. It also confirmed his reservations about subordinating NATO airpower to UN decision-makers. He had opposed the use of American power in the Balkans; the Bush administration was reluctant to get involved in the conflicts that erupted after Slovenia and Croatia declared independence in 1991, and Bosnia the following year. But McCain's own reluctance was more attributable to his distrust of what he viewed as the Clinton administration's irresolute approach to international problems, particularly to questions

about where and how to use force, than it was to the previous administration's hesitation to get involved in a Balkan quagmire. He also
doubted the Bosnian military's ability to take back territory from the
Serbs even with the assistance of U.S. airpower. The daily reports of
indiscriminate sniper killings during the siege of Sarajevo and of other
atrocities in Bosnia and Croatia had tested his opposition to U.S. military involvement, and he had joined with colleagues on the other side
of the issue to support lifting a UN arms embargo in Bosnia. But it
wasn't until Srebrenica that he reconsidered his position.

Bosnia would also mark an evolution in McCain's views on the use
of force. He previously believed the use of force should be reserved
to protect vital U.S. security interests. That was one of the lessons he
drew from Vietnam. After Srebrenica, he saw a role for military force
in the mitigation of human suffering and to prevent crimes against
humanity. The simple view of McCain held by some of his critics is
that in every dangerous international conflict, he wanted to shoot first
and ask questions later. That was never true. When he argued for military intervention, it was usually a carefully considered case intended
to avert greater bloodshed and suffering, using no more means than
were necessary to achieve that end.

During the early years of the North Korea nuclear crisis, as the
administration fitfully negotiated an ultimately failed deal, McCain
argued for a more rigorous sanctions regime and, if all else failed, for
an air strike on the reactor complex in Yongbyon, which at that time
might have produced enough weapons-grade plutonium for two small
nuclear weapons. Then as now, Seoul, a metropolis of ten million people, was within range of enemy artillery and essentially a hostage to
North Korean threats to incinerate the peninsula. That understandably made offensive action to cripple North Korea's plutonium production distressing to contemplate, if not unthinkable. McCain did
contemplate it, however. In the longest speech he ever made on the
Senate floor, well over an hour in length, he gave a detailed analysis
in which he argued that the risks posed by air strikes on North Korea's nuclear facilities were very serious "but not insurmountable." He
believed a tougher sanctions policy could obviate the need for such

drastic action, but his willingness to address all contingencies caused critics to dismiss him as a reckless "überhawk." A *New York Times* editorial denounced "Mr. McCain's Risky Korea Strategy." I worried about his reaction, wondering if he would feel he was too exposed to criticism. Few Senate Republicans appeared to share his opinion, or at least they didn't publicly share it. When I walked into his office to discuss a reaction, all he said was: "Don't worry about it. As long as they get the name right." Then he suggested sending a note to the *Times* editorial-page editor, Howell Raines, jokingly thanking him for the notoriety.

McCain viewed North Korea's acquisition of nuclear weapons and its eventual possession of the means to deliver them as such a dire threat to the security of the United States that prevention warranted taking all necessary measures. Much of his criticism of Clinton administration policy focused on what he viewed as the weakness of its negotiating strategy, which he complained was long on carrots and short on sticks. But he did make a case for air strikes if all else failed. He was joined in that view by General Brent Scowcroft—who is not an überhawk in anyone's estimation—whom he frequently consulted at the time. For the better part of three decades, the crisis has continued to worsen. Today the North Koreans have accumulated an arsenal of nuclear warheads and long-range missiles to deliver them. The gravity of the threat, along with North Korea's destabilizing brinkmanship, make it the most acute immediate danger confronting the U.S. and its allies. The problem would have been very dangerous to solve in 1993. It's nearly insoluble now. McCain forecast that predicament a quarter century ago. You have to concede that much to him, even if you think a military solution was never feasible.

Political considerations complicated his deliberations on Bosnia. His friend Phil Gramm was running for president, and McCain had agreed to serve as the campaign's national chairman. Gramm had publicly argued against U.S. military involvement in the Balkans. Gramm's primary Republican opponent, Bob Dole, was shocked by Serbian atrocities from the beginning of the conflicts in the former Yugoslavian republics; he was the leading Republican proponent of military intervention. When I became McCain's administrative assistant in 1993, I continued to serve as a foreign policy aide, and I don't remember him anguishing over the decision to reverse his opposition to direct U.S. military involvement. I do remember he was aware it would come as a surprise to allies on both sides of the question. In addition to Dole, his friend Joe Lieberman was a strong advocate of U.S. military intervention, and John had gotten into a heated exchange over the issue on a Sunday-morning show with his friend Joe Biden, another leading proponent. It would be an unwelcome surprise to Phil Gramm. But, as was often the case with McCain, once he began contemplating a change in position, he wouldn't leave it alone until he had made up his mind. In this case, he very quickly decided he would reverse himself and support intervention, and once he made the decision, he was all in. He felt pulled to come to Bob Dole's aid.

He respected the majority leader and admired him as someone who answered to an innate sense of justice. A majority of congressional Republicans opposed intervention. Most public opinion polls reflected the same split among Republicans nationally. Dole was in a predicament. Most presidential candidates would have taken the easier position or at least tried to stay noncommittal. But the Dayton Accords were announced in November 1995, and they included a provision for the deployment of U.S. peacekeepers to Bosnia. The Clinton administration wanted political cover for the deployment and sought a resolution authorizing the deployment from the Senate. Dole was majority leader, and McCain knew he felt morally obliged to help. The New Hampshire Union Leader, a prominent conservative voice in New Hampshire, was already criticizing Dole's position.

I remember discussing Bosnia with McCain in his office at the end of November, when he affirmed that he was ready to support the deployment. No more than a few minutes had passed from his declaration until he said, "Let's go see Bob." We went to the Senate floor, where a vote was under way. McCain pulled Dole aside and said, "I know you want to help Clinton with the resolution. It's the right thing to do. I want to help." A surprised Dole suggested the two of them announce their intention to reporters outside the chamber, which they did, and they spoke on the Senate floor the next day in support of an authorizing resolution. The *Union Leader* denounced them as "yellow-bellied cowards." The Republican whip at that time, Trent Lott, led opposition to the resolution along with another member of the leadership, Don Nickles. Texas Republican Kay Bailey Hutchison drafted a counter-resolution disapproving the deployment but professing support for the troops.

Phil Gramm asked McCain to meet him in his office a few days later. I went with him, and Gramm's foreign policy aide joined us as well. Though Gramm and McCain were close friends, and McCain respected his political talents and enjoyed his company, he told me on our way to the meeting that Gramm was not just wrong on the issue, he knew he was wrong and was opposing the resolution purely to gain an advantage over a rival. McCain was disappointed in his friend, and it put steel in his spine when Gramm entreated him to back down. Gramm argued that Dole could get the resolution passed on his own: "He's a big boy. He doesn't need your help, John." He complained that the press was already "making a thing" out of the fact that "my national chairman is working with my opponent. It's making me look bad." McCain was adamant that he had made up his mind and couldn't be persuaded to change it. He wasn't testy. On the contrary, his tone was oddly unemotional. He was very direct but not impassioned until Gramm's aide tried to make a policy case for opposing the peacekeeping mission. That angered him. "Go ahead and take a politically expedient position," he said afterward, "but don't bullshit me it's for the good of the country." By the end of the meeting, Gramm was left pleading for John to stay more in the background of the debate even if he was determined to support the resolution. That didn't work, either. McCain brought the meeting to an end when he said, "I'm not on the wrong side of the issue, Phil. You are."

Debate on three resolutions began on the evening of December 13. Two opposed the peacekeeping mission, and the Dole-McCain resolution supported it. Bob Dole was an able vote counter, and he made sure he had the votes to defeat the opposing resolutions, though one of them had the support of a majority of the Republican caucus. It was very late when debate on the Dole-McCain resolution commenced. McCain spoke before Dole. "This is not about a Democratic president and a Republican Senate," he said. "This is about a lot of frightened young Americans who are in Bosnia or on their way to Bosnia. They may not think of it directly, but they are going to look back one day to see if they had the support of those who represent them in Congress."

When Dole spoke, he explained the provisions of the resolution and then thanked McCain for his support. He took John completely unawares by saying, in a voice thick with emotion, that he had worn on his wrist a POW bracelet bearing John's name twenty years earlier, when he had argued on the Senate floor against cutting off aid to South Vietnam. McCain was emotional as he listened. The vote was sixty-nine to thirty in support of the resolution: Twenty-four Republicans and all but one Democrat had voted for it. The next day, the *Arizona Republic* ran an editorial cartoon depicting McCain and Dole walking into an open grave labeled: "Dead-end Bosnia policy." But the peacekeeping mission in Bosnia would succeed.

Bob Dole won the Republican presidential nomination the following year. Phil Gramm had raised enough money to challenge him but was eclipsed by the more populist conservative Pat Buchanan. Gramm dropped out of the race just before the New Hampshire primary, which Dole lost to Buchanan. Once Gramm was no longer a candidate, McCain endorsed Dole and logged thousands of miles and hundreds of hours on the campaign trail, with Dole and separately, as Dole slugged it out with Buchanan and Steve Forbes before clinching the nomination in March. Dole resigned his Senate seat in June, and McCain called his farewell speech to the Senate—with its emphasis on friendships and bipartisan cooperation—"one of the most inspiring I ever heard here." Two decades later, he told me to "go look at Dole's goodbye speech" when we were working on the speech he would give to the Senate after returning from brain surgery. McCain was on Dole's vice presidential short list and agreed to be vetted by campaign lawyers. Just before the Republican convention, Dole announced he had chosen Jack Kemp as his running mate. John didn't appear disappointed or even surprised to be passed over; he figured being a finalist would elevate him as a national figure in the press's estimation.

He got a call from Dole on Tuesday morning, the second day of the Republican convention in San Diego, which would raise his national profile even more. McCain had just finished an editorial board meeting with *Newsweek* magazine when an aide handed him his cell phone. For years afterward, McCain would delight in recounting the brief exchange in a passable impersonation of Dole's clipped speech pattern. Dole got right to the point, no greeting or how are you, just a question: "You want to nominate me?" John answered, "I'd be honored." Dole responded, "All right, my people will be in touch," and then hung up. The nominating speech was scheduled for prime time the next night. "Better get to work, boy," McCain said to me after explaining what Dole wanted. My hotel room was next to his, and he barged in repeatedly that afternoon as I sat chain-smoking on the balcony and hurriedly wrote a first draft. He actually read the pages over my shoulder as I typed them. It was distracting. Nevertheless, between the two of us, we managed to produce a ten-minute speech.

The convention chairman that year was the governor of Texas, George W. Bush, already rumored to be considering a presidential bid of his own. He introduced McCain, who began his speech with "In America, we celebrate the virtues of the quiet hero," and cast Bob Dole in the role of the selfless patriot, a role he had played for real during his World War II service in the 10th Mountain Division, as he recovered from his crippling wounds, and in his decades of public service. I was concerned that the applause during the first half of the speech wasn't resounding, but McCain eventually had the audience's full attention. Near the end, he recalled the story of Dole wearing his POW bracelet and never telling him until the Bosnia debate. "He never sought my thanks. He never imposed on me an obligation to him for the support he gave me at a time when I needed it most." He closed by offering Dole his gratitude "for myself, for my comrades who came home with me to the country we loved so dearly, and for the many thousands who did not." His voice cracked on the word "comrades," and he paused for a beat to collect himself. The speech was widely praised in the next day's commentary. McCain was ecstatic. Bill Safire called it "a brief gem from a brave man."

McCain hit the campaign trail for Dole almost every day the Senate wasn't in session that fall. He got to know Dole campaign aides who would later join his own presidential campaigns, including his future campaign manager, Rick Davis, and Greg Stevens, his lead ad maker. During the brief Gramm campaign, he had gotten friendly with the campaign's political director, John Weaver, who would also play a key role in McCain presidential campaigns.

Facing almost certain defeat at the end, Dole ordered round-the-clock appearances for the final ninety-six hours, napping on the plane between stops. McCain joined him and, years later, fondly recalled his impromptu late-night speeches in bowling alleys and diners as the candidate looked on. "He never deceived himself," McCain said. "He knew he was going to lose. But he was going to give it everything he had right to the end." McCain admired fatalistic heroism above other virtues. He said about Dole's last stop of the campaign, an emotional homecoming in Russell, Kansas, "every person in town showed up, and neighbors brought all this food to Bob's sister's house. How could you not be moved by that? It was so genuine."

The Republican caucus had elected Trent Lott majority leader after Dole left the Senate. McCain had supported his election. He and Lott liked each other and got along well. But McCain was coming into his own as a national figure in the late 1990s, and he used his greater prominence to exert his independence as a legislator, which couldn't help causing consternation among the leadership. He was making a name for himself as a reformer, sponsoring a line-item veto to curtail appropriations earmarks, proposing restrictions on lobbyists, and introducing his first bills to outlaw the unlimited sums, so-called soft money, that corporations and labor unions donated to the two political parties.

In the lead-up to his first race for president, a few Washington commentators—who relied on an excess of Beltway wisdom rather than original reporting—trafficked in the myth that John McCain in the 1990s was more show pony than workhorse. It used to annoy the hell out of me when I heard that tired metaphor applied to McCain; I doubt there was a harder-working or more accomplished Republican legislator in the Senate in that decade. As I worked on this book, I read an article on the comparative effectiveness of senators, referencing research conducted by Vanderbilt University and the University of Virginia, that confirmed my conviction. The study used more than a dozen metrics to determine effectiveness, including the number of bills sponsored by a senator, their importance, and how far they got through the legislative process. The study was cited by Senator Amy Klobuchar's presidential campaign because it found her to be one of the five most effective senators serving today, the only member of the minority to enjoy that distinction, and only the second to do so since John McCain did it in 1994.[31]

Two of his favorite legislative partners at the time were midwestern liberals, Russ Feingold and Paul Wellstone, who joined him in various ethics reform efforts. Feingold, of course, would cosponsor McCain's signature legislative success, the Bipartisan Campaign Reform Act, otherwise known as McCain-Feingold. I remember dismissing Wellstone as a middle-aged hippie when he was first elected to the Senate in 1990. I was surprised to find him waiting in our office's reception room not long after he had arrived in Washington. Suddenly, John burst into the room and said, "Let's go, Paul," and the two walked together out the door. "Where are you going?" I called after him. "To see Mo," McCain answered. Wellstone had approached John on the Senate floor and told him he'd long been an admirer of Mo Udall's, and asked to go along the next time John visited him.

"Had you talked to him before he came up to you?" I asked when he returned.

"Yeah, why?"

"I didn't know you knew him."

"He's a good guy."

Paul Wellstone was a good guy, unfailingly courteous to everyone he encountered, as nice to custodial workers in the Capitol as he was to his Senate colleagues. I used to see him on occasion driving one of the little underground trolleys that run between the Senate office buildings and the Capitol; he had made friends with the operator, who let him drive when he asked. McCain was very fond of him. They joined forces with Carl Levin and Russ Feingold to tighten restrictions on lobbyists, a two-year battle that concluded with a compromise in 1995. The proposed rule changes prohibited senators and staff from accepting from lobbyists gifts valued over fifty dollars, and ended the widespread practice of lobbyist-funded junkets. They also cooperated on related legislation requiring lobbyists to register and disclose their clients and fees.

The leadership of both parties hated the legislation and sought to soften its effects. Trent Lott got an amendment passed that blew a hole in the new limits, and Wellstone and Feingold threatened to withdraw their support of the bill. McCain worked to keep them on board, telling them he thought they could get Lott to agree to a compromise. A meeting was convened in Lott's office. McCain told me as we walked to the meeting, "I need to show Paul and Russ that I won't let Trent sabotage the whole thing if we have to agree to a deal with him." He had a good sense of the personalities involved. Both Wellstone and Feingold were ardent reformers, and Wellstone in particular could be as impassioned on the subject in private conversations as he was in public debate. McCain thought Lott would take offense if subjected to a tirade from a first-term senator of the other party. All parties were already seated at the table in Lott's conference room when the whip joined them.

Lott had barely settled in his seat when McCain accused him of bad faith for deceptively promoting his amendment as ethics reform when its effect would be to protect the status quo. "So, let me tell you what's not going to happen today, Trent. We're not going along with something you can call a victory but that won't do shit. We'll walk." When he had finished, he reached over to Wellstone, seated next to him, and patted his knee as if to say, "That's how you talk to the bosses, my friend." McCain's eruption seemed to quiet everyone. Lott might not have taken abuse like that from a couple of freshman Democrats, but it wasn't the first time he had received it from McCain, nor was he the only senator who had. He also took seriously McCain's threat that the legislation's sponsors would blow it all up if Lott's amendment remained in the bill unaltered. Wellstone and Feingold didn't feel the need to add to the passions in the room. Everyone settled down to good-faith negotiations, which ultimately produced a compromise acceptable to all.

McCain's first encounter with Russ Feingold had been brief and not pleasant. Not long after Feingold first arrived in the Senate in 1993, he sponsored an amendment to cut funding in the defense appropriations bill for a new aircraft carrier. McCain charged to the floor, sought recognition from the chair, and began peppering his new colleague with questions along the lines of "Has the senator from Wisconsin ever visited an aircraft carrier? Has he ever even seen one? Has he seen a carrier's air wing operate? Does he understand how carriers project power?" He didn't wait for Feingold to answer any of the queries before offering a concluding thought: "Perhaps the senator from Wisconsin could find out what an aircraft carrier does before he decides we don't need one." He didn't remain on the floor to listen to Feingold's response. It was unnecessarily rude and unwarranted behavior.

The next time he spoke to Feingold it was in private conversation. He had noticed Feingold's voting record and observed that he usually supported McCain amendments striking earmarks from appropriations bills. "He just called me out of the blue," Feingold recalled about the day in 1994 when McCain approached him, said he admired his voting record, his emphasis on spending reforms and tightening ethics regulations, and asked if he would be interested in working together on some things. Feingold cosponsored McCain's main domestic legislative initiative at the time, a line-item veto bill that passed in 1996 and was ruled unconstitutional by the Supreme Court two years later. Their first collaboration was on a 1995 op-ed in *Roll Call* calling for the abolition of soft money. They introduced their first campaign finance reform bill that same year, beginning a seven-year campaign to pass meaningful restrictions on campaign donations that would have to overcome multiple setbacks as the two legislative partners became friends and admirers.

McCain and Feingold's early attempt at passing a soft-money ban was defeated by filibuster. A bare majority supported it, but they never got close to the sixty votes they needed to cut off debate. Lott allowed them two weeks of debate in 1998. The public opponents of McCain-Feingold were Republicans led by Mitch McConnell. But a soft-money ban wasn't universally popular in Democratic Party leadership, either. Democrats relied on soft money more than Republicans did, and much of McCain's argument in favor of a ban relied on media coverage of Clinton campaign finance controversies, Al Gore's appearance at a Buddhist temple, and Lincoln-bedroom overnights to reward soft-money donors.

McCain's most ambitious undertaking of the 1990s was a complicated effort to federalize a settlement agreement between the major tobacco companies and the attorneys general from forty states who had sued to recover smoking-related health care costs. The legislation would have imposed a stiff tax on a pack of cigarettes to fund a massive campaign to discourage smoking, especially among teens; increase health care research; and compensate impacted tobacco farmers.

McCain had assumed the chairmanship of the Commerce, Science, and Transportation Committee in 1997. He was an energetic chairman, and the committee's broad oversight of all interstate commerce, forms of transportation, communication, communications technology, consumer protection, the Coast Guard and Merchant Marine, and various other enterprises gave him enormous latitude to explore almost anything that interested him. He liked to convene hearings on topics to educate himself and other committee members on subjects they might have little knowledge of, a practice he would continue as chairman of the Armed Services Committee.

Commerce wasn't the obvious choice to be given responsibility for the tobacco settlement. The Judiciary and Health committees had competing claims to jurisdiction. But McCain, a former two-pack-a-day smoker who, as far as I knew, had no prior interest in tobacco policy, somehow cajoled Trent Lott into assigning the entire effort to Commerce. Once he had the reins in hand, McCain drove the committee, the White House, and a collection of competing interests toward what he hoped would be a grand compromise that would be acceptable enough to all parties concerned. Initially, leading liberals in the Democratic caucus, including Ted Kennedy, were suspicious of McCain's intentions and pushed the White House not to agree to major compromises. They believed the politics of the bill favored Democrats and could help them regain the majority in the November elections, and ultimately produce a more ambitious tobacco bill than Republicans would accept. The White House chief of staff, Erskine Bowles, and domestic policy counsel Bruce Reed believed McCain was on the level, and his expressed willingness to negotiate a bill that he could get through his committee and satisfy the administration might present a genuine opportunity to settle the issue now. Over the objections of Kennedy and others, Bowles directed Reed to negotiate with McCain in good faith.

The bill ultimately failed because one party to the dispute, the tobacco companies, did not find it acceptable and spent millions of dollars on a lobbying and advertising campaign that encouraged opposition by a majority of Republican senators, unwittingly assisted by a handful of progressives. Although the effort ended in defeat, it gave Washington its first full look at John McCain's dogged leadership style.

He negotiated an agreement with the White House on the provisions they wanted included in the bill, becoming friends in the process with Bruce Reed. Commerce was the Senate's largest committee, and its membership in 1998 included tobacco-state senators, anti-tobacco progressives, business-oriented conservatives, a former state attorney general, and some of the Senate's longest-tenured veterans. After multiple sets of negotiations with committee members, administration officials, state attorneys general, trial lawyers, tobacco companies, and others—led by committee staff and by McCain personally—they had the elements of a bill to take to the full committee with the understanding that it would be substantially revised by amendments offered during the markup.

The markup lasted all of April Fools' Day, 1998. The committee clashed, sometimes heatedly, over differences, but found ways to bridge them and balance competing interests while McCain played the roles of trail boss, disciplinarian, mediator, idealist, and pragmatic solution broker. At the end of what McCain jokingly called "the longest day" (a reference to the movie about D-Day), when the committee voted nineteen to one to report out a tobacco bill, politicians and pundits praised McCain's mastery of the markup as a virtuoso performance. Dan Inouye, the long-serving senator from Hawaii, proclaimed it "a great day for the committee, a great day for the Senate. This was a presidential performance." Another committee member professed she "would never have believed that anyone could have gotten the forces together as you have." Another called him "the bionic man." One veteran columnist confessed that while he had always considered McCain a brave man and able politician, he had not realized before that McCain could be a "master legislator."

At one point during the markup, as a proposed tax hike on a pack of cigarettes increased to $1.10, and penalties imposed on the tobacco industry rose billions beyond what it was prepared to pay, committee staff and the chairman realized the companies would likely withdraw support for the bill. But they reasoned that if they could keep the administration on board, and the White House delivered the Democratic caucus, they could corral enough Republican votes to get it out of the Senate and into negotiations with the Republican House, where they would try again to square the circle. That was a miscalculation.

To kill the bill, the tobacco companies launched a $50 million advertising campaign, much of it specifically targeting supporters, including McCain. A tobacco-funded "issue advocacy" group calling itself the National Smokers Alliance ran attack ads against him in Arizona, where he was up for reelection that year, as well as in New Hampshire and Iowa, in case the rumors of a 2000 presidential candidacy were true. For two months after the committee reported out the bill, as McCain continued to negotiate with the White House and various other interests, the companies pounded television and radio airwaves, promising Republicans they would continue advertising through the November elections. Opposition within the Senate Republican caucus hardened. While Lott claimed, if not neutrality, a willingness to let McCain try to negotiate his way through the array of obstacles, the rest of the Senate Republican leadership was implacably opposed, including Don Nickles, the majority whip, and Mitch McConnell, who chaired the Senate Republican reelection committee and assured the caucus of significant financial support from the industry if they defeated the bill. At a weekly Tuesday Senate Republican lunch, leadership staff produced a chart detailing a Rube Goldberg scheme of regulatory oversight that it claimed the tobacco bill would create. McCain denounced the chart as "chickenshit." The incident would be featured in many subsequent stories about John McCain's notorious temper.

He fought back as hard as he could, becoming a scourge of the tobacco companies, which he hadn't been before, and a genuinely ardent advocate of smoking cessation efforts, which he also hadn't been before. Floor debate on the bill began on May 18. It lasted a month, and for much of that time the outcome was unclear. McCain was on the floor most of every day it was pending, scurrying around to shore up support, brokering deals, trying to prevent alliances against it. Republican opponents formulated a shrewd strategy to exacerbate complaints about the bill by proposing amendments that would further penalize the tobacco companies, and luring the most progressive Democrats to support them. When the decisive votes were scheduled for June 17, one a cloture vote and another requiring a supermajority to send the bill back to committee, the bill's supporters lost the first one by three votes and the second by seven.

McCain addressed the chamber right before the final vote, which he knew he would lose. He didn't have written remarks or even notes. He pleaded with his party near the end of his statement to "understand that our obligation first of all is to those who can't care for themselves in this society, and that includes our children. Isn't it our obligation— shouldn't it define the Republican Party that we should do everything we can to handle this scourge, this disease that is rampant throughout young children in America?"

All Democrats in the chamber rose to their feet to applaud him; a few Republicans joined them. Ted Kennedy told friends afterward that it was the moment when he realized McCain had become a Senate power. McCain's maverick reputation was established and would assume greater dimensions in the years ahead. The *New York Times* published a story the day after the defeat under the headline "Though His Bill Is Dead, McCain May Be Enlivened."

McCain was elected to his third term that November, defeating a little-known Democrat opponent by a margin of 40 percent; 55 percent of Hispanics voted for him, as did 40 percent of Arizona Democrats. The McCain family spent Christmas in Fiji that year. I spent it in my hometown, in a hospital room, keeping vigil as my father was dying. A brave man who lived a good life spent his last few days unconsciously drifting away. To pass the long hours at the hospital, I reviewed page proofs of the book McCain and I had recently finished writing, the first one, *Faith of My Fathers*. A year earlier we had been approached by a literary agent, Philippa "Flip" Brophy, with an idea for a book. McCain had turned down previous offers to write about his Vietnam experience. Flip suggested he write about his family's military history, which would include his navy service. He liked the idea but had a caveat: He wanted me to be his collaborator. Some publishers passed on the book for that reason, because both writers were amateurs. A senior editor for Random House at the time, Jonathan Karp, liked the book proposal we had written and decided to gamble on our producing something that wouldn't embarrass all of us. The friendship with agent and editor begun then continued for seven books, and continues with this one, to the gratitude of the amateurs.

On December 20, other McCain aides were registering a John McCain for President Exploratory Committee with the Federal Election Commission, the first 2000 candidacy to do so.

STRAIGHT TALK
EXPRESS

Insufficient executive experience is a common deficiency in the résumés of senators running for president. Governors are thought to be better prepared to take on the responsibilities of the commander in chief. McCain's response to the criticism was to point to his service as commander of VA-174, the navy's largest squadron, at Cecil Field in Jacksonville, which trained replacement pilots and aircrews for carriers. Thanks to postwar defense budget cuts, it was in a state of disrepair. As many as half the squadron's planes weren't operational, and some of them hadn't flown in two years, when McCain arrived in the autumn of 1974. Discipline and morale suffered as well.

Not for the first time in McCain's navy career, skeptics speculated that his assignment as the squadron's executive officer in 1975, and then in 1976 as its skipper, was a benefit of his famous navy lineage even though his father had been retired for four years. McCain was by then too senior in rank for the job. Fleet squadrons have twelve planes, sixteen pilots, and about a hundred support personnel. VA-174 had more than fifty aircraft and a thousand people. Skeptics also wondered how he could have regained flight status, given the extent of his war injuries. He had suffered through two operations when he first returned from Vietnam, and spent his first five months back in the States on medical leave. He persevered through long, excruciating hours of physical therapy to get back 90 percent of the flexibility in his right knee; when he left Vietnam, he had less than 10 percent. A physical therapist, Diane Rauch, had volunteered her services to him when he was assigned to the National War College at Fort McNair in Washington. She recounted with admiration his determination to overcome his disability and his tolerance for pain in their two-hour, twice-a-week sessions. She told Bob Timberg that the pain McCain had experienced "was ten on a scale of ten." When he reached his limit, he would put his hand over his face and say, "That's it, honey."[32] I rely on Timberg and other McCain biographers for descriptions of his physical rehabilitation. When I asked McCain about it as we collaborated on our second book, all I got was something along the lines of "I wanted to fly, so I did what I had to do." When I pressed him for more, he said the sessions lasted "a couple hours and hurt like hell." Then he volunteered that he had introduced Rauch to her future husband, Bill Lawrence, his senior ranking officer in the Hanoi Hilton, whom McCain once described to me as "probably the best commanding officer I ever served under."

New York Times reporter Nicholas Kristof wrote about this period in McCain's life in an affecting 2000 profile. He recounted McCain's kindness to another of Rauch's clients, twelve-year-old Ann Jones, who had terminal brain cancer. He would arrive early at the clinic "to cheer up Ann and came to her home when she was dying." I had never heard the story before reading Kristof's account.[33, 34]

Thanks to Diane Rauch's dedication and his perseverance, his knee was rehabilitated enough to regain flight status in the spring of 1974—although, he joked to Timberg, his arm and shoulder injuries would have made it difficult for him to reach up and "pull the curtain" if he'd needed to eject.[35] The pilots in VA-174 flew A-7 Corsairs, which McCain had never flown. He would have to train and qualify in the plane if he were to remain in the squadron. Kristof reported that senior officers in the air wing who had criticized McCain's appointment were "delighted" when he failed his first attempt to land an A-7 on a carrier deck. He quoted one of McCain's instructors, who reported "two senior officers taking him and a co-worker aside and ordering them to make sure McCain did not make it." But the junior officers "were mesmerized by 'the Skipper'" and made sure he qualified in his second attempt at a carrier landing.[36]

Carl Smith was an instructor in VA-174 and eventually became McCain's executive officer. He followed him to Washington some years later, when McCain was the navy's Senate liaison, and landed a staff position on the Senate Armed Services Committee. Smith recalled how the squadron "had become rather stagnant," how some of the maintenance chiefs had been in their jobs too long, and repair parts for grounded aircraft were unavailable. "Then McCain came in," Smith remembered, "and you had this incredible transformation."

McCain's doubters included the commanding officer of his air wing, Captain Marvin Reynolds. Shortly after assuming command of the squadron, McCain went to Reynolds and asked for permission to "cannibalize" the grounded A-7s, moving parts from one aircraft to another, which was expressly forbidden at the time. He promised Reynolds that in exchange for an exemption from the rule, he would have every plane in the squadron in the air before he finished his tour in a year. Reynolds told him it couldn't be done. No skipper had ever had all the squadron's planes operational. But he gave him permission to try.

McCain got to know everyone under his command, officer and enlisted, teasing them, barking at them, encouraging them, delegating to them, and inspiring them, Smith and other pilots recalled. He was congenial but direct. He told them what he expected from them and held them to account. He met with the heads of the maintenance departments, asked what they needed, and instructed them to put together a schedule for the repairs to get the grounded planes in the air. "He got them fired up or he fired them," Smith said. Kristof interviewed an instructor who had helped train McCain in the A-7. He was an admiral by then and commanding a carrier battle group. He told Kristof he had never intended to stay in the service, but he decided to make a career in the navy because of McCain's inspiring example. "Morale went through the roof," remembered Smith. "Man, we just loved the guy." McCain described the squadron to me as "the best pilots and maintenance crews in the navy."[37]

On the day before he transferred command of the squadron, Carl Smith flew the last of the grounded A-7s—barely. He had to fly with the plane's landing gear down, but he got it in the air. The squadron had kept McCain's promise to Captain Reynolds. It hadn't suffered a single accident during McCain's command, and earned its first-ever Meritorious Unit Commendation.

Near the end of the Kristof profile, Dick Stratton, who had been in prison with McCain, recalled a conversation the two had when they were in the Hanoi Hilton. "We asked John what he wanted to be—chief of naval operations? He said no, the best job in the navy is commander-in-chief of Pacific forces [his father's last navy job], because then you're chief warrior. But he said what he really wanted to be was president."

The initial plan conceived by McCain's small presidential campaign staff had targeted April 1999 for a formal announcement of his candidacy. But as would be the case in his second presidential run, war would affect the campaign's message and scheduling. In this instance, it was the NATO air war against Serbia's Slobodan Milošević regime, in retaliation for Serbia's invasion of Kosovo and bloody suppression of Kosovo's independence movement.

The first NATO air strikes were measured and ineffective, and Serbia responded to them by cleansing Kosovo of ethnic Albanians, sending hundreds of thousands of refugees teeming into neighboring Albania, Macedonia, and Montenegro. The Clinton administration's starting presumption had been that Milošević would back down soon after the first shots were fired. That was a mistake, and McCain knew it was a mistake. He supported military action against Serbia but had argued against publicly identifying the limits of the force the West was prepared to use to achieve its objectives of getting Serbia out, refugees back, and peacekeepers into Kosovo. The day the air campaign began, President Clinton explicitly stated that ground troops were off the table. "Never tell the enemy what you're not prepared to do to win," an angry McCain complained. He urged the administration to let Belgrade know it had changed its position, that nothing was off the table. It was an argument he made more stridently with each passing day that

Milošević rid Kosovo of more Kosovars. He didn't think ground forces would prove necessary, he told me, but the threat of them was. At a minimum, McCain observed, "You have to drop the bridges and turn off the lights in Belgrade to have any chance of changing Milošević's mind." Even when NATO missiles hit Belgrade for the first time on April 3, Clinton was still doubling down—inexplicably, to McCain—on his insistence that no ground operations were under consideration. At the time McCain was getting calls from senior government officials in other NATO countries, as well as from General Wesley Clark, whom Clinton had appointed supreme allied commander in Europe, sharing that they, too, were mystified by the administration's position, and urging him to keep up his criticism.

McCain was where he liked to be, in the middle of a big Washington debate over a critical national security issue, and he preferred to remain there until it was concluded one way or another. He also worried it would appear unseemly for him to withdraw from a debate that was getting more intense by the day to go to New Hampshire and other early primary states on a campaign announcement tour. So he made the decision to postpone until the fall a formal announcement of his candidacy. A more cynical justification, the one campaign aides discussed among ourselves, was that McCain, who wasn't then as well known nationally as he would be after the campaign, couldn't hope to get as much attention from the announcement of his underdog campaign as he was presently getting in daily media attention to the war in Kosovo. He liked to joke that at the start of the campaign, he had "three percent name ID in polls with a five percent margin of error." So, for the first and not the last time, Candidate McCain's campaign team adapted to Senator McCain's policy priorities. We became skillful at making a virtue of necessity. Sometimes we saw the inherent wisdom in letting McCain be McCain, and other times we realized he would sabotage any attempt to get him to be someone else.

Milošević threw in the towel in June, after NATO sorties had dropped the bridges and turned out the lights in Belgrade. The unannounced McCain campaign was already under way, with the candidate making appearances to small crowds and little interest in the early states, particularly New Hampshire and South Carolina. The decision to launch an underdog campaign for president had evolved over two or more years. The seeds had been planted by McCain's campaign experiences in 1996, first with the Gramm campaign and then flying around the country with Bob Dole. He had observed what had worked for each candidate and what hadn't. He formed relationships with key Dole and Gramm aides. Some of them—John Weaver, Gramm's political director; Greg Stevens and his partners, Paul Curcio and Rick Reed, Republican ad makers who ran Dole's media campaign; and Bill McInturff, McCain and Gramm's pollster—had urged him to run and informally advised him since late 1997. With Carla Eudy, finance director for McCain's reelection campaigns, and two prominent Washington establishment figures, former Minnesota congressman Vin Weber and former Reagan chief of staff Ken Duberstein, they formed the early nucleus of a McCain campaign team. When McCain gave his consent to proceed, Greg Stevens approached Dole's deputy campaign manager, Rick Davis, who had been asked to manage Elizabeth Dole's campaign, to see if he had any interest in managing the McCain campaign. Rick consulted a few friends but hadn't made up his mind when he left for a business trip to Spain. He took a copy of *The Nightingale's Song* with him. He was seated next to John Glenn on the return flight, who noticed the book Rick was reading, and proceeded to deliver "A five-hour briefing on what a great American hero and statesman John McCain was and how lucky the country would be if he ran." Rick called Greg Stevens that evening and told him he was in.

The field was crowded with big names at the outset, including former vice president Dan Quayle; former cabinet official in the Reagan and George H. W. Bush administrations Elizabeth Dole; former Tennessee governor and Bush education secretary Lamar Alexander; McCain Senate colleague Orrin Hatch; McCain friend and House freshman classmate John Kasich; and publishing executive Steve Forbes. Both Forbes and Alexander were running for the second time, having lost to Bob Dole in the 1996 primaries. A few lesser-known Republican figures joined the race as well, including prominent social conservative Gary Bauer and conservative gadfly Alan Keyes.

From the beginning, the field had an acknowledged front-runner, the governor of Texas, George W. Bush, around whom most of the party establishment appeared to be coalescing. The Bush campaign attracted most of the party's big bundlers, wealthy donors who commit to raising large sums from other wealthy donors; and most of the high-profile endorsements, including many of McCain's Republican Senate colleagues. At times it appeared as if Governor Bush had established a government-in-waiting, since the party's most respected statesmen, smartest policy minds, and much of the professional consulting class had migrated to Austin or visited there regularly while his campaign smartly portrayed the governor as preparing to become president.

Most of the candidates left the field before the first votes were cast, including Dole, Quayle, Alexander, and Kasich. Alexander's exit in August 1999 yielded an addition to the thin ranks of the McCain campaign leadership team, veteran GOP ad maker and strategist Mike Murphy, whose quick mind and sharp wit entertained reporters, colleagues, and the candidate for the duration of the McCain campaign. Murphy had signed on with Alexander out of loyalty, having been a top aide in his 1996 bid. But he expected Alexander to drop out early and had been informally advising us for months. The most important advice Murphy offered was not to play in Iowa, and to concentrate most of our resources and the candidate's time in New Hampshire and South Carolina.

It wasn't clear how much money McCain could raise for the race, but we knew it wouldn't approximate the Bush campaign treasury. The Iowa caucuses are money and labor intensive, and we would have a lot less of both than the Bush campaign. They are also dominated by social conservatives, who clearly favored Bush over McCain. And McCain, in his perpetual battle against pork barrel projects, had long targeted ethanol as a prime example of wasteful spending, an unpopular opinion in the state that produced the most corn in the country. Finally, the Iowa Republican Party had an annual summer event known as the Ames Straw Poll that drew almost all national political reporters and most of the candidates. It was a fund-raising racket for the state party. Campaigns had to pay to compete in the poll, and to cover the logistics of bringing their supporters there—including, allegedly, voters with dubious Iowa origins. We didn't have the resources or the organizational strength to win the straw poll, so we made the decision not to try.

The decision not to compete in Iowa was a harder one to make. Friends and advisors were divided on the question, and it took a couple months before a firm decision was made. No nominee had ever won without finishing at least in the top three in Iowa. But Murphy made a compelling case that the attempt would fail and likely kill a McCain bid. Most of McCain's senior aides were convinced, and so was the candidate, who thought of himself as a risk-taker and liked the idea from the outset. He did want to make a few appearances in Iowa, but just to make it clear that we had no intention of spending resources there. He would use the appearances to criticize the expense and debatable environmental benefit of government-subsidized ethanol production.

When we were working on our second book, the year after that first presidential campaign, I asked McCain what the main factors had been in his decision to run. His answer was banal but honest: "I guess I thought I was in the right place and the right age to give it a shot." I had hoped for something more inspirational and asked if that was all he wanted me to write. "Just write that running for president became my ambition." Still trying to draw him out, I asked, "When?"

"When what?"

"When had it become your ambition?"

"I don't know, sometime before I decided to run."

I had been around him long enough to know when I was on a fruitless search for psychological insights. But I kept at it for a bit. I told him I had seen quotes from guys he was in prison with, saying he had presidential ambitions even back then. He dismissed the idea: "Not serious ones, daydreams, kid stuff."

"Did you give any thought to it when you were elected to the Senate?"

"Again, not seriously," he reiterated. "I didn't start thinking seriously about it until Phil's campaign and Dole's. I guess I thought I could probably do this, maybe do it better, do it differently, anyway. I thought the opportunity might be there, I was getting better known. I thought I was a good age to run. And I didn't think the competition—at least the people we knew were probably going to run—were impossible to beat."

"Is that all there was to it?" I asked.

"Well, no, I also thought I'd be a good president. I don't think anyone should run for president if they don't believe that."

Unexpressed in that conversation was his conviction that he would be a better president, specifically a better commander in chief, than any of the other candidates running. As his campaign message evolved, it would concentrate more on domestic policy issues, especially public ethics issues, than on foreign affairs and national security. But his desire to be president, as opposed to his decision to run for president, was based in his aspirations to be a world leader and influence world history. His decision was as practical as he had made it sound to me. And in the McCain tradition, his outlook on his prospects was fatalistic. To veteran *Washington Post* political reporter David Broder, he repeated his approach to the campaign: "Look, I'm sixty-two years old. There will not be another point in my life. If I didn't run and somebody else won the race, I would always wonder if I could have done it. But, I would hasten to add, this is not the alpha and omega to me."[38]

That attitude could frustrate campaign aides, including me. It's not the most inspirational message to voters or campaign volunteers. McCain had a tendency, not a rare one among politicians, to lapse into punditry. Most pols are avid consumers of political horse-race commentary, so it's a natural avocation for them. But his fatalistic "don't concede you care too much" attitude was a defense mechanism that allowed him to undertake improbable quests. It helped keep him steady in adversity, all manner of adversity, the kind politicians encounter, and the kind soldiers do.

Despite his occasional attempts at color commentary, his campaign message suited him and the times. It evolved quickly and out of necessity. Much of McCain's national profile in 1999 was shaped by his outspokenness on defense and foreign policy issues. His positions on domestic issues were mostly a grab bag of political and government ethics reforms he was identified with; his opposition to earmarked spending in appropriations bills; lobbying restrictions; and, of course, his and Russ Feingold's efforts to pass sweeping campaign finance reform. At the time, McCain-Feingold consumed more of McCain's attention and the media's focus on him than any other non-international issue. He talked about it all the time in the Senate and in his first forays in New Hampshire and other early states, which posed a messaging problem. Bill McInturff explained that while voters responded to general promises to reform Washington—and still do, even to the emptiest promise to "drain the swamp"—fewer than 3 percent of voters listed campaign finance reform as a priority that would influence their choice of a candidate. But it was a priority for our candidate, and a waste of time for anyone to try to dissuade him from talking about it so much.

McCain himself provided the formula to make the issue a more compelling message for a presidential campaign. His advocacy of campaign finance reform was not simply, as many commentators suggested, an effort to repair his reputation from the damage inflicted by the Keating scandal. It was in part a reaction to that experience, but as much or more so, it was a reaction to how current campaign finance rules—specifically, the unlimited sums from corporations and unions—corrupted the legislative process and discouraged members of Congress from acting on their principles. He often cited the Telecommunications Act of 1996, the first overhaul of telecommunications law in over half a century, as the legislative effort that really opened his eyes to the need for a soft-money ban. The purpose of the bill, from his free-market perspective, was to promote competition among the major telecommunications commercial entities because competition provided the consumer more choices and lower costs. But, he said, every commercial interest affected by the legislation had given hundreds of thousands of dollars in soft-money donations to both parties. So, instead of a bill that promoted competition to the benefit of the consumer, in which there would ultimately be winners and losers among competing companies, "we got a bill that stifled competition and cut the same size piece of pie for everybody."

McCain recalled, too, the painful memory of how tobacco companies had encouraged Republicans to vote against his tobacco bill by promising to spend huge sums defending them and attacking the bill's supporters. He saw the influence of campaign donations in every appropriations bill, where dozens of unauthorized earmarks were awarded to interests, which hadn't been selected through competitive bidding or any kind of meritorious process.

How to make the voters care wasn't clear to us. The candidate responded to claims of the public's disinterest in campaign finance reform by arguing that he "couldn't get anything big done on stuff that should matter to people," on spending, taxes, health care, acquisition reform, and government programs in need of overhauling, "unless we take on the influence of special interests by stopping them from buying influence." So, in McCain's pitch to voters as a candidate for president, campaign finance reform became the gateway reform through which he would deliver reforms that were bigger priorities for them. It was difficult to get McCain to repeat his core message—to maintain message discipline, in campaign parlance. He would repeat the same jokes over and over for years until everyone who worked for him could recite them backward. But for some reason, he resisted repeating for an entire campaign the main points of a central campaign message. If it began to bore him, he assumed it was boring to his audience. It was odd that he never had the same worry about the jokes. But framing all government reforms as products of campaign finance reform was an idea he embraced. It allowed him to add new elements ripped from the headlines, so to speak, and to improvise wisecracks, and in the end, it imposed a kind of discipline on his daily communications, something he had instinctively resisted.

It also helped differentiate his conservativism from the conventional orientation of small government, low taxes, and less regulation that had lapsed in the modern era into a reflexive anti-government ideology. He was drawn to the idea of national-greatness conservatism articulated by Bill Kristol and David Brooks, mocked by its conservative critics as "big-government conservatism." National-greatness conservatism took its inspiration from one of McCain's favorite historical figures, Teddy Roosevelt. Its object was the improvement of the country through pragmatic problem-solving rather than the drown-government-in-a-bathtub goal of libertarian conservatism, achieved in part by restoring the public's faith in the credibility and capabilities of government, a cause McCain described as a "new patriotic challenge."

The international corollary of national greatness was a muscular foreign policy that championed American values as purposefully as it defended American interests. McCain outlined a compatible world-view in a speech at Kansas State University in March 1999, which was remembered, and criticized, for its advocacy of "rogue state rollback." The speech wasn't, as critics exaggerated, a call to arms to democratize the world's worst autocracies. McCain's views on the use of military force had evolved from post-Vietnam reservations, apparent in his opposition to the marine deployment in Beirut and his initial skepticism about military involvement in the Balkans crisis. He was more open to the use of force where he thought it could achieve worthwhile objectives. The change in his attitude was attributable to several factors. The collapse of the Soviet Union meant the U.S. no longer had a superpower rival able to oppose or assist others in opposing U.S. military intervention to defend our interests. The growing technological prowess, especially of American airpower, and the professionalism of America's all-volunteer armed forces greatly improved the prospects for obtaining objectives quickly and with fewer casualties, as demonstrated in the success of Desert Storm. Finally, McCain's empathy with oppressed peoples moved him to publicly champion their cause, and to urge whichever administration was in office to use diplomacy and economic influence to do likewise. Sometimes, in situations of extreme inhumanity, as in Srebrenica, he would support military intervention to stop or prevent a slaughter.

McCain's rogue-state-rollback proposal was not an argument for the use of force to "liberate" subject populations from regimes that threatened the world's peace and stability and were the world's worst human rights offenders. Rather, it was a call for the U.S. to use soft power, public diplomacy, and economic sanctions to support popular resistance to "odious regimes" and, where possible, by supplying them with arms and material support. McCain cited North Korea and Iraq as examples, but he had other regimes in mind as well, including Iran, Libya, and Afghanistan. It was a reformulation of the Reagan Doctrine. In the same speech, McCain warned against using military force as a substitute for diplomacy.

As I write about McCain's support for a different kind of conservatism, I've resisted the use of the term "governing philosophy." I'm not sure McCain's view on government and government service could be described as a philosophy. It was more an ethos, a commitment to probity in government from a man who was raised to obey a code of conduct. To the extent that it was some kind of philosophy, it could be summarized thus: America isn't merely a tribe or collection of tribes or a geographic entity. It is an idea that forms the greatest cause in human history, the idea that self-government is the only moral government, and that all people everywhere possess equal dignity and a natural right to their freedom and to equal justice under the law. The American people distrusted their government because they had less influence on its behavior than did wealthy special interests. The public's cynicism about government was hardening into alienation, which threatened America's cause at home and abroad. To address that threat, patriots should act to improve government, ethically and operationally, to restore the public's faith in America's system of government and the cause of freedom. That was it in a nutshell, and it more or less remained for the rest of his life what I guess you could call the guiding principle of John McCain's public service.

While campaign finance reform was a critical component of the McCain campaign's message, it was not the organizing theme. That, too, developed sort of organically. Near the end of a meeting in spring 1999, Vin Weber asked me to explain the main message of the McCain memoir we had just finished writing. I hadn't given thought to planting a political message in an account of the McCain family's military history. The only question about the book's impact on the campaign at that time was scheduling. McCain had agreed to give the publisher,

Random House, two full weeks of book promotion, including book signings in states around the country, not one of which was an early primary state. John Weaver had complained there was no way McCain could take that much time off the campaign trail.

Skeptics will scoff, but the book was not written as a campaign biography. It was written as a family memoir, and the timing was purely coincidental. We didn't suggest any of the contract terms, including the date of publication. September 1999 proved to be fortuitous, and I admit to the campaign's quick realization that the book had a political utility. But at the time we sat down to write it, near the end of 1997, McCain had not decided to run for president. Neither of us considered how the book could convey a campaign message. Obviously, the story of his and his family's sacrifices for the country distinguished him from other candidates. By the time we turned in the manuscript in early 1999, I assumed that if the book sold well, it would help promote a heroic image of him that was the surest way to draw attention to his candidacy. But that had not been a consideration in the timing or writing of the book.

So Weber's question caught me off guard, though a response came immediately to mind. I adapted a line in the book: "Nothing in life is more liberating than to fight for a cause larger than yourself, something that encompasses you, but is not defined by your existence alone." The book's message, I told Weber, "is about the importance of serving a cause greater than self-interest." I wished I'd copyrighted the phrase and the variations of it that McCain delivered in stump speeches and town halls and media interviews. I've heard it regularly echoed for the last twenty years by politicians of every persuasion in campaigns for everything from city council to the presidency. I don't claim to be its original author. Its genesis likely preceded our formulation. But I don't remember ever hearing that particular construction in such common usage. "I'm running for president," McCain proclaimed, "because I want to inspire a generation of Americans to serve causes greater than self-interest." Every part of McCain's message, as long as he stayed on message, fit comfortably under that theme. It struck a chord with voters, who might have rejected it as pretentious if it had not described the arc of his story. And his campaign mirrored that authenticity. His message was echoed in rolling press conferences, sometimes ten hours a day in the back of a bus, taking all questions. He would try to slip a punch now and then by turning to Murphy for comic relief, but mostly, he gave an honest answer if he had one. It was reaffirmed in the way he campaigned, in open, lengthy, often raucous questions and answers with voters, speaking bluntly to them, unafraid to disagree with them, and undisturbed by their disagreement with him. They were two-way exchanges in which voter and candidate learned what was important to each other. McCain's work with Joe Lieberman on climate change legislation originated in his observation that one or more voters raised the issue at every one of his town halls.

We took a cue from the candidate's own shrewd understanding that his military background was more deftly used when referred to with humor and modesty. "It doesn't take a lot of talent to get shot down," began his routine dismissal of compliments about his war record. He worried that he had told prison stories so often and for so many years that he had worn out the public's interest in them.

In March 1999 he appeared at the Gridiron Club dinner, an annual gathering of Washington reporters and the politicians they cover, wherein the latter are lampooned by the former in skits that are occasionally funny. McCain stood before an immense American flag like in the opening scene in *Patton*. The lapels of his tuxedo jacket were covered in comically large medals as he described himself as "an incredibly self-effacing guy. The question I ask myself every morning while shaving in front of the mirror is: 'Okay, John, you're an incredible war hero, an inspiration to all Americans. But what qualifies you to be president of the United States?' "

That same month he received a more serious honor when he and Russ Feingold were notified by the Kennedy Presidential Library that they had been chosen to receive the 1999 Profile in Courage Award for their work on campaign finance reform. The award ceremony, hosted by Ted Kennedy, Caroline Kennedy, and John F. Kennedy Jr., was held at the library on May 21, which happened to be Jimmy McCain's eleventh birthday. Senator Kennedy arranged for a Coast Guard cutter to

take the McCain family on a tour of Boston Harbor, complete with a
birthday cake for Jimmy, and he led a booming rendition of "Happy
Birthday." At the award dinner that evening, another birthday cake
appeared, along with another round of "Happy Birthday." McCain was
genuinely moved by Kennedy's thoughtfulness.

The Kennedys held a lunch the next day on the library's top floor in
rooms reserved for the Kennedy family, which are filled with photographs and memorabilia. Ted Kennedy again played the convivial host,
and he and McCain swapped Senate stories, including an exaggerated
version of their notorious shouting match in the well of the Senate.
McCain laughed as hard as Kennedy did. Some weeks afterward, Mc-
Cain again recalled Kennedy's kindness to Jimmy and how much he
had enjoyed the two days in Boston. "You know what I was thinking
during that lunch," he asked, "when Ted and I were joking around?"

"What?"

"I was thinking Kennedy was treating me like we had the same
stature. That there were guys who come and go in the Senate, and then
there are the guys who last and get things done, and we were those
guys."

The Gridiron Dinner and McCain's speech at the Kennedy Library
presented two sides of an appealing image, the politician who wants
to be a hero but doesn't take himself too seriously. And it wasn't manufactured. That was who he wanted to be.

Five months later, in mid-October 1999, McCain and Feingold
tried to pass a version of their bill stripped of most provisions other
than the soft-money ban. Trent Lott had given them a week to get
the sixty votes they needed to overcome a filibuster, which neither
supporters nor opponents of the measure believed possible. Mitch
McConnell planned to use the debate to rally Senate Republicans to
oppose the bill and, in the process, embarrass its sponsors. The episode, in addition to further straining relations between McCain and
McConnell, accelerated McCain's sense of independence from his
caucus, which had been growing since the tobacco bill's defeat, just as
he became a credible challenger for the Republican Party's nomination for president.

To the surprise of many Washington observers and, to a lesser extent, to ours, the McCain campaign was on a roll. He rose slowly but steadily in national polls over the late summer and early fall, and much more rapidly in New Hampshire, where he was practically living at the time. He had managed over the summer and early fall to make campaign finance reform an appealing issue for New Hampshire Republicans and especially to independent voters. By tying other reforms to the necessity of reducing the influence of special interests, he remade a process issue into a populist one. The freewheeling nature of the candidate and his campaign had gone from a novelty noted by a comparatively small number of reporters to a major subject of interest in the national press. We christened the McCain campaign bus the "Straight Talk Express," and took every opportunity we could find to contrast McCain's ragged authenticity with the more cautious Bush campaign. Now our press contingent had grown to the point where editors, nationally prominent columnists, and news anchors were parachuting into the ranks of beat reporters to bounce briefly along the back roads of New Hampshire in the back of a bus with a candidate who appeared to be genuinely enjoying the experience. His crowds were getting bigger, too, and not just in New Hampshire and South Carolina.

Faith of My Fathers had been published around Labor Day, and its popular and critical success was a pleasant surprise to the campaign and its authors, one of whom had theretofore never earned more than a modest government salary. The book tour, which had initially caused consternation among senior campaign staff, was now embraced as an opportunity to draw national attention to the candidate's heroic backstory. The first few book signings were unexpectedly large, with long lines outside the stores as people queued to get in. McCain would talk briefly about serving causes greater than self-interest, then proceed to write inscriptions, exchange a few words, and take a picture with anyone who asked for one. Some of the signings lasted for hours; he never cut them off before everyone had a chance to talk to him. Campaign aides and a few reporters referred to the signings as "Salter fund-raisers." One Thursday night in early November, in miserable freezing rain and sleet, fourteen hundred people braved the elements to come to a Presbyterian church in a Kansas City suburb and hear McCain talk about the book. I think that was the first time I believed he might actually have a puncher's chance at pulling off the upset. The crowd was almost worshipful. "Something's happening," I said in a phone call with Rick Davis and John Weaver later that night. "Something you can't manufacture."

George W. Bush was still seen by the press and his rivals as the well-resourced front-runner and the choice of the Republican establishment. The Bush campaign was a rich, disciplined effort, organized in most of the primaries through Super Tuesday, and run by a talented group of professionals. Bush's announcement tour had kicked off with an impeccably staged event in Iowa in June affirming the conventional wisdom that he was the prohibitive favorite. In contrast, McCain didn't formally announce his candidacy until late September. The day began with a stop at the Naval Academy, where he made impromptu remarks. "Let me remind you," he said to midshipmen, "as a U.S. senator, unless you're under indictment or detoxification, you automatically consider yourself a candidate for president." He had told the same joke in a speech at the academy two years before, repeated it constantly throughout the 2000 campaign, and recycled it in 2008.

The main announcement was held that same day in a park in Nashua, New Hampshire, where he issued his "new patriotic challenge" to fight "the pervasive cynicism that is debilitating our democracy," starting with campaign finance reform. He followed the call with a quick litany of issues where we thought he could draw a distinction with Governor Bush, including tax cut proposals that were smaller and more focused on the middle class than those the governor supported. That wasn't the only position McCain would take over the course of the campaign that tactful conservatives would call "counterintuitive" and the less generous would denounce as "apostasy."

He saved the national security portion of the speech for the end, implicitly contrasting his more extensive experience with defense and foreign policy issues with Bush's. "No matter how many others are involved in the decision," he said of ordering Americans into harm's way, "the president is a lonely man in a dark room when the casualty reports come in." The line was meant to suggest that his time in uniform had given him the strength for the awesome responsibilities of the job. "I am not afraid of the burden" was his closing mantra. Other advisors lampooned the line, which I had written: "Salter taking McCain down another dark, lonely road," as Weaver described it. I laughed at his dig, but McCain laughed harder.

The optics of the event were fine, an enthusiastic and good-size crowd for New Hampshire, around a thousand people, although it wasn't as polished and ready-made for gauzy television ads as Bush's Iowa announcement. But the improvised, organic nature of the McCain effort emphasized his biggest advantage over Bush: The latter was running a traditional front-runner's campaign; McCain was putting on a show. Smart and cautious as Bush and his strategists were, they sensed McCain had a slight but growing potential to cause them trouble, and they weren't the type to leave anything to chance. The day after McCain's announcement, Bush flew to Phoenix to collect the endorsement of Arizona's Republican governor, Jane Hull, and other prominent Arizona Republicans. Polls at the time showed McCain in danger of losing his home state's primary to Bush. The state's leading newspaper, the *Arizona Republic,* which McCain considered antagonistic toward him, regularly raised the prospect that Arizona voters might embarrass their senior senator. The front-page story of Bush's September visit was headlined: "Bush's Juggernaut Rolling into Arizona." We joked at the time that we would be lucky to survive until the state's February 22 primary. Hull's endorsement implicitly emphasized the weakness of McCain's support among party leaders, and fed the impression that McCain's temper was the cause. Governor Hull would make the insinuation explicit when she told the *New York Times* that she had often been the object of McCain's wrath. She demonstrated for the reporter how she had to hold the telephone receiver away from her ear while she waited for an angry McCain to calm down and lower his voice.

I think Hull was distorting some incident when McCain had criticized her, making it appear a matter of temperament rather than an ordinary disagreement. Oftentimes stories about McCain's temper recounted by colleagues didn't amount to more than complaining about his criticism of them and how, from their perspective, McCain made himself look good at their expense. Some Senate Republicans had felt that way after the tobacco bill, when he chastised Republicans over their lack of concern for children's health. Many of his colleagues, Republicans and Democrats, had at one time or another been on the receiving end of a McCain pork-barrel-spending attack. He had staff scour each appropriations bill and put together a list of the most easily ridiculed earmarks, and then he would go to the Senate floor to do just that—ridicule them. He would single out a few of the funnier-sounding expenditures, mostly for the laughs he would get. A six-figure appropriation to study the DNA of bears became a staple of his stand-up routine for a decade. "I don't know if that was about a paternity issue," he would say, laughing, "or a criminal one." But he also used earmarks to stress his broader point that campaign finance rules were making government reforms, including fiscal restraint, harder to achieve. That bred resentment among the sponsors of the earmarks.

Support for campaign finance reform was more bipartisan in those days than it is today. McConnell had shrewdly decided to use the resentment felt by some members about McCain's anti-earmark crusade to undermine the campaign's signature issue. With the late senator Robert Bennett of Utah and Washington senator Slade Gorton, McConnell hatched a scheme to engage McCain in a colloquy on the Senate floor, demanding that he specify which campaign donations had led to corrupt acts and name the offenders.

We had an inkling something was up when McCain received a note the day before from Slade Gorton, whom McCain considered a friend, informing him that he would object to McCain singling out an earmark Gorton had sponsored. But none of us anticipated how sharp and personal the confrontation was intended to be. The debate began with McConnell quoting McCain railing against the corrupting effect of big money in one campaign speech after another. "Who's corrupt?" McConnell demanded to know. "Someone must be corrupt for there to be corruption." Bennett jumped in with a reference to unauthorized spending for Utah—which would host the next Winter Olympics—that he and McCain had been fighting about for the better part of two years. He demanded McCain identify the soft-money donation that had resulted in the earmark. McCain tried to dodge their demands by explaining that he wasn't accusing any colleague of violating laws or ethics, but that a political system awash in unregulated money had the effect of impairing the institutional integrity of Congress. They pressed him repeatedly to name specific corrupt acts, and he continued to decline to do so. I was on the floor with him, sitting on a staff bench at the back of the chamber while he argued from his desk twenty feet in front of me. At one point, he turned to face an antagonist, and I saw what looked like a genuinely pained expression on his face. I felt in that instance, if just for a moment, he was at a loss as to what to do. That wasn't normal for him. His instinct in a fight was to slug away until an opponent was defeated or got tired of the exchange. But in this debate, criticism he could marshal in his defense was used against him to suggest he was slandering his colleagues, and the longer he refrained from personalizing the argument, the more it seemed he had been guilty of falsely accusing fellow senators.

McConnell and Bennett were getting the better of him, and he knew it. At one point, Paul Wellstone, who had been watching the proceedings with fascination, attempted to intervene, asking how long the senators planned to continue attacking Senator McCain. When I saw McCain suddenly tense his shoulders and back, I knew he was done with rope-a-dope and was going on the attack. I can't remember his exact words, but he finally gave them what they claimed they wanted, recalling the time during the debate on the tobacco bill when "a colleague" told the caucus that the tobacco companies would support their campaigns if they voted against the bill. The colleague, of course, was McConnell, but McCain didn't mention him by name. McConnell was prepared for the accusation and admitted to being the unnamed colleague. But he insisted the tobacco companies had promised only that they would keep running ads against the bill for the rest of the year. They certainly had not offered campaign donations in exchange for votes, he insisted.

The fight sort of petered out after that exchange. But it had sent a signal that party leaders in Congress were 100 percent behind the front-runner in the Republican primaries and were prepared to make life difficult for their colleague should he become a real threat for the nomination. Like the Hull controversy, and the fact that only four of his Senate colleagues had endorsed him, the ambush on the Senate floor reinforced the emerging media narrative that McCain might be a politician with principles, but he didn't work and play well with others, raising the question of whether he had a "presidential" temperament.

The experience was an eye-opener for McCain, too. Until that incident, he hadn't given much thought to how his colleagues viewed his candidacy. He hadn't seemed especially troubled by the fact that most Senate Republicans had endorsed Bush. Bush was the likely nominee, and most senators prefer to bet the favorite when there is one. Only his Arizona colleague Jon Kyl; his friend Mike DeWine, who had been a member of McCain's freshman class in the House; and his friends Fred Thompson and Chuck Hagel had endorsed him. He wasn't the most motivated candidate when it came to asking for endorsements, either. You got the impression he was okay with losing Senate supporters to Bush if it absolved him of the need to ask for their help.

I don't think he was different from most of us in our wish to be well thought of by our associates, and I believe he was sincerely bothered on occasions when it was apparent his colleagues were offended by something he had said or done. He didn't always take it seriously. Sometimes he wrote it down to envy over his media appearances or sour grapes about a past skirmish or to the offended party's inability to take a joke. But when he discovered a colleague disliked him for legitimate reasons, it distressed him. I suspect he worried that McConnell's ploy exposed a deeper vein of genuine dislike for him than he had thought existed. He was angry in the immediate aftermath of the confrontation, angry with the three senators, angry with himself for not being ready for the attack, but it was anger with an edge of anxiety. That was evident in his attitude going forward. He was on the verge of being a serious rival for the nomination, but if his long-shot candidacy were to succeed, he would have to beat not just the governor of Texas but the Republican establishment. That was a bigger task than he had planned on undertaking. An anonymous wit on the Republican National Committee likened it to a "hostile takeover" of the party. Or as McCain, in his zest for battle and fondness for cinematic heroes, characterized the final months of the contest, "I'm Luke Skywalker taking on the Death Star." Behind the scenes, though, he was more solemn and serious than was typical for him. He knew he was in for the political fight of his life, and he could count on few people outside his immediate circle for help.

McCain dismissed the Bush campaign's venture into Arizona, insisting he wasn't the least bit worried about winning his home state. He said Governor Hull's accusations about his temper were a sign the Bush campaign was worried about him. "We're up to within twelve points of him in New Hampshire," he bragged. A 12 percent deficit in the polls isn't the most persuasive boast, but to the campaign, which began as a statistical nonentity, it registered a momentum shift in the Granite State that we were seeing for ourselves as we approached the Christmas holidays. McCain's town halls were getting bigger and rowdier and more fun for the candidate, the voters, and our press contingent, which was also growing in size. McCain had committed to more town hall appearances in the state than any previous candidate had attempted in a single campaign.

What the campaign lacked in establishment endorsements, it made up for in friends the candidate could rely on in New Hampshire. Warren Rudman had retired from the Senate but was still widely respected in his home state. He was our highest-profile supporter there. The talented and well-liked former executive director of the New Hampshire Republican Party, Mike Dennehy, had signed on to manage the McCain effort in the state. A popular local politician from Hopkinton, Peter Spaulding, was the campaign's state chairman. Paul Chevalier, retired marine and commander of the New Hampshire VFW, chaired New Hampshire Veterans for McCain, a key component of McCain's coalition in the state. More than a hundred thousand New Hampshire residents are veterans; their percentage of the state population is about double their share nationwide. The state party chairman, Steve Duprey, was officially neutral but friendly. As elsewhere, the Bush campaign had gathered support from many of the state's leading political figures. But the McCain effort had recruited enough local supporters that we weren't at a serious disadvantage as we were in other state primaries.

The candidate's biggest advantage, though, was himself. He suited New Hampshire, and the state suited him. The scrappy, irreverent, blunt politician and underdog candidate with the military background had a natural appeal to direct and iconoclastic Granite Staters. McCain repeated in private and public, so often it seemed like a personal mantra, that he would outwork the opposition. Nowhere was that more clearly the case than in New Hampshire. As important, it was clear to New Hampshire voters, and to reporters, friends, and family, that he was enjoying it, all of it, every one of his 114 town halls, and the endless, rollicking back-of-the-bus press conferences, where it was obvious, as campaign communications director Dan Schnur observed, that the candidate would "rather hang around with them [reporters] than us." It also underscored, had his critics paid attention, that for all his irascibility and displays of anger, McCain, in circumstances that would have exhausted anyone mentally and physically, was very even-tempered. He might argue with reporters as he would with voters, even briefly appear a little cross at times, but never in the months of constant questions and challenges and disagreements did he once lose his cool.

He loved New Hampshire's micro-retail politics: house parties, VFW and American Legion hall visits, stops at firehouses and diners. He loved talking with 101-year-old Neil Tillotson, patriarch of the family who owned the famous Balsams Resort in Dixville Notch, where the first primary votes were cast at midnight. McCain asked Tillotson who his favorite presidential candidate had been, and Tillotson had answered, "Mr. Roosevelt." McCain assumed he was referring to FDR, and Tillotson corrected him: "No, *Theodore* Roosevelt. Teddy." McCain was entertained by local eccentrics who showed up at his events, especially the ones who followed him from town hall to town hall, the kid dressed in the shark costume and notorious Vermin Supreme, who wore a fishing boot on his head and flippers as shoulder boards. McCain would call them up on the stage and have them give their pitch or ask him a question. He loved the laughs he got from his opening stand-up routine or when he said to a kid who asked a tough question, "Thanks for the question, you're drafted, you little jerk," or when he pointed to the swelling ranks of reporters, scribbling away in the back and laughing under their breath, and called them "Trotskyites and Leninists and other kinds of Communists." He'd bound onto the bus every morning, an aide would hand him his first coffee and doughnut of the day, and he would bark, "Are we having fun yet?" The underdog maverick was having a hell of a good time in the state he thought valued the kind of politician he wanted to be. Authentic. No posing. No hiding. "A lot of people were laughing at us and said this thing was a done deal," he reminded a crowd of New Hampshire veterans in Hudson about his early forays into the state. "Thanks to you, my dear friends . . . it ain't any done deal! We're having a great time, and we're on a roll!"

In speech after speech, he committed himself to strict honesty, a claim that would have sounded laughable from almost any other candidate, but he seemed to pull it off. "You may agree or disagree with me," he told audiences, "but you will always hear the truth from me, no matter what." He meant it. It's a nearly impossible standard to uphold in politics, and he was setting himself up to disappoint people who believed him, which included himself. "Spinning is lying" was one of the campaign's more arrogant mottoes, as we pretended we were above the exaggerations and dissembling of politics. We weren't, but we risked candor and honesty more than was usual in those days or today. We followed the candidate's example. No sweating the small stuff, no dressing up his image or toning down his manner of speech or orchestrating his interactions with voters and reporters and critics. Did he have a temper? Yeah, so what. He was just screaming about that yesterday. By the middle of November, New Hampshire polls were tightening, and insiders were speculating that McCain's Iowa gambit might actually work. To make sure everyone got the point, he hammered away routinely at ethanol subsidies as a perfect example of how special interests controlled politics. And the campaign sent a letter with McCain's signature to the chairman of the Iowa Republican Party, saying essentially that, except for debates that were scheduled in the Hawkeye State, McCain would not campaign, advertise, spend money in the state, or so much as breathe Iowa air.

We weren't hands-off when it came to defending him from attacks we thought could do lasting damage. Whispers from anonymous Washington detractors—which, it was reported, included some of his Senate colleagues—insinuated that his temper raised questions about his mental health. We made sure reporters realized what the "chicken-shits" were actually suggesting: that being a prisoner of war, suffering for your country, had made him nuts. We allowed pool reporters to review thousands of pages of medical reports from his navy records after the war, including psychiatric reports. The records disclosed that he had scored 133 on an IQ test, which, *Time* magazine noted, "would rank him among the most intelligent presidents in history."[39] There were a few less flattering items included in the documents. He exhibited a "histrionic pattern of personality adjustment" was one such observation. As explained to his aides, it meant he was easily excitable, which we could attest to. But every psychiatrist who had examined him after the war found him remarkably well adjusted and free of the effects of noticeable trauma. One psychiatrist actually wrote that McCain's years in a prisoner-of-war camp had helped him "control his temper better, to not become angry over insignificant things." In the middle of the whisper campaign, Admiral Stockdale, who had run on Ross Perot's ticket in 1992 and had been one of McCain's senior ranking officers in prison, rushed to McCain's defense on his own initiative, sending an op-ed to the *New York Times* that claimed:

> His experience in Vietnam actually made McCain more balanced than he had ever been. He has been brought up in a family of very high principles. He is a guy who can handle a crisis and not feel sorry for himself.

Though we succeeded in putting a negative spotlight on McCain's anonymous accusers, the insinuation that McCain, poor man, had been driven crazy in prison circulated sub rosa in fits and starts for the next decade. Even in recent years, the calumny made an occasional appearance. Vladimir Putin, whom McCain regularly assailed as a thug and a thief, and who detested McCain in return, took a shot at him in 2011, dismissing with faux sympathy criticism from McCain that had obviously upset him: "They kept him . . . in a pit for several years. Anyone would go nuts."

The voters who responded to McCain seemed to be having as good a time as he was. By December, his New Hampshire town halls were routinely drawing overcapacity crowds, anxious fire marshals frequently attested. Voters roared their approval as soon as the candidate issued his first good-natured insult of the event, and laughed harder at his jokes than they had the last time they'd come to see the show. It wasn't unusual to meet people who were attending their seventh or eighth McCain town hall. There is nothing more valuable to a campaign in a small state than supporters who become so enamored of the candidate that campaign events are consuming most of their free time. You know they're talking about their candidate all the time to friends and family. Word of mouth in a small state is more effective than advertising. McCain had a lot of favorable word of mouth in the last months of the New Hampshire campaign. We started calling his most dedicated supporters McCainiacs. Eventually, we began to call ourselves the same. Because even his underpaid and overworked campaign staffers and senior aides—the shrewd Rick Davis, who kept the whole ruckus running; the steady Carla Eudy; the wiseass Murphy; the worrying pollster, McInturff; the best political adman of his time, Greg Stevens; the New Hampshire Sherpa, Mike Dennehy, doubling as the guy who combed and sprayed in place the disabled candidate's wispy white hair (Salon Michelle, we called him); even the naturally gloomy souls like Weaver and me—were having the best time of our professional lives. We didn't want to leave the bus. I used to joke that the McCain 2000 campaign was the last good time in politics. That was a conceited thing to say. I'm sure the candidates and staffs of every winning presidential campaign look back with fond nostalgia at the experience. But I'm willing to bet no other losing campaign ever enjoyed itself quite as much as McCain's did, at least in those heady weeks of his ascent in the state of New Hampshire.

For all the fun he was so plainly having on the stump, there was a reserve about McCain in private that was unfamiliar to those who knew him well, and it became more pronounced as he gained more traction in the race. He seemed to be more self-contained, inside his own head more, less demonstrative than usual. I was used to McCain the Senate dealmaker who, once he decided on an objective, could focus on little else as he urged, hectored, and pleaded with his colleagues and pushed his staff constantly until he got a deal or it fell apart, the McCain who couldn't hide his joy or disappointment. He demonstrated more patience in the campaign than I thought he possessed. He wasn't easily distracted or upset by criticism or attacks. He made the most of every day, but he didn't react to the ups and downs of a single day or week. He was looking down the road to the hazards ahead.

Maybe he had an earlier sense than the rest of us that he might actually make the triple bank shot his success was premised on—survive not placing in Iowa, win New Hampshire, decide the race in South Carolina. Maybe he was content that, win or lose, he had exceeded expectations, enhanced his stature, and become more of a power in Washington. Maybe it was related to his superstitious nature. He was on a roll and didn't want to jinx it by overreacting to good news. He was the most superstitious person I ever knew. Throughout the campaign, he kept acquiring odd talismans, lucky feathers, coins, shells, things pressed on him by supporters, which he would associate with something favorable that had happened at the time he acquired them. He would empty his pockets when he got back to his hotel room at night and spread his collection out on a dresser. He appeared to be his most composed when things were their most chaotic and his more excitable aides were losing our cool. "Steady strain," he cautioned whenever we were too full of ourselves or angry about something. The year after the campaign, as he and I worked on his second book, *Worth the Fighting For,* I asked if he really had made a conscious effort to be more self-contained during the primary or if it had been my imagination. He laughed and answered, "It was your imagination."

"No, seriously," I said, "you definitely seemed more reserved, especially when things started to get going in New Hampshire. You seemed to keep more things to yourself."

He laughed again and said, "Shit, all I did every day was talk, talk, talk, to reporters, town halls, to you guys. What was left that I could keep to myself? Maybe I was just tired of talking and taking a breather. Don't confuse it with being moody."

"I didn't say you were moody. I said you seemed more reserved than I was used to seeing you."

"Whatever. Don't read something into nothing is what I meant."

Running for president is a monumental undertaking. It takes a level of concentration and self-restraint that would be unusual for even the most disciplined person. That is probably the affect I was witnessing in McCain's personality as a presidential candidate—his steady resolve to see this big, all-consuming thing through to the finish. I also think McCain only pretended to be introspection-averse. Though he didn't have a hidden side, that doesn't mean he didn't have an interior life. He really was who he appeared to be. But he was too perceptive of dualities in human nature not to be aware of his own, and too appreciative of how others had shaped his personality not to have spent time in self-examination. The report of one of the navy psychiatrists who had interviewed him after the war is full of examples of McCain's self-reflection. He knew who he was, he knew his strengths and flaws, he knew what helped him and what hurt. He didn't let any of it stop him from being who he wanted to be. And he didn't like to talk about what went on in his head, which is what he was trying to convey to me in my attempt to get him to open up. He looked back on that first New Hampshire campaign as one of the best times of his political life. That was all he cared to share of his feelings about the experience. New Hampshire was his "second favorite state." Eight years later, he would look back at his second New Hampshire primary win with pride, if not with the same extent of warm nostalgia he felt for the first one. "There's nothing quite as exciting," he reflected two years before his passing, "as those last couple of weeks before the primary, in all of American politics."

I can't speak for their entire hard-fought campaign for the White House, but Governor Bush and his aides didn't seem to be having as much fun as we were. Bush had sat out earlier candidate debates, the cattle-car events that multiply with every election and are as taxing on the candidates and staff as they are uninformative to the voters. Bush was getting criticism for ducking them, even from some of his own supporters. He made his first appearance in an early-December debate in Manchester, New Hampshire, when McCain was clearly building momentum in the state. Bush seemed rusty and uncomfortable but committed no gaffes that I remember. None of the candidates seriously mixed it up during the ninety-minute exchange except for Alan Keyes, who was enraptured by his own oratorical skills and couldn't resist showing them off by hogging more airtime than is usually controlled by marginal candidates. In every debate, he would denounce one or more of his opponents for moral cowardice and then soar into the heavens to the sound of his own voice. It ate up the clock, which was fine with us. Another debate was held four days later, this one in Phoenix; Bush's prominent Arizona supporters were in the audience and gave interviews in the spin room afterward praising the governor's performance. McCain was too busy in New Hampshire to make the trip home and joined the debate by satellite. Again, nothing memorable occurred, no sign of outward hostility between Bush and McCain, but the rivalry between the campaign staffs was another matter.

For a few heady days between the New Hampshire and South Carolina primaries, we let ourselves believe we might win. Prior to that, we had an underdog's fatalism and shared a notion that we would likely lose and ought to get some enjoyment out of it anyway. We took a perverse pride in being seen as an annoyance by the Bush camp, or at least we imagined they saw us that way, and we made fun of every glimpse of irritation or fatigue revealed by McCain's opponent and his senior aides. We were making them work for it. We had read or heard somewhere that the governor traveled with a pillow from home. I don't know if the anecdote was apocryphal or not, but it amused us to no end. We worked the pillow into the daily derisive observations we shared with each other and a few reporters. When Bush looked testy in an exchange with someone, we blamed it on poor advance work: "Someone left the pillow on the plane again." When he looked at a loss for an answer to a reporter's question in a debate or interview: "Rove, quick, get the pillow!" Sometimes we referred to the pillow as his binky. It was juvenile, of course. But what are you going to do? We knew how formidable they were. We were far outmatched in resources, money, and labor. We would probably lose. We used to call the Bush campaign Jurassic Park, and whenever we thought we had gotten their attention, we mimicked the heavy footfall of a dinosaur approaching us slowly from behind. Wisecracks, playground taunts, gallows humor, they're the balm of dark-horse campaigns, where the prospect of getting your ass kicked is never far from mind. The candidate mostly ignored or didn't react to our attitude. An occasional chuckle was all we got out of him. The exception was Mike Murphy, who could crack McCain up in an instant, imitating Karl Rove taking calls from jumpy donors and party leaders after a positive McCain poll was reported. He would get Murphy to do it on the bus in front of reporters. "Murph, what do you think they're doing in the Bush campaign today?" And Murphy would go into his routine: "Governor Engler on line one! Karl." McCain never tired of telling the same jokes. And he never tired of listening to his favorite comedy riffs, either.

One of the most important events of the New Hampshire primary that was underappreciated, considering its impact on the race, was a joint appearance in Claremont by McCain and Bill Bradley, who was challenging Al Gore for the Democratic nomination. Independents can vote in either party's primary in New Hampshire, and the strategies of both the McCain and Bradley campaigns relied on winning the independent vote. We knew it would be exceedingly difficult to win Republican voters in the state by anything more than a narrow margin, if that. We thought we had a better shot with independents, who responded more enthusiastically than did Republican loyalists to McCain's campaign finance reform argument. But you can't vote in both parties' primaries, and Bradley, with his Hall of Fame basketball career, wasn't viewed by independents as a typical politician. Neither was McCain at that point, but we couldn't afford to split independents with Bradley.

Bradley, like McCain, was an outspoken supporter of a soft-money ban. In 1995 President Clinton and the new Speaker of the House, Newt Gingrich, had shared a town hall–style event in Claremont, during which they shook hands on a commitment to form a national commission that would propose reforms of the campaign finance system. Neither man was sincere, and the pledge went unfulfilled. But the false glimpse of progress had given heart to reform advocates, only to leave them disappointed again. We pitched to the Bradley campaign an idea to resurrect the promise of the Claremont handshake, and to attract the notice of independent voters we both were courting—a joint press conference in the same spot Clinton and Gingrich had held their event, where both candidates would sign a pledge affirming their commitment to reform. Bradley agreed, and the event was scheduled for December 16.

Two nights earlier, at a debate in Des Moines, Bush had argued against McCain's campaign finance proposals, asserting that they would give an advantage to labor unions, which supplied manpower for the Democrats' turnout operations. McCain responded that labor unions gave the DNC seven-figure checks just as corporations provided the same to both parties. In my memory, it was the first time the front-runner and leading challenger directly debated the issue. It wasn't a harsh exchange, and neither appeared to gain an advantage at the debate. But Bush's apparent opposition to a soft-money ban strengthened McCain's hand as he framed the primaries as a contest between change and business as usual, an enviable position in an election that was expected to be a reaction to voters' fatigue over Clinton administration scandals. After Bush took a position on the issue—albeit a somewhat nuanced one—McCain could refer to "big money in Washington" rallying to stop his candidacy, and everyone knew that big money was backing George Bush.

The Claremont event was staged on the grounds of a senior citizens' center. The two candidates stood on a platform lined with Christmas trees, bearing two podiums and a table and two chairs, where they were supposed to sign a written pledge. It began with McCain and Bradley giving each other a copy of their recently published books. A laughing McCain held up *Faith of My Fathers,* asked for "more pictures, please," and wisecracked about its availability on "Amazon.com." Then he proceeded to give stage directions to Bradley: "I think they want us to sign this," pointing to the poster-size pledge card and telling Bradley which pen to use. "Now I think we're supposed to shake hands," he instructed, gripping Bradley's hand as he grinned from ear to ear for the cameras. McCain staff were chuckling under our breath within the first minute. Both men wore overcoats, and Bradley, at six-five, towered over McCain. But the shorter candidate dominated the event. The peppery, fast-talking McCain paced the stage or rocked on his heels or bounced on the balls of his feet, waiting to answer another question or answer one asked of Bradley, whose thoughtful demeanor and slow drawl made him appear more formal and aloof. At times Bradley seemed to fade into the background, while McCain, who jousted with reporters for hours every day, appeared more at ease and in command, firing off brief, sharp answers to questions and teasing rejoinders to skeptical comments. Each did the other a favor by criticizing their rival for the nomination. McCain mocked Al Gore for his tone-deaf explanation that "no controlling legal authority" had stopped him from taking a six-figure check from a Buddhist monastery. It was just one event among many that provided the subject for our two-minute package on the evening news. But its effect, as we suspected, was to help McCain capture the lion's share of the independent vote. Politics is a cruel business, and McCain aides joked afterward that Bradley, whom we all respected, had left Claremont never to be seen again. Sure enough, we immediately began seeing trend lines in public polling and our own that showed independents breaking heavily for McCain.

After the holidays, as the January 24 Iowa caucuses loomed and with polls tightening, the Bush campaign began to shed some of the former friendliness toward rivals and started "drawing contrasts" with the candidate Bush aides complained was getting a free ride from the media. It was typical issue-based negative campaigning, nothing out of the ordinary and nothing like the storm to come after the New Hampshire primary. But people in both camps started getting their backs up as game day neared. Speaking for McCain aides, we were spoiling for a fight, though we wanted to conduct it in earned media—debates, press conferences, town halls—mindful that we could be crushed in an artillery battle of paid advertising. But the pace of incoming hits we were starting to get, most of which we assumed had originated with Bush campaign research, was keeping us busier on defense than we wanted to be. Much of it was aimed at making McCain the reformer look like a hypocrite.

In early January, the *Boston Globe*, the most widely read newspaper in New Hampshire, published an investigative story about a McCain letter to the Federal Communications Commission (FCC) urging they expedite a decision regarding the acquisition of a television station by a telecommunications committee, Paxson Communications, whose CEO and other executives contributed generously to his campaign. McCain had also used the Paxson corporate aircraft on four occasions, paying the equivalent of first-class airfare, as specified by law. After Keating, we took considerable precautions to avoid the appearance of impropriety when it came to McCain's dealings with regulators. But he was chairman of the Commerce Committee, and in that capacity, he was in frequent communication with the FCC and other regulators. In the letter regarding the Paxson acquisition, he insisted he did not care which decision they made, but that they had taken long enough to reach a conclusion. The letter concluded with a standard caveat appended post-Keating to every McCain letter to a regulatory agency, essentially urging that no action be taken that could be construed as showing unfair favoritism to one party or another. Staff used to joke that the boilerplate language gave permission to regulators to ignore any request from our office.

The controversy was raised in moderator Tim Russert's first question to McCain at a New Hampshire debate on January 6. McCain responded that it was "my job to make the bureaucracy work for people." McCain, with his intuitive appreciation for responding to a bad story with a flood of information, authorized the release of hundreds of letters he had written to regulators as chairman of the Commerce Committee, many of them merely urging fair and prompt action, all with our standard caveat. He also canceled another scheduled fundraiser with Paxson executives. We got through it, but we were on notice that the game was getting rougher in a hurry. Although we never would have admitted it to each other, McCain aides, at least—if not the candidate, who appeared unruffled by the story—were starting to experience the first taste of dread. Other attempts at painting "the chairman," as Bush now routinely called McCain, as a hypocrite came at a regular clip over the rest of the campaign. We had a small but talented group of professionals on our communications team, led by the capable Dan Schnur, talented press secretary Howard Opinsky, McCain's unflappable Senate press secretary, Nancy Ives, and traveling press secretary Todd Harris, who managed the ceaseless flow of journalists on the bus with efficiency and good humor. They kept the Bush team's opposition research from swamping us before we could ignite our campaign with a New Hampshire win, and they gamely fought a lot of little fires every day, as well as some big ones.

McCain and Bush had a few more arguments at that debate. Again, their exchanges were on the issues and without much evidence of personal animus. Bush had fired the first volley in an appearance in Bedford, New Hampshire, two days earlier, when he criticized McCain for an insufficient commitment to tax cuts. He repeated the attack in the debate. Bush's proposed tax cuts were twice the size of McCain's proposal, most of which focused on the lower and middle class, while Bush's, among other things, lowered top marginal income tax rates, which McCain opposed as too expensive. It was a legitimate point of contention, and I doubt either candidate resented the other's criticism. Bush complained that McCain's campaign finance reform proposal would hurt the Republican Party. We never minded that criticism because it reinforced McCain's image as a reformer, and we figured we could make up for any New Hampshire Republicans who would be swayed by it with independents who would be convinced ours was the biggest change on offer. It never got too testy between the two candidates. There were four others on the stage with them, and they frequently interrupted Russert's attempts to get McCain and Bush to fight. Bush had taken a pass at using the Paxson controversy to score a point, although we assumed his "Mr. Chairman" routine was meant to accentuate an image of McCain as a Washington wheeler-dealer.

Things were livelier at a debate the next night in Columbia, South Carolina. It was held before a capacity crowd at a state party fundraiser in a cavernous warehouse with one working portable toilet, after the audience had finished dinner and were ordering more drinks. They were animated and loud, and some of them were more interested in expressing their opinion than they were in listening to the candidates. Referring to the audience, McCain said afterward, "They weren't there to be spectators." When one of the reporters raised the subject of the Confederate battle flag that flew over South Carolina's state capitol, he was greeted with a storm of boos. The issue was roiling the state's politics at the time. The NAACP had called for a boycott to protest the official support for an emblem of the South's rebellion over slavery. The large crowd of white Republicans at the dinner clearly felt aggrieved. When Bush was asked about the controversy, he said to loud applause that it was a matter for South Carolinians to settle. When the moderator, NBC's Brian Williams, asked how, "as an American citizen," he felt about the flag, he responded, "As an American citizen, I trust the people of South Carolina to make the decision for South Carolina," indicating he had said all he intended to on the matter. "I thought they were going to carry him out of there on their shoulders," McCain said of the audience's reaction. Bush had clearly won them over with his deference to their sensitivities. Bush and McCain crossed swords again over tax cuts and campaign finance, but it was Bush's answer to the flag question that was the debate's most memorable moment.

The last debate before the Iowa caucus was scheduled for Tuesday, January 11, in Grand Rapids, Michigan. McCain spent part of the weekend in Washington, where he appeared on Face the Nation that Sunday. He was always comfortable on Sunday shows even when the questioning was aggressive. He had done them so many times, and he had been in so many other stressful situations in his life that the thought of being intimidated by a television interview seemed ridiculous to him. He might get a little hot under aggressive questioning, he might misstate things on occasion, but he almost always arrived in the studio relaxed and in good humor. He was so unconcerned, almost lackadaisical, about the shows that he rarely prepared vigorously for them. In the early years, we used to write memos for him that attempted to anticipate questions and suggest responses. Sometimes he read them. By the year 2000, Sunday-show prep usually consisted of me riding with him to the studio and discussing what points he wanted to make in the interview, guessing at a few questions the moderator would ask, listening to his answers, and suggesting an alteration here and there. That rarely took the entire car ride, and he would go back to reading the newspaper.

I went with him to *Face the Nation* that Sunday. I don't remember what we talked about in the car, but I'm pretty sure neither of us considered one of the questions Bob Schieffer asked. That was my fault. I should have seen it coming. It was a variation on the question that had caused the uproar at the Columbia debate. "What does the Confederate flag mean to you?" Schieffer asked. McCain hemmed and hawed a little as he considered his response. He decided on an honest answer without a lot of wiggle room. He said the flag was offensive "in many, many ways. As we all know, it's a symbol of racism and slavery." When Schieffer followed up by asking if he thought it was a matter South Carolinians should decide for themselves without outside interference, as Governor Bush had insisted, McCain acknowledged they would decide it for themselves, but we can "urge them to come to some reasonable conclusion."

John Weaver had joined us at the studio. By the time McCain emerged from the interview, arching his eyebrows as he usually did to elicit our opinion of his performance, Weaver had fielded several calls from our South Carolina team, pleading for McCain to "clean up his answer" before it ignited a firestorm among the state's Republican voters. I searched for a way to tell him he had answered a question honestly but wrongly, lighting on the phrase "You were a little less artful with that answer than you probably could've been." What a pathetic way to put it. If you're going to advise a candidate to lie, and take a position you both know is wrong, don't pretend it's just a matter of phrasing. We told him he needed to put out a statement immediately that acknowledged the flag had other meanings. When we started suggesting wording he could use, he told us to stop. "That's not cleaning it up. That's taking it back. I can't do it." We told him he had to, that he couldn't win South Carolina if he didn't. Independents could vote in the GOP primary in South Carolina, but they were a smaller share of the vote than in New Hampshire. McCain had to do well with registered Republicans there, and by a substantial majority, they supported flying the Stars and Bars over the state capitol. He was polling fairly well with more moderate Republicans along the coast, but he needed to perform better in conservative upstate counties, which were where the pro-flag sentiment was strongest. The controversy was so intense at that point, with passions on both sides peaking, that the McCain team in South Carolina thought the candidates' position on that issue alone could be the deciding factor for many primary voters. We argued with him on the ride back to his condo. He was adamant that he couldn't retract what he had said. Weaver, Davis, our South Carolina advisors, and I were adamant that he had to placate the people who believed the flag was, as the argument went at the time, "a symbol of heritage." We kept pressing him that afternoon and wore him down.

We were flying to New Hampshire the next morning. The first stop on the day's itinerary was a town hall in Dublin, New Hampshire. He agreed to read a prepared statement "clarifying" his flag comments to reporters outside the event. Press were pestering us all day for further comment on his comments, and a scrum would be waiting for him at Dublin. We released the statement a few minutes in advance. We had drafted it Sunday afternoon and gotten it to him right away. He read it without comment. The next morning, on the way to the Dublin stop, I asked him to read it aloud so I could offer advice on his delivery. "No," he responded, and didn't elaborate further.

He stepped off the bus, a boom mike and cameras pressed in on him. Some reporter asked him to clarify "your position on the Confederate flag," and instead of stopping to read the statement, he replied, "I've already done that." The reporter tried again, and McCain, visibly irritated, repeated, "I've already done that."³⁹ "Can you tell me what that is?" the reporter tried once more, and McCain said, "Yes, I'll give you the piece of paper." Then he retrieved the statement he had crumpled into a ball and stuffed in his pocket when we gave him another copy that morning. He bent his head down to read it. The camera zoomed in on the wrinkled piece of paper rather than his face, which was just as well. He read it as quickly as he could spit out the first four sentences, with no more inflection than a man making a hostage tape, stopping about halfway through it, and angrily jamming it back in his pocket. "As to how I view the flag, I understand both sides. Some view it as a symbol of slavery. Others view it as a symbol of heritage. Personally, I see the battle flag as a symbol of heritage."

Twenty years have passed since the incident. I still laugh every time I think of his performance. He was doing everything he could to have his demeanor signal to anyone who observed him that he was lying. Honestly, I think he would have preferred to have concluded the statement with "I'm lying."

The statement went on to note that he had Confederate ancestors "who fought honorably," but that was a bridge too far for him. He was pissed off at us and himself, and at the temptations of political ambitions to make moral compromises he had promised to resist but had not. On the subject of the Confederate battle flag, voters had not always heard the truth from him, and he felt ashamed about it. His campaign would continue for another two months, through triumphs and defeats. The flag issue wasn't uppermost on his mind through it all. He managed to suppress the memory of his embarrassment most of the time. But from time to time, when he was campaigning in South Carolina, he would suddenly remark out of nowhere, "I shouldn't have done it." It happened often enough for us to realize that the matter wasn't really closed. His conscience was a persistent nag, and it played a long game. He told me once that for a few days after reversing himself on the flag, he felt awkward around reporters on the bus: self-conscious, he said. It hadn't been noticeable to me, but I took his word for it.

We couldn't buy as much airtime in New Hampshire as the Bush campaign could, especially on expensive Boston stations. But we had money enough, thanks to Carla and Rick and McCain's resignation to start attending fund-raisers, to get Greg Stevens's ads on the air in decent rotation, and to finance a first-rate organization in the state. While the Bush New Hampshire team included most of the state's Republican establishment, led by Senator Judd Gregg, we were better organized in the state. Warren Rudman played the role of godfather to our New Hampshire team. Mike Dennehy and John Weaver built and oversaw the operation. They and Peter Spaulding and Paul Chevalier and dozens of staff and supporters made sure we had a decent turnout operation everywhere we needed one, from the North Country to Nashua. Both parties had competitive primaries, and by January, McCain was far and away the hottest ticket in the state and building a small lead in the polls. Bush didn't start campaigning there in earnest until the middle of the month. He had to campaign in Iowa, of course, and I'm sure he and his team resented that the press was letting us get away with not competing there.

As McCain was building momentum in his state, Judd Gregg complained to the *New York Times* that McCain was a one-state pony. He wasn't running a national campaign. He could win New Hampshire, but he wouldn't go further than that. We were pleased to read Gregg's criticism. It was the first time any senior Bush supporter had raised the prospect of a McCain victory in New Hampshire, which meant McCain was probably looking good in their internal polling. We couldn't afford to do as much polling as they could, so we were happy for the confirmation that McCain was the candidate to beat. And Gregg was wrong in one respect: We didn't have a one-state strategy. We had a two-state strategy—actually, two and a half states.

We had a good organization in South Carolina, another state with a big veteran population. We had recruited two up-and-coming South Carolina pols, Congressmen Lindsey Graham and Mark Sanford, who had liked our pitch that with most of South Carolina's Republican leaders behind Bush, they could only hope to be foot soldiers in the governor's campaign. They would be big dogs with us. They brought their political operations with them. In South Carolina, feuds between rival Republican political consultants long outlast resentments between rival candidates. Bush had the services of popular former governor Carrol Campbell's political machine, which included Lee Atwater associate Warren Tompkins as the lead local consultant. His rival in party politics was Richard Quinn, who consulted for Lindsey and had signed on with us. For an interlude, the Bush-McCain contest was the main event in a local rivalry that preceded it and carried on afterward.

We believed if we won New Hampshire, we would have enough momentum for a good shot at beating Bush in South Carolina. And if we won there, three days later we would likely win Michigan, where we were somewhat organized, and in quiet discussions with Teamsters officials and some African-American churches to turn out their not necessarily Republican rank and file for McCain in the state's open primary. If we ran the table—New Hampshire, South Carolina, Michigan, and Arizona (which held its primary the same day as Michigan)—Bush's support would collapse, no matter how many states he had operations in, as the party establishment reluctantly turned to McCain, who at that point would appear to be the most popular politician in the country. First we had to survive an abysmal showing in Iowa. Our small New Hampshire lead could disappear in a wave of media attention to the winner of the Iowa caucus. But that's not what happened.

Iowa Republicans rendered their verdict, or a portion of them did, as the caucuses are poorly attended political exercises. I grew up in Iowa. My parents and grandparents were civic-minded and always voted in general elections, as did their friends and associates. I lived in the state until 1979, and I never knew a soul who participated in either party's caucus. The thought of joining strangers for a political debate in a school basement on a freezing winter night didn't appeal to most Iowans I knew. But eighty-eight thousand of them, in a state with a population of a little under three million, showed up on January 24 to caucus for one of the Republican candidates. Thirty-six thousand Iowan Republicans chose Governor Bush. Four thousand picked McCain, who finished not only far behind Bush but behind Forbes, Keyes, and Bauer as well. We had thumbed our nose at the caucus, and caucus-goers—except for a small defiant bunch of iconoclastic

Hawkeyes—had thumbed their noses at McCain. We braced for the impact of Bush's Iowa triumph in New Hampshire, where Granite Staters would make their decisions one week later on February 1.

We were coasting, and nothing in the public polls showed McCain's momentum slowing. We believed we had a three- or four-point lead. Bush's campaigning suddenly seemed to acquire a frantic quality. In an attempt to make up for time spent in Iowa, the Bush campaign scheduled a quick succession of mostly photo-op stops, Bush on a snowmobile, Bush bowling, Bush making pancakes, Bush at a big rally with his parents, who were popular in the state. McCain was hell on wheels that last week, sensing victory and relishing what would be his favorite memory of his political career. He hammed it up in every jam-packed town hall that week, hauled out every joke and wisecrack he had in his inventory, teasing reporters, his staff, and voters, giving a double dose of straight talk to anyone who asked for it. In the last debate before the primary, on Wednesday, he and Bush took shots at each other on taxes and campaign finance, as they were now doing routinely. But the only memorable exchange of the night was when Alan Keyes, summoning his bottomless reservoir of outrage, blasted McCain for being wishy-washy on abortion. Some days earlier, McCain had answered a reporter's question about what he would say to his daughter should she be contemplating having an abortion. He gave the impression that he would leave the decision to her. He cleaned up later by adding that he would counsel her to have the child. Keyes couldn't resist, but McCain was ready—we hadn't discussed it with him in debate prep, but his answer was perfect: "I've seen enough killing in my life, Alan. I know how precious human life is, and I don't need a lecture from you."

"I didn't lecture you," Keyes protested.

"Yes, you did. Next time, use decaf," McCain retorted.

We had suggested the decaf line, but weeks earlier, as an all-purpose rebuttal to the excitable Keyes.

McCain held his 114th and final town hall on Sunday, two days before the primary, in Peterborough, where he had held his very first town hall, when he was at 3 percent in the polls. This time it was packed to the rafters, people jamming the aisles and cheering every

McCain joke and jibe. More than a hundred reporters were there to record the enthusiasm, and some were smiling at McCain aides, acknowledging the obvious: We were going to win. The next day at an outdoor rally in Portsmouth, near the naval shipyard, a fired-up McCain was just winding up his remarks when the captain of a tanker leaving the harbor signaled his support by blasting the ship's horn twice. McCain loved it, shaking his fist in front of his face and yelling, "Yeah!" in response. "A good omen," he said later, "for an old sailor." The last stop on primary eve was in Bedford. With Warren Rudman at his side, McCain spoke from the top of the town hall's stairs. The crowd spilled out of the building and filled the streets for blocks in all directions. Crowds that size, in the thousands, are hard to come by in New Hampshire. I was with Bill McInturff, watching in disbelief. We looked at each other, and Bill forecast the next day's result by mimicking Mr. T. "Prediction: Pain!" he shouted. Senator Rudman hosted a dinner for the McCain family, a few friends, and aides at his family's home in Hollis. We toasted to tomorrow. It was a lovely evening, and you could tell McCain was soaking in the experience.

We woke up the morning of the primary confident of victory, although we had gone to bed the night before disappointed by the midnight news from Dixville Notch, where a dozen or so residents had cast their votes at the Balsams Resort, with a slight majority for Bush. The Straight Talk Express made four stops that morning, starting in Keene and ending in Manchester, where we made an unscheduled visit to the *Union Leader*. The paper had endorsed Steve Forbes, but Joe McQuaid was clearly pleased that we had come, and showed McCain around the premises, introducing him to every employee of the paper they encountered. People seemed as delighted to see him as he was to meet them. Many of them volunteered that they had voted for him. We were full of ourselves that day.

Weaver and I were having a late lunch with a couple of reporters at the Crowne Plaza in Nashua, where we were headquartered, when we heard the results of the first wave of exit polls. McCain was comfortably ahead, but first exits are notoriously unreliable, so we tried to keep our cool. When the next wave came in a little past five o'clock, we couldn't help ourselves. They had McCain winning by 20 percent, a bona fide landslide that we knew would upend the race. We would end up tying or barely losing Republican voters to Bush, but we were beating him with independents two to one. I went to my room to finish McCain's victory speech and then went up to his suite to give him the news.

He was in the bedroom practicing the speech an aide had just given him. The superstitious McCain would never let me write election-night speeches more than a couple of hours in advance; I always had to wait until at least the second wave of exit polls. If the vote was close, we gambled on the outcome. He wouldn't let me write two speeches; that could jinx a win. If the exits proved wrong, we would have to cobble together some talking points at the last minute and hope for the best. To be honest, I'd been writing that first New Hampshire victory speech in my head all week. But I didn't tell him that.

When I entered the room, he was standing in front of the window, the speech in his hand. I told him, "We got the last exit polls."

"And?"

"You're going to win."

"How much?"

"A lot. You're going to clobber him. Twenty points, maybe."

He turned to look out the window and, with not a trace of excitement in his voice, mused, "That has implications." I snorted a laugh and said, "Yeah, I guess. Like, you might be president. That might be one of the implications."

He gave me one of his looks, eyes boring into mine, but the rest of his face inscrutably composed. It meant, "Don't get cocky or you'll jinx it. We've got a long way to go."

The suite filled with family, aides, friends, and a few young reporters who had covered McCain throughout the primary and to whom he had taken a shine. Everybody was hugging and high-fiving waiting for Bush to concede as the reporters looked on. Karl Rove called Weaver to concede on behalf of Bush and offer his congratulations to McCain. Weaver, who had a long-running feud with Rove, told him consultants don't concede to consultants. Moments later, Bush called

McCain, and they had an unmemorable but amicable exchange. Then we went downstairs to the ballroom, crowded with wildly cheering McCainiacs, where he gave his victory speech. The first people he noticed were a group of his POW buddies, including Orson Swindle and Bud Day. They looked like they were going to cry. "You've sent a powerful message to Washington, my friends," he congratulated the exuberant crowd, "that change is coming!" Weaver, Davis, Stevens, and I were all standing on the riser to his left, yelling and jumping up and down like excited teenagers, and when McCain delivered the "change is coming" line, I roared in response, "Burn it down!" in earshot of reporters. I'm not really the revolutionary type, but the spirit of rebellion was strong that night, and we were having a hell of a good time. We went with John and Cindy to a nearby bar filled with McCain volunteers. It was pandemonium in there, too, and the McCains could barely navigate through the excited throng to the microphone stand where he thanked them. He repeated a few of the lines from his speech, gave an emotional thank-you, exhorted them to keep up the fight, and concluded with a promise that he would be the nominee and would "beat Al Gore like a drum." Everyone, volunteers and aides, went nuts.

I wished we could stay there all night, but we got on a plane to Greenville, South Carolina, where a couple hundred college kids— who had evidently washed down the pizza the campaign had provided them with a little too much beer—were waiting to greet the weary McCains. We wanted to get an early start on the next contest, and we wanted to make clear we were in it to win it—in the words of the candidate, there would be "no slacking off." But there were nineteen days before South Carolinians made their choice, almost three weeks, a lifetime in political campaigns.

During a joint TV interview two days before the New Hampshire primary, Rick Davis had bet Karl Rove that if we won in New Hampshire, we would be leading in South Carolina the next day. At that point, we were around ten points behind Governor Bush in most South Carolina polls. But as Rick had predicted, the first flash polls from South Carolina after the New Hampshire primary gave us a five-point lead. McCain's New Hampshire upset led the news. His picture was on the cover of all three leading newsweeklies. In George Bush's father's words, McCain had the "Big Mo."

Rick and Carla expected a wave of new donors, caught up in the excitement of McCain's blowout win, would want to contribute immediately. Internet fund-raising was in its infancy then. Rick had petitioned the Federal Election Commission to let us accept credit card donations, which had never been allowed in federal campaigns. Prior to New Hampshire, the campaign had raised about $14 million and had spent most of it. Schnur had joked to a *New York Times* reporter that the McCain financial strategy was to "spend everything he had in New Hampshire's primary . . . and South Carolina's . . . and then rob a bank." The Bush campaign, which had declined federal matching funds so that it didn't have to comply with spending limits, had raised almost $70 million in 1999 and had spent about half of it. We didn't have to rob a bank. Millions poured in online, over half a million the first day. Those were unheard-of sums of "cyber-cash" for a political campaign, and we bragged to reporters. Message and momentum had been our strategy for running the table of early primaries, and now we added a third "M": money. We would never match the governor's totals, but we believed we would have enough to knock him out of the race.

In his gracious concession speech in New Hampshire, Bush called his loss a bump in the road and reminded listeners he was prepared to campaign in all fifty states. But no serious observer believed he would survive losing the next two consecutive primaries. He had to adapt his message. Prior to the New Hampshire primary, he had been the "compassionate conservative" with a thoughtful plan for improving public education. After New Hampshire, he styled himself as a "reformer with results." We took it as a compliment and an affirmation that McCain had made the race into a referendum on reform. It was also an implicit criticism of McCain, insinuating that the governor of Texas had enacted reforms, while the senator only talked about them.

The Bush campaign and its supporters, on background and on the record, directed the attention of reporters to aspects of McCain's record that they contended made him a Washington insider and exposed his reformer image as bunk. McCain took money from industries his committee oversaw. McCain had lobbyists working on his campaign. McCain was one of the Keating Five. Their efforts generated some unfavorable coverage and made us try to custom-fit the necessities of financing a competitive presidential campaign with the spirit of reform. Sometimes the effects were comical. After the New Hampshire landslide, a number of lobbyists and their corporate clients who had maxed out to Bush decided it would be prudent to hedge their bets a little. We scheduled a Washington fund-raiser for February 11; McCain wouldn't attend in person. It presented a golden opportunity, of course, for the Bush campaign and its allies to accuse McCain—who daily inveighed against the Washington "iron triangle of money, lobbyists, and legislation"—of brazen hypocrisy. We proceeded anyway. That night a couple hundred lobbyists entered the Willard Hotel wearing buttons that read "McCain Voted Against My Bill." McCain appeared via satellite feed from another fund-raiser in South Carolina and addressed both crowds on the evils of soft money, then reiterated his pledge to take the special interests out of Washington, to the good-natured applause of most attendees.

McCain aides were cocky and full of ourselves that first week after New Hampshire. We knew what was coming, a full-on assault from the much richer Bush campaign, and from everyone who had a vested interest in preventing McCain from being president. That included organizations such as the National Right to Life Committee (NRLC). McCain had a solid pro-life record, and there wasn't much in his votes or positions for religious conservatives to complain about except his support for "Don't Ask, Don't Tell." But Pat Robertson and the Christian Coalition, like the NRLC and other social conservative groups, were indirect beneficiaries of Republican Party soft money. Some of them, especially Robertson, in interviews and automated voter calls, would go after McCain as if he were the Antichrist. So did the National Rifle Association and various conservative activists, who rushed to prevent the apostate McCain from capturing the nomination. In addition to Bush's attempts to grab the mantle of reformer and the insinuation that McCain wasn't one, their campaign was going to make emphatically clear to conservative Republicans in the state that there was only one conservative with a chance to win, and his name wasn't McCain. Bush's first post–New Hampshire speech in the state was at ultraconservative Bob Jones University, where he referred to himself as "the conservative candidate" and criticized his "chief rival" for supporting the same tax policies as Democrats.

We did our usual gallows-humor routine, with the wisecracks about Jurassic Park. We were so excited by the margin of the New Hampshire victory that we weren't as worried as we should have been. For the first time, we believed the nomination was actually in reach. So did the candidate. And he wanted it. The residue of confidence and ambition was pugnacity. We thought we were ready to slug it out with the Bush campaign however they wanted to fight. What we failed to appreciate was the way we fought back and how it would affect our message; it would practically become our message. And while Bush and company were spreading skepticism about McCain's reformer credentials, sub rosa activities—conducted mainly but not exclusively via push polls, flyers, faxes, and emails by unaffiliated but supportive entities—took negative campaigning to new lows.

The Bush campaign also made clear they weren't going to concede the veterans' vote to McCain. Bush's first rally, two days after New Hampshire, was held on the courthouse steps in Sumter, South Carolina, with a group of decorated veterans and one known McCain antagonist (known to us, anyway), Tom Burch. Burch was the head of a gadfly veterans' group with a small following who traded in POW/MIA conspiracy theories. Burch had attacked not only McCain but Bush's father. At the rally, he lied that McCain opposed assistance for veterans suffering the effects of exposure to the defoliant Agent Orange, and made several other false accusations, ending with the charge that McCain had "abandoned veterans. He came home and forgot us." We scurried to rebut Burch's allegations with facts from McCain's record, which convinced reporters. But sensing an opportunity for attention, Burch's deprecation of McCain's record on veterans' issues brought the whole "Manchurian Candidate" crowd—including my old sparring partner, Ted Sampley—out of the woodwork and onto the

Internet, where they reissued the slander that McCain had betrayed his fellow POWs. John Kerry organized a letter signed by him and four other Vietnam veterans in the Senate denouncing the calumny. We demanded an apology from the Bush campaign. None was forthcoming. Bush himself, when pressed by reporters for comment about Burch's attack, allowed that "John McCain served our country very well."

We were outraged, and we helped get the candidate worked up about it. When a reporter asked him about Bush's claim to be a "reformer with results," McCain wisecracked, "If that's true, it's his first day on the job." But wisecracks weren't a sufficient defense against the onslaught coming our way. We were deluged with negative ads from the Bush campaign, which had bought time on television and radio to go after McCain on taxes, ads that were complemented by negative ads run by allied entities, including a front group for the tobacco companies. We wanted to show them we weren't afraid to fight. By the end of the week, we were airing our own ads in response, taking Bush to task for breaking his promise to campaign on a positive message.

To another Bush ad—which accused McCain of pressuring government agencies on behalf of campaign donors—we responded with a tough spot of our own. It accused Bush of lying about McCain's record, with the tagline that Bush "twists the truth like Clinton." You would've thought we'd burned someone with a red-hot poker. In the course of the South Carolina primary, McCain would be accused of everything from being a brainwashed Russian agent to siring a child with a prostitute, the notorious rumor circulated in emails from some creep on the faculty of Bob Jones University. The son of BJU's president, Bob Jones IV, wrote an article in *World*, a magazine published by Marvin Olasky, who authored the "compassionate conservative" label borrowed by the Bush campaign. The piece criticized not just McCain's positions but the McCains' marriage, Cindy's wealth, and her struggle with painkiller addiction. But accusing Bush of Clinton tactics was apparently the equivalent of accusing him of murdering puppies. The intensity of the attacks over the next two weeks, and our attempts to fight back, would make that particular South Carolina primary legendary in the annals of political brawls. Some of McCain's aides were fuming from the moment we woke up until we drank ourselves to sleep at night. I was one of the worst offenders.

I had just walked outside a rally venue on a Saturday when I spotted some kid handing out flyers near where two of the McCain children were standing. The flyers accused Cindy of stealing drugs, a reference to her addiction to painkillers in the early 1990s following two difficult operations on her spine. I charged at the kid, and he ran. I caught him after twenty or thirty yards, spun him around, and started screaming at him, holding him with my left hand, my right hand balled in a fist. I would have hit him if I hadn't noticed that a camera crew with a boom mike had caught up with us and was recording the whole thing. As it was, my performance made part of our coverage that night on ABC's evening broadcast.

McCain wasn't incensed by the heavy barrage of incoming attacks as much as he was distracted by it. He was angry when he got wind of under-the-radar attacks that involved his family, angry enough that I thought he might have a volatile public reaction. But he never appeared more than agitated. More often, he seemed to be sort of at sea with the campaign and himself. He looked like he knew what we were doing wasn't working, and we sure weren't enjoying ourselves, but he didn't know what else to do.

He decided to reverse course after a town hall in Spartanburg on the morning of February 10. As he was taking questions from the audience, a woman stood up and told him he'd been the hero of her fourteen-year-old Boy Scout son. She then told how the boy had answered the phone the day before and been informed by the person on the other end that "McCain is a cheat and a liar and a fraud." She was in tears as she recounted the push poll. McCain looked rattled as he condemned "the disillusionment of a young boy" as shameful. He spoke to the boy's mother privately after the town hall and asked for permission to call her son. Then he conferenced with us and told us he wanted to pull all our negative spots and challenge the Bush campaign to do the same, which he proceeded to do in a quickly arranged press conference. "I'll pull down every negative ad I have," he promised, and pleaded with Bush to take down his. "We're not in the business of harming young people." He repeated the offer multiple times that day and the next before finally announcing that he was taking his negative ads off the air irrespective of what his opponent did. His opponent, Governor Bush, complaining McCain had "challenge[d] my integrity," declined to take down his.

The last week was the worst. The Bush campaign had spent millions on airtime, most of it attack ads. The hardest hits were on the radio. To illustrate to senior aides how profuse the attacks were, a South Carolina staffer turned the knob on a car radio from one AM station to the next: Each station on a commercial break was airing an anti-McCain ad, as many as five or six at the same time. Bush campaign allies kept up their attacks as well. The National Right to Life Committee paid for a mass mailing accusing McCain, who supported stem cell research, of voting for taxpayer-funded "experiments that use body parts from aborted babies." We were a combination of punch-drunk and infuriated, including the candidate. Polls showed our support was evaporating. The press was characterizing us as beleaguered, and it was easy to detect a note of sympathy in the tone and substance of their questions, and in their off-the-record personal interactions with McCain aides. They believed we would lose.

Two days before the primary, CNN's Larry King hosted the three remaining candidates, Bush, McCain, and Keyes, for an hour-long exchange of recriminations. It was a miserable hour. Both men sounded petulant and petty.

McCain ended the primary with a final burst of positive energy in a rally on the campus of the College of Charleston. It was held in a gym packed with enthusiastic college kids. It must have been a hundred degrees inside, but McCain, dressed in a College of Charleston sweatshirt a student had presented him, didn't appear to mind as he beseeched "independents, Democrats, Libertarians, vegetarians" to vote for him. Nevertheless, the expected ass-kicking arrived a little after five o'clock the next day, when an aide read the exit poll numbers to the McCains in their hotel suite. Bush had won by a landslide, beating McCain by eleven points. Cindy burst into tears, more from the strain and hostility of the last two weeks than from the defeat. John tried to comfort her, encouraging her to keep her game face on. Then he called Governor Bush and congratulated him.

I can't say how McCain did with South Carolina Libertarians and vegetarians, but Democrats and independents had turned out for him in record numbers. George Bush, however, had cleaned his clock with Republican voters, who had also set a turnout record. We had three days to fight for Michigan. If Bush won there, he would force McCain out of the race. We had hopes of encouraging a bigger independent and Democratic turnout in Michigan's open primary; we were working with labor officials interested in embarrassing the Republican front-runner as well as with several popular African-American ministers in Detroit.

We were tired of litigating Bush's campaign tactics. It hadn't done us any good in South Carolina, and we sounded like a bunch of whiners. But we believed it would motivate non-Republicans to vote against Bush in Michigan. We made the decision not to be gracious in defeat. The candidate agreed, and I quickly banged out a draft that congratulated Governor Bush and swore to fight him "with every ounce of strength I have." McCain criticized Bush's "negative message of fear" and, in another obvious knock on the governor, promised he "would never take the low road to the highest office in the land." The media reaction was harsh. Some pundits derided his concession as the least gracious in living memory.

I was a little concerned that the harshest of the commentary would mitigate the speech's intended effect on Michigan voters, but I wasn't seriously rattled until I called my wife, Diane, and the first words out of her mouth were something like: "Oh, Mark, why did you write that?" After I failed to convince her it had been necessary, I laid down on a bench in the plaza outside the venue, stared up at the stars, and thought, "You fucking idiot." Other McCain aides weren't as worried as I was, or as one of them put it, "We don't have time to worry about it." Someone must have spoken to the candidate and told him I had been upset by criticism of the speech. McCain took me aside the next morning and assured me the speech had been the right message in the moment, then told me to "stop stewing about it and get to work."

We tore around Michigan for two days as the candidate delivered the same combative and, at times, serio-comic message.

We spent Election Day in Phoenix, where McCain voted for himself in Arizona's primary. As Cindy made grilled cheese sandwiches for us in the McCains' kitchen, Davis, Weaver, and Murphy were getting positive reports about turnout from our allies in Michigan. The gambit had worked. He beat Bush by eight points, 51 percent to 43 percent. The record turnout of Democrats and independents that we'd hoped for had materialized. Half the electorate had been crossover voters, and they had swamped our opponent's margin with Republican voters. Governor Engler, a Bush campaign national chair, practically accused us of stealing the primary. McCain was happy, too, that he had won his own state's primary in a landslide.

The victories seemed to reset the race again. Some in the media resumed covering it as a neck-and-neck down-the-stretch contest. A "Humdinger," blared the cover of the *Economist*. But shrewder observers knew that our best—and probably our only—hope had been to knock Bush out one-two-three before we had to square off in a war of attrition against him in the big delegate-rich Super Tuesday states, including California, New York, and Ohio, on March 7.

Two competitive primaries preceded Super Tuesday, Virginia and Washington, both on February 29. We had some hope of doing well in one or both. They had large veteran populations, and substantial segments of their electorates were more moderate and receptive to McCain's reform message. However, he lost both of them, Washington by less than a point and Virginia handily. Since the South Carolina primary, the candidate and his aides had been discussing ways to rebuff attacks by self-appointed Christian-right leaders and make a case for McCain's conservatism. We didn't have any hope of beating Bush with evangelicals, but we needed to do better with them. We decided on a very McCain approach of appealing to religious conservatives over the heads of some of their leaders. The best way to do that, we reasoned, was to attack the sincerity and stature of prominent anti-McCain Christian-right figures.

The day before the primary, McCain traveled to Virginia Beach,

Pat Robertson's hometown, with social conservative Gary Bauer, who had endorsed McCain after dropping out of the primary. McCain gave a speech there expressing his support for the values of religious conservatives and defending his conservative record. He argued that conservative leaders who opposed his candidacy had not done so for any moral principle but because of his support for campaign finance reform. He likened them to "union bosses who have subordinated the interests of working families to their own ambitions." The most quoted passage of the speech, however, was his warning that "neither party should be defined by pandering to the outer reaches of American politics, and to agents of intolerance, whether they be Louis Farrakhan or Al Sharpton on the left, or Pat Robertson and Jerry Falwell on the right."

I wrote the first draft of the speech and sent it to colleagues before showing it to the candidate. My original draft hadn't called out anyone by name. Someone included Robertson and Falwell, and Gary Bauer recommended we add Farrakhan and Sharpton. I didn't have a problem with the addition. I found Robertson repulsively hypocritical. I was pleased after the speech when we heard reports that he was apoplectic after McCain had attacked him in his own backyard. And while Falwell struck me as very transactional, he hadn't been nearly as malicious in South Carolina as Robertson had been. It was fine by me if John agreed to call them out by name. But, no other part of the message, including the defense of his conservative record, would be remembered. The attack on Robertson and Falwell dominated the coverage, and Bush accused him of trying to divide people by religion.

As it turned out, Michigan really had been our last gasp. We were short on funds and organization. McCain was the king of New England on Super Tuesday, winning Massachusetts, Connecticut, Rhode Island, and Vermont, but not Maine, where the Bush family spent summers. Bush won everything else. After the concession speech, we left California and headed for the McCains' cabin to consider what to do. Aides discussed the feasibility of waging some sort of guerrilla campaign through the remaining primaries, picking up delegates where we could so that we might have enough strength at the convention to influence the platform. It was all nonsense, of course. We just didn't want to concede the race. We were angry and hurt, and we wanted to make trouble for the Bush campaign as payback. The next morning, McCain cut through the nonsense: "I lost," he announced. There is "no point to postponing the inevitable." He instructed us to set up a place and time the following day for him to announce he was quitting the race. We staged it on the tarmac of Sedona's little airport, on top of a mesa, looking out at the red rocks that make the area so popular.

A couple days later, we went back to Washington, and I returned to my old job in McCain's Senate office. He spoke on the Senate floor the first day he was back. Typical of him, he spoke about an international affairs topic—the situation in Kosovo—and to the disappointment of the reporters who observed it, ones who don't normally spend their day in the Senate press gallery, he made only the briefest mention of the campaign he had lost. That was by design. We had suggested he reflect on the public's desire for a different kind of politics, which he had tapped into, and express his gratitude to the McCainiacs, who had stuck with him throughout the campaign. "I've already done that," he responded. "I want to get back to work." He also declined to let us notify his Republican colleagues that he was coming to the floor to speak. Trent Lott said afterward that, had they known McCain was going to speak, many of his Republican colleagues would have come to the floor to welcome him back. McCain didn't want anyone to make a big deal about his return. That same day, at the weekly Republican caucus lunch, his colleagues welcomed him back with a standing ovation.

One piece of unfinished business from the campaign remained. We couldn't have been back in town more than a couple days when McCain announced he wanted to go back to South Carolina. He had received an invitation to speak at a conservative think tank in Columbia. He told us he was going to accept it and use the occasion to apologize for lying about the Confederate flag. No one tried to talk him out of it. He gave me a general idea of what he wanted to say, instructing me to "lay it on thick, boy." In what the *Washington Post* would call "an extraordinary act of contrition," he confessed he had "broken his promise to always tell the truth," and had done so because he didn't think he could win the South Carolina primary without lying. As to his real feelings about the Confederate battle flag and whether it symbolized southern heritage, after acknowledging his Confederate ancestors, he stated: "I don't believe their service, however distinguished, needs to be commemorated in a way that offends, that deeply hurts, people whose ancestors were once denied their freedom by my ancestors." He went on to concede that apologizing after the primary wasn't hard. He had nothing left to lose. "I will be criticized by all sides for my late act of contrition," he acknowledged. "I accept it, all of it. I deserve it. Honesty is easy after the fact when my own interests are no longer involved."

His act of contrition might have been as easy for him as he claimed it was, but it was unusual. It was also unusual for the candidate who had lost his party's nomination to have as much influence as McCain was now perceived to have. The general election between Governor Bush and Vice President Al Gore was expected to be close, and pundits considered McCain's support for his victorious rival to be important. McCain's stature was elevated; a recent Gallup poll indicated that he was one of the most popular politicians in the country. There was also the effect of McCain and the press's practical codependency. McCain had so thoroughly captured the media's attention during the primaries that he and they were reluctant to part company. Some of McCain's conservative critics would soon mockingly refer to him as Senator John McCain (R-Media). In the weeks after he withdrew from the race, there was often a camera crew stationed outside his office, and a scrum of reporters would usually pepper him with questions as he walked from his office in the Russell Building to the Capitol.

He went to Vietnam that April. Cindy and his son Jack accompanied him, as did *Today* anchor Matt Lauer, who interviewed him on the twenty-fifth anniversary of the fall of Saigon and the reunification of the country. So did several other reporters: Jake Tapper, then with *Salon*; *Time*'s Jay Carney; *Newsweek*'s Howard Finema; Roger Simon with *U.S. News & World Report*; and Tucker Carlson at *The Weekly Standard*. At Hao Lo, McCain entertained the group while they toured the little museum that occupied the remnants of the prison. As they looked at photographs of American POWs playing volleyball and celebrating Christmas, McCain wisecracked, "Now, that's entertainment." In Saigon, when a foreign reporter asked why he had come to celebrate the fall of Saigon, he snapped, "I'm not here to celebrate it. I think the wrong side won," agitating, not for the first time, his Vietnamese hosts.

Most of the media's attention on him in April 2000 was focused on the question of when and how enthusiastically he would endorse Governor Bush. McCain had every intention of doing so, and to campaign for Bush if he were asked to, but he allowed aides to negotiate the particulars of the event. I don't really remember what we were trying to accomplish, whether we were playing for a big role in the convention or to secure assurances of Bush's support for campaign finance reform in the next Congress. But we dragged out discussions of what should have been a pretty straightforward affair, where the runner-up endorses the winner, and everybody pretends there are no more hard feelings. We left it uncertain in media reports whether their first meeting, scheduled for May 9 in Pittsburgh, would even include an endorsement. Speculation in the press was so extensive, it was as if they were anticipating a summit meeting between two antagonistic foreign powers. At one point, we even discussed postponing the meeting over some perceived slight I no longer remember. When Al Gore asked to meet with McCain in Washington for a few minutes, reporters were intrigued, and exasperated Republicans grumbled. I have no idea what the hell we expected him to do other than endorse Bush, but we were the center of attention, and some of us, including me, were still sore about South Carolina.

The press would report that the Bush-McCain meeting produced a tepid endorsement from a reluctant McCain. The two men met alone for almost an hour and a half, much longer than we expected, while their aides caucused in separate holding rooms. After they emerged and held a brief joint press conference, McCain did not debrief us in detail about their discussion. He said Bush had apologized for Tom Burch's attacks in South Carolina, and that McCain had committed to campaign for Bush in the fall. He also mentioned they had discussed campaign finance reform, and while Bush appeared open to supporting a soft-money ban, he hadn't firmly committed. When we asked how tense the meeting had been, he said it hadn't been. "Really?" we asked skeptically.

"Really," he responded.

"How did you get along?"

"Fine. Fine."

We couldn't get any other details out of him. He probably didn't trust us to keep our mouths shut.

At the press conference, which the *Guardian* described as "scrutinized in forensic detail for signs of healing of the Republican wounds left by the primaries," McCain promised to campaign for Bush "enthusiastically." He didn't utter the word "endorse," and a reporter asked if his omission was purposeful, to which McCain responded, "I endorse Governor Bush," repeating the phrase six times. He did it in a droll way that reporters interpreted as signaling his discomfort with the formal ritual of pledging support for his former rival. It was actually McCain's sarcastic attempt at teasing the media for making a big deal about one word. He had just "said I was going to campaign for the guy," he complained to us afterward. "Isn't that an endorsement? I didn't know I had to use the magic word." Ever the wise guy, he made matters worse when a reporter asked him if his endorsement was heartfelt or a decision to "take your medicine now?" Laughing, McCain said it was "take my medicine now."

The Bush campaign gave McCain a prime-time speaking spot on the second night of the convention, which was held in Philadelphia. The day before, in an emotional speech to his delegates and as a gesture to party unity, McCain had released them from their pledge to vote for him on the first ballot. They responded with a chorus of nos. McCain cried as he urged them to make the vote for Governor Bush unanimous. He wholeheartedly endorsed Bush in his speech the next night, so there wouldn't be a repeat of taking-his-medicine speculation, and he made a case for uniting the country by enacting political reforms. The address was warmly received by Bush and McCain delegates.

McCain seemed to have a permanent press scrum accompanying him wherever he went in Philadelphia, and much of the television media coverage focused on him. Without rancor or disrespect, Bush aides asked us if we would consider leaving town Wednesday morning so that the media's attention would focus on the nominee. They asked that we stay away until Thursday night, when McCain would appear with Bush in the traditional party unity picture onstage after Bush's acceptance speech. McCain understood and agreed, and we caught a train that morning for Washington.

Since the Senate wasn't in session, and he had nothing else scheduled, he decided to use the rare day off to go to Bethesda Naval Hospital to have a spot on his left temple looked at. He had suffered from skin cancer before and was usually careful to have anything questionable looked at by his dermatologist. But he had been so busy with the campaign, and now with a hectic schedule that reflected his new status as a national political celebrity, he had been negligent about getting this one looked at. They removed two spots on his temple. When he appeared onstage Thursday night, a Band-Aid covered the excision. A week later, his doctor called with the biopsy results. The spots were melanoma. He kept a commitment to campaign with Governor Bush in California, Washington, and Arizona, and to welcome the Bushes to the cabin for barbecue, where he told Bush about his diagnosis. On August 16, he had surgery to remove a melanoma tumor and surrounding lymph nodes. The news broke during the Democratic National Convention, a few hours before his friend Joe Lieberman gave a speech accepting the vice presidential nomination. Had the Bush people not requested he leave Philadelphia, or had he been the party's nominee, it's likely he would have put off the doctor's exam until it was too late. Lucky guy.

MAVERICK

The conventional take on John McCain in the first few years after his 2000 presidential campaign was that he returned to the Senate as one of the country's most popular politicians—perhaps, for a brief time, *the* most popular—and one of the more aggrieved, still angry about the tactics used to defeat his bid for the presidential nomination. His crossover appeal to Democrats and independents seemed a tonic to voters wearied by the angry Florida recount saga that delayed the election results, and it gave him outsize influence in Washington. But his political independence in what is remembered as his maverick heyday was frequently interpreted as payback for the Republican establishment's collaboration with attacks on his character and family. That's a simple explanation for actions taken by a politician with an unguarded personality and a sardonic sense of humor. And it's a false one, or it so exaggerated his motivations that it distorted the reality.

I don't suggest there were no hard feelings affecting McCain's relations with the new president and his administration. He wouldn't forgive attacks that involved his family, even if they weren't the work of the Bush campaign itself. And during the transition and first months after President Bush's inauguration, John Weaver and I were quick to report to him every example of what we characterized as a Bush administration hiring ban against people with McCain connections. That would set him on edge a little. But whatever grievances he might have had, they did not drive him to take positions contrary to administration policies. Though they might have contributed to his sense of himself as a more independent political player, that was a role he had grown increasingly comfortable in before he ran for president.

McCain's mind-set in those years shouldn't be a mystery to anyone who knew him. He had acquired national celebrity status and more crossover political appeal than any other politician at that time, with the possible exception of Colin Powell. But he was popular with most Republicans, especially in the years between his two presidential campaigns. He campaigned with Governor Bush in multiple states, everywhere the Bush campaign asked him to appear. At the Republican congressional campaign committee's behest, he campaigned for more than forty Republican House candidates in 2000. He had rock-star status at fund-raising dinners the Republican National Committee asked him to attend; excited party activists queued in long lines to have their pictures taken with him.

The fact that a Republican political celebrity was regarded favorably by a surprisingly large percentage of Democrats, and had off-the-chart support from independents, while maintaining solid approval ratings within his own party, should have indicated to Republican leaders that McCain was onto something, both in his personal style and his championing of reform-oriented conservatism. It certainly indicated that to him. Contributing to his wide appeal was his conviction that political capital should be spent as if it were drawn from an inexhaustible supply. He returned a more influential member to a Senate that was divided fifty-fifty between the two parties, with newly inaugurated Vice President Cheney's tiebreaking vote giving Republicans the barest of majorities. That increased the bargaining power each senator possessed, as one defection could result in a legislative defeat. The sweep and pace of McCain's legislative activities in the 107th Congress was in part a reaction to the empowerment derived from an evenly divided Senate in a country that had just endured an evenly divided general election. He knew he was more influential in that Congress than he might ever be again, and he intended to take full advantage of it.

His differentiation from positions that were considered staples of Republican orthodoxy at the time *was* shaped by his experiences as a presidential candidate, but not from his reaction to losing. He did not get a kick out of bucking his leadership or enjoy being criticized as disloyal. He believed when he found himself in that situation that his policy differences with colleagues were ultimately in the best interests of Republicans as well as the country at large. But it wasn't easy for him to be at odds with his caucus—to be considered, as he often worried, "the dog in the manger again." At one point in 2001, Senate Republican leader Trent Lott expressed concern in the press that McCain's reform agenda had expanded beyond campaign finance rules, and while the caucus was prepared to tolerate his apostasy on his signature issue, the increasing number of other incidents of policy nonconformity could strain his relations with Republicans beyond repair. McCain mentioned the criticism several times to me, and I dismissed it as an empty threat from leadership that would need his support in every close vote. But it bothered him. He would sometimes return from the weekly Republican caucus lunch on Tuesdays to report, without his typical bravura, that a colleague had criticized him or snapped at him or sneered when he had addressed the caucus.

However, he did not let colleagues' antipathy deter him from the objective he had set for himself: to use his influence, and the opportunity presented by a fifty-fifty Senate, to make progress on the issues he had introduced into the campaign, including campaign finance reform and more modest, middle-class-focused tax cuts; and the issues he acquired as voters made clear to him their priorities, including concerns about global warming and health care. If he was working out grievances from the heated nomination contest, it was through the act of keeping promises he had made to voters. If Republicans in Congress or the Bush administration wanted to fight with him about that, fine, he would fight.

The first promise he would act on was campaign finance reform. He and Senator Feingold introduced the latest version of their bill on January 22, two days after President Bush's inauguration, with a new cosponsor and recent convert to the cause, Mississippi Republican Thad Cochran. There was speculation in the press that the incoming administration had requested McCain postpone reintroducing

McCain-Feingold until their legislative priorities had been addressed. I don't recall requests of that nature coming from the president or White House officials. The story was likely an exaggeration from a White House aide annoyed by McCain's public campaigning for his own agenda while the new president was preparing his.

In a subsequent meeting at the White House, held two days after McCain and Feingold had introduced the bill—and reported in the press before the White House had called to invite McCain—he, Bush, and Cheney briefly discussed timing. Bush reaffirmed his support for the bill's main provision, the ban on soft money, but he wanted to add a provision pertaining to labor unions' use of membership dues for political donations. This provision would have lost Democratic support for the bill. Cheney, McCain recalled afterward, "acted like he was completely against the bill," adding, "I hope he's not calling the shots on this." During the meeting, Bush said he would appreciate it if McCain wouldn't push for a vote on McCain-Feingold until after the debate on the budget and his proposed tax cuts. McCain wouldn't commit to a delay without the White House committing not to oppose the bill. But he was generous in comments to the press after the meeting about finding common ground and about the president's commitment to reform. He would wait until March to see if their common ground could be turned into actual agreement on the issue. If nothing had happened by then, he would do what he usually did when facing delaying tactics by a resistant leadership: He would try to force the debate.

Long a familiar presence on news shows and in newspapers, McCain became practically ubiquitous in the media after 2000, to the frustration of his detractors. We couldn't keep him off the air. There were times when he figured in a political controversy that was dominating the news, or when he hadn't decided what position to take on the issue of the day, that we advised him to decline a request from a Sunday show. I can't remember an instance when he took our advice. He would pay the price now and again for his lack of caution; he would screw up an answer or get pinned down in an untenable position or just seem off his game. But he believed those occasional penalties were insignificant compared to the benefits he got from his recurring media appearances. They broadcast his message to bigger audiences over the arguments and obfuscations of opponents in the conservative press and on talk radio. I remember talking with him in his office one morning when he suddenly yawned and complained he was tired, blaming his fatigue on a BBC radio producer who had woken him up when she called his cell phone at two in the morning for a comment on a breaking news story. He couldn't remember the producer's name when I asked for it. I told him I would track her down anyway to chew her out and let her know we would turn down all interview requests from the BBC for the foreseeable future. Then we were going to change his cell phone number, I added; he had given it out to scores of reporters, and that was untenable. "No, you won't," he told me. "It would take too long for me to give them my new one." Then he told me not to threaten the BBC producer but just ask her to refrain in the future from calling him in the middle of the night.

There was persistent press speculation that first year about the disaffection between McCain world and Bush world leading to an irreversible break. McCain criticized administration decisions and policies, as he did with every administration from Reagan's to Trump's. He prized the Senate because its rules and traditions granted members considerable autonomy, and he resented attempts from any quarter to curb his independence. There wasn't a lot of trust between him and the White House in the early years of the Bush administration. He didn't take their word for anything, frequently quoting Reagan's "trust but verify" maxim when we came to terms with the White House on an issue. And they didn't accept his assurances at face value. Our mutual skepticism fluctuated over the course of the Bush presidency, with regular setbacks but enough progress that a disagreement never truly threatened to cause a permanent breach in relations. Contrary to conventional wisdom, McCain didn't complain or appear to register as personal anything said about or done to him. Nor did he talk about grudges left over from the campaign. While he would spar with the administration over policy disagreements, he had bigger plans than prosecuting grievances from the South Carolina primary.

In February 2001, McCain introduced the Bipartisan Patient Protection Act with Ted Kennedy and John Edwards, commonly referred to as the Patients' Bill of Rights. His interest in the issue began during the campaign with complaints from voters about their HMOs, the relatively new managed health care plans that were frequently accused of unfairly restricting access to care. The bill was similar to legislation passed in the Republican-controlled House the previous year. Its central provisions allowed HMO patients to seek emergency care and see medical specialists without a referral. It set up an adjudication process for patients who believed they had been wrongly denied care by their HMO. Their complaints would be considered by an independent panel of medical experts, after which they could sue their HMO in state or federal court. Most Senate Republicans opposed the measure, as did the White House. They contended that it would trigger an avalanche of litigation. The White House endorsed an alternative bill sponsored by surgeon-turned-legislator Senator Bill Frist. Like the McCain-Kennedy-Edwards bill, Frist's measure granted HMO patients freer access to specialty care, but it differed significantly on the liability issue, allowing patients to sue only in federal court, a slower and more expensive proposition, and capping awards for pain and suffering at half a million dollars.

McCain was in Kennedy's office frequently that month, negotiating provisions of the bill and trying to get Edwards to agree to more significant litigation restrictions, worried that without greater constraints, they wouldn't attract enough Republicans for a veto-proof majority. Over time, he would grow to distrust Edwards, but even then he had mixed feelings. He grumbled that all Edwards (a successful trial lawyer) appeared to care about in the bill was protection for the income of trial lawyers. McCain didn't want to block patients from suing their HMOs in state court, as the Frist bill did. Neither did he want to ban punitive damages, as the Frist bill also did. But he did want a ceiling on punitive damages. All he could get Edwards to agree to was a $5 million punitive cap in federal lawsuits. "I swear to God," McCain muttered after returning from one meeting, "he'd let us change anything we want in the bill as long as we don't touch the lawyers."

He got a call from Senator Kennedy late one morning, asking him to come to his office for what McCain assumed was another discussion about the bill. I accompanied him to the meeting but sat in the reception area while the two men conferred behind closed doors. When McCain emerged a half hour later, he gave me the wide-eyed, arched-eyebrows signal that he had news to share. He didn't explain until we were in the hall and out of earshot of eavesdroppers. Kennedy had pitched him on switching parties. Democrats had identified three Republican senators as possible party switchers: two New England liberal Republicans, Jim Jeffords of Vermont and Lincoln Chafee of Rhode Island; and the reform-minded conservative John McCain. The Democratic leader, Tom Daschle, had tasked Kennedy with reaching out to McCain first. Kennedy told McCain he would have more influence in a Democratic majority than he did with Republicans. He assured him he would retain his seniority in their caucus. McCain would still be in line to chair the Armed Services Committee, his long-held ambition. Kennedy was a member of the committee and had more seniority than McCain. But he promised to step aside when the time came and let McCain assume the chairmanship. As things stood, and assuming Republicans retained control, he would succeed the current chairman, John Warner, in 2005.

"What did you tell him?" I asked.

"I told him no. But he wants to talk again, with Daschle, too, and I said okay."

"Are you seriously considering it?"

"No, but I'm interested that they're interested."

I was as intrigued as he was. We were a little full of ourselves in those days, and I welcomed the Democrats' overture to McCain as another confirmation that I worked for one of the most powerful politicians in town, who could influence events in Washington more than most members of Congress could. I didn't think he should and never thought he would change parties. He was a pragmatic problem solver who had working partnerships and friendships with members in both parties and was a center-right rather than a base conservative. But he was still a conservative. He had conventionally conservative views about most issues—federal spending, taxes, regulations, and the inefficiencies of government. He was a defense hawk. He was pro-life. McCain's differences with his Republican colleagues in the years between his presidential campaigns were fewer than he would have had with Democrats if he'd joined their caucus. But Democrats argued the point, as did a few center-left commentators, who thought his positions were more in line with Democratic orthodoxy.

There was a second conversation with Kennedy, which Daschle joined. I believe there was a third meeting as well, but I don't remember the last one with certainty. The meetings were off the books, and there isn't a record of them. McCain told me Harry Reid, then the Democratic whip, had a word with him on the subject as well, and for all I know, he had similar sidebar conversations off the Senate floor that he neglected to share with me. But McCain never got close to agreeing to change parties. He was flattered, and enjoyed the attention, and used it to secure Democrats' cooperation with his initiatives. But he knew he would have looked opportunistic, not principled, had he agreed to switch sides. As far as I knew, no McCain advisor counseled him otherwise.

Despite his repeated rejections of the idea, McCain didn't bring the talks to a permanent end by insisting Democrats let the matter go. But the talks sputtered out inconclusively anyway. Republican Senate leaders and the White House had assigned Judd Gregg the responsibility for managing Bush's No Child Left Behind education initiative in the Senate, bypassing Jim Jeffords, the chairman of the Health, Education, Labor, and Pensions committee. Jeffords complained it was the latest example of what he viewed as attempts to intimidate him into conforming to the caucus's more conservative views. On May 24, he announced that he was changing parties, giving Democrats a 51 to 49 majority. McCain's defection was no longer necessary to gain control of the chamber, and the efforts to recruit him ceased, for the most part. McCain reacted to the news by releasing a statement criticizing the way Republican leaders had treated Jeffords. He was no doubt defending his own independence as well as Jeffords when he argued, "Tolerance of dissent is the hallmark of a mature party, and it is well past time for the Republican Party to grow up."

Word about the Democrats' discussions with McCain would eventually leak from both sides. Although I was among the likely suspects, I had managed to keep quiet to reporters, mostly because McCain kept reminding me to keep my mouth shut. By May 2001, he was at odds with the White House over HMOs, McCain-Feingold, and a bill he'd introduced with Joe Lieberman that would have closed the so-called gun show loophole by requiring background checks for firearms sales at gun shows. He maintained over and over that the initiatives were commitments he had made to voters and not a personal vendetta against the president. But obviously, the environment was ripe for speculation that McCain was contemplating leaving the party, possibly to mount an independent or third-party bid for president in 2004. No serious consideration was ever given to such a thing, but McCain world didn't bother to throw cold water on the idea, so the speculation reached a fever pitch when he voted against the president's tax cut package on May 27, one of only two Republicans to do so.

His argument defending his vote was the one he'd made during the campaign: The cuts were too generous to the wealthy at the expense of the middle class. During debate on the legislation, he had offered amendments to address his concern, one of which would have lowered the top marginal income tax rate by just 1 percent rather than the 4.6 percent cut the White House proposed. In exchange for the higher top rate, the amendment raised the level of income taxable at 15 percent, effectively lowering middle-class tax rates. It nearly passed. The vote was 49 to 49. Cheney broke the tie. After the vote, McCain declared he wouldn't go along with a top rate any lower than 36 percent. The White House stuck to its 35 percent proposal, and as he had threatened, McCain voted against the bill.

Most observers thought he had done so unhesitatingly. But it was a closer call than reporters knew. He was genuinely torn about it. Lincoln Chafee was the only other Republican voting against the bill, and he was perhaps the most liberal Republican in Congress. McCain was a conservative who had supported Ronald Reagan's tax cuts. Phil Gramm and other friends whose advice he respected lobbied him, warning him that he was making a big political mistake.

Cheney called and said he thought he could make a case for the bill
that would convince him. McCain was genuinely worried he would
permanently damage his standing not only with Senate Republicans
but with Republicans generally. Democrats, on the other hand, weren't
working him aggressively, sensing, I suspect, that it was better to let
him come to his own conclusion without risking irritating him with a
heavy lobbying campaign. Daschle talked to him regularly, but more
often than not to discuss McCain's ideas for amendments. McCain advisors were divided. I argued that he had laid down his marker, a 36
percent top rate and no lower, and he would damage his reputation
for straight talk, possibly irreparably, if he reversed himself. Others
worried he would aggravate tensions within the caucus and make it
harder for him to find Republican votes for McCain-Feingold. When
defending his vote, he kept his game face on and appeared unboth-
ered by his decision. But he wasn't as sure of himself as he pretended
to be. The president and first lady invited the McCains to dinner at
the White House, a gesture intended to lower tensions and assure the
public the two weren't enemies. It had been scheduled for May 24 but
was postponed as votes on amendments to the tax bill kept the Senate
in session into the night.

After the final vote on the bill, McCain planned to spend the weekend at his cabin. He often invited colleagues in both parties to join him
for a couple of days of recreation and barbecue. The office kept a block
calendar of scheduled guest visits. Months earlier McCain had invited
Tom and Linda Daschle, as well as former Clinton domestic policy
advisor Bruce Reed, whom McCain had become friends with while
working on the tobacco bill. The addition of Reed made it impossible
for Washington cynics to accept our protestations that the occasion
was strictly social. As it happened, their arrival was scheduled for Saturday, June 2, the same day the *Washington Post* published on its front
page a story headlined: "McCain Is Considering Leaving GOP." It was
written by two reputable journalists, Tom Edsall and Dana Milbank,
and it was about 70 percent exaggeration and invention, although that
wasn't all Edsall and Milbank's fault. I'm sure they had credible sources
for the article's boldest assertions, including their lede:

"Maverick Republican Sen. John McCain of Arizona, in a widening rift with President Bush and his party's dominant conservative wing, is talking with advisers about leaving the GOP and launching a third-party challenge to Bush in 2004."

No such discussions had occurred, not between McCain and his advisors. He had told us about the Democrats' approach. But at no point did he convene a meeting or engage in serious discussions with an advisor or advisors about the pros and cons of changing parties or running for president as an independent. The story did quote him affirming he had "no cause to leave the Republican Party, period!" But it also quoted various McCain associates, some on the record, contradicting him. The reporters referenced a lunch meeting that week that John Weaver had with Bill Kristol, editor of *The Weekly Standard*; McCain's legislative director, Dan McKivergan; and future McCain staffer Marshall Wittman, to "debate whether McCain should quit" the party. One or more of them had obviously tipped the reporters about the lunch, and Kristol and Wittman were quoted in the piece.

McCain was unhappy, all the more so when news helicopters started flying over the cabin trying to get film of the McCains hosting the Daschles. Then a White House operator called the cabin with the president on the line. McCain had to assure him the *Post* story wasn't true. "It was embarrassing, Mark," he barked at me. "Goddamn embarrassing." Weaver argued internally that the more concern there was that McCain might bolt parties, the less the White House and congressional leaders would obstruct McCain-Feingold. It was a valid point, but it didn't lessen McCain's displeasure. When news of the Daschles coming to the cabin had broken several days earlier, we had put out a statement maintaining the "purely social" purpose of the visit. Now McCain dictated the gist of a statement he ordered me to release that day:

I have not instructed nor encouraged any of my advisors to begin planning for a presidential run in 2004. I have not discussed running for president again with anyone. As I have said repeatedly, I have no intention of running for president, nor do

I have any intention of or cause to leave the Republican Party. I hope this will put an end to further speculation on this subject.

He might have enjoyed the extra attention brought by all the speculation about his plans, as long as he could treat the whole thing as a joke and dismiss it with a wisecrack. He might have bought into the idea that both caucuses competing for his allegiance increased his influence. But the uproar kicked up by the *Washington Post* article and the Daschles' visit had him worried that he had lost control of the story and that he was burning bridges he had never intended to destroy. Conservatives nationally and in Arizona were becoming increasingly hostile to him, and Senate Republicans were whispering to conservative journalists about his isolation in the caucus.

Finally, he worried he was reinforcing criticism that he was a sore loser. A few years after these events, he told a *New Yorker* reporter, Connie Bruck, that he had read a biography examining the last years of Teddy Roosevelt's life, the period from his failed Bull Moose bid for the presidency to his death in 1919. McCain said Roosevelt had been a broken man after the death of his son, Quentin, in World War I, the war Roosevelt had been adamant the United States enter. "He was never the same after that," McCain said, recounting a weeping Roosevelt moaning, "Quinty, Quinty," as he patted his dead son's pony in the stables at Sagamore Hill, and how Quentin's death and T.R.'s political defeats had soured the great, dynamic, lively personality that had been an inspiration to McCain. "Roosevelt was very bitter at the end of his life," he told the reporter.

And I took a lesson from that. I would not be bitter. Americans don't like sore losers. They want you to move on. And that's what I did. I didn't complain, didn't express outrage. I moved on.[40]

There's more truth in his assertion than many McCain observers— bred to skepticism by familiarity with the genus *Politico Americanus*— believed. Had I not been personally involved in the preceding events, I wouldn't have taken his protestations seriously, either. But he didn't gripe about the campaign once it was over, and he did want to move on. It's just that the things he wanted to move on to, a bigger voice in Washington politics and action on his agenda, were mostly things Republican leaders and the White House would have preferred he not accomplish. He didn't have any intention of lowering his profile or easing up on his legislative ambitions. But he did want to lower the heat in his relations with the White House. He told aides he suspected were taking shots at the White House in the press (including me) to knock it off. And he made an effort to refrain from sounding angry or acerbic in reaction to something the administration had said or done. A compulsive wiseacre, he succeeded in keeping the anger more in check than the acerbity.

Dinner with the Bushes was rescheduled for June 5, two days after he returned to Washington from his weekend with the Daschles. Press interest in the dinner was understandably intense. It was on the early side: I believe the McCains were expected to arrive around six thirty for drinks, with dinner served soon after. I was having dinner downtown that night with friends and didn't expect to hear from him until nine o'clock. My phone rang at seven forty-five. The McCains were in the car and on their way home. I struggled to suppress a note of alarm in my voice. "You're done already? What happened?"

"Nothing. It was fine. Fine."

"Fine? You were barely there an hour."

"We finished dinner. It was fine. No problems. He was tired. I'm tired. So we went home. I promise you, it was fine."

Still skeptical, I asked what they had talked about. "Oh, you know, what you might expect." McCain's inadequacies as a debriefer could be maddening. I asked if they had talked about McCain-Feingold. "A little," he replied. "As you know, Bush can be pretty likable when he wants," he added. "It was nice." I thought I might get more out of him in the morning and was preparing to hang up when he suddenly interjected, "Oh, Mark, I almost forgot, I talked to him about Carlos."

"Carlos?"

"Yeah, Carlos. Your friend Carlos."

My friend's name was not Carlos. It was Adolfo. We had gone to school together and been close friends for over twenty years. Out of friendship to me, Adolfo had volunteered on the 2000 McCain presidential campaign. A lifelong Republican with years of experience in international development, he was slated for a job as an assistant administrator at USAID, and it was rumored that someone in the White House was blocking him. I had mentioned it to McCain a few days earlier.

"Adolfo, his name is Adolfo."

"Oh, shit."

McCain added that Bush had written down the name and promised he would take care of it. I imagined the president handing the name to an aide and the aide futilely searching for a prospective political appointee named Carlos without a last name.

The next day McCain spoke to the conservative columnist Bob Novak, a persistent critic for whom McCain had a soft spot, and told him the dinner had been "very congenial. I had forgotten how effective the president can be one-on-one." Subsequent events and continued sniping on background from aides on both sides would keep the story of enduring antagonism between Bush and McCain worlds alive. McCain made fun of the tensions between the camps, wisecracking on talk shows that the White House dinner had been an intimate affair— just the six of them, the Bushes, the McCains, and their food tasters. But the interactions between the two principals remained respectful, and speaking for McCain, the same attitude prevailed in private, too.

As I had hoped, he was more forthcoming in the morning and filled me in on a few subjects he had discussed with the president. They had talked about foreign policy, reforming the Pentagon's procurement policies, and reining in earmarks, subjects important to McCain and where he thought he and the administration could find common ground. He said he had also talked to Bush about the patients' bill of rights, which was scheduled for debate and votes on the Senate floor that month. He came away from the conversation believing he had a shot at finding a compromise with the administration on HMOs, if not in the Senate version, then in conference with the House version. That view proved unduly optimistic.

The Senate passed the Kennedy-McCain-Edwards Bipartisan Patient Protection Act shortly before adjourning for the July Fourth recess. It was approved by a respectable margin, 59 to 36, with eight other Republicans joining McCain, but it wasn't a big enough majority to override a presidential veto, and a veto threat, albeit a politely worded one, was immediately forthcoming. Minutes after final passage, the White House released a statement from the president, complimenting "the good-faith efforts of those who worked to improve the bill by narrowing some loopholes and giving greater deference to state patient protections." But the statement went on to complain that the bill did not do enough to prevent "excessive, unlimited litigation," and Bush intended to veto it because "it puts the interests of trial lawyers before the interests of patients." McCain disputed the administration's argument but added that he would cooperate "in any sincere effort to reach fair compromises on the issues that still divide us."

The House was scheduled to take up their version of the bill a little under a month later, just before Congress adjourned for the August recess. The White House hoped it would produce a bill closer to the administration's wishes than the Senate measure. The HMO bill passed by the House in the previous Congress—cosponsored by Republicans Greg Ganske of Iowa, a surgeon, and Charlie Norwood, a dentist—had been supported by sixty-eight Republicans. Ganske and Norwood were part of a bipartisan group of members leading the effort to pass virtually the same bill over the opposition of the Republican House leadership and the White House. Someone in the White House sensed that Norwood was susceptible to presidential persuasion. He was invited to the Oval Office, where, purportedly, the president spent hours getting him to agree to a White House proposal that severely restricted HMO litigation in state courts. Norwood had neither informed his bipartisan cohort that he was negotiating a compromise with the president nor sought their buy-in before announcing his support for it, and they didn't hide their displeasure. "Charlie cut his own deal with the White House," Ganske objected. "He didn't share any information with us." McCain publicly opposed and disputed the talking points released by the White House. Privately, he complained, "Charlie screwed the whole thing up."

McCain knew the bill's supporters eventually would have had to reach an accommodation with the White House on the issue of liability to forestall a veto. But he expected those discussions to begin after the House passed its bill and went to conference with the Senate, when the sponsor would be in a stronger position than the White House, and he would be the one brokering the deal. Thanks to "Norwood's cave," the liability provisions in the House bill that went to conference were too restrictive for Senate Democrats. Instead of negotiating with Democrats for a cap on punitive damages to avoid a presidential veto, McCain would have to appeal to the White House to walk back part of their deal with Norwood, and the White House would have no incentive to do so. The president didn't have to worry about vetoing the bill. He could get Republican House conferees to hold firm on the liability provisions in the House bill, and let the conference end in a stalemate, which was just what occurred after the House passed the Norwood-Bush compromise legislation. McCain and Kennedy tried to negotiate an agreement informally with the administration, but the White House wouldn't budge on the state court restrictions, and the sponsors abandoned the effort for that Congress.

McCain was disappointed, but he didn't dwell on the defeat, confident they could resuscitate the effort in the second session or the next Congress. As involved as he was in the HMO debate and other issues that engaged his wide-ranging interests, his main occupation that year was getting campaign finance reform across the finish line after six years of obstruction and defeats. With the heightened public attention from his presidential campaign, and the addition of Thad Cochran to the list of eight other Republican supporters, McCain was confident he could bulldoze McCain-Feingold through the Senate that year. The deciding battle would be in the Republican-controlled House, where the bill's primary sponsors, Connecticut Republican Chris Shays and Massachusetts Democrat Marty Meehan, would have to overcome the opposition of Speaker Denny Hastert and Majority Whip Tom DeLay, whose nickname, "the Hammer," had been bestowed in recognition of his talents at strong-arming Republicans who strayed from the Republican consensus. President Bush had told McCain that DeLay had asked Bush for a commitment to veto the bill. Instead, the White House assumed a passive-aggressive approach to the debate: They wouldn't publicly oppose the bill, but they wouldn't support it, either, and would quietly cooperate with efforts to undermine it.

As he had promised in the meeting with the president and vice president, McCain gave the White House until March to figure out whether they would be a help or a hindrance. In the meantime, he ramped up his public campaign for the bill, giving scores of interviews on the subject, featuring it in almost every speech he gave, and conducting a series of televised town halls nationwide with Russ Feingold. To lobby for the bill, he helped form an umbrella organization—Americans for Reform—with Common Cause, the League of Women Voters, and other advocates. With no White House agreement forthcoming, his strategy was to pass the bill as quickly as he could. He wanted the Senate to act on it before the Easter recess in April. He figured the sooner it went to the White House, the harder it would be to veto. The president, he reasoned, would likely be stronger later in his term, further from his hotly contested election. He might not believe he had the political capital to veto a popular reform bill now, but who knew what he would do after he had a few legislative wins on tax cuts and education under his belt.

Republican leaders in the House would almost certainly bottle up the Shays-Meehan bill in the Rules Committee, from which, if they had their way, it would never emerge. It would take some time to force Hastert and DeLay to let them have a vote. It would probably require a rare discharge petition, which needed 218 signatures, a majority of the House, to force a bill out of Rules and onto the House floor. It had been nine years since the last successful discharge petition. Members of the majority, even if they supported a bill that was blocked in committee, were extremely reluctant to risk seriously offending their leadership by signing a discharge petition, knowing how easily an angry leadership could exact punishment.

As early as January, McCain began pestering Lott for time in

March for a debate and vote. Almost daily he queried Mark Buse, the long-serving McCain aide with responsibility for the issue, wanting to know if Lott had offered a date yet. Each time Buse told him, "Not yet," McCain made a point of going up to Lott at the next vote and lobbying him some more, and as was often the case when McCain was at his most intense and felt he was being stonewalled, his lobbying contained the implicit threat of trouble. Lott knew if he continued putting off debate, McCain could try to force a vote on the bill as an amendment to another measure. Or he could block leadership from bringing a different measure to the floor in retaliation. In a fifty-fifty Senate, as long as McCain had Daschle's and the Democrats' support for his procedural moves, which he did for the time being, he could stop consideration of any Republican bill.

Lott first offered him a vote in May with the promise of no filibuster. He would need only a simple majority if he would let the president's agenda take precedence until then. But there was little in the president's agenda that would be ready for floor debate and a vote before May, which McCain pointed out to Lott as he reiterated his insistence that McCain-Feingold be given floor time in March. Indeed, floor debate on Bush's tax cuts wouldn't begin until May, and his education initiative wouldn't be voted on until the end of the year. Lott eventually relented and gave McCain the last two weeks of the month, with debate on amendments proposed by either side limited to three hours.

The final iteration of McCain-Feingold contained—in addition to the ban on soft money—a prohibition on using corporate or labor union money sixty days before an election to run so-called issue ads, which mentioned a candidate's name and were actually electioneering ads. The sponsors of the bill assumed correctly that if soft money to the parties were banned, it would flow to independent expenditures instead. There was broad support among members in both parties for restricting third-party ads. Candidates not only don't like being attacked by entities in addition to their opponent, they don't always appreciate others running ads on their behalf, as those ads often contradict the message the campaign is trying to communicate. There was also widespread support for raising the hard-money limits that individuals were allowed to donate to a candidate. The thousand-dollar limit on a donation to a candidate in the primary and general elections had been set in the 1970s, and inflation had eroded two-thirds of its value. McCain and Feingold hadn't included a hard-money increase in the bill, but the sponsors were prepared to accept a higher limit in exchange for support on a soft-money ban.

In addition to opposition from the usual Republican-aligned interest groups such as the National Right to Life and the National Rifle Association, McCain and Feingold now had to contend with criticism from Democratic-aligned groups, the most significant being the AFL-CIO, which was vehemently opposed to the restrictions on "issue ads." Labor also wanted to preserve the use of soft money in state elections even if it were banned for federal elections. In truth, opposition among Democrats to campaign finance reform, including the soft-money ban, was substantial, if not as widespread, especially among Democratic Party campaign committee officials, consultants, and election lawyers. Bob Bauer, a leading Democratic attorney close to Tom Daschle, was outspoken in opposition to McCain-Feingold. Democrats raised as much soft money as Republicans did, and it was more important to Democrats, since they raised considerably less hard money from direct-mail appeals than Republicans.

McCain was sometimes caught off guard by the cynicism of politicians. But his equanimity during this final push for the bill never seemed disturbed by the discovery of a purported ally's bad faith. This was the rare bill that personally affected every member of Congress voting for or against it. If there had been a secret vote, the bill would have gone down in defeat one hundred out of one hundred times. He expected insincerity and even joked about it. "I don't know for sure where his heart is," he said to me about one Democratic ally when I first raised the possibility of hidden sabotage. "But his balls are on our side right now." He asked John Edwards to help defend the bill against Republican charges that it violated the First Amendment; Edwards readily agreed. When I reported to McCain that I had been sitting on the staff bench on the Democratic side of the Senate floor, and had overheard Edwards complaining to Daschle that McCain-Feingold was going to pass, he just laughed and said, "Figures," then told his very old joke about the difference between catfish and lawyers. Despite all the grumbling in the Republican cloakroom about McCain's ubiquity in the press, editorial support for the bill in the leading newspapers and his extensive campaigning for the bill in the media had much more impact on Democrats than Republicans. The latter are more used to being on the wrong side of *New York Times* editorials. Democrats aren't.

McCain was a little more upset when his friend, fellow Vietnam veteran, and one of four senators to have endorsed him for president Chuck Hagel worked with Karl Rove and other White House political aides on an alternative to McCain-Feingold that would have effectively gutted the soft-money ban. Even then he didn't get angry or remonstrate with Hagel; in fact, I don't think he bothered to appeal to him to back down or negotiate a compromise. "Why don't you?" I asked him. "Because he doesn't have the votes," he answered dryly. He later explained that all he wanted from Hagel was for him to bring up his amendment early. "Beating it will show guys on the fence the train is leaving," he added. "That's all I'm going to ask him. Bring it up soon." Again, he was confident of getting the bill through the Senate, sensing that the pro-reform political zeitgeist, the media attention, and his ability to influence events were all at their zenith, and there would never be a more propitious moment for reform. The real fight was in the House, he kept repeating.

Debate on the bill began on March 19. Chris Dodd, the ranking Democrat on the Rules Committee, which had jurisdiction for the issue, managed the debate for the Democrats, and McConnell, the committee's chairman, managed debate for the Republicans. McCain acted as sort of a third manager, the manager for the reform side of the Senate. At his instruction, I included in his opening statement tributes to both the president and McConnell. McCain instinctively grasped that the more unexpected the courtesy, the greater its effect. Though complimenting opponents won't stop them from trying to beat you, it makes it easier to get their cooperation on things that might not materially affect the outcome of a debate but can expedite it.

Whenever McCain was a leading player in a legislative debate, he was intense and hyperactive, seemingly wanting to be in the middle of every dispute and brokered deal. But he kept a steady strain throughout. I don't remember one time during the two weeks the bill was on the floor when he truly lost his temper. I don't even remember him snapping at anyone. He was sensitive to personal relations, hiding any hard feelings when a friend voted the wrong way on an amendment. He was savvy about the larger dynamics that gave reformers the advantage. He didn't overreact to setbacks or drop his guard when they won a vote. He pushed and prodded but mostly with good humor, smiling as he implored a colleague to offer his or her amendment or to accept a compromise and a voice vote. He convened daily meetings in the president's room off the Senate floor to plot the day's tactics, and to assign roles in the debate even to members he suspected were secret reform skeptics.

Despite his hyperactivity, he was sensitive to the potential drawbacks of letting the debate become entirely the John McCain show. Lowering his profile didn't come naturally to him, and he wouldn't cut back on media appearances that gave him an advantage in shaping public impressions of the debate. But he knew the more voices he enlisted in the debate, the harder it would be for anyone to desert the bill on the pretext that the other side's amendments had ruined it. By the end of the first week, Daschle was warning that too many changes to the legislation would "change its character." Schooled by the tobacco bill experience, McCain was alert to the possibility that the effort could be undone by his purported allies as readily as by his opponents.

He worried about the number of amendments making it hard to get to the final vote in the allotted two weeks. He seemed to physically will his colleagues to speed things up as they offered and debated amendments, as he paced the chamber within their eyesight, occasionally interjecting the suggestion of a shortcut to a resolution or urging managers to accept uncontroversial amendments without a vote. He preferred to take one or two of the toughest votes early, believing that if you beat back the first few dangerous amendments, it would discourage sponsors of other contentious amendments, a few of whom might decide against offering them.

McCain's biggest concern was an amendment he expected from McConnell to plant a fatal vulnerability in the bill, a non-severability clause, which meant if the courts found a single provision of the bill unconstitutional, the entire bill would be struck down. McCain had expected all along that some amendments to the bill would prove constitutionally dubious. The one he anticipated as the likeliest to draw judicial scrutiny was the so-called millionaires' amendment, expected from several senators, including his friend Mike DeWine, which raised limits on hard-money donations for candidates facing a self-financing opponent, as DeWine once had. McCain wanted the heart of the bill, the soft-money ban and the restrictions on corporate and union-funded independent expenditures, to survive challenges to other parts of the bill.

"They tipped their hand too early," McCain suspected, and he hoped greater media attention would make it harder for Democrats who secretly wanted to kill the bill to publicly drive a stake in it by voting for the non-severability amendment. He deployed his political operation led by Rick Davis and John Weaver, along with Mike Dennehy, who had directed McCain's New Hampshire primary campaign and now managed his political action committee, into what McCain believed would be the climactic Senate battle for reform. They flooded senators' offices, particularly Democratic senators' offices, with calls from McCain voters. They focused the energies of Reform PAC allies on rallying opposition among their rank and file, and from politicians who relied on their support. McCain made it clear in his media appearances that a vote for non-severability was a vote to kill reform. He would make the same point one-on-one to Senate Democrats, usually with a friendly "I really need you on this one" appeal, but sometimes, when he thought it useful, with a hint of menace in his approach that went something like: "There are no free votes on this one. If Mitch kills it again, we're going to make famous the guys who helped him do it."

Daschle committed to McCain that he would urge his caucus to oppose non-severability. He kept his word, identifying the vote on the amendment as a do-or-die test for campaign finance reform. We drew up a list of wavering senators in both parties, and Dennehy had the

PAC mass-email hundreds of thousands of McCainiacs, urging them to call the targeted offices. When debate on the amendment began on March 29, the lobby off the Senate floor was filled with reform activists. Bill Frist actually offered the non-severability amendment with John Breaux, one of the few avowed Democratic opponents of McCain-Feingold, but McConnell was believed to be the amendment's author. In a bid to give wavering senators a reason and disingenuous senators an excuse for voting for the amendment, McConnell had limited non-severability to two provisions, the soft-money ban and the independent-expenditures restriction. Now, Frist and McConnell argued, the bill's supporters needn't worry that a court finding a minor provision unconstitutional would toss out the entire law. McCain asked Fred Thompson to rebut his Tennessee colleague's argument, which he did effectively. So did other senators who had practiced law, including, somewhat to my surprise, John Edwards. Thompson made the case for how rare non-severability clauses were, suggesting its sponsors had not been motivated by a good-faith desire to improve the bill. McCain's argument was blunter: "If you are voting for this amendment, you are voting for soft money." Period.

Daschle worked suspect Democrats individually, and in the end, forty-five Democrats joined twelve Republicans in opposing the amendment. When McCain and Feingold left the floor together, they were greeted with loud applause from the crowd of reform advocates who filled the reception lobby outside the chamber. The first battle was over, although the vote on final passage wouldn't be held until the evening of the following Monday, April 2, after senators returned from the weekend. Fifty-nine senators voted for it and forty-one against, one vote shy of a filibuster-proof majority. McCain assumed Republican leaders had worked one or two Republicans to vote no and send a signal that they could kill reform with a filibuster if they didn't like the iteration that came out of conference with the House. Senator Hagel voted against the bill in the end, even though he and McCain had remained on friendly terms, and McCain had made a point of including him in negotiations over various provisions. If McConnell and others were trying to worry him that they still had the votes to block reform,

McCain didn't take it too seriously. "If they really tried to block it," he explained, "some of those no votes would've been a lot harder to get." The bill's sponsors and their staffs were in a celebratory mood, but just for that night. The hardest part still lay ahead, getting it through the House of Representatives, where the leadership has greater authority to impose its will, and individual members don't have the same power to cause trouble that a single persistent senator possesses if he or she isn't afraid to use it.

McCain assumed Tom DeLay would never agree to allowing the Shays-Meehan bill a vote. He liked Chris Shays a great deal, and trusted him, but remarked more than once that "Chris is too nice a guy." When Shays reported optimistic takeaways from conversations he had with Speaker Hastert and with the chairman of the House Rules Committee, David Dreier, McCain would bang the drum he regularly banged. Shays and Meehan would have to get 218 of the bill's supporters to sign a discharge petition and force the Rules Committee to send it to the House floor. They would never get a vote otherwise. "You have to hammer the Hammer," McCain repeated. Months passed with no progress on the bill other than an informal promise by Hastert that it was his intention to schedule the bill for debate after the July Fourth recess. McCain was frustrated by Shays's willingness to take the Speaker's word when everyone in town had heard reports of DeLay swearing he wouldn't let legislation leave the House that bore any similarity to McCain-Feingold. The sponsors' plan was to pass something so close to the Senate version that there wouldn't be a need for a conference committee to reconcile differences between the two measures. The Senate could just take up and pass the House bill.

McCain started having discussions with House Democratic leader Dick Gephardt, who promised his full support and agreed that a discharge petition was necessary. McCain didn't have a relationship with Gephardt, as he did with his Senate colleague Tom Daschle. He knew Daschle and especially some of Daschle's political advisors had reservations about a soft-money ban. He had counted on the media attention and the political appeal of reform proving a stronger inducement than Democrats' reliance on soft money, and he had been grateful when Daschle held the line in his caucus against non-severability. He suspected Gephardt, famous for his prowess as a fund-raiser and for his close ties to organized labor, might not be the most genuine of reformers, either, but again he trusted the politics of the issue to serve as motivation where idealism was lacking. As it turned out, Gephardt proved to be such a shrewd and diligent ally in the cause that McCain soon trusted him completely. Gephardt's good faith surprised some observers. Many House Democrats blamed McCain, who had campaigned for forty Republican candidates in close races in 2000, for saving the Republican majority in the House. Except for Tom Davis, who led the House Republicans campaign committee, no one in the Republican leadership credited him with the same. And some, including Hastert and DeLay, were angry that McCain reminded candidates he had campaigned for that they had committed to support campaign finance reform. Hastert accused him of "bullying" members. If Democrats believed McCain's support had been so beneficial to Republican candidates, perhaps Gephardt recognized the power of McCain's reform message.

Whatever brought Gephardt to the cause, his knowledge, political skills, and unaffectedness made a big impression on McCain, who considered Gephardt's help indispensable. He relied on Gephardt for advice on whom he should lobby among House Democrats, some of whom, as mentioned, resented his involvement in dozens of House races; others, susceptible to institutional resentments between the two legislative bodies, were offended by the thought of a senator big-footing their deliberations. Still other Democrats had more or less open reservations about banning soft money, especially in the influential Black Caucus, whose members relied on money from the party to turn out the vote in their districts. One member of the Black Caucus had already signed on to the Republican-alternative campaign finance reform bill that did not ban soft money, sponsored by Ohio congressman and chairman of the House Administration Committee Bob Ney. But another member, legendary civil rights activist John Lewis, would pledge his full support for Shays-Meehan. "More than any other group in Congress," Lewis told the *New York Times*, "we should be for reform, for a way to level the political process." Lewis would make a speech during debate on the bill that deeply affected McCain, who admired Lewis a great deal and insisted we include a chapter about him in the book about courage we wrote in 2003, *Why Courage Matters: The Way to a Braver Life.*

Various Democratic constituencies weighed in with reservations about the bill. In addition to the financial concerns of the Black Caucus, there were renewed objections from organized labor about restrictions on their advertising. There were also growing concerns among longtime reform advocates about increases in hard-money aggregate amounts, and about an amendment to McCain-Feingold that let the parties raise some soft money for state elections rather than campaigns for federal office that Carl Levin of Michigan had sponsored, and his brother, Representative Sander Levin, proposed to the House bill. Gephardt believed he needed to raise hard-money aggregates more than the Senate had to keep enough Democrats on board, and that soft money to state party entities would have to remain in the bill, causing liberal supporters and folks at the nonprofits with whom McCain and Feingold had long been allied—Common Cause, Democracy 21, and others—to balk.

Republican leaders, aware of the contradictory interests affecting the bill, had the Rules Committee, which sets the terms for debate, issue a rule that required the last-minute fixes devised by Gephardt and the bill's sponsors to be voted on individually rather than as one large correcting amendment. That would greatly increase the likelihood that the fragile coalition of supporters would come apart under the pressure of competing amendments. Gephardt realized the danger and told McCain the rule had to be defeated. That's an awfully big move against the leadership, a cardinal sin against the tribal traditions of the two parties, and Chris Shays had strong reservations about doing it. But McCain immediately accepted the necessity of it and urged Shays, who reluctantly went along, to accept the fact that for Shays-Meehan to succeed, its supporters would have to defeat Republican leaders, not persuade them.

Debate on the bill was scheduled to begin on Thursday, July 12, and conclude the next day. Davis, Weaver, and I put together a list of members for John to lobby. There was no hope of getting all Republican supporters of the bill to risk leadership's wrath by voting against the rule. But we needed about twenty. Gephardt believed he could deliver the rest. He would have to convince some of the Democrats who didn't support Shays-Meehan to vote against a rule that would make it easier to defeat it. He also had to help Shays and McCain convince Republican supporters of the necessity of defeating the rule. Getting opposition members to oppose the majority's rule isn't a huge lift, in the ordinary course of things; getting members of the majority to do it, even when they are on the opposing side of an issue from their leaders, is quite another thing. There was also the concern raised by some of the reformers that if the rule were defeated, Hastert would preempt debate on the bill indefinitely, which is what happened.

Shays tried cutting a deal with an annoyed but resigned Hastert that would have given leadership a face-saving way to back off the rule. But there wasn't enough time for Gephardt to vet the compromise with his caucus, while restive Republican conservatives, who hated the bill, didn't like Gephardt, and liked McCain even less, were threatening rebellion. In their rump caucus meeting, several of the louder mouths were heard excoriating McCain, as well as Shays, as traitors, but the abuse for McCain was more venomous. One of the abusers was McCain's Arizona colleague J. D. Hayworth, who had pleaded with McCain to help in his last campaign, which McCain had done generously. We got word of Hayworth's attack hours after he made it. I wrote an intemperate note to Hayworth's chief of staff to let them know we had heard, and there would be repercussions. He squawked about it to conservative journalists, which I should have expected. When I explained to McCain what I had done after one conservative writer had criticized me and him for threatening Hayworth, he had a one-word reaction: "Good."

DeLay convinced Hastert and the caucus to let the rule be defeated and then blame reformers for killing campaign finance reform for the year. The vote was 228 to 203. Gephardt delivered all but one Democrat. Nineteen Republicans voted with the majority. Most of the freshmen Republicans McCain had campaigned for had, under pressure from leadership, voted for the rule. Lindsey Graham told us that if you listened to conservatives in the caucus, you would "think McCain's first name was goddamn." Hastert pulled the bill from consideration, and dejected reformers pondered their next move.

There was really only one move left—force the bill onto the floor with a discharge petition, an action that would surely rile up leadership and conservatives even more than collaborating with Democrats to defeat the rule. McCain was ready for that fight. Some of his House allies weren't eager for another confrontation with leadership, although most of the bill's supporters accepted that it was probably the only way they would get a vote on it. McCain wanted to push the fight forward as much as possible, knowing that with every week that passed, more differences would crop up among various constituencies affected by the bill, which would necessitate more deal-making, which ran the risk of not just mollifying the complaining party but attracting new opponents. He hoped that at some point before they got to the magic number of 218 signatures on the petition, Republican leaders would relent and schedule the debate rather than suffer another public defeat. We gave McCain daily call lists to work through, urging the bill's supporters to sign the petition. He was mostly gentle in his persuasion. There was very little strong-arming involved. McCain knew that emotions about him were running high among conservatives, and many of the members he called had been exposed to it. "We're in the friend-making business," he repeated constantly, as if to remind himself he had already made all the enemies he needed. That didn't mean he pulled his punches in public against the enemies he already had. He was immersed in a fight, and as usual, he was enjoying it. He had a line he repeated often, which never failed to amuse him. He set the joke up by noting that a majority of Americans wanted campaign finance reform. The Senate had passed campaign finance reform. A majority of the House wanted campaign finance reform. But the response from House Republican leaders was "First Ney, then DeLay, then Doolittle." It was a play on the names of McCain-Feingold's top House opponents, Tom DeLay, Bob Ney, and

California congressman John Doolittle. Then he would chant it: "Ney, DeLay, and Doolittle. Ney, DeLay, and Doolittle," until he cracked himself up.

McCain increasingly relied on Lindsey Graham for intelligence on which member needed encouragement and about the temperature in the caucus regarding him. Lindsey can be blunt about what others would consider sensitive issues; once or twice, I saw McCain wince as he talked to him on the phone, and I assumed Lindsey had just shared another unflattering quote with him. Rick Davis and Trevor Potter, a former federal election commissioner and longtime McCain campaign counsel, helped organize the public lobbying campaign with the reform community. Some of the members McCain and allies had lobbied begged off on signing the petition until Congress returned after Labor Day. Two hundred signatures were deemed sufficient to convince supporters and opponents that the necessary number was within reach. By the time McCain boarded a flight for Arizona, the petition had 203 signatures. Finding the last fifteen would be a laborious one-at-a-time process, but few doubted it would be done. McCain told me before he left that he expected Shays-Meehan would be debated and passed before the end of September.

His prediction seemed certain to come true when seven more members signed the petition within a week of Congress's return. The day after the 209th and 210th members signed the petition, two passenger jets seized by terrorist disciples of Osama bin Laden destroyed the World Trade Center, another slammed into the west side of the Pentagon, and a fourth, following a struggle between passengers and their murderers, crashed in a field near Shanksville, Pennsylvania. The history-making tragedies would consume the attention of Americans and most of the world for months into the future. Congress, reminded that Americans' political differences were insignificant compared to the dangers we faced and the responsibilities we shared, focused most of its energies for the rest of the congressional session on working with the administration to respond to the attacks and prevent new ones from occurring. Compared to the urgency of those tasks, campaign finance reform was an occupation for a less dangerous time, although the public disclosure of the Enron scandal in October of that year was a reminder not to leave the job unfinished for long.

When Congress adjourned sine die in late December, the discharge petition was still three signatures short. The last three were secured just a few days before President Bush's State of the Union address. Hastert scheduled debate on the bill to begin on February 13, and it would conclude in the early-morning hours of February 14. McCain's objective was to help pass a bill in the House that was close enough to the Senate version that he could get it through the Senate intact, obviating the need for a conference, where hidden dangers would lurk. McCain tended to the public campaign with his usual crowded schedule of media appearances, while privately he was in the middle of several negotiations to find compromise solutions for clashes between competing interests among the bill's supporters. He was reluctant to do many public events on the House side, mindful of how his presence in the company of Gephardt had been used by Tom DeLay and others to provoke a tribal reaction. He decided he would remain in his Senate office during the debate and use the phone for any one-on-one persuasion. Gephardt and Graham convinced him he needed to be physically present to shore up shaky supporters in both parties and lend his approval to the few remaining deals that had to be brokered. Gephardt found a room on the House side of the Capitol, and McCain, with a small retinue of staff and political advisors, camped there for the next twenty-four hours.

Opponents filed various amendments intended to exacerbate fault lines among the bill's supporters, a few that would be hard for Republican reformers to vote against. One would have excluded the NRA from the prohibition on electioneering ads financed with soft money. The NRA is adept at intimidating politicians who dare to cross them, and it appeared for a brief time that the amendment might succeed, but it was narrowly defeated. None of the other amendments was as close. There were eighteen roll call votes in all. The Ney alternative was easily defeated. At 2:48 a.m. on Valentine's Day, 2002, the Bipartisan Campaign Reform Act of 2002 passed the United States House of Representatives by a vote of 240 to 189.

The bill was sent to the Senate, where majority control had transferred to the Democrats after the Jeffords defection. Daschle committed to passing the bill before Easter. McCain was confident there weren't enough votes to filibuster it, but he worked on recruiting a few new Senate supporters just in case. Later that same day, the Senate passed the House bill 60 to 40. Five days later, President Bush signed the bill into law in a small ceremony to which none of the bill's authors were invited.

The law would be subjected to repeated court challenges. After emerging intact from its first U.S. Supreme Court review in 2003 by a narrow 5 to 4 vote, subsequent court challenges filed after changes to the Court's political composition would significantly erode its impact. The 2010 *Citizens United* decision overturned the restrictions on corporate and union spending on electioneering ads. McCain was an observer in the Court during oral arguments for *Citizens United*. There he encountered lead counsel for the complainant, Ted Olson—who, as U.S. solicitor general, had successfully defended the bill before the Court in 2003—and accused him of hypocrisy. "What did he say?" I asked when McCain told me the story. "He said, 'I'm a lawyer,'" he laughingly recounted.

Those battles were far in the future. On the day of his greatest legislative triumph, McCain was subdued. He responded to President Bush's low-key signing ceremony with a low-key one-sentence statement: "I'm pleased that President Bush has signed campaign finance reform into law." He had been the driving force in a seven-year battle to pass a law that affected every person who voted for or against it, as well as the president who had signed it. He had done it over the formidable opposition of his party's leaders, objections from Republican-allied interest groups of considerable influence, and the disguised opposition of Democratic interest groups. But all that was in the past, even mere hours after the final vote. His influence grew even greater in the years after McCain-Feingold was enacted into law, a period of constant commotion for him as a legislator during which he seemed to play some role in almost every major Senate debate, discovering, he once said, that "the funny thing about political capital is the more you spend, the more you make." He had his nose in everything and an overworked staff to prove it.

The Enron scandal in October 2001 was followed by accounting scandals at Arthur Anderson, Global Crossing, Tyco, and other corporations. McCain called for the resignation of Bush-appointed Securities and Exchange Commission chairman Harvey Pitt and gave a much publicized speech at the National Press Club in July 2002, denouncing the scandals as "crony capitalism" and calling for stronger reforms than even those offered in legislation sponsored by the Democratic chairman of the Senate Banking Committee, Paul Sarbanes. "To love the free market," he argued,

> is to loathe the scandalous behavior of those who have betrayed the values of transparency, trust, contract and faith that lie at the heart of a healthy and prosperous free enterprise system and the patriotism that sustains an aspiring and confident free society.

He called for disciplinary hearings before an accounting oversight board proposed in the Sarbanes bill to be public, and for "executives who intentionally misstate their companies' financial reports" to "go to jail." He criticized exemptions to a Sarbanes rule to prohibit accounting firms from providing consulting services to companies they audit. And he made the case for stronger government oversight generally. "The current threat to our prosperity comes not from overregulation," he argued, "but from diffident regulation." President Bush had given a speech about the scandals a few days earlier. William Saletan, writing in *Slate*, compared the two addresses and the politicians giving them: "Where Bush looks for conscience and good behavior, McCain looks for a fight."[41]

Over the next two years, McCain would provide examples of the scrupulous government oversight he was calling for as he used his committee assignments to launch investigations into corruption that would trigger criminal prosecutions. The first example began with a routine McCain exercise. Staff had scrubbed the 2002 Defense Appropriations bill and given him a list of earmarks and examples of policy making that should have been left to the authorizing committee—in this case, the Senate Armed Services Committee, whose jurisdiction McCain zealously protected. He reviewed the list, asking routine questions about several items, and then paused when he noticed a $30 billion rider to lease from Boeing as many as a hundred 767s for the air force to use as refueling tankers. "What the hell is this about?" he asked an aide. "Not sure," came the reply. "Why lease them? Don't you think for this amount of money they could buy them?"

Those questions were the first of many. Initial digging by staff discovered that the tanker leases not only had not been authorized by Armed Services, they had hardly been discussed at all. The program wasn't included in the president's budget or in the list of unfunded priorities the Defense Department sends Congress every year. Finally, an "analysis of alternatives," typically prepared for acquisition programs of this size, hadn't been done. McCain's suspicions were raised by the program's abnormalities and his usual skepticism about unauthorized spending. Recognizing the need for scrutiny of something that Defense Department officials had gone to considerable lengths to slip past Congress was also attributable to the fact that his judgment was informed by decades of experience with defense spending. He could grasp in a glance that something was off about the earmark. Additional queries were met with silence from the senior air force procurement officer in charge of the acquisition, Darleen Druyun, who insisted that staffers and McCain himself sign a nondisclosure agreement before she would consent to briefing them on the program. That was a terrible mistake on Druyun's part. McCain directed Pablo Carrillo, a new Senate investigator and former New Orleans litigator, to find out what she was hiding. As it turned out, it was quite a lot.

The tanker leasing deal appeared to be on a fast track, and Pablo and his team worked against the clock to uncover how it had come into being. President Bush signed the Defense Appropriations bill into law, and air force officials began immediate negotiations with Boeing for a lease agreement that would cost taxpayers $6 billion more than if they had purchased the 767s outright and refitted them. Air Force Secretary Jim Roche sent a report on the deal to the four congressional defense committees, appropriators, and authorizers for approval. Although McCain was a senior member of Armed Services, he conducted his investigation from his perch as the Commerce Committee's chairman, which led Defense Department officials to mistakenly believe they could be unresponsive to him. Three of the four committees approved the lease after only a cursory review of the contract. McCain asked Armed Services Committee chairman John Warner to withhold approval until the Defense Department responded to his inquiries and demands for relevant documents. To his credit, Senator Warner agreed and allowed McCain to lead the investigation from the Commerce Committee in coordination with Armed Services.

Recognizing the mounting danger McCain posed to the deal, Boeing and its allies at the Pentagon undertook—through a small army of lobbyists and public affairs representatives—a public pressure campaign against McCain, which produced attacks such as "John McCain's Flying Circus," a *Wall Street Journal* editorial that appeared the morning of the committee's first hearing on the tanker lease in September 2003. The editorial either gullibly or disingenuously swallowed whole a Boeing–air force disinformation campaign. Central to that campaign were complaints about the age of the air force's existing tanker fleet and an alleged "corrosion problem" threatening their sustainability. McCain, the former military pilot, sensed that the corrosion concern was fabricated. He understood what the *Journal's* editors did not grasp, despite being self-proclaimed fiscal hawks. There was enough life left in the tankers that there was no urgency to replace them. It could be done in an ethical and fiscally responsible way.

McCain didn't flinch in the face of criticism, and there was a lot of it. When it came to fighting battles in the media, he was as experienced as any Boeing flack. He waged his own public relations campaign that proved more effective than the one waged against his investigation. He did scores of interviews on the subject, made countless statements, and shoehorned updates on the investigation into interviews and public appearances convened to discuss other topics.

In the end, the Commerce Committee investigation exposed one of the biggest defense procurement scandals in recent history. It demonstrated that the air force had invented the fleet-wide corrosion problem, grossly misrepresented the costs of the tanker lease contract, and used deception to avoid public and congressional scrutiny. It discovered that top officials in the Pentagon, the White House, and the air force general counsel's office had raised objections to the deal that were ignored by senior air force leaders. It also revealed that air force officials had colluded with Boeing to wage an aggressive public campaign against McCain's oversight. McCain's effort instigated investigations by the Defense Department inspector general's office, the General Accounting Office, the Congressional Budget Office, and the Congressional Research Service. The IG investigation found that the air force had let Boeing, which had been suffering a downturn in its business, write the specific requirements for new tankers to suit its 767s. Evidence that McCain's investigation helped to uncover resulted in Druyun's criminal prosecution as well as the prosecution of Boeing chief financial officer Michael Sears on public corruption charges. Druyun had gone to work for Boeing, and she and Sears had discussed her employment requirements while she was still overseeing the tanker negotiations for the air force. A Boeing vice president had purchased her home as well. In her plea agreement, Druyun confessed to overpricing the 767s as "a parting gift" to "ingratiate herself" with her future employer, and to help two relatives secure employment with the company. Both Druyun and Sears served prison sentences. Phil Condit, Boeing CEO, was forced to leave the company, which was ultimately fined over $600 million. Jim Roche, secretary of the air force, was cited for ethics violations.

The *Seattle Times* described McCain having "outmaneuvered Air Force brass and Boeing's 35 person Washington lobbying operation in a classic Washington power play and a media blitz worthy of Madison Avenue." A leading Washington government watchdog organization pronounced McCain's scrutiny of the tanker deal "congressional oversight at its best, something we rarely see anymore."

In his relations with Arizona's large Native American population, McCain tried to emulate Mo Udall's example and represent their interests conscientiously. He chaired the Senate's Select Committee on Indian Affairs in the 104th Congress from 1995 to 1997, and again from 2005 to 2007 in the 109th Congress. He was the ranking Republican on the committee for several years when Democrats were in the majority. He had ups and downs in his relations with the tribes, but on the whole, he was accepted by them as a friend to Indian country. One of my first off-hours trips with McCain was on a cold Saturday night in March 1990, to Gallup, New Mexico, where the alcoholism epidemic on the nearby Navajo reservation was on vivid display. On Saturdays, convoys of vehicles streamed off the reservation into Gallup, where the passengers purchased beer and spirits at convenience store drive-up windows and the bars that had proliferated in the town. The drunk tanks in the town jail were full by ten o'clock. On Sunday, when alcohol sales were banned, many Navajos remained in town and drank "Ocean," a toxic concoction of alcohol distilled from hair spray mixed with cheap fruit juice. Alcohol-related deaths were common occurrences. An intoxicated woman had given birth recently on a bar floor. McCain wanted to witness the problem for himself and write about what he had seen, so he brought me with him.

He was an active chairman of Indian Affairs, as he would be on other committees he chaired, and he was central in all major issues affecting Native Americans. He sponsored legislation to resolve land disputes, codify water settlements, boost tribal economies, and address alcoholism and drug abuse on reservations and various other concerns. Chief among them was the burgeoning Indian gaming industry, which he supported, sponsoring the Indian Gaming Regulatory Act of 1988 as a source of desperately needed revenue to impoverished tribes. During the years when he was bankrupting his Atlantic City casinos, Donald Trump was an outspoken opponent of casinos on Indian reservations, which he claimed were controlled by organized crime, an accusation that had less basis in reality than it did in Trump's hostility toward his competition. He repeated the charge at a 1993 House hearing, where McCain was also scheduled to testify, and Trump waited to buttonhole him. McCain walked briskly past the casino owner, pretending not to notice as Trump tried to get his attention. Frustrated, Trump shouted after him, "I gave money to your campaign." Looking over his shoulder, McCain yelled back, "Oh yeah? See what that will get you."

In February 2004, McCain read a front-page exposé by *Washington Post* investigative reporter Susan Schmidt, titled "A Jackpot from Indian Gaming Tribes: Lobbying, PR Firms Paid $45 Million Over 3 Years." The article's allegations concerned misconduct by well-connected Republican lobbyist Jack Abramoff and an associate, former aide to Tom DeLay Michael Scanlon. As the scandal developed, it would implicate prominent Republicans with ties to the Bush White House political operation and administration officials. McCain was chairman of the Commerce Committee at the time. When he finished reading the article, he called Pablo Carrillo, the committee counsel who had led the Boeing investigation, into his office and told him to start looking into the story. Then he went to see Ben Nighthorse Campbell, who chaired the Indian Affairs Committee, and got his authorization to investigate it.

The investigation lasted two years. Campbell retired in 2005, and McCain assumed the Indian Affairs Committee chairmanship. He convened five dramatic hearings, covered live on television, in which Abramoff, Scanlon, and others implicated in the scandal were called to testify. He subpoenaed 750,000 pages of documents and took sixty depositions to ascertain whether Abramoff and Scanlon had ripped off six different tribes, as alleged. The investigation exposed Scanlon as Abramoff's secret partner. Abramoff, who had lobbying contracts with the tribes, persuaded them to hire Scanlon as a "grassroots specialist" to handle public affairs as they sought casino licenses. The two men hatched a scheme they called "gimme five," in which they split many millions of dollars in kickbacks and grossly inflated fees and costs that they charged the tribes. Some of the contracts they landed were made possible by assisting the campaigns of winning candidates in tribal council elections. One of the more brazen abuses was a successful effort by Abramoff and former Christian Coalition leader Ralph Reed to persuade Texas legislators to shut down a casino operated by a tribe, to whom they then pitched their services in a multimillion-dollar contract to help them recover their casino license. In emails discussing his clients, Abramoff derided them as "morons" and "monkeys."

In the committee's opening hearing, McCain reminded listeners of the "long and lamentable chapter" in American history that concerned the exploitation of Native Americans.

> It began with the sale of Manhattan, and has continued ever since. Every kind of charlatan and every type of crook has deceived and has exploited America's native sons and daughters. While these accounts of unscrupulous men are sadly familiar, the tale we hear today is not. What sets this tale apart, what makes it truly extraordinary, is the extent and degree of the apparent exploitation and deceit.

The various swindles uncovered by the investigation were documented in a 350-page report. Criminal prosecutions ensued. Abramoff went to prison. Scanlon cooperated with prosecutors and avoided jail time by paying a nearly $20 million fine. A total of twenty guilty pleas or convictions were secured, including against two administration officials, one in the Interior Department and the other a procurement officer in the Office of Management and Budget, who were sentenced to prison. Bob Ney, former congressman and chairman of the House Administration Committee, was convicted of lying to John McCain's investigators and sentenced to prison. A prominent Washington law and lobbying firm where Abramoff worked was deluged with civil suits filed by cheated customers. McCain and staff had successfully navigated the shoals of what could have been a highly partisan investigation, implicating prominent Republicans in the biggest Washington scandal of the decade, enhancing McCain's reputation for integrity and as an independent power in Washington, and improving his prospects for another presidential bid. The newspaper *Roll Call* said the committee's investigation "set the standard for what congressional oversight should be, but often isn't."

In 2003, McCain opposed the administration's second round of tax cuts. He was open to using tax cuts to stimulate the weak economy, "but not at this time," he said in a Senate speech given two months before the vote and days before the United States invaded Iraq. The costs of the war in Afghanistan and the coming war in Iraq were "simply not knowable at this time," he explained. But what was "already clear to me is we will need to spend substantially more on our national defense in the long term than is currently envisioned . . . in the budgets being marked up by House and Senate budget committees." Considering the mounting costs of homeland security and the fight against Al-Qaeda, it was irresponsible, he argued, to support increased spending for purposes other than national defense or additional tax cuts.

A few months earlier, acting, as he'd promised he would, on the concerns conveyed to him by New Hampshire voters, he introduced, with Joe Lieberman, the Climate Stewardship Act of 2003. The bill would have mandated reductions of greenhouse gas emissions across major sectors of the U.S. economy, capping them at 2000 levels, and instituted a cap-and-trade system, allowing businesses to trade and borrow emissions credits to meet compliance levels. The bill was defeated in the Senate in October 2003. McCain and Lieberman sponsored a revised bill in the 2005 Congress, keeping most of the provisions of their original climate legislation and adding the requirement that the U.S. government play the leading role in researching new energy technologies, especially nuclear power plant designs. Over the objections of some environmentalists, McCain was adamant that support for nuclear power be an important part of any serious climate change remedy. That version of cap-and-trade was defeated on the Senate floor as well, by a wider margin than their first bill had lost. They offered their third and final version in 2007, which preserved the cap-and-trade credits and the government mandate for researching new technologies but required deeper cuts in emissions than the first two versions had. That bill never got a vote. It died in committee. Three serious efforts, each one more ambitious than the last, each one suffering a worse defeat than the last. McCain was as persistent as any member of Congress, and capable of playing a long game. But I think the course of his climate change bill raised doubts in his mind that there would be in the foreseeable future sufficient political support for a cap-and-trade approach to the problem, and it aggravated his disagreements with some parts of the environmentalist movement over nuclear power. Nevertheless, he continued campaigning for it throughout the 2008 presidential election.

In 2005, the Bush White House and Senate Republicans, who were returned to the majority in the same election that had reelected President Bush and were now led by new majority leader Bill Frist, were frustrated with the Democrats' obstruction of judicial appointment confirmations. Frist, encouraged by White House aides, threatened to resort to the "nuclear option," a change to the Senate's rules that would require only a simple majority to cut off debate on judicial nominations and not the sixty votes needed under existing rules. As the crisis neared a climax, Democrats had blocked or were blocking ten different nominees.

McCain was, for all his irreverence and independence, an institutionalist with a deep appreciation for the Senate rules that gave him and the other ninety-nine members of the body considerable autonomy. He was alarmed at the prospect of those rules being weakened to strengthen the power of the majority, and what he feared would be reactions from the minority that would launch a spiral of changes that could turn the Senate into a version of the House of Representatives. He jumped into the middle of the fight, stealing the initiative from Frist and the White House and recruiting thirteen like-minded members from both parties to solve a problem their leaders appeared likely to make worse. Republicans had a fifty-five-member majority, which meant six Republicans were needed to stop Frist from instituting the rule change. McCain convinced six Republicans and seven Democrats to join him in what became known as the Gang of Fourteen. The group's negotiations held the entire town in suspense, including the leadership of both parties and the White House. A main component of McCain's influence in the first decade of the twenty-first century and a major irritant to his detractors was his uncanny ability to dominate media coverage for every major activity he was involved in. During the Gang of Fourteen episode, camera crews camped outside his office and followed his every movement, an environment he treated as normal and in which he appeared completely at ease.

The Gang of Fourteen included several senior senators, chairmen, and ranking members of committees, and up-and-coming newcomers. But there was no doubt who led the effort. The negotiations took place in McCain's office. He suggested most of the elements of the compromise. The other members of the gang deferred to him. Former majority leader and Senate eminence Bob Byrd praised his leadership as "worthy of history's notice." In the end, they produced an agreement that freed all but one nominee. Three filibustered appointments had already withdrawn their nominations. In exchange for the seven Republicans' commitment to oppose a rule change, the seven Democrats committed to support filibusters only in "extreme circumstances," the definition of which was left to each gang member's discretion. The deal and its authors were celebrated in the media and by voters exhausted with partisan squabbling and gridlock, but excitable activists on the left and right considered them traitors to the cause.

Most of McCain's critics lived in Washington or New York, but their hostility toward him gave rise to wishful thinking among them that perhaps McCain, whom they derided as a RINO—Republican in name only—could be challenged from the right in Arizona. Stephen Moore, who ran the Club for Growth in those days, boasted he could raise $1 million from his members, who "loathe John McCain," for a credible conservative challenger. Their hopes focused for a time on persuading a new congressman, Jeff Flake, a thoughtful and candid libertarian, to run against McCain. McCain liked Flake, and the two of them would grow to be good friends, especially after Flake succeeded Jon Kyl as Arizona's junior senator. But the first favorable impression Flake made on McCain was when he responded to overtures from Moore and others, noting that, while he would like to be in the Senate, "after much soul searching, I came to the conclusion I'd get whipped." McCain, whose problems with Arizona's far right persisted, was nevertheless immensely popular in the state, and never more so than when he ran for a fourth term in 2004. No serious Republican primary opponent emerged for the very reason Flake gave: McCain would have whipped them. His problem with the base meant that a credible challenger could count on a quarter, maybe a third, of Republican primary voters; McCain would win the rest.

More to the point, at that time McCain had greater crossover appeal to independents and Democrats than any other living politician. Arizonans in both parties knew that. No experienced Democratic candidate challenged him that year. Stuart Starkey, a well-intentioned Phoenix public school teacher, volunteered for the job. After their one and only debate in Flagstaff, the McCains invited Starkey and his family to dinner. McCain was reelected that year with 77 percent of the vote. According to exit polls, he won over 70 percent of the Hispanic vote and a majority of Democrats.

In May 2005, McCain and Ted Kennedy, in consultation with the Bush White House, introduced their first iteration of comprehensive immigration reform legislation, the Secure America and Orderly Immigration Act. It had three major components: greater resources for border security; a temporary worker program; and a path for legalizing the status of the estimated ten to twelve million immigrants who had entered the country illegally or overstayed their visas. The path required undocumented immigrants who had been in the country for at least five years and hadn't committed any other crimes to pay a fine of two thousand dollars and any back taxes they may have owed; to learn English; and to wait another six years to apply for citizenship. The bill was referred to the Judiciary Committee, then chaired by Senator Arlen Specter. It emerged from committee the next year with its main provisions intact as the Comprehensive Immigration Reform Act, with Specter as the primary sponsor alongside McCain and Kennedy, and Republican senators Sam Brownback, Lindsey Graham, Chuck Hagel, and Mel Martinez as original cosponsors. On May 25, 2006, the Senate easily passed the bill by a vote of 62 to 36, with the support of the White House, the majority leader and whip, Senators

Frist and McConnell, and twenty-one of fifty-three Senate Republicans. Ted Kennedy, as the principal Democratic sponsor, kept his word time and again by voting with Republicans when Democrats proposed amendments that would have undone some of the compromises he had made. His good faith and good humor made a lasting impression on McCain, and deepened their friendship, which had grown close in the years after he and Russ Feingold received the Profile in Courage award. In a press conference with the other sponsors after the vote, McCain devoted most of his remarks to praise Kennedy, whom he called "the last lion of the Senate."

The House had passed an immigration bill the previous December known as the Sensenbrenner bill, named for its sponsor, House Judiciary Committee chairman Jim Sensenbrenner, which provided for improved border security but not a path to legalized status for undocumented immigrants. It would have made finding employment a little more difficult for them, but it otherwise left their status unaffected, which, McCain would constantly argue over the next seven years, was itself "de facto amnesty." The House bill triggered Latino protests that began in Chicago but quickly spread elsewhere, including to Phoenix. The demonstrations featured undocumented immigrants, including teenagers and twentysomethings who had been brought to the country when they were infants or toddlers, and were, McCain said, "as American as I am." He and the other sponsors of the Senate bill, including Kennedy, knew and were prepared to support a compromise bill in conference with the House that would have tightened border security and immigration controls even more than the House had approved already. They also expected to make more difficult the path to citizenship for the undocumented. But House Republicans rejected any path at all, and as a result, there would be no compromise measure emerging from conference.

McCain's positions on various domestic policy issues had irritated Republican establishment types, and his leading role after his 2004 reelection in Congress's attempts to pass comprehensive immigration reform would undeniably antagonize parts of the Republican base.

But the nation's attention, and his, was increasingly focused on the wars Americans were fighting. McCain's position as one of the most prominent national security voices in the country made him one of the Bush administration's most useful allies and one of its most influential critics.

WAR

"This is war," quoted in various accounts as McCain's first re-action to the September 11 attacks, isn't quite accurate. It's missing the indefinite article I remember him using. We were in my office staring at the television screen, he and I and a few other aides, moments after American Airlines Flight 11, which had originated at Boston's Logan Airport, struck the North Tower of the World Trade Center. It was nearly nine o'clock in the morning when McCain arrived in the office, late for him. He had flown back from an event in Boston late the night before and had decided to sleep in. He had heard the news about the North Tower on the radio as he drove to the Capitol, and he came straight to my office. We all assumed in that moment that the first plane strike had been a horrible accident. We were processing the magnitude of the disaster, like every other television viewer that September morning. No one said anything much, or anything memorable, anyway, just a handful of slack-jawed people trying to get our minds around what had happened. And then United Airlines 175, also from Logan Airport, slammed into the South Tower. I don't remember how much time elapsed—twenty seconds, maybe, or thirty, as we registered the atrocity with gasps—before McCain spoke, the first of us to say anything intelligible. "This is a war," he said in a low voice.

I'm not sure it makes a difference, "This is a war" or "This is war." I'm likely ascribing meaning to the phrase that he didn't intend. But I thought I caught a note of a question in his tone, and softness rather than a declaration, as if the enormity of the act—deliberately targeting civilians at a site with no military significance—had so transgressed the law of war that an attack pilot, who had dropped bombs on a power plant in the city of Hanoi, couldn't recognize it. I never asked him about it, probably because I expected him to laugh at me for reading nuance into the remark that hadn't existed. Still, when I think of our reaction in those first moments after the South Tower was hit, I always have a sense that we were both befuddled as well as shocked, and that the self-possessed "To arms!" quality of the declaration didn't accurately represent his state of mind.

If I'm correct, and he was in that instant perplexed, it was a momentary condition, as his attention quickly turned to what he should say about the attack and when he should say it. Should we hold off until we had more facts, or should he make a short statement condemning the atrocity and affirming the nation's resolve? As we were talking, we learned that another plane had been hijacked and had just hit the Pentagon. Soon after, we heard Capitol Hill police calling out in the hallways for everyone to evacuate the building, and we hurriedly finished our discussion. McCain decided on a short statement of condemnation and resolve. If he had any doubts in his initial reaction, they were no longer in evidence. He condemned "the enormity of these attacks" and declared that "These are not just crimes against the United States, they are acts of war." He had stressed in our conversation that he wanted to go on record insisting that our response not be solely the province of law enforcement and the intelligence services, but that America's armed forces would ultimately deliver justice to the people who had organized and enabled the attacks. We settled on the emphasis that they were acts of war. The statement closed with his assurance "We will prevail in this war, as we have prevailed in the past," and the invocation that God "make our justice swift and sure."

As I was emailing the statement to his press secretary, Nancy Ives, two fighter jets scrambled from Andrews Air Force Base crossed the sound barrier, and the resulting sonic booms sounded like explosions. Outside my office window, I saw people react to the sound by throwing themselves on the ground. Staff exchanged rumors about which government building had just been hit. Most of us felt our blood pressure spike, except McCain, who hardly reacted at all, either to the loud sound or the alarmed speculation about its cause that immediately ensued. While Nancy distributed the release, McCain and I made sure the rest of the staff left the office, then we left and eventually reconvened at Sonya Sotak's apartment. When the Fourteenth Street bridge across the Potomac was reopened late that afternoon, we went to my house in Alexandria, Virginia, taking I-395 past the burning Pentagon, black smoke rising from the debris, plane wreckage visible. "Jesus" was all McCain said as we stared at it.

By the end of the day, he had done over fifteen media interviews with national and Arizona news outlets. In all of them, he emphasized that the attacks were acts of war. After he heard that Phoenix officials had closed the city's schools, he started urging listeners not to panic, assuring them that the government had grounded air traffic and was taking other necessary precautions to keep people safe. The president had been visiting a school in Sarasota, Florida, when the attacks occurred. The Secret Service, fearing further attacks, thought it best to keep him out of Washington that day, mostly aloft in Air Force One. As news reports speculated about the president's whereabouts, McCain remarked to us: "All the Secret Service in the world couldn't keep me out of Washington right now. And I'd go to New York, too." That was unfair of him, he acknowledged to me a couple of years later as we were discussing our third collaboration, *Why Courage Matters*, and unrealistic. Bush was reported to have chafed at the decision to keep him away from Washington, as McCain would have if he had been president, but I doubt very much that he would have overridden the decision. Fear and confusion prevailed at the highest levels of government that day. Until the intelligence services and the military had greater confidence that the last threat of the day had ended at the hands of the heroic crew and passengers of United Airlines Flight 93, it would have been reckless to bring the president back to Washington. And it would have been irresponsible in the extreme for the president to have added to the burdens and confusion in New York, a city in ruins and chaos, where ashes covered the living and the dead. McCain would have understood that, no matter how much he barked about not being where the action was.

To McCain, action and leadership were almost synonymous. His desire to lead, to behave and be seen as a leader, was never more acute during the decades I knew him than it was in the days, weeks, and months after September 11. I would say it drove him to hyperactivity, but he was already hyperactive. Two weeks before the attacks, he had surgery to reduce an enlarged prostate. His doctor's orders to take it easy were forgotten in the urge to be relevant. He looked a little tired at the end of some days, but on the whole, he wasn't much the worse for wear as he hustled through his crowded schedule of interviews, meetings, hearings, and speeches.

He never said so, nor would he have acknowledged it if I had asked him (which I never did), but I'm sure he wished he were president then. I think he was envious of President Bush, heavy as his burdens were. History had come calling, and the president got to rally the nation's response. The first principle of McCain's brand of leadership and his general attitude to most crises was "Do something just as soon as you can." His heedless remark about President Bush coming back sooner to Washington was an expression of both his aspiration to lead and his bias for action. I think McCain would have been more deliberate if he were president. He was capable of caution, but his instinct was: Show people you're acting swiftly in an emergency even before you're entirely sure that what you're doing is effective.

In the policy battles and actual wars that followed September 11, McCain's natural sense of urgency was never more apparent, in part because he recognized that the national unity and spirit of bipartisanship in Congress engendered by the attacks presented a unique opportunity to get big stuff done. For the first time since he came to Congress, the two parties' weekly caucus lunches were held together that week. He knew that the comity wouldn't last forever. The closer they got to the midterm congressional elections the next year, the more partisanship would revert to the norm, and legislation would succumb to Congress's usual sclerotic pace. He asserted himself centrally into post–September 11 debates by his usual means, driving bipartisan legislative activity and dominating the media, which few members of Congress—even those in top leadership posts—did as effectively. McCain was again ubiquitous on television and radio and in print, one of the most prominent voices in the country as critical decisions were made about who and how we would fight the so-called war on terror, and how we would prevent other attacks.

He managed to involve himself in just about every major national security debate of the period. His accomplishments would prove more impressive than even his ambitious domestic policy agenda was over the same years. He joined those debates frequently as one of the administration's defenders and just as frequently as one of its critics. Early on, he had nothing but praise for the president and his cabinet, even officials he would eventually lose confidence in (such as Defense Secretary Rumsfeld) and those (such as Vice President Cheney) he would oppose in what he believed was a battle for America's exceptionalism. But in those first weeks and months, they were, as he told CBS's Bob Schieffer, part of "the strongest national security team ever assembled." The president's speech from the Oval Office the evening of September 11 had been "just what the country needed to hear," and his leadership since, "magnificent." McCain helped shape the Senate resolution authorizing the administration's use of military force in response to the attacks. But he played a critical role with John Kerry in getting language removed from the resolution that could have been construed as a blank check for the administration to take military action against entities that weren't involved in the attacks. They made certain the authorization was restricted to "nations, organizations, or persons [the president] determines planned, authorized, committed or aided the terrorist attack that occurred on September 11, 2001."

As the ranking Republican on the Commerce Committee, McCain helped put together a financial bailout for the airline industry, $5 billion in emergency assistance and another $10 billion available as loan guarantees. He was normally skeptical about spending public money for purposes that could be derided as "corporate welfare," and he had been critical of the airlines in recent years for consolidations that suppressed competition and for their often inconsiderate treatment of passengers. These were not normal times, however. The airlines, some of which were barely solvent before the attacks, were obviously essential to the national economy, and they had been staggered by the four-day nationwide shutdown and the continued reluctance of Americans to travel by air. McCain played his customary role of prodding the legislative process along faster than it typically proceeded, helping negotiate the bailout package with the White House—including telephone calls with President Bush and with House and Senate members—imparting his intensity to colleagues who were already working with a sense of urgency. The final bill was sent to the president just eleven days after the attacks.

McCain kept an eye on the $40 billion emergency disaster relief bill that included $20 billion for devastated New York City, which was passed within three days of the attacks, a blink of an eye in congressional time. McCain, the scourge of earmarks, feared that a bill of such size, passed with such speed, would prove an irresistible target for members seeking garden-variety pork barrel projects unrelated to the attacks. It took guts, though, to take a position that could be misconstrued as criticizing emergency relief for the places that had been devastated by the deadliest attack on American soil. But he was so offended by the idea of exploiting a national emergency of that magnitude for what he considered the pettier prerogatives of Congress that he risked it, and his vigilance helped keep the relief package reasonably clean of nonemergency spending.

His most important legislative work of the period focused on understanding how the country's defenses had failed and preventing it from happening again. In an appearance with Joe Lieberman on *Meet the Press* in October, McCain told Tim Russert: "I absolutely believe we have to go back and see what happened, not in order to hang somebody from the yardarm or disgrace anyone, but so we will not make the same mistakes again, . . . [and] do everything in our power to prevent a recurrence."

In December, he and Lieberman introduced a bill to establish the National Commission on Terrorist Attacks upon the United States, known thereafter as the 9/11 Commission Act. In his statement introducing the bill, McCain cited as models blue-ribbon commissions appointed after the Pearl Harbor attacks and the assassination of John F. Kennedy. Working closely with the families of 9/11 victims, and with clear public support for a commission, they overcame resistance from the Bush administration and congressional Republicans acting on its behalf. Lieberman got the bill through the Government Affairs Committee—which he chaired at the time—in March the following year, but a final iteration of the legislation wouldn't reach the president's desk until November. The administration had insisted on an eighteen-month time frame for the commission to investigate and report its conclusions, ending on May 27, 2004, so that any politically damaging conclusions would be disclosed over five months before the next presidential election. It was a concession that the legislation's sponsors accepted, knowing that the administration was threatening to create the commission by executive order, which McCain believed would make the panel not only less independent but less responsive to Congress's concerns.

To McCain's applause, President Bush originally appointed Henry Kissinger as chairman and former Senate majority leader George Mitchell as vice chairman of the ten-member commission, but both men stepped down within weeks out of concern for potential conflicts with their private work. Former New Jersey governor Tom Kean and recently retired chairman of the House Foreign Affairs Committee Lee Hamilton were then appointed chair and vice chair, respectively. McCain knew and respected both men and had close relationships with a number of the commissioners, as well as with members of the commission's staff, one of whom, John Raidt, had served as his legislative director and staff director for the Commerce Committee. McCain saw to it that the commission received the support it needed, both in time and in resources, and pressured the administration, publicly and privately, to allow access to all the classified information commissioners and staff believed they needed to form sound conclusions. "Every time we ran into a problem, he was there by our side," Kean remembered in an article published after McCain's death that described McCain as "adept at making backroom deals, and knowing just when to go public with a crucial demand."[42] McCain used much of the testimony he gave the commission in its first hearing to criticize administration stonewalling and warn that "Excessive administration secrecy on issues related to the September 11 attacks feeds conspiracy theories and reduces the public's confidence in government."

I remember how riled up he got in public and private conversations with administration officials and Republican congressional leaders whenever he suspected the administration of foot dragging. He wasn't surprised that Bush aides had wanted to deal with fallout from the commission report before the general election. Nor did he resent it. He was a politician, too, and understood the value of putting as much distance as possible between bad news and Election Day. But he was adamant that the commission be given the resources, time, and information it needed. "They're trying to run out the clock," he insisted when I suggested he tone down some of his comments to the press, "and I'll be damned if I'm going to let them."

The commission's public hearings would dominate the news, but they didn't begin until March, and they continued until June 2004. Commissioners and staff complained they were being stonewalled by officials, especially at the Pentagon and in the Federal Aviation Administration, if not outright lied to. Kean asked for more time and money to complete their work, substantially more than the $3 million originally appropriated. McCain and Lieberman made sure they got it. When they learned that Speaker Hastert, presumably at the behest of the White House, was working behind the scenes to block funding the commission needed to continue, McCain called the Speaker and asked him directly if that were the case. According to Lieberman, Hastert didn't confirm or deny it, provoking McCain to declare, "Denny, you know, I'll be as direct as I can with you: If our bill doesn't pass and that commission isn't funded, there's not another fucking bill from the House that's gonna go through the Senate, because I'm gonna object to everything." When an incredulous Hastert responded with something to the effect that McCain wouldn't dare do anything so extreme, Lieberman said, "McCain shot back with 'You're damn right I would.'"[43] I don't recall being in the room when that conversation

occurred, but I have no reason to doubt Lieberman's account. I overheard many like it.

While McCain pushed the 9/11 Commission bill, he was simulta-
neously working with Commerce Committee chairman Fritz Hollings
on politically complicated legislation to federalize airport security that
would establish the Transportation Security Administration. Administration officials and House Republicans in Congress preferred that
private contractors be hired to provide airport security, partly for fear
that the TSA would provide fresh recruits to public sector unions. But
McCain joined Democrats and some Senate Republicans in insisting that the security of the American people was the government's
responsibility and not one that should be dismissively relegated to
the private sector. He did not add "for political reasons," but he believed politics was the primary motivation for Republican opposition
to the federal government running airport security. While the White
House appeared willing to negotiate, the House leadership acted like
it wanted to fight. "They can't win," McCain maintained. "Try explaining that we won't make airports safer because we don't want the government in charge of the security. Try making that stick." His view
prevailed, but not without compromise. The Aviation and Transportation Security Act, which passed shortly before Thanksgiving in 2001,
established a three-year trial period during which the TSA, under the
U.S. Transportation Department, would run security at the nation's
airports. At the end of three years, Congress would reassess whether
private companies would assume the responsibility, and during the
trial period, TSA employees would not be entitled to all the civil service protections afforded other government employees. McCain took
the deal, and when the three-year period concluded in 2004, Senate
Republicans were in the majority, and McCain was again chairman
of the Commerce Committee with oversight jurisdiction for the Department of Transportation. Airport security remained a government
responsibility.

I'm sure that would have been the case had Hollings still been
chairman. He and McCain got along quite well. McCain's partnerships with the ranking Democrats on his committees were probably

the most productive he had in the Senate. He made a point of being honest and playing fair, being willing to compromise, understanding what was important to the other side in a negotiation, and "just being normal," he used to say, by which he meant as considerate as you would be if you weren't in politics. His small courtesies to Democratic counterparts were well known; they included scheduling hearings on subjects they were interested in, and letting them chair the hearing when he had to leave rather than handing the gavel to the next ranking Republican, which is customary. Things like that don't go unnoticed.

McCain's demeanor in the media was usually self-assured and relaxed, even if the message he conveyed was pointed or urgent. He spoke with authority, and especially in those days, he gave people the sense that he knew his business, knew what he was talking about. He spoke hard truths to the public in a way that didn't alarm but imparted resolve. The day after the attacks, he told a media scrum on the front lawn of the Capitol, "I say to our enemies, we are coming. May God forgive you. The United States will not." He gave his first Senate address on the attacks on Wednesday, September 12, contending that Americans were unified in common purpose "not just to punish but to vanquish our enemies." He spoke, too, of Americans coming together in love of our common values and in service to the nation founded on them. He urged Americans not to let their justified anger devolve into racial prejudice or religious bigotry. The following Monday, McCain was the only guest on a special broadcast of *The Tonight Show with Jay Leno*, an intentionally serious, not lighthearted, show. "We are a beacon of hope, liberty and freedom," McCain told the show's national audience, "to everybody . . . including Arab countries where the majority of people are good and decent and peace-loving." He went on to note, "No other nation on earth would react with the nobility that this nation reacted with; it's a sign of our strength and our greatness." Then he encouraged patience, explaining that it would take time to defeat our enemies, and firing a few cruise missiles wouldn't cut it. "But remember, our motive is not revenge. Our motive is to keep this from ever happening again."

On Friday, September 21, McCain, at Mayor Rudolph Giuliani's invitation, went to New York for the first time after the attacks to see the devastation for himself. The man who would succeed Giuliani as mayor, Michael Bloomberg, accompanied them to Ground Zero. McCain and Giuliani were veteran pols, demonstrative, at ease in crowds, voluble in conversations with strangers. Bloomberg, new to politics, hadn't the same demeanor. He and McCain became quite good friends; he would ask Bloomberg to be a pallbearer at his funeral. And Bloomberg would become a successful politician, an accomplished three-term mayor of America's greatest city, whom McCain admired as a leader as well as a friend. But that day, I could see him watch Bloomberg, skeptical that the businessman was cut out for politics. Bloomberg walked gamely behind them, speaking when spoken to, but otherwise quiet, observant, exhibiting a reserve the two extroverts rarely if ever possessed. McCain and Giuliani glad-handed their way past the ruins, holding their dust masks in their hands as they called out encouragement to emergency workers, stopping for handshakes and photographs, offering consoling words to people, some with tears in their eyes, who told them they had lost family or friends. When they walked onto the floor of the New York Stock Exchange, someone introduced McCain to a young trader who had lost his brother in the attacks. As others crowded in to greet them, McCain put his hand on the young man's shoulder and leaned in to whisper something to him. It was too noisy to hear what he said, but he took his time, and when he finished speaking, he pulled back and, extending his arm again, cupped the boy's face in his hand and kept it there while the kid wept. Everyone watching was affected by the scene.

The next morning, John and Cindy flew to California. He had been asked by the family of Mark Bingham, one of the passengers who had fought the terrorists for control of United Flight 93, to give a eulogy during his memorial service at UC Berkeley. Bingham had been a McCain supporter in the 2000 campaign and had met McCain at a San Francisco fund-raiser. John didn't remember him, but someone told him that Bingham had a photograph of the two of them prominently displayed in his office. McCain was very touched by that, and solemn as we talked about what he would say at the service. On the day of the

service, he struggled to get through his eulogy, which was characterized in various press accounts as "tearful." The terrorists on Flight 93
were believed to have targeted the White House or the U.S. Capitol. "I
love my country . . . but I cannot say I love her as well as Mark Bingham did," he said. Referring to the terrorists' plans, he acknowledged,
"I may very well owe my life to Mark. Such a debt you incur for life."
He nearly broke down when, looking at Bingham's mother, he told the
five hundred mourners, "To all of you who loved Mark and were loved
by him, he will never be so far from you that you cannot feel his love.
As our faith informs us, you will see him again, when our loving God
reunites us all with the loved ones who preceded us. Take care of each
other until then, as he would want you to."

From the outset, McCain made the case that to be a decisive war, it
would be a long one, possibly fought over decades. We could no longer fight terrorists half-heartedly or intermittently. If they were willing to commit atrocities that killed thousands, then they were willing
to kill tens of thousands, should they manage to get their hands on
weapons of mass destruction. He argued that Osama bin Laden and
Al-Qaeda had been emboldened by what they perceived as a lack of
resolve in the American reaction or inaction to previous attacks on
the marine barracks and our embassy in Beirut in 1982, the routine
kidnappings and assassinations of the period, Libya's destruction of
Pan Am Flight 103, the 1993 World Trade Center bombing, the Kho-
bar Towers bombing in 1996, and Al-Qaeda's attacks on our embassies
in Kenya and Tanzania, to which the Clinton administration had responded with ineffectual cruise missile strikes on mostly empty terrorist training camps. McCain told Bob Schieffer the war "wouldn't be
over if we got bin Laden tomorrow." His appeal to commit to the long
haul was partly for propaganda purposes, to discourage the enemy,
as he conceded in one interview. "The longer we tell them it's going
to take," he maintained, "the shorter it will be." It was an extension of
his argument during the Kosovo debate: "Never tell your enemy what
you won't do to win." Another purpose was to prepare the American
people: The country's morale and fortitude, he always believed, was
best served by giving people the hard truths.

Prior to September 11, when McCain was asked in interviews which national security challenges concerned him the most, he usually included on his short list of priority concerns "Muslim fundamentalism" fomenting terrorism and threatening the stability of the Middle East. But most of his focus in the 1990s was on the problems and opportunities associated with the end of the Cold War, the wars in the former Yugoslavia and NATO enlargement, principally, as well as on Latin America, Southeast Asia, North Korea, and, after he traveled to the country for the first time in 1997, on the human rights struggle in Burma. His main preoccupation in the Middle East was Saddam Hussein, who he believed had violated the terms of the Gulf War cease-fire by shooting at American planes patrolling no-fly zones over Iraq; had committed mass atrocities against the Marsh Arabs in the south and the Kurds in the north; and had a secret chemical, biological, and possibly nuclear weapons program. I don't believe McCain anticipated operations by Al-Qaeda or any terrorist organization anywhere close to the scale of the catastrophic attacks on New York and Washington. Before and after September 11, he frequently identified the lack of liberty and economic opportunity in the autocracies of the Middle East as the main drivers of alienated young men joining the ranks of the extremists. The assertion was more a feature of his evangelizing for democracy and human rights than it was an analysis of an imminent threat. Like most of the government and most of the country, he hadn't seen something like September 11 coming. But he had strong views about how we should respond to it.

"We have to change the way they see us," he said. He worried that America had acquired a reputation among our enemies for being irresolute despite the West's victory in the Cold War and the success of Operation Desert Storm. This he mostly attributed to Clinton administration policies he criticized as "vacillating, feckless," and to the impression that Americans had the stomach for only very short wars, as in Grenada, Panama, and the Persian Gulf. In a commencement speech the following spring, McCain talked about the mind-set that had encouraged bin Laden to attack us. "They believed liberty was corrupting," he said. ". . . Spared by prosperity from the hard uses of life, bred by liberty only for comfort and easy pleasure, they thought us no match for the violent, cruel struggle they planned for us. They badly misjudged us."

He believed our response to September 11 needed to confound that dangerous impression by being tenacious. He was on the lookout for signs that the Bush administration didn't share his resolve. Offensive operations in Afghanistan began on October 7, and McCain was outspoken in his support. But within weeks he was worried that Secretary Rumsfeld wasn't committed to the war against Al-Qaeda and their Taliban hosts that he believed was necessary. He thought Rumsfeld was trying to fight Afghanistan on the cheap, reluctant to commit a sizable infantry force to the battle, satisfied with SEAL teams lighting targets for bombers and cruise missiles, and forming tactical alliances with tribal opponents of the Taliban.

Near the end of October, McCain published an op-ed in the *Wall Street Journal* that began with an acknowledgment of the terrible costs of war and a warning not to fight it incrementally. "Our enemies harbor doubts that we will use force with a firm determination to achieve our ends," he warned. "We must persuade them otherwise, immediately."

He went on to maintain that destroying Al-Qaeda required the destruction of the Taliban as well, and toward that end, we should help with "air support and other assistance" the Northern Alliance and other Afghans who were "committed to the destruction of our enemies." He closed the piece with a widely quoted line: "War is a miserable business. Let's get on with it."

He had a network of advisors, in and out of government, who kept him well informed on the state of affairs in Afghanistan. It's fair to say that there was sensitivity among some political appointees in the Bush administration, especially in the first term, about confiding in John McCain. But McCain had to be reckoned with as a senior member of the Armed Services Committee whose opinion on national security issues was valued by the media. He also had relationships with military and civilian defense officials cultivated over years, some from as far back as his days as the navy's liaison to the Senate. It wasn't practical to try to keep him in the dark. He knew that most of the military's top leadership thought it would take a substantial ground force to achieve our objectives in Afghanistan.

Though McCain had been friends with Colin Powell for years, they didn't have much contact in the years Powell served as secretary of state. I'm sure there were a few conversations, but I don't remember any of importance in the first Bush term. We assumed Powell, no slouch when it came to navigating Washington's political shoals, was wary of appearing to Bush political aides as too chummy with McCain. He seemed to have delegated McCain outreach to his deputy, Rich Armitage. McCain didn't seem to mind (although he was amused when Powell called him out of the blue years later, as he was leaving office, to complain about the White House); Armitage was a friend, too, who regularly stopped by to brief him on developments in Afghanistan and elsewhere.

I liked Rich as well. We shared an enthusiasm for Georgetown University's men's basketball team and had seats very near each other at the arena where the team played its home games. At a game one Saturday afternoon in December 2001, a distracted-looking Armitage told me he was unsure about the outcome of a battle under way in the mountains of eastern Afghanistan. He provided no other details but told me to "let John know, it might be bad." He was referring to the ten-day battle in the Tora Bora region near the Khyber Pass. Kabul had fallen in November, and Kandahar the following month. Most of the remaining Al-Qaeda fighters were thought to be gathering in Tora Bora to mount what looked for a time to be the last stand. Osama bin Laden was believed to be among them, as were other members of the terrorist group's leadership. Tribal militias did most of the fighting, assisted by American airpower and American and British special operators who were helicoptered in, with designated targets for American bombers to strike. Though the actual number of Al-Qaeda fighters proved to be fewer than initially believed, and the cave complex where they sheltered less sophisticated and formidable than reported, bin Laden and the other Al-Qaeda leaders managed to escape and make their way through mountain passes to Pakistan. With only special forces teams and a few CIA paramilitary fighters, the U.S. didn't have infantry to secure the area around the terrorists' positions and prevent their breakout. The failure confirmed McCain's unease about Rumsfeld's light-footprint strategy, which relied on local proxy fighters, special forces, CIA paramilitaries, and American airpower. "He thinks he's avoiding the mistakes the Soviets made there," he told me, adding with a laugh, "He's hell-bent on making his own."

Although McCain had urged Americans to go on with their normal lives, he took offense at appeals from national leaders that urged only that. He thought they missed an opportunity to encourage greater volunteerism and commitments to military and civilian service in the swell of patriotism that often occurs during moments of national crisis. Years later, he was sarcastic in his criticism of leaders who limited their public pleas to exhortations to consume more: "We had a once-in-a-generation opportunity to call Americans to serve, and we told them to go shopping. Take a vacation. That's the spirit," he added derisively.

In the early years of his Senate career, he opposed legislation that created national service programs such as AmeriCorps, citing fiscal conservatism as his motive, and he supported amendments in subsequent appropriations bills that would have zeroed out funding for them. Writing almost a decade after those votes, he explained the concerns that led him and other conservatives to oppose new national service programs. "We feared it would be another 'big government program,'" he wrote in *Washington Monthly*,

that would undermine true volunteerism, waste money in "make-work" projects, or be diverted into political activism. We were wrong.

McCain the fiscal hawk gave way to McCain the national-greatness conservative, with patriotic appeals to strengthen civil society and serve causes greater than self-interest. "Americans didn't fight and win World War II as discrete individuals," he observed in the magazine.

Their brave and determined energies were mobilized and empowered by a national government headed by democratically elected leaders. That is how a free society remains free and achieves greatness.[44]

Even before September 11, McCain had come around to the idea that all Americans should have an opportunity to serve their country in some capacity. By the time of his 2000 campaign, he was an advocate for AmeriCorps and other programs. In the weeks after September 11, he exhorted audiences to "volunteer in your communities, join the Peace Corps, enlist in the army, give blood, do something. You and our country will be better for it." In 2003, at an annual convention of the AmeriCorps subsidiary City Year, he acknowledged his past skepticism and attributed his change of heart to "exposure to AmeriCorps, Peace Corps, and other volunteer organizations."

He and Evan Bayh of Indiana introduced the Call to Service Act, which would have quintupled AmeriCorps from fifty thousand participants to a quarter million, with half of the additional AmeriCorps members assigned to work in projects related to homeland security. McCain tried again with Ted Kennedy two years later. The bill also included a provision that offered military volunteers a short enlistment option, "18-18-18," an eighteen-thousand-dollar bonus for eighteen months of active duty and eighteen months of reserve. McCain was adamant that any national service plan should encourage military service as ardently as it encouraged civilian volunteers. He wanted to revive ROTC programs on college campuses and even talked about withholding federal assistance from schools that shut their gates to ROTC. "It's outrageous," he said, "that some colleges receive federal aid while forbidding access to an organization that protects our freedoms."

McCain advocated in both his presidential campaigns for a national service program open to all Americans with inducements to encourage participation. Libertarians denounced it as compulsory service or at least a big step in that direction, and in the 2008 race, liberal critics dismissed his advocacy as insufficient when compared to candidate Obama's proposals. But over the rest of his life, McCain maintained his commitment to expanding opportunities for national service. With Mike Bennet of Colorado, and the public support of retired general Stan McChrystal, he authored legislation to establish the 21st Century Conservation Service Corps, a public-private partnership that sought to enlist returning veterans and young Americans in the maintenance of public lands and waters. He wrote an op-ed with General McChrystal, describing the bill's national service choices for young people "as opportunities to elevate the nation while elevating themselves." They introduced the bill in 2015, in 2017, and again in 2018, a little over two months before McCain's death. It was signed into law in February 2019, after he was gone.

He took his first trip to Afghanistan with eight other senators, including regular traveling companions Joe Lieberman, Fred Thompson, Susan Collins, and Chuck Hagel, in January 2002, just a few weeks after Tora Bora. I didn't accompany him; I had stopped routinely traveling with him overseas by then, as my daughters were still young but nearing an age when they might start resenting my absences. I explained to him that I spent sixty or more hours a week in the Senate office, and our new book-writing sideline kept me busy after work and on the weekends. He was gracious about it, and said he understood, although I'm not sure he did understand. He wasn't disappointed by the request—more like confused. He couldn't understand why anyone would want to miss out on the interesting places and experiences to be found in the far-flung corners of the world. Though I still traveled overseas with him now and again, one of my chief regrets in life is that I did miss out on some memorable experiences abroad, and I never witnessed John McCain in the two places he traveled to most often for purposes that meant more to him than most, Afghanistan and Iraq. His recounting of that first Afghanistan trip made me wonder whether I might have overstated my preference for domesticity.

McCain, of course, had wanted to travel to the country weeks earlier. The Bush administration had resisted allowing congressional delegations in-country, which was perfectly understandable. They were a security headache, and you couldn't count on members of Congress to stick to whatever message the administration was emphasizing in public no matter how carefully you briefed them. You especially couldn't count on John McCain, who had his own opinions, informed by his own sources and his own knowledge, and constant contact with reporters. But he was irrepressible, and if he wanted to see the war he was expected to support, you could delay the inevitable only so long.

They flew first to Tashkent, the capital of Uzbekistan, where they met with Islam Karimov, the absolute ruler of the former Soviet republic from the dissolution of the Soviet Union to his death in 2016. The U.S. and our coalition partners in Afghanistan relied on an air base in southern Uzbekistan—Karshi-Khanabad, or K-2—for use in reconnaissance, logistics, and special forces missions to Afghanistan, so the U.S. mostly tolerated Karimov's despotism. At a press conference after the fact, McCain pronounced the delegation's meeting with the Uzbek president "excellent" and thanked him for his cooperation. Karimov would prove to be an especially brutal tyrant. His security forces were reported to have once boiled to death two political prisoners, and in 2005 they fired into a large crowd of protestors in the city of Andijan, killing hundreds. McCain would divert to Tashkent a CODEL he led to the region not long after the massacre, so he could hold a press conference there to denounce the atrocity and the oppression of the Uzbek people by their despotic ruler.

McCain had a thing about the "Stans," as he called them, which encompassed in his mind more than the countries with that suffix, and included other former Soviet republics Armenia, Azerbaijan, and Georgia. He had read histories of Central Asia, seen the exotic names of its cities in fiction and poetry—much of it from the nineteenth and early twentieth centuries—and was thoroughly intrigued. The first planning meeting for any McCain foreign trip began with him holding an atlas open on his lap as he recited names familiar to him from his school days. He once stabbed a finger at a point on a map of Uzbekistan and practically sang out the name "Samarkand," then proceeded to recite from memory the poem "The Golden Road to Samarkand" by long-gone British diplomat and poet James Elroy Flecker:

> We travel not for trafficking alone,
> By hotter winds our fiery hearts are fanned.

For lust of knowing what should not be known,
We take the Golden Road to Samarkand.

His peripatetic mother, Roberta, and her twin, Rowena, had visited Samarkand in 1999, and he had been envious. At some point in his life, McCain had acquired a fascination with the fourteenth-century Central Asian conqueror Tamerlane, remembered for the apocalyptic devastation his horde brought in its wake as he built an empire that encompassed parts of modern-day Iran, Iraq, Turkestan, Uzbekistan, Afghanistan, Syria, and Georgia; he had even occupied Moscow and invaded India. Tamerlane was born in Uzbekistan, and his tomb is there. McCain intended to visit it on a later trip to Uzbekistan. For some reason, although he returned twice to Uzbekistan, he never made it to Samarkand, to his eternal disappointment. After Karimov's death, he thought he might be allowed into the country again, and said to me about Samarkand, "I might get there yet, boy."

The delegation flew at twilight the next day to Dushanbe, Tajikistan, where they waited for nightfall and the arrival of an air force C-130 that ordinarily carried special forces teams in and out of Afghanistan. For security reasons, they had to fly at night to Bagram Airfield, forty miles outside Kabul, would be on the ground for less than six hours, and would depart for Pakistan in the early-morning darkness. There were no lights on inside the C-130; glow sticks were used for illumination. A quiet man dressed in black flew with them. He had an attaché case stuffed with cash and handcuffed to his wrist. "For the fuel," he explained. After a wild landing—the pilots having taken evasive maneuvers in anticipation of being fired upon—they reached Bagram a little before midnight. A convoy of Humvees drove them from the plane to the tent where they would be briefed by U.S. military and civilian officials, and meet for the first time with the Afghan in whom the U.S. and U.K. had placed their faith as the next leader of Afghanistan, Hamid Karzai. The Humvees passed men with long beards dressed like mujahideen, watching them. "Who are they?" asked McCain's aide, Dan Twining. "They're our guys. Special forces," an escort officer replied.

Years later, a still-animated McCain recalled his first night in Afghanistan with the zest of someone reciting a favorite adventure story. He said he had been captivated by the experience. They were seated on sandbags in "a tent in the desert night" when Karzai "appeared out of the darkness in his flowing robes. He turned out to be a prickly character, but you couldn't tell that night. He was charming. Spoke English with American slang, talked about his vision of a modern Afghanistan. He sounded confident and smart. He seemed like the right guy for the job. The setting was exciting, as striking, as it could be. The whole experience was kind of surreal and captivating."

McCain was well versed on the history of the country, particularly pre-twentieth century. He knew the stories of imperial powers that had come to grief "in the graveyard of empires," starting with Alexander the Great; then Great Britain's failed attempts to subdue the country, its army massacred in its first war there; and the Soviet Union's demise in the wake of its adventurism in Afghanistan. McCain didn't expect America's war there to last the two decades it has, although very early on he envisioned a relationship with a democratic Afghanistan that might include a small, more or less permanent, American military presence in the country, similar to our troops stationed in South Korea almost seventy years after the Korean War ended. Karzai proved to be a disappointment, a corrupt, venal, and unreliable leader. But that night, he convinced nine U.S. senators, including the history buff John McCain, that he had a vision of how to make a modern, democratic Afghanistan. A council of Afghan regional leaders selected him as president of a transitional national government the next summer, and he was subsequently elected president by popular mandate. His deficiencies became apparent pretty quickly, McCain acknowledged, "but I went to great lengths to continue getting along with him," he explained. "I managed to have a relationship with him where I could try to talk sense to him, pretty strongly sometimes, even if he spent the entire time complaining about 'you Americans.'"

The delegation departed for Pakistan while it was still dark, landing in some remote location that looked "like a moonscape," Twining recalled, and drove from there to Islamabad. They met with Pakistani president Pervez Musharraf and spent a long time discussing the campaign in Afghanistan and Pakistan's support for the U.S. military. Musharraf talked about the pressure he was under from extremists in Pakistan, and the risks he was taking with his personal security by supporting the U.S. military campaign in Afghanistan. We would eventually realize that Musharraf was playing a double game in deference to Pakistan's Inter-Services Intelligence (ISI), which wanted to protect their assets in the Taliban. But that night, both McCain and Twining told me, Musharraf came off as sincere in wanting to help us. And he was helpful to a considerable extent, especially in the early months of the war in Afghanistan, as evidenced by Al-Qaeda's multiple attempts to assassinate him, one of which would have succeeded had the U.S. not supplied him with signal-jamming technology that stopped a cell phone–triggered IED from blowing him up.

From Pakistan they flew by helicopter to the Arabian Sea, where the aircraft carrier the USS *Theodore Roosevelt* was on station. There McCain, by his own admission, did "a really fucking stupid thing." The news about it reached me and the rest of the world days before McCain returned to Washington and explained what he had done. Speaking on the deck of the carrier to an enthusiastic crowd of sailors, McCain got carried away and shouted, "Next up, Baghdad." I want to say he immediately regretted it, and he might have. But he certainly regretted it when the press reported the remark. "I look like an idiot, like I'm cheerleading for a war," he told me when he got back. When I responded by predicting that the incident would be quickly forgotten in the busy news environment, he said, "It will come back to bite me. Watch." And it did, after the invasion of Iraq, when it was discovered that Saddam Hussein didn't have the stocks of WMD that the administration and McCain had argued he had, and when the insurgency took hold and the war went south. Then McCain would wince at every reference to his gung ho performance on the *Roosevelt* that he saw in print or on television. I think what bothered him most was that he had always been careful before to talk about war, any war, in solemn and compassionate ways. He had always emphasized that wars, all wars, those he supported and those he did not, were unmitigated disasters. It would have been another thing if he were an officer rallying his troops for battle. "I'm a U.S. senator, for chrissakes. I don't get to fight them. I'm supposed to say if we *should* fight them." His visit to the *Roosevelt* occurred over a year before the United States invaded Iraq. We were still in the diplomatic phase of our conflict with Saddam; the administration and international community were pressing Saddam to give weapons inspectors access to suspect sites. It would be ten months before Congress passed an authorization for the use of force against Iraq. McCain should have kept his rah-rah routine focused on the war at hand, in Afghanistan, and he knew it.

McCain had advocated for military measures against Saddam well before September 11. He was one of the authors of the Iraq Liberation Act, which Congress passed in 1998 and President Clinton signed. The act cited Saddam's many transgressions against international law and agreements ending the Persian Gulf War; declared it was the policy of the United States to support regime change in Iraq; and outlined a program of support for Iraqi opposition groups. McCain believed the conclusions reached by U.S. intelligence agencies and by allied countries that Saddam had weapons of mass destruction—chemical weapons, surely, and probably biological weapons—and was trying to reconstitute his nuclear program. Saddam was behaving like a guilty man, too, refusing access to weapons inspectors no matter how many UN Security Council resolutions demanded it.

McCain also felt by then that the first President Bush had ended the first war with Iraq too soon. He hadn't felt that way at the time; on the contrary, he had supported George H. W. Bush's decision to suspend hostilities. But in the intervening years, when U.S. overflights were routinely fired at by Saddam's air defenses, McCain began to believe we should have demanded Saddam's removal from power, either by voluntary departure or forced overthrow, as a condition of a ceasefire. And he was sickened by brutal reprisals against popular uprisings in Iraq that had been ignited by Saddam's defeat, especially the Marsh Arabs in southern and eastern Iraq.

Finally, McCain believed—and believed until his death, despite evidence to the contrary—that a liberated, democratic Iraq in the heart of the Arab world "could strike a blow as great as any force of arms against extremism and despotism in the Middle East." Some might interpret that mentality as an example, a costly one, of McCain's stubbornness. He could be a stubborn man, there's no disputing that. But he believed first and foremost that freedom protected by governments derived from the consent of the governed was the natural aspiration of all people. The right to choose for yourself the direction of your life, to express yourself freely, to worship God as you saw fit, to follow your own ambitions—all were aspirations that inhabited every human heart, "and from there they cannot ever be wrenched," no matter the kind of culture you lived within or the hostility of regimes that suppressed your rights. He thought freedom and democracy were communicable conditions, and Iraq could be the example that inspired the transformation. He felt that way before the Arab Spring and after, when, in one country after another, the promise of freedom heralded by the popular uprisings in the Middle East was corrupted and crushed.

He and I were talking over dinner once about the tragedy of Syria, which preoccupied him the last seven years of his life. I asked whether he thought things might have turned out differently in Syria if Iraq had become a functioning democracy and pluralistic society. "It still might," he replied. "Why do you think Assad and the Iranians are trying to make sure it doesn't? It's the only way out of Iraq's misery. It's the only way out of Syria and Iran's misery, too." He wasn't referring to the chaos and dislocations often associated with the transition from autocracy to democracy, but to the anger and despair afflicting the populations of Middle Eastern autocracies, where "generations of young people have no opportunities, no hope, no future."

All those reasons aside, the war was fought on the grounds that Saddam had weapons of mass destruction that he would not relinquish, and in the age of 9/11, that posed an unacceptable threat. Whatever other purposes he hoped to achieve by getting rid of Saddam, McCain, too, had made the WMD threat the basis of his support for the war. When it turned out there were no WMD, and the ramifications from the mismanaged war began to materialize, it was incumbent on supporters of the war to acknowledge it had been a mistake, a very costly one. McCain was reluctant to do that publicly. He wasn't eager to concede it privately, either, but he did. He never argued that the war hadn't been a mistake, and he conceded that it had been when pressed. But in his mind, the way to compensate for the mistake was to prevent compounding it by losing the war, so he focused his attention on that. I remember a conversation I had with him years after I had left his staff in which he was critical of President Obama's decision to withdraw all U.S. forces from Iraq. I agreed with McCain, but I also observed that the politics of keeping troops there "were impossible considering most of the country has believed the war was a mistake ever since they found out there weren't WMD there." "Of course it was a fucking mistake," he shot back heatedly. "But so is pulling everybody out after all they did to stop the place from falling apart completely." We discussed the subject of Iraq again when we were working on his last book, and he told me: "Put in there that it was a mistake, and I was as responsible as anyone else for it."

McCain wouldn't return to Afghanistan until August 2003, on the same trip that took him to Iraq for the first time and opened his eyes to the fact that the war in Iraq, contrary to the assurances of political and military leaders, was not nearing its conclusion; it was becoming a debacle.

He had been a prominent supporter of the October 2002 resolution that authorized the use of force against Iraq, and which cited the Iraq Liberation Act he had cosponsored as one of its premises. Five months elapsed between passage of the authorizing resolution and the start of Operation Iraqi Freedom. As U.S. forces staged for battle and the world tensed for a war that looked increasingly inevitable, McCain worried that the wait would exhaust the public's patience and adversely affect the military's morale. Some U.S. allies, France chief among them, opposed the decision, as had a minority of Senate Democrats and a majority of House Democrats. By the war's start, a solid majority of Americans expressed support for it, but that hadn't been the case in the fall, when the resolution was passed. There was also opposition within the administration, critically from the State

Department. Despite his famous UN Security Council speech asserting Saddam's possession of WMD, making the case in February, Colin Powell had argued internally against the decision, and leaks that he remained a skeptic were common. McCain was invited to the White House to discuss Iraq early in 2003, before Powell's UN speech, and was seated next to Vice President Cheney. He asked Cheney if Powell, who was also in the room, was on board with the decision or still arguing against it. Cheney confirmed it was the latter, and he asked McCain, "Could you talk to him?" On the day the invasion of Iraq was launched, McCain said on the Senate floor: "The wait is over. The liberation of the Iraqi people is under way, and the world is witnessing the end of one of the most horrible regimes in history, and with it, the end of the threat Iraq for too long posed to its people, its neighbors, and the world."

By the time McCain arrived in Iraq in August 2003, the swift defeat of Saddam's regime had been followed by looting and general lawlessness, intensifying sectarian hostilities, and an incipient Sunni insurgency, as the U.S. seemed unprepared for the challenges of being an occupying power. The general commanding the invasion, General Tommy Franks, had retired and been replaced by Lieutenant General Ricardo Sánchez. President Bush had flown to the USS *Abraham Lincoln*, where he announced, "Major combat operations in Iraq have ended. In the battle of Iraq, the United States and our allies have prevailed." Secretary Rumsfeld was describing the armed opposition in Iraq as "a few dead-enders." The Coalition Provisional Authority (CPA) head, Paul Bremer, had cashiered the Iraqi army and issued his edict that former Baathists could not serve in the new Iraqi military or the government. The public had been informed that no weapons of mass destruction had been located in Iraq, and it no longer appeared that they would be.

McCain traveled to Iraq in a large House and Senate delegation that was not allowed to remain in the country overnight. They traveled to three cities over three days and returned each night to Kuwait City. They were meeting in Baghdad with Bremer and Defense Department official Walt Slocombe, whom McCain respected, when they heard an explosion. An Al-Qaeda operative had driven a truck bomb into the lobby of the Canal Hotel, which housed the UN headquarters. The UN mission was led by one of its most able diplomats, Brazilian Sérgio Vieira de Mello, who was killed in the blast. McCain described to me his first and subsequent impressions of Iraq as "grimmer, more depressing," than Afghanistan. The Shia and Sunni politicians he met with were all "dour" and "suspicious" and "angry." Only Kurdish officials had seemed to him "open and trustworthy." He had a bad feeling that Iraq was on the verge of total disarray, he said, before the delegation went to Basra in the Shia south, where they witnessed widespread dysfunction and lawlessness and were briefed by a British colonel who convinced McCain "our strategy was the opposite of what we needed there."

McCain talked for years about that colonel and British soldiers based in Basra, about the impression they had made, and how much he admired them. "Every day they leave their base and engage with locals who are pissed off about power outages, no water, and garbage everywhere, no work." He couldn't remember the colonel's name, which is odd, since he claimed he could quote verbatim whole passages of the colonel's bracing presentation. "'I'm going to tell you the truth,'" he said the colonel had begun. "'No one with stars on their shoulders will tell you what I'm going to tell you. No one at CPA or coalition headquarters. You're in their chain of command. You're not in mine. I won't see any of you again. So I'm going to tell you the truth.'

"You could tell the guy had just had it," McCain recalled, "the place was going to hell and we weren't doing what had to be done, and he was sick of the bullshit." The colonel documented the myriad problems—economic, security, and infrastructure—afflicting the Iraqis, then announced "We're not winning" to the wide-eyed American politicians. He went on, "These people are prepared to give us the benefit of the doubt for a limited period of time if we improve their lives. If we don't, they'll turn against us like they've turned against everybody else who's occupied this country. They're already starting to." When McCain asked how long he estimated it would be before the situation was irreversible, he answered, "You have four to six months. After that you'll lose."

The whole performance was riveting, McCain remembered. He had admired the officer's style as much as he admired his candor. "He was an impressive character. Didn't suck up. Didn't bullshit," and he drove home that "the strategy we had was doomed to fail." He was referring to the policy that kept coalition forces on their bases, venturing out for quick missions at night looking for bad guys and weapons, while we trained a new Iraqi military and Iraqi police force and mostly left local populations to fend for themselves in the ruins of their communities as Sunni insurgents or Shia militia fought for control. "We need to protect these people, give them security and a decent environment to live in," the colonel said. After returning from Iraq, McCain began immediately to spread the colonel's warning in speeches, interviews, and editorials, calling for a switch to counterinsurgency tactics. He warned against drawing down our forces, insisting that the war was far from over. He heard some months later that the British colonel had cut short his tour. It was unclear whether he had done so voluntarily or been summoned home, but McCain suspected the latter. He also heard that CPA or coalition headquarters had ordered that no future congressional delegations were to receive briefings from British soldiers.

By November, McCain was arguing strenuously to "deploy at least another full division" to Iraq, "to conduct a focused counterinsurgency campaign across the Sunni Triangle that seals off enemy operating areas, conducts search-and-destroy missions, and holds territory."

He told me he thought General Sánchez would have welcomed more forces. "He didn't say that to us, but he gave me the impression that he knew he didn't have enough, that they were facing a real insurgency and could be overwhelmed." But Sánchez was gone by the following summer, replaced by General George Casey, who would command coalition forces in Iraq for almost three years, until he was replaced by General David Petraeus in February 2007. Casey was as opposed to a counterinsurgency and increased force levels as was the man who recommended his appointment, Secretary Rumsfeld. "The longer . . . U.S. forces continue to bear the main burden of Iraq's security," Casey argued, "it lengthens the time that the government of Iraq has to take the hard decisions about reconciliation and dealing with the militias."

McCain traveled to Iraq at least twice a year while Casey was in charge, and with each trip he said, "the security situation had worsened noticeably since the last time we were there." He often talked about how, in 2004, he could walk unescorted by security back to his hotel from a meal in a restaurant without fear that he would be "shot, kidnapped, or blown up." By 2006, "our plane had to do a corkscrew landing, we were driven everywhere in armored vehicles, and we had to wear Kevlar."

Sunni insurgents—religious, secular, and foreign jihadists—had launched an offensive in the spring of 2004, attacking U.S. forces in dozens of locations all over Anbar Province. The first battle for Fallujah occurred during this time. Marines experienced the most difficult urban fighting of the war, trying to clear the city building by building, until the Iraqi government protested the high casualties and prevailed on the coalition to agree to a cease-fire. Sunni insurgents were gaining ground in areas outside Anbar as well. In Shia strongholds, Muqtada al-Sadr's Mahdi army battled the U.S. for control. By November, the marines were back in Fallujah and successfully cleared the city of insurgents, but at the cost of very high casualties. Near the end of the year, Casey announced he had ordered coalition forces to concentrate on training the Iraqi army, which henceforth would do most of the fighting. The downward spiral accelerated, and by 2006, Iraq, in McCain's opinion, was on the verge of being "a hopeless cause." Al-Qaeda had bombed the Al-Askari mosque in Samarra, one of the holiest Shia sites in the country, and the Shia reaction turned the sectarian conflict in Iraq into full-scale ethnic cleansing. Bodies littered empty Baghdad streets. Casey turned security over to the Iraqi army and the recently elected Maliki government for every province except Anbar, which was almost completely controlled by Sunni insurgents. As he became more and more frustrated, McCain's exchanges with Casey were increasingly confrontational. Every time they met, McCain would ask Casey—each time more incredulously, since the situation had obviously become even more dire—did he now need more forces to restore control? Invariably, Casey answered in the negative, and "it drove John crazy," recalled Lindsey Graham, who witnessed many of the exchanges. "It's all falling apart," McCain told me when he returned from one trip, the only time he appeared on the verge of despair during his years of intense involvement in the war.

As soon as he returned from that first trip to Iraq in 2003, he started assembling a network of people who shared his view of the war and agreed with the necessity of switching to a counterinsurgency approach to the conflict. His associates included Lindsey Graham and Joe Lieberman; Fred and Kim Hagan, military historians at the American Enterprise Institute; Ken Pollack, a former CIA analyst; Andy Krepinevich, who wrote an influential essay in *Foreign Affairs* that made the case for counterinsurgency; and several retired flag officers, led by the former vice army chief of staff, General Jack Keane. They provided McCain insights and arguments that he made publicly and privately with administration officials he hoped to persuade, forming a counterinsurgency plan for Iraq that looked a lot like the basic elements of David Petraeus's counterinsurgency plan, which would be known as "the surge." Critically, the group was also a source of encouragement for McCain. They gave him a sense of fraternity, that he wasn't fighting a lonely battle with no chance of success as the situation in Iraq grew bleaker; also, they were working contacts in the administration.

They all knew that the first step to getting the president to change directions in Iraq was to "get Rumsfeld out at DoD." By the end of 2004, McCain began stating in press interviews that he had "no confidence" in Secretary Rumsfeld's leadership. When pressed on if he wanted Rumsfeld fired, he would respond, "That's up to the president," and then repeat that he had no confidence in the secretary of defense, hoping that the president was listening. He chastised Vice President Cheney, who was seen as Rumsfeld's main supporter, for saying in early 2005 that the insurgency was in its "last throes." Asked to comment, McCain advised waiting "until we achieve the successes, then celebrate them."

McCain also resisted attempts to intimidate or punish outspoken opponents of the war. When Natalie Maines, a member of the popular country music trio the Dixie Chicks, told a London audience days before the Iraq invasion that she was ashamed to hail from the same state as the president, the group was besieged by criticism and banned from country music radio stations. It was a stupid remark, but it's a free country, McCain believed. When he invited the CEO of the radio chain that had shunned the group to testify to the Commerce Committee on the issue of new media ownership regulations, he chastised the CEO for violating the Dixie Chicks' rights. "To restrain their trade because they exercised their right of free speech is remarkable," he contended. "If someone offends you," he continued, "and you decide to censor those people . . . the erosion of our First Amendment is in progress." For good measure, he tossed in a warning that "it's a strong argument about what media concentration has the possibility of doing."

In March 2004, John Kerry approached McCain with a hypothetical offer of the vice presidential nomination, not as a Democratic convert or an independent but as a Republican, in what would be billed as a unity ticket comprised of two Vietnam War veterans. Kerry later claimed to have been encouraged by McCain advisor John Weaver, who denied it and claimed Kerry had approached him. I remember being intrigued by the novelty of the idea when McCain told me about it, and by its validation of McCain's national stature. But I didn't believe McCain would or should seriously consider the idea. Neither did he. When he recounted their first conversation, McCain stressed he had made clear to Kerry that the idea was unworkable. They were too far apart politically, disagreeing on too many issues. "I said if something happened to him," he told me, "Democratic voters were going to be pretty surprised how big a Republican they had made president." There were additional calls from Kerry to McCain and to a few people who had John's ear. I know Kerry called Cindy, and their mutual friend Warren Beatty, and me. I assume he was also in contact with Weaver; some person or persons were regularly leaking word of the discussions to the media. In at least one conversation with McCain, and possibly in others, Kerry had promised to give John a substantial role in national security policies should they end up running together and getting elected, even entertaining the idea of nominating McCain as secretary of defense.

When Kerry called me, it was late at night, and I had already gone to bed. I like and respect Secretary Kerry and am always happy to talk with him. But I laugh when I recall him asking if he had woken me, and I replied yes, and without skipping a beat, he proceeded to talk for ten minutes or so, pitching me on the idea. I was polite but non-committal and just wanted to get off the phone as quickly and courteously as I could. I sensed that Kerry assumed I would be an obstacle, or someone had told him that I'd advised McCain against the idea. He ended the call by asking me to keep an open mind and saying we would talk again. I hadn't advised McCain one way or another. I didn't need to. He was as skeptical as I was. He had made the thing worse in a television interview at the height of the speculation, when he said he "would obviously entertain it." He had prefaced the declaration by dismissing the speculation: "It's impossible to imagine the Democratic Party seeking a pro-life, free-trading, non-protectionist deficit hawk." But Kerry was a friend, he explained, and out of friendship, he would listen to him. That's all he meant, but it set off a flurry of press calls to the office. I told McCain that I thought I should slam the door on any further Kerry-McCain fantasizing, and he agreed. I called a reporter for the Associated Press with a one-sentence declaration: "Senator McCain will not be a candidate for vice president in 2004." The hubbub died down after that, although it would be resurrected when McCain started running for president again three years later.

Two months after the Kerry VP controversy subsided, a rapprochement was achieved between feuding Texans Karl Rove and John Weaver, with Mark McKinnon, President Bush's media strategist, acting as intermediary. McCain told Weaver to let Rove and other Bush operatives know he would be happy to campaign for and with the president. He had several reasons for extending the offer: He was worried the publicity surrounding the discussions with Kerry had damaged his standing with Republican voters. He had not decided on another presidential run, but he wanted to demonstrate his Republican bona fides to preserve the option of running at least until after the coming election, when he would give it serious consideration. He also wanted to have more influence with the White House on national security issues, especially on Iraq. He wouldn't refrain from criticizing the administration's mistakes in the execution of that war, or from stating his disagreements on other issues. But he thought he could keep the disagreements from getting personal if he proved his commitment to the president's reelection. He knew he had something of value to trade—his unmatched popularity with independents, who could decide the outcome in swing states. He believed, too, that he and Bush would draw closer if they traveled together, which was typical of him, with his unshakable belief in the road's magical, friendship-forming properties.

The odd thing about him was that he never seemed to worry that criticism—even persistent, sharp criticism of a fellow politician's actions or policies—would prove a barrier to friendship, as long as you kept things generous and lighthearted in your private dealings. Months after their first campaign swing together, we heard that the president was irritated by McCain's continued criticism of Rumsfeld, whose strategy in Iraq was the thing McCain most wanted to persuade Bush to reconsider. But you took what you got from John McCain. His offer was welcomed, and he did everything asked of him with enthusiasm, while he continued to speak his mind on subjects important to him, no matter who he displeased.

Their first joint appearance was in June at Fort Lewis, near Tacoma, Washington, where McCain introduced the president and extravagantly praised his leadership in the war on terror. From there they flew together to a political rally in Reno, where McCain again introduced and praised the president. Before they left for Reno, Bush and McCain met separately with wounded soldiers and the families of soldiers from Fort Lewis who had been killed in action. Both men were reported to have wept.

Their next campaign swing together was in August, and it occasioned a greeting that became notorious. McCain had joined the president in Pensacola, Florida. The two approached each other on an

airport tarmac with arms extended. The hug that was captured in photographs was instant fodder for late-night comics, an irresistible metaphor for reporters, and, according to McCain, "the dumbest fucking
shit I've ever had to deal with." The shot was snapped in an instant
when McCain's face was awkwardly pressed into Bush's shoulder, and
their arms were wrapped around each other. A split second before or
after, the camera might have captured a more dignified embrace. One
reporter called it "one of the odder embraces in American politics
since Sammy Davis Jr. hugged Richard Nixon." But the hug had been
simply a natural expression of each man's genuine unreservedness.
It was so trivial a thing to McCain. Had they hugged in private, he
wouldn't have remembered it five minutes after the fact. "They act like
it was some kind of big moral choice I made. It was a fucking hug, for
chrissakes," he complained.

On the same campaign trip, McCain repeated his earlier condemnation of a controversial ad that disparaged John Kerry's service in
Vietnam, sponsored by an independent organization of Vietnam veterans who called themselves Swift Boat Veterans for Truth and included several former POWs, including Bud Day, one of McCain's
dearest friends in the world. The ad was produced by the same political
media team that made McCain's ads, Stevens, Reed, and Curcio. When
he'd first seen the ad a week or so earlier, he had released a statement
forcefully criticizing it and calling on the White House to disown it.
He'd followed up by doing an interview with the Associated Press re-
emphasizing his disgust. He thought Kerry's anti-war activities were
fair game, although he didn't consider them much of a vulnerability;
but questioning Kerry's heroism in the war "crossed a line," he told
me as he dictated the statement he wanted released that day. He didn't
hold the president responsible for the ad, he told the AP reporter, but
he thought Bush's campaign should denounce it just the same. Hours
after the hug, reporters again pressed him on the appropriateness of
the ad. McCain called the ad "dishonest and dishonorable," as he had
in his statement, and answered "yes" when asked if the White House
should condemn it. He was talking to reporters on Air Force One at
the time, while the president stood next to him. That made news, of

course, but his condemnation of the Swift Boat ad would be mostly forgotten in time. A year after the campaign, McCain and Bud Day, who loved each other, were still squabbling about the Swift Boat ad at a restaurant in New Orleans. Their back-and-forth was pretty testy and made two reporters who observed it uncomfortable.

McCain had a high-profile role in the Republican National Convention that year, speaking in prime time on Monday night, doing interviews and making appearances before delegates and donors wherever the Bush campaign asked him to. In his speech, he had full-throated praise for the president's leadership and talked movingly about the war and the Americans who were fighting it. He didn't take a single shot at Kerry. He did numerous other campaign events for the president's reelection that year. The Bush campaign's political director, Terry Nelson, called him "our most important surrogate." After the election, when both men were returned by the voters to Washington, residual tensions between White House and McCain staff appeared to relax, as did some of the press's fascination with the subject. But an improvement in personal relations—the "era of good feelings," as an anonymous McCain associate described it—didn't prevent McCain from speaking his mind, publicly and privately, when he opposed an administration policy or disagreed with an administration official. He continued to criticize Rumsfeld and argue for more troops and counterinsurgency in Iraq. And in 2005 and 2006, McCain fought two of his most contentious battles with the administration, clashing with an array of national security professionals in the CIA, the National Security Council, the Justice Department, the Pentagon, and the office of the vice president.

In April 2004, *60 Minutes* and investigative reporter Seymour Hersh, writing in the *New Yorker,* broke the news, complete with shocking photographs, about systematic abuses by the U.S. Army military police who guarded prisoners at an Iraqi prison twenty miles outside Baghdad called Abu Ghraib. Around the same time, CIA inspector general John Helgerson completed a confidential review of CIA interrogations of captured terrorists, and his conclusions, which were kept classified for five years, found that interrogators were complicit in the death of at least three detainees. He referred to the Justice Department eight instances of homicide and severe mistreatment. His report warned that intelligence gained from mistreated detainees was unreliable, and the techniques used to coerce them was likely a violation of the Convention against Torture.

The Senate Armed Services Committee convened a hearing a little over a week after the *60 Minutes* broadcast. McCain was stunned by the disclosures, as were the other committee members. "I shouldn't have been," he said. He faulted himself for not paying attention to how detainees were being treated, citing his support for the war and his experiences as a POW as reasons he should have been vigilant. He knew he had moral authority to take on the issue that no other senator possessed, and he started exercising it at the hearing.

Secretary Rumsfeld was scheduled to testify first on a panel with the chairman of the Joint Chiefs; the army chief of staff; the deputy commander of CENTCOM, the combatant command with authority for military operations in the Middle East; and several other Defense Department officials. McCain, Richard Fontaine, his foreign affairs aide at the time, and I had discussed the day before how McCain should question Rumsfeld. McCain suspected the military would try to confine their response to punishing the MPs who had committed the abuses, and issuing reprimands to officers in their immediate chain of command in Iraq. He wanted to know if "their sadistic behavior . . . had been influenced by instructions from or the example set" by U.S. officials interrogating the prisoners at Abu Ghraib. He also worried that the guards and those right above them in the chain of command were emboldened by the negligence of senior officials who should have been explicit with orders on the treatment of prisoners and watchful that they were carried out. "If all we end up doing is throwing a few knuckleheads in the brig, this shit is going to happen again and again," he predicted.

Normally, I would have advised McCain on his demeanor in the hearing. We could see how fired up he was, which sometimes meant he was going to come off too heated and bullying as he sought answers from a witness he believed was being evasive. The hearing was carried live on all the cable news networks. We expected Rumsfeld to be evasive. He had a technique, honed in exchanges with reporters, of giving answers to questions he hadn't been asked to avoid answering ones he had been asked. I knew it drove McCain crazy. But we figured if he didn't emphasize through aggressive questioning how important the matter was to Congress, no one else on the committee would, either. McCain anticipated that Rumsfeld, who would be seated on a panel with five other witnesses, would try to defer as many questions as he could to his associates, and he was determined not to let him. I don't remember actually advising John to "go get him," though another McCain advisor said I had. I think I said something like "Keep cool, but don't let him wiggle off the hook." I needn't have said it. He did keep his cool, but he was dogged and pointed. He didn't register as angry or beside himself. He appeared exasperated at times, which was exactly the right way to appear in response to Rumsfeld's evasiveness.

McCain's first question was a simple one, a setup for more pointed follow-ups. He asked Rumsfeld to explain the chain of command from the MPs to their most senior military and civilian superiors. Rumsfeld replied that he had ordered a chart depicting the chain of command, but an aide had left it at the Pentagon. General Lance Smith, the deputy CENTCOM commander, tried to intervene with his own description of the chain of command. McCain cut him off, curtly instructing him to "submit it for the record," and returned his attention to Rumsfeld. "What agency or private contractor was in charge of the interrogations?" he asked. "Did they have authority over the guards?" Rumsfeld cleared his throat and referred again to the missing chart that he wished he had at hand so he could be accurate in his responses to the senator. Committee chairman John Warner asked General Smith to answer, but McCain stopped him. "Secretary Rumsfeld, with all due respect, you've got to answer this question," he instructed. "This is a pretty simple, straightforward question. . . . What agencies or private contractors were in charge of the interrogations, and what were their instructions to the guards? This goes to the heart of the matter."

Rumsfeld started speaking words that were so muddled you suspected he was being deliberately incomprehensible. Again Smith jumped in, risking McCain's wrath, but McCain let him speak. He said the commander of the military intelligence brigade had responsibility for the interrogators and "tactical authority" over the guards. McCain turned to Rumsfeld and asked why he couldn't answer fundamental questions he should have been prepared to answer. Then he pressed him again for the instructions that had been given to the guards. Rumsfeld kept demurring, but McCain wouldn't let it go. Finally, Rumsfeld offered that the guards had been instructed to follow the Geneva Conventions.

McCain's grilling of the defense secretary got quite a bit of media attention. Within days of the hearings, the office began to receive a number of unsolicited calls and emails from people with credible information about interrogation abuses, some of which had resulted in the deaths of detainees. Most of the calls went to Fontaine, although the senator's military legislative assistant, Chris Paul, was contacted by a few purported whistleblowers. Fontaine had worked on the National Security Council prior to coming to the McCain office. He knew about the CIA's black-site rendition program and briefed McCain about it; the *Washington Post* broke the story of the black sites the next year. News reports of abusive interrogations were starting to appear, as was information about the so-called torture memos prepared by various Justice Department lawyers to justify the CIA's use of abusive interrogation methods that McCain and others would denounce as "torture," especially the most sensational of them, waterboarding. McCain knew all about waterboarding. He knew it had been used by the Japanese in World War II and by the Khmer Rouge in Cambodia, and he was revolted by the thought that Americans in the twenty-first century would resort to what he characterized as a "mock execution" and "exquisite torture." "They're supposed to have a 'shock the conscience' standard for judging these things," he complained. "Waterboarding doesn't shock their conscience? Well, it sure in the hell shocks mine."

He was already talking to a few colleagues about doing something legislatively that would prevent further violations of the Geneva Conventions when he received a letter from a captain in the 82nd Airborne Division, a West Point graduate who had served in both Afghanistan and Iraq. Captain Ian Fishback had reported abuses of prisoners by soldiers in his division to his chain of command and waited seventeen months in vain for a meaningful response. He asked Tom Malinowski at Human Rights Watch, who had worked with McCain and McCain staff, for an introduction, and Tom had him write to Richard Fontaine. Fontaine gave McCain the letter, and it made quite an impression on him. Fishback wrote that the conduct of his superiors had "led me to believe that United States policy did not require application of the Geneva Conventions in Afghanistan and Iraq," and he chronicled his many unsuccessful attempts "to get clear, consistent answers . . . about what constitutes lawful and humane treatment of detainees." He closed by declaring that he "would rather die fighting than give up even the smallest part of the idea that is 'America.'" McCain must have quoted that line hundreds of times, it so moved him. He met with Fishback soon after and promised that he was working on legislation that would address the issue, and he would see to it that "you get the answers you seek, the answers you have not just a need but a right to know."

That legislation was the Detainee Treatment Act of 2005, which McCain introduced with Lindsey Graham and John Warner. It had two main provisions: The first enjoined all members of the U.S. Armed Forces and Defense Department civilian employees to adhere strictly to standards prescribed in the Army Field Manual for treating captured enemy combatants, standards that are completely in accord with the Geneva Conventions. The second provision—the most contentious, as it turned out—was a simple instruction to all other agencies of the federal government, including the CIA, to refrain from treating any prisoners, no matter their nationality or location, in "cruel, inhuman or degrading" ways.

Opposition from the administration was intense, mostly driven by the CIA and Vice President Cheney. DCI Porter Goss and Cheney asked to see McCain shortly after he had introduced the resolution. They met in the secure facility in the basement of the Capitol, where Goss described some of the enhanced interrogation techniques (EITs) the CIA had employed and Justice had signed off on, soft-pedaling their severity to a skeptical McCain, whose personal experience of some of the techniques made it hard for Goss to pull the wool over his eyes. They also maintained that the techniques were responsible for getting intelligence from bad guys that had led to the capture or death of bigger bad guys. That turned out to be bullshit, though McCain wasn't then in a position to dispute it. But when they coupled the claim with an insinuation that the resolution as written would have the effect of keeping some of said bad guys at liberty to kill more Americans, McCain got angry, suspecting that every other claim they had made was dubious.

He told me many times that the most important thing he had to remember to keep himself from going insane during the period when he was regularly mistreated in prison was that if the positions were reversed, if he were the interrogator and his captors were the prisoners, he would never treat them the way they had treated him. Americans would never torture their enemies. In essence, that was his notion of American exceptionalism. He believed Americans are obliged by our founding ideals to respect the dignity of every human being, even our enemies. That's the origin of the much publicized formulation he used to summarize his views on torture: "It's not about them, it's about us." I didn't suggest the line to him, nor did anyone else I know of. It came from him, I believe in an interview he gave around this time, and it expressed the deepest political conviction he held. America is different, it's an ideal, a universal ideal worth serving and suffering for, and we keep faith with it by our actions and our restraint.

Before the meeting ended, Cheney aide David Addington handed McCain a revised resolution that would have exempted only the CIA from the prohibition on cruel, inhumane, and degrading treatment, thereby rendering the resolution pointless. Cheney continued to lobby Republicans to oppose it, mostly unsuccessfully. Eventually, the president called Cheney off and delegated his national security advisor, Steve Hadley, to negotiate with McCain. Fontaine had worked for Hadley and told McCain the move signaled that the president was ready to compromise. Hadley signed off on the resolution after McCain and his cosponsors agreed to a few minor changes to the text, and it passed the Senate in December as an amendment to the Defense Appropriations bill by a vote of 90 to 9.

Despite the huge Senate majority in support of it, the White House released a statement from the president when he signed the bill that effectively declared he was not bound in all circumstances to obey its restrictions. When McCain heard that, I thought for a moment we were going to have another donnybrook with the White House. He was upset, not only as the author of the bill, but because Congress had clearly spoken, and he believed the president was obliged to respect it. Although he publicly expressed his disappointment with the signing statement, and complained about it privately in rougher language, he managed not to let it get out of hand and disrupt the progress he hoped to make on other issues with the administration, particularly on Iraq. He told us we had to look for another way to "make them give it up." "Give what up?" I asked. "Waterboarding," he answered, "and whatever else they're doing that will destroy our reputation."

Common Article 3 of the Geneva Conventions prohibits the abuse of prisoners of war, including "violence to life and person . . . [and] torture." It also forbids "outrages upon personal dignity, in particular humiliating and degrading treatment." In 1999, Congress had amended the War Crimes Act, making violations of Common Article 3 a war crime. In June 2006, the U.S. Supreme Court announced its ruling in *Hamdan* v. *Rumsfeld*, which, among other things, held that Common Article 3 governed our treatment of Al-Qaeda prisoners. The Court also ruled that detainees had the right of habeas corpus to challenge their detention. The administration had to come to Congress for authority to establish military tribunals they hoped could satisfy the habeas ruling, and to circumvent what administration officials never admitted—but clearly believed was now the case—were the prohibitions of the CIA's enhanced interrogation techniques under Common Article 3. Their solution was to get Congress's help in weakening the prohibitions by revising the article.

McCain was incensed by the notion. Although the American POWs in Vietnam were refused Geneva Convention protections by their captors, the POWs frequently invoked them in their day-to-day struggles with the Vietnamese, and they were sacrosanct to McCain. He would fight any attempt to weaken them. We worried that the necessity for congressional action after the *Hamdan* ruling regarding habeas would make it harder to prevent the administration from acquiring the authorities McCain hoped the Detainee Treatment Act had denied them. So, while he was infuriated by the administration's intention to undermine Common Article 3, he knew he could lose a showdown vote in the full Senate on an administration proposal if the practical effect of defeating it left *Hamdan* unaddressed. Congress had to act, so McCain committed to negotiating with administration officials. His goals were to prevent any changes to the Geneva Conventions, and stopping the further use of interrogation techniques he believed violated them. In exchange, he was prepared to accept protections for administration officials against prosecution for the past violations.

The ensuing negotiations and dealmaking consumed all of Fontaine's time and much of McCain's and mine. McCain had so many irons in the fire that summer and fall that he couldn't devote all his attention to the issue despite its importance to him. The administration initially focused its discussions with him on the establishment of military commissions to address the habeas problem. But McCain was more intent on protecting the Conventions, and he deferred to Lindsey Graham, an air force JAG lawyer, and his Arizona colleague Senator Jon Kyl to negotiate the terms of the military commissions.

The administration dispatched rotating casts of officials to lobby him to change his mind about the morality and efficacy of the EITs, all to no avail. Once they brought in a young officer who had waterboarded one or more detainees. He assured McCain that the technique was safe and did no lasting harm to the detainee. Neither Fontaine nor I was at the meeting. When McCain debriefed us later, he said he had responded to the officer politely but firmly, "Son, it might be safe, but it's still torture, and with all due respect, you don't have any idea what lasting harm you might have done."

Occasionally, in our discussions with administration officials about potential legislative fixes, McCain, as well as Fontaine and I, got bogged down in the details of proposals. We weren't lawyers, and the administration's lawyers knew it. But every time they thought they had steered McCain in their direction, he would ask if what they had proposed still required changing the Geneva Conventions. When they answered in the affirmative, McCain invariably gave them a one-word answer: "No." He would not permit so much as a comma being moved in Common Article 3, and in our separate discussions with administration officials, Fontaine and I kept that as our bottom line as well.

At one point, CIA Director Michael Hayden asked to meet with Fontaine and me in the Capitol's Sensitive Compartmented Information Facility, the SCIF, I assume because he suspected we were advising McCain not to accede to the CIA's requests. It was, of course, the other way around. We took McCain's unconditional refusal to accept changes to the Conventions as our instruction. It was one of those occasions, and there were many of them in my years with John McCain, when I found myself wondering how in the hell I had wound up in situations where the director of Central Intelligence would ask to meet with me and spend an hour very agreeably trying to change my mind, or where senior White House officials and even one or two presidents knew me by name. I hadn't the experience, the intellect, or the political skills to mix with such company, and as exciting as that could sometimes seem, it was more often the case that I had to suppress feelings of insecurity. But something in McCain's regard for me, and mine for him, encouraged me to think I could keep the masquerade going indefinitely.

Fontaine and I couldn't give Hayden any cause for hope that McCain would come around to his point of view, and answered every idea floated in the meeting by reiterating McCain's bottom line: There could be no alterations to Common Article 3. After that, Hayden gave up lobbying McCain and McCain staff. Hadley and Bradbury led the negotiations, which continued off and on for weeks and culminated in an all-day-and-into-the-evening session in a Senate hearing room the last week of September. We agreed on an approach that involved amending the War Crimes statute but left Article 3 untouched. There are two classifications of Common Article 3 violations, grave and nongrave breaches: The former are prosecutable as war crime violations (and theoretically punishable by death); the latter are not. We agreed that the president could enumerate the non-grave breaches as long as they exceeded current standards. The grave breaches, prosecutable as war crimes, were the focus of our negotiations that long day. McCain was present for most of them, as was I. Fontaine was there the entire time.

In the weeks leading up to the marathon negotiation, Fontaine was in frequent communication with the representatives of human rights groups, including Tom Malinowski at Human Rights Watch and Elisa Massimino at Human Rights First. We were fixated on protecting the Geneva Conventions, and after several attempts at finding a solution to our impasse with the administration, we proposed changes to the War Crimes Act that we believed would prohibit the CIA from employing extreme interrogation techniques. The act identified nine offenses as grave breaches. Torture was the first crime, defined as methods that were intended "to inflict *severe* physical or mental pain and suffering." The second breach was "cruel and inhuman treatment," which included "*serious* mental pain and suffering," which must be "prolonged." We thought the qualifier "prolonged" was ambiguous enough to justify or rationalize all manner of abuses. After all, the principal torture memo in 2002, written by Assistant Attorney General Jay Bybee to White House counsel Alberto Gonzales, had maintained that for treatment of detainees to be considered torture, it had to cause "serious physical injury, such as organ failure, impairment of bodily function or even death."

The three of us talked, and at Fontaine's suggestion, McCain told Hadley and Bradbury that he wanted to replace "prolonged" with "non-transitory (which need not be prolonged)." They agreed to "non-transitory" but initially refused the further clarification. They finally relented when we agreed the new definition wouldn't apply retroactively, which they expected would protect CIA personnel from prosecution for abuses already committed. McCain thought it was a fair exchange. He wasn't there to punish anyone, but to stop the government from doing something he believed offended American values. When we'd settled on the compromise, McCain turned to Bradbury and Hadley and asked if they believed that "these changes mean waterboarding and some of the other things would be illegal?" Both men nodded. "I'd like to hear you say it," he followed up. Bradbury went first and acknowledged, "Yes, I don't think it will be allowed going forward." Hadley simply said, "I agree." By then the agency had stopped using the worst of the EITs, and waterboarding didn't appear to have been used since 2003. But McCain was negotiating to restrain not just the current government from torturing captured combatants but future governments, too. He was satisfied that he had achieved his objectives—the Geneva Conventions had been protected, and water-boarding was no longer permissible.

The 2006 congressional elections were a disaster for Republicans, as voters who were clearly fed up with the war in Iraq—which, as was plain to all, had descended into a debacle—took out their dissatisfaction on the party in power. The day after the elections, President Bush relieved Secretary Rumsfeld. Former director of Central Intelligence Robert Gates would replace him. Years later, when Gates remained secretary of defense in the Obama administration, McCain told me he considered Gates "the finest secretary of defense I've worked with, bar none." General Casey was relinquishing his command in Iraq and returning to Washington to serve as army chief of staff. General David Petraeus, the officer McCain and his fellow counterinsurgency advocates all believed was the best man for the job, would succeed him. McCain traveled to Iraq a month after the elections. The situation had never appeared worse to him. When he returned, his frustration level was off the charts, relieved only by the knowledge that command changes in Iraq would replace some of the sources of his frustration.

When McCain's delegation arrived that December, they all heard a loud explosion as their plane landed. "It was so loud, I thought a bomb had gone off at the airport," he told me in a phone call from Baghdad. They heard a second big boom as they disembarked. They helicoptered from the airport to the city. McCain described the scene below to me: "No cars, no people, just the people who were doing the bombing and shooting. No commerce, no security, no sign of a functioning society. Bleak. Bleak."

His first meeting in Baghdad was with Lieutenant General Peter Chiarelli, Casey's deputy and commander of U.S. ground forces in Iraq, and with his replacement, Lieutenant General Ray Odierno. True to form, McCain pressed Chiarelli to concede finally that the command needed more troops to lower the rampant violence and take back some of the vast amount of territory the insurgents now controlled. Also true to form, Chiarelli repeated his and Casey's usual rebuttal, that all would be well when they had trained enough Iraqi units to take over the fight. "They're fighting now," McCain pointed out, "and the violence is only getting worse." He turned to Odierno, who would assume command that afternoon, and asked what he thought. Without a second's hesitation, he answered, "I think we need more troops in this country," earning McCain's eternal respect and gratitude. "I could've kissed him," he told me afterward. Odierno went on to tell a nodding McCain where he would deploy the five additional brigades he wanted. Fontaine, who was with McCain, told me another officer had taken him aside after the meeting and told him that Casey would shoot down any request for more troops, so Odierno had been candid in the hope that the senator would repeat to his colleagues and to the White House that they needed five more brigades. Fontaine assured him they could rely on it.

The meeting with General Casey followed a predictable pattern: McCain arguing for more troops, Casey arguing for more training. At one point, Casey declared, "We are winning in Iraq," and McCain "nearly went through the roof," Fontaine recalled. "What are you talking about?" McCain demanded. "There are like a thousand bodies showing up every week on the streets of Baghdad. There's no political activity, no economic activity. People are afraid to leave their homes. Our guys are getting killed every day."

Casey responded by insisting they were making progress toward their strategic objective: standing up the Iraqi army and going home. McCain scoffed and asked to see the most recent casualty figures. Casey couldn't produce them. "We're losing, General," McCain told him. After they left Casey's headquarters, they learned another suicide bomb had just been detonated, killing scores. McCain turned to Lindsey and Joe Lieberman and remarked, "This is winning."

Their most encouraging experience of the trip was their meeting with Colonel Sean McFarland, who commanded the mixed force of marines, army infantry and armored, navy SEALs, and two Iraqi brigades, who were taking control of Ramadi one block at a time in the heart of the Sunni insurgency. McFarland was one of the most innovative, risk-taking commanders in Iraq, and McCain thought very highly of him. He was operating in Ramadi according to the principles of counterinsurgency, and it was working. "He takes the initiative, and he takes responsibility for it," he explained to me, "and he doesn't wait to be blessed by Baghdad." McFarland told him of the outreach he had received the previous August from local sheik Abdul Sattar Abu Risha, who said he and many other sheiks and their people were tired of the extremism and violence that the insurgents brought with them. They were ready to fight alongside the Americans if the Americans were willing to give them protection. McFarland hung up the phone, he told McCain, and immediately dispatched a tank to the sheik's house. It was the beginning of the Anbar Awakening, which, along with the arrival of Petraeus and Odierno and the surge of troops, would, in McCain's estimation, win the war in Iraq.

President Bush announced the surge and his appointment of General Petraeus to command it the next month. McCain said it was "Bush's finest hour." Ryan Crocker was appointed the new U.S. ambassador in Iraq, and McCain would come to consider him "the country's most capable diplomat." He took satisfaction and relief in knowing that at last, the plans and the people he had long thought would make the difference between winning and losing would be in place, and he had played a major role in making it happen.

Those were such hectic days. Really, when I think back to the years between his two presidential races, I usually imagine one long, frenetic day that began very early and ended God knows when, crowded with confrontations, arguments, and negotiations about dozens of different interests. He was involved in so many issues. It gave you a charge, working like that for a guy like that, and it propelled you to perform at a pace you might have previously thought beyond your skills and endurance.

John S. McCain III on the day of his christening with his grandfather, John S. McCain Sr. (right), and his father, John S. McCain Jr., Panama Canal Zone, 1936 *ALAMY*

Lieutenant Commander John S. McCain III (front right) with members of his squadron, 1965 *ALAMY*

Lieutenant Commander John S. McCain III (right) inspects bomb damage to the USS *Forrestal*, July 30, 1967 GETTY

Lieutenant Commander John S. McCain III departs Hanoi in Operation Homecoming, March 14, 1973 *ALAMY*

President Richard Nixon welcomes Lieutenant Commander John S. McCain III to a White House reception for returning POWs, May 24, 1973 *ALAMY*

Captain Howard Rutledge and his wife, Phyllis, Nancy and Governor Reagan, and actor Michael Landon talking with Commander John S. McCain III at a POW reunion dinner, Los Angeles, May 28, 1978 *ASSOCIATED PRESS*

Senator John McCain with his wife, Cindy, and children Bridget, Meghan, Jack, and Jimmy, October 14, 1999 *GETTY*

Senators John McCain and Edward Kennedy (seated), along with, from left to right, Secretary of Homeland Security Michael Chertoff, Secretary of Commerce Carlos Gutierrez, Senator Ken Salazar, and Senator Johnny Isakson, announcing their bipartisan immigration legislation, May 17, 2007 *GETTY*

President Bill Clinton shakes hands with Senator McCain after announcing the restoration of diplomatic relations with Vietnam as Senator John Kerry, Secretary of State Warren Christopher, and Secretary of Defense William Perry look on, July 11, 1995 *GETTY*

To MY FRIEND MARK —
WITH DEEP APPRECIATION FOR THE OUTSTANDING
QUALITY OF YOUR WORK AND THE PLEASURE OF YOUR COMPANY,
BEST REGARDS, John McCain.

Senator McCain with the author on the shore of Trúc Bach Lake, Hanoi, where the senator was taken prisoner, next to the monument that erroneously refers to him as an air force major, 1991 *MARK SALTER*

The author with Senator
McCain in Hanoi, 1991
MARK SALTER

Senator McCain in his first bid for the presidency, taking questions at the VFW post in Franklin, New Hampshire, while fellow POWs Orson Swindle, Everett Alvarez, Bud Day, and his Naval Academy roommate, Frank Gamboa, look on, January 30, 2000 *ALAMY*

Senator McCain surrounded by reporters in the U.S. Capitol after leaving a briefing on the situation in Syria, September 4, 2013 *GETTY*

Senator McCain introduces President George W. Bush to soldiers at Fort Lewis
in Washington State, June 18, 2004 *ALAMY*

Senator McCain campaigning in Nashua, New Hampshire, on January 8, 2008, the day he won the New Hampshire primary for the second time *ALAMY*

The author sitting on the corner of the stage as Senator McCain delivers his New Hampshire victory speech, holding a copy of the speech marked up by the senator, January 8, 2008
ASSOCIATED PRESS

Senator McCain with his mother, Roberta, and other family members after delivering his acceptance speech at the Republican National Convention in Saint Paul, Minnesota, September 4, 2008 *GETTY*

President Barack Obama discusses immigration with Senators McCain and Chuck Schumer at the White House, July 11, 2013 *ALAMY*

Senator John McCain speaks with a U.S. Special Operations Forces team member in Mangwal Village, Khas Kunar District, Konar Province, Afghanistan, July 4, 2011 *ALAMY*

Senator McCain speaks to anti-regime protestors in Independence Square, "the Maidan," Kiev, Ukraine, December 15, 2013 *ALAMY*

Senator McCain warning against "spurious nationalism" at the National Constitution Center after receiving the Liberty Medal "for his lifetime of sacrifice and service," October 16, 2017. He had been diagnosed with brain cancer three months earlier *GETTY*

Horse-drawn caisson carrying the body of United States Senator John S. McCain III to his final resting place in the United States Naval Academy Cemetery, Annapolis, Maryland, September 2, 2018 *ALAMY*

FRONT-RUNNER

Twelve years after its conclusion, I still have mixed feelings about the 2008 campaign. That isn't surprising. I wasn't opposed to McCain running for president again, and I never argued against the idea. But I had a kernel, maybe more than a kernel, of doubt that it was the right decision for him. I encouraged him to weigh the decision carefully. He was one of the most popular politicians in the country, with an independent political base, and one of the most influential people in Washington. He would be putting that at risk if he ran for president again. McCain himself felt some ambivalence prior to his decision to run, and occasionally expressed skepticism to me, Rick Davis, and John Weaver, which he usually conveyed in the form of a question: "Can we bottle lightning twice?"

I don't remember him actually making the decision to run for president again, or announcing it to us. Maybe he did to others. But I don't remember him coming into the office one morning and telling me directly, "Hey, I've decided to do it." I don't know why that bothers me. It's possible that, with my poor memory, I've just forgotten it. But I have this weird sense that we started a campaign that the candidate eventually joined. His window for making the decision was between his 2004 reelection and the 2006 congressional elections. By the time the latter arrived, he had a campaign structure in place, a headquarters, and a growing campaign staff of old McCain hands and new arrivals from President Bush's campaigns, including Terry Nelson, who was the campaign manager. Rick, the campaign chairman, and

Weaver, the chief strategist, had been building the campaign infrastructure and assembling a team years before he formally announced
his candidacy.

McCain led some of the polls of likely prospects before and, for a
while, after he began the campaign, and was treated by the press as
the front-runner. That's where the trouble started. He had been the
clear favorite in every one of his Senate elections, so it wasn't like he
was unfamiliar with the experience. But being the early favorite in a
presidential campaign isn't the same advantage it is in a Senate campaign. In most of McCain's Senate races, his solid approval ratings,
fund-raising advantages, and national prominence scared off serious
competition in the primaries and the general election. By 2007, his
national approval ratings had declined from their record heights prior
to his 2004 reelection. The 2006 midterm elections gave us an indication why.

Republicans were routed all over the country, most a casualty of
the country's dissatisfaction with the war in Iraq, though the federal
government's deservedly criticized response to Hurricane Katrina
didn't help much, either. Then, as in 2000, New Hampshire was central to the McCain campaign's strategy. For various reasons, the Iowa
caucuses were a harder lift for McCain than New Hampshire. In the
2006 midterms, every Republican in statewide office had been defeated for reelection. Granite Staters had turned decisively against the
war, and they took it out on every Republican candidate they found,
even though most of them had played no role whatsoever in the Bush
administration's Middle East policies. No member of Congress was
more identified with that war than John McCain, and he was the most
outspoken congressional voice supporting the surge.

We didn't advise him to start distancing himself from the surge he
had so long advocated. It would have been pointless to try. He had
publicly warned that the transition to a counterinsurgency in Iraq
would initially result in a spike in casualties as U.S. forces started
"clearing and holding," taking back territory from insurgents, and providing protection to local populations rather than returning to base
after an offensive operation. Petraeus routinely acknowledged the

same. As anticipated, when five new brigades started deploying to Iraq and U.S. forces began taking back the streets of Baghdad and other cities from Sunni insurgents and Shia militia, casualty rates did spike: Americans were deluged with even more bad news from the war they no longer wanted any part of. It was in this period of escalating violence and higher casualties that the "McCain for President" campaign launched, a period in which nothing preoccupied the candidate more than Iraq. "Iraq," he would recall years later, "was on my mind every day of that campaign." The runner-up for his attention—in the short term, anyway—was the new comprehensive immigration bill he had put together with Ted Kennedy and Jon Kyl, who had opposed the last Kennedy-McCain effort. McCain liked and respected his Arizona colleague. He and Kennedy had worked hard to get Kyl to join forces on new legislation, and they hoped the changes to the bill they negotiated with Kyl and the White House would make it acceptable to more conservative members. For the time being, running for president would be McCain's third priority.

I left the Senate office and joined the campaign headquarters in Arlington, Virginia, as a senior advisor a few days before McCain appeared on *Late Show with David Letterman,* where he acknowledged he was running. He formally announced his candidacy two months later, in Portsmouth, New Hampshire, on April 25, 2007. In between his informal and formal announcements, he went where his head and heart were, Iraq. He arrived in Baghdad on April 1. The surge had been under way for three months, roughly. Not all the additional brigades were in-country. The increase in violence and casualties wouldn't peak for another month or so. But McCain saw in that trip that the situation was noticeably better than it had been when he was there four months earlier. He ticked off some of the progress he had seen to a reporter there: "The drop in murders; the establishment of security outposts throughout the city; the situation in Anbar; the deployment of additional Iraqi brigades who are performing well."

Petraeus and Crocker confirmed the progress and were as encouraged as he was. McCain had never professed a public doubt that a counterinsurgency would not work. But after his last trip to Baghdad in December, he privately worried that it was too late, that things had gone so far downhill that maybe nothing could be done to reverse it; that maybe all the surge could hope to accomplish was to stabilize Iraq's dystopian reality at current levels of anarchy and violence. He wasn't convinced that would be the case. But I think he was preparing himself for the possibility that he would be proven wrong, so he was relieved by the signs of progress he observed and by Petraeus's and Crocker's guarded optimism.

I trust those who dismissed McCain as a knee-jerk hawk wouldn't have felt the same had they known how heavily he felt his responsibility for advocating a war that had caused the deaths of three thousand American servicemen and -women, and now a counterinsurgency that would require an even greater sacrifice. He went to Walter Reed hospital regularly to visit with the most seriously wounded who could receive visitors. He would be a wreck sometimes when he returned to the office, unable to describe what he had seen. When he returned the following July from another trip to Iraq, he broke down as he tried to recount a reenlistment ceremony he had attended in Baghdad. Over six hundred soldiers and marines, some of whom had served multiple tours in Iraq and suffered the worst conditions, were signing back up, knowing they would likely serve another tour. I know what detractors will say: Poor McCain, he had to see the human consequences of his views; he didn't have to do the fighting and suffering and dying. Others did, the maimed and disabled and killed in action who had no say in the wars he helped send them to. He would have agreed with that. His responsibilities were not anywhere near the burden imposed on the troops in Iraq and Afghanistan. But I know he felt their suffering deeply. His empathy was acute and humbling, informed as it was by his own experiences of war. He knew the feeling of terror in war, the pain of wounds received in war, the prolonged suffering, the death of friends. It was an enormous relief to him that, for the first time in years, he had cause to hope that the sacrifices Americans made in Iraq would not be in vain.

McCain saw commerce coming back to life in Baghdad neighborhoods. Petraeus wanted to take him to an outdoor market in downtown

Baghdad "where we couldn't have gone the previous December"; they would have been fired at by snipers, and no one was selling or buying anything there anyway. The market had revived when people felt safe enough to shop there. They traveled there in armored Humvees, McCain and Lindsey Graham and two congressmen, Rick Renzi of Arizona and Mike Pence of Indiana. They had a military escort while helicopter gunships patrolled overhead. They wore Kevlar vests as they walked through the market, attempted to talk to some of the merchants, and made a few purchases, all of it captured on camera. In an interview afterward, McCain talked about the encouraging progress he had seen and claimed there were areas in Baghdad where, weeks earlier, Americans would have come under fire, where they could now walk safely; when asked for an example, he mentioned the market. War opponents and McCain critics pounced and ridiculed the statement, citing the heavy security that had protected them. Mike Ware, an Australian journalist working for CNN who had a lot of attitude and not much objectivity, practically mocked him on air. Other critics, too many to list, insisted he was arguing the surge had succeeded. He had not—he had simply maintained that "things are better, and there are encouraging signs." I watched the controversy unfold from the office, and I knew how embarrassed he would be by the coverage. He was still angry about it when he got back to Washington, at the reporter who had mocked him, at the media pile-on that followed, and at himself for giving them the opening.

His relationship with the press changed for the worse in the course of his second presidential bid. The mostly positive coverage he had enjoyed as the high-spirited challenger in 2000 with an open-access media policy, and as the candid, readily-available-for-comment senator who liked few things better than bantering with reporters, became much more adversarial in the scrutiny accorded to McCain, the perceived front-runner for the nomination. There was an almost universal presumption among reporters that McCain would transform himself into a more conventional establishment candidate if he ran as the favorite for the nomination. Also, like many voters, many journalists were convinced the Iraq war had been a colossal blunder, and deeply skeptical that it could be salvaged by the counterinsurgency McCain advocated. When it became clear that the new phenom in town, the eloquent Barack Obama, who had burst on the national scene only two years earlier, was going to challenge the expected Democratic nominee, Hillary Clinton, reporters gravitated toward his campaign. In McCain world, we knew what press favoritism looked like. McCain had been the beneficiary of it in 2000. We could see in an instant that Obama would have that advantage for as long as he was in the race.

When McCain accepted an invitation from Jerry Falwell's Liberty University in 2006, reporters took it as confirmation that McCain was, as they presumed, going to reinvent himself as the establishment candidate. He had strongly criticized Falwell and Pat Robertson in his Virginia Beach speech in 2000, and now he was perceived as courting favor with one of the very same "agents of intolerance" he had denounced six years earlier. McCain had agreed to meet Falwell at his request in 2005, and John Weaver had brought him to the office. During the meeting, Falwell insisted the attacks by religious conservatives against McCain in South Carolina had been Robertson's doing, not his. McCain dismissed it as beside the point. Whatever disagreements he had with Falwell or Robertson weren't personal, he insisted. I don't think that was entirely true. But it is fair to say that for McCain to move on from an experience, which he was psychologically wired to do, he had to do his best to leave any bitterness behind as well. You could tell he felt he had something to prove in South Carolina in 2008, he was so intently focused on winning the state this time. But he wasn't doing it to settle scores; he was doing it to prove he could.

Falwell went on to assure McCain that religious conservatives weren't irreversibly opposed to a McCain candidacy in 2008. It was an amicable exchange, and near the end of their discussion, when Falwell asked if he would consider giving the commencement address to Liberty University's 2006 graduates, McCain answered, "Sure, I'll do it." Nothing else happened or was sought in the meeting. McCain didn't ask Falwell to endorse his candidacy. Falwell didn't ask McCain to change his position on any issues. No one apologized for anything. Falwell's invitation was the only request made by either man.

McCain had accepted two other commencement invitations that year: one at Columbia University, where his daughter, Meghan, was graduating; and the other at the New School in New York, which was run by his friend and former senator Bob Kerrey. McCain decided he would give essentially the same speech to all three graduating classes. He would use the occasions to emphasize Americans' common values and appeal for tolerance of opposing views, using divisions over Iraq as a case study. "Americans deserve more than tolerance from one another," McCain told graduates of all three schools. "We deserve each other's respect, whether we think each other right or wrong in our views, as long as our character and our sincerity merit respect."

The Liberty University address on May 13 was received with polite applause. In addition to the graduates, their families, and faculty, the auditorium hosted an unusually large contingent of political reporters, including some of the most respected journalists in the profession: Dan Balz, senior political correspondent for the *Washington Post,* was there, as was Adam Nagourney, his counterpart at the *New York Times.* No one criticized the content of McCain's speech. To the extent it was quoted, the analysis was mostly favorable. But it wasn't really featured in most of the coverage, and barely at all in television news reports. Almost all the reporting presented McCain's appearance as evidence he was courting religious conservatives and transitioning to a more conventionally conservative political persona. Obviously, a candidate for his or her party's presidential nomination is in the friends-making business and, where possible, will want to repair relations with constituencies where they might have some weakness. But McCain's acceptance of the invitation hadn't been the result of a political calculation. His campaign aides hadn't convened a meeting to discuss the idea. McCain didn't ask for our opinion. We hadn't known Falwell was going to ask him to speak. I'd seen him give an immediate reply to an invitation hundreds of times. He was asked on the spot, and answered on the spot because he liked to conduct business that way, he could use the opportunity to convey an important message, and he didn't think there was anything controversial about giving a commencement address.

Around the same time as his college tour, McCain gave observers more evidence to substantiate the allegation that he was remaking his political identity. He voted to extend the Bush tax cuts he had opposed in 2001 and 2003, and to lower rates on capital gains and dividend income. It's hard to argue that the critics weren't, more or less, correct in this instance. It was a political move made out of concern that our candidate was carrying into Republican primaries one item of baggage too many. Campaign finance reform, comprehensive immigration reform, the Gang of Fourteen compromise on judicial nominations, his frequent criticism of administration policies, and his reputation for bipartisanship, all offended one or more segment of Republicans. His vote against tax cuts had been his worst defection in the eyes of the Republican establishment. So we recommended that he reverse his position when he had to vote on their extension.

Though I would like to say he resisted the idea, that would be an exaggeration. He hesitated a little, anticipating the blowback he would receive. But he willingly went along in the end. The policy explanation he gave to defend his change of heart: He hadn't wanted to cut taxes as much as President Bush had, but he didn't want to raise them, either, which is the practical effect of opposing the extension. "American businesses and investors need a stable and predictable tax policy to continue contributing to the growth of our economy," he argued. "These considerations lead me to the conclusion that we should not reverse course by letting higher tax rates take effect." He mostly convinced himself that his rationale was his honestly held belief, but there was no escaping the media's judgment that his reversal was, in the words of the fact-checking website PolitiFact, "a Full Flop." Guilty as charged.

As we would soon discover, his tax cut reversal wasn't enough to placate some of the most conservative elements in the party. Neither was it a magic antidote to McCain resistance within the party establishment and among major donors. The candidate who would prove to be his toughest challenger, Mitt Romney, had stronger appeal in those quarters. Changes in the political media universe were a challenge as well. The new do-it-yourself medium for political commentary on the Internet, blogs, which had exploded in the first decade of the new century, was mostly unfriendly territory for McCain. Many of them were dominated by dogmatic voices on the right and left, who imitated the style of insult comics rather than the sober punditry favored by old media. In the spring of 2007, as the surge was under way and the public was growing more tired of the war, Iraq roused the left's antipathy to McCain. At the same time, McCain's newest bipartisan project, the Kennedy-McCain-Kyl comprehensive immigration bill, was lighting fires among the hard right.

Immigration reform was supported by many party leaders and donors, especially after the crushing defeat Republicans suffered in the 2006 election, and it was as much of a priority for the Bush White House as it was for McCain and Kennedy. Republican immigration opponents in the Senate were in the minority. But the conservative "base" of the party was no more enamored of the president's support for immigration reform than it had been by his unsuccessful nomination of White House legal counsel Harriet Miers to the Supreme Court. Despite ideological differences among McCain, Kennedy, and Kyl, they were all practical legislators. Their goals were grounded in political reality. They addressed national problems with modest expectations and a willingness to compromise. Conservative opponents of the legislation had a bottom-line demand for immigration reform that was irreconcilable with the reality that around twelve million people had immigrated to the United States unlawfully, most by overstaying their visas and not by crossing the southern border illegally, and almost all of them were never going to leave. No practical immigration proposal could refuse to address their status, but every attempt to do so was met with hostility by intransigents on the right. No matter how long and arduous a process was prescribed for undocumented immigrants to attain some form of legalized status, it was denounced as amnesty by the loudest voices on talk radio, on the Internet, and in Congress, who preferred the informal system of de facto amnesty that has existed for over thirty years. Their protestations to the contrary, it isn't merely impractical to round up twelve million people—many of whom have children who are native-born Americans—and load them on buses bound for Mexico. It's impossible.

There was opposition to the bill on the left as well, mostly from organized labor, which opposed the legislation's guest worker provisions. The two Democratic presidential candidates, Hillary Clinton and Barack Obama, supported the McCain-Kennedy bill in 2006 and the McCain-Kennedy-Kyl bill in 2007. During floor debate on both iterations, Senator Obama occasionally joined the small group of Senate supporters who met every morning to plot floor strategy for the day. The bipartisan group was bound by a commitment to act by consensus and oppose proposals that either side considered unacceptable. Neither in 2006 nor in 2007 did Senator Obama adhere to that commitment. In his defense, he never promised he would. He voted for amendments offered by Democrats to address labor's concerns. Many Republican opponents of the bill voted for them as well, hoping that by making the bill less business-friendly, they could drive off some of its Republican support. Obama offered one of the amendments that McCain, Kyl, Lindsey Graham, and others declared could be a deal breaker. It failed, but he cosponsored another amendment the group objected to, which would sunset the guest worker program, and it passed with the support of conservative opponents. McCain chafed at Obama's unreliability, but he left it to Kennedy to discipline his side. During both immigration debates, Kennedy had scolded his Democratic colleague. I witnessed the rebuke in 2006: Kennedy barked at him something along the lines of: "Why don't you help instead of getting in the way." It was a sharp but brief reprimand. When Kennedy chastised Obama the second time, McCain and I were on a bus in New Hampshire, but Lindsey Graham cheerfully recounted it to McCain on the phone.

McCain might have been irritated by Senator Obama, but he did not consider him an adversary. In the spring of 2007, Obama was still considered the underdog in the contest for the Democratic presidential nomination. McCain, like most observers at that time, was impressed by Obama's rhetorical skills, intelligence, and equable manner. He didn't resent the freshman senator's ambitiousness, either, as some colleagues did. He admired the boldness of Obama's risk-taking. He had been a young man in a hurry, too, when he was first elected to

Congress, and he recognized the type. But however impressed he was, he didn't believe Obama had a realistic chance of wresting the nomination from Hillary Clinton, whom McCain knew much better than he knew Obama.

McCain had formed a friendship with Clinton, who had impressed him as a member of the Armed Services Committee. Veteran senators in both parties had anticipated her 2001 arrival in the Senate with a mix of curiosity, condescension, and envy. She brought with her greater national prominence than most senators ever have, and a Secret Service detail that none of them had. The expectation was she would be a celebrity senator but not an influential one. She had confounded those expectations by staying initially out of the spotlight to the extent that the media allowed her to remain in the background. In McCain's estimation, she was a quick, diligent student of the issues within her committees' jurisdiction. Unexpectedly, she also proved adept at forming personal relationships with her colleagues. She was careful to show deference to her more senior colleagues, which went a long way toward alleviating premature ill will. But more than flattery was at the heart of her appeal. She was warm and engaging in conversation, and considerate in social interactions with her colleagues. McCain, who traveled overseas with her on several trips, described her to me simply as "a lot of fun." A 2004 dinner in Estonia's capital, Tallinn, led to a vodka drinking competition. "We didn't empty the bottle," McCain pointed out as he defended the respectability of the contest and his reputation for modest drinking. Ask any of the participants—who included Susan Collins and Lindsey Graham, you get four somewhat altered versions. Lindsey said he tossed his vodka in a nearby planter but egged on his companions. McCain said Clinton matched him ounce for ounce, but their total consumption was limited to "three, maybe four shots," and he insisted they left the table "no worse for wear, although I can't say the same about Susan."

Whatever the truth of their Baltic adventure, McCain clearly respected Clinton and enjoyed her company. He wanted to run against her, believing their friendliness could translate to a general election campaign different in tone from the negativity that voters say they detest but don't seem able to resist. That hope was probably naive. The Clintons weren't known for their gentility in the slash-and-burn of presidential campaigns. But when he let himself imagine winning the nomination, which the superstitious McCain didn't often do, he envisioned joint campaign appearances with Clinton. He had been captivated by stories that Jack Kennedy and Barry Goldwater had discussed traveling the country on the same plane and stopping at various locations to debate each other. It was the romantic in McCain who envisioned such an unlikely demonstration of public-spirited amicability. The practical politician in him knew better. Nevertheless, once he secured the nomination, he was disappointed when Obama rejected his offer to fly together to a series of informal town hall–style debates. Obama was leading in the polls at the time, and he was getting more attention than McCain was. The novelty of joint town halls and shared transportation would have attracted extraordinary attention, with each candidate sharing the spotlight equally. Moreover, it would have associated McCain with political change, the message monopolized by Senator Obama, despite our efforts to appropriate it. McCain said he understood why Obama would be reluctant to agree. Front-runners are risk-averse; challengers are risk-takers. But McCain's disappointment was real and lasting. Years after the election, long after he had let go of other disappointments, he still lamented the lost opportunity to have "a campaign that people would always talk about, that changed the rules."

Early in his brief Senate career, Obama had approached McCain on the floor to profess his admiration and his desire to work together. McCain was very receptive to the overture. He was usually on the lookout after every election for new senators in either party with whom he could forge productive relationships, and Obama was the star of his freshman class. Like many observers, McCain thought Obama was unusually talented and that working with him would bring positive attention to projects they undertook. In early 2006, when McCain was looking to form a bipartisan group that would develop a package of lobbying and congressional ethics reforms in the wake of the Abramoff scandal, he approached Obama. He talked to Russ Feingold, too, his usual partner in such efforts, and his close friend Joe Lieberman. Paul Wellstone had died in an airplane crash in 2002, to the sorrow of everyone who had ever met that lovely man. But McCain was particularly interested in employing Obama's star status and communication skills. He thought Obama's involvement made it likelier that a bipartisan bill would overtake competing bills proposed by both parties' leadership.

Harry Reid, the Senate Democratic leader, had other ideas. He believed fallout from the Abramoff scandal would help the Democrats take back their majority in the 2006 elections, and he wanted to retain the issue as a weapon against Republicans. That meant making sure McCain didn't pull off another Gang of X compromise that circumvented partisan proposals. McCain recognized an authenticity in Reid, who came from humble origins, that he respected even when it manifested itself in ways that McCain didn't like. But he was under no illusions about what Reid, who shared McCain's affinity for boxing, was up to. "Harry's a brawler," he often observed, "as partisan as they come." Years later, Reid would infuriate McCain when he changed Senate rules to stop Republicans from filibustering President Obama's judicial nominees. McCain went to the Senate floor to vent but approached Reid before he spoke to let him know: "Harry, I'm going to beat the shit out of you." In McCain's retelling, an unconcerned Reid smiled and responded mildly, "John, I would expect nothing less from you." McCain was genuinely angry at the time; he said to me, "Harry's going to ruin this place." But Reid's coolness when confronted impressed him, and he smiled as he recounted it admiringly to staff.

Reid managed to dissuade Senator Obama from joining the McCain-led effort. McCain had succeeded in getting Obama to meet with a group of like-minded Republicans and Democrats to discuss priorities they thought should be included in the new ethics legislation. But not long afterward, Obama sent McCain a very formal letter saying, in effect, thanks but no thanks. "I know you have expressed an interest in creating a task force to further study and discuss these matters," the letter stated, but I and others in the Democratic Caucus believe the more effective and timely course is to allow the committees of jurisdiction to roll up their sleeves and get to work on writing ethics and lobbying reform legislation that a majority of the Senate can support. Committee consideration of these matters through the normal course will ensure that these issues are discussed in a public forum and that those within Congress, as well as those on the outside, can express their views, ensuring a thorough review of this matter.

This is not how members of the Senate typically communicate with each other privately. I knew at a glance it was meant for public consumption. McCain didn't take it seriously, and I wouldn't have, either, had it not arrived after Reid or Obama staff had given it to the press. Reporters were calling about it as I read it. McCain was out of town. When he called to check in, I gave him the news, describing Obama's letter as "a press release probably written in Reid's office" before I read him its contents. "Harry got his hooks into him," McCain said, laughing, and told me to brush him back in response. I was more annoyed than he was, and I discharged my assignment with more enthusiasm than the offense warranted. The letter I wrote Senator Obama under McCain's signature was drenched in sarcasm and accused Obama of "self-interested partisan posturing."

I succeeded in turning a story that would be little noticed outside the Capitol into a feud that got the attention of the whole town. "You overdid it, Mark," McCain rebuked me, using my first name to underscore his displeasure, rather than "boy" or "my friend" or the other forms of address he typically used. I knew I had. I thought Obama's letter had been deliberately disrespectful of McCain's sincere intentions. I knew that it was Harry Reid's doing and I shouldn't have taken it personally. McCain hadn't. It was just election-year politics, nothing out of the ordinary, and I was forced to concede that I had exceeded my instructions to brush him back; I had beaned him. McCain and Obama talked on the phone to assure each other of their continued respect. At a Rules Committee hearing where both men testified about their ideas for ethics reform, Obama referred to McCain as "my new pen pal." McCain laughed as hard as everyone else in the room.

Some pundits speculated that the incident had caused an iciness in relations between the two politicians that would persist indefinitely. But it hadn't. They both remained friendly in their interactions, and McCain welcomed Obama's participation in the immigration effort the following year. He had tried to be in the Senate during debate on the bill, which started in early May and lasted almost a month, as often as he could be, which wasn't very often. He was campaigning full-time by then, having formally announced his candidacy in April, as was Obama. He talked with Kennedy, Lindsey Graham, and Jon Kyl several times a day while the bill was pending, and McCain legislative staff were present in every meeting and for every major decision. He had been very confident going into the debate that advocates of comprehensive reform would prevail. With Kyl's involvement and Kennedy's assent, the bill was much more focused on border security than was its predecessor. It authorized $4 billion in spending for thousands of new Border Patrol agents, seven hundred miles of new fencing on the border, infrared cameras, drones, and sensors that detected footsteps. It increased penalties on employers who knowingly hired undocumented workers. It replaced existing family reunification rules with more restrictive ones. It also included provisions of the DREAM Act, detailing a path to citizenship for immigrants who were brought to the country when they were children, and who were attending college or serving in the military.

McCain was convinced that the legislation's concessions to conservative critics would win at least some support in that quarter. He was wrong. Any bill that did not maintain the fiction that all undocumented immigrants could and should be removed from the United States was denounced as amnesty. The fire-eaters on conservative talk radio continued to condemn it daily and excoriate McCain personally as "John McAmnesty." Progressives disliked the greater emphasis on security, the restrictions on family reunification, and the guest worker provisions. As debate dragged on, more marriages of convenience formed between conservative and progressive critics, weighing down the legislation with amendments that cost more votes than they attracted. McCain grew more anxious about its fate, and frustrated that he was on the campaign trail rather than on the floor, trying to navigate between all the competing interests at play. He began almost every address to voters and every press interview with a defense of the bill. Whenever he was able to get back to Washington, he worked feverishly to get the bill moving, seeming to insert himself into various policy disagreements all at once. He was quick to lose his temper with colleagues, who appeared to be trying to sabotage the bill rather than improve it. In one heated exchange, he told a Republican senator to "go fuck yourself." He quickly apologized for the outburst, but word of it spread to reporters, and his indiscretion didn't exactly improve the bill's chances.

After a month of debate, the measure was effectively dead. McCain was upset by the result, feeling disbelief at first, then guilt that he hadn't been there for more of the debate, and concern that the politics of immigration reform would not allow it to be addressed comprehensively but only piecemeal. He had been pummeled for his position by rivals for the nomination. His most caustic critic was an immigration restrictionist, nuisance candidate and congressman from Colorado Tom Tancredo, who never shut up about the subject. Tancredo once ordered a plate of chips and salsa delivered to McCain's table in a South Carolina restaurant. We assumed it was Tancredo's attempt at a joke or an insult. The guy was weird, and it was hard to tell what he meant to convey by the gesture. The most effective criticism came from Mitt Romney, McCain's chief rival for the nomination. Romney was smarter, better spoken, more telegenic, and more prominent than Tancredo. He had the resources to put his attacks on air, which he did. Between the hell McCain was catching in debates, the hostility from conservative radio, and Romney ads in key early states, the issue was hurting McCain's standing not only nationally (Rudy Giuliani was now leading most national polls) but acutely in New Hampshire and South Carolina. His support for the surge was hurting him, too, we worried, although none of his opponents whom I recall—except isolationist Ron Paul—criticized him for that. But it wasn't a popular position with the country at large. It linked him closely to the increasingly un-popular Bush administration. If McCain was still the front-runner, he appeared to be a weak one to his opponents, to party regulars and donors, and to the press.

He continued to defend his position on immigration in speeches, debates, and interviews. In almost every utterance on the subject, he stressed that undocumented immigrants were "God's children," who should be treated with compassion and respect. He never stopped insisting that removing all of them from the United States was prac-tically impossible and morally objectionable. When he mused after the bill's demise about finding another route to comprehensive re-form, possibly pursuing it in stages, Democrats would point to it in the general election as evidence that McCain had abandoned real reform to placate conservative critics. The Obama campaign would run ads in Arizona accusing McCain of adopting Rush Limbaugh's anti-immigrant views.

Adding to McCain's agitation over immigration and his anxious-ness about the surge was his growing dissatisfaction with his cam-paign. The campaign was built with a view to taking advantage of his front-runner status. We had hired a lot of talented staff, hoping to deprive rival campaigns of their services. We were building a bat-tleship campaign with an expansive headquarters, a fully staffed pol-icy shop, communications operations, and field offices in the early primary states. We had interviewed several media firms, and rather than choosing one, we assembled a team with principals from three of them. We expected the size of the campaign to attract greater financial support and discourage support for his opponents. But small-dollar donations to the campaign from grassroots Republicans had fallen off significantly during the immigration debate, and doubts about McCain's viability among the donor class increased by the day.

We had a somewhat rocky announcement tour in April. McCain seemed off his game in the delivery of his speeches and in his ex-changes with the press. He got testy a couple times under aggressive questioning. The weather was lousy at a couple of outdoor events. The crowds didn't impress reporters in terms of size or enthusiasm. At an appearance in South Carolina a few days before the announcement, McCain answered a voter's question about the threat posed by Iran by jokingly substituting "Bomb, bomb, bomb, bomb, bomb Iran" for the lyrics of the Beach Boys song "Barbara Ann." It was just McCain playing the cutup again. He had not advocated military action against Iran. But denizens of the blogosphere and the new social media site Twitter took it seriously, or pretended to, as did liberal critics in old media, and used the joke to denounce him as a warmonger. Nothing bugged McCain more than having his attempts at humor—successful or unsuccessful—scrutinized for intentions other than getting a laugh. He vowed, "I don't care what they say. I'm not going to stop having a sense of humor. Fuck 'em." The bomb-Iran controversy followed him for years. Whenever he saw a reference to it, he would shake his head as if still astonished by the injustice of it.

We raised $13 million in the first quarter of 2007, which I'm sure was at that time a personal best for McCain. But it was a little better than half the figure Mitt Romney had raised and less than Giuliani reported. McCain worried that the campaign's expenditures weren't sustainable, and repeatedly pressed Terry Nelson, Rick Davis, John Weaver, and me to make economies. Almost every discussion with him about the campaign began with "We're too big" or "We can't afford this" or "Goddammit, we're going broke." The first presidential campaign I'd ever worked on had been McCain 2000. Other than helping manage communications, I was mostly useless to him. I had agreed with the strategy that had brought us to this point, and I didn't offer realistic suggestions to get us past it.

Compounding his agitation, his senior aides were fighting among ourselves, which he was aware of, and which appeared to be a battle for control of the campaign. Weaver wanted most authority vested in him and Terry, but Rick still had McCain's confidence. Carla Eudy, McCain's longtime finance director and to whom he was very close, was being marginalized as well. Several times he instructed us to stop feuding and start working by consensus, as we had in 2000, when we were, in his words, "a band of brothers." We'd had our disagreements then, too, but they were mostly mild and short-lived, nothing like the rifts that existed in 2007. I was friends with all parties concerned, which caused me to argue on behalf of the status quo. But I knew McCain well enough to know that sooner rather than later he was going to demand big changes to the campaign. None of the others was satisfied with the way things were. I was afraid of the image of chaos conveyed by a shake-up. I was afraid of losing valuable staff. And I was afraid of losing friends. I hoped we could stop the feuding, make the economies he expected, and otherwise continue as we were. As I said, I was useless to him then. I was naive and afraid to confront reality. That was never more apparent than when we reported our second-quarter fund-raising in June. We had raised less than last quarter, and Governor Romney's campaign had again surpassed us. Some staff cuts had been made, but the campaign's expenditures had not been reduced to the level McCain expected. The campaign was in fact going broke, and the candidate was furious. He pulled me into his office and told me he had decided to make the changes. He wanted Rick in charge. He assumed Terry Nelson would leave the campaign in response. He wasn't clear about what he expected from Weaver, other than he had to report to Rick, but he knew that could cause Weaver to bolt, too.

I went to his condo that night to plead with him some more. We had an emotional discussion, our voices raised at times, and we were both distraught. It was unlike any conversation I had ever had with him. I begged him to not take actions that would precipitate more turmoil in the campaign. He was leaving for Iraq in two days, and this would not only distract attention from the trip, it would look like he was making a getaway after blowing up his campaign. I told him Terry had a plan to downsize the campaign drastically, and I promised him I could get John and Rick to reconcile. After almost an hour, when we both felt drained, he relented. He met Terry the next morning to go over the new budget and staff layoffs. When he and Lindsey left for Iraq the next day, I thought he was, while unhappy with the current state of affairs, satisfied that his concerns were now being addressed. That wasn't the case.

On the flight to Iraq, he told Lindsey he was considering dropping out of the race, something he hadn't said to me. He was miserable, he told his friend. His heart wasn't in it. He would rather be working on Iraq. He was embarrassed by the campaign's insolvency. He didn't feel like himself, and nothing about the campaign felt authentic to him. "I felt like a phony," he told me a decade after the fact, "like I was pretending to be someone I wasn't." Lindsey encouraged him to make changes he felt were necessary, campaign the way he wanted to—like an underdog rather than a front-runner—and stick it out awhile to see if he could turn it around. McCain listened, but when the plane landed in Baghdad, he was still leaning toward getting out.

He was briefed by Petraeus and Crocker with encouraging news. The worst of the violence had peaked in May and had been declining since. Americans were taking back more territory from the insurgents, and bringing a measure of security and order to Iraqis living there. Progress in Anbar Province, the heart of the insurgency, had been astonishing. McCain could see the progress in Baghdad: Once-deserted streets were clogged with traffic and people. Shops were open. McCain trusted Crocker and Petraeus not to sugarcoat reality, and he was relieved by their cautious satisfaction that the surge was working as expected.

The experience that made the biggest impression on him, which he would later struggle to describe to me, was the reenlistment of approximately six hundred servicemen and -women, many of whom had been in the thick of some of the worst fighting—which included a naturalization ceremony for 161 soldiers, most of them Hispanic immigrants—who had risked their lives for the country while waiting to become citizens. McCain described in our last book together how he felt while watching these "brave kids sign up for more sacrifices."

They had seen their friends killed and wounded. Some had been wounded themselves. They had seen firsthand the failed strategy that had allowed the insurgency to gain strength, and had risked their lives to reinforce what they knew was a mistake. They had retaken the same real estate over and over again. They had conducted raids night after night looking for insurgents and caches of arms. They had been shot at by snipers and blasted by

IEDs, and buried friends who hadn't survived the encounters, while month after month the situation got worse. And here they were, re-upping again, choosing to stay in harm's way.

"I was in awe of them," he told me. "They were so damn good." When Petraeus spoke, he directed the audience's attention to two chairs on which sat two pairs of boots, representing two soldiers of Hispanic heritage who had planned to become American citizens that day but had been killed in action the day before. "They died serving a country that was not yet theirs," Petraeus reflected.

No other experience in McCain's long political career and world-wide travels had ever moved him as much as that ceremony, he claimed. In a candidate debate a few weeks later, as Tom Tancredo was complaining about the Mexicans invading our southern border, I could see McCain stiffen. I knew he was remembering the naturalization ceremony and the two pairs of boots. He responded to Tancredo by advising the other candidates to go to the Vietnam Veterans Memorial the next time they were in Washington and see for themselves all the Hispanic names carved in its black granite panels.

On the flight home, McCain told Graham he was staying in the race. "If those kids can stick it out," he observed, recalling the sacrifices of the reenlisted soldiers, "so can I." He told me essentially the same after he arrived in Washington, then informed me that he had made up his mind to put Rick in full charge of the campaign with instructions to reduce it to a size that we could realistically find the financing to run. He knew Terry and John would likely leave, but if they wanted to remain, they would report to Rick, and like all top staff, including me, they would have to volunteer their services until he had won or lost the nomination. He would rather run as an underdog, he insisted, if for no other reason than to "defend the surge, to defend what we're doing in Iraq."

I tried pleading with him again, assuring him everyone had gotten the message about the spending and the infighting and would respect each other's roles in the campaign. I warned him the move would dominate the news and not in a good way. Within hours, he

was scheduled to give a speech on the Senate floor about the situation
in Iraq, and another in New Hampshire in a couple of days. "No one
will pay any attention to you," I said. "This will overshadow everything." But he was informing me of his decision, not discussing it with
me. He wasn't angry; he was determined. He spoke firmly, and his jaw
was clenched when he held up his hand to cut off my protests. "I'm not
going to debate, Mark. I'm not happy. I wasn't happy. And I won't be
happy until we're running the campaign I want to run. Period." I stood
up from my chair next to him in his Senate office. I was worked up and
worried that the staff could hear us. I told him if his mind really was
made up, then I should probably resign, too. I had given him my best
advice, and he had rejected it, as he had every right to do. The honorable thing to do was resign. I wasn't sure Rick would want me in the
campaign, either, since I had argued against the shake-up that put him
in undisputed control. Finally, while I couldn't speak for the others, I
couldn't work without a salary for eight months or more.

McCain was shaking his head, and before I could turn to leave, he
told me to sit down. Without any resentment in his tone but with the
same firmness, he laid into me. This is from memory, and subject to its
increasing unreliability over twelve years after the fact. I didn't scribble notes while he spoke or write it in a diary afterward. But nothing
he ever said to me before or since made the impression this did. "First,
you told me before I went to Iraq, no matter what happened, you
weren't going to leave," he reminded me. "So don't talk to me about
what the 'honorable thing to do' is. The honorable thing is to keep
your word. You've told me what you're going to do. Now let me tell you
what I'm going to do. I've made my decision, and I'm going to take the
consequences like a man. I'm going to go to the floor and talk about
what really should matter to us, what brave Americans are doing in
Iraq, and just like you said, no one is going to pay any attention to
it. All the press will want to know is if I'm quitting. I'm going to go
back to New Hampshire Friday, and every reporter in town will show
up to see if I announce that I'm done. I'm going to be criticized, ridiculed, pitied, and embarrassed, and I'm going to take it. I'm going to
go out there every damn day and talk about what I believe we should

be talking about with my head up. I'll beg people for money. I'll talk to small crowds about the most unpopular subject in politics. And then in six or seven months, I'll probably get my ass kicked and go home. So tell me, Mark, why are you being such a wimp?"

Shamefaced and on the verge of embarrassing myself, I nodded that I had gotten the message. "Okay," he said, "I'll see you later, boy." I left the office and went back to campaign headquarters. He called our agent, Flip Brophy, and told her to assign to me all the remaining advance we were owed for our latest book, which would be published the following month.

His decision impacted the campaign as expected. John and Terry left. Some people left out of loyalty to them, and some people agreed to stay. I tried convincing as many as I could to remain, at least until things stabilized a little. Some agreed to remain temporarily, and some wound up staying for the duration. I didn't think McCain had a very good chance at winning the nomination after that. I can only speak for myself, but I'd be surprised if many of the remaining staff thought the opposite. Rick appeared to, though, and he quickly came up with a plan to finance the campaign that involved a sizable bank loan but would buy McCain time to make his case. McCain came to the headquarters later that afternoon to encourage the remaining staff, and he said a few words about several of us. When he mentioned me, his voice cracked. I put my head down to hide my reaction. We were close friends. But while he still valued my opinion, he never trusted it again as much as he once had, and I couldn't fault him for that.

That Friday, I found myself at Reagan National Airport boarding a flight to Manchester, New Hampshire, with John McCain and his son Jimmy, a marine who was scheduled to deploy to Iraq in a week; John wanted to spend Jimmy's last few days stateside with him. At each public event that weekend, press aides asked reporters not to report Jimmy's presence or his imminent deployment. The McCains were naturally worried that were Jimmy's situation widely publicized, he would become even more of a target in Iraq. Every reporter we asked agreed to the request.

The media reaction to the campaign's implosion was brutal, as expected. The respected political analyst Charlie Cook pronounced McCain a corpse. Reporters had seen him in the airport carrying his own bag, and used the image as a metaphor for the campaign's falling fortunes, despite the fact that it was hardly out of the ordinary: McCain often carried his own bag in good and bad times. His first scheduled event that weekend was in Concord, where he gave a speech about Iraq to the local chamber of commerce. The room was crowded with reporters, including the top political journalists for the major newspapers and networks. They had come, as McCain had predicted they would, to see if he was going to drop out of the race. "Like crows on a wire," he described them afterward, good-naturedly, considering the circumstances. "They thought maybe I'd clutch my chest and drop dead right there in front of the cameras."

That night, McCain, Jimmy, three press aides, and I had dinner in a Concord restaurant. McCain was in a surprisingly expansive mood and feeling nostalgic. He regaled the party with stories from his navy years; one involved his romance with a Brazilian model while he was a Naval Academy midshipman. In a few weeks' time, nothing would worry him more than his son's presence in the war he had argued to escalate. But that night he was relaxed. He loved having Jimmy with him. He had done a hard thing that felt right to him. He would, as he'd told me, accept the consequences with dignity.

The next two months would test his resolve. Down in the polls, most of the press ignoring him, living off the land, scrambling for every dollar, defending an unpopular war, while he was, as he'd known he would be, dismissed, mocked, and criticized. The smaller war room at headquarters emailed the daily take of abuse to our BlackBerrys, which McCain would demand we share with him. I remember handing him the clips one morning not long after the shake-up. It included a transcribed joke Jay Leno had told the night before: "Senator John Edwards began what he's calling his poverty tour today," the joke began. "He's visiting people who have no money and no hope. His first stop: John McCain's campaign headquarters." It made McCain laugh.

His sheer cussedness got him through those first couple months, along with his conviction that he had done the right thing. He was feisty and adamant and, importantly, felt he had nothing else to lose. By Labor Day, our press hadn't gotten much better; his polling numbers had stabilized but weren't much improved; fund-raising was still anemic, although Rick had secured the bank loan that would keep the operation going; and all the candidate wanted to talk about was the situation in Iraq. He restricted his campaigning to the early primary states, New Hampshire and South Carolina. But he spent a little time in Iowa, more than he had eight years earlier, hoping to do better there than he had done in 2000. He declined to participate in the racket known as the Iowa Straw Poll, and he was careful not to spend so much time in Iowa that he would be expected to finish in the top three. Michigan would follow New Hampshire. Mitt Romney had grown up there, and his father had been governor, so our expectations were modest; but since McCain had won it in 2000, we dedicated some resources to it, and he spent a few days campaigning there as well.

At a town hall in August in Wolfeboro, New Hampshire, a woman stood up to ask McCain a question. She seemed rather shy, and spoke in a low voice, and he had to listen closely to hear her. McCain said afterward that he had a feeling she was going to criticize him, he assumed for his position on Iraq. She told him she had worn a POW bracelet during the Vietnam War. Then she announced, "Today I unfortunately wear a black bracelet in memory of my son who lost his life in Baghdad." McCain braced himself for the denunciation he expected. He thought "she would hold me responsible for her loss, and she would be right to do so," he remembered. But that wasn't her purpose. She asked only that he wear her son's bracelet to "remember your mission and your mission in support of them." He took the bracelet from her and managed to say he would be "honored and grateful" to wear it. Reading the name inscribed on the bracelet, Matthew Stanley, McCain asked how old Matthew had been when he died. "Twenty-two," she answered. "Twenty-two," he repeated as his eyes welled with tears. "Yes, ma'am, I'll wear this. Thank you." He wore Matthew Stanley's bracelet through the entire campaign and for years afterward.

Steve Schmidt, a communications strategist on President Bush's campaign and Arnold Schwarzenegger's reelection campaign manager, had been an informal advisor to the McCain campaign and agreed to come on board as the campaign's strategist after the July shake-up. He and McCain discussed an idea the candidate was instantly taken with: the "No Surrender Tour," which was essentially a renamed Straight Talk bus tour with McCain, a few political friends, and whichever buddies from the navy and prison he could recruit, defending the surge to any voters who would listen. It didn't start on a bus, since we couldn't afford one full-time yet; we traveled from one sparsely attended event to the next in an SUV.

The No Surrender Tour made stops in Iowa and South Carolina, but most of its itinerary was centered on the Granite State. There was no path to the nomination for McCain that didn't depend on winning New Hampshire. The crowds were really small at first. I remember one stop where no more than a dozen people gathered in a garage to listen to him. I felt embarrassed for him, but he betrayed no unease about his situation, plunging into the task, stumping for the surge and himself with enthusiasm and humor. He did more events each day than any of his opponents, priding himself on his determination to outwork the competition. He was scheduled to speak at a VFW hall on a Friday night. Lindsey was with him. They arrived to discover a large crowd in attendance. "You're starting to catch on," Lindsey told him. But it turned out his stump speech wasn't the draw. It was the regular Friday-night fish fry that the locals had packed the hall for; one cheerful diner explained to us, "It always gets a good crowd." McCain got a bigger kick out of that humbling discovery than he would have had the crowd lifted him onto their shoulders. Thereafter, he often worked the story into his opening monologue, the ten minutes or so of old jokes and stories he used to warm up a town hall audience before he got to the serious stuff and to their "questions, comments, or insults."

He was happy. Or at least happier than he had been. He was the underdog, fighting for a cause he believed in, his reduced fortunes a worthy sacrifice. It showed. He was talking to voters in the way that felt most natural to him, close up, in informal settings, not in big venues with big speeches. He had his old dynamism back, relying on his unconventional candor and humor, the qualities that conveyed his authenticity, telling the fish-fry story on himself, making fun of his economy-class campaign, calling a young man who had questioned his age "a little jerk." Voters responded. In New Hampshire first, then even in Iowa, we started seeing his numbers tick up and his crowds increase a little. Giuliani still led most of the national polls. Romney led in Iowa and New Hampshire. Fred Thompson, who had entered the race late, when it looked like McCain was going to be an early casualty, was doing better than McCain was in Iowa, as was Mike Huckabee, whose Southern Baptist credentials attracted religious conservative voters who dominate the Republican caucus. But we could feel a little movement, enough to raise our hopes.

At an annual Republican gathering on Mackinac Island in Michigan, McCain had the crowd on their feet cheering his passionate, upbeat defense of the surge. Even New Hampshire voters who challenged him on the war seemed to respect his sincerity. "I'd rather lose an election than lose a war," he told them. And they believed him. At a debate late in October, he brought up a recent news story involving a $1 million appropriations earmark Hillary Clinton had secured for a museum to house memorabilia from the Woodstock music festival; he regularly mocked earmarks on the stump. At the debate, he introduced a new element to the routine that the campaign debate coach, Brett O'Donnell, had suggested to him. McCain referred to the festival as "a cultural and pharmaceutical event." "But I wouldn't know," he added, "I was tied up at the time." It took barely a second for the audience to get the joke, and get to their feet in unison, and, along with his opponents, cheer him loudly for a full minute. He was beaming while they applauded. I don't think I'd ever seen him more pleased with himself.

By the end of the year, he had caught Romney in New Hampshire and had a slight lead. The *New Hampshire Union Leader*, the bastion of Granite State conservatism, had endorsed him. The newspaper's endorsement didn't have the clout it had in years past, when its choice of candidates could prove pivotal in the primary. But it still had influence with Republican voters. With the endorsement came the paper's daily commitment to bashing the hell out of the opponents, Governor

Romney in this instance. We still were worried that our small advantage wouldn't hold up if Romney won Iowa the week before. New Hampshire voters are famous for rejecting the verdict of Iowa voters. But in a contest as close as it was in New Hampshire, we reckoned a Romney victory in Iowa could prove decisive, worth at least two or three points in a neck-and-neck race. Huckabee was surging in the Iowa polls, though, and we were rooting for him. Giuliani, who had looked formidable in the national polls, and who we worried could have strong appeal in New Hampshire, didn't campaign very seriously there, to our surprise. He had seemed to settle on a novel strategy of ignoring the earlier states and betting all his chips on a big-state win in Florida, where he led in the polls, to give him momentum going into Super Tuesday. Sam Brownback, McCain's Senate colleague and erstwhile rival for the nomination, had dropped out of the race in October and endorsed McCain a couple of weeks later, which, considering Brownback's clout with social conservatives, we hoped would help a little in Iowa.

Huckabee won Iowa on January 3 by an unexpectedly big margin, nine points. We were as ecstatic as Huckabee's campaign was. We were confident he couldn't capitalize on his Iowa win in New Hampshire; Huckabee had practically no ground operation to turn out his vote there. We did. When McCain called that night to congratulate him, he did so knowing that Huckabee's victory had likely ensured his own. Huckabee knew it, too, telling McCain, "Now it's your turn to beat him." He didn't need to explain who "him" was. McCain had liked Governor Romney before they competed for the nomination, and he liked him after their competition ended. Romney was one of McCain's best surrogates in the general election, and McCain would return the favor by endorsing Romney in the 2012 primaries and campaigning enthusiastically for him. But in 2008, McCain had worked up what we described later as "situational antipathy" for his main rival for the nomination. Most of the other candidates shared it to one extent or another. McCain admitted that a lot of the resentment was just envy. Romney was "really good at raising money, and he looks like a movie star," he said. After a year on the road, candidates can start to look a little bedraggled. Romney, on the other hand, always arrived at candidate debates in a motorcade worthy of an incumbent president, and, McCain joked, "looking like he'd just got back from a two-week vacation at the beach." Having clawed his way back into contention in New Hampshire, with everything riding on the outcome there—not to mention having overcome the onslaught of Romney's attack ads lashing his immigration position—McCain wanted to charge into the center of the ring and throw punches until someone went down.

The news from Iowa was exceptionally good. Not only had Huckabee won in a landslide, but McCain had practically tied his friend Fred Thompson for third place, despite spending the week before the Iowa caucus on a bus in New Hampshire. His showing surprised the press, who awarded him the "beat expectations" prize for the night. We had hoped the results in Iowa wouldn't hurt him in New Hampshire. Now we wondered how much the results might help him. We had to wait only five days to find out.

"These people have been so good to us," McCain remarked to Cindy after he was declared the winner of New Hampshire for the second time on January 8. As he had been eight years earlier, he was poker-faced and nonchalant about the victory, which must have come as an immense relief. It had been a merciless, exhausting crawl back from being the butt of jokes to presumptive front-runner, the achievement of an extraordinary force of will intended to prove a point as much as it was to win the nomination. McCain couldn't turn off his tenacity even in the celebration of a desperately fought victory.

It hadn't been a blowout, as it had been eight years earlier. McCain beat Romney by five points. He was already looking down the road to South Carolina, which he believed, even if some of us did not, was a must-win primary for him. Romney wasn't competing there; his campaign believed resistance from evangelical voters in the upstate was too great a handicap to overcome. Huckabee was likely to be as popular there as he had been in the more conservative counties in Iowa.

At the time the race in New Hampshire was called for McCain, the Democrats' contest was still undecided. Barack Obama had won a decisive victory in Iowa and given an inspiring victory speech. Hillary had narrowly lost second place to John Edwards. We assumed New Hampshire would effectively crown Obama the nominee. By "we" I mean me, other senior McCain staff, and just about every campaign reporter I knew. I'm not sure about McCain. He admired Clinton's toughness and remarked on it often. Given New Hampshire's legendary contrariness, I suspect he thought she had a puncher's chance to pull off an upset there. But I don't remember him prognosticating one way or another. He was focused on his race. We had originally prepared a victory speech for him that recognized the historic significance of Obama's victory. But with the Democratic outcome in doubt, we had to rewrite his victory speech. "I'm past the age when I can claim the noun 'kid,'" McCain began, "but we sure showed 'em what a comeback looks like." McCain had instructed me to focus the speech on New Hampshire, on what the state's voters had meant to him: "I could have only done this here," he told me. "These people let you be who you are." In the speech, he explained why he put his fate in the hands of Granite State voters. "When the pundits declared us finished, I told them, 'I'm going to New Hampshire, where the voters don't let you make their decision for them.' When they asked, 'How will you do it? You're down in the polls, you don't have money,' I answered, 'I'm going to New Hampshire, and I'm going to tell people the truth.'"

Win or lose the nomination, McCain planned to return to Iraq in March; he hoped to see Jimmy and share a meal with him. Jimmy told him that his squad was digging an armored personnel carrier out of a muddy wadi in Anbar Province the day of the New Hampshire primary. His sergeant called out his name. "Yes, Sergeant," Jimmy answered.

"Your dad won New Hampshire."

"Did he?"

"Yeah. Keep digging."

McCain loved the story.

Thanks in part to native-son bona fides in the state and in part to McCain's heedless candor, Governor Romney won a decisive victory in Michigan a week later. The automobile industry was hurting, laying off thousands of workers. At the time, Michigan suffered the highest unemployment rate in the country. As McCain was talking with a Michigan audience about the need for high-skill worker training in light of the advances in robotics and other technology, he conceded, "Let's face it, there are some jobs that aren't coming back to Michigan." It was an honest observation but an impolitic one. Romney pounced on it, calling McCain a defeatist and assuring Michigan voters he knew how to bring jobs back to the ailing state. McCain reacted by doubling down on his blunt statement, of course, although he tried to decorate his straight talk with a touch of optimism. "Detroit once saved the world in World War Two," he reminded one Michigan audience. "They can do it again." Romney took 39 percent of the vote to McCain's 30 percent.

Romney's decision not to contest South Carolina meant that the outcome there wouldn't determine the nominee. But if McCain could win it, he would have the momentum going into Florida, the state that could effectively decide the race. Fred Thompson did us a favor by staying in the race and cutting into Huckabee's support among social conservatives. While McCain was his usual casual, wisecracking self in his interactions with South Carolina voters, I have an image in my memory of him behind the scenes—unusually serious, teeth gritted, tight-lipped, no joking, no goofing around, his attention fixed on his task. There was a lot at stake, of course. He would be hard to stop if he won the state that had cost him the nomination eight years before. He would demonstrate strength in the South, the region believed to be the least supportive of his candidacy. But there was something else that seemed to drive him. Although he never said it, and I doubt he would have admitted it, I think winning South Carolina was a point of personal pride. He wanted to prove to the country and to himself that he could come back from a crushing defeat there to win the state on his second try. He left nothing to chance, insisting we add more stops every day to his already crowded schedule.

It was a long, tense primary night. The McCains, top aides, friends, and family were all gathered in a crowded hotel suite in Charleston, staring intently at various televisions as the returns came in. A small McCain lead seemed to rise and fall by slight percentages, up and

down, much of the night. At one point, someone took a call from a reporter who advised him that the Associated Press was about to call the
race for McCain. Word spread quickly through the room, and cheers
broke out. McCain sternly waved them off, calling for quiet and warning, "It's not over." A few minutes later, the reporter called to say that
something they saw in the returns had caused them to delay the call,
and worry etched the faces of the premature celebrators. Except for
McCain. He remained as he had been, glowering at a television screen,
trying to tune out the rest of us. He relaxed after the race was finally
called an hour later. Soon after the call he exulted in the cheers of
a fired-up crowd of South Carolina McCainiacs who had stuck with
him for the better part of a decade. He stood on the stage surrounded
by his family, including his mother, who tried to hide at the back of
the throng. He took her by the hand and guided her to the front, kiss-
ing her check and giving her a smile as broad as any I'd ever seen him
wear. "Well, it took us a while," he observed to the crowd, "but what's
eight years among friends."

We never understood why Giuliani didn't contest New Hampshire
and chose to make Florida the first primary he would try to win. He
was popular there, but the race would be strongly affected by earned
media. Florida was too big a state to win with just ad buys and campaign appearances. Rudy hadn't factored in the news for weeks, as
McCain, Romney, and Huckabee were posting their wins and soaking
up all the coverage. Romney had a strong presence in Florida and the
means to compete in both earned and paid media. He also had the
business credentials to be a more credible authority in a debate on
the economy. He was having some success at pressing his advantage
over McCain, who was getting barraged daily by an assortment of Fox
News personalities and conservative talk-radio hosts who sounded
desperate to stop him from winning Florida. "Jesus, I listened to
Limbaugh for five minutes today," McCain told me one afternoon. "I
thought the fat bastard was going to have a heart attack. McCain this.
McCain that."

He fought to keep the debate focused on Iraq and national security. In the meantime, Rick Davis was assiduously working political

aides to secure the endorsement of Florida governor Charlie Crist. Crist had apparently promised Giuliani his support, and we heard he had given Governor Romney some reason to hope. I know Rudy and his people were furious with Crist when, the night before the Florida primary, he endorsed McCain. But they didn't take out their anger on us. Giuliani knew that night he was going to lose. He and McCain were friends, and his people had already reached out to discuss when Rudy would endorse McCain, who won Florida the next day by a five-point margin.

Super Tuesday was a week later. Many of the biggest prizes were at stake, including the biggest, California. McCain was the prohibitive favorite, and the candidate and his aides were brimming with confidence. We started the day in New York City at a rally with Giuliani, before flying cross-country for a rally in San Diego with Schwarzenegger. Then we got to spend a relaxing Super Tuesday night at the Biltmore Hotel in Phoenix. When the night was over, McCain had won eight states in addition to his own, including the biggest ones, California, New York, and Illinois. Romney won seven smaller contests, and Huckabee took five southern primaries. But McCain's delegate lead was practically unsurpassable now. Governor Romney suspended his campaign two days later. McCain asked to see him in Boston a week after that. Sensitive to the resentment that can linger after a campaign's defeat, McCain wanted to visit the Romney campaign headquarters and personally pay his respects to the governor and his aides. The visit concluded with Governor Romney's endorsement. It was the end of a rivalry and the beginning of a friendship.

Over the course of eight months, McCain had summoned every ounce of his toughness to crawl from the wreckage of his front-runner's campaign and the almost certain end of his presidential ambitions to become the Republican nominee for president. It was an extraordinary comeback, and it was mostly overshadowed by the bigger story of the Democratic race.

NOMINEE

The Obama-Clinton contest wouldn't be settled for another four months. Obama was the clear favorite by then, but the two candidates were going at it hammer and tong. We took that as mostly good news for us, but we realized it would be hard for McCain to get more than a fraction of the exposure accorded the battling Democrats. We had some hope that our coverage, even if it didn't match the volume given the Democrats, would improve. At the start of McCain's campaign, we received a good share of the media's attention, but it had been mostly negative. A study by Harvard's Shorenstein Center on Media, Politics and Public Policy reported that in the first half of 2007, McCain received more negative coverage than any other presidential candidate in either party. And that was before the campaign imploded in July. After that, it was hard to get any attention at all, and his day-to-day media interactions were mostly with the young press embeds, the local papers, and more junior reporters from the national press.

That changed for the better late the next fall, when reporters perceived that McCain might still have a chance to win New Hampshire. All along he had kept his open-access policy with reporters and spent hours in the back of the bus taking all comers. He didn't enjoy it as much as he had eight years earlier. There was more reliance on gotcha questions than we remembered. A candidate with McCain's candor, irony, and humor was an easy target for that style of journalism. But it was important to his self-respect to be, and to be seen, as accessible and candid as possible. He got testy with reporters more often in 2008. But he got even testier with us when we tried restricting his encounters with sparring partners in the press corps. Late in the general election campaign, when our frustration with press coverage was peaking, aides (including me) tried to convince him to let us communicate for him. He would go along with it for a few hours or even a day or two, and then he would blow and demand we let him talk. If we were on the plane we leased for the general election campaign, with our regular traveling press corps seated in the back, he would just get up without saying a word and walk to the back of the plane and start taking questions. Nicolle Wallace, who had been President Bush's communications director, joined the campaign and traveled regularly with the candidate. She laughingly recounted an experience during the fall campaign after she had successfully kept McCain from doing impromptu press conferences for a day. "Nicolle, you see that tree over there?" he said, pointing. "I'm going to walk over to it and stand there until they come over and start asking me questions."

We weren't under any illusions about the favoritism the press showed Senator Obama. Every campaign feels ill used by the press, an observer might say. But that doesn't mean you can't discern when your candidate is held to different standards than the other candidate. We'd known in 2000 that we were the beneficiaries of press favoritism. We might have felt we had earned that favor for the manner in which our candidate related to reporters. But we recognized while it was happening that some of the press's coverage of McCain had crossed from appreciative to boosterism. Now Obama was getting that kind of treatment by the press, in both his primary contest with Senator Clinton and in the general election. Clinton and McCain received far more critical coverage. Some of that was understandable. Obama's campaign was exceptionally well run. He raised the most money and made the fewest mistakes. He was an excellent candidate and excited his supporters more than any presidential candidate I can remember. The Clinton and McCain campaigns made more mistakes, raised less money, often operated at less than peak efficiency, and suffered in comparison to Obama's, which was fair. But Obama also received less scrutiny for his positions than did his opponents. He was the subject of far fewer investigative stories. Many of the investigative pieces we endured certainly originated in Obama campaign opposition research. Questions were raised about McCain aides, associates, and friends almost weekly. If we tried to raise questions about Obama associates, we were usually rewarded with indignation from editorial writers, which frequently included insinuations and sometimes explicit accusations of racism.

I'm not blaming any of this on the reporters who covered the McCain campaign. They were professionals, and while we argued regularly, I respected their commitment to objectivity. I consider many of them friends. I do believe editors for the most influential news outlets, who shaped the coverage of the 2008 presidential campaign, were biased toward Obama and tried to protect him from our attacks. Pew Research analyzed the reporting each candidate received from the party conventions to their final debate in mid-October: 14 percent of McCain's coverage was deemed positive; 57 percent was negative; the rest was neutral or mixed. Obama's ratio of positive to negative press was 36 percent positive to 29 percent negative. I suspected what was coming as I watched the Democratic nomination fight play out. But that didn't make it easier to shrug off when it came.

The frequent accusations that our attacks on Senator Obama were blatant or subtle appeals to racists were the most frustrating part for McCain and his aides. I don't argue that racism wasn't a factor in some voters' hostility to Obama; I'm certain that it was. But we believed we took every precaution to avoid our exploitation of that fault in our country. We prided ourselves on it. The chief enforcer of the edict to avoid doing anything that might be construed as racist was the candidate himself. Fred Davis, the Republican ad maker who produced most of the campaign's general election advertising, created an ad that attacked Obama's association with his pastor, Reverend Wright, some of whose sermons had been divisive and controversial. McCain forbade him to run it, even going so far as saying, "Obama addressed the issue. We're not going to reopen it." When a Cincinnati talk-radio personality warmed up a crowd in advance of McCain's arrival, took a lot of cheap shots at Clinton and Obama, and repeatedly stressed Obama's middle name, Hussein, McCain chastised the guy publicly, apologized for the disparaging remarks, and called his opponents "honorable." When the Republican Party in North Carolina ran an ad using video of one of Reverend Wright's more incendiary sermons, McCain denounced it as divisive. There were no racist dog whistles or subterranean smear campaigns emanating from our campaign. The candidate wouldn't have it, and he made sure we knew it.

In May, not long before Obama clinched the Democratic nomination, *Newsweek* ran a cover story speculating on how Republicans would use racist appeals to win the election. I was incredulous and upset and fired off an angry email to Jon Meacham, the magazine's editor and a friend. My point was that using the tactics of past Republican campaigns to generalize about the current one was unfair. This wasn't just a Republican campaign. It was John McCain's campaign, and he was a candidate who had never played politics that way, who believed it would demean him and the country if he did. The Republicans managing his campaign had names and reputations, too, and we took offense at being presumed racists.

We ran our famous or infamous (depending on your politics) "celebrity ad" in August for the purpose of raising doubts about Obama's readiness to be president. That was its only purpose. It was just after Obama had returned from his tour of European capitals, where he had been greeted rapturously by heads of state and massive crowds chanting his name. He was leading in the polls, raising unbelievable sums of money, and had rejected federal spending limits. He was a phenomenon, but he had been in federal office less than four years. We thought if we emphasized his celebrity status and likened it to the celebrity of pop stars, we might be able to raise doubts about his qualifications for office. "He's the biggest celebrity in the world," the tagline began as a crowd cheered, "O-bam-a! O-bam-a!" "But is he ready to lead?" There was no comment on race, expressed, implied, or intended. The ad got a lot of attention, and it appeared to work. The polls tightened, and references to Obama's inexperience appeared in many of the verbatim responses in our polling. It was denounced as "crypto-racist" by one liberal writer, a view echoed by many of his like-minded peers.

It felt like an impossible predicament to us sometimes, which I appreciate was a situation created by centuries of transgressions against African-Americans by white politicians. But it's hard to keep that perspective when you're getting the shit kicked out of you regularly for sins you didn't commit. The other side could attack us twenty-four hours a day. We couldn't attack them without being labeled racist. Sometimes we took it personally, including the candidate. I think if you had asked McCain what the lowest moment of the campaign was for him, he would have said when civil rights hero John Lewis, a man he revered, likened him to George Wallace. He was deeply hurt by it. I worried when it happened, shortly before the final general election debate, that it would knock McCain badly off his stride and it would be all he talked about. It did preoccupy him for a few days; he talked about it to reporters and at the debate, but not to the exclusion of other issues. He really did admire Lewis. I regret that the two never reconciled.

McCain left for Iraq in mid-March. When he returned, relieved by further evidence that the surge was succeeding, we presented him a plan to use this time before the Democrats had a nominee to reintroduce himself to voters. That's not the easiest thing to do when the candidate has been in public life for more than twenty years, and a national figure for a decade, and he was skeptical that he needed reintroduction. But he went along, even if he wasn't entirely persuaded by our argument that he needed to get voters to see him as something other than a familiar Washington figure. He didn't underestimate the challenge Obama posed. "That guy's got something going, doesn't he," he observed appreciatively as he watched a clip of an Obama rally on TV. McCain was almost seventy-two years old, a nationally known commodity, a Republican running to succeed a Republican incumbent who was at the nadir of his presidency in an environment where three-quarters of voters thought the country was on the wrong track. McCain was competing with a dashing, eloquent opponent who was twenty-five years younger, who personified change, who was an African-American inspiring people of every background and ethnicity to believe he would deliver the change they were looking for. McCain had to get people to see him as more than a career politician to have a chance of convincing them that he, too, would be an agent of change.

Our first gambit was to launch what we informally referred to as the bio tour and formally called the "Service to America" tour. McCain had one of the best stories in politics, and we thought we could use the intermission between our primaries and the general election, when reporters assigned to us didn't have anything more exciting to cover, to retell it to the country. He began at the Naval Academy on March 31 and continued to Episcopal High School that same day, then on to Pensacola, where he had earned his aviator wings. The next stop was McCain Field, named for his grandfather, in Meridian, Mississippi, his family's ancestral home. The tour ended on the courthouse steps in Prescott, Arizona, where McCain had finished every one of his campaigns.

He gave a speech at each stop, culled mostly from material in the two memoirs we had written, offering interesting, sometimes spicy, and inspiring details of his cinematic life story. It seemed like a good idea at the time, and I think it might have helped a little. But it seemed to bore the guy who owned the story. I know that because McCain said to me, "This is kind of boring," after the Pensacola speech, in which I'd included an oblique reference to an old flame of his, an exotic dancer with the stage name Marie the Flame of Florida. He had more stops on the tour, but he didn't seem to have his heart in it, and reporters and audiences probably picked up on it. He seemed more engaged at the last stop in Prescott, where he talked about Arizona history and the inspiration Mo Udall and Barry Goldwater had been to him.

He was considerably more enthusiastic about his next venture, which we tried to brand the "It's Time for Action" tour, conceived to differentiate McCain as much as possible from previous Republican presidential candidates. McCain had come to like and respect President Bush, but his unpopularity at the end of his presidency was a tough challenge for a potential Republican successor. The president had formally endorsed McCain at the White House in early March, and he and his staff had been exceedingly gracious. McCain was appreciative, but he knew he had to distance himself from the president. He was already, for better or worse, closely identified with the president's Iraq policy. He couldn't persuade anyone that he was a change candidate if he didn't make clear what needed to change. And so he embarked on a tour of hard-pressed, mostly Democratic communities—places, we boasted, where no Republican presidential candidate had spent time. McCain would stress by words and deed, over and over, that he was an unconventional Republican who cared about issues Democratic voters cared about and was committed to working with politicians in both parties to address them. He wasn't running to be "president of the Republicans," he insisted, but of all his countrymen. "My fellow Americans," he said repeatedly, "that kinship means more to me than any other association."

He went to a shuttered steel mill in Youngstown, Ohio, and to the Florida Everglades to witness the impact of climate change. He went to Selma, Alabama, and gave a speech on national unity at the foot of the Edmund Pettus Bridge, in which he praised the courage and patriotism of John Lewis. He went to New Orleans's Ninth Ward and excoriated the Bush administration's response to Hurricane Katrina. He talked to coal miners in Inez, Kentucky, where Lyndon Johnson had announced the War on Poverty. He went to Baton Rouge and Little Rock. "There must be no forgotten places in America," he repeated at every stop. At a town hall in Youngstown, he joked about his stumbles during the primaries: "I've been left recently in the unfamiliar position of facing no opposition within my own party. And as you might recall, it was a different story last year, when I could claim the unqualified support of Cindy and my mother—and my mom was starting to keep her options open. Back then, there were some very impressive front-runners, there was a very formidable second tier of contenders, and then there was me."

As he had done in Michigan, he didn't pull punches about the challenges facing places like Youngstown. "I can't tell you that these jobs are ever going to come back to this magnificent part of the country," he told a questioner. "But I will commit to giving these workers a second chance. They need it, they deserve it. I know that's small comfort to you, but I can't look you in the eye and tell you those steel mills are coming back."

He went to a junior college in Thomasville in Alabama's Black Belt and to a small isolated community of quilt makers in Gee's Bend, Alabama. That was his favorite stop on the tour. The elderly ladies who sewed the highly prized quilts greeted his bus, singing old gospel songs and dancing, and took the McCains by the hand, pulling them into their circle. They were delightful and he was delighted. He awkwardly danced a step or two, looking a little sheepish, but smiled and laughed, admired their quilts, and bought three of them. He promised them he would be back. "I know none of you are going to vote for me," he told them. "But if I'm elected president, I'm coming back here anyway. Hold me to it." He rode the ferry across the river with them to the nearest town on the opposite bank, where reporters quizzed him on why he had voted against an appropriations bill that had contained an earmark for the ferry, a fact Democratic researchers had dug up and helpfully shared with reporters.

The only community McCain addressed where he was likely to find votes were the coal miners in Inez, some of whom were openly hostile to Obama and didn't hesitate to say so. *New Yorker* reporter George Packer was there and wrote afterward that McCain "refused to take the bait." The line that closed the article is one I remember all these years later, more for its discernment about McCain than for its modest optimism about his prospects: "McCain says to audiences, Here I am, a man in full, take me or leave me. That might be the only Republican who could win in 2008."[45]

I believed McCain had a decent shot at winning that spring, and I believed it for a brief period after the Republican National Convention. Most of the rest of the time I was pessimistic, owing partly to my natural negativity and the rest to events beyond our control. But I loved his tour to America's forgotten places. So did he. Whatever its value to our project to differentiate him from the administration and associate him with political change, it was the kind of thing McCain lived to do, to ignore conventions and flaunt his profile as an independent thinker, a man who had character rather than ideology. He was who he wanted to be on that tour. Democrats sneered at his pretension; the press examined it through the prism of professional skepticism that often looks quite like cynicism. But he was happy and proud of it, and he deserved to be.

Hillary Clinton quit the race in early June, and the victorious Obama could now concentrate on his Republican opponent. They had ample resources to do so and still enjoyed more media attention than McCain could attract. McCain kept at it, trying to make voters and reporters see him not through standard political expectations or the Obama campaign's framing but as someone as indifferent to the conventions of politics as Obama claimed to be. He had limited success in that endeavor, but he didn't quit trying. He was genuinely disappointed when Obama declined his offer of joint town halls, and angry when Obama dropped out of the public financing system and the press paid it little notice.

We made a mistake by scheduling an event on the same night Obama captured the nomination and gave his victory speech. McCain congratulated Obama in his speech, but we should have given Obama and his supporters the night; they had earned it. That was the authentic McCain move. But we were always thrashing around trying to get the press to pay as much attention to us as they were to Obama. What we received that night was mostly derision for trying to steal the spotlight, but also for the odd-looking green backdrop behind McCain, which we had intended to underscore his concern for the environment.

He tried hard to project optimism on the stump, but he didn't seem to inhabit the quality like Obama did. He took pride in speaking hard truths, and that sometimes got in his way. We worked to create situations in which he could project his faith that a McCain presidency would tackle big challenges. He gave speeches on a wide array of issues. He gave a speech in Columbus, Ohio, looking ahead four years to the end of a first McCain term, and ticked off all the progress he hoped to have made. Real progress against climate change, with cleaner energy sources proliferating. A peaceful Iraq, setting a democratic example for the Arab world. An America not dependent on foreign sources of energy. Greater access to more affordable health insurance. A budget nearly balanced.

McCain had traveled often to the Republic of Georgia, from the earliest days of its independence from Russia to as recently as 2006. He had cheered on its peaceful Rose Revolution and admired Georgia's young, pro-Western president, Mikheil "Misha" Saakashvili, whom he had known since the early 1990s, when Saakashvili was a political activist studying law at Columbia University. When Russian forces invaded Georgia the first week of August, McCain released a very detailed statement, demonstrating the depth of his knowledge of the country and the nature of its crisis with Russia. He made clear who the aggressor was, Vladimir Putin, and called for the West to demand that "Russia unconditionally cease its military operations and withdraw all its forces." Obama's initial statement was milder and declined to blame Putin for the war. He would do so a few days later, when it was clear to almost everyone that Putin had caused the crisis. But he still refrained from the blunt denunciations McCain favored. McCain talked by phone to Saakashvili many times over the ten days or so until a cease-fire was agreed to and Russia began withdrawing its forces. He was preoccupied with another overseas crisis, as he had been persistently with Iraq, and using his campaign to publicize it. Senator Obama and Obama surrogates criticized him for his rhetoric and his positions, while McCain claimed to speak for "every American when I say today, we are all Georgians." Most Americans couldn't have found Georgia on a map, and he knew that. But his concern over Russia's attacks on "a tiny, struggling democracy far away from the United States of America" was genuine, and he wanted to impart it to Americans while he had their attention. Despite differences in tone and emphasis, McCain's and Obama's positions on the subject were not all that dissimilar. But their exchanges over Georgia would begin a long debate between the two about how to confront Putin's troublemaking and hostility to the U.S., a debate that would peak six years later during Putin's invasion of Ukraine.

The summer wore on, Obama went on his successful overseas tour, and nothing we did seemed to close either the polling or the enthusiasm gap. Then we ran the celebrity ad, the polls tightened, and we got an infusion of hope. We hunkered down to endure the Democrats' convention and work on the planning for ours, which immediately followed. We had a major piece of business outstanding: McCain hadn't made up his mind about a running mate. The decision was pending in August when I left the campaign for a week in Maine to write his acceptance speech.

Not long after I sent McCain a first draft and was preparing to return to campaign headquarters in Arlington, Virginia, I received a call from the candidate, who was in Phoenix. "I need you to come out here," he instructed. "I need you to go with Schmidt to Flag [Flagstaff, Arizona] and meet Sarah Palin tomorrow night." I tried not to show my surprise as I listened to him explain that Steve Schmidt and I were to, in effect, give the governor of Alaska a job interview, followed by a long (almost all night) discussion between the governor and A. B. Culvahouse and the lawyers vetting prospective vice presidential candidates. We would meet with her in a borrowed condominium located on a Flagstaff golf course.

I hadn't discussed the vice presidential selection or anything else with McCain for days. I had been busy with the speech and chastened by his frustration in conversations he had a week earlier with Rick, Steve, and me, when we had persuaded him that he could not have the person he wanted, his friend Joe Lieberman. We all liked Senator Lieberman and loved the idea of a bipartisan ticket as a signifier of real political change. But when word started leaking, Rick, Steve, Charlie Black and other top aides were deluged with panicked calls from party leaders warning that the choice of a pro-choice Democrat would rip the party apart, and would be challenged on the convention floor and possibly rejected. Rick thought we could win a floor fight over the nomination, but at what cost? McCain would leave St. Paul (where the convention was held that year) wounded by the fight over his VP nominee and leading a badly divided party. It took days to convince him that picking Lieberman would in the end do more harm than good to his prospects. He wasn't happy, and he wasn't receptive to other suggestions for a few days, seemingly in a funk over opposition to doing the thing that "felt right to me." But the Democrats' convention in Denver had already started. The plan was to announce the

McCain VP pick the day the Democrats left Denver, three days before our own convention was to begin.

When I had left for Maine, I thought the choice had likely come down to Governor Romney or Governor Tim Pawlenty of Minnesota. I was past any situational antipathy I might have felt for Governor Romney. I respected him and thought he would be an effective messenger for the ticket, especially on the economy. Should they win, I thought he would be a valuable counselor to President McCain. But we all knew that from the moment Romney was announced, the Democrats would showcase clip after clip of Romney and McCain from the primaries, beating each other up in debates, interviews, and television ads, and the press would eat it up. We worried the shelf life of the blasts from the recent past could last through the convention and into the precious first week after, when campaigns sought to capitalize on the boost they got from being lionized in prime time for four days. On account of those concerns, I had decided that should McCain ask me to weigh in again on the vice presidential choice, I would recommend Governor Pawlenty.

Schmidt had business clients in Alaska and traveled there regularly. He was the most familiar of us with the governor and impressed by what he knew of her. Schmidt recommended her to McCain, who had met her once briefly but did not have an opinion about her. She also had admirers among other conservatives who were sympathetic to McCain. The conventional wisdom about the Palin pick is that McCain did it to motivate a Republican base that was unenthusiastic about his candidacy. That's crap. The circle of people who were involved in her selection, besides John and Cindy, was limited to Schmidt, Davis and me, and a few staffers, sworn to secrecy, who had to arrange the logistics of covertly getting her to Arizona. We were determined to avoid seeing another choice leaked before we were ready to confront opposition to it. Not one of us, at any point, recommended her to McCain on the basis of how her selection would energize the base. We didn't even emphasize her conservative bona fides. She wasn't well known nationally, and none of us knew how popular a figure she would prove to be with conservatives nationally. I had to google her when I hung up with McCain to get the basics of her biography. Steve and Rick had done some research and thought Palin merited a closer look. Her appeal was basically twofold—she personified change, a small-town mayor who had taken on the Republican establishment and the oil companies, beaten them, and gotten herself elected governor. Her second, not inconsiderable, quality was that she was a woman in an election where a good number of women voters were disappointed by Hillary Clinton's defeat for the Democratic nomination. Palin was a working mother of four who related easily to other working women and reportedly had exceptional retail skills. Her youngest child, Trig, had Down's syndrome, which we thought conveyed a strong image of maternal devotion and commitment to pro-life values. But that was it. We had no other considerations. She was a reformer, a woman, a mother, and a relatable politician with natural campaign chops.

She struck me on first acquaintance as one of the most self-assured people I'd ever encountered. For someone so new to politics, she gave no indication that she was overawed by the prospect of being McCain's running mate and becoming an overnight celebrity. By the end of the campaign, I would revise my opinion of her self-assurance. I never thought she was the insecure wreck some of her caricatures portrayed her as, but I saw her get rattled by her press coverage—probably no more than other candidates who had never competed at that level of politics, but enough to contrast with the confident, unflappable person she struck me as that night in Flagstaff. My main concern then and later was that she did not have the experience in government or national politics to debate an array of issues in the white-hot intensity of a presidential campaign. I thought her inexperience would be a self-inflicted injury to McCain's message of putting the country before politics, and to his subsidiary message that he was readier to be president than Obama was. He was seventy-two years old the day he asked Sarah Palin to be his running mate; he certainly was more experienced than his opponent and ready to be president. Governor Palin was self-evidently neither of those things.

For two or more hours, she talked knowledgeably with Schmidt and me about natural resources and basic economic issues. On the whole,

I thought she could appear credible on most domestic issues. She had opinions on a lot of things, a few of which clashed with McCain's, but she stressed that she understood her subordinate role and assured us she was a team player. She emphasized her reformer credentials and said she had always been impressed with McCain's maverick reputation. When asked any questions about foreign policy and national security issues, she conceded she knew very little, and if that were a priority qualification for the VP, she wouldn't be the right choice. She would have to be "coached up," she said, but assured us she was a fast learner and could learn enough to defend McCain's views. I had heard she was an evolution skeptic, which I thought would be disqualifying, and I asked for her opinion on the subject. She told me her father had been a science teacher, and he had shown her fossils and other evidence that species evolve, but she believed the hand of the Creator was at work in all of it. That was a perfectly suitable response to me. Schmidt and I belabored the point that no matter how tough she was, nothing would prepare her for the kind of pressure she would face as McCain's running mate. I don't think she believed us.

Our charge from the candidate was to make a determination—after our interview with her, in consultation with Rick, and after A.B. and his team had gone through their issues with her—about whether or not it was worth his time to meet with her. If we thought it was, we were to arrange for her to come to the cabin in the morning. If not, we were to thank her on his behalf, tell her we would be in touch, and fly her back to Anchorage. She spent hours with the lawyers going over various concerns, which I mostly observed and Schmidt weighed in on from time to time. She might have left out some details of the controversies she and her husband featured in, but I think every one of them was at least mentioned. She volunteered information we didn't have that her daughter Bristol was pregnant. When the lawyers finished, A.B. summed up for McCain his judgment on choosing the governor: "Big risk, big reward," he told him, which is not something you should say to McCain if you want to discourage him from doing something. Schmidt was confident she was the right choice—not without risk but the best choice of the available options—and could change the direction of the campaign. I worried she wasn't ready for the challenge of the campaign or the presidency and that it would be clear to the press and public. Nevertheless, I agreed that McCain should interview her.

We left her a couple of hours before dawn to get to the McCains' place. We gave John and Cindy a brief summary of the night's discussions, then watched as Palin's SUV bumped down the steep road to the cabin. After introductions and brief small talk, John and the governor walked to his favorite spot on the property at a bend in the creek, where they sat and talked for about an hour. McCain, ever the tight-lipped debriefer, didn't share with us many details of their discussion, but mentioned that she had stressed her record as a reformer and was passionate about fighting corruption. "She's got a lotta confidence," he added. After they had talked, he and Schmidt and I walked to another house on the property to talk privately, while Palin chatted with Cindy on the deck of the McCains' house. Schmidt and I debated the choice. He made a convincing argument that she was our last chance to shake up the race. He told McCain we could have a good convention and good debates and run a mistake-free general election campaign, and none of those things would prevent us from losing in an environment so politically toxic for Republicans. I argued McCain would be putting his "Country First" pledge at risk, because Palin was a strictly political pick who didn't have the knowledge or experience to be president.

I wasn't angry or morose when Schmidt's advice prevailed. Schmidt can be a persuasive fellow, and his argument had merit. We were on a trajectory to lose if we didn't somehow grab a piece of the change message. Neither was I certain Palin's deficiencies couldn't be addressed in time, and supported enough by staff in the meantime to prevent them from doing lasting damage to her and McCain's reputation. I was certain, though, that however fast a learner she was, and however confident a candidate she proved to be, her selection would wreck McCain's advantage on the experience question. But McCain, who ended our debate with a curt "I'm gonna offer it to her," believed whatever she lacked could be supplied and shaped to reflect his views and values. He called to talk it over with Rick and then rejoined Cindy and the governor. That is how Sarah Palin found her way into the national spotlight.

Schmidt and I flew with Governor Palin and her aide to a private airfield outside Dayton, Ohio, and registered under assumed names at a nearby hotel. McCain would reveal his choice the next day before a packed auditorium at Wright University. We were joined that night by Nicolle Wallace, who would help prepare the governor for the national exposure she was about to receive, and Matthew Scully, one of the best speechwriters in the profession, who would help draft her remarks for the announcement. Neither Nicolle nor Matt had been told before they left Washington whom they were being summoned to assist. As soon as I got to the hotel, I went to my room to write McCain's remarks for the next day. I sat at a narrow desk in my room and hammered away at my laptop, while in the background, the TV broadcast Obama's acceptance speech, delivered in the football stadium they had chosen for the venue.

I was anxious about the announcement, which was a symptom of my anxiety about the Palin choice. But when McCain introduced to a cheering crowd "the next vice president of the United States, Governor Sarah Palin from the great state of Alaska," and she made her entrance surrounded by her family, and then delivered her speech with verve and an almost cocky self-assurance, I felt relieved. I turned to Nicolle, smiled, and said something like "Well, maybe she is up to it." The next week Palin would hit it out of the park again in her acceptance speech at the convention, another Scully gem, and I would be relieved again. But there were signs even that week that my optimism was unwarranted. She might not have believed our warnings about the intensity of the exposure she would have to withstand. Maybe I really hadn't, either, or I would have been slower to conclude she could withstand it. I'm sure she took strength and confidence from the rapturous reception her acceptance speech received, and she survived the first round of furious scrutiny she got at St. Paul, which included the disclosure of her daughter's pregnancy and offensive rumormongering about whether she or Bristol was baby Trig's real mother. She was tough—at one point, she asked Schmidt, "Do they want to see my stretch marks?"

After the convention, Palin seemed distracted by coverage of ethical controversies that involved her family, especially by Alaska news outlets. Later, after she received negative reviews of an interview with Katie Couric in which she had appeared unready for the office she was running for, and was daily confronting critical coverage of various subjects concerning her, and a lot of nasty commentary, she was, as most people would be, upset. All the while she was getting tutored hours a day on a host of foreign policy issues and McCain's positions on them. It was too much to expect from her.

To prep for her one debate with Joe Biden, we sent her to the McCains' cabin, where she could rest and get exercise in a beautiful, relaxed environment. She acquitted herself respectably, to the enormous relief of her running mate and his aides. I watched it in McCain's hotel suite with several other aides, each one of us so nervous we couldn't speak. McCain wasn't as nervous in his own debates with Obama as he was while watching Palin debate his old pal Joe Biden. The tension in the room was memorable, as was the relief we felt when it was over and we judged that she had held her own. McCain never conceded he had made a mistake in choosing Palin. He felt responsible for putting her in the position, and he thought it ungracious to do anything other than defend her. "She didn't put herself on the ticket," he snapped at me once. The most he ever allowed was that he wished he hadn't listened to us, and had gone ahead and picked Joe Lieberman. In his last book, he agreed to describe Governor Palin as a "skilled amateur performer asked to perform on Broadway twice a day." She really was a natural at the retail side of politics. I'd never seen anyone play a roomful of strangers as warmly and attentively as she did. She was always running late because it took her so long to finish a rope line: She had a kind word and a photograph for everyone on it. She was game for challenges and could handle herself well when confronting unexpected problems. When her teleprompter went dark during her acceptance speech, she winged it until it came back. No one could tell there had been a problem. But she was not ready for presidential-level scrutiny, nor was she ready for the presidency. He shouldn't have chosen her.

We didn't think that coming out of St. Paul. McCain was on a roll for the first time since he had sewn up the nomination. His own acceptance speech had gotten mixed reviews, although the nicer ones outnumbered the negative ones. I was proud of it, and so was he. He stumbled a couple of times in the beginning, but in the second half of the speech, he was rolling, and he delivered the end with aplomb and had the audience roaring approval. I was seated right in front of him, where he had instructed me to sit so I could motion for him to speed up or slow down if needed. As he started to pick up speed and force, and the crowd started getting into it, I kind of forgot myself and the television cameras trained on him and us, and I stood up and started whirling my upstretched right arm in circles as if twirling an invisible lasso, trying to motion him to ride the crescendo of cheers. I must have looked like an idiot. I didn't remember doing it until laughing colleagues described my behavior to me. But he left St. Paul happy, with the crowd's applause still ringing in his ears.

He and Palin appeared together at the first few stops after the convention, before they divided forces and campaigned in separate locations. Press accounts of their separate rallies often included an observation that Palin's crowds were bigger and livelier than McCain's. If that bothered him, he never said so. He knew she was a phenomenon and didn't resent it. He got the bump we hoped for from the convention, and the polls gave him a consistent lead over Obama for the first time since the two candidates had secured their nominations. Different polls put McCain's advantage at a few points, five points, and ten points in one really encouraging Gallup poll. The polls had tightened a little by September 11, when McCain and Obama took time out from hammering away at each other to appear at a commemorative event with their wives, where, in an expression of national unity, they laid a wreath at Ground Zero. I watched the ceremony with an old friend from campaigns past, former ABC reporter and then Obama communications aide Linda Douglass. It was a brief but welcome reminder that a society existed outside the campaign and in a couple of months

I would rejoin it. I asked McCain afterward what he and Obama had talked about during their time together. I had observed him talking to his opponent quite animatedly and patting him on the back a couple of times. "Oh, what you might expect," he answered.

"I don't know what I'd expect, what did you talk about?"

"Just small talk, boy, small talk."

Had their conversation been so inconsequential that it bored him to recount it? Probably. Was he reinforcing his image as a lousy debriefer? Maybe. Or had he said something to Obama that he didn't want to share with me? I wondered. I asked him about it when we were working on his last book, and he acted like he didn't know what I was talking about.

Four days after the temporary cease-fire, Lehman Brothers filed for bankruptcy. The real estate bubble had burst, and the global credit crisis was under way. The race was even at that point. McCain would never have a lead again. The next day, hoping to reassure voters—many of whose mortgages were about to be underwater as housing prices collapsed—he ad-libbed his remark, "The fundamentals of our economy are strong." The Obama campaign and the press pounced, exploiting the impolitic claim to make him look clueless as more bankruptcies were announced and the stock market plunged hundreds of points a day. I was watching his appearance on television in the Arlington headquarters with Matt McDonald, who was helping craft the candidate's messaging on the economy. "Did he say the fundamentals of the economy are sound?" I asked McDonald, who just nodded in reply. We were both on the campaign plane the next day, where McDonald furiously worked on statements to address the financial disaster, and all of us struggled to get a sense of the growing dimensions of the crisis and when it might bottom out. McCain's senior economic advisors warned him that we might be approaching a point when people wouldn't be able to withdraw cash from their ATMs.

The Bush administration was working on their response to the crisis, the $700 billion Troubled Asset Relief Program (TARP) to rescue financial institutions that were teetering on the edge of the abyss. They had yet to send it to Congress for approval when McCain aides in charge of congressional relations started picking up indications that it was likely to meet with resistance from conservative House Republicans. For two weeks, the news had gone from bad to worse to incomprehensible. We didn't have a very persuasive response. McCain called for a 9/11-style commission to figure out what had happened, and for reckless CEOs at bankrupt financial institutions to be prosecuted. But that wasn't a reassuring message to voters whose savings and homes were in jeopardy. We had to do something big, we reasoned, in response to the calamity before something really big and bad happened to us.

We were in New York on September 24, planning to spend the afternoon there doing debate prep. The first candidate debate in Oxford, Mississippi, was scheduled for September 26. Obama called McCain to suggest they issue a joint statement supporting the administration's plan. A little while earlier, Schmidt, Davis, and I had pitched McCain an idea we hoped would knock over the chessboard before we were checkmated: We recommended he suspend the campaign for a few days, including his participation in the debate, so he could fly to Washington to help address the crisis. We thought the move would underscore his "country first, politics second" message. More urgently, we didn't know with certainty how devastating it would be to the economy were Republicans in Congress to reject the Bush rescue plan, but we were certain it would mean the end of any chance of a McCain victory. So we appealed to him to return to Washington, meet with the Republican leadership in the House, and ask the president to convene a meeting with both parties' congressional leaders, the two candidates, Treasury secretary Hank Paulson, and the Bush economic team to discuss ideas for a relief package that could win congressional approval. We thought McCain, as the party's presidential nominee, would have a positive influence on restive House Republicans. So we essentially put McCain's destiny in their hands. It was a stupid mistake, as we would soon discover and, if we had been honest with ourselves, probably suspected all along. Conservative opponents of TARP in the House did not want to give $700 billion to CEOs who had bankrupted their companies, and they didn't care if their party's nominee for president did.

McCain proposed to Obama that they both suspend their campaigns to focus on the crisis. "Do you think he'll agree?" we asked McCain when he had hung up. "Doesn't sound like it," he answered. We plunged ahead anyway, called the president to ask for the meeting, and made arrangements to return to Washington. For good measure, McCain called Harry Reid to encourage him to participate in a White House meeting. They had known each other a long time, both having arrived in the Senate in 1987. They butted heads from time to time, but liked each other and talked informally and frankly together. Reid was ready for his call and read woodenly from a prepared script criticizing McCain's "stunt." McCain knew right then, he told me later, "that this thing was going to blow up in my face." The Obama campaign also denounced it as a stunt, and Obama promised he would be in Oxford the day after next to debate McCain or his empty chair; he gave the impression that it didn't matter to him. An overworked Hank Paulson was reportedly infuriated by McCain's proposed interference in the plan he was begging Congress to approve.

McCain's first stop in Washington was Republican leader John Boehner's office. That was almost as discouraging as the call with Reid. Boehner wasn't very forthcoming as McCain asked questions about what it would take to get his caucus on board with a rescue package. I don't think Boehner knew then what it would take. His whips were likely trying to determine that as they spoke. Maybe he didn't want to share with us intelligence he needed to keep confidential for the time being, suspecting that we would blab it to the press. He knew his caucus a lot better than we did. We had experienced House political hands on the campaign, and they advised that it would be a big lift to convince conservatives to support anything like Paulson's bailout plan.

The White House meeting was a bust. Obama had spoken briefly and, according to McCain, had not been confrontational. Reid and Speaker Pelosi had been, he reported, and had practically shouted at him and the president, who then asked McCain to speak. McCain demurred, saying he wanted to hear what Leader Boehner had to say, which I'm sure puzzled the president and other participants, since McCain had asked for the meeting. But he explained his reasoning to us afterward: If Boehner didn't say what it would take to get his caucus on board, "then I don't know what I'm supposed to be doing. What am I supposed to ask Bush for? I don't know what he needs." Within minutes of the meeting's conclusion, Democrats reported McCain's reticence to the press—further evidence, they said and the press conveyed, that McCain was erratic in a crisis. By the end of that first day in Washington, we were making plans to end the campaign's suspension and fly to Mississippi to debate Obama.

As feared, the House rejected the plan on September 29. The Senate passed a revised version of the legislation two days later, which the House reluctantly went along with two days after the Senate action. Critics of TARP, which would prove enormously unpopular with conservatives and with the public at large, advised McCain to vote against it. The Obama campaign was worried he would join the critics and gain at least a short-term advantage over Obama, who had committed to vote for it. But McCain didn't consider it. On October 1, he and Obama walked up to the Senate clerk and voted yea. All our campaign suspension had managed to achieve was an opening for the Obama campaign to call McCain erratic.

Whatever McCain or his aides thought about his chances at that point, we kept it to ourselves. I suspect each of us had a different point when we, at least privately, conceded it was hopeless. Mine occurred after the second debate, in Nashville, billed as a town hall debate. The press's pre-analysis was that the format favored McCain. Obama was the better orator, but McCain was a natural in town hall exchanges with voters and had done more of them than any living politician. The problem was that town hall–style presidential debates weren't anything like the town halls familiar to McCain. They were quiet and formal. No cheers or boos or laughs. There wasn't the usual back-and-forth with voters; his answers were limited to two minutes and the moderator asked the follow-ups. No comments, jokes, or insults, the improvised exchanges of ideas and attitudes that McCain loved. It was just as unnatural a setting for him as debates with podiums and a panel of journalists refereeing, even more so. He had at least done plenty of those debates. This pretend town hall was a new experience, and I watched him struggle to find his rhythm and get a rapport with the audience. He kept trying and failing to elicit a reaction from them. It threw him, and Obama had the better debate. It wasn't a disaster, and we had another debate to go. I thought McCain won the last one on points. I thought their first encounter was a draw. But a draw is the same as a loss for the candidate who's trailing.

I went for a walk in the rain after the Nashville debate. I wanted to get away from the circus for a while. I walked into a bar selling bottles of beer in buckets, four to the bucket. I ordered a bucket. Schmidt called, and I told him where I was. The circus found us, and a couple hours later, Schmidt, a dozen or more reporters, and I were drinking buckets of beer and singing karaoke. I ran through the bar's Dylan catalog and made a new friend, a guy who did a Dylan tribute act. He gave me his card in case I was ever interested in performing as a duet next time I was in town.

The Obama campaign spent three times more on advertising than the McCain campaign, handicapped, as we were, by our acceptance of public financing. Most of it was negative, as was our advertising for most of October. But we couldn't hope to match the volume of income we were taking, so McCain had to take shots at Obama himself rather than rely on our advertising exclusively, while Obama could stick to mostly positive messages on the stump. We were handicapped further by the Democrats' and the press's readiness to discredit any personal attack by alleging it was racist. When Fannie Mae tottered on the brink of bankruptcy, Obama campaign researchers pointed out to reporters that Rick Davis had consulted for the mortgage giant. When we responded by pointing out Fannie Mae's CEO, Franklin Raines, was on Obama's team, we were accused of race baiting because Raines is black.

The last debate was held on October 15 at Hofstra University. Moderator Bob Schieffer challenged both candidates to take the same shots at each other in person that their ads were taking. McCain responded first and criticized Obama for not repudiating John Lewis's demagogic attack. Obama accused McCain of running ads that were 100 percent negative, which was technically true of the last few weeks, but ignored the many positive spots we had run for most of the campaign and the fact that the volume of our attacks never neared the Obama campaign's spending on attack ads. Obama's most effective associational attack was tying McCain to President Bush's policies, which he continued to do in that last debate. McCain had a good line that he used to try to slip that punch: "If you want to run against President Bush, you should have run four years ago." He was scrappy throughout the entire debate and landed many of his shots effectively. But winning the debate on points wouldn't affect the trajectory of the campaign. Obama had led in all the polls since the last week of September, a lead he never surrendered.

The last twenty days of the election were a blur. All of us, including the candidate, were aware that his chances of winning were negligible, though we didn't acknowledge it to reporters or ourselves. McCain fought like hell until the end of the campaign, with as much energy as if he were on the cusp of an upset. Win or lose, he didn't know how to campaign any other way. We all kept our game face on and our energy level up as we raced through the intensely crowded schedule of a campaign's final weeks. For me, the thought of the end being near was sort of a morale booster. I wanted my life back. I wanted McCain to win, of course. But if you had told me a McCain victory could be had at the cost of another six months of campaigning, I don't think I would have taken the offer. I'm not sure McCain would have, either. But you couldn't have told that from the hustling figure he cut on the campaign trail those final weeks. In exchange for the long hours and stress, we were privileged to witness again the resilience and extraordinary drive of a man who had no quit in him, who would campaign his heart out in a race he knew he had lost.

Some of McCain's rallies got pretty raucous in October, with the crowd booing mentions of his opponent's name. Small numbers of people at some of the events shouted offensive insults and even racial epithets. McCain didn't hear anything of the kind over the general noise of the crowd. But reporters picked up on them, and journalists covering Governor Palin were alleging her crowds were even more hostile. Some commentators asserted McCain was inciting his supporters with his campaign's negative attacks on Obama. That aggravated me. No pundit accused Obama of inciting the gross abuse of McCain that some of his supporters shouted. Be that as it may, as we often lamented to ourselves and to reporters, "It is what it is." We knew we had to address the problem, especially after a McCain rally in Albuquerque, where a sizable contingent of the crowd had been hateful, and Rick, Steve, and I had heard people shouting racist insults. We mentioned it to McCain, and he said in a quiet voice, "I'll take care of it." Four days later, in a Minneapolis suburb, he did.

McCain wanted to win, but win or lose, he wanted to be proud of his campaign. He had defended Obama before from unfair abuse by his supporters. After the Albuquerque rally, he was especially vigilant. During a question-and-answer in Minnesota on October 10, McCain rebuked an elderly lady who had expressed her concern that Senator Obama was an Arab: "He's a decent family man [and] citizen that I just happen to have disagreements with on fundamental issues, and that's what this campaign's all about. He's not." Some in the crowd booed him. To another supporter who said Obama scared him, McCain insisted, "Senator Obama is a decent person and a person you don't have to be scared of as president of the United States." More boos and a shout of "liar" were heard. Several people told McCain they wanted him to fight harder. He promised them he would fight as hard as he knew how, "but I will be respectful. I admire Senator Obama and his accomplishments, and I will respect him." McCain's forthright response to those slurs would be remembered in later years and after his death as one of the finest—if not the finest—moments in his political career.

On the evening of October 16, the day after their last debate, a relaxed McCain enjoyed himself at the Al Smith Dinner in New York, an annual white-tie fund-raiser for Catholic charities, where both candidates are expected to gently roast each other. McCain spoke first, and his routine—most of which was Matthew Scully's work—was the hit of the night. After landing a series of mostly funny jokes ribbing Obama, he paid him elaborate tribute. "It's not for nothing that he has inspired so many folks in his own party and beyond," McCain observed.

MARK SALTER

"Senator Obama talks about making history and he has made quite a
bit of it already. . . . [He] has achieved a great thing for himself and his
country, and I congratulate him." Before he surrendered the mike, he
comically raised expectations for Obama, who followed him, claiming
he had seen an advance copy of Obama's speech. "You are all about
to witness the funniest performance in the sixty-three-year history of
this event," he promised the audience. "Let's not add to the mounting
pressure he must be feeling. Just prepare yourself for nonstop hilarity,
the funniest fifteen minutes of your life or any other. I think he knows
that anything short of that will mar the evening and insult our host,
and perhaps even cost him several swing states. Senator Obama, the
microphone is all yours."

The last week of an underdog presidential campaign can be an ex-
ertion of will unequaled in other political experiences. The days are
exceptionally long and include as many as five stops at different airports to give the same rally-the-troops speech over and over. Within a
few days, the candidate's voice is so hoarse he can't speak above a whisper in conversation, but he has to keep shouting his speeches. McCain
was his most exuberant, bouncing on the balls of his feet as he spoke,
hitting his closing "fire 'em up" lines in his cracked voice with all the
vigor he possessed, plunging into the crowds to shake a few hands and
pat a few backs, then getting on the plane for an hour or two-hour or
three-hour flight to another airport hangar rally to do it all again. To
do that every day for a week while knowing you are almost certainly
going to lose requires exceptional fortitude. McCain had to do it to
limit the damage his loss would cause to down-ballot races. He did it
without complaint. I was with him the entire time, and I can't remember an instance when he was cranky or lost his temper. I don't even
remember moments when he seemed wistful, as he had on a few occasions when he relaxed his stoicism for a moment and you assumed he
was anticipating his defeat. He just focused on what he had to do, and
he did it with everything he had until time ran out. He was still doing
rallies in Colorado and New Mexico on Election Day before finally
retiring to Phoenix's Biltmore Hotel to wait for the results.

They came quickly. By late afternoon Arizona time, three hours behind the East Coast, we knew it was over when returns in Virginia and North Carolina were indicating an electoral college landslide for Senator Obama. McCain was stoic the whole night. He didn't permit a mournful moment to pass. He made small talk with close friends and family. He invited various friends to come with him and Cindy to their cabin the next day. He greeted Sarah Palin and her husband, Todd. He had given me leave to write his concession speech earlier in the day, deciding just that once not to stand on his superstitious ceremony. But I waited until the outcome was certain anyway. We had discussed what he wanted to say off and on for days, and it didn't take me long to write it. As with any intense experience, good or bad, McCain wanted to turn the page the moment it was over. Life wouldn't end, the world would still excite him, joy and adventure were in the offing. He wanted to impart to the country his need to move on. He instructed me to make it as gracious as it could be, to pay respect to the new president. "We should say something like 'He was my opponent, now he's my president,'" he told me. "And write how lucky I am," he added, "nobody has to feel sorry for me." I did as he instructed. When I showed it to him, he read it silently once and didn't rehearse it. He wanted it to feel fresh to him when he read it off the teleprompter. "Let's get out there as soon as California closes," he ordered.

He took the stage with Cindy and the Palins at eight fifteen. He quickly quieted the crowd and began speaking. His delivery was very good that night. Disappointed supporters in the crowd booed when he mentioned at the beginning that he had just called President-elect Obama to congratulate him. He insisted they stop, and then he resumed his remarks. Near the close, he remarked, "I would not be an American worthy of the name should I regret a fate that has allowed me the extraordinary privilege of serving this country for half a century. Today I was a candidate for the highest office in the country I love so much. And tonight I remain her servant. That is blessing enough for anyone, and I thank the people of Arizona for it. Tonight more than any night, I hold in my heart nothing but love for this country and for all its citizens, whether they supported me or Senator Obama. I wish Godspeed to the man who was my former opponent and will be my president."

It was as gracious a concession as either of us had in us. He wanted to be remembered for it, and he has been. He wanted to turn a page in his life and in the history of the country he loved, and he did.

He invited me to come to the cabin, but I declined. I needed to be back in Washington the next day; I had booked a flight to Maine the day after that. I intended to spend a week alone and with my phone turned off. McCain wanted to rest and recreate for the rest of the week before he plunged back into public life. After a day, he started getting restless. On the third day, he called his foreign affairs aide, Richard Fontaine, to tell him he was bored. "Time to take a trip, boy," he informed Fontaine, who had taken a leave to work on the campaign and was as exhausted as the rest of us. Fontaine replied, "Geez, John, I didn't think you'd be ready so soon to be stuck on an airplane for hours again."

"Don't worry, we won't make it a death march. We'll go somewhere easy, somewhere fun."

The resulting trip took McCain and his two amigos, Lindsey Graham and Joe Lieberman, to eight countries in nine days. Iraq, Afghanistan, Kuwait, and Pakistan were on the original itinerary, but the State Department urged him to make a stop in India, which had just suffered the Mumbai massacre, when terrorists had killed close to two hundred people. Bhutan, Bangladesh, and Malta were also added to the schedule. By all accounts, including his own, the defeated presidential candidate enjoyed the experience.

THE SENIOR SENATOR

McCain's December trip with Lieberman and Graham included a brief stopover in Dhaka, Bangladesh. They arrived late at night and left the next morning. They had scheduled the stop only because they had to refuel before continuing on to Bhutan. The delegation had time for one meeting, which turned out to be breakfast with the entire government cabinet. A period of widespread political unrest had gripped Bangladesh in 2006 and led to the imposition of a state of emergency and the installation of a caretaker government, headed by a technocrat, until a general election was held two years later. As it happened, the election would be held later that month. In the course of McCain's discussions with the ministers, one of them informed him that the government had played a video recording of McCain's concession speech on Bangladesh national television to demonstrate to supporters of the country's political parties how you react to defeat in a democracy. He was proud of that, he told friends.

Before he left for the trip, McCain met with President-elect Obama in Chicago. Lindsey Graham accompanied him, and incoming White House chief of staff Rahm Emanuel participated in the discussion. The two were designated by McCain and Obama to serve as their intermediaries. By all accounts, including McCain's, it was a good meeting, and he seemed very pleased with it. "Very friendly," he told me, "and substantive." They discussed a host of issues, including earmark reform, immigration, weapons procurement, corporate welfare, and closing Guantánamo. They talked about Iraq, too, McCain said, and he was hopeful that he could influence the president-elect to reconsider his commitment to withdrawing all U.S. forces from the country. Obama paid him tribute at a dinner held in McCain's honor the night before the inauguration. Praising McCain as "an American hero I have come to know very well and admire very much," Obama reminded the audience that "John is not known to bite his tongue, and if I'm screwing up, he's going to let me know. And that's how it should be." McCain was touched by the president-elect's graciousness and pledged again "to my former opponent and my new president, I will do the best I can to help you in the hard work ahead."

Conventional wisdom in Washington, particularly among his conservative critics, was that McCain would be a frequent Republican ally of the new president. That did not turn out to be true. Although he cooperated with the Obama administration to a greater extent than I think is generally appreciated, he was much more frequently a critic, at times an adamant and caustic critic, of administration policies. I have a few thoughts about why that was. But the reader should be advised that not all of my account of this period of his life is the product of firsthand scrutiny, due to the alteration in my association with John McCain after 2008. I did not return to his Senate staff after the election. I had completed twenty years of government service and decided to claim my pension, work for myself, and see more of my wife and kids than I had for the last ten years. For the next ten years, I was on retainer to McCain's campaign committees, continuing to advise him and write speeches for him. We would collaborate on two more books. I spoke to him a couple times a week and met with him in his office often, and we regularly got together for lunch or dinner or a basketball game. We remained close friends for the rest of his life. But I was no longer his chief aide or daily confidant. And my memories of him in the last decade of his life, except for his last year, are not informed by uninterrupted personal observation.

Critics of McCain's combativeness with the Obama administration, especially early in Obama's first term, usually attributed it to McCain's bitterness over his defeat. That was not accurate or fair. I saw few traces of resentment in McCain in that period, privately or publicly, directed at Obama for winning the election. On the contrary, I was surprised in the weeks immediately following the election by how little anger or disappointment McCain displayed. From his concession speech to his interactions with Obama before and just after his inauguration, Mc-Cain was gracious to his former opponent and appreciative of Obama's graciousness to him. That's not to say he didn't bear any grudges from the campaign. He had felt ill used on the immigration issue by former allies who had not come to his defense when the Obama campaign ran ads comparing him to Rush Limbaugh. "I knew they weren't going to vote for me," McCain complained, "but they could have stuck up for my record." His hard feelings over immigration didn't last long, though, and in meetings with President Obama before and after the election, he stated his willingness to work with him on the issue. He did, however, expect the administration to come to him with a plan, which did not happen. He wasn't ready to take another major po-litical risk unless others did as well. Other disappointments, mostly over friends he thought had turned their back on him or hadn't been straight with him, dissolved in time, too.

The election did, however, affect his sense of his political identity. He had been the Republican nominee for president, and though he lost the election, he believed his nomination had conferred on him party leadership responsibilities that gave his role in Washington de-bates a more partisan cast than had previously been the case. It's fair to say that his sense of party loyalty was strengthened by the expe-rience of having his friends on the other side of the aisle attack him during the election, while his Republican colleagues—even some with whom he wasn't on the best of terms—defended him. That's human nature. Intellectually, he understood it hadn't been personal, but it's shirts and skins twenty-four hours a day in a presidential election. He would side with his party on close votes more often in the years ahead than he had in the past. That said, I cannot think of a single friendship with a Senate Democrat that McCain considered forsaken by the friend's rhetoric during the campaign. I was visiting with him in his office one afternoon just two or three months after the Obama inaugural, and he told me he had gotten coffee with John Kerry that day. I thought Kerry had been unnecessarily rough on McCain during

the campaign, especially in his speech at the Democratic National
Convention, whereas McCain had been very gentle with his criticism
of Kerry in 2004, when Kerry was his party's nominee. "Ah, life's too
short, boy" was all he offered by way of explanation. When Obama
nominated Kerry for secretary of state four years later, McCain agreed
to introduce him at his confirmation hearing, just as he had introduced Hillary Clinton at her confirmation hearing four years earlier.
He asked me to write his statement recommending his friend's nomination, which I did without complaint.

What was clear to me, and to anyone else who knew McCain well,
was that he was determined to remain on center stage. He never saw
losing the presidential election as a turning point in his public life.
He wasn't going to retire or stay in the background while his wounds
healed. If you had suggested that to him, he would have looked confused and asked, "What wounds?" The election had been one event,
a big one that had not worked out in his favor, in his lifelong pursuit
of one great ambition, one driving purpose: to play as large a role in
national and international affairs as he could, to be part of history. He
would do that as a senator and not as president, but he was no less intent on it. He would do it by working with the administration at times,
and other times he would do it by fighting the administration.

Two big and early legislative battles cast McCain in the role of
Obama adversary, but they shouldn't have surprised observers.
McCain was a fiscal hawk with a well-known aversion to appropriations earmarks. The stimulus spending bill the administration proposed to jump-start the economy was far in excess of what he would
support. He was in favor of a more modest stimulus bill that was generated by middle-class tax relief rather than by spending. He proposed
a Republican alternative that was less than half the cost of the administration's proposal; nevertheless, he was open to negotiating and said
so. Republicans were "prepared to sit down, discuss, negotiate a true
stimulus package that will create jobs," he insisted after introducing
his alternative. But Democrats weren't willing to go halfway or even
a third of the way to meeting Republican concerns. They didn't need
to. Democrats had huge majorities in both houses of Congress. They

could avoid a filibuster in the Senate by picking off a couple Republican moderates or by using the budget process to move legislation that couldn't be filibustered. In this instance, they cut the cost of their stimulus bill by a little over 10 percent, which satisfied three moderate Republicans, and the administration's plan prevailed. The next month, though, McCain led the successful opposition to an omnibus appropriations bill, which he argued "was stuffed with egregious earmarks."

He was furious with the three Senate Republicans who had supported the stimulus bill and let them know it. He blamed their defection for the administration's unwillingness to negotiate seriously, but he was intemperate in his reproach. I didn't say anything when he told me about it some days after the fact. But I imagined how he would have reacted if a Republican colleague had dressed him down for breaking with the party on an important vote. That said, his fiery opposition to administration-backed spending bills was as predictable as his subsequent outspoken opposition to the Obama administration's signature accomplishment, the Affordable Care Act (ACA), Obamacare.

During the campaign, McCain and Obama had been miles apart on health insurance reform. During the 2008 primaries, McCain had criticized Governor Romney for the individual mandate and the mandate on small business employers required in the reform he had successfully negotiated with the Massachusetts legislature. So it's hardly surprising that McCain opposed Obamacare. Most Republicans did. As Democrats were nearing final passage of health care legislation, which they would achieve in part by using budget rules to avoid the need to win any Republican votes, the president and administration officials convened a televised bipartisan health care summit at Blair House with forty members of Congress from both bodies. Obama proved more adept at defending the provisions of Obamacare than most Republicans were at attacking it, and he was not above taking swipes at Republicans he thought were making political statements rather than debating the merits of the bill.

The meeting had already lasted over two hours when McCain spoke. He thanked Obama for convening the meeting, and then, calmly and without rancor, he spent five minutes criticizing the process by which the legislation had been assembled, as well as some of its substance, which he faulted for buying off special interests, among other deficiencies. He made several references to campaign promises he and Obama had made. Obama tried to interject with a comment, and McCain cut him off with "Can I just finish, please." When he had finished, Obama said dismissively, "Let me just make this point, John, because we're not campaigning anymore. The election is over." McCain jumped in and said with a laugh, "I'm reminded of that every day."

I watched the exchange on television. I worried McCain would flash some anger over the president's curtness. As Obama tried to turn to another speaker, McCain defended his criticism of the process: "Mr. President, the American people care about what we did and how we did it. And I think that's a subject we should discuss." Obama briefly disagreed and then moved on. A second exchange occurred an hour later: McCain complained that the bill allowed seniors in Florida to retain a benefit that was not allowed seniors in other states. Obama acknowledged, "I think that's a legitimate point." McCain started to resume his argument before he realized Obama had just agreed with him. He stopped himself and said, "Thank you." They both seemed in better humor then. I didn't talk with him that day, but when I dropped by his office a day or two later, he shook his head instead of commenting on his back-and-forth with Obama. The experience probably stuck in his craw for a while, but he didn't mention it, not to me, anyway.

Reporters had a hard time pegging the role McCain intended to play. Not long after he had helped defeat the omnibus spending bill, McCain stressed to a New York Times reporter that he would support the administration when he thought they were right and oppose them when he thought they were wrong. "I'm the . . . loyal opposition, and both words, I think, are operative." Ross Baker, a political scientist and longtime McCain observer at Rutgers University, predicted "His support will come at times and places of his choosing," which proved to be mostly true.

Obama called McCain several times in the first months of his administration for his advice on a few nominations and to discuss various issues, including Iraq. McCain was pleased that Obama had retained Robert Gates as secretary of defense, and he initially endorsed the outline of an Obama plan to gradually withdraw U.S. forces from Iraq. He met several times with Obama's first White House counsel, Greg Craig, to discuss cooperating on a plan to wind down prison operations in Guantánamo, although they never reached the point where the administration presented him with a plan. He worked on weapons procurement reform with Carl Levin, who chaired the Armed Services Committee at the time, and he and Levin sponsored legislation that would restrict corporate tax deductions of stock options. He defended the administration's decision to cut production of the F-22 Raptor fighter jet. He pushed for drug re-importation from Canada with Democrat Byron Dorgan. He supported an anti-tobacco bill written by liberal House chairman Henry Waxman. He worked with Russ Feingold to ban earmarks, and on a proposal for a revised line item veto that he and Feingold had put together in the hope of giving the president greater authority to control spending excesses. He and Feingold continued to collaborate on political reforms. They proposed a constitutional amendment requiring that vacant Senate seats be filled in special elections and not appointed by governors, and they sponsored a bill to replace the Federal Election Commission with a new agency that wouldn't be paralyzed by partisanship. He joined with Democrat Maria Cantwell to restore the Glass-Steagall Act's separation of commercial and investment banking, and he was the only Republican to support it.

These and other initiatives in 2009 and early 2010 were indicators that McCain was still the bipartisan dealmaker he had been before 2008. But they went largely unnoticed in part because they were obscured by McCain's more publicized opposition in other debates, and by the frequent stridency of his arguments. His style of argument had been described as fiery long before President Obama's administration. But his ferocity did occasionally strike me in the first couple years after the 2008 election to be more disproportionate to its provocation than had been the case in the past. McCain was incensed when Democrats succeeded in getting Obamacare passed in February 2010 by using the budget process to prevent Republicans from killing it by filibuster, a novel but not unprecedented tactic. He pledged that no other major legislation would pass the Senate that year, an ill-considered threat that he didn't believe and didn't have the power to make good on. He had the charge-to-the-center-of-the-ring mentality, which often resulted in declarations he would later regret. It was a defect, but it wasn't the residue of sour grapes.

There were two positions McCain took in the 111th Congress, the first one ambivalently and the other too emotionally, that I struggled to understand and for which I still cannot offer a satisfying explanation. He delayed his decision on whether to support Sonia Sotomayor's confirmation to the Supreme Court for quite a while. I think he was genuinely uncertain, and I was surprised by that, even more so when he eventually decided to oppose her confirmation. I argued with him about it. His initial defense was "She's too liberal," which was hardly convincing, as I pointed out, given his previous vote to confirm President Clinton's appointment of Justice Ginsburg. For most of his Senate career, McCain usually deferred to the president on judicial nominations. There were exceptions, of course, but he didn't think political ideology should be the deciding factor; barring some obvious disqualification, the president's preference should be respected. He acknowledged that Sotomayor was very well qualified by experience, intellect, and temperament to serve on the Court, but he was going to "defer to Kyl." Jon Kyl is a serious, intelligent lawyer, and he was a fine senator whose judgment McCain respected and whose friendship he valued. But McCain had never deferred to another senator's judgment on judicial appointments. He had been the leader of the Gang of Fourteen, whose achievement had been to facilitate the confirmations of all but the most ideologically extreme nominees to federal courts. He relied on Senator Kyl's judgment on water rights issues in Arizona, a subject Kyl had great expertise on and McCain had little; that was understandable. But while McCain wasn't a lawyer, or as versed as Kyl in the judicial philosophies of various nominees to the federal bench, he had a point of view about such appointments that granted wide latitude to the president. That changed in 2009 and did not revert back, although it should be noted that he voted to confirm most of Obama's appointments to federal district and appellate courts.

The following year, McCain would vote against confirmation of Elena Kagan, someone he knew and liked. He premised his opposition on her refusal as the dean of Harvard Law School to allow military recruiters on campus in reaction to the military's Don't Ask, Don't Tell policy, which Kagan considered abhorrent. I didn't argue with him about that vote. I knew it would be pointless. Earlier that year, I had a couple of difficult conversations with him about Don't Ask, Don't Tell. By 2010, a social transformation was under way that would broaden respect for the dignity and rights of gay men and women. I don't think McCain had a serious concern that letting gays serve openly in the military would disrupt good order and discipline. He had a live-and-let-live attitude about human relationships that didn't allow personal prejudice against gays. He had gay friends, had hired gay staff, and I had never heard him make so much as a thoughtless joke about gays. I didn't (and don't) understand how he got himself trapped in passionately defending the policy.

His stance wasn't a flip-flop from his past position, as some critics alleged. He had supported the policy at its inception and believed that the policy, while not a perfect solution, addressed a controversial subject and caused the least amount of repercussions. He explained his opposition benignly to me as a question of timing. He had always allowed that if military leaders came to him and said the policy should be changed, he would support their position. The Joint Chiefs were currently conducting a study of the impact that ending Don't Ask, Don't Tell would have on military readiness. The chairman of the Joint Chiefs, Admiral Mike Mullen, had endorsed ending the policy, as had Secretary Gates. But McCain knew the commandant of the Marine Corps disagreed with the decision, and the JCS study hadn't been finished, so he argued the decision should be delayed. As the debate wore on and he became increasingly bellicose, few paid attention to McCain's reasoning, which sounded like hairsplitting to many observers. It was a doomed cause to begin with. With the president, the secretary of defense, and the chairman of the Joint Chiefs all in favor, the policy's change was inevitable.

The conversations I had with John were tense. When I told him he had looked petty and unfair at times, he snapped back at me, "I. Don't. Care. I have to do what's right." With every accusation that he was homophobic or unfair or an angry old man, he put up a stouter defense and got angrier. Perhaps he knew he was wrong, but he had boxed himself in and didn't know how to back down without embarrassment, and it was making him crazy.

Maybe I'm giving him too much credit in this instance for an unquiet conscience. But I don't know how else to explain it. Maybe he just mysteriously got stuck fighting on the losing side of an issue I had never heard him discuss with any strong view. He revisited the issue three years later in an interview with Isaac Chotiner for *The New Republic*. He argued again, but mildly, that he had only wanted to wait for the JCS report on how readiness would be affected. When Chotiner asked him if readiness had suffered, he responded, "I think it has worked out." In 2017, when President Trump ordered the Pentagon to ban transgender people from military service, McCain, as chairman of the Armed Services Committee, denounced it and co-sponsored legislation to thwart Trump's instruction. That might indicate that all the passion he exhibited in his defense of Don't Ask, Don't Tell had been misdirected.

While the stimulus debate and the debate over Obamacare occasioned the first strong clashes, McCain's strongest disagreements with the administration were over reactions to world events. The first of those occurred in June 2009, when McCain faulted the administration for its muted response to Iran's Green Movement, when Iran's president, Mahmoud Ahmadinejad, stole his reelection and the ensuing protests were brutally suppressed by the regime. Nothing roused McCain's fighting spirit more than an oppressed people bravely confronting their oppressors. He was deeply concerned with the fate of the protestors, and outraged by the paramilitary thugs who kidnapped, tortured, and murdered them.

Again, contrary to some of his detractors' accusations, McCain's support for freedom movements around the world rarely included calls for military action. But he did expect that at a minimum, the American president would lend moral support in defense of American values. He thought Obama was deliberately pulling rhetorical punches about the regime's crackdown, which certainly appeared to be the case in the first weeks of the protests. He wanted Obama to denounce the election as a sham. On June 20, the world watched a video of a young demonstrator, Neda Agha-Soltan, dying on a Tehran street from a sniper's bullet to the heart while her friends tried to comfort her. On the Senate floor, McCain denounced her murder, graphically described her last moments, and eulogized her as the "brave young woman who was trying to exercise her fundamental human rights and was killed on the streets of Tehran." He called on Obama with increasing vehemence to speak up in support of the protestors. "People are being killed and beaten . . . all over Iran, we should stand up for them," he urged, "the way we stood up for the Polish workers in Gdansk, the way we stood up for the people of the then Czechoslovakia in the Prague Spring, the way we have stood up for freedom in every part of the world. We're not doing that."

Obama explained his reticence by arguing that it would be seen by Iranians as meddling in their affairs. "Meddling?" McCain repeated sarcastically. "They're being shot, tortured, but for God's sake, don't meddle in their business by demanding they stop being killed and tortured." By the last week of June, in response to intensifying violence, the president toughened his criticism of the regime. He praised the protestors and, referencing Neda Agha-Soltan, declared, "Those who stand up for justice are always on the right side of history." McCain seemed briefly satisfied that the administration was on the right course, until he learned that the CIA had been instructed to sever contacts with protestors.

In September, as part of a "reset" with Russia, and in response to Putin's threats, the administration announced that it was halting construction of ballistic missile defense installations in Poland and the Czech Republic. The governments of the two NATO allies had braved considerable opposition when they agreed to host the installations, including large demonstrations and heavy-handed attempts at intimidation by the Russians. Obama had previously insisted the sites would remain as a deterrent to Iran's nuclear program, and the Poles and Czechs felt blindsided by the decision. So did McCain, and he was quick to denounce it, calling it a "victory for Putin" that "calls into question the security and diplomatic commitments the U.S. has made to Poland and the Czech Republic" and undermines "American leadership in Eastern Europe."

By the end of the summer, McCain was urging the administration to decide on its Afghanistan policy. By necessity, the U.S. had been muddling through in Afghanistan while it waged a resource-intensive counterinsurgency in Iraq. Now that the situation in Iraq had been stabilized, the U.S. could afford to shift more resources to Afghanistan. McCain argued that the situation in Afghanistan was so dire that substantial increases in forces were required to get off defense and back on offense against the Taliban. At a White House meeting in October, he complained to the president that the administration was engaged in a "leisurely process," which Obama, understandably, took offense at.

McCain had been pleased by Obama's initial deployment early in 2009 of twenty thousand additional troops, and he publicly praised the decision. He had also cheered the June 2009 appointment of General Stan McChrystal to command coalition forces. McChrystal was tasked with conducting a thorough review of the war before submitting his recommendations for troop levels. His report leaked in September, and it called for thirty to forty thousand more troops. The president was said to be displeased with the request, preferring a smaller force, but felt compelled by the public disclosure to go along with McChrystal's recommendation. In a December speech at West Point, Obama announced he had ordered thirty thousand more troops to Afghanistan to "bring this war to a successful conclusion." That was the low end of McChrystal's request, and McCain worried it wasn't sufficient, but he praised the decision anyway. In the next breath, he berated the president for imposing what he considered an "arbitrary" nineteen-month deadline on withdrawing the new forces. "How do you break the enemy's will to fight," he asked rhetorically, "if they know they only have to wait a year and a half before they don't have to fight us?"

It would become a pattern with McCain: He would try to influence an Obama national security policy by public advocacy and in direct talks with Obama or with cabinet officials and military commanders. When the policy was decided, he would praise the parts of the policy he approved and excoriate those he didn't, usually in the same statement. If he later had doubts about the efficacy of the policy's execution or subsequent decisions, he started the process over again. I'm sure it could rankle the decision-makers, but it was in good faith.

Six months after his West Point speech, Obama relieved McChrystal of his command after the general's aides had been quoted in a *Rolling Stone* article complaining about administration policies and officials, complaints they said McChrystal shared. As soon as McCain had heard about the article, he'd worried that it would cost McChrystal his job at a pivotal moment in the war. He would later recall that he had "expected the loss of this intelligent and inspirational commander would be a setback for our efforts in Afghanistan." Nevertheless, he issued a statement right after news broke about the article, criticizing the comments attributed to McChrystal aides as inappropriate, and he made clear he would support whatever the president decided to do about it. He was true to his word. When Obama summoned McChrystal to Washington and relieved him, McCain refrained from criticizing the decision, and he was ecstatic when the president appointed David Petraeus to succeed him.

McCain's confidence in Defense Secretary Gates and, to varying extents, in other administration national security officials, including Secretary of State Hillary Clinton, didn't calm his mounting doubts about the administration's policies any more than his respect for many Clinton administration officials had made him less of a critic of President Clinton's statecraft. As he had during the Clinton years, McCain often operated on the assumption that the problem resided with White House officials, including the president, and not with cabinet officers. He heard reports from Afghanistan that the White House was micromanaging the conflict. Reports like that set him on edge, as they recalled instances of Lyndon Johnson and Robert McNamara picking bombing targets and, in the words of his old commanding officer Jim Stockdale that McCain often quoted, "making gestures with our airplanes." McCain's criticism of the administration began to echo the rhetoric he had used to castigate the previous Democratic president, "feckless" being his adjective of choice about both administrations' policies.

During his congressional tenure, McCain criticized decisions made by all five presidents who were in office, beginning with Reagan's decision to send the marines to Beirut. He argued with Jim Baker about George H. W. Bush's Central American policies. He was a constant scourge of Clinton policies, quoting Jim Stockdale to characterize the Clinton administration's worldview as "who are we and why are we here." He was an early and persistent critic of the Bush administration's management of the Iraq war; he called on the defense secretary to resign; and he led opposition to the administration's detainee policies. Nothing bugged McCain more than the almost constant assertions that his opposition to Obama foreign policies was attributable to hard feelings over his defeat. "It was okay when I criticized Bush," he often complained, "what a maverick I was then. But I'm a bitter old man when I criticize Obama." Some critics replied that they now considered his criticism of the Bush administration to have been sour grapes as well. McCain went so far as to confess to a few reporters that such criticism hurt him, a rare admission for a proud man. "I admit . . . it bothers me from time to time," he told a *Washington Post* reporter, "I wish that it didn't. But it does."

That was not how he saw himself, and it wasn't how he wanted to be seen. He wanted to be who he believed he was that day in the Kennedy Library when he reflected on himself and Ted Kennedy as "the guys who last and get things done." He wanted to be useful to the world, and he knew that would sometimes require he be useful to the president when their purposes were in accord. Even during policy arguments when McCain was his most impassioned and relentless, I don't think he would have spurned an offer to work together and get something done that they both believed was important.

Ted Kennedy died in August 2009 of the same brain cancer that claimed John McCain's life nine years later to the day. McCain spoke at his public wake at the Kennedy Library. Calling his deceased friend "excellent company" whom he would miss "more than I can say," McCain described the legislator Kennedy had been in terms that would describe the kind of legislator McCain would be remembered as: "a fierce advocate," "hard to ignore," "the best ally you could have," "a man of his word." Kennedy had "an uncanny sense for when differences could be bridged and his cause advanced by degree. . . . He took the long view. He never gave up. And . . . he taught me to be a better senator." He promised to return to Washington determined to be "as persistent as Ted was, and as passionate for the work. I know I'm privileged to serve there. But I think most of my colleagues would agree, the place won't be the same without him."

Challenges to America's interests and values in the world were the issues McCain cared about the most, on which he worked hardest. In his stormiest clashes during the president's second term—over Syria especially but Ukraine, too—his convictions estranged him from friendships, even some begun before the Obama presidency. But his criticism wasn't meant to gain political advantage or to retaliate for a perceived slight. He never intended it for any purpose other than the cause that had roused his passion.

McCain was up for reelection in 2010, and barely a week had passed since the 2008 election when he announced he intended to run for reelection to the Senate. No matter how gracious he was in defeat, he didn't like losing, and I think he harbored in those years an urge to win something or, more accurately, to beat someone. Fortunately, he didn't have to wait too long to satisfy it. J. D. Hayworth volunteered for the assignment when he announced his primary challenge to McCain in February 2010. Hayworth had lost his seat in the 2006 Democratic wave and was currently hosting a local talk-radio show. The bombastic Hayworth was the ideal opponent for McCain, who would enjoy beating him a little more than was warranted given the disparities between the two candidates.

That didn't mean Hayworth didn't pose a danger. A Rasmussen poll the previous November, which we suspected was weighted to boost the former congressman's prospects, had a hypothetical McCain-Hayworth race within the margin of error. Our polling didn't, but it did reveal that somewhere between a quarter and a third of Arizona conservatives didn't much care for McCain. Arizona had been hard hit by the recession, and the devastated housing market caused real estate values to collapse. Unemployment in the state was as high as it had ever been during his years in Congress. The Tea Party movement, which would never embrace a veteran legislator with a reputation for bipartisan compromises, was in full flourish. McCain knew that outrage was still building and that it posed dangers for incumbents in both parties. He took nothing for granted. He started early and ran an aggressive, hard-hitting campaign, defining his opponent and keeping Hayworth off-balance to discredit his attacks. McCain transferred millions of dollars left over from his presidential campaign, using the money to dominate the airwaves with positive and negative ads, build an extensive voter-contact operation, and fund deep research into Hayworth's record in Congress and his activities after he lost reelection.

I don't know what Hayworth was thinking when he decided to challenge McCain. McCain's political operation had been battle-hardened by a grueling national election. He had access to much more money than Hayworth could hope to get his hands on. McCain was still popular with most Republicans and with centrist independents, who could vote in the Republican primary. Despite appreciating the danger posed by any credible primary challenge, McCain practically goaded Hayworth into running. He had the campaign's lawyers file complaints with the FCC that Hayworth was an all but announced candidate for office who was using his radio show to attack his opponent. McCain knew some conservative was going to challenge him, and he preferred it be Hayworth. No other serious challenger emerged, although a little-known Tea Party conservative, Jim Deakin, would run, too, and take votes from Hayworth.

McCain's baiting of his former congressional colleague should have been a clue to Hayworth that he might be undertaking a fool's errand. But he likely paid more attention to the anti-McCain grumbling on the right and the fulminating from conservative talk-radio heavyweights. He probably made the same mistake people make about Twitter today, believing those guys have the power to affect elections just by turning up the volume in their echo chambers. Most of their audiences were already anti-McCain. They weren't going to convince a lot of Republicans and independents who liked McCain to change their mind.

McCain would be accused, with justification, of tacking right in the primary on immigration. To ward off Hayworth's attacks, he emphasized the aspects of his immigration record that were more conservative than others. After months of trying to avoid taking a clear position, McCain endorsed SB 1070 hours before the controversial measure passed the state senate. The bill empowered local law enforcement officers to determine the immigration status of anyone they had lawfully detained and suspected was in the country illegally, then arrest those unable to produce immigration papers. Both McCain and Arizona governor Jan Brewer had remained mostly silent about the measure publicly. McCain, and I assume the governor, knew that passing SB 1070 would stigmatize Arizona nationally, would have serious political and economic consequences, and would be challenged in the courts. Huge protests were staged in reaction to its passage. Hispanic groups of every political persuasion were enraged. The Catholic Church and most other organized religions opposed it. There were calls for economic boycotts. Tourism was hurt. Companies refused to hold their conventions in the state. McCain explained that he acceded to the necessity of the measure because lawlessness at the border and drug trafficking–related violence had become an emergency. But it was a bad law that codified racial profiling.

McCain did not abandon his support for immigration reform that included legalizing the status of immigrants who came to the U.S. unlawfully but were otherwise law-abiding residents. But he did stress the parts of his immigration bills that focused on improving security at the border. Every immigration bill he sponsored had spent money on border security, and some of that money had always been targeted for new fencing. The last measure he had sponsored with Jon Kyl and Ted Kennedy authorized $4 billion in new border security spending, much

of it on fencing. At the time that legislation was pending, McCain explained to a reporter for *Vanity Fair* how the sponsors of the bill were
trying to placate border security hawks. He dismissed fencing as the
least effective barrier on the border but added, "I'll build the goddamn
fence if they want it."

McCain worked to wrap up as many endorsements as quickly as
he could to deny Hayworth support that might translate into money
and votes. The entire Republican congressional delegation endorsed
McCain, including archconservatives who had served with Hayworth
in the House. He was endorsed by the National Right to Life and the
NRA despite sticking to positions each group opposed, support for
stem cell research in the case of the former and closing the gun show
loophole in the case of the latter. He won the backing of the Arizona
Police Association and most of Arizona's county sheriffs. In filmed endorsements with six sheriffs, Pinal County sheriff Paul Babeu attested
to McCain's commitment to border security, assuring voters that he
would "complete the dang fence." Babeu's endorsement received the
most attention.

Fred Davis used the "dang fence" line in the script for a thirty-
second spot he cut with McCain and Babeu walking beside the border, discussing whether McCain had the "right plan" to address the
spike in illegal crossings and related problems. Babeu ticked off a few
provisions, and McCain added, "And complete the dang fence," which
Babeu followed up by observing, "Senator, you're one of us." I winced
when I first saw it, and I winced when I watched it again as part of my
research for this book.

I was part of a group of McCain's friends and political advisors who
served as the campaign's trustees, for lack of a better term. We met
regularly at the senatorial committee's headquarters to discuss messaging and strategy. We received ad scripts, to which we could suggest
changes, and reviewed the spots themselves before they aired. I suggested Fred cut the "dang fence" line from the script for the Babeu ad.
It made McCain look like he was pandering. When I saw the spot, I
discovered it hadn't been cut. I thought the whole ad looked contrived

and McCain's performance was affected. "Dang" sounded as natural coming out of McCain's mouth as "by Jove" would have. Fred pushed back, claiming the spot was the best they had produced, and the "dang fence" line was its most memorable moment. Others, including McCain, thought it was okay because he was quoting Babeu to Babeu. But those who hadn't seen the sheriff's endorsement ad wouldn't know that.

Hayworth reacted to McCain's tacks to the right by calling himself "a consistent conservative" and labeling McCain "a political shape-shifter." It hardly mattered. Hayworth's record was a dream assignment for opposition researchers. Unlike the fiscal hawks he served with in the state's congressional delegation, Hayworth was an avid pork-barrel consumer. He had also been entangled in the Abramoff scandal. He had returned the lobbyist's donations to his campaigns but not the money he had received from Abramoff's clients; nor did he pay compensation for the use of luxury sky boxes Abramoff made available to him at Washington sporting events. Fred produced tough ads hitting both controversies, and Hayworth struggled to defend himself. The most devastating attack featured an infomercial Hayworth had done in 2007 for a shady group, National Grant Conferences, that claimed it could help consumers gain access to "free government money." When Hayworth was asked about it, he conceded he had promoted the company, but he blamed consumers for not being more vigilant. It was a case of "buyer beware," he maintained. The McCain spot capitalized on Hayworth's dismissive response as much as it did on the image of a self-proclaimed "consistent conservative" promoting "free government money." The ad's closing line was "J. D. Hayworth. Pork Barrel Spender. Lobbyist. Huckster. Voter Beware."

The contest wasn't close in the end. McCain beat Hayworth by nearly twenty-five points, and he breezed through the general election campaign against little-known former Tucson city councilman Rodney Glassman. Three days after the election, McCain flew to Halifax for a security conference he attended every year. From Halifax, he and Lindsey flew to Iraq and Afghanistan. When he returned to

Washington for the lame-duck session of the 111th Congress, he was
as intent as ever at being in the center of things, and 2011 would give
him abundant opportunities to do so.

The year began with a tragedy. On January 8, a mentally disturbed
man diagnosed as a paranoid schizophrenic shot and killed six people, including federal district court judge John Roll and nine-year-old
Christina Taylor Green, in a supermarket parking lot where Tucson
congresswoman Gabrielle "Gabby" Giffords was meeting with her
constituents. The man shot Congresswoman Giffords, his primary target, point-blank in the head. Early and erroneous reports announced
she had succumbed to her wounds. McCain was in South America at
the time of the shooting. Like everyone, he was stunned by the news
and called for updates on Giffords's condition. He didn't learn about
Judge Roll's death until later that day, and he was devastated. The judge
was a friend, and McCain had been responsible for his appointment in
1991. He was also very fond of Gabby Giffords, a Democrat just starting her third term. He liked working with her more than he did with
some Republicans in the delegation. He liked her husband, astronaut
Mark Kelly, quite a lot, too.

McCain returned to Arizona to attend a memorial service for the
victims the following Wednesday, and funerals for Judge Roll and
Christina Taylor Green. The University of Arizona auditorium where
the service was held was crowded with political figures from Arizona
and Washington. President Obama had flown out the day before and
visited Giffords in her hospital room. He was the main speaker at the
service. McCain called me afterward to see if I had watched Obama's
speech. I had. It was a moving tribute to the victims and a plea to
keep our politics in perspective and constrained by the best qualities
of human nature, love, compassion, generosity, and kindness. He used
the loss of the little girl to summon our better angels. "So curious, so
trusting," he said, ". . . so full of love, and so deserving of our good
example." McCain was more impressed by that speech than any other
he had heard the president make. Its message struck the chords of
McCain's own idealism. He said he wished he had Obama's "gift" for
oratory and that he wanted to do something to reinforce what the

president had said. We talked over what format he should use and decided on an editorial because, he said, "I don't speak as well as he can."

The piece appeared in the *Washington Post* that Sunday. "President Obama gave a terrific speech Wednesday night," it began. McCain praised Obama for encouraging "every American who participates in our political debates . . . to aspire to a more generous appreciation of one another and a more modest one of ourselves." He demonstrated what he meant by offering an example of his own. "I disagree with many of the president's policies, but I believe he is a patriot sincerely intent on using his time in office to advance our country's cause," he wrote.

I reject accusations that his policies and beliefs make him unworthy to lead America or opposed to its founding ideals. And I reject accusations that Americans who vigorously oppose his policies are less intelligent, compassionate or just than those who support them.

Striking the same theme Obama had, he observed,

There are too many occasions when we lack that empathy and mutual respect on all sides of our politics, and in the media. But it is not beyond us to do better; to behave more modestly and courteously and respectfully toward one another; to make progress toward the ideal that beckons all humanity: to treat one another as we would wish to be treated.

Some commentators interpreted the editorial as McCain signaling his return to form as the independent-minded maverick who worked with Democrats. If you asked him—as many reporters did—he would argue that he already had been working across party lines. After the editorial appeared, the president called and invited him to the White House the following week. They discussed several issues where they might work together, including immigration, and talked about the stunning events in the Middle East.

Mohamed Bouazizi's self-immolation in December 2010 to protest government corruption had acted as a catalyst for mass protests in Tunisia as thousands took to the streets, demanding accountability from the government. The police counterattacked, the protests spread nationwide, and the Tunisian military refused to intervene. In under a month, the government was deposed; the autocrat who had ruled Tunisia for a quarter century, Zine El Abidine Ben Ali, fled to Saudi Arabia; and mass movements demanding the overthrow of corrupt, unresponsive regimes were ignited throughout the Middle East, in Algeria, Egypt, Morocco, Yemen, Syria, Bahrain, and elsewhere. McCain was gripped by the chain reaction of revolutions sweeping through the region. It appeared to him to be the moment democratic internationalists had long anticipated, when "the autocracies of the Middle East come undone [as] generations of young people without jobs, without hope, and without recourse finally had enough and revolted."

McCain talked of little else at the time and was hopeful that the contagion of protests would result in democratic transformations of repressive societies in the Middle East and beyond. "The winds of change are blowing," he observed in an appearance on *Face the Nation*. "It's going to spread throughout the world." Even China and Russia should be worried, he said. Mass protests in Cairo's Tahrir Square began January 25. A week later, just a few days after meeting with Obama in the White House, McCain called on Egypt's long-ruling president, Hosni Mubarak, to hand over power to a transition government that included the army and pro-democracy parties. "The best opportunity for a pro-democracy government and not a radical Islamic government," he advised, "is an open, transparent process." The Arab Spring, as it came to be called, would end in the Arab winter of crushed democratic dreams. But McCain was immensely hopeful in the beginning that, as had happened after the collapse of the Soviet Union, a global upsurge of democratic self-governance was under way. His faith that the desire for self-determination inhabited every human heart was affirmed. "This virus spreading through the Middle East," he maintained, "proves the human yearning [for freedom]." He wanted to see it for himself.

He and Joe Lieberman arrived in Tunisia on February 21. They met

with the head of the caretaker government established after Ben Ali's
overthrow. But the meeting in Tunisia that fascinated McCain the most
was his dinner with a group of young pro-democracy activists who explained to him how social media had facilitated the rapid proliferation
of protests throughout the country. The government had censored the
Internet but not, curiously, Facebook, which became their preferred
communications platform. "If it wasn't for Facebook," they insisted,
"there would have been no revolution." McCain promised to contact
Mark Zuckerberg on their behalf to convey their appreciation and invite him to go to Tunis to meet with them. As promised, he called
Zuckerberg as soon as he returned to Washington. He told me afterward that Zuckerberg "couldn't have been less interested." A year or
two after his unproductive call to Facebook's CEO, McCain referred
to him as "that little prick." He didn't elaborate, but I assumed it was
related to Zuckerberg disappointing the young Tunisians who revered
him. "Those kids should be *his* heroes," McCain remarked, "not the
other way around."

Lieberman and McCain flew from Tunisia to Lebanon and from
there to Jordan. On the flight from Beirut to Amman, they discussed
whether they should issue a joint statement calling on NATO to intervene militarily in Libya, where anti-regime protests that began on February 15 and were limited mostly to Benghazi had reached the capital,
Tripoli, in five days' time. Muammar Qaddafi was violently confronting the uprising. Hundreds were dead and a civil war was under way
by the time McCain and Lieberman boarded their flight to Jordan.
The rebels held Benghazi and most of eastern Libya. The regime's
air and naval forces were bombing and shelling the city, and infantry and armored columns were on their way. Qaddafi had threatened
to "cleanse Libya house by house." McCain told me later that he and
Lieberman were worried they would be tagged with the usual "neocon
warmonger" label if they called for military intervention before the
administration had decided on a policy and before other members
of Congress had done so. He said they also weren't sure how much
of the threat was real. They thought it possible that, in the interest of
self-preservation, Qaddafi would follow Ben Ali's example and flee to

a friendly country. But McCain and Lieberman had met Qaddafi at his desert compound outside Tripoli in 2009. They both thought he was crazy, and the fear that Qaddafi was capable of deciding to go out in a blaze of glory, killing as many of his enemies as he could, convinced them to support the use of NATO airpower to impose a no-fly zone over eastern Libya. "The Qaddafi regime's ongoing slaughter and military oppression is deplorable and must end," they declared. They didn't call for ground forces to intervene. They advocated a U.S.-led air campaign to ground Qaddafi's planes and helicopter gunships that he used to slaughter rebels and civilians indiscriminately. McCain emphasized those points in an interview on *Meet the Press* two days later from Tahrir Square in Cairo, where they had traveled after leaving Jordan. It was the first of seven trips McCain would make to Egypt over two years, as a transition government yielded to an elected government headed by a member of the Muslim Brotherhood, which was deposed by yet another Egyptian strongman. He was trying "to figure out if there was more the U.S. could do to stop it [Egypt] from totally going to shit."

McCain would make six trips to Libya after the start of the insurrection. His first, to rebel-controlled Benghazi, happened in April over the Obama administration's objections, which were reasonable. The war was still raging; Qaddafi remained at large and his forces were still dangerous; a NATO air campaign had been under way for a month; and the U.S. Sixth Fleet was blockading Libya's ports. It wasn't out of an abundance of caution, as the cliché goes, that the administration refused to facilitate McCain's trip to Benghazi. Just a small dose of caution would argue against letting a heedless, internationally recognized U.S. senator make himself an object of curiosity in a war zone where the U.S. was a party to the hostilities. But the senator in question refused to be deterred. When his fourth or fifth petition to the administration was rejected, he made plans with the government of Qatar, which had offered to fly him to Benghazi courtesy of the emir. When he informed the State Department of his plans, they relented and agreed to fly him there, although they forbade his military escort, a navy captain, to accompany him. McCain flew to Libya from Crete in an old turboprop plane.

McCain and John Kerry sponsored a bipartisan resolution authorizing the administration to use force in Libya. U.S. planes joined France and the U.K. in initial air strikes on regime targets, but after a little over a week, the president announced in a televised speech on March 25 that the U.S. would thereafter play a "supporting role" in the operations. McCain described for me his reaction when his foreign policy aide, Chris Brose, brought him the news that the administration was giving command of the air campaign to NATO: "I thought about Bosnia, when France and the Brits let things get so screwed up." In an Armed Services Committee hearing that same day, McCain asked a Defense Department witness to confirm the news and was told, "We're acting in support of NATO." McCain repeated the answer before thundering, "We are NATO!"

He met Chris Stevens for the first time on that trip to Benghazi. Stevens was the administration's special envoy to the provisional rebel government in Benghazi, and he arranged McCain's meetings with rebel leaders and, as McCain put it, "saw to it that I didn't wander into any real harm." Over the course of McCain's half dozen trips to the country, he and Stevens would become friends, and McCain held the career diplomat in very high esteem. Writing years after Stevens was murdered by terrorists, McCain hailed him as "an exceptional human being." "I was bound to like him," McCain remembered. "We had the same hopes for Libya and the same . . . optimism they could achieve them. He was a go-getter, a risk-taker, who didn't wait on events but tried to shape them. He was positive, good-humored and fun to be with. . . . I miss him very much."[46]

Human Rights Watch representatives were in Benghazi, and Tom Malinowski arranged for McCain to meet with activists trying to lay the foundations of the civil society they hoped would replace the regime. Meeting people as they confronted danger and the discouragement of societies wrecked by decades of misrule always roused McCain's empathy as they struggled to build a modern, functioning democracy, believing themselves and their country capable of it. "If ever there was a spirit of the Arab Spring," he wrote, "that Americans could relate to—a people's confident belief in their ability to shape their own destiny—it was present in Benghazi." He felt a connection to them, as his hopes had once defied his circumstances, too.

Malinowski and a rebel leader escorted McCain to Benghazi's main square, where photographs of rebel casualties covered a wall. A crowd there chanted, "Thank you, McCain. Thank you, Obama." He knew the demonstration had been organized for his benefit but enjoyed it nonetheless. He noted to his escort that he had often heard the president's name chanted and had once or twice heard his own name chanted, "but it's usually just one or the other of us." He returned to Libya in September after Tripoli had fallen and Qaddafi was besieged in his hometown of Sirte. He asked to inspect a prison where, Human Rights Watch believed, Libyans detained by various rebel militia were being physically abused. McCain wanted to signal to militia commanders and to the provisional government that one of the most outspoken American defenders of their revolution cared about the lives of prisoners. When he toured "Martyr's Square" in Tripoli, he was welcomed by a spontaneous demonstration of Libyan gratitude, with the crowd chanting, "We love America. We love Obama."

In May, McCain and Lindsey Graham went to Iraq to lobby Prime Minister Maliki and other Iraqi political leaders to agree to a smaller U.S. force in Iraq after the current Status of Forces Agreement (SOFA) expired, a mission they believed was blessed by the administration. The year before, President Obama had announced an end to U.S. combat operations in the country, and the last combat brigade had left Iraq. Fifty thousand U.S. forces remained to train Iraq's armed forces and run counterterrorist operations. Though the president had campaigned on the promise to bring the troops home from Iraq, all indications were that he was agreeable to keeping some there as a stabilizing force. Prime Minister Maliki, bowing to his Shia constituencies, demanded that any U.S. soldiers who remained in Iraq after the expiration of the current SOFA and had been accused of felonies had to be tried in Iraqi courts, a nonstarter for the U.S. Lindsey claimed

Secretary Clinton had asked him to see if Maliki would back down, and to determine whether Maliki; his main rival, Ayad Allawi; and the political boss of Iraqi Kurdistan, Masoud Barzani, would support a new SOFA without the offending condition.

For months, McCain had discussed with contacts in the military and elsewhere the prospects of a residual U.S. force in Iraq. He knew most military leaders, including General Lloyd Austin in Iraq, believed it would take ten to fifteen thousand troops for the force to be effective. He had heard reports that the White House was resisting recommendations for a force level that size, having in mind a much smaller presence—a few thousand at the most—which McCain considered pointless. Nevertheless, he left for Iraq in high spirits, on a mission, he believed, to prevent Iraq from descending back into anarchy.

They first met with Allawi, who spent most of the time, McCain said, complaining about Maliki. But Allawi believed his fortunes depended on good relations with the U.S., and he promised to endorse a new SOFA. Maliki was a harder sell. Backtracking on his demand would risk offending his political base. General Austin and Ambassador Jim Jeffrey, whom McCain trusted and liked, accompanied McCain and Graham to the meeting. McCain and Graham did most of the talking; Maliki listened rather than responding. McCain said they stressed to Maliki how essential it was for Iraq's security and the stability of his government that a U.S. force remain to cooperate with the Iraqi military in counterterrorism operations. The meeting had lasted three-quarters of an hour, McCain remembered, when Maliki asked his first question: How big a force were they proposing? Graham asked General Austin to respond; he deferred to Ambassador Jeffrey, who said he didn't have an answer yet. The administration was still considering different options. McCain told me you could tell from Maliki's reaction that he wasn't going to risk his political hide "for a force that was too small to do him any good." Nevertheless, after they had flown to Irbil and secured Barzani's support for a new SOFA, McCain felt he could faithfully report to administration officials that Iraq's leaders were willing to negotiate a new agreement that would allow U.S. troops to remain in the country.

Upon his return, McCain put a call in to the president and ended up talking to the national security advisor, Tom Donilon. He called White House chief of staff Denis McDonough, too, assuring him that the Iraqis were ready to make a deal. He talked several times to both men and was confident the administration would settle on a force size that Austin and the Iraqis could live with. He checked in periodically with friends in the Pentagon and heard nothing that discouraged his confidence. News broke in October that the administration had decided to pull all remaining troops out of Iraq by January; the president made the announcement the next day. No one in the administration had given McCain a heads-up or had thought at any time that summer and fall to reengage him on the question. He was blindsided and furious about it. When the last American soldiers exited Iraq in December, McCain noted their sacrifices and warned that "the gains made possible by brave Americans in Iraq, at such great cost, are now at risk." He was proved right almost immediately: By the end of 2012, Iraq teetered again on the brink of civil war. The following year, Iraq was pulled into the Syrian civil war, and by the end of 2013, ISIS controlled most of Anbar Province. McCain's anger over the Iraq decision subsided faster than I thought it would, although it would spike episodically when the news from Iraq was particularly discouraging. But there were too many other world events for which he wanted to have some influence with the administration in order to effect.

McCain went back to Libya a third time in February 2012, after Qaddafi had been caught and killed. He asked to meet with the commander of one of the strongest militias, Abdel Hakim Belhaj, an Islamist militant who had led a Libyan rebel group since the 1990s. Belhaj had fought against the Soviets in Afghanistan, where he acknowledged meeting Osama bin Laden. Tom Malinowski advised McCain that Belhaj had played a constructive role, helping to calm tensions and lawlessness in Tripoli as various militias roamed the city. He suggested McCain encourage Belhaj's transition from military commander to political leader committed to the rule of law. Malinowski also told him that when Belhaj had been a fugitive from a regime arrest warrant seven years earlier, he and his wife, Fatima, had been apprehended by the CIA as they were about to board a plane from Kuala Lumpur to London. They were flown to a secret site in Bangkok, where Belhaj was stripped naked, submerged in ice water, and kept awake for several days. They stripped Fatima, who was six months pregnant, and photographed her naked and bound, with duct tape covering her mouth, while American interrogators stood next to her. They showed the photograph to Belhaj before they turned him over to Qaddafi's secret police, who tortured him and imprisoned him for six years.

The meeting with Belhaj was the first thing McCain mentioned when I asked him about the trip after his return. He explained Belhaj's background and said the militia commander had been cordial but serious as he met with McCain and four Senate colleagues. They discussed the military and political situation in Libya, and McCain thanked him for his efforts to restore order in the city. He assured him America would respect any Libyan leader who was committed to governing the country democratically. As the meeting was nearing an end, McCain told Belhaj he knew what the CIA had done to him and that it was wrong and shouldn't have happened. He told him he had worked to stop the mistreatment of prisoners. McCain said Belhaj "didn't say a word, but his eyes were staring into mine the whole time I was talking." When McCain told him he was aware his wife had been mistreated, too, he said Belhaj had teared up. "As an elected representative of my country, I apologize for what happened," McCain offered, "for the way you and your wife were treated, and for all you suffered because of it." Belhaj thanked him for the apology and assured him "we don't think of revenge," and that "our actions will be governed by law." McCain said the CIA station chief in Libya had taken strong exception to McCain's apology. "I don't care, he was owed one," he said he told the agent.

He and Belhaj never met again, but McCain recalled their encounter whenever he discussed the subject of detainee abuses. He had been incensed months earlier when former attorney general Michael Mukasey, and other defenders of the CIA's systematic abuse of detainees, credited the abuses with yielding intelligence that led to the discovery of bin Laden's location and his death in May 2011. Almost nothing the agency's

apologists claimed about the program as it pertained to the hunt for
bin Laden or other alleged intelligence breakthroughs proved true, and
McCain said so at the time. He believed the so-called enhanced interrogation techniques (EITs) were a moral and practical failure, having
offended our values and done little to protect our interests. The truth
of his conviction was revealed in 2014 in a declassified summary of a
four-year investigation into the program by the Senate Select Committee on Intelligence, chaired by Dianne Feinstein. The report was written
by Dan Jones, a former FBI officer who directed the investigation and
whose dedicated search for truth won McCain's admiration and was the
subject of the critically acclaimed film *The Report*.

At Senator Feinstein's instruction, Jones kept McCain and his aide,
Chris Brose, informed of the investigation's progress throughout its
long, arduous course, which the agency did its best to confound. CIA
personnel hacked the computers used by Jones and his team, which
McCain denounced as "clearly unconstitutional, and some ways,
worse than criminal." DCI John Brennan even filed a criminal referral
against Jones, alleging that he had illegally accessed an internal review
of the program inadvertently given to investigators by agency personnel. The investigation was based entirely on thousands of agency
memos, emails, and texts detailing the program's failures and the dishonest representations made by agency officials to hide its deficiencies
from top Bush administration officials, including the president. Some
of the emails mentioned McCain's involvement in the issue, much to
his amusement. His favorite concerned an email exchange between an
agency official who had just briefed him on the EITs and a colleague
back at Langley who asked if McCain was now "on board" with the
program. "Not totally," the briefer replied.

"Was it painful?"

"Very much so."

"Is the issue the EITs still?"

"Yep."

The report was finished in 2012. For sound practical reasons, the
Obama administration declined to prosecute officials responsible for

detainee abuses, including the former head of the CIA's clandestine service, Jose Rodriguez, who ordered the destruction of videotape recordings of two interrogations rumored to have been so disturbing that they would have discredited the program and the officials who defended it. His action had violated instructions from the White House counsel to preserve the tapes, and it alarmed Feinstein and McCain when it was reported by the *New York Times*. The abuses had ended years before President Obama was inaugurated, and he ordered that only the interrogation techniques detailed in the Army Field Manual would be permissible in the future. He and Attorney General Eric Holder were convinced by arguments from intelligence community heads to consign the controversy to the past. McCain didn't object. But he did object to burying the truth about the program, which was why he had so vehemently rebuked Bush administration alumni for falsely attributing bin Laden's death to intelligence acquired by torture. And it was why he supported Senator Feinstein in her two-year battle with the administration to release the unclassified summary of her committee's report.

As the ranking Republican on the Armed Services Committee, McCain was entitled to ex officio status on the Intelligence Committee. He could attend the committee's hearings and deliberations, though he did not have a vote in its decisions. But his moral authority on the subject of torture as well as his prominence in national security debates made his support invaluable. Republicans on the committee, presumably in defense of the Bush administration policies, had withdrawn their participation in the investigation and prepared an alternative report. Only one committee Republican, Susan Collins, was expected to support releasing the report. DCI Brennan and other top intelligence officials urged the White House to oppose publication, and it did for two years, dragging out the redacting process, lobbying Feinstein and other committee members to keep their conclusions confidential, and warning that the committee could have blood on their hands if they went through with the disclosure. But on December 9, 2014, the committee's Democratic majority and Senator Collins voted to release the redacted summary of the report. McCain went to the Senate floor to defend the decision from Republicans, who denounced the release as a partisan attack that would jeopardize national security.

McCain had called me a few days earlier to tell me the committee would vote to release the summary. He asked me to come to his office to discuss in person rather than on the phone what he should say in his remarks about it. He wanted to incorporate the line he used whenever arguing against torture—"It's not about them, it's about us"—although, for the first time, he expressly directed me to make reference to the fact that he had been a victim of torture. This was the only time I recall him specifically asking me to invoke it. The final product, which was as much his work as mine, is one of our collaborations that I'm proudest of. I was gratified when I watched *The Report* and saw that the film ended with McCain delivering it on the Senate floor. I hope he'll be remembered for it as an example of his idealism and his innate decency.

He had clearly rehearsed the speech and delivered it carefully, mindful, it seemed, of the dignity the occasion required. "The truth is sometimes a hard pill to swallow," he reminded the senators listening to him. "It sometimes causes us difficulties at home and abroad. It is sometimes used by our enemies in attempts to hurt us. But the American people are entitled to it nonetheless." He thanked Senator Feinstein and the committee for providing answers to the questions Americans had a duty to ask about such controversial practices. What damage did they do? Were they worth it? He made his case disputing the efficacy of torture. "I know from personal experience that the abuse of prisoners will produce more bad than good intelligence. I know that victims of torture will offer intentionally misleading information . . . will say whatever they think their torturers want them to say if they believe it will stop their suffering."

Then he addressed the ideal that meant the most to him. Torture's failure "wasn't the main reason to oppose its use," he contended. "[T]his question isn't about our enemies; it's about us. It's about who we were, who we are and who we aspire to be. It's about how we represent ourselves to the world.

"We have made our way in this often dangerous and cruel world, not by just strictly pursuing our geopolitical interests, but by exemplifying our political values, and influencing other nations to embrace them. When we fight to defend our security, we fight also for an idea, not for a tribe or a twisted interpretation of an ancient religion or for a king, but for an idea that all men are endowed by the Creator with inalienable rights. How much safer the world would be if all nations believed the same. How much more dangerous it can become when we forget it ourselves even momentarily.

"Our enemies act without conscience. We must not. This executive summary of the committee's report makes clear that acting without conscience isn't necessary, it isn't even helpful, in winning this strange and long war we're fighting. We should be grateful to have that truth affirmed.

"Now let us reassert the contrary proposition: that it is essential to our success in this war that we ask those who fight it for us to remember at all times that they are defending a sacred ideal of how nations should be governed and conduct their relations with others—even our enemies.

"Those of us who give them this duty are obliged by history, by our nation's highest ideals and the many terrible sacrifices made to protect them, by our respect for human dignity to make clear we need not risk our national honor to prevail in this or any war. We need only remember in the worst of times, through the chaos and terror of war, when facing cruelty, suffering and loss, that we are always Americans, and different, stronger, and better than those who would destroy us."

The speech was praised by some of his most persistent critics. I went to see him that evening at his hideaway office in the Capitol, and he was pleased with the reaction to it. He told me when he had read the line about "how we represent ourselves to the world," he had thought about Abdel Hakim Belhaj, the proud, hard man whom Americans had humiliated. "Who does he think we are?" he asked rhetorically.

McCain returned to Libya in July 2012. No other senators went with him, just his aide Chris Brose and his navy escort Captain Jim Loeblein. He told me afterward that it was one of the most memorable experiences of his career. I think it was one of two foreign trips that most inspired McCain's idealism, and one of those experiences that made him feel as if he were, as his father had been, swept up in history. He went to observe Libya's first free election. He spent two nights there. On previous trips, the State Department had refused him permission to remain in the country overnight. He insisted he be allowed to stay this time. Chris Stevens was the newly appointed U.S. ambassador, and the McCain party stayed in his residence. Stevens made him a cappuccino the morning of the election, and Brose took a picture of him preparing it. McCain kept the picture in his office. They spent the entire day visiting polling sites. McCain was elated by the huge turnout, and the festive spirit the Libyans expressed as they exercised their franchise for the first time, laughing and cheering each other, honking their car horns, shooting off fireworks in jubilation. He told me the experience reminded him of the time in 1990 when he and I had gone to Prague to observe the first elections in Czechoslovakia since the collapse of the Warsaw Bloc. We wandered the winding streets of that beautiful city for hours, crossed its ancient bridges, drank beer, and celebrated the joy of people who had been suddenly liberated and given back their right to choose their government.

McCain had dinner that night in Libya at an outdoor restaurant Stevens chose, next to the ancient arch the Romans had built and named for Marcus Aurelius. They went for a walk after dinner as Libyans continued their celebrations. McCain said they were stopped constantly and asked to pose for pictures. Recalling the evening in our last book, he said he didn't think any of the celebrators had known who they were. "They just seemed to know we were Americans and had helped make this day possible." It made him feel proud, he told me, and the "lovely, hopeful evening" would be one of his "favorite memories."

When Chris Stevens was killed in Benghazi two months later, McCain mourned the loss personally. He described himself in the immediate aftermath as "just saddened, not angry with the administration." He sent a note to Hillary Clinton praising her remarks at a memorial service for Stevens. Soon, though, he was issuing harsh recriminations. Citing mistaken talking points used by UN ambassador Susan Rice in television interviews, McCain and others accused the administration of trying to obscure that Stevens had been deliberately targeted by terrorists. The riots in which he and three other Americans were murdered had been organized and led by extremists and were not, as administration officials appeared to allege, a spontaneous reaction to an anti-Muslim video produced in the U.S. McCain was angry about it, which I understood. But after administration officials conceded their error, I thought McCain should move on. He stayed white-hot for a while. He threatened to block Ambassador Rice's nomination to be secretary of state if, as rumored, Obama was considering appointing her to succeed Hillary Clinton. As the controversy inevitably played into the partisanship of the times, and House Republicans went on their Captain Ahab quest to affix all the blame for the tragedy to Hillary Clinton, I thought McCain risked being lumped together with them. He relented eventually, but not as soon as I wished he had.

Later, when Libya was disintegrating as Islamic extremists preyed on its anarchy, factions feuded, and militias clashed, McCain wrote elegiacally of the country and the American diplomat who had helped nurture Libyans' hopes for freedom, and about the controversy surrounding his death. "Anger subsides, politics move on, but sadness remains. Chris Stevens deserved better from all of us."[47]

If his fury over the Benghazi attacks slackened, and Libya's falling fortunes consumed him less in the years that followed, it was likely because the situation in Syria and its unimagined horrors consumed his attention and his outrage. I can think of no other conflict in which the U.S. was not a belligerent that preoccupied McCain to the extent Syria did or that he seemed more emotionally invested in. It was the last great public passion of his life. He had notorious disagreements with administration officials over Syria policy. But I think more than anything else, it was a feeling of hopelessness that drove him nearly to despair, emotions he rarely succumbed to in his life, that so disturbed him. The stygian blackness that descended on Syria with the onset of civil war—the mass atrocities, the chemical weapons attacks, the deliberate targeting of civilians, hospitals, and aid workers, the executions of women and children, the territory and populations taken captive by ISIS nihilists, Putin's ruthless ambitions in Syria and Iran, the five hundred thousand killed and the five million made homeless—the evil was on as grand a scale as any witnessed in his lifetime. He couldn't believe how little the world was doing to stop it. "Just when you think that's the worst thing they could do, they do something even worse," McCain lamented about the Assad regime and its allies. "And what are we doing then to stop them from committing more atrocities? Nothing, nothing, nothing."

He first called for U.S. and NATO air strikes to ground the Syrian air force in March 2012, after the regime killed thousands in the city of Homs and was indiscriminately bombing population centers. A British reporter who had fled Homs described the regime's offensive as "medieval siege and slaughter,"[48] a phrase that caught McCain's attention and which he quoted often. In a speech on the Senate floor, he argued the conflict was at a "decisive moment"; the time to act was now. In hindsight, that is hard to argue with. ISIS hadn't established its caliphate yet. The Russians had not intervened militarily, and while Hezbollah and some Revolutionary Guard officers were on the ground in Syria, Iran had not fully committed itself to the war. McCain believed ever after that if we had used air power to stop Assad from flying his bombers; created a safe haven in northern Syria for refugees and opposition groups; and provided arms to the Free Syrian Army (FSA), which mostly consisted at the time of defectors from the Syrian military, the regime would have collapsed. Many critics of McCain's recommendations believed Assad was internationally isolated and on the verge of collapse anyway. The Obama administration had deftly organized international opposition to Assad, imposing diplomatic and economic sanctions that their proponents believed would cost Assad support within the regime, but that proved to be wishful thinking. Also, at the time McCain spoke, the consequences of our intervention, he argued, were easier to predict and manage. Foreign jihadis hadn't flooded the country in the numbers they eventually would. Al-Qaeda was there, but it didn't dominate other armed opposition groups as it would later. All these horrors, McCain fervently believed, would not have come to pass had the world used force then to confront the aggressors.

The administration leaned heavily on objections to McCain's proposals from some senior military leaders, the gist of which was that it would be a costly and time-consuming operation to destroy all of Assad's air defenses, his airfields, and his command and control. It would take months before we could create and protect a safe haven. For over a year, "in every conversation, every . . . hearing, every private discussion I had with senior members of the administration," McCain complained, "I was told over and over that a no-fly zone was practically impossible. . . . [It] was too complex and dangerous for the greatest airpower in the world to manage safely and quickly."

McCain was frustrated but undeterred, believing the administration would ultimately come around to the necessity of intervention. He pressed on. He made several trips to Turkey to meet with Syrian opposition leaders, and with humanitarian workers risking their lives to bring relief to suffering Syrian civilians. In Washington, he met with the group that would come to be known as the White Helmets. He had been introduced to them by a young Syrian he had met with several times in Turkey, who was helping supply the FSA. I never met the guy, who went by the assumed name of Abu Salim, but McCain really admired him and talked about him a lot. By the time we started working on our last book together in 2017, he had lost track of Salim's whereabouts and wasn't even sure he was alive, though I learned subsequently that he is alive, and still committed to the cause. After McCain was diagnosed with brain cancer, he told me he wanted to include a reference to Salim in the book: "Say that I admire him and wish him well." It struck me as I did that McCain was singling out this one Syrian to whom he wanted to say a personal goodbye. I was touched by the gesture. It was as if this one brave and compassionate Syrian had embodied all of McCain's hopes for Syria, his unvanquished hopes, even though that wretched country descends further into the abyss with each passing year. He believed in Abu Salim, and he held on to his hopes for Syria.

By the new year, the regime had bombed Aleppo, Syria's largest city, as well as Damascus. Seventy thousand civilians had been killed, and three-quarters of a million to a million refugees had fled Syria and were burdening neighboring countries. Two years later, millions more would flee and roil the politics of Europe. Insurgents seemed to have the upper hand early in 2013, but Hezbollah came to the rescue of Assad's beleaguered troops and checked the rebels' advance. More Russians were on the ground. Worrying McCain, too, was the increase in foreign fighters: A few hundred Al-Qaeda–linked jihadis the year before now numbered in the thousands. The one development that could change President Obama's calculation, he maintained in private and public, was for Assad to use chemical weapons. McCain was convinced that Assad would resort to the drastic measure because nothing the West had done had threatened his hold on power. "We emboldened him," he observed.

McCain was back in southern Turkey in May 2013. By then the administration had agreed to provide defense assistance to the FSA, but only nonlethal assistance such as body armor and communications equipment. McCain convinced the State Department to allow him a few hours in Syria for a meeting he had arranged with representatives of the FSA and another opposition militia. Before he left, he hadn't mentioned anything about a Syria trip to me or anyone besides Chris Brose, the aide who would accompany him, and the Syrians who were facilitating the meeting. When I heard on the news that he had slipped into the country, I expected a cloak-and-dagger description of how McCain became the highest-ranking U.S. government official to visit Syria since the war's inception. "There wasn't much to it," he acknowledged when I asked him about it. He had met the FSA's military commander in Turkey, and he, Chris Brose, and two other Syrians loaded into a couple of SUVs, drove a mile to a border crossing, where the guards waved them through, and then another few miles to the building where they met with rebel commanders. The rebels told him they were desperate for ammunition, anti-tank weapons especially, and air defenses of some kind. McCain said he would keep pushing the administration. The meeting had been brief, he said, and after posing for a few photographs, he then returned to Turkey. The whole experience had taken barely an hour. I couldn't tell if he was disappointed the trip had not been more eventful.

Later that day, McCain forwarded the pictures he had taken with the FSA commanders to his press office in Washington, with the instruction to choose one to put in a tweet. Some days later, a Hezbollah-associated Beirut television station broadcast the photograph and alleged that two of the men were members of an Al-Qaeda-linked militia. It wasn't true, as we quickly established, but falsehoods can live forever in the age of the Internet. Soon the story was embellished to include ISIS leader Abu Bakr al-Baghdadi in the picture. No amount of third-party fact-checking or authoritative denial could stop its spread. Even McCain's Senate colleague and conspiracy-minded antagonist Rand Paul accused him of meeting with ISIS. "Here's the problem," Paul told the *Daily Beast*. "McCain did meet with ISIS, and had his picture taken, and didn't know it was happening at the time." The persistence of the smear frustrated McCain, as it was apparently immune to refutation, but after a couple of years, he tended to laugh it off, especially after someone doctored the photo with a plainly Photoshopped head of Baghdadi superimposed on an FSA fighter's body. I mentioned the photograph to him once, and he burst into a rendition of Paul Simon's "Me and Julio Down by the Schoolyard," substituting Abu for Julio.

On August 21, 2013, the Syrian army fired rockets with warheads containing sarin gas at rebel positions in Damascus, killing as many as fifteen hundred civilians. Video recordings of the atrocity included children writhing in agony as they died. Assad had crossed President Obama's red line. McCain had no doubt the president would retaliate militarily, although he worried the response wouldn't be proportionate to the severity of Assad's crime. Obama surprised everyone when he announced he would seek congressional authorization first. Shortly after his announcement, he invited McCain and Lindsey Graham to the White House to be briefed on his proposed response. McCain was impressed with the plan, which included air strikes on targets that the administration had previously argued couldn't be undertaken without destroying the regime's air defenses. It also provided lethal weapons to the FSA. McCain and Lindsey held a press conference on the White House driveway to endorse a congressional resolution, intimating they were satisfied with the plan as it had been described to them.

They had been told the strikes would launch in two days. A day after their White House meeting, JCS chairman General Martin Dempsey called to let them know the strikes had been delayed, without explaining why. That same day the Senate Foreign Relations Committee voted 10 to 7 to approve a resolution, amended by McCain, authorizing the use of force against Syria. Nothing happened. The president had his famous conversation with his chief of staff, Denis McDonough, and called off the strikes. Russian foreign minister Sergei Lavrov, with whom McCain often sparred at security conferences over the years, had offered to broker a deal in which Assad would surrender his chemical weapons stocks. No one from the administration had called McCain or Graham to let them know the president had a change of heart.

"He was lying, of course," an infuriated McCain would later say in reference to Assad's agreement to abandon his chemical weapons. Assad gave up some stockpiles but kept others and used them again. McCain was not alone when he contended that Obama's Syria reversal was "the worst decision of his presidency . . . and its consequences are felt to this day," he wrote. "His administration's credibility in the region was lost and with some of the region's worst actors. . . . It shook the confidence of our allies and emboldened our adversaries, no one more so than Vladimir Putin. For the next couple years, the administration's policy for Syria was reduced to pleading with Russia to help convince Assad to negotiate a settlement to the war."

McCain's anguish over the plight of Syrians and his anger over what he considered inconstant and unreliable American leadership colored his relations with members of the administration ever after. At times he felt powerless to affect the situation, and became distraught, and confessed he was, which was unlike him. "I don't know what else to do," he lamented once. "I don't know if there's anything I can do to stop it from getting worse." And worse it got. ISIS established its caliphate.

Russians intervened in full force by 2015, insisting they were there to fight ISIS but targeting the FSA for destruction. In the process, they bombed hospitals and relief workers and established "permanent" air and naval bases in Syria, reestablishing a presence in the Middle East they had not had since Anwar Sadat had kicked them out of Egypt. The death toll hit a half million. The refugee crisis was destabilizing the region and beyond, not to mention the intense human suffering it caused. To McCain, Syria was his personal failure as well as a failure of the United States and the West. He wouldn't live long enough to get over it. A Syrian human rights group showed him photographs of the mutilated corpses of Syrians who had been tortured and killed by the regime. "I keep copies of these pictures on my desk," he said in impromptu remarks at the U.S. Holocaust Memorial Museum, "so that every single day, when I come to my office, I will be reminded of the horrific crimes that have been committed and are being committed as we speak against innocent Syrian men, women, and children."

Toward the end of the administration's tenure, the hostility McCain felt over Syria did cool to something closer to strong but civil disagreement. The president invited him to the Oval Office for a private meeting, no aides, just the two of them. It lasted about a half hour, McCain told me, during which "I let him have it, and he let me have it." They argued with voices raised, he said, neither man yielding his position, and in the end, McCain gave credit to his former rival. "I respect him for doing it. He's wrong, but he listened." There had been other occasions when he and the president met privately, and their conversations had been informal and friendly. President Obama would refer to them in his eulogy for McCain. Curiously, the senator never related the contents of those conversations to me or anyone else, as far as I know. He kept them confidential. He did, however, make a point of telling some of us about their private, heated exchange over Syria. I think he appreciated the respect implicit in the president's willingness to have at it with him.

The fate of Syria, its endless savagery and suffering, and the Arab winter wrought by reactionary regimes that crushed the aspirations for self-determination throughout the Middle East almost drove

McCain to permanent despair. But as he faced his own mortality, he clung to his hopes for the peoples of the region. He told me he wanted to close the chapter about these events in his last book "on a realistic but a hopeful note."

So he did, writing that the White Helmets and Syrians fighting for their human rights embodied "the eternal promise of the Arab Spring, which was engulfed in flames and drowned in blood, but will, like all springs, come again."[49]

MR. CHAIRMAN

The Republican Party was changing under the influence of elected officeholders identified with the Tea Party movement, and it was an increasing concern to McCain. Their maximalist, uncompromising politics, as well as their suspiciousness of government that bordered on conspiracy-nuttiness, offended McCain's practical, problem-solving approach to governing and taxed his short supply of patience. But what worried him most about the new conservative populists in the House and Senate were the strains of isolationism and protectionism he detected in their America First chauvinism, which he would reject years later and in another context as "spurious nationalism."

He seemed at times to take pleasure in poking them, though he must have been mindful of the problems they could cause legislation he sponsored or even his own reelection in 2016. I don't know when McCain decided to run for a sixth term, but I doubt he ever seriously considered retiring. With the Democrats in control of the Senate in the 112th Congress, he had yet to achieve his ambition to chair the Armed Services Committee. No one who knew him well was surprised he didn't want to leave the Senate before he had that honor. He often referred to the example of long-gone senators who had remained in Congress after they were clearly mentally and physically enfeebled, and he implored his friends, "Don't let me overstay my welcome." But McCain in his late seventies seemed hardly changed from a decade before, as energetic, enthusiastic, and curious as ever, and seemingly immune to the infirmities that usually accompany old age. None of us would have dared suggest it was time to retire.

In his travels with Hillary Clinton when she was a member of the Senate, McCain had gotten to know Clinton's aide Huma Abedin. In the summer of 2012, Abedin was the undeserving subject of a conspiracy theory originating in a far-right think tank that warned darkly of a "civilization jihad" waged in the U.S. by Muslim extremists. It was embraced by Michele Bachmann and four other House Republicans. In a letter to the State Department inspector general, Bachmann et al. alleged that Abedin's family was connected to "Muslim Brotherhood operatives" and further insinuated that Abedin herself was some kind of secret agent for the Brotherhood, responsible for proposing State Department policies they claimed were intended to benefit Islamic extremists. For reasons unknown, Bachmann had a seat on the House Intelligence Committee, so her ridiculous smear of Abedin, who served at the time as Secretary Clinton's deputy chief of staff at the State Department, got some notice in the press and gained currency in the fever swamps of the Internet.

When aides informed McCain about Abedin's vilification, he went that day to the Senate floor to denounce it. McCain had known Frank Gaffney, the author of the report that started the campaign against Abedin, since he had been employed on Scoop Jackson's staff. McCain had worked with him a little in the 1990s, but Gaffney's intellectual trajectory had taken a turn toward Islamophobia and crackpot conspiracy theories years ago, so McCain had written him off as a "wack job," a category to which he likely assigned Michele Bachmann and a couple of the other signatories to the letter. "These allegations about Huma and the report from which they are drawn are . . . an unwarranted and unfounded attack on an honorable woman, a dedicated American, and a loyal public servant," McCain fumed in what *The Atlantic* described as "McCain's furious speech." He went on: "Put simply, Huma represents what is best about America: the daughter of immigrants, who has risen to the highest levels of our government on the basis of her substantial personal merit and her abiding commitment to American ideals that she embodies so fully."

THE LUCKIEST MAN 479

Then he returned to the recurring theme of so many of his public addresses, American exceptionalism. "Ultimately, what is at stake in this matter is larger than the reputation of one person. This is about who we are as a nation and who we aspire to be. What makes America exceptional among the countries of the world is that we are bound together as citizens not by blood or class, not by sect or ethnicity, but by a set of enduring, universal, and equal rights that are the foundation of our constitution, our laws, our citizenry, and our identity. When anyone, not least a member of Congress, launches specious and degrading attacks against fellow Americans on the basis of nothing more than fear of who they are and ignorance of what they stand for, it defames the spirit of our nation, and we all grow poorer because of it."

Earlier that year, Bachmann had been a candidate for the Republican nomination for president, and in August 2011, she had managed to win the Iowa Straw Poll. Iowa wasn't as kind to her in January, when she came in sixth in the caucuses. The day after, McCain overruled the objections of some friends who thought that, as the party's last nominee, he should stay neutral in the 2012 presidential primaries. He wanted to endorse Governor Romney, who he thought was the best candidate in the field and would make the best president. He didn't think the governor's two closest rivals, Rick Santorum and Newt Gingrich, could defeat President Obama, and I doubt he would have wanted them to; he didn't care for Santorum, and he thought Gingrich was full of himself and talked too much. There were a couple other candidates in the race who were his friends, former governors Jon Huntsman and Buddy Roemer, but they trailed far behind Romney in the polls. Just two days before the primary that McCain had twice won, he appeared at a Romney town hall in Peterborough, New Hampshire, and announced to the audience that he was there to make sure "we make Mitt Romney the next president of the United States of America." He urged New Hampshire, the state he considered his other political home, to "catapult him to victory in South Carolina." As Governor Romney had done for him four years earlier, McCain made clear he was willing to do anything the Romney campaign asked of him for the duration of the campaign. He saw Romney as a Republican who, if he won the White House, could check the ideological drift of the party toward xenophobia, mercantilism, and isolationism, and McCain was sorely disappointed when Romney lost.

The election occurred in the midst of the Benghazi controversy, when McCain was at the forefront of the administration's critics. But with Governor Romney's defeat, and the election to Congress of more Tea Party adherents, McCain would make his own efforts to push back against the direction they were leading the party. Some of those efforts were in the form of legislation or formal addresses and debate, and others were the product of his sarcasm and natural pugnacity, which he could never entirely restrain. He grew increasingly exasperated by attacks from Republicans "who've been here for five minutes" on traditional Republican views of national security, foreign policy, and trade policy. Rand Paul, who was elected in 2010, and Ted Cruz, elected two years later, were the two who seemed to irritate him the most, as well as Paul's fellow libertarian in the House, Justin Amash. While Paul's and Amash's views were the most antithetical to McCain's, Cruz was a junior member of the Armed Services Committee and in a position to annoy him more frequently. McCain clashed with Cruz during the confirmation hearing for Chuck Hagel's nomination as secretary of defense. McCain was planning to oppose Hagel's nomination over their differences on Iraq policy, and had grilled the nominee on the subject in a pretty harsh exchange. He was way too aggressive, and I worried people would think he had a personal grievance with Hagel. But he was furious when Cruz made an unsubstantiated accusation that Hagel had taken money from terrorist groups. Looking at Cruz, McCain stated, "Senator Hagel is an honorable man, and no one on this committee at any time should impugn his character."

Rand Paul, supported by Cruz, filibustered John Brennan's nomination in March 2013 over what McCain dismissed as "ludicrous" fears about the military's use of drones. At one point, Paul speculated about a drone strike on an innocent American sipping coffee at a Starbucks. McCain popped off, not for the first or last time, at his Republican antagonists. When a reporter asked him if Paul, Cruz, and Amash were "positive forces in the Republican Party," he first damned them with faint praise: "They were elected, nobody believes there was a corrupt election," before giving in to his usual temptation to wisecrack: "But I also think that . . . it's always the wacko birds on the right and left that get the media megaphone. I think it can be harmful if there is a belief among the American people that those people are reflective of the views of the majority of Republicans. They aren't."

When the reporter asked him who he meant by "wacko birds," McCain replied, "Paul, Cruz, Amash, whoever." Amash had tangled with him before on Twitter, for which McCain had recently acquired an affinity as a forum for wiseasses. Amash tweeted a mocking response to the wacko bird reference: "Bravo, Senator. You got us. Did you come up with that at #DinnerWithBarack?" The quip was a reference to a dinner held by President Obama with Republican senators at the Jefferson Hotel; McCain and Lindsey Graham had suggested the idea to him. "Just fine" and a thumbs-up was all reporters managed to get out of McCain after the dinner, and he wasn't much more forthcoming with aides and friends. Amash's tweet puzzled him. "Is that supposed to be an insult," he asked when he showed it to me, "that I had dinner with Obama?" The question suggested the trouble McCain was having adjusting to the new brand of Republican opposition to the Obama administration that scorned all dealmaking and, if Amash's tweet was any indication, even social interaction with Democrats. In a speech at the Center for New American Security, he signaled his concern with the isolationist orientation of both parties' fringes by expressing solidarity with Obama. "The President and I have had our differences," he observed. "Many of those differences will persist. But there are times these days when I feel I have more in common on foreign policy with President Obama than I do with some in my own party."

McCain and Democratic senator Chuck Schumer had been in discussions since the beginning of 2013 about the feasibility of another attempt at comprehensive immigration reform. They eventually recruited six other senators, three from each party, to negotiate with the Obama administration the provisions of a sweeping overhaul of immigration laws. The Gang of Eight (as they were styled in the media)

included on the Democratic side, in addition to Schumer, Michael
Bennet of Colorado, Robert Menendez of New Jersey, and the Democratic whip, Dick Durbin of Illinois. Republicans joining McCain included his Arizona colleague Jeff Flake, his pal Lindsey Graham, and
Marco Rubio of Florida. McCain, like much of Washington, had his
eye on Rubio, the son of Cuban immigrants, whose intelligence and
communications skills had garnered quite a lot of attention. Although
he had been backed by the Tea Party and was an underdog winner in
2010 over the establishment's choice, Governor Charlie Crist, Rubio
seemed free of the intransigence and fervor of self-identified Tea Party
conservatives, and his views on national security, unlike those of his
libertarian peers, impressed McCain as close to his own. As McCain
had once believed Jon Kyl's involvement would crack conservative opposition to immigration reform, he was now convinced that Rubio's
support would signal to other newly arrived conservatives that this
latest iteration had prioritized border security and rationalized the
immigration system while still addressing the other components of
immigration reform. When the battle was joined, and opposition
to the bill built in quarters that were usually friendly territory for
Rubio—particularly among House conservatives—he appeared to
back off some of the provisions he had agreed to, or so it seemed in
some of his comments to the media, and he proposed concessions to
Republican critics without informing the bill's other sponsors. McCain
was irritated but mostly kept his peace. Complaints were made to staff
privately. "He'll probably be president someday," McCain remarked to
me, "but he'll need more guts than this."

The press knew by the end of January that a new immigration bill
was in the offing, as the Gang of Eight negotiated its provisions among
themselves and with administration officials, who were intentionally
keeping a low profile. McCain on several occasions remarked to me
how shrewd he thought Obama was in the way he was approaching the
issue. "They're involved in every discussion," he observed, "but they're
not bragging about it. They're hardly talking about it," recognizing,
McCain said, that "the more it looks like Obama's bill, the more the
crazies will go after it." The important role the president would play,

McCain said, "was keeping Democrats on board when this thing gets loaded up with stuff for Republicans."

The bill's authorized spending for border security greatly exceeded the money provided for the same purpose in the previous immigration reform bills: new fencing and other barriers; more money for Immigration and Customs and the Border Patrol; an elaborate employment verification system. An amendment offered during floor debate to attract more Republican support for the measure would surge forty thousand additional Border Patrol agents to the border. The bill proposed a new merit-based immigration system that would grant green cards to high-skill immigrants. No temporary work visas would be granted for areas with high unemployment. The legalization of undocumented workers was even more exacting in restrictions than previous bills had imposed. Dreamers—immigrants who came here as children—could apply for a green card after five years. But undocumented immigrants who came here as adults had to wait ten years, and their path to citizenship would be suspended if certain markers weren't met that indicated the border was secure, including a 90 percent apprehension rate for illegal crossings. "The bill," McCain argued, "was a balanced, conservative, scrupulously thorough, and fair attempt to settle the immigration problem in a way that would satisfy economic needs, the interests of American workers, justice, and human decency."[50]

McCain and Romney had both lost the Hispanic vote by big margins, despite the fact that McCain had been a champion of reform. The Republican Party obviously had a problem with the fastest-growing demographic in the country. The Republican National Committee had undertaken an autopsy to analyze reasons for the Republican defeat in 2012, and the failure to attract Hispanics and other minorities was highlighted as one of the party's major weaknesses. Most of the party's leaders accepted the reality that as long as Republicans were, in their noisy opposition to practical immigration reform, perceived as not wanting Hispanics in the country, the liability would remain. But Republican leaders in Congress were not prepared to incite the base by backing a comprehensive bill that legalized immigrants who had come here illegally.

The Border Security, Economic Opportunity, and Immigration Modernization Act of 2013 was introduced on April 16 and denounced by the usual suspects in the House and Senate and in the media as "amnesty," the accusation that reliably inflamed grassroots conservatives. A ludicrous and quickly discredited Heritage Foundation study projected that the bill would cost taxpayers $6.3 trillion. The Congressional Budget Office, which still prides itself on conducting serious analysis, projected that it would actually save $175 billion over ten years.

Most of the bill's details had been known since February, and opposition had been gaining steam ever since. McCain, who was never shy about confronting opposition face-to-face, scheduled town halls in Arizona to try to blunt it, though he knew it was likely a fool's errand. At this point in the long saga of his attempts to reform immigration laws, he didn't believe anything would placate opponents who rejected any path to citizenship. But he didn't believe it absolved him of the responsibility to respond to their criticism. The town halls were described by different reporters who observed them as "rowdy," "testy," and "very rough." McCain seemed to take a curious satisfaction in them, mixing it up aggressively with critics who pilloried the bill and him. One persistent constituent attending a town hall in a Phoenix suburb kept alleging that McCain had broken his promise to build "the dang fence." McCain kept repeating that the bill included miles and miles of fencing, but the guy wouldn't take yes for an answer. Finally, McCain called him a "jerk" and said listening to him was "an Orwellian experience." Despite his give-as-good-as-he-got approach to constituent relations, McCain seemed good-humored about the raucous town halls. It was a format where he was so at ease that even hostile receptions didn't throw him. I didn't witness any of his town halls that winter and spring, but he recounted a few of the highlights for me, chuckling as he did. For all but the last year of his Senate career, he continued to hold question-and-answer sessions with his constituents, knowing that the encounters would be lively, to say the least. He never screened the people who attended, never tried to fill the venue with supporters, never put a topic off limits, and never had prepared answers. He prided himself on it.

Opposition to the bill within the Senate wasn't formidable, and it passed easily, 68 to 32, on June 27. Harry Reid had instructed all senators to vote on final passage from their desks, a rare occurrence meant to convey the moment's importance. Vice President Biden presided from the chair. Immigration activists filled the Senate gallery and erupted in cheers when the tally was announced. Fourteen Republicans had joined all Democrats in voting for the bill. Supporters, including McCain, had wanted to secure seventy votes for the bill, believing that would signal to Republican leaders in both the House and Senate—who McCain believed all secretly supported it—that they could summon the courage to get reform done in that session of Congress. Though they had fallen two votes short, McCain still believed reform had enough momentum that the House would have to pass something they could go to conference with. He was wrong. The House did nothing. Speaker Boehner, whom McCain considered a friend and who he knew supported reform, didn't feel he had the support within his conference to force the issue. Even the Senate's version of the bill would have passed easily if brought to the House floor, with almost all Democrats in favor and a substantial minority of Republicans as well. But at this point in his speakership, Boehner was constantly harassed by Tea Party detractors dedicated to his ouster, and who took the view that government in a closely divided country never required compromise. They would eventually form their own ultraconservative Freedom Caucus and succeed in driving Boehner into retirement two years later.

Given his past experiences with the House leadership's attempts to ignore legislation he sponsored, it's a little surprising that McCain didn't expect the same treatment in this instance. He kept lobbying Boehner and others to pass some kind of immigration reform, anything that could form the basis for negotiations with the Senate. When House Republicans released a statement in June declaring, "We will not go to conference with the Senate's immigration bill," he was as

discouraged as I had ever seen him after a legislative defeat. The thing
that bothered him the most, he said, was that the problem itself wasn't
that hard to solve. It had multiple components, each of which involved
competing constituencies, but it wasn't complicated by trade-offs as
difficult as those in other policies. "I don't know why we can't get this
done," he complained years later. "It's not Medicare, for chrissakes." He
was confounded by the absurd notion that there was a realistic way
to get eleven million or more immigrants, many of whom had been
in the country for decades, to leave the country. The politics of the
issue give an advantage in many Republican primaries to immigration
hardliners, and until that changes, every sensible immigration reform
proposal will be met by cries of "amnesty."

Despite the third discouraging defeat for reformers, he would try
again five years later, introducing another immigration bill with his
friend Senator Chris Coons of Delaware, "the nicest guy in this place."
He knew it had no chance of succeeding while Donald Trump was in
the White House and he was in Arizona fighting cancer. It was a statement more than a battle plan, an act of defiance aimed at the nativism
he believed was behind Trump's hostility toward immigrants.

McCain continued butting heads with Tea Party stalwarts, especially senators he believed were trying to make the Senate like the
more polarized House. In July, he joined forces with progressive Elizabeth Warren to revive banking regulations in the Glass-Steagall Act
that had been repealed in 1999, which McCain believed had contributed to the financial crisis in 2008. That same month, he and Chuck
Schumer negotiated a truce in the standoff between Harry Reid and
Mitch McConnell over Obama administration appointments blocked
by Republican filibusters. The deal allowed seven blocked nominations
to be confirmed in exchange for Reid backing down from his threat
to change the rule to end the filibuster. The truce lasted until December, when, in retaliation for more Republican obstruction, Reid went
ahead and exercised the nuclear option, killing the filibuster for executive calendar votes, and McCain went to the floor to inform Reid he
was "going to kick the crap" out of him. He spoke out against the government shutdown forced by House Republicans over their demands

to defund Obamacare. When Ted Cruz staged a twenty-one-hour filibuster to draw attention to those demands, and disparaged Republicans who disagreed with his tactics as appeasers, McCain rebuked
him. He was one of only nine Senate Republicans to vote for the Bipartisan Budget Act in December, though its continuation of the onerous
sequestration cap on defense spending worried McCain, a worry that
became a nightmare in years ahead, when he chaired Armed Services
and the spending cuts severely impacted military readiness.

Predictably, his actions prompted a new round of punditry about
the return of the maverick. But all the while McCain was cutting bipartisan deals or criticizing the maximalist demands of Republican
bomb-throwers, he was routinely criticizing the administration over
Syria and a host of other foreign and defense policy issues. He was
who he had always been, an idiosyncratic, boundlessly energetic legislator driven to be in the center of action and to make things happen.
His detractors on both the right and left could find him maddeningly
inconsistent ideologically and attributed changes in his attitudes to
changes in his politics or his adversaries. He was hard to explain, and
he wasn't very good at explaining himself. But the search for a psychological or political explanation overlooks the most obvious one: He
wanted to be one of the guys who last and make things happen. He
wanted to live his "crowded hour," as he often said, quoting his political hero Teddy Roosevelt.

In retaliation for McCain's support on immigration reform and
various other alleged apostasies, the Arizona Republican Party passed
a resolution at its annual meeting in January 2014 censuring McCain
and calling his record in the Senate "disastrous and harmful." His detractors were the legislative district committees elected by Republican
precinct committeemen. The minor status of the posts meant that in
most cases, only conservative activists invested time and effort campaigning for them, which gave them control of the state party's annual
meeting. McCain had ignored them over the years, and under their influence, the state party drifted increasingly toward the far-right fringe.
He responded publicly to the censure by saying it made him more
likely to run for reelection in two years. "I've won every election in

Arizona by very large margins, quite often with the opposition of that element of the party," he told a reporter. "If anything, it fires me up."

Privately, he acknowledged it had been a mistake for him and other party leaders to leave these local party posts uncontested, and he thought it was time to correct that. Aides from his presidential campaign and his 2010 reelection campaign formed a PAC to raise money and recruit mainstream Republicans to run for them. The small but influential and decidedly pro-McCain Vietnamese-American community in Arizona proved a ready source of local Republicans willing to run for and back candidates at the precinct and district level. By the end of the year, ousted McCain antagonists were complaining about a McCain "purge" of conservatives, including the fellow who had authored the censure resolution and lost his district committee chairmanship. They swore revenge in 2016, when McCain would seek the party's nomination for another term. As he had claimed in his reaction to the censure resolution, it made him more inclined to run again.

In April 2013, Harry Reid convened a bipartisan lunch in the Kennedy Caucus Room to commemorate the fortieth anniversary of McCain's release from prison. Nearly every senator attended. He was so moved by his colleagues' tribute that he spoke at length about his captivity, which few of them had heard him do. He told them stories of his suffering and stories of times when he had been treated with compassion. He talked of the men who had inspired him and the two men who had saved his life. Some days later he told me about the lunch. By then, I had already received an email from a Republican senator telling me how McCain had held the entire Senate spellbound for almost an hour, "not a dry eye in the house."

Three months later, Bud Day, veteran of three wars and Medal of Honor recipient, McCain's commanding officer in prison, whom he credited with saving his life, and one of his dearest friends, died at the age of eighty-eight. McCain spoke at his funeral, and when he returned to Washington, he delivered part of his eulogy on the Senate floor in tribute to the "bravest man I ever knew." He recounted all Bud had done to bring him back to life and to show him how to keep his honor under duress. He talked of their lasting friendship and campaigning together in the years after Vietnam. "I'm going to miss him terribly," he said in a wavering voice. "Even though Bud had reached advanced years, I could never imagine him yielding to anything, even to the laws of nature. Tough old bird that he was, I thought he would outlive us all." With that, he broke down and closed his remarks through tears. "He's gone now," he continued. "To a heaven I expect he imagined would look like an Iowa cornfield in early winter filled with pheasants. I will miss Bud every day for the rest of my life. But I will see him again. I know I will. I'll hunt the field with him, and I look forward to it."

The next year, 2014, Republicans won a majority of Senate seats. At last, John McCain would be chairman of the Senate Armed Services Committee, successor to the statesmen he had admired and envied all those years ago, when he watched them scribble on scraps of paper instructions that would profoundly impact national security. He would not live long enough to serve a full six-year term as chairman. But he would make the most of the three years when he had the gavel.

He scheduled committee hearings to educate members on all manner of subjects affecting national defense, from defense acquisition to the history and politics of countries where Americans faced security challenges. He was a fierce interrogator of witnesses, even those he liked. He was the scourge of defense contractors for cost overruns and schedule delays. Flag officers, even four-stars, took extra care to prepare for McCain's hearings and steeled themselves for confrontation. Disagreeing with the chairman could be unpleasant but unlikely to cost you his respect. Evading his questions, however, was a whole other category of misery. He would be merciless if he thought a witness was trying to obfuscate an issue. And if you lied to him, he'd "have your ass for a grape." Even Secretary Jim Mattis, the legendary marine general, acknowledged after McCain's death his trepidation every time "I sat at his witness table." Once in a while, I'd catch him terrorizing a witness in a televised hearing and mention it to him the next time I saw him, suggesting he might have been a little too hard-assed. Rarely did he defend his behavior by saying he had been provoked. Most times, he seemed honestly surprised that I had that reaction, looking puzzled and protesting, "I didn't think I was too tough on the guy."

Ferocity was just his style, though I doubt many witnesses knew that while they were experiencing it.

One of his first hearings was with former secretaries of state Henry Kissinger and George Shultz, whom he asked to share their strategic visions for U.S. leadership. When protestors with the anti-war group Code Pink noisily took over the hearing, McCain had security remove them, yelling after a protestor who had put her hands on Kissinger, "Get out of here, you lowlife scum." He defended his outburst afterward as rallying to the aid of old men. "Henry's ninety-four, who the hell tries to rough up someone who's ninety-four. I'd do it again, goddammit," he barked. I hadn't even criticized him for it.

Writing in the *Wall Street Journal* after McCain's death, former Clinton White House aide and Brookings Institute fellow Bill Galston reflected on McCain's leadership of the committee:

> The hearings McCain conducted as a member and then chairman of the Armed Services Committee were always tough and not always entirely fair. But no one could doubt his commitment to the nation's defense, and especially to the men and women in uniform whose lives were on the line. He wanted the defense budget to be large enough to ensure that American forces had the best training and equipment. But he loathed the Pentagon's waste and, worse, its failure to terminate weapons that cost too much and delivered too little. On more than one occasion he ruthlessly exposed a military commander's lack of strategic clarity and failures of candor about battlefield progress, knowing that evasions and half-truths would cost lives on the front lines. He was never cowed by the rank and reputation of the military leaders arrayed before him. Like President Eisenhower, his experience gave him a BS detector sharp enough to cut through Pentagon jargon and acronyms to reach the often uncomfortable truth.[51]

McCain was the leading critic of five expensive acquisitions. He condemned the $400 billion F-35 cost overruns, and the Defense

Department's cozy relationship with the plane's manufacturer, Lockheed Martin, as "the kind of cronyism that should make us all vigilant against . . . the military-industrial complex." He opposed the acquisition of the F-22 stealth fighter, another Lockheed contract that blew past cost estimates, as an unaffordable non-necessity "that may very well become the most expensive corroding hangar queen in the history of modern military aviation." He applauded Secretary Gates's 2009 decision to terminate further production. He got in a contentious back-and-forth with Obama's secretary of the air force, Deborah Lee James, over a cost-plus contract the air force negotiated with Northrup Grumman for the new B-21 long-range bombers; the funding mechanism would guarantee the contractor a specific profit in addition to the agreed-upon purchase price. McCain threatened to block the acquisition even though the contract had already been signed. "They can do whatever the hell they want," he said dismissively of the air force, "we have to authorize that procurement."

He didn't spare the navy from abuse when it offended his frugality and priorities. He was a relentless critic of the navy's acquisition of three new littoral combat ships, when "cost overruns more than doubled the cost of each LCS," and the ships' "warfighting capabilities . . . have fallen years—I repeat years—behind and remain unproven." And he opposed the acquisition of a new aircraft carrier, the USS *Gerald Ford*. Carriers are the crown jewels of the navy's fleets. McCain, who had served as a pilot on four different carriers and gone to war on two of them, considered carriers essential platforms for projecting American power. But he thought the navy could make do with smaller, less expensive carriers. The *Ford*'s costs were so over budget that he blasted it as "one of the most spectacular acquisition debacles in recent memory—and that's saying something."

McCain's primary concern as chairman, in addition to inefficient and wasteful acquisition practices, were the spending limits imposed under the so-called sequestration agreed to in the 2011 Budget Control Act, which had ended a partisan standoff over increasing the debt ceiling. McCain said he had "swallowed hard" and voted for the agreement because of the urgency of the debt crisis, but he had done so with grave reservations about the defense caps. As chairman of the committee that authorized defense spending, he could direct funds from one purpose to another to address critical deficiencies caused by the caps, but the caps themselves could be lifted only by a new budget agreement, outside the jurisdiction of his committee. He used his gavel to focus media attention on examples of where sequestration was damaging national security. Obama vetoed the first defense bill produced under McCain's leadership because he had tried to circumvent sequestration by authorizing more money for an emergency fund exempt from the limits. McCain complained but quickly stripped out the problematic provision and sent the White House a revised bill that the president would sign. He kept pressing through the end of the Obama administration and the start of the Trump administration to get rid of sequestration.

Within weeks of assuming the chairmanship, McCain launched a review of the Goldwater-Nichols Act of 1986, which had created the modern military command structure and was meant to fix chronic problems caused by service rivalries. Goldwater-Nichols had streamlined the chain of command, vested more authority in combatant commanders, and given the chairman of the Joint Chiefs of Staff the principal advisory role to the president and the secretary of defense rather than the various service chiefs. McCain and many defense policy experts had begun to worry that the "jointness" instituted by the Goldwater-Nichols reforms was producing "lowest common denominator recommendations to senior leaders," or the "tyranny of consensus," as Michèle Flournoy, a top Obama defense official, called it. Under McCain's leadership, the Armed Services Committee would mandate changes to the acquisition process by transferring authority for managing service-specific acquisitions from an undersecretary of defense, where it had produced bottlenecks that "slowed acquisitions to a crawl," back to the services themselves.

When its review of Goldwater-Nichols was completed, the committee proposed what McCain described as the "most sweeping reforms of the organization of the Department of Defense in a generation." The proposals encountered strong opposition from the Pentagon but had the backing of prominent former military commanders and civilian defense officials. The most contentious proposal addressed concerns with unimaginative, sluggish decision-making in the Pentagon. It required the secretary of defense to produce a plan for reorganization that included cross-functional "mission teams," which were meant to be more collaborative, innovative, and results-oriented than the "excessively parochial, duplicative," and innovation-resistant functional bureaucratic structures. Other reforms included a reduction in the number of flag officer billets, as well as limits on the size of the National Security Council, which had expanded with every new administration. McCain's first two years as chairman were among the most productive of his career. He told me he was worried that Democrats would retake the Senate, and he wanted to get started on, if not finish, all of his priorities. Anything outstanding, "I can work on with Jack if he's chairman."

As he had when he chaired the Commerce and Indian Affairs committees, McCain forged a productive partnership with the ranking Democrat on the committee, Senator Jack Reed of Rhode Island, a West Point graduate. Bipartisan cooperation was the norm for Armed Services, one of the last redoubts in Congress where partisanship usually takes a back seat to committee business. But it was particularly true with McCain's leadership as chairman or ranking Republican. He and the recently retired Carl Levin, who had chaired the committee when Democrats were in the majority and McCain was the senior Republican, were particularly close and had compatible views on most issues within the committee's jurisdiction. It was the same with Reed. That's not to say McCain steered clear of subjects in which there were differences between the parties' positions. He used his chairmanship to focus attention on issues that were his most urgent priorities. Some were controversial, and some were the subject of disagreement between the chairman and whichever administration was in office. He convened hearings on Syria in which he made abundantly clear his disapproval of Obama administration policies. After Russia invaded Ukraine, he used the committee to rally public opinion, the Obama and Trump administrations, and U.S. allies to provide Ukrainians the weapons they needed to defend themselves from Russian aggression. In the first defense authorization bill the committee reported under his chairmanship, he included, over the Obama administration's objection, funding authorization for arms shipments to Ukraine. He denounced the administration's prohibition on lethal assistance, calling it "a shameful chapter in American history" to a *New York Times* reporter.

Ukraine was John McCain's last great overseas cause. Ukraine's president, Viktor Yanukovych, had negotiated an agreement with the European Union that would put Ukraine on a path to membership. Under the terms of the agreement, Ukraine had to institute political and economic reforms that addressed the country's endemic corruption and lapses into authoritarian politics. Yanukovych was an unlikely figure to lead Ukraine toward a European future. He was notoriously corrupt himself, had thrown political rivals in jail, and was a member of Ukraine's ethnic Russian minority. He was internationally regarded as the Kremlin's man, the Ukrainian whom Vladimir Putin expected would return Ukraine to a reconstituted Russian sphere of influence. Putin demanded that Ukraine join the customs union Russia was forming with two other former republics, Belarus and Kazakhstan, which the Kremlin boss had unrealistically conceived of as a rival to the EU. As EU and Ukrainian officials negotiated the terms of Ukraine's association, Putin put intense pressure on Yanukovych to turn east rather than west, threatening a cutoff of natural gas supplies and reportedly issuing private warnings of a more personal nature. For a while, it appeared Yanukovych would confound the skeptics and sign the agreement with the EU. Ukraine was broke and in debt, and the EU promised loans, investments, and access to European markets. The vast majority of Ukrainians wanted a European future and abhorred the idea of a return to the Russian past. U.S. and EU diplomats mounted a lobbying campaign to persuade Yanukovych to stay the course. McCain had wanted to lead a delegation to Kiev to encourage the same, but Vice President Biden and Assistant Secretary of State Victoria Nuland asked him to hold off.

On November 21, 2013, Yanukovych succumbed to Russian intimidation and announced he would not sign the EU agreement. Rumors abounded that Putin had summoned Yanukovych to his dacha in Sochi and made various political and economic threats until Yanukovych gave in to his demands. Kiev erupted in protests, which grew in size and intensity after police used force to try to shut them down. Kiev's Independence Square, the Maidan, where the largest protests were held, gave a name to what would soon become a revolution: the Euromaidan. Police and regime goons attacked demonstrators on November 30. Within a week, more than eight hundred thousand people occupied the square and swore they wouldn't leave until Yanukovych resigned and Ukraine signed the EU association agreement. On December 11, Yanukovych again ordered his security forces to clear the Maidan, precipitating an eight-hour battle during which veterans of the Soviet war in Afghanistan formed a militia to fight off the attackers. McCain was desperate to get involved. The administration finally relented, and he and Democratic senator Chris Murphy of Connecticut arrived in Kiev three days later. Nothing he had experienced in all his years of travel, McCain told me, had ever moved him as much as the Maidan protests. Years before, he had been captivated by a press account of a demonstration in Prague's Wenceslas Square as the Soviet empire was coming apart. A million Czechs had listened as a young man had taken the mike and proclaimed their independence in borrowed words: "We hold these truths to be self-evident, that all men are created equal, that they are endowed by their Creator with certain unalienable rights, that among these are life, liberty and the pursuit of happiness."

McCain had referred to that inspirational moment in dozens of speeches in the 1990s. Now, he said, he got to witness a similar moment himself.

Their first meeting, after a briefing by embassy staff, was with the patriarchs of the Ukraine and Russian Orthodox Churches. McCain and Murphy had put in a request to see Yanukovych but hadn't received a response yet. They met with oligarchs who hadn't decided whether to back the regime or break with it, and with the Klitschko brothers, the famous boxers, heavyweight title holders, and prominent opponents of the regime. McCain, the fight fan, had gotten to know the older brother, Vitali, years before, during one of his efforts to clean up the sport, and greeted him like a long-lost friend. McCain and Murphy went to the Maidan for the first time that night. He said an estimated half million people were occupying it on a bitterly cold and snowy night as he looked down from the balcony of a building next to the square: "Men, women, and children, young and old, from all parts of the country." It was a joyous celebration, he said, as the crowd cheered the various speakers and waved their mobile phones in the air, "LED lights glowing in the swirling snow."

McCain filmed a short video of the demonstration that night on his iPhone. For weeks afterward, he showed it to everyone he encountered. He must have shown it to me half a dozen times. I think he played it for people so often because he never tired of watching it himself. There was his cause, he said, the one he had described for so many years as greater than self-interest, the cause that gave him the sense he was "a small part of something larger than myself." His various campaigns for the rights of people to live with dignity in freedom and justice—in Burma and the Balkans, in the former republics of the Soviet Union, in Russia itself and China, during the Arab Spring, in the country that had imprisoned him and the country that had sent him there—all crystalized into one. He told me that everything those causes meant to him was brought home to him in the Maidan. "I tell you, I've never been so damned inspired in my life," he said to me after he returned from the trip. Four years later, we were discussing his visit to the Maidan for a chapter in our last collaboration, *The Restless Wave*. He said he wanted his account of the experience to be as special to the reader as the experience had been to him. He had been diagnosed with cancer, and he knew his time was short. He told me exactly the sentiments he wanted to express. I suggested a phrase that President Obama often quoted, and he said, "Start with that."

Martin Luther King, Jr., had called it the "fierce urgency of now," the transformational moment when aspirations for freedom must be realized, when the voice of a movement can't be stilled,

when the heart's demands will not stand further delay. I saw it
that night. I felt it. It was thrilling and affirming. If you told me
I would choose to retain only a handful of memories from my
long life, that night at the Maidan would be one of them. . . .
The fervent political movements of our age seem so often to
be the workings of religious fanaticism or injured ethnic pride
or dehumanizing ideologies of one kind or another, and the
power seekers who profit from them. That night I witnessed a
fervent mass movement for the universal ideas of freedom and
justice. That's what a European identity meant to those people.
It was humankind I saw in that square, in all its impossibly resilient dignity, known to God, and striving to be recognized
and answered to by the powerful forces who had set themselves
above them. Those ideals were my cause, the cause that gave
meaning to my eventful life, a life that might otherwise have
been squandered.[52]

McCain went back to the Maidan the next day to address the demonstrators. He stood on the stage with Senator Murphy, Vitali Klitschko, and a group of demonstration leaders. He made a brief speech
consisting mostly of one-line exhortations that were translated into
Ukrainian. He said he couldn't remember the last time he had gotten
as big a response for a speech in the U.S. When he declared, "America
is with you," the crowd roared, "Thank you. Thank you." He had asked
his aide Chris Brose, who had traveled with him to Ukraine, to find
some appropriate lines of Ukrainian poetry he could use. Brose found
a verse by the Ukrainian poet Taras Shevchenko: "Love your Ukraine,
love her in cruel times, love her in cruel moments, pray to God for
her." McCain said that the crowd's reaction had exceeded his expectations but allowed that it was "for the message, not the man." After he
finished, he walked around the square, offering praise and encouragement, joking around, and posing for pictures with the demonstrators.

That night, the senators received word that Yanukovych would
see them at the presidential palace. It had been a long day and they
were tired, he said, by the time the meeting convened around eight

o'clock. The room was overheated, and after introductions were made, Yanukovych spoke without pause for an hour. "I couldn't keep my eyes open," McCain recalled. "Chris, thank God, finally interrupted him and said we had some things to say, too." Their host detailed the many ways in which he believed he had been unfairly treated by the West and by the demonstrators. He told his American guests that he had offered to resume negotiations with Europe, but the EU had rejected the offer. "It was obvious he was trying to stall for time," McCain said, "hoping the protests would peter out." They went back and forth for another hour, until "we told him for the fifth or sixth time, the independence movement couldn't be stopped. If he tried to stop it with more violence, he'd be swept out of power," and the meeting adjourned.

Yanukovych didn't heed their advice. His attempts to suppress the demonstrations with force incited riots, and regime thugs responded by killing some of the demonstrators. Putin threatened to intervene, and someone planted a bomb in the building where McCain had watched the protests on the first night of his visit. A massive crowd marched on parliament on February 18. Security forces and armed irregulars fired on them. The marchers fired back, and dozens on both sides were slain. Yanukovych fled to Russia a few days later. A week later, Putin's soldiers, disguised as Ukrainian civilians, seized Crimea's legislature. Putin's "little green men" soon controlled the entire peninsula, which Russia annexed after orchestrating a phony referendum.

To McCain, Putin was a villain representing all the lying, murdering tyrants in the world who, for the sake of their own enrichment and glorification, crushed human aspirations for self-determination. He was every big guy who preyed on little guys because he cared for no one but himself. Putin deliberately bombed hospitals in Syria, McCain believed, because crimes against humanity are effective deterrents in war. McCain despised him. He had gotten under Putin's skin at the Munich Security Conference in 2007, and it had delighted him. Every now and again, Putin would insult McCain by name, thereby reassuring him that he had Putin's attention. He mocked Putin's pretenses to be a great power. Russia, under Putin, was "a gas station masquerading as a country." Putin is "the head of a mafia family, not a great power."

While anti-Putin demonstrations were under way following the autocrat's return to the Russian presidency in 2012, McCain tweeted, "Dear Vlad, the #Arab Spring is coming to a neighborhood near you." He argued that Russia was overextended and Putin was acutely vulnerable thanks to his adventurism in the Middle East and Ukraine. "China," he argued, "is the big challenge, the challenge of the century. But Putin is the immediate threat." He responded to Putin's propaganda that he hated Russians by insisting, "I'm more pro-Russian than the regime that misrules you today."

With Ben Cardin of Maryland, McCain sponsored the Magnitsky Act, named for Sergei Magnitsky, the Russian lawyer who worked for Bill Browder's hedge fund in Russia and uncovered widespread government corruption, for which he was murdered. The legislation that bore his name denied U.S. visas and access to American banks to Russians implicated in his arrest and murder. It infuriated Putin, who raised it constantly in communications with the Obama administration. The administration initially resisted the legislation, but after a two-year campaign, it was passed and enacted into law. Putin's response was to ban American adoptions of Russian orphans, typical of his indifference to the suffering of others. He imposed equivalent sanctions on a list of Americans, with McCain's name prominently among them. McCain and Cardin joined forces again to pass the Global Magnitsky Act, enacted in 2016. It imposed similar sanctions on human rights abusers in other countries. The two laws were arguably the most important human rights legislation passed by Congress in two decades.

In 2011, McCain had begun a warm friendship with former Russian elected official and leading Putin opponent Boris Nemtsov and his associate Vladimir Kara-Murza. McCain and Joe Lieberman had issued a statement condemning Nemtsov's arrest during a New Year's Eve protest, and Nemtsov asked to meet McCain when he traveled to Washington after his release from jail. They had hit it off instantly. Nemtsov and Kara-Murza were courageous defenders of the dream of a democratic Russia. The former had been one of the leaders of some of the biggest demonstrations against Putin's autocracy, and had gone to Ukraine to protest Putin's invasion. He specialized in getting under Putin's skin, documenting the Kremlin boss's personal corruption. McCain loved him but worried that he was too reckless and urged him to be more cautious. Putin had proved time and again his homicidal tendencies. Boris "was funny, irreverent, and full of himself, a big man with a big personality," McCain wrote admiringly, and he told me, "He's making himself a big target." Boris "rationalized he wouldn't be murdered because it would set a bad precedent" to murder a former elected official. When McCain told him he was concerned anyway, the Russian responded by saying, "My mother is worried, but I'm not worried."

They met for the last time in McCain's office in January 2015. McCain had heard reports that threats against Nemtsov's life had proliferated in recent months. He pleaded with his friend, who was planning another large demonstration against Putinism, not to return to Russia. "That's exactly how I said it," McCain told me sometime after their last meeting. "He was sitting in the same chair you are. I said, 'Boris, I'm begging you, please don't go home. Not now. Please.'" He said Nemtsov hadn't reacted with his usual bravado but with a note of resignation. "What can I do?" he had asked rhetorically. "It's my country." The following month, a gunman shot Boris Nemtsov four times in the back as he walked with his girlfriend across a bridge near Red Square on an unusually warm February night.

Eulogizing his friend a few months later, McCain described Nemtsov as unafraid. "He knew his enemies," he continued. "He knew what they were capable of, but he would not be oppressed . . . by unjust laws or by violence and fear. . . . [H]e lived for love of justice and truth. He had been threatened repeatedly and demonized. . . . Yet when his enemies took his life in the shadow of the Kremlin, they found him walking in the open air, enjoying the evening, unafraid."

Two years later, Vladimir Kara-Murza was poisoned and near death, surely by order of Vladimir Putin. He survived, and McCain saw him many more times, and begged him to be more careful, too. As a final gesture of solidarity, when his own life was nearing its end, McCain asked Kara-Murza to be a pallbearer at his funeral.

McCain rushed back to Ukraine with a delegation of eight senators in March "in a show of bipartisan solidarity" as Ukraine sought Western help in repelling the Russian invaders. Putin's "little green men" had turned their attention to the Donbass in eastern Ukraine, where the country's largest ethnic Russian population resided. McCain argued strenuously for the U.S. and NATO to provide weapons to Ukraine, but the Obama administration, influenced heavily by German chancellor Angela Merkel, declined to provide lethal defense assistance for fear of igniting a wider war. The U.S. and Europe imposed more sanctions on Russia, targeting some of Putin's closest confederates. They kicked Russia out of the G8, which McCain had advocated since the early 2000s. While McCain supported the policies, he knew their impact wouldn't change Putin's behavior, not in the near term, anyway. Only defense assistance, he constantly argued, could deter Putin from further aggression, and not providing assistance would encourage him to escalate. "Weakness is provocative" to Putin, McCain wrote in the *New York Times* following the Russians' invasion of the Donbass a few weeks after the Senate delegation's visit.

McCain went back to Kiev in June for the inauguration of Ukraine's new president, Petro Poroshenko, and he returned to Ukraine several more times after that. He was the beleaguered country's most outspoken advocate in the U.S. and in various international security conferences in the West. He pushed relentlessly in legislation and in rhetoric to get weapons to Ukraine's defenders, although he never convinced the Obama administration. He made his last trip to Ukraine in late December 2016, after the election of Donald Trump to the presidency. Legislation passed in the incoming Congress would succeed in getting the new administration to announce in December 2017 that it would provide arms to Ukraine. McCain praised the move. Ukraine has used them to fight Russians to a near stalemate, exacting casualties on Russia that Putin goes to great lengths to hide from the Russian people.

McCain returned from his last visit to Ukraine deeply affected by two events. In my recollection, his description was the last time he effused to me about a conviction that he had been a witness to some of history's most poignant moments. He had attended with President

Poroshenko a meeting with families of fallen Ukrainian soldiers where the president pinned a medal for valor on a soldier's mother. "She was very stoic," McCain described, "very quiet, and trying to stand still, although she was trembling a little. She wasn't that old, but the effort seemed to take all her strength." She said nothing in reply when Poroshenko said something to her in Ukrainian as he pinned the medal on her. "But tears were streaming down her face." As usual, the memory prompted McCain's own emotions, and he slowly shook his head to punctuate his story of a woman's dignified grief and the solemn privilege it had been to observe it.

He spent New Year's Eve with Ukrainian marines on the front lines in eastern Ukraine. He was accompanied by Lindsey Graham, Amy Klobuchar, and Masha Yovanovitch, the U.S. ambassador to Ukraine, whom he regarded highly. He showed me a photograph of the four of them, surrounded by marines in what looked like some kind of bunker, laughing and appearing to have a good time. He said he had made a few off-the-cuff remarks to the marines praising their courage and patriotism. They in turn gave him a captured AK-47 with a full magazine and a round in the chamber that was discovered by an aide only after they had boarded the air force transport plane for home.

McCain was a longtime advocate of NATO expansion, and outspoken in support of the accession of the last country to enter the alliance, Montenegro. Putin, unfatigued by his aggression in Syria and Ukraine, was determined to stop the small country on the Adriatic from joining NATO. Montenegro's beaches were a favorite destination for rich Russians who owned nearly 40 percent of the country's real estate. Putin himself was believed to have investments there. Of greater concern to the Russian autocrat was the worry that Montenegro's accession might encourage other western Balkan nations to align with the West. At the same time he was meddling in our elections, Putin was plotting to subvert Montenegro's democracy. McCain had heard reports as early as February that Russia was interfering with Montenegro's parliamentary elections, scheduled for October, and the vote on NATO accession that would follow. McCain sent committee staff to Montenegro to investigate. They returned with reports that Putin could be up to something more alarming than election tampering. There was real concern in Montenegro that he might orchestrate the government's overthrow in advance of the elections.

On the morning of the election, Montenegrin police arrested twenty Serb nationals in the country and charged them with plotting a coup. Their plan, which a defector had tipped to the authorities, involved staging a phony protest demonstration in front of the parliament, while fifty Serbs dressed as policemen entered the building and killed the actual security guards there. The fake protestors would respond by storming the parliament and proclaiming a new government. They would probably have killed the incumbent pro-NATO prime minister. Two Russian military intelligence operatives in Belgrade had organized the coup and hired an assassin. They absconded to Moscow when the coup was uncovered. A month passed before *The New York Times* reported the details of the failed plot and Montenegrin officials conceded Russia's role in it. They had been reluctant to publicize it lest Putin retaliate by trying again.

McCain believed the best way to forestall another coup was to accelerate Montenegro's accession into NATO. The Montenegrin parliament, post-coup, voted to join the alliance. Now the legislatures of current NATO members had to ratify the accession treaty. McCain pushed the Senate to do so quickly, but Rand Paul, supported by fellow libertarian Mike Lee, objected to bringing the treaty to a vote. McCain lost his temper with Paul and accused him in a floor speech of "working for Vladimir Putin." When I talked to McCain that week, he knew it had been an intemperate thing to say, but "it's true," he maintained. "That fool doesn't know who he's hurting and who he's helping. And the worst thing is, he doesn't even want to try to find out. He doesn't give a shit."

With Mitch McConnell's help, Paul and Lee's hold was cleared, and the Senate voted 97 to 2 to ratify Montenegro's accession. McCain flew to Montenegro a few days later and received a copy of the indictment issued by the government for those responsible for the coup attempt, which included the names of the Russian intelligence agents. McCain had the U.S. embassy translate the entire 135-page document, and brought it back to Washington, where he disseminated it to colleagues and reporters. Montenegro joined NATO on June 5. McCain held a hearing the next month to publicize the coup attempt. He warned Americans and our allies that Putin would continue to attack all our democracies, and it was past time we joined together to fight his aggression. "We must take our own side in this fight," he pleaded.

For the book, I asked how he wanted to respond to questions that his exertions in so many of these cases hadn't persuaded Putin to stand down or the U.S. government to stand up. McCain looked a little wounded by the question and brought up Nadiya Savchenko, a Ukrainian army pilot who had been captured in the Donbass and handed over to the Russians. They accused her in a rigged trial of murdering two Russian journalists and sentenced her to twenty-two years in prison. When the judge pronounced the verdict, she stood up defiantly and sang a patriotic Ukrainian hymn. The Obama administration protested her conviction, as did the EU and the Red Cross, and John McCain. He made two statements calling for her release and urged Secretary of State Kerry to bring up her case on his visit to Moscow. She would be released in a prisoner swap between Ukraine and Russia two years later, after which she traveled to Washington and asked to see McCain. She thanked him profusely, "more than I deserved," McCain said. "I hardly did anything for her." He told her he admired her courage, and when he offered, "I do know a little of what you went through," she started to cry. "What has any of it meant," we wrote in the book.

> All these trips, all these speeches, op-eds, press statements, interviews, professing support for Ukrainians and Georgians and Estonians and Montenegrins, condemning Putin, criticizing my own government? Did it change anything, improve anything? I hope so. But I know for certain it meant something to the people I meant to help because they've told me it has. It meant that Americans were on their side, that we hear them, we acknowledge the justice of their cause, they aren't forgotten.[53]

It had mattered to Nadiya Savchenko. When John McCain died, the *Kiev Post* published an editorial describing him as beloved in Ukraine:

"When Ukraine faced some of its darkest and most dangerous times, it was often not the voice of a Ukrainian politician who lifted the spirits of the nation. It was the voice of U.S. Sen. John McCain."[54]

Given McCain's ardent support for Ukraine's independence, I imagine the question occurs to readers, as it does to the author: What would the senator have said about the controversy involving defense assistance to Ukraine that resulted in President Trump's impeachment? I'm going to resist speaking for the senator in absentia; it wouldn't be fair to him or the reader for me to do otherwise. On Trump the man and his various controversies, I can only describe the views John McCain publicly or privately expressed when he was alive, as well as observe pertinent facts that would have influenced his views. I will leave readers to draw their own conclusions.

I can offer these relevant observations about President Trump withholding military assistance to Ukraine in order to pressure the Ukrainian government to investigate his prospective opponent in the 2020 election, former vice president Joe Biden. McCain was Congress's most outspoken advocate for that assistance, which was lawfully appropriated by Congress and signed into law by the president. McCain believed that without the assistance, Russia would eventually annex eastern Ukraine as it did Crimea, and the rest of Ukraine would submit to Putin's dictates. McCain was very protective of Congress's role in shaping national security policy. He had immense respect for the judgment and professionalism of Ambassador Maria Yovanovitch, who was disgracefully mistreated by Rudy Giuliani and his client. He had a forty-year friendship with Joe Biden, whom he knew to be an honest and honorable man. Finally, he repeatedly expressed in the strongest terms his concern with President Trump's affinity for autocrats generally and Vladimir Putin specifically.

McCain did not hide his disdain for Donald Trump; he made it clear in press interviews and public statements and privately. "The appearance of toughness or a reality show facsimile of toughness," we wrote in *The Restless Wave*, "seems to matter to him more than any of our values. Flattery secures his friendship, criticism his enmity."[55] He usually dismissed Trump's boorishness, especially when he was the object of it, trusting the voters to punish it. When Trump dismissed his heroism as a POW with the infamous "He's not a war hero . . . I like people who weren't captured" insult, McCain's family and friends were incensed. I called him and cussed prolifically as I condemned Trump's character, intelligence, and appearance. McCain advised me to take it easy. "All he did was get people to talk about what a hero I am all weekend. That's not my problem, it's his." McCain did, though, take issue with Trump's stated views on issues that most mattered to the senator, such as the treatment of captured enemies, relations with Putin and other autocrats, America's advocacy of human rights, refugee assistance, respect for immigrants, our alliances, and global leadership. His criticism was often derisive.

His encounters with Trump prior to his election to the presidency were so few that I can't remember hearing him express views one way or another. He treated Trump's candidacy as a novelty, as most people did in the beginning. He had endorsed his friend Lindsey Graham's underdog bid for the nomination, but there were several Republican candidates he liked and respected. When it became clear that Trump could actually win the nomination, and when he became the prohibitive favorite, McCain was in the middle of another contested Republican primary for his Senate seat, and the Trump effect in Arizona was proving to be a challenge.

In April 2015, to the surprise of almost no one, John McCain announced he would run for a sixth term in the U.S. Senate. Polls, including one conducted by his own longtime pollster Bill McInturff, showed he would again start a campaign with 25 to 30 percent of Arizona Republicans firmly opposed to him. His decades-long estrangement from far-right Arizona voters hadn't improved when he sponsored another immigration bill in 2013. We initially worried that one of the more conservative members in Arizona's congressional delegation would challenge him, possibly David Schweikert of the 6th congressional district or, of greater concern, Matt Salmon from the 5th. Neither chose to do so. McCain faced former state senator and Trump supporter Kelli Ward, who waged a spirited campaign but one that was handicapped by her inexperience and some goofy views she espoused. Nevertheless, given his vulnerability with the base, and the political environment in that election cycle, McCain could not take the race for granted. Neither was he assured of an easy race in the general election. A Democratic member of congress from Arizona's 1st district, Ann Kirkpatrick, announced she would challenge him. He had to run for the nomination mindful not to hurt his prospects in the general election. Trump complicated things.

McCain being McCain, he wasn't reticent about discussing his political challenges in the media. He gave an interview to *The New Yorker's* Ryan Lizza in July 2015, a few days after Trump—who was leading all national polls then—held a campaign rally in Phoenix. McCain complained to Lizza that Trump "fired up the crazies." He mentioned how the Arizona GOP had censured him in 2014 and how, after considerable effort, "we did to some degree regain control of the party" from those he described as a "very extreme element within our Republican Party."[56] Now Trump had "galvanized them. He's got them really activated." Trump had been responding to those comments when he made the "He's not a war hero" crack.

Henceforth, McCain's campaign advisors would prevail on him to show more discretion about the Republican front-runner. He was squeezed between the competing demands of his primary and general election challenges. By ignoring Trump's crude attacks on various American constituencies, he risked, among other things, alienating Latino voters in November. In May 2016, he told a group of supporters, "If Donald Trump is at the top of the ticket, here in Arizona, with over thirty percent of the vote being the Hispanic vote, no doubt this may be the race of my life." But criticizing every outrageous Trump statement and position risked driving up the turnout of hard-right Trump fanatics. When it was clear Trump would be the nominee, McCain was pressed repeatedly on whether he would support him, and repeatedly, he responded that he would support the nominee of the party. He also made clear that he would be skipping the Republican National Convention, and that supporting the nominee didn't mean campaigning with him, as he steered clear of every Trump appearance in the state. McCain spouted off every now and again about something Trump said that contradicted his position on an issue—the use of torture, crude depictions of immigrants, and the virtues of Vladimir Putin, for example. In March, McCain endorsed Mitt Romney's forceful criticism of Trump and added that he had grave concerns about "Trump's uninformed and indeed dangerous statements on national security." But he labored with unusual discipline to keep his balance, and his campaign was the most buttoned-down and disciplined he had ever run.

Jim Newell wrote a perceptive analysis in *Slate* of McCain's situation less than two months before the late-August primary:

> Neither of these threats is catching McCain by surprise, and both the campaign he's assembled and the candidate it's tasked with re-electing are skilled operators. He is running a tight, merciless campaign, one at odds with the caricature of McCain as a hopeless old fud and with the spontaneity of his campaigns of yore. This is John McCain, in a bind of his own devising, doing what he needs to do to squeeze another six years out of history.[57]

I spent the summer of 2016 in Maine, watching with dread as Trump won my party's nomination for president, and played only a small role in the campaign. I helped a little with communications and occasionally piped in my two cents of advice to the campaign manager, Ryan O'Daniel, or to Rick Davis, who chaired the effort, or to the candidate himself. Typically, my interventions weren't the product of rigorous analysis or self-discipline, and they weren't always helpful. I despise Trump, and my reactions to him were often impulsive and emotional. In May, as Trump was wrapping up the nomination, I tweeted that I would support Hillary Clinton. It got a fair amount of attention in the press and gave Kelli Ward another talking point to use in her attacks against McCain. It could have been used by the Kirkpatrick campaign as well. I got some grief, appropriately, from a close friend working on the campaign who observed that I had made myself feel better at John's expense. The candidate, graciously, never said anything to me about it.

I worried that McCain's endorsement of Trump, half-hearted though it was (I don't think he actually ever strung together the words "I support Donald Trump"), was injuring his reputation for candor. I also thought he was making himself miserable. He was frequently terse and irritable when we spoke. He was testy with reporters when they barraged him with questions about Trump. He was clearly frustrated, and I suspected his conscience was pestering him. I told him in one conversation that I thought some of the things he was saying and doing were "good for the candidate but not so good for the man." He responded that, as a previous Republican presidential nominee, "I have to respect the process," which I think he genuinely believed. "I'll criticize him when I disagree with something he says, but I can't refuse to accept him as the nominee, and I can't spend every day reacting to him."

My wife and I were driving back from a visit with friends in New Hampshire on Sunday, July 31, when McCain called my cell phone. "Did you see him?" he asked.

"Who?"

"Trump. What he said about the Khans."

The previous Thursday, Khizr Khan had spoken at the Democratic National Convention with his wife, Ghazala, by his side. Born in Pakistan, the Khans had emigrated to the U.S. almost four decades earlier. Their son, Captain Humayun Khan, a decorated officer in the U.S. Army, had died bravely in Iraq in 2004. Khan's remarks, in which he excoriated Trump for, among other things, proposing an unconstitutional ban on Muslims immigrating to the U.S., received an enthusiastic reception but not from Donald Trump. In an interview with ABC News's George Stephanopoulos on Saturday, Trump had complained about the criticism, claiming he had been "viciously attacked," raised questions about why Ghazala Khan had remained silent at the podium, and whined about the sacrifices he had made as he "created thousands and thousands of jobs" and "built great structures." The interview aired Sunday morning. McCain watched it and was revolted, which was what had prompted his call to me.

McCain wanted me to write a statement for him that denounced

Trump, and he began describing the points he wanted to make and some of the language he wanted to use. I told him I was on the road and wouldn't be home for three hours, but I would write something as soon as I arrived. "At the end, I want you to write that I'm withdrawing my support," he instructed. "Yes, sir," I replied. As promised, as soon as we reached home, I dashed off a statement for him in under a half hour. I emailed it to Cindy, who printed it out for him. He called to let me know that he was still going to release a strong statement criticizing Trump. But "I'm not going to withdraw my support at this time," he explained, emphasizing the last three words. "Everybody here thinks that would be a bad idea." I was disappointed, but I didn't argue. I knew it was a tough call.

I saw the revised statement when it hit the wires Monday morning. It was described in the press as "powerful," "blistering," and "furious," but as he'd warned me, it did not announce he was rescinding his endorsement.

The Republican Party I know and love is the party of Abraham Lincoln, Theodore Roosevelt, Dwight D. Eisenhower, and Ronald Reagan.

I wear a bracelet bearing the name of a fallen hero, Matthew Stanley, which his mother, Lynn, gave me in 2007 at a town hall meeting in Wolfeboro, New Hampshire. His memory and the memory of our great leaders deserve better from me.

In recent days, Donald Trump disparaged a fallen soldier's parents. He has suggested that the likes of their son should not be allowed in the United States—to say nothing of entering its service. I cannot emphasize enough how deeply I disagree with Mr. Trump's statement. I hope Americans understand that the remarks do not represent the views of our Republican Party, its officers, or candidates.

Make no mistake: I do not valorize our military out of some unfamiliar instinct. I grew up in a military family, and have my own record of service, and have stayed closely engaged with our armed forces throughout my public career. In the American system, the military has value only inasmuch as it protects and defends the liberties of the people.

My father was a career naval officer, as was his father. For hundreds of years, every generation of McCains has served the United States in uniform. My sons serve today, and I'm proud of them. My youngest served in the war that claimed Captain Khan's life as well as in Afghanistan. I want them to be proud of me. I want to do the right thing by them and their comrades.

Humayun Khan did exactly that—and he did it for all the right reasons. This accomplished young man was not driven to service as a United States Army officer because he was compelled to by any material need. He was inspired as a young man by his reading of Thomas Jefferson—and he wanted to give back to the country that had taken him and his parents in as immigrants when he was only two years old.

Captain Khan's death in Iraq on June 8, 2004, was a shining example of the valor and bravery inculcated into our military. When a suicide bomber accelerated his vehicle toward a facility with hundreds of American soldiers, Captain Khan ordered his subordinates away from the danger. Then he ran toward it.

The suicide bomber, striking prematurely, claimed the life of Captain Khan—and Captain Khan, through his selfless action and sacrifice, saved the lives of hundreds of his brothers and sisters. Scripture tells us that "Greater love hath no man than this, that a man lay down his life for his friends."

Captain Humayun Khan of the United States Army showed in his final moments that he was filled and motivated by this love. His name will live forever in American memory, as an example of true American greatness.

In the end, I am morally bound to speak only to the things that command my allegiance, and to which I have dedicated my life's work: the Republican Party and, more importantly, the United States of America. I will not refrain from doing my utmost by those lights simply because it may benefit others with whom I disagree.

I claim no moral superiority over Donald Trump. I have a long and well-known public and private record for which I will have to answer at the Final Judgment, and I repose my hope in the promise of mercy and the moderation of old age. I challenge the nominee to set the example for what our country can and should represent.

Arizona is watching. It is time for Donald Trump to set the example for our country and the future of the Republican Party. While our party has bestowed upon him the nomination, it is not accompanied by unfettered license to defame those who are the best among us.

Lastly, I'd like to say to Mr. and Mrs. Khan: Thank you for immigrating to America. We're a better country because of you. And you are certainly right; your son was the best of America, and the memory of his sacrifice will make us a better nation— and he will never be forgotten.

That same day, Donald Trump renewed his criticism of the Gold Star parents of Captain Humayun Khan. McCain would formally withdraw his support for the Republican nominee on October 8, in reaction to Trump's bragging about sexual assault to Billy Bush on *Access Hollywood*. He said he would write in a qualified Republican. He never told me whom, and I never asked him.

McCain won the Republican primary by a wider margin than pundits expected. In November, he defeated Ann Kirkpatrick by an even bigger one. Donald Trump defeated Hillary Clinton in the state by only three points. I had flown to Arizona for the election. For a candidate who had just won a landslide reelection in a race he had expected to be a tough one, McCain was subdued in victory. We all were as we watched the returns from the presidential election, stunned, like everyone else, that Donald Trump had won. I don't remember any of us saying anything memorable. Muttered expressions of disbelief were all any of us seemed capable of articulating. I'm sure McCain said something, but I've lost the memory. No one else in the room that night whose recollections I asked for can remember what he said, either.

He was back in Washington during much of the transition, planning a trip right after Christmas to Montenegro and Ukraine, as well as the Baltic states, all countries that felt threatened by Vladimir Putin. Before that trip, he flew to a security conference in Halifax, Nova Scotia, that he attended every year. I saw him in between trips, and he seemed in a good frame of mind. Trump had announced that he was going to nominate General Jim Mattis to be his secretary of defense and General John Kelly to head Homeland Security. McCain was an admirer of both men, as he was of his Senate colleague Dan Coats, the incoming director of National Intelligence. "They'll keep a lid on things," he assured me as I indulged my habit of fretting about Trump's presidency. "They'll do what's right." He didn't know Rex Tillerson and was skeptical due to the relationship with Putin that Tillerson had formed while Exxon's CEO; and he wasn't impressed by Trump's incoming national security advisor, General Mike Flynn. He was appalled to learn that Flynn had contacted Russia's ambassador to the U.S. to intimate that the incoming administration might lift the sanctions imposed by the Obama administration to punish the Kremlin's interference in our election. McCain was relieved when Lieutenant General H. R. McMaster, whom he also knew and admired, was selected to replace Flynn.

Trump's seeming indifference to Flynn's behavior, as well as to Russia's attack on our democracy, made McCain wonder whether Trump knew which side America was supposed to be on. "Does he know any history all?" he asked rhetorically. Nevertheless, whenever I launched into an anti-Trump diatribe in his presence, he would listen good-naturedly for a few minutes before encouraging me to settle down. As if reassuring a fellow passenger on a turbulent flight that all was well if you could hear the engines, he reminded me again that as long as Mattis, Kelly, McMaster, Coats, and other adults were on the job, we would be fine. "This too shall pass, my old friend," he assured me. "Don't get yourself so worked up about it."

Trump called him not long after the inauguration. As McCain recounted it, the conversation started off rocky. Trump began by saying how hurt he had been when McCain withdrew his endorsement.

McCain told me he didn't respond to the complaint at first, "but he kept repeating it—three, maybe four times, like he wanted me to apologize before we talked about something else. So I told him how offended I'd been when he attacked the Khans."

"No," Trump protested, "you unendorsed me over the *Access Hollywood* thing."

"Well, that's the real reason I unendorsed you," McCain retorted.

He told me that Trump appeared to calm down after that, and they had a short conversation "about nothing important," and at the end of the call, Trump gave McCain his cell phone number.

"Did you write it down?" I asked.

"Yeah," he answered.

"Can I see it?"

"No."

"Why not?"

"I don't know what I did with it."

At some point after that call, McCain and Lindsey were invited to a meeting at the White House to share their priorities with the new administration. McCain had started to say the Armed Services Committee would be proposing major acquisition reforms on which he hoped to work with the administration, when the president's son-in-law, Jared Kushner, cut him off and informed him, "Senator, we're going to change everything about how the government does business." McCain said he responded, "Well, good luck with that," and didn't say another word. He enjoyed impersonating Kushner's supercilious response to friends. I saw the performance multiple times.

I was in McCain's office frequently in those weeks, and not just to seek reassurances that the Trump presidency wasn't the start of the end-times. We were beginning our last book, and I came to see him regularly to discuss the subjects he wanted to cover. Invariably, though, the conversation would turn to something Trump or someone had said or done that had bothered one or both of us. At no time did he tell me about or even vaguely allude to an encounter he'd had at the Halifax conference. A British diplomat, Sir Andrew Wood, had asked to meet with him to discuss a confidential matter, and McCain had agreed.

McCain aide Chris Brose and David Kramer, a former assistant secretary of defense who was working for the McCain Institute, joined the meeting as well. After a brief discussion of Russian interference in the U.S. election, Wood informed McCain that he knew a former MI6 officer, Christopher Steele, who had been commissioned to look into the Trump campaign's connections with Russian agents as well as compromising information that Moscow was rumored to possess about the new president. Wood had seen the report Steele compiled and had found it alarming. While much of it was raw and unverified intelligence, both Wood and Steele were convinced it warranted further investigation and were worried that it would be dropped after Trump took office. Wood asked McCain if he wanted to see a copy of the report, and if he saw fit, perhaps there was something he could do to make sure the proper authorities were looking into it.

McCain asked David Kramer to go to London and meet with Steele and, if he found him credible, to bring back a copy of what would soon be referred to as the "Steele dossier." Several days later, Kramer returned with the dossier and handed it over to McCain, who read it and then locked it in his office safe. The next day, he called the FBI and asked for a meeting with Director Comey. He told Comey how the dossier had come into his possession and mentioned that its contents were disturbing, but he had no way of ascertaining whether all or any of them were true. He might have known in advance that the FBI already possessed the dossier, but he thought a member of Congress bringing his copy to Comey's attention would ensure that it was investigated.

I got a call the second week of January from Jake Tapper at CNN, asking me if I knew anything about McCain possessing a so-called dossier that asserted unsavory connections between Trump and the Kremlin. I said I didn't, and he told me CNN was about to report that McCain had a copy. I hung up and called McCain. "Did someone give you some intelligence report or something about Trump and Russia?" I asked him.

He paused before answering, "Yes." I started to ask him another question, and he cut me off. "I've already said too much on the phone. Come to the office and I'll tell you about it."

So I did, and so he did. "Do you think any of it's true?" I asked him. BuzzFeed had published the entire dossier, including its most salacious content. "How the hell would I know," he answered. "I certainly think it ought to be checked out." What impressed me most about McCain's conduct was how untypically discreet he had been. Clearly, it was a serious matter, and he had treated it as such. When Trump sycophants criticized his role in the controversy, he was defiant. "What would people say if I had just ignored the whole thing? Who the hell do they think I am?"

He genuinely didn't have a sense of whether the dossier's contents were true, but they worried him. And despite his frequent assurances to me that we were in capable hands with Mattis et al., he was also clearly concerned that Trump, with his ignorance about world events and indifference to Western values, was going to damage our alliances and the international order built by the United States and its allies. It was the great historic enterprise of McCain's lifetime, and he felt a personal responsibility to defend it. Over the next half year, he would fly around the world, literally, to reassure America's allies, as he had reassured me, that we would weather the storm, that our relations were built on firm ground. He began his mission at the Munich Security Conference, which he had faithfully attended for forty years. It would be his last time there, and his speech renounced the nativism and moral indifference inherent in Trump's worldview, and gave a resounding defense of liberal values. It would be remembered as the finest the attendees had ever heard him deliver. They gave him a huge ovation at the end, and some who cheered him had tears in their eyes. "These are dangerous times," he began,

but you should not count America out, and we should not count each other out. We must be prudent, but we cannot wring our hands and wallow in self-doubt. We must appreciate the limits of our power, but we cannot allow ourselves to question the rightness and goodness of the West. We must understand and learn from our mistakes, but we cannot be paralyzed by fear. We cannot give up on ourselves and on each other. That is the definition of decadence. And that is how world orders really do decline and fall.

That is exactly what our adversaries want. This is their goal. They do not have meaningful allies, so they seek to sow dissent among us and divide us from each other. They know that their power and influence are inferior to ours, so they seek to subvert us, and erode our resolve to resist, and terrorize into passivity. They know they have little to offer the world beyond selfishness and fear, so they seek to undermine our confidence in ourselves and our belief in our own values.

We must take our own side in this fight. We must be vigilant. We must persevere. And through it all, we must never, never cease to believe in the moral superiority of our own values—that we stand for truth against falsehood, freedom against tyranny, right against injustice, hope against despair . . . that even though we will inevitably take losses and suffer setbacks, through it all, as long as people of goodwill and courage refuse to lose faith in the West, it will endure.

That is why we come to Munich, year in and year out—to revitalize our common moral purpose, our belief that our values are worth the fighting for. Because in the final analysis, the survival of the West is not just a material struggle; it is now, and has always been, a moral struggle. Now, more than ever, we must not forget this. . . .

Even now, when the temptation to despair is greatest, I refuse to accept the end of the West. I refuse to accept the demise of our world order. I refuse to accept that our greatest triumphs cannot once again spring from our moments of greatest peril, as they have so many times before. I refuse to accept that our values are morally equivalent to those of our adversaries. I am a proud, unapologetic believer in the West, and I believe we must always, always stand up for it—for if we do not, who will?

I had no hand in that speech. I wish I had.

THE LUCKIEST MAN

Afriend texted to ask if I had seen it and if there was something wrong. I had not seen it; I hadn't watched the live broadcast of FBI Director Comey's testimony before the Senate Intelligence Committee. As ex officio member of the committee, John McCain had been the last senator to ask questions. His confused and confusing interrogation of Comey had Washington buzzing. I watched a recording of the exchange and called the Senate office. "What was he trying to get at?" I asked.

What had happened was that Lindsey Graham had texted a McCain aide a line of questioning he wanted John to pursue with Comey. The aide had passed his phone with Lindsey's text to John. The purpose of the question was to contrast the director's handling of the Clinton email controversy with the FBI's investigation of Russian connections to the Trump campaign. Months later, McCain explained to a reporter that the text had faded from the screen before he fully understood the question. I know he didn't believe the FBI had taken it easy on Secretary Clinton or that it was unfairly pursuing the Trump campaign. Whatever he thought he was asking Comey, it came out a mangled mess of fractured syntax and a disjointed predicate, and he had mixed up the witness's name with Trump's. I suggested to the McCain press office that they make light of the incident, joking that he had stayed up late watching the Diamondbacks game, which he probably had.

I stopped in the office to see him later that week. I was dropping in frequently that spring. I'd been having a hard time getting him to focus on the book we were writing. He kept promising he would turn his attention to it, but he hadn't really done much more than agree on an outline. I had already interviewed aides and colleagues for information he hadn't gotten around to providing me, and I was regularly pestering him now. I didn't bring up the Comey hearing. He did. He was angry about it. Angry with the staff member who had relayed Lindsey's question to him. Angry with Lindsey. Angry with himself. He was embarrassed and believed he had looked like a confused old man. I tried reassuring him that it would be forgotten by the next week. "You're probably right," he said, trying to convince himself to believe me. But he wasn't buying it.

I don't remember being terribly concerned about his state of mind. I thought he was probably tired and cranky. He had complained about feeling fatigued, blaming it on an exhausting trip the previous month to Australia and Southeast Asia. "I can't shake it," he said, as if it were a virus. It wasn't like him to complain of feeling worn down for weeks. I had never heard him say more than "I'm a little tired. I stayed up too late." But it wasn't until I got a call from his legislative director, long-time aide and friend Joe Donoghue, a week later that I began to worry something else might be wrong.

Joe had become alarmed by John's recent inability to get over what in the past would have been minor irritations. He described incidents of irrational anger, trivial things that became major obsessions. "I don't know why he can't let anything go," Joe worried. That was enough to concern me. And when Joe added that John had also been showing up late for work, sometimes arriving in the office later than ten o'clock in the morning, I was stunned. He had always been the first to arrive for work, usually around seven o'clock. He liked to get an early start, reading his newspapers and drinking his cappuccino, before things got busy. The idea of him sleeping until midmorning was inconceivable.

Not long after my conversation with Joe, I called Rick Davis to see if he had heard similar concerns. He had, and he had already discussed them with Cindy. John was scheduled for his semi-annual physical at the Mayo Clinic in Phoenix during the August recess. Cindy was going to have them add a CT scan to the examination. Rick, Carla, and I had subsequent discussions with members of the staff. John's new chief of staff, Truman Anderson, wasn't scheduled to start the job until the last week of June, but he had picked up on the concerns. Everyone was worried enough that Cindy had the physical moved up to a weekend in July. On June 26, John was scheduled to fly with Lindsey and Senators Sheldon Whitehouse, Sonny Perdue, and Elizabeth Warren to Dubai, Pakistan, and Afghanistan, where he kept his annual commitment to spend the Fourth of July holiday with the troops. It would be his last visit there.

I went to see him again shortly before he left. He didn't reiterate his complaints from our last meeting, and I didn't detect any signs that there was something seriously off. I would describe our concerns to have been more in the nature of perplexity about his odd behavior rather than fear that he might be gravely ill. If it had been the latter, we might have made a run at persuading him against undertaking more foreign travel (though he wouldn't have paid us any mind).

We talked a little about the book, and more about the subject that was never far from mind, Donald Trump's presidency. "We'll get past it," McCain promised, the same message he was traveling great distances to convey to allies. Before I left, he mentioned that he wanted to get involved in the health care debate. He was upset that Republican leaders in both houses were going to impose a solution that would be strictly partisan, instead of letting committees of jurisdiction develop something that might attract bipartisan support, to which all senators would have a chance to contribute. "We need to get back to doing things by regular order," he snapped. He said he wanted to give a speech on the subject when he got back, and told me to start thinking about how to frame it. I didn't talk to him again until after a surgical team at the Mayo Clinic in Phoenix had removed a mass from his frontal lobe.

McCain had finished his physical, including a CT scan of his brain. He had mentioned to his doctor his persistent fatigue and something he hadn't raised with any of us, that he had recently experienced episodes of double vision. He was driving alone on I-70 on his way to their cabin for the weekend. Cindy was in San Diego. She had participated in a McCain Institute event in Los Angeles that morning and was going to spend the night at their place in Coronado. John was about an hour into the drive north when he received a call from his doctor at Mayo, telling him to return to the clinic immediately. "Can't it wait until Monday?" he asked. "No, the CT scan showed something. We need to do an MRI to get a better look, and then we'll probably have to operate." Unbeknownst to John, the neurosurgeon who would perform the operation had been about to leave on vacation. Mayo located him at Sky Harbor Airport as he was about to board his flight.

McCain turned around and called his top aide in Arizona, Michelle Shipley, at his Phoenix office to let her know what was happening. He wasn't very specific, just said that Mayo wanted him to come back so they could check something. He instructed her not to say anything to Cindy yet. There was nothing to worry about. Michelle called Rick Davis, who was also in L.A. for the McCain Institute event, to let him know John had finished his physical and had been on his way to the cabin when Mayo told him to come back; she couldn't say more. Minutes later, John called Rick and gave him an idea of the situation—"They think they found something. They don't know what it is. Might need an operation"—and he instructed Rick, too, not to call Cindy. "It's probably nothing." Rick hung up and called a public affairs official at Mayo who acted as a liaison to the McCains and helped ensure that the family's wishes for discretion were respected by hospital staff. She told him that John would be operated on that night. She didn't say they suspected a tumor, but Rick got off the phone believing that was their fear. At that point, Rick assumed that if John had a brain tumor, it would be related to his bouts with melanoma. Rick called Cindy, and they both booked flights to Phoenix. Then he called me.

The MRI confirmed the mass on John's brain, and he was prepped for surgery. The four-hour operation, a minimally invasive craniotomy with an incision over his left eyebrow, removed the two-inch "blood clot." A pathologist was present in the operating room to collect a biopsy sample. A battery of surgeons and neuro-oncologists would later testify to the surgeon's skill. He had removed all the matter that had been visible. "Very clean" was the consensus. When John awoke from the anesthesia, he answered every question put to him by doctors to test his cognitive ability: "What day is it? Who's the president?" He boasted later that one of them told him they'd never had a patient as mentally acute as he was just after brain surgery. He was prouder still when another doctor marveled at his threshold for pain, assuring him they'd never had a patient who could "tolerate that much." He was still telling people about the compliment months later, as the disease and its treatment were wearing him down.

He started pushing hospital staff to let him go home almost as soon as he was out of post-op. When Rick arrived, John tried to enlist him in his lobbying campaign to persuade the doctors not only to discharge him but to let him return to the Senate the next week. Rick sensibly refused, and John sent him off to find a cappuccino. The doctors somehow managed to keep him there until Sunday. On Wednesday, the doctors came to his condo and broke the news to John and Cindy. He had a primary glioblastoma tumor. They explained the gravity of the diagnosis but put off a more detailed discussion of his prognosis and treatment options until the following day.

I got a call from him that afternoon. It began with "Hi boy," like every other call with him began, "I need you to start working on—"

I interrupted him. "John, did you get the lab results back."

"Yes."

"And?"

"Not good."

"Define 'not good.'"

At that point, he said something unintelligible, possibly a mispronunciation of the word "glioblastoma." I had no idea what he was talking about. Then he said, "Tumor." I assumed melanoma, which I knew could be treatable. Jimmy Carter had just survived a melanoma tumor in his brain. As I started to mumble some reassurance, he cut me off. "Listen," he ordered, "we'll know more tomorrow. But I need you to start working on that speech. I'm coming back to Washington. They haven't agreed yet, but they will. I want to give it as soon as I'm back. They're writing this thing in Mitch's office. They're going to drop it on us at the last minute. They won't let us amend it. It's not right. They ought to let Lamar and Patty mark up a bill in committee."

The legislation in question was a replacement for the Affordable Care Act. Senate leadership staff were still drafting it, and the details were as yet unknown. Leadership was looking to put together any vehicle that could win a majority vote and make it to conference with the House. McCain, a veteran lawmaker skilled at forging bipartisan compromises, believed the right thing for the Senate and the country was for the chair and ranking member of the committee with jurisdiction over health care law, Senators Lamar Alexander and Patty Murray, to use their committee to negotiate and report out a bill. Senator McConnell had already announced that the Senate would delay a vote until the senior senator from Arizona was well enough to return to the Senate. John's would prove to be the deciding vote. Republicans had a fifty-two-seat majority, which meant they could lose just two votes, assuming no Democratic defections. Vice President Pence would be in the chair to break a tie. Three dissenting Republican votes would defeat the bill.

That John McCain could concentrate on any of that just after receiving his diagnosis astonishes me to this day. I've tried to imagine what was going through his head: *I have a terminal illness. Okay, thanks. I gotta get back to work.* His business-as-usual attitude deceived me into thinking that whatever he had, which was still unclear to me, could be treated and beaten. I told him I'd get going on the speech, and we hung up. Cindy had overheard our conversation and knew John had buried the lede. She texted Rick and had him call me to explain the seriousness of the diagnosis. "It's really bad," he began, then he explained the prognosis for someone with this kind of brain cancer. When he told me it was the same cancer that had killed Ted Kennedy and Beau Biden, I didn't need to hear any more. The air seemed to go dead as neither of us could think of what more to say. Finally, Rick recommended I fly out there. "We're probably headed for the cabin after tomorrow. He wants to go back to Washington, but they're not going to let him. He has a hole in his head." We hung up, and I booked a flight to Phoenix.

On Wednesday, John, Cindy, their daughter Meghan, and Rick met with his doctors at the Mayo Clinic. Using a series of charts, they went through the variables that would affect his prognosis: his age, physical fitness, cancer history, and other factors. They explained the known life expectancy ranges for people with glioblastomas. No one made a prediction about how much time he had left. There were some cases, a few, of people diagnosed with glioblastoma who were still living after three or four years. The average range, though, was twelve to eighteen months. They discussed treatment options and decided on the standard treatment for glioblastoma tumors, a combination of radiation and chemotherapy, which he would begin at Mayo the first week of August. They weren't gloomy in their presentation, Rick said, but they didn't pull any punches. Cindy and Meghan were understandably upset. John didn't appear to be. Rick said he went in there for answers: "He wanted to know exactly how long he had." He kept coming back to it—"Tell it to me straight," he repeated—and they kept demurring, saying they couldn't be more specific. How he would tolerate the radiation and chemo was also unknown. But those of us who knew him well assumed he would likely be above average in that department.

I landed in Phoenix on Saturday afternoon, expecting to rent a car and drive to the cabin. I called Rick, who alerted me to a possible change of plans. "He's adamant about going back to Washington. They don't want him to, but he's not letting it go." It takes most patients four to eight weeks to recover from brain surgery. His doctors insisted he get another brain scan on Monday before they would clear him to fly. They warned him he was at risk of a cerebral hemorrhage. He had an air pocket where they had operated, a common occurrence after a craniotomy. He really shouldn't fly until the air pocket had closed, they argued. He agreed to the brain scan. Rick said his doctors were confident it would show the air pocket was still a problem, and they thought they could then convince him to stay put. "But he's getting on a plane no matter what they tell him," conceded Rick, who was working on locating a private jet to take him back. To placate Mayo, John agreed to have a nurse on the plane. I checked in to a hotel near the McCains' condo and spent Sunday working on a draft of the speech. They were coming back to Phoenix that afternoon with a plan to fly to Washington on Tuesday, July 25. John and I would finish his speech on the plane.

He had the MRI on Monday. The air pocket was still there. His doctors again advised him not to fly. He thanked them and told them, "I'll be fine." We left from the private terminal at Sky Harbor late the next morning, John and Cindy; Meghan and her fiancé, Ben Domenech; Rick; Cindy's friend and associate Meghan Latcovich; the traveling nurse; and me. I had finished most of the speech but spent an hour or more revising it with John on the plane. He was anxious about it. He hoped it would make an impression on his colleagues. He was genuinely distressed about the state of the Senate. He had served in the institution for thirty years. He had made fun of it. He had tested its decorum and teased its more pompous inhabitants. But he revered it, its traditions, its empowerment of each senator, the necessity it made of collegiality and cooperation, the opportunities it presented to influence world events and to make history. He worried it was all at risk in the continued decline of regular order, as the Senate began operating more and more like the House of Representatives, where the majority rides roughshod over the minority, and where a handful of leaders decide the contents of legislation without going to the bother of forging consensus in committees. Each senator was being robbed of his or her authority with every change in the Senate's filibuster rules, with the decisions of majority leaders of both parties to block amendments from the floor to protect their caucus from tough votes, to move legislation intact or to pull it from consideration.

I had a feeling that McCain also hoped the speech would make an impression on him, reassuring him that he still had a role to play in the nation's affairs, that he still had the time and opportunity to make news and history. He reminded me that Ted Kennedy had stayed engaged in Senate business after his cancer diagnosis, though mostly out of sight. "I don't want to do that," he told me. "I want to keep working—and for people to see me working." He started to tick off items of pending business. "I want to get DoD done," the annual Defense Department spending authorization bill that he prided himself on sending to the White House every year on schedule and with the support of a bipartisan Senate majority. "I want to get started on an immigration bill," he added.

He had other plans as well, including more foreign travel. He wanted to go to the Munich Security Conference in February, he said. He had made many friendships in Munich over the years, and his prominence at the conference, as well as his high profile in national security debates in Washington, had elevated him in the eyes of world leaders. He was as outspoken in Munich as he was on the Senate floor or in a New Hampshire town hall, funny, candid, blunt, passionate, and pugnacious in the defense of the values and interests of the West. He loved to mix it up in any venue. He was delighted when Vladimir Putin had given a threatening, bombastic speech in Munich excoriating the United States and the West, while glaring the whole time at a smiling McCain seated in the front row. He wanted to go back one more time to say goodbye.

He looked wan and tired and had a nasty scar along his eyebrow. He didn't joke much on the flight to Washington. But neither was he noticeably solemn. He read his newspapers, talked about the speech, seemed uninterested in discussing his health, and napped a little. He was annoyed by our frequent admonishments to drink more water. He let the nurse take his pulse and temperature with a look that hinted he might soon grow tired of that routine as well.

There were cameras waiting for him at Reagan National. That seemed to enliven him. Back in the spotlight, time to perform. He went straight to the Capitol, while the rest of us filed into his office to watch him on television. He walked through the doors to the Senate floor and discovered the entire Senate turning to greet him with sustained applause. They had to vote on a closely contested motion to open debate on the Obamacare replacement that Republican leaders had not yet finished writing. All Democrats voted against it. All but two Republicans voted for it, including John, who would be sharply criticized by liberal critics for, in their view, voting for a process he was about to condemn in his speech. Had his critics listened more closely to him and taken him at his word, they wouldn't have been so surprised by his subsequent vote to defeat the legislation.

Leadership had reserved floor time right after the vote for him to deliver his speech, and he sought recognition as soon as the final tally had been announced. He began by noting that while he was proud of his naval career, his "service here is the most important job I have had in my life." He decried the tribalism that was overwhelming Senate traditions that had served the nation well, and he called for a return to an open legislative process and the compromises it required. "Our responsibilities are important, vitally important, to the continued success of our republic," he said. "And our arcane rules and customs are deliberately intended to require broad cooperation to function well at all."

He said he had voted to allow debate to begin and for amendments to be offered but that he "will not vote for the bill as it is today. It's a shell of a bill right now," and he decried the leadership's exclusive control of legislation that would affect the lives of every single American. He urged his colleagues to take control of the process, to work out a proposal that would represent genuine if modest progress. "Let's return to regular order," he pleaded.

Incremental progress . . . just plain muddling through to chip away at problems and keep our enemies from doing their worst isn't glamorous or exciting. It doesn't feel like a political triumph. But it's usually the most we can expect from our system of government, operating in a country as diverse and quarrelsome and free as ours. Considering the injustice and cruelties inflicted by autocratic governments, and how corruptible human nature can be, the problem solving our system does make possible, the fitful progress it produces, and the liberty and justice it preserves, is a magnificent achievement.

"This place is important," he reminded them. "The work we do is important. Our strange rules and seemingly eccentric practices that slow our proceedings and insist on our cooperation are important." He tried appealing to pride for their constitutional authority, urging his colleagues to remember, "[W]e are not the president's subordinates, we are his equals."

He closed by thanking them for their expressions of concern. He intended to remain in Washington for the duration of the health care debate and, he hoped, to manage debate on that year's defensive authorization. He planned to go home after that, he told them. But he had every intention of returning and "giving many of you cause to regret all the nice things you said about me." And he added that he "hoped to impress on you again that it is an honor to serve the American people in your company."

The speech, however unlikely it was to be heeded, was welcomed with appreciation for a Senate lion who, in a moment of personal crisis, had thought of the Senate and the country first. One senator told me months after the fact that being on the floor watching him give the speech was the kind of experience you imagined could happen here but never did. "You felt privileged to see it." They lined up after he had finished, almost all of them, to hug him, tell him they loved him. He was deeply affected. He couldn't stop talking about it afterward. "Amazing," he said. "I've never seen anything like it." Some of them had been crying when they talked to him. "Amazing," he repeated.

The legislation introduced by leadership repealed central provisions of Obamacare without providing an alternative. They said it was intended as a placeholder, something that could get them to conference with the House, where the actual bill would be written. That would mean even fewer senators would have input on the final bill, but at least it would have to go back to the Senate for a final vote. McCain was worried that House negotiators would abandon their own bill and accede to the Senate's "skinny repeal," killing Obamacare without replacing it, which they could send straight to the president's desk without another Senate vote. He sought assurances from Speaker Paul Ryan that the House wouldn't do that. The speaker told him that wasn't his intention, but he did not give an ironclad commitment.

I wasn't sure how McCain would vote on the bill. It clearly wouldn't be improved before the vote. It would still be the "shell of a bill" he had denounced. But over the next forty-eight hours, he came under pressure from Republican colleagues, who would enlist Arizona's governor, Doug Ducey, in the campaign to persuade him, and other friends whose views on the subject he respected. As I argued earlier, McCain didn't seek opportunities to break with his fellow Republicans on issues where there was wide consensus in the caucus. Politics had gotten so tribal that it demanded orthodoxy on issues large and small. That bothered him. But that's not to say he didn't feel obligated to be a team player. There were times when I or other aides counseled him to go his own way, and he refused for no reason other than "I don't want to be the dog in the manger again." For the next two days, he listened to appeals to party loyalty, and he could not easily dismiss them. But on something like this, something that involved a fifth of the nation's economy and touched the lives of most Americans, the appeal of conscience should be stronger than appeals to party loyalty. He knew that. He knew, too, that his time was short, and he was in earnest about encouraging the Senate to return to its best traditions.

He was also alert to the criticism he would receive were he to vote to repeal Obamacare and, contrary to Republican promises, fail to replace it with something that could be argued was an improvement. His detractors on the left were already leveling the charge that he had excellent government-subsidized health insurance as he faced a health crisis, while voting to repeal Obamacare would leave millions of Americans with health emergencies of their own and no or inadequate health insurance. In fact, McCain did not have government-subsidized health insurance. He did have an excellent insurance plan that he and Cindy paid for themselves. He didn't expect the distinction would convince his critics. It didn't even convince him. He knew he would fight for his life with the resources of a wealthy person, and he felt the unfairness that left others to suffer the same disease with a lesser standard of care.

The day of the vote, he met with Dr. Mark Gilbert, the head of neuro-oncology at the National Institutes of Health, and an associate. John and Cindy decided after the meeting that they would ask Gilbert to lead his medical team. It wasn't intended as a slight to Mayo. They were grateful for the care he received there, and his doctors at Mayo would continue to be part of the team. But McCain wanted to continue working in Washington for as long as he could, and so it was decided that he would receive radiation and chemotherapy treatments at NIH in Bethesda, Maryland, rather than fly back and forth to Arizona.

He heard from friends who supported Obamacare as well. Several Democratic senators, including Minority Leader Chuck Schumer, lobbied him. His good friend Joe Lieberman had talked to him every day since John had called with the news of his diagnosis. Joe was on the phone with him again the day before the vote; at the end of the call, he gently urged McCain to vote no. McCain talked to the two known Republican defectors, Susan Collins and Lisa Murkowski, who encouraged him to join them in voting no. He had a long conversation with his old friend Joe Biden. Two years earlier, Biden had buried his son, Beau, who had died from the same disease. John had known Beau since he was a boy, and he knew how hard his friend had taken the loss. They eventually got around to discussing the Obamacare repeal bill. "I know you'll do the right thing" was all John recalled Biden telling him.

I was reasonably confident he would, too, but I was not certain. His Senate staff were divided. Some wanted him to vote for it; others, including his communications director, Julie Tarallo, and chief of staff, Truman Anderson, thought he should vote no. Longtime McCain confidants were split as well, and some were agnostic, advising him to vote his conscience. He asked my opinion. I said he ought to vote against it, and that he should stop the pressure campaign by announcing that day his intention to oppose it, which he declined to do. When I had my last conversation with him Thursday evening, the night of the vote, I knew he was leaning toward a no vote, but I also knew he had left himself space to change his mind. I left for our northern Virginia home, where I was on my own; my family was in Maine. I made myself dinner and ate it in front of the television, switching between cable news channels. A few hours later, I fell asleep on the sofa and was awakened by a call from Truman a little before two o'clock in the morning. "Well, he did it."

"What?"

"He voted no."

I looked at my phone and saw that I had missed several texts and phone calls, including one from John McCain. I turned on CNN and watched replay after replay of him walking into the chamber, the last member to vote, colleagues on both sides holding their breath and straining to see what he was going to do, the majority leader standing in the well of the Senate, arms folded, looking at McCain as he thrust out his right arm to get the clerk's attention and turned his thumb down. Democrats gasped and started applauding before Schumer motioned them to be quiet. You couldn't beat it for drama. You might have suspected he had staged it that way.

When McCain had walked to the Senate floor, he had told a group of reporters who asked him how he would vote, "Wait for the show." People interpreted that as McCain building suspense for his star turn. But he told me afterward that he had made the "smart-ass" remark because he wanted to give himself a little more time to make up his mind. What actually happened is that an hour or so before the vote, McCain talked to Collins and Murkowski as they sat at their desks, and he told them they were doing the right thing. Then he walked over, smiling, to a group of Democrats, including Schumer, put his arm around Dianne Feinstein, and let them know they would be happy. Everyone was buzzing with anticipation in the chamber and in the press gallery. Majority Leader McConnell was aware he was prepared to vote no, and stalled the vote while Republicans furiously lobbied him to change his mind. Someone got Governor Ducey on the phone. John listened politely as Ducey let him know that, his previous concerns about the bill notwithstanding, he would advise a yes vote. Others circled around him with the same message. He was twice buttonholed by Vice President Pence, who was there to break a tie. The second time Pence pulled McCain off the floor, he handed him his phone: President Trump was waiting to talk to him. That's why he was the last member in the chamber to vote. He had just finished rebuffing Trump when he walked back onto the floor to vote. The thumbs-down thing was a common practice. On most votes, a throng of senators is vying for the clerk's attention, and many will give a thumbs-up or -down because they aren't certain the clerk heard their yea or nay. It was just a habit for McCain. He didn't intend it as a theatrical gesture. He was amused, though, in the aftermath of the vote as reporters diagrammed the Senate tableau at the moment of his thumbs-down, analyzing it, as one reporter described, as if it were "a Renaissance painting."[58]

He was amazed by the reaction and relieved to have done what he knew was the right thing. A quiet conscience makes for a light heart. But he wasn't gleeful. He didn't care that he had disappointed Trump. But he knew he had disappointed his Republican colleagues, many of whom he considered close friends, and that was not a cause for celebration. He and Majority Leader McConnell were depicted as each other's nemesis during campaign finance reform fights. They were adversaries then and on other occasions, and quite hostile adversaries at times. But they had served in the Senate nearly the same length of time. Their offices were once across the hall from each other. They had compatible views on foreign policy and worked together to advance them. As majority leader, McConnell had acknowledged McCain as the caucus's leading voice on national security. When you work with someone for thirty years, it's hard not to form an attachment that will survive disruptive disagreements, even occasional meanness. They had shared decades of experiences, grown old in each other's company, and cooperated in enough common pursuits that neither of them let a fight every now and again cause a permanent rupture. That's how human nature works in other professional settings. I'm always surprised when people are surprised that it works that way in politics, too. McCain and McConnell each considered the other a friend, as was apparent when they met alone in the majority leader's office after John first returned. It was an emotional meeting, he told me afterward, as would be their last meeting two months before John died, when McConnell went to Arizona to say goodbye.

The majority leader had agreed to call up the defense bill before the Senate adjourned for the August recess so John could manage debate before starting his treatment. However disappointed he was by John's vote, he kept his word and asked for unanimous consent to turn to the bill the next morning. Rand Paul, who tended to be a nuisance by temporarily impeding defense bills that ultimately passed with overwhelming majorities, objected. They were nearing the start of the recess, so his objection effectively killed any prospect of finishing the defense bill before the break. I'm sure Paul's supporters would defend him by saying it was an act of principle to delay debate on a bill he opposed. But it's hard not to see it as an act of spite to prevent a Senate veteran with terminal cancer from doing the job he took pride in completing every year. "Why do you think he did it?" I asked John. "Because he hates me, and he's an asshole," he replied.

I flew back to Arizona with him and spent a few days at the cabin. As he grilled dinner one night, he told me he wasn't going to let himself expect any outcome at that point, good or bad, but he was ready for the worst. He didn't want to upset his family, but "I don't want to deceive them, either." He was trying to prepare himself for the end, to make peace with the prospect. He could be a little insensitive to those of us who couldn't match his fatalism. He recalled the last days of a friend with terminal cancer whose family kept hoping for a miracle and didn't want to let him go. "He had all these tubes and wires hooking him up to machines," he described. "Any spot they could stick something in him, they did. And he was zoned out from the morphine. That's no way to go."

I left for Maine the next day, and John and Cindy drove to Phoenix for him to start chemo and radiation. I came back near the end of the month to help prepare for the *60 Minutes* and HBO interviews. In both lengthy interviews, held over two days, he's relaxed and engaging, funny at times and wistful at others. He and Cindy are seen strolling the shaded lawns of the property beneath sycamores and cottonwoods, his dog, Burma, trailing after them, chasing tennis balls John threw underhand into the creek. In both interviews, he is brave and fatalistic, insisting that, rather than sympathy, he wanted people "to celebrate, as I celebrate, a life well lived." He is a picture of a man at ease, taking life and death as they came.

Off camera, he had an urgency about him. Before the Senate adjourned, he had convened Rick, Carla, Truman, and me to discuss his funeral arrangements and the disposition of his papers, the first of many conversations on those subjects. Right away we began preliminary planning for private and public memorial services and for a McCain archive. The topics were never off his mind. We discussed details with him weekly, sometimes daily. His first notion was to have a public memorial in Phoenix and a private one at the Naval Academy, where he wanted to be buried, in a plot his pal Chuck Larson had reserved for him. We suggested he have a public service in Washington as well, in the National Cathedral, which could accommodate the thousands of people he had developed relationships with over the four decades he had worked in Washington. Once he agreed to a Washington service, he immediately started thinking about the political message he wanted it to convey. As was often the case on the biggest stage, he liked the grand gesture.

I was with him when he came up with the idea of asking Presidents Obama and Bush to give eulogies at the cathedral. What grander gesture of national unity could he have made than by asking the two men who had denied him his highest ambition to speak on his behalf and on behalf of the idea of America they had all served? He tasked me with finding out whether President Obama would be receptive to the request, and Rick or Carla with reaching out to President Bush's people. I emailed Obama confidant David Axelrod, who quickly replied with an answer in the affirmative. President Bush was agreeable as well. McCain called both men to ask them formally and to thank them. They told him they were honored to be asked.

In several meetings on the subject, we raised the delicate issue of whether or not to invite the incumbent president. Neither man liked or respected the other. Yet neither would have been the first person in Washington to pay insincere tribute to someone he disliked. Many of the values of public service John wanted his funeral to commemorate were antithetical to Trumpism, and he intended that contrast to be clear. The last time we raised the question, McCain remarked, "I'm sure he would rather play golf." We took that as a no.

His other priority was finishing the book we had been working on before his diagnosis, which he had intended to be mostly a record of his involvement in world affairs. He now wanted it to be a more personal reflection on his life and career, "summing up," he put it, "and showing gratitude." From the beginning of his final illness to its end, he insisted again and again that he be remembered as "the luckiest

man you ever met" and the most grateful. We talked about how the
book could convey that as we sat in the gazebo next to the bend of the
creek. "Just think of everything that's happened to me, good and bad.
Who wouldn't be grateful. Look at this place," he said, sweeping his
arm in front of him. "Look at my life."

Burma was competing for his attention, and he tossed her a tennis
ball a few times. When he resumed talking, it was about a visit made
the previous weekend by his children from his first marriage. "I really
enjoyed seeing them," he said. "They all turned out well. Cindy and
my kids turned out well. See what I mean? What more could I ask for
from life."

When the camera crews departed, he returned to Phoenix for another round of chemo and radiation treatments. He was finished in
time to fly with Cindy to a conference at Lake Como in Italy on Labor
Day weekend, one he had attended for several years and wanted badly
to return to again, not as much for the conference as for the location.
"I want to see Lake Como one more time," he explained. There he
repeated the message of his last several overseas trips, emphasizing
the importance of America's alliances and acknowledging the pressure
they were under from Donald Trump's antagonism and those of his
supporters who endorsed his skepticism about the international order
the West had built. "[T]he future of the world," McCain prophesied,
"will turn, in large part, on how this debate in America is resolved."
He offered as encouragement the strength and decency of Americans,
referencing recovery efforts in Texas and Louisiana from Hurricane
Harvey, and the young woman, Heather Heyer, who had been murdered for protesting the white supremacist rally in Charlottesville.
"This is America at its best—ordinary people, despite long odds, rising to master moments of extraordinary challenge, powered by their
belief in that most simple and audacious of ideas—that all people are
created equal."

We reconvened in Washington after the holiday. He was in good
spirits. They'd had a wonderful time, he said. "You really have to go
there someday, boy. One of the most beautiful places." Leslie Stahl
for *60 Minutes* and the Kunhardts for the HBO film interviewed him

again in his Senate office. If you watch both programs and you're looking for it, you can see the difference from the Arizona interviews to
those filmed a month later in Washington. He's thinner, and there is a
first glimpse of frailty. Still, for a guy who had brain surgery six weeks
earlier, and just endured weeks of chemotherapy and radiation, he appears in pretty good shape.

He was scheduled for an MRI at Walter Reed hospital on September 11. Glioblastoma is a sneaky cancer, concealing its tentacles
in the canals of the brain, undetected by modern diagnostic imag-
ing. The radiation and chemo were intended to kill remnants of the
tumor that hadn't been visible when they operated. He and his doctors
would decide on the next course of treatment after the MRI. There
had been preliminary talk of considering newer cancer treatments—
immunotherapy, for example—once they had confidence that the radiation and chemo had achieved their desired effect. Unfortunately,
the MRI on September 11 discovered the existence of another tumor
in a different part of his brain. It had been too small to detect in July,
and it wasn't operable. It's rare for glioblastoma to produce a second
tumor distant from the first. The MRI signaled that John McCain's
luck might have finally run out.

He didn't despair; neither did his doctors. He intended to keep
working and fight the cancer as long as he could. He informed Gilbert
and the other doctors that he did not expect to be kept in the dark
about his chances. "Tell me the truth. I want to know how long I have,"
he insisted. They promised him they would be candid when they knew
enough to give him those answers. But now, they maintained, wasn't
that time. He was still strong enough to fight. Further rounds of chemo
and radiation to kill the new tumor were prescribed, as well as doses
of steroids, at times very high doses, to prevent the treatment from
killing him. He went back to work that afternoon.

By the end of September, the toll on him was starting to show. He
had dropped more weight, and his usual quick gate through the Senate
halls, as aides trotted to keep up, had slowed to a more normal pace for
an octogenarian. He complained of fatigue, and he went home at night
right after the last vote of the day. But he kept pressing, kept showing

up. He managed debate on the defense bill, which passed the Senate on September 16. He introduced legislation to block President Trump from imposing a ban on transgender people serving in the military. He sponsored with Amy Klobuchar a bill to apply to political advertising on the Internet the same disclosure rules governing television, radio, and print ads. He announced he would oppose another Republican attempt to repeal Obamacare, this one proposed by his friend Lindsey Graham. The president of the United States attacked his position via Twitter, the medium for the witty and the witless, where Trump likes to air his many grievances. In McCain's *60 Minutes* interview, which had aired a few days earlier, he responded to a question about Trump's antagonism by noting in a voice that didn't convey the contempt his words seemed to imply, "[W]e're very different people. Different upbringing. Different life experiences. He is in the business of making money, and he has been successful. . . . I was raised in a military family. I was raised in the concept and belief that duty, honor, country is the lodestar for the behavior that we have to exhibit every single day."

After the discovery of the second tumor, McCain seemed largely indifferent to Trump's attacks, and he advised me to follow his example. I often resorted to Twitter to vent my dislike of Trump, and whenever the conversation turned to the occupant of the Oval Office, I had a tendency to go from cold to boiling in mere seconds. "I don't know why you let him get you so worked up," McCain chastised me. "That's not how you beat him." He preferred instead to take on Trumpism, if such a peculiar mix of personal insecurity, resentment, mercantilism, and nativist demagoguery amounts to a governing philosophy. He would spend time that was now precious to him opposing Trump's most noxious views, mainly his nativism and affinity for autocrats, and making the case for the international order founded on the values of free people and free markets.

Well before his cancer diagnosis, McCain had agreed to accept an award, the Liberty Medal, from the National Constitution Center. The event was scheduled for October 16 in Philadelphia. Former vice president Joe Biden would give him the award. He wanted to use his acceptance speech to attack Trump's "America First" nationalism without mentioning him by name, and the lines he spoke to that end brought the audience to their feet:

> To fear the world we have organized and led for three quarters of a century, to abandon the ideals we have advanced around the globe, to refuse the obligations of international leadership and our duty to remain 'the last best hope of earth' for the sake of some half-baked, spurious nationalism cooked up by people who would rather find scapegoats than solve problems, is as unpatriotic an attachment as any other tired dogma of the past that Americans consigned to the ash heap of history.

Of all the speeches we worked on together, that is one I hope will be remembered with his concession speech in 2008 and his speech on the Senate floor in 2014, defending the release of the Senate Intelligence Committee's torture report. The poignancy of his delivery in Philadelphia was equaled only in his last formal address two weeks later to the Brigade of Midshipmen at the Naval Academy. It will stay with me as one of my most affecting memories of him, as I suspect it will for anyone who watched it. He looked in failing health. You could practically see him tap his last reserves of strength to give a rousing call to arms for the cause he had dedicated his life to. He became emotional while expressing his gratitude for having been "a bit player in the extraordinary story of America." And the look on his face when he had finished, as the crowd applauded not only the speech but the life of the man who had given it, was one of relief to have found himself, near the end of his life, still brave enough to be the man he always wanted to be.

Events seem compressed in my memory after that speech. When I next saw him a week later, he was a guest on *The View*, the talk show cohosted by his daughter Meghan. Both my wife and I were surprised at his appearance. He moved with deliberate care; his voice, like his body, was weaker and thinner; the flesh on his face was taut; and his eyes looked bigger. He and Meghan were both in tears as he handed her a framed photograph of the two of them sitting on top of their hill, looking down on their valley. We saw him in person a few days later at a barbecue at Rick Davis's house, and he was much livelier as he and Cindy held court in a crowd of old friends. His appetite was good, and he laughed quite a bit. He was seated more than was his habit at parties, and they were the first to leave, but not unusually early for him. He was clearly enjoying himself, and I remember feeling relieved that he hadn't deteriorated as much as I had worried. Two days later, he was ill at a Pentagon memorial for the sailors who had lost their lives on the *John S. McCain*. But he didn't excuse himself until he had finished his remarks and shared a few words individually and taken photographs with any of the bereaved families who wished to speak to him. That evening he mustered enough strength to make the trip to Annapolis to speak to the Brigade for the last time. He spoke to them of the ideals they would defend, and exhorted their political leaders to "fight isolationism, protectionism, and nativism. We have to defeat those who would worsen our divisions. We have to remind our sons and daughters that we became the most powerful nation on earth by tearing down walls, not building them," he exclaimed as the midshipmen thundered their approval.

As he reached the end of his speech, he recalled again his "complicated" initial relationship with the Academy, but stressed that he had embraced the Academy's values nonetheless. "I arrived a rebel without a cause, and left much the same," he told them. "But I would discover that a sense of honor had been imparted to me here that would speak to me in the darkest hours. And so I come back again and again, to the place where I learned to dread dishonor and from where I embarked on an eventful life, in good company, in the service of my country and its great cause. May your lives be as lucky as mine."

He spent the next weekend at Walter Reed hospital. He had looked and felt run-down that Friday, and he complained of something wrong with his right foot. His blood sugar was off the charts. He was diagnosed with diabetes, and he had ruptured his Achilles tendon. Both conditions were likely caused by the steroids he was receiving to reduce brain swelling from the radiation treatments. When he returned to the Senate on Monday, he was wearing a boot on his right foot and using a cane, which he detested. He had the press office tweet a picture of him, and he dictated the caption: "I can't tell you how much I hate wearing this boot."

The cane was soon replaced by a wheelchair, which he hated even more, but it was difficult for him to navigate on his own the Capitol's crowded corridors. Despite his irritating infirmity, his morale was pretty good, and he remained unfailingly kind to members of the public, welcoming every greeting and request for a photograph. I had lunch with him that Veterans Day at a barbecue joint near his Washington condo. We met at his place and walked the block to the restaurant together. He hadn't yet been consigned to a wheelchair. He was wearing the boot and using the cane, leaning on my arm for support, and shuffling slowly. He was clearly frustrated with his condition, but he set his jaw and persevered. When we entered the restaurant, diners began applauding him, and he brightened considerably, wearing a wide grin and tapping his chest to return the affection. He stopped at a few tables to chat and take pictures. Some people wished him "Happy Veterans Day" and thanked him for his service. He said the same to several servicemen present. After we finished eating, he resumed his rounds and continued until he had exchanged a few words with every person in the place who had looked even slightly interested in meeting him. By the time we got back to his condo, he was exhausted but in good spirits.

A few days later, army chief of staff General Mark Milley hosted a Twilight Tattoo for him at Fort Myer and presented him with the army's Outstanding Civilian Service Award. The Tattoo is a military pageant featuring the U.S. Army Band and soldiers from the 3rd U.S. Infantry, the Old Guard. The pageant and presentation took close to two hours. They were preceded by a lovely reception in General Milley's quarters. John was very touched by all of it, but it was fatiguing. He was on his feet for quite a while, frequently rising from his seat to applaud the performance, and spending a half hour or more afterward mixing with soldiers and their families, signing autographs, and taking photographs. His left Achilles tendon ruptured the next day.

He flew to Arizona the following week for Meghan's wedding in Hidden Valley. The ruptured Achilles prevented him from walking her down the aisle, but he did give her away. It was a beautiful, fun wedding, and he was a convivial host. I sat at his table during the rehearsal dinner, and he teased people and conversed animatedly throughout while sipping a single vodka. When he toasted the couple and thanked the guests for coming, his eyes welled with tears, but he obviously enjoyed himself that weekend. It was a pleasure to see him so cheerful. He looks happy in a wedding photograph the couple released, seated next to Cindy and smiling broadly as Meghan rests her hand on his shoulder. Conspiracy theorists noticed he was wearing the boot on his left foot, and a legion of Achilles Truthers furiously launched their crazy notions into cyberspace, much to his amusement.

McCain came back to Washington after Thanksgiving looking pretty worn out. He had decided he would vote in favor of the Republican tax cut bill, which was the pending business. I argued that he shouldn't because one of its provisions removed Obamacare's individual mandate. But he countered that leadership had addressed the process arguments he'd objected to during the health care debate. The bill had been debated, amended, and approved by the Finance Committee, and amendments were in order on the Senate floor. However, McConnell had added substitute amendments before the vote that Democrats rightly complained they hadn't had time to review, which weakened his case. The other two Republicans who had voted against the Obamacare repeal, Murkowski and Collins, were going to vote for the tax cuts, and McCain didn't want to be the lone Republican holdout. It was the last major vote he cast in the Senate.

Ten days later, he was rushed to Walter Reed by ambulance. The doctors suspected a pulmonary embolism, but it turned out to be a children's virus in his upper respiratory tract that caused pneumonia, which his immune system was too compromised by chemotherapy to fight. Cindy called me from the hospital, and when I arrived, they still suspected an embolism. We were distraught and feared the worst. He had a very high fever and difficulty breathing, and he was delirious. Family and close friends gathered at the hospital. His children flew in from different parts of the country. Word leaked out that he was in serious condition. By the next day, his press office was receiving calls from reporters asking, as gently as they could manage, if he was dying. But the hospital put him on a course of antiviral medicine and pumped him full of fluids, and after a few days, his fever was down and his delirium started to clear. I was standing in his room at one point when he was confused. I didn't think he knew it was me; we had to wear surgical gowns and face masks when we entered his room. But he looked at me and started gesturing at his right arm and the various tubes and wires attached to it, and he shook his head as if to remind me of our conversation about his friend who had spent his last days in similar circumstances.

His NIH doctors conferred with the family. They thought the crisis had passed but his recovery would take a while. The decision was made to fly him home to the cabin, and Rick and Carla started looking for a private plane. The Senate was still in session, and he would miss the final vote on the tax cut bill. He was weak and not very communicative. But he acquiesced as long as we assured him he would come back to the Senate when it reconvened in January. President Trump called Cindy to wish them well and intimated that he had heard John's condition was grave. She told him John was responding well to treatment. Trump told reporters later that John would return from Arizona if they needed his vote for the tax cuts. We heard rumors that he had told people privately that John was near death.

John was taken by ambulance to Dulles in the late afternoon on December 17. I don't remember if any of us thought then we would be able to keep our word and see him back in the Senate by January. But it was usually foolish to bet against him. Rick and I flew to Arizona after the holidays and were impressed by how much progress he had made. As soon as he had shaken off the pneumonia, he started physical therapy to regain his strength, several sessions every day. While he was still seriously underweight, he had recovered his appetite and was eating well and getting appreciably stronger as a result. His Achilles had healed, and he was using a walker to get around. The day after we arrived, he walked with us and his son Jimmy from one end of the property to the other. He stopped a couple of times to rest, but it was a good half-hour walk. Rick and I both believed then that he would get back to the Senate at some point, and we began discussing how we could get him to Munich the next month. John and I spent a few hours that afternoon going over the manuscript of our last book before I sent it to our publisher. He seemed a little down. I told him again how much better he looked. He stared at me for a second and then nodded in the direction of the steep road that climbed out of their little valley to the highway. "Five months ago, I hiked that hill," he said, remembering a trek he had made with Meghan in August. He paused for a few seconds as he looked at the hill. "I'll never do it again."

He kept up a daily routine with his Senate and Phoenix offices, nine o'clock conference calls five days a week. They discussed the Senate schedule, what bills were pending, which he should publicly support or oppose. They went over requests from colleagues to cosponsor legislation, and committee hearings that he couldn't chair but for which he needed to approve the witnesses and give staff guidance on what questions he wanted to submit for the record. They updated him on the progress of an infrastructure project in Maricopa County, the Rio Salado Project, that he had taken a lead role in promoting. They kept him informed on the planning for his archives. They gave him the latest gossip and passed on encouraging and worrying news from overseas. He managed to stay current on most news on his own. He read the papers every morning and *The Economist* every week. He watched the news on television. He read the clips and memos the Phoenix office delivered to him every weekday. He stayed active, physically and mentally, and we were encouraged that he still had time and opportunity to, as he put it, "stay relevant."

Rick and I came back for another visit two weeks later. He was keeping up with his physical rehabilitation, but he didn't seem to have progressed any further; in fact, I thought he had declined a little. I can't remember if he was between chemotherapy courses at that time or receiving them. The general consensus seemed to be that the high doses of steroids were debilitating him more than the chemo, and periodically, his medical team would reduce the dose. But soon after, the effects of brain inflammation caused by the radiation used to kill the second tumor became apparent, so the steroids were increased.

We were nearing the point where we had to make a decision about whether he would go to Munich. His doctors at NIH and Mayo were united in opposition to the idea. As more than one of them pointed out, there was a bad flu contagion under way, and "if he gets it, it could kill him." Cindy called me not long after I returned to Washington and asked me to break the news to him, which I did. I blamed the flu.

"You can't risk it, John."

"I can't?" he responded.

"No, I'm really sorry. Cindy's agreed to go and read your speech for you. You and I can start working on it. I'll send you something soon."

He didn't argue or complain. I would have felt better if he had roared at me or at his doctors or at fate. It was the mildness of his reaction that got to me, his weary acquiescence that conveyed he wasn't experiencing mere disappointment but something worse, despair. It was a terribly sad moment I haven't been able to forget. It was the right call, the only call, really. But I felt lousy about it then, and I feel lousy as I write about it.

In the hope that it would restore his spirits, Cindy started plotting a clandestine trip to Las Vegas a few weeks later with a small group of family and friends. She hired a private plane, arranged with the owner of the MGM Grand for a private room, and formed a plan to get John in and out of the casino discreetly to avoid embarrassing headlines about the senator whose illness prevented him from traveling to Washington but not from shooting craps. It worked. The twenty-four-hour excursion boosted his morale. Rolling dice with family and friends even in a private setting, and not the crowded tables he had long enjoyed, proved a tonic, even if he had to confine himself to an hour or so at the table rather than a marathon session like he once routinely managed. It worked so well, there was talk of attempting another trip.

It was not to be. Rick and I went to see him every few weeks. Each time we found him weaker than the last. He wasn't fighting as hard. He was spending less time at physical therapy. He kept up some of his daily routines and welcomed friends, who arrived regularly to check on him and tell him they missed him. Two public appearances were under discussion: the first, a trip to the Grand Canyon in March, when a memorial to the work he and Mo Udall had done to protect the natural wonder was to be dedicated. The other was the McCain Institute's annual Sedona Forum in late April, held at a resort just fifteen minutes from the McCains' Hidden Valley ranch. The HBO documentary about him was nearly finished, and one of the filmmakers, Teddy Kunhardt, was coming to Sedona to play part of the film for the invited guests. The plan was for John to remain at the cabin, where some of the attending senators would stay. And on Friday night, as the film clips were playing, we would smuggle him into the auditorium, and when the lights came up, there he would be, waiting to say hello to his friends.

Those plans were abandoned when he was medevaced to the Mayo Clinic in the middle of the night of April 15. Some days earlier he had complained of a gut ache, and his doctors had increased the steroids. The steroids and his high pain tolerance masked the intestinal infection he was suffering. He became increasingly confused over the next several days but was uncomplaining. On the fifth day, his intestine ruptured, his fever spiked, and his heart rate jumped, and his nurses feared he might be having a heart attack. He was operated on that night, and a section of his intestine was removed. I arrived in Phoenix two days later and joined the group of family and friends keeping vigil at his side. He was weak but alert, and you could tell he hadn't given up. He didn't want to be there and was trying to rally, and each day he seemed to get a little stronger.

He was still in the hospital when the Sedona Forum started on April 20, and we took turns shuffling between Sedona and the hospital. I introduced Teddy Kunhardt the first evening, when he screened the documentary. Most of the audience members were in tears by the end. The next day, I went with Teddy to Phoenix to show the film to John. I don't think Teddy was prepared to see him in that condition. They had last met in the early fall, when they had recorded their final interview with him, and John was still vigorous and in control. Teddy is a good guy from a family of good people, all of whom John liked from the start. They chatted amiably as Teddy connected a DVD player to the television in John's room. Neither John nor anyone else present said anything while the film ran. When it was finished, and we had turned on the lights in the room, I could tell John had been moved, as had Teddy, who struggled a little with his emotions as he told John it had been an honor to make the film and that he was his hero. John grabbed his arm and cut him off. "Well, you're my hero. Thank you."

Cindy took John home to the cabin on April 23, in time to enjoy another sunset in Hidden Valley. He had had enough of hospitals and made it clear he did not wish to return. There would be no more serious efforts to treat his illness, just its effects. The next months passed peacefully. He stayed engaged in public affairs as long as he could. He still talked to aides daily, although the calls were shorter now and not always productive. He decided in June to endorse a bipartisan effort in the House to get a vote on an immigration reform bill that would protect from deportation immigrants who came here as children. He was so incensed by President Trump's sycophancy to Vladimir Putin at their Helsinki press conference that he authorized the harshest statement I ever heard him make about an American president: "Today's press conference in Helsinki was one of the most disgraceful performances by an American president in memory," it began, and went on to blast Trump's "naïveté, egotism, false equivalence, and sympathy for autocrats." It was a corker, and much deserved. I wish I had helped write it.

Guests continued to arrive regularly, old friends and newer ones; many were repeat visitors who now came to say a last goodbye. His children were often there. He and his son Jack had parted for the last time just before Jack, a navy pilot, deployed to Afghanistan. Longtime aides took turns visiting. Through it all, Cindy constantly attended him. He liked to sit in a chair on the deck outside their bedroom for as many hours a day as he could, gazing at the creek and watching the birds. He was still in thrall to the pair of black hawks that returned every spring to their nest in a sycamore on the property. As the summer progressed, he spent more time in the hospital bed Cindy had purchased. We would wheel it out on the deck for him so he could keep taking in the beauty of the place he loved so much. And Cindy never left his side—literally. All those weeks and months, she sat next to his chair or his bed and saw to his every need, kept his spirits up, made sure his meals were to his liking and he ate them. She managed the team of nurses and physician's assistants who cared for him, and monitored his meds. She welcomed their guests and made sure they were well fed and comfortably situated. She kept in constant touch with their children while she watched news shows and movies with him, and she consoled him when he was down and soothed him when he was anxious. I've never seen a more devoted spouse.

I spent a few days with him in May. *The Restless Wave* would be published later that month, and for the first time, I would have to do the book promotion, the television, radio, and print interviews that he had always done and for which I was a poor substitute. "Any advice?" I asked him. "Don't screw up," he offered. I would spend the rest of May and most of June in Washington and New York. Then I planned to go to our home in Maine. I would see him again, I promised, in July if not sooner. I wasn't worried at the time that he would be gone before I could get back. He was stable and determined to "beat the over/under," he said. Rick and I expected him to be around into the next year, and we had discussed the depressing prospect of having to advise him to resign his Senate seat. Neither of us wanted that job. In early August, Rick had to convince him to resign his chairmanship of the board of the International Republican Institute, the democracy-promoting NGO he had chaired for a quarter century. We had wanted him to give it up when he would still have influence in the choice of a successor. "That was hard enough," Rick lamented. I'm glad neither of us had to break his heart again.

When I was there in May, I mentioned a letter McCain received from Samantha Power, who had been the UN ambassador in the Obama administration. She was the author of a book about genocide, *A Problem from Hell,* that John had read and admired. He respected Power as a fellow warrior in the defense of human rights. As happened in some of his friendships with other Obama administration officials, theirs had run aground on the issue that would be one of his last great, passionate fights—Syria. Power's letter to him had somehow been routed to me. I had read it and sent a copy to Arizona, then brought the original with me. I wanted to make sure he had seen it. He had seemed uncertain when I mentioned it, so I read it to him.

It was an unusual letter, to say the least, and powerfully affecting. I can't recall having seen other correspondence that expressed in so straightforward a manner an appreciation for someone from whom the writer was estranged. It touched him very much. She recalled the "bad phone call" they had when she'd hoped to help persuade him to lift his objections to Tony Blinken's nomination as deputy secretary of state. "[Y]ou not only refused to change your position on Tony," she wrote,

but you demanded that I resign as well. "How can you defend this?" you asked, speaking of Syria. I did my best to answer but given what was happening to Syrian civilians, I knew how hollow my words sounded to you. What struck me most in our call was how sincere you were—no public gallery or journalists were listening to you confront an Obama official. You were just incredibly sad for the people who had believed in the power of their revolution and who had hoped that the United States would do everything in its power to protect them. And you cared so much that you eventually couldn't stand talking to me, so you hung up. Strange though it may sound, I don't think I have ever admired you more than I did at that moment. What for many in Washington is often merely a policy or political debate, for you, because lives are at stake, is deeply personal.

Power's observation was exceptionally perceptive. I have reread it often since. And I'm very glad he saw it. It *had* been personal to him. All of it. The policy debates and political fights, the successes and defeats. What others would write off as McCain hotheadedness, she knew was something more. Other people's suffering mattered to him. It infuriated him. It stirred him to act. It broke his heart. When you saw people being made to suffer, he believed, you didn't just sympathize with them, you fought for them. He wanted to do good in the world. He wanted to fight on the side of the persecuted, and he had. And here someone with whom he had clashed, but whom he respected, had told him she saw what he had done and who he was, and had thanked him for it.

Her letter went on to cite other instances when he had distinguished himself in the service of others, and she closed by thanking him "for insisting that we Americans find our better angels. And . . . for demonstrating the importance of trying every day to ensure that the world we leave to our children and grandchildren is kinder and gentler than the one we found."

During that same visit, McCain told me he wanted to have a statement from him ready to be released, kind of a last testament. He asked me to draft it, and he mentioned passages from some of his speeches that he wanted to include. I wrote it per his instructions and showed it to him before I left for Maine. He handed it back to me without detectable emotion and said, "Good. Put it in a drawer until the time comes." Rick Davis would read it at a press conference the day after John passed away, struggling to control his emotions when he got to "I lived and died a proud American."

He hung on through much of the summer, lucid and still paying attention to the world. In July, he began to suffer aphasia and struggled to remember words he wanted to use in conversations with friends. It was hard to have a conversation with him on the phone. Cindy called me the second week of August to let me know he was failing. She promised to give me enough notice to get there before the end. She called me on August 22 and told me the time had come to say goodbye. I had already booked a flight for August 24 and decided to keep the reservation. Our oldest daughter was living abroad, and we hadn't seen her in a year, and she was home for a week's visit. On August 23, Rick called me in the middle of the night. Family and friends were gathered around his bedside. They didn't think he would make it through the night. I was racked with guilt and couldn't get back to sleep. My flight was scheduled to depart at six-thirty in the morning, so I drove in darkness to the airport to wait for it. When I boarded my connecting flight for Phoenix, I worried he would be gone by the time

I landed. I didn't order Wi-Fi on the flight. I didn't want to learn the news on a crowded airplane. When I landed, I saw I had a voicemail from Rick. I assumed the worst, but to my relief, he had called to tell me nothing had changed. The tough old bird had beat the over/under. I got to the cabin two hours later. I whispered my goodbye to him and took my place in the vigil at his bedside.

The end came the next afternoon. We had wheeled his bed onto the deck outside his bedroom and pointed him toward the creek he loved. He was surrounded by loved ones as the intervals between his breaths grew longer. Just before four-thirty p.m., one of the black hawks flew over his bed to the other side of the creek, settled on a sycamore limb, and looked down on the scene. He never drew another breath. The music playlist Cindy had made for him, an eclectic mix of his favorite pop songs and jazz standards, was running. A moment after he passed, the mourners heard Sinatra's voice singing "My Way."

Two hours later, while another Arizona sunset colored the western sky, we climbed the bumpy road up their hill in a small convoy of state police vehicles, SUVs, and a hearse. A throng of people was waiting at the top, hands over hearts, saluting, holding flags. People lined the entire route, the county roads and the interstate entrance ramps. They lined the city blocks in Phoenix around the funeral home. They lined up to pay their respects as John McCain lay in state at the Arizona capitol and the United States Capitol, where he had served his country for thirty-four years. They gathered at the Vietnam Veterans Memorial to watch his widow lay a wreath in remembrance, and they gathered around the cathedral where he was eulogized by presidents. Vietnamese, young and old, including at least one of his captors, stood in a long line at the U.S. Embassy in Hanoi to sign the condolence book, and heaped flowers at the foot of his monument on the shore of the lake where he had been captured. They lined the streets of Annapolis as his hearse passed on its way to the Navy Academy Chapel. Midshipmen in their summer uniforms lined the route from the chapel to his final resting place, each of them in turn giving a slow-motion salute as the horse-drawn caisson went past.

In the same year John McCain was dying, my daughter, who was serving as a Peace Corps volunteer in a rural province of Cambodia, listened to a local colleague complain about his government. "We need freedom," he told her, and he didn't appear optimistic about the prospects for achieving it. "But we have friends in America," he said, brightening. "John McCain wants to help us." He hadn't any idea my daughter had a connection to McCain, and she didn't volunteer it. A random guy living in the back of beyond not only knew John McCain's name but knew him to be a friend who would help if he could. I told John the story when I next saw him. "You should be proud," I told him, "that's quite a testament to your value to the world." He smiled and nodded but didn't have a comment on the subject. He asked how my daughter was doing and when she would be coming home.

It *was* quite a testament to him, but he was past needing affirmation. All his life, John McCain believed we redeemed ourselves by our work in the world to sustain the unvanquished hopes of the suffering. He died believing it.

His last filmed interview was for a documentary on the life and works of his favorite author, Ernest Hemingway, directed by Ken Burns and Lynn Novick. I attended a screening of the unfinished film a year after John died. He had been noticeably frail when the interview was filmed. But you couldn't tell that from his appearance on-screen. There he was again, lively and engaging, forthright, expressing himself in the way he had of seeming wry and earnest at the same time. Though I knew it was coming, when he appeared in the film, it took me a little by surprise. *There you are, old man. It's good to see you.* His moments on-screen are moving. He pays tribute to his role model, Robert Jordan, Hemingway's protagonist in *For Whom the Bell Tolls.* Near the end, commenting on Hemingway's suicide and the life of the troubled soul who could be selfish and cruel, McCain was generous. "He was a human being," he said, by which he meant someone who, for all his "many vices," had used his art to understand mankind, and represent mankind, and take the side of mankind in battles against injustice. "And that, my friend, erases a whole lot of other what may be failings in life." Just hearing him say again "my friend," that old familiar salutation, brought a lump to the throat.

I remember an experience over a decade before, in October 2008, near the end of the presidential campaign we knew he was losing. We were a small party, gathered in his hotel suite in La Crosse, Wisconsin. The candidate and his wife, and a few aides and traveling companions. It was an unusually early end to the day, maybe five or six o'clock. Most campaign days ran eighteen hours, and I picture us almost out of sorts, as if none of us knew exactly what to do with the time other than check BlackBerrys and cell phones. It was kind of a gloomy end to the day, despite the room's cheerful view of the fall foliage along the Mississippi that reminded me of the river town where I grew up. Ruminating about old times isn't an activity much indulged in the last weeks of a national election, nor is feeling gloomy or unexpectedly idle or nostalgic. It's all frenetic energy, bad diets, and stress. But I do remember the moment that way, a touch of autumn melancholy, an idle few hours, each of us occupied with our own thoughts.

Should we get something to eat? someone asked. Why not. "See what they have for room service," the candidate instructed. I located a menu, which had photographs of the fare on offer. I started flipping through it and stopped when I came to the dessert page, and marveled at the confections pictured, pastries heaped with ice cream and whipped cream. "Oh, the short, happy lives of midwesterners," I remarked. McCain smiled as he caught the reference to Hemingway's story "The Short, Happy Life of Francis Macomber."

"That's a great story," he said, "one of his best." I agreed. "Not his very best, though," he added. "Not 'Snows of Kilimanjaro.' Did you ever read it?" I told him I had but not since high school. He reached into his battered briefcase, stuffed with books and magazines and memos he meant to read later, and extracted a paperback volume of Hemingway stories. "Listen to this," he ordered, and he began to read the story. This is how it begins:

> Kilimanjaro is a snow-covered mountain 19,710 feet high, and
> is said to be the highest mountain in Africa. Its western summit
> is called the Masai "Ngaje Ngai," the House of God. Close to
> the western summit there is the dried and frozen carcass of a

leopard. No one has explained what the leopard was seeking at that altitude.

He read the entire story aloud. It's long for a short story, more than nine thousand words. It took him over an hour to read, and he was hoarse when he finished. For those who have never had the pleasure, it's the story of a writer on an African safari, dying of gangrene, aware of his predicament, and reflecting back on his life's choices. I had always considered it a story of heartbreaking regret. An odd choice, or maybe not, for a candidate in a presidential election. But I don't think McCain's impulse to read it had a thing to do with his present circumstances. I don't think for him the story was about regret. It was a story of aspiration. At the end of it, in his delirium as death approaches, the protagonist believes he is aloft in an airplane, flying through a violent storm until he sees the "square top of Kilimanjaro," looking "as wide as all the world, great, high, and unbelievably white in the sun." McCain struggled to finish the story's last paragraphs as his small audience, frozen and silent, shot furtive glances at each other. He had read the story a hundred times, by his account. And on the hundred and first time, he cried at the end. "It's beautiful," he explained, "beautiful."

What was the leopard seeking at that altitude? To leave below the regrets of a life. To make up for its failings. To ascend by courage and good work and sacrifice until your conscience was quiet in appreciation of the steep climb. What was the leopard seeking at that altitude? Its best self. Its honor.

EPILOGUE

I joined the staff of Senator John McCain in August 1989, having met him a year earlier at the Republican National Convention, which was held in the New Orleans Superdome. I was working at the time for former ambassador to the United Nations Jeane Kirkpatrick. She had given a speech at the convention in support of George Bush's nomination and had agreed to do several press interviews afterward, but when we had trouble finding our way through the Superdome, I asked for an escort.

That escort was Victoria "Torie" Clarke, who was John McCain's press secretary at the time and had been volunteering at the convention. We didn't know each other, but Torie and I hit it off instantly. We made plans to meet for a drink after I had gotten the ambassador back to her hotel. We joined a throng of other Republican revelers hitting the nightspots on Bourbon Street, where she introduced me to McCain's personal assistant, Diane McClellan, and to other McCain staffers we bumped into that evening.

Before we parted company, Torie invited me to join the Arizona delegation, which occupied prime real estate near the front of the convention floor, for Vice President Bush's acceptance speech on Thursday. I showed up with the floor credentials Torie had secured for me, and she introduced me to various McCain aides and friends, and to the man himself, a white-haired guy about my height whom I had watched three days earlier deliver a good speech that had been memorable for its account of Mike Christian, the POW who had sewn an American flag on the inside of his shirt.

I got a handshake and approximately twenty seconds of McCain's time. "Torie tells me you're a good speechwriter," he volunteered, and I mumbled something in reply. "Maybe you could write something for me sometime," he added before turning his attention elsewhere. A month or so later, Torie called with an assignment. The speech that resulted was well received, and she soon called with another assignment, and another after that. A year later, I sat in John McCain's office listening as he offered me a job on his staff.

I had been directionless for much of my early life, short on ambition and long on attitude. For four years after high school, I worked on a railroad section gang and sang backup vocals in a rock band. I was twenty-six when I graduated from college. I stumbled into a couple of job opportunities without really looking very hard. Each had played out before I moved on, and I was nearing another dead end in a career that lacked imagination when I met John McCain, and all that changed.

Thirty years later, after a multitude of adventures with John McCain—during which I married his assistant, Diane McClellan, and we had two daughters—a young woman in a college audience asked me what my career plan had been in the beginning. "I got lost in the Superdome," I told her, "and the rest of my life happened."

Profile writers now and again observed that John and I shared a sensibility that tended to look on the dark side of things. That wasn't fair, or not fair to him, at least. He recognized the dark side but resisted it as a force in human affairs. I saw the dark side and assumed it was in charge.

We shared a similar taste in literature. We both admired the late William Trevor, whose stories are often characterized as tragedies, though that isn't quite fair, either. They are stories of people beset by misfortune, to be sure, caused by their own mistakes or just bad luck. But they usually end in the characters reaching an understanding or accommodation with their fate that lets them and the reader appreciate the poignancy of lives enduring loss and grief. Trevor loved his characters, no matter their misadventures or shortcomings, and his compassion for them stays with the reader after the story ends.

McCain had that kind of compassion. He understood the world as it was, with all its corruption and cruelty. But he believed it a moral failure to accept injustice as the inescapable tragedy of our fallen nature. He was a fatalist but never a pessimist. He never believed the world couldn't be made better or wasn't worth trying to make better. He believed we could use whatever shaped our psychologies, the strengths and weaknesses of our personalities, the codes we tried to live by, to help make it better.

I grew up in a stable, comfortably middle-class, loving family and, unlike him, without the burden of great expectations. I was a pessimist for no better reason than the impression made when I was a boy by the Catholic Church's emphasis that we have to die before we can have eternal life. I tended to see efforts to avert the world's doom as admirable but as futile as the hope of immortality on earth. McCain showed me what a fool I had been to miss that hopefulness made every tragedy bearable and all progress possible. Hope made every beautiful thing in this world and stood as a rebuke to every bad thing, the things within us and outside of us.

I'm a lucky bastard, as John McCain would say, and I know it. Every meaningful thing I did, everything I have, my dearest loves, came from that chance encounter with a man everybody knew and few can imitate. What can you say to someone to whom you owe that much? Nothing close to what it meant.

Near the end, while he still could, John would read aloud to close friends and family the closing lines of our last book, tapping his finger on the page as he read: "What an ingrate I would be to curse the fate that concludes the blessed life I've led. . . . I hope those who mourn my passing, and even those who don't, will celebrate as I celebrate a happy life lived in imperfect service to a country made of ideals, whose continued success is the hope of the world. And I wish all of you great adventures, good company and lives as lucky as mine."

He reached a point where speaking more than a few words became difficult. In one of our last visits, he pointed at the passage and gestured for me to read it. I did as he wished, and fighting tears, I managed to say, "Thank you, John, thank you for everything."

ACKNOWLEDGMENTS

How to convey John McCain's singular personality and which episodes to illuminate from his crowded life are questions that would challenge the skills of any biographer. They certainly challenged mine. Luckily, I could rely on Jonathan Karp's impeccable judgment to point me in the right direction. I am as grateful today for his guidance, confidence in me, and his patience as I was when our association began more than two decades ago. John McCain's and my literary agent, Flip Brophy, was responsible for facilitating that association. I remain indebted to her for that and for all her support and advice these many years.

I relied, too, on the memories and insights of scores of McCain alumni from his senate staffs in Washington and Arizona, and from his senate and presidential campaigns. There are too many to name, but I owe all a debt of thanks for their help and friendship. Those whose recollections proved invaluable included Truman Anderson, Steve Biegun, Chris Brose, Ellen Cahill, Pablo Carrillo, Mark Delich, Joe Donoghue, Sonya Sotak Elling, Carla Eudy, Richard Fontaine, Dan McKivergan, Arjun Nijhawan, Virginia Pounds, John Raidt, Randy Scheunemann, Nancy Ives Schroeder, Doug Smith, Julie Tarallo, Becky Tallent, Jake Terrell, Dan Twining, and Grant Woods. Lee Carosi Dunn hosted a dinner for various McCain aides to share their favorite McCain stories with me. It became a very funny trip down memory lane, and provided a lot of the material for the book's first chapter. Truman Anderson and Rick Davis, whose memories are in better shape than mine, kept me straight about the order of events in the last year of John McCain's life, and Rick offered valuable insights about other, happier times in our long association with the old man. New Hampshire McCainiacs, Mike Dennehy and Steve Duprey, drove five hours to my town in Maine at a time when I was falling behind schedule and could not see the book's end very clearly. A good dinner and a few good McCain stories later, and I was back at it.

I am grateful as ever to Kevin and Roxanne Coady, for their advice and cherished friendship.

My thanks, too, to all at Simon & Schuster who graciously tolerated my late delivery of the manuscript, and under a tight deadline helped make it a better book, especially Stephen Bedford, Kayley Hoffman, Larry Hughes, and Maria Mendez who, among other courtesies, put up with my poor photography skills and ignorance about securing the rights to photographs taken by professionals. And finally, to the discerning Beth Thomas, the copy editor who almost made me cry when she told me she cried at the end of the book.

I'm indebted to Cindy McCain, the entire McCain family, and their closest friends for their many kindnesses to me over the years, and for allowing me the privilege of spending time with John when the time that was left with him was very precious.

Finally, to Diane, Molly, and Elizabeth—thanks for putting up with me, and for not believing me when I complained for the thousandth time that I would never finish writing this book. I love you.

NOTES

1 John McCain and Mark Salter, *The Restless Wave: Good Times, Just Causes, Great Fights, and Other Appreciations* (New York City: Simon & Schuster, 2018), 12.

2 Mark Salter, "John McCain Spent His Life Serving the Dignity of His Fellow Man," *Washington Post*, August 26, 2018, https://www.washington post.com /opinions/john-mccain-spent-his-life-serving-the-dignity-of -his-fellow-man/2018/08/25/ca68d8da-4346-11e8-ad8f-27a8c409298b _story.html.

3 Elizabeth Spencer, *Landscapes of the Heart* (New York City: Random House, 1997), 9.

4 Jake Tapper and Suzi Parker, "McCain's Ancestors Owned Slaves," *Salon*, February 16, 2000, https://www.salon.com/2000/02/15/mccain_90/.

5 Spencer, *Landscapes of the Heart*, 12.

6 Barry R. McCain, *Finding the McCains: A Scots Irish Odyssey* (Oxford, Mississippi: Ulster Heritage, 2015).

7 The confusion is attributable to the fact that there were apparently two William A. McCains living in Mississippi at the time. I've seen conflicting accounts about which is the John McCain ancestor. The cavalry trooper is believed to have died in Memphis, in a Confederate hospital or possibly a prison, where he was held for desertion. The other William McCain is believed to have died at home after enlisting in the militia. (*Admiral John S. McCain and the Triumph of Naval Air Power*, William F. Trimble; Finding Your Roots, Series 3, aired February 9, 2016.)

8 Spencer, *Landscapes of the Heart*, 11.

9 Max Boot, *The Savage Wars of Peace: Small Wars and the Rise of American Power* (New York City: Basic Books, 2002), 183.

10 William F. Trimble, *Admiral John S. McCain and the Triumph of Naval Air Power* (Annapolis, MD: Naval Institute Press, 2019), 21.

11 John McCain and Mark Salter, *Faith of My Fathers: A Family Memoir* (New York City: Random House, 1999), 3.

12 Ibid, 2.

13 Ibid, 66.

14 Ibid, 166.

15 Ibid, 103.

16 Jonathan Weisman, "McCain's Maverick Side: Grandpa Would Be Proud," *Washington Post*, July 22, 2008, https://www.washingtonpost.com/wp-dyn/content/article/2008/07/21/AR2008072102653.html.

17 John McCain and Mark Salter, *Character Is Destiny: Inspiring Stories Every Young Person Should Know and Every Adult Should Remember* (New York City: Random House, 2005), xi.

18 Claudia Grisales, "The McCains: A Military Legacy," *Stars and Stripes*, August 26, 2018, https://www.stripes.com/news/special-reports/featured/mccain/the-mccains-a-military-legacy-1.532541.

19 Robert Timberg, *The Nightingale's Song* (New York City: Simon & Schuster, 1995), 304.

20 Ibid, 365.

21 Ibid, 530.

22 Ibid, 382.

23 Ibid, 521.

24 Ibid, 330.

25 Bernard Weinraub, "Start of Tragedy: Pilot Hears a Blast as He Checks Plane," *New York Times*, July 31, 1967, https://www.nytimes.com/1967/07/31/archives/start-of-tragedy-pilot-hears-a-blast-as-he-checks-plane-tragedys.html.

26 Stephen A. Rowan, *They Wouldn't Let Us Die: The Prisoners of War Tell Their Story* (New York City: Jonathan David Co., Inc., 1973).

27 Stuart I. Rochester and Frederick T. Kiley, *Honor Bound: American Prisoners-of-War in Southeast Asia, 1961-1973* (Annapolis, MD: Naval Institute Press, 1998).

28 John McCain and Mark Salter, *Worth the Fighting For: A Memoir* (New York City: Random House, 2002), 125.

29 Larry Margasak, "Lessons From Keating Scandal Applied to McCain Presidential Campaign," *Associated Press*, March 24, 2008, https://www.fosters.com/article/20080324/NEWS81/986895248.

30 John McCain and Mark Salter, *Worth the Fighting For*, 162.

31 Jennifer Rubin, "What Do Other Moderates Have over Klobuchar?" *Washington Post*, December 1, 2019, https://www.washingtonpost.com /opinions/2019/11/25/what-do-other-moderates-have-over-klobuchar/.

32 Timberg, *The Nightingale's Song*, 233.

33 Nicholas Kristof, "P.O.W. to Power Broker, A Chapter Most Telling," *New York Times*, February 27, 2000, https://www.nytimes.com /2000/02/27/us/pow-to-power-broker-a-chapter-most-telling.html.

34 Forty-four years later, it came to mind as I watched McCain stop to talk to a mother and her five-year-old son at Walter Reed Hospital. McCain had just finished discussing treatment for his second brain tumor, and he looked a little defeated as we rode the elevator down to the lobby. But he brightened as soon as he saw the mother and son coming toward us to thank him for his vote to save Obamacare. She told him her son was also suffering from glioblastoma, and she couldn't have afforded his treatment if she had lost her insurance. He bent down to talk to the boy, as if it were just the two of them there, and cheerfully asked him a few questions. McCain became for a moment his usual lively, positive self, telling us to get out our phones and take a picture of the three of them, stage-directing their pose, hugging mother and son two or three times, before the mother apologized for taking up his time, and he assured her there was nothing he would rather be doing. Before we left, he gave her his number and insisted she call him if she needed help with anything.

35 Timberg, *The Nightingale's Song*, 233.

36 Kristof, "P.O.W. to Power Broker, A Chapter Most Telling."

37 Ibid.

38 David Broder, "McCain Begins Complicated Quest," *Washington Post*, May 23, 1999.

39 James Carney, "The Diagnosis: Stable," *Time*, December 5, 1999, https://www.washingtonpost.com/wp-srv/politics/campaigns/wh2000/stories /mccain052399.htm.

40 Connie Bruck, "McCain's Party," *New Yorker*, May 23, 2005, https://www .newyorker.com/magazine/2005/05/30/mccains-party.

41 William Saletan, "Compassionate Corporatism," *Slate*, July 11, 2002, https://slate.com/news-and-politics/2002/07/mccain-vs-bush-on -corporate-corruption.html.

42 Mike Kelly, "John McCain and Tom Kean: How the 9/11 Commission forged an unlikely political partnership," northjersey.com, September 1,

2018, https://www.northjersey.com/story/news/columnists/mike
-kelly/2018/09/01/john-mccain-tom-kean-9-11-commission-unlikely
-partnership/1150638002/.

43 Anthony Toth, "Another Reason to Celebrate John McCain Was His
Critical Role in Establishing the 9/11 Commission," History News
Network at George Washington University, September 10, 2018, https://
historynewsnetwork.org/article/169960.

44 John McCain, "Putting the 'National' in National Service," *Washington
Monthly*, October 1, 2001, https://washingtonmonthly.com/2001/10/01
/putting-the-national-in-national-service/.

45 George Packer, "The Fall of Conservatism," *New Yorker*, May 19, 2008, https://
www.newyorker.com/magazine/2008/05/26/the-fall-of-conservatism.

46 McCain and Salter, *The Restless Wave*, 171.

47 Ibid, 179.

48 John McCain, "It's Time to Use American Air Power in Syria," *New
Republic*, March 5, 2012, https://newrepublic.com/article/101405
/mccain-speech-america-airpower-syria.

49 McCain and Salter, *The Restless Wave*, 194.

50 Ibid.

51 William A. Galston, "McCain Championed a Strong Senate," *Wall Street
Journal*, August 28, 2018, https://www.wsj.com/articles/mccain-cham
pioned-a-strong-senate-1535495359.

52 McCain and Salter, *The Restless Wave*, 281.

53 Ibid, 288.

54 Brian Bonner, "Who Will Fill John McCain's Void for Ukraine?" *Kyiv
Post*, August 26, 2018, https://www.kyivpost.com/article/opinion/op-ed
/brian-bonner-who-will-fill-john-mccains-void-for-ukraine.html.

55 Ryan Lizza, "John McCain Has a Few Things to Say About Donald
Trump," *New Yorker*, July 16, 2015, https://www.newyorker.com/news
/news-desk/john-mccain-has-a-few-things-to-say-about-donald-trump.

56 McCain and Salter, *The Restless Wave*, 325.

57 Jim Newell, "Can John McCain Survive the Year of Trump?" July
10, 2016, http://www.slate.com/articles/news_and_politics/cover
_story/2016/07/can_john_mccain_survive_the_year_of_trump.html.

58 David Mack, "Watch the Shocking Moment John McCain Killed the
Republican Health Care Bill," *BuzzFeed*, July 28, 2017, https://www.buzz
feednews.com/article/davidmack/back-and-to-the-left.

INDEX

About the Author

Mark Salter has collaborated with John McCain on all seven of their books, including *The Restless Wave, Faith of My Fathers, Worth the Fighting For, Why Courage Matters, Character Is Destiny, Hard Call,* and *Thirteen Soldiers.* He served on Senator McCain's staff for eighteen years.